systems of fifty-eight African political entities.
Part Two describes and appraises broadcasting
in Africa as a whole, discussing such subjects
of common interest as foreign aid, training,
research, and educational uses of broadcasting. Also covered are international broadcasts
aimed at Africa from the rest of the world,
religious broadcasting, and broadcasting and
commerce. Part Three is a critique and an
agenda for further study. The bibliography of
over five hundred entries is the most extensive
to date on the subject.

SYDNEY W. HEAD is Professor of Commu-
nications, Temple University. He has spent
nine years in Africa working in Ethiopia,
Ghana, Kenya, Liberia, Malawi, Nigeria,
Sierra Leone, Southern Rhodesia, the Sudan,
Tanzania, and Zambia. He is the author of
Broadcasting in America, the definitive work
in the field.

Broadcasting
in Africa

International and Comparative Broadcasting
A Series Edited by Sydney W. Head

Broadcasting in Africa

A Continental Survey of Radio and Television

Edited by
Sydney W. Head

Temple University Press
Philadelphia

Temple University Press, Philadelphia 19122

© 1974 by Temple University. All rights reserved
Published 1974
Printed in the United States of America

International Standard Book Number: 0-87722-027-1
Library of Congress Catalog Card Number: 73-79478

Contents

Preface   xv

1. Introduction   3
    1.1 Why This Book?   3
    1.2 Organizational Framework   5
        1.2.1 *Individual Systems*   5
        1.2.2 *Cross-System Functions*   6
    1.3 Delimitations   7
    1.4 African Broadcasting in Brief   8
        1.4.1 *Signal Propagation*   8
        1.4.2 *Parameters of Development* 9
        1.4.3 *Descriptive Summary of Systems* 10
    1.5 Bibliographic Conventions   12

Part 1. National Systems

2. Egypt and the Maghreb   15
    2.1 Egypt, by *Timothy Green*   17
        2.1.1 *Introduction*   17
        2.1.2 *History*   18
        2.1.3 *Domestic Radio Services* 20
        2.1.4 *External Services*   23
        2.1.5 *Television*   24
    2.2 The Maghreb, by *Ali Z. Elgabri*   28
        2.2.1 *Libya*   28
        2.2.2 *Tunisia*   30
        2.2.3 *Algeria*   31
        2.2.4 *Morocco*   34

3. The Horn   37
    3.1 Ethiopia, *by Sydney W. Head*   37
        3.1.1 *Development of Radio*   38
        3.1.2 *Radio Programming*   39

           3.1.3 *Television*   40
           3.1.4 *Autonomous Status*   41
           3.1.5 *The Audience*   43
           3.1.6 *Technical Aid*   44
           3.1.7 *Radio Voice of the Gospel*   45
     3.2 The Sudan, *by Ali M. Shummo*   46
           3.2.1 *Radio*   47
           3.2.2 *Television*   49
     3.3 Somalia, *by Sydney W. Head*   50

4. East Africa   53

     4.1 Kenya, *by John Stewart Roberts*   54
           4.1.1 *Broadcasting History*   55
           4.1.2 *Radio*   57
           4.1.3 *Television*   57
           4.1.4 *Audience Data*   58
           4.1.5 *Training and Development*   59
     4.2 United Republic of Tanzania, *by Graham L. Mytton*   62
           4.2.1 *Historical and Political Background*   62
           4.2.2 *Facilities*   64
           4.2.3 *Programming*   65
           4.2.4 *Audiences*   68
           4.2.5 *Educational Broadcasting*   68
           4.2.6 *Training*   70
           4.2.7 *Zanzibar Broadcasting*   70
     4.3 Uganda, *by Edward M. Moyo*   71
           4.3.1 *Regionalization of Services*   71
           4.3.2 *Language Problems*   72
           4.3.3 *Television*   74
     4.4 Burundi and Rwanda, *by James M. Kushner*   75
           4.4.1 *Burundi*   75
           4.4.2 *Rwanda*   77

5. Anglophone West Africa   78

     5.1 Nigeria, *by Christopher Kolade*   78
           5.1.1 *Federal and Regional Services*   79
           5.1.2 *Control and Structure*   80
           5.1.3 *Finance*   80
           5.1.4 *Technical Facilities*   81
           5.1.5 *Programs*   82
           5.1.6 *Educational Broadcasting*   83
           5.1.7 *Commercial Broadcasting*   84
           5.1.8 *External Service*   85
           5.1.9 *Television*   85

          5.1.10 *Audience Relations*   86
          5.1.11 *Training*   86
          5.1.12 *The Past and the Future*   87
    5.2 Ghana, *by John Kugblenu*   89
          5.2.1 *Broadcast Services*   89
          5.2.2 *Specialized Units of the GBC*   90
          5.2.3 *Training*   93
          5.2.4 *Receiver Assembly*   95
    5.3 The Gambia, *by Swaebou J. S. Conateh*   96
          5.3.1 *General Description*   96
          5.3.2 *Radio Syd*   97
          5.3.3 *Radio Gambia*   98
          5.3.4 *Programming*   99
          5.3.5 *Future Plans*   101
    5.4 Liberia, Sierra Leone, and Cameroon, *by Sydney W.*
          Head   102
          5.4.1 *Liberia*   102
          5.4.2 *Sierra Leone*   104
          5.4.3 *Cameroon*   105

6. Francophone West and Equatorial Africa, *by R. Arnold*
    Gibbons   107

    6.1 The Francophone Colonial Legacy   107
          6.1.1 *Geography*   107
          6.1.2 *Broadcasting Policies*   108
          6.1.3 *French Aid*   110
          6.1.4 *Postcolonial French Influence*   111
          6.1.5 *Belgian Colonial Policy*   112
    6.2 French West Africa   113
          6.2.1 *Senegal*   113
          6.2.2 *Ivory Coast*   114
          6.2.3 *Guinea*   115
          6.2.4 *Togo*   116
          6.2.5 *Dahomey*   117
          6.2.6 *Mali*   117
          6.2.7 *Mauritania*   118
          6.2.8 *Niger*   118
          6.2.9 *Upper Volta*   119
    6.3 Francophone Equatorial Africa   119
          6.3.1 *The Congo*   119
          6.3.2 *Chad*   121
          6.3.3 *Central African Republic*   121

      6.3.4 *Gabon* 122
  6.4 Zaïre 122

7. South-Central Africa 125
  7.1 Zambia and Southern Rhodesia, *by Jon Powell* 125
      7.1.1 *Pre-Independence Radio* 125
      7.1.2 *Zambia* 128
      7.1.3 *Southern Rhodesia* 131
  7.2 Malawi, *by William E. Mackie* 133
      7.2.1 *Facilities* 134
      7.2.2 *Governance* 135
      7.2.3 *Programming* 136
      7.2.4 *Special Services* 137
      7.2.5 *Finances* 138

8. Southern Africa, *by Peter B. Orlik* 140
  8.1 Radio in the Republic of South Africa 140
      8.1.1 *Afrikaner Hegemony* 140
      8.1.2 *SABC Founded* 141
      8.1.3 *Development of FM* 143
      8.1.4 *Commercial Services* 144
      8.1.5 *External Service* 146
      8.1.6 *Domestic Programming* 146
  8.2 South African Television 147
      8.2.1 *Political Maneuvers* 148
      8.2.2 *TV Plans Announced* 149
  8.3 Conclusion 150
  8.4 Swaziland, Lesotho, and Botswana 151
      8.4.1 *Swaziland* 151
      8.4.2 *Lesotho* 152
      8.4.3 *Botswana* 153

9. Islands and Territories 155
  9.1 Independent Islands, *by Sydney W. Head* 155
      9.1.1 *Malagasy Republic* 155
      9.1.2 *Mauritius* 156
      9.1.3 *Equatorial Guinea* 157
  9.2 Portuguese Dependencies, *by Alexander F. Toogood* 157
      9.2.1 *Ownership and Control* 158
      9.2.2 *Programming and Finance* 160
      9.2.3 *Angola* ·161
      9.2.4 *Moçambique* 163
      9.2.5 *Other Territories* 165
  9.3 British Insular Dependencies, *by Sydney W. Head* 167
      9.3.1 *Seychelles* 167

9.3.2 *South Atlantic Islands* 167
9.4 French Dependencies 168
    9.4.1 *French Territory of Afars and Issas,* by
        James M. Kushner 168
    9.4.2 *Indian Ocean Islands,* by Sydney W. Head 169
9.5 Spanish Dependencies, *by Sydney W. Head* 170

Part 2. Cross-System Functions

10. International Broadcasts to African Audiences, *by Donald R. Browne* 175

    10.1 Colonial Period 175
    10.2 Postcolonial Scramble for the Ether 177
    10.3 African Audiences for International Services 180
        10.3.1 *Physical Aspects of Reception* 180
        10.3.2 *Psychological and Sociological Receptivity* 181
        10.3.3 *Audiences in Actuality* 183
    10.4 International Services from the West 184
        10.4.1 *BBC External Services* 184
        10.4.2 *Voice of America* 186
        10.4.3 *Deutsche Welle* 187
        10.4.4 *Office de Radiodiffusion-Télévision Française* 188
    10.5 International Services from Communist Sources 189
        10.5.1 *Radio Moscow* 189
        10.5.2 *Radio Peking* 190
        10.5.3 *Radio Berlin International* 190
    10.6 International Services from African Nations 191
        10.6.1 *Radio Ghana* 191
        10.6.2 *Voice of Nigeria* 192
        10.6.3 *Radio Tanzania* 192
        10.6.4 *Lourenço Marques Radio* 193
        10.6.5 *Republic of South Africa* 193
        10.6.6 *Radio Cairo* 195
        10.6.7 *Other African Services* 196
    10.7 Conclusion: Some Strategic Considerations 197
    10.8 United Nations Radio, *by Athmani R. Magoma* 199

11. Religious Broadcasting 201

    11.1 Islam and Christianity, *by Sydney W. Head* 201
    11.2 Christian Broadcasting in and to Africa, *by E. H. Robertson* 204
        11.2.1 *Religious Programming on Government Systems* 205
        11.2.2 *Production Centers* 205

11.2.3 *Church-related Stations in Africa*   207
11.2.4 *Church-related Stations outside Africa*   209
11.2.5 *Training*   210
11.3 A Program Philosophy for Religious Broadcasting, *by Sigurd Aske*   211

12. Bilateral Foreign Aid   215
12.1 Great Britain, *by J. F. Wilkinson*   216
12.1.1 *Colonial Broadcasting Policy*   217
12.1.2 *Development of Colonial Systems*   219
12.1.3 *Programs Transmitted to Africa*   221
12.1.4 *BBC Programs Transmitted by African Stations*   223
12.1.5 *Future Prospects*   224
12.2 The United States   225
12.2.1 *Agency for International Development*, by Sydney W. Head   226
12.2.2 *United States Information Agency*, by James M. Kushner   230
12.2.3 *The Peace Corps*, by James M. Kushner   234
12.2.4 *Exchange of Persons*, by Wayne Towers   236
12.3 Canada, by *Cynthia E. Bled*   240
12.3.1 *Canada's Aid Philosophy*   240
12.3.2 *Direction and Extent of Canadian Aid*   241
12.3.3 *Educational Broadcasting*   242
12.3.4 *Community Development*   244
12.3.5 *Training*   245
12.3.6 *Advisory/Feasibility Studies*   247
12.4 The Federal Republic of Germany, *by Laura Gläser-Weisser*   247
12.4.1 *German Policy on Aid to the Mass Media*   247
12.4.2 *German Government Media Projects*   249
12.4.3 *Nongovernment Aid*   251

13. Multilateral Aid   252
13.1 UNESCO, *by Francis Bebey*   254
13.1.1 *Meetings, Seminars, Training Courses*   255
13.1.2 *Experts, Projects, Experiments*   257
13.1.3 *Longer-Term Projects*   258
13.2 International Broadcasting Unions, *by Charles E. Sherman*   259
13.2.1 *International Telecommunication Union*   260
13.2.2 *Union of National Radio and Television Organizations of Africa*   262
13.2.3 *Arab States Broadcasting Union*   262

13.2.4 *European Broadcasting Union*   263

13.2.5 *International Radio and Television Organization*   264

13.3 The Commonwealth Broadcasting Conference, *by Kenneth Adam*   264

13.4 The World Bank, *by James M. Kushner*   267

14. Training   270

14.1 Introduction   270

14.2 British Training   271

14.2.1 *British Broadcasting Corporation,* by Geoffrey Seymour   271

14.2.2 *Centre for Educational Development Overseas,* by Alexander B. Edington   276

14.2.3 *Thomson Foundation Television College,* by Sydney W. Head   280

14.3 Training in Africa, *by James F. Scotton*   281

14.3.1 *Traditional Methods*   281

14.3.2 *Broadcast Training in African Higher Education*   285

14.4 A German-sponsored Radio Training Center in Ethiopia, *by Laura Gläser-Weisser*   290

15. Educational Uses of Broadcasting, *by Robert Nwankwo*   292

15.1 Modes of Application and Their Differentiation   293

15.1.1 *Content and Its Organization*   294

15.1.2 *Target Audience*   295

15.1.3 *Production Style*   295

15.1.4 *Scheduling*   296

15.1.5 *Reception Conditions*   296

15.1.6 *Feedback*   297

15.1.7 *Assignment of Responsibility*   297

15.2 Some Practical Examples   298

15.2.1 *Transplanting Farm Forums: Ghana*   298

15.2.2 *Pioneering ITV: Nigeria*   300

15.2.3 *First Success with ITV: Niger*   301

15.2.4 *A Ministation for ETV: Senegal*   302

15.2.5 *Literacy Training: Tunisia*   302

15.3 The Unfulfilled Promise   303

15.3.1 *Limiting Factors: Information/Guidance Programming*   304

15.3.2 *Limiting Factors: Instructional Programming*   306

15.4   Case History: Ethiopia's Mass Media Center, *by John Gartley*   309
    15.4.1   *Educational Television Service Initiated*   311
    15.4.2   *Mass Media Center Established*   312
    15.4.3   *ETV Research*   314
    15.4.4   *Educational Radio*   315
15.5   Case Study: Ivory Coast ETV, *by Stephen H. Grant*   315
    15.5.1   *A Radical Solution*   315
    15.5.2   *Five Publics*   316
    15.5.3   *Evaluation: Pros and Cons*   318

16.   Research, *by Sydney W. Head*   320

16.1   Role of Research   320
16.2   Development of Research   322
16.3   External Sponsorship   323
    16.3.1   *Advertiser-oriented Research*   323
    16.3.2   *Foreign Government Sponsorship*   324
    16.3.3   *Educational Sponsorship*   326
    16.3.4   *Religious Broadcasters*   327
16.4   Self-Study   328
16.5   Methodological Problems   330
16.6   Needed Research   332
    16.6.1   *Information Infrastructure*   332
    16.6.2   *Developmental Role of Media*   334

17.   Broadcasting and Commerce, *by Sydney W. Head*   336

17.1   Broadcast Advertising   336
    17.1.1   *Commercial Efficiency*   336
    17.1.2   *Advertising Agencies*   338
    17.1.3   *Limits on Revenue Potential*   339
17.2   Commercial Practice   339
    17.2.1   *Salience of Commercials*   340
    17.2.2   *Rate Policies*   340
    17.2.3   *Miscellaneous Rate-Card Provisions*   341
17.3   Construction and Management Contracts   342

Part 3.   Conclusion

18.   An Agenda for Further Study, *by Sydney W. Head*   347

18.1   Audience-building Strategies   347
    18.1.1   *Artificial Impediments to Audience Growth*   347
    18.1.2   *Polylingualism*   350
    18.1.3   *Localized Service*   352
    18.1.4   *Legal Status of Broadcasting*   353

18.2 Aspects of Programming   355
    18.2.1 *Quality and Motivation*   355
    18.2.2 *News*   355
    18.2.3 *Indigenous Arts*   357
    18.2.4 *Status of Artists*   358
18.3 Personnel Recruitment, Training, and Utilization   359
    18.3.1 *Overseas Training*   359
    18.3.2 *University Broadcasting Education*   360
    18.3.3 *Capacity to Utilize Trained Personnel*   361
18.4 Problems Inherent in Foreign Aid   362
    18.4.1 *Aid Tying and Donor Ethnocentrism*   363
    18.4.2 *Defective Reciprocation*   364
    18.4.3 *Are the Premises Wrong?*   365
18.5 Two Technical Questions   367
    18.5.1 *Frequency Modulation: The Coming
          Thing?*   367
    18.5.2 *Satellites: How Soon?*   368

Appendixes

1. Technical Problems of Spectrum Utilization, *by Alfred F.
   Barghausen*   375
    A1.1 The Radio Spectrum   375
    A1.2 The Broadcasting Service   377
    A1.3 Medium-Frequency Broadcasting   378
        A1.3.1 *Ground-Wave Primary Service Area*   379
        A1.3.2 *Sky-Wave Secondary Service Area*   380
        A1.3.3 *Summary*   383
    A1.4 High-Frequency Broadcasting   386
        A1.4.1 *Equatorial Sporadic E*   387
        A1.4.2 *Low-Latitude Spread F*   388
        A1.4.3 *Low-Latitude Regular F Region*   388
        A1.4.4 *Summary*   389
    A1.5 Broadcasting at Very-High and Ultra-High
          Frequencies   390
        A1.5.1 *Factors Affecting FM and Television*   390
        A1.5.2 *UHF Television*   392
        A1.5.3 *Summary*   393
    A1.6 Satellite Broadcasting   393

2. Broadcasting and Political Crisis, *by William A. Hachten*   395

3. Historical and Demographic Data   399

4. Summary of System Facilities   401

5. Languages Used in Broadcasting   406

Bibliography   415

Index   443

Preface

Not being able to undertake the extensive field work it required, I had about given up the idea of a book on broadcasting in Africa when Gordon L. Gray, chairman of my department at Temple University, suggested instead my editing a book of essays on the subject. With encouragement from the Temple University Press, I took up this challenge—little realizing that I was letting myself in for two full years of continuous correspondence, research, and writing. What with topics for which in the end no contributing authors could be found, and contributing authors who, once found, ultimately disappeared without having contributed, the task grew far more demanding than I had thought possible.

The contributors who did contribute as scheduled deserve both thanks and great sympathy, for they tolerated my committing many editorial indignities on their prose as I struggled to bring the subject matter under control. Many colleagues, friends, and even complete strangers generously gave time and expert attention to the critical reading of particular chapters and sections. They caught many errors and made many wise recommendations. Without meaning to undervalue the help of still others not mentioned by name in the following list, and without holding to account those mentioned for errors of fact or interpretation on my part, I should like to thank particularly Ismail al Faruqi, Alfred Barghausen, Vernon Bronson, Andrew Hess, John M. Kittross, John Kugblenu, James Kushner, F. A. Leary, William Minette, Graham Mytton, John Ohliger, Everett Rogers, Sayre Schatz, Lavay Sheldon, Christopher Sterling, and Stanley F. X. Worris.

For bibliographical research, for manuscript typing, and for handling seemingly endless correspondence, I am grateful to John Vilanilam and Sharon Foster, my graduate and undergraduate student assistants, respectively, at Temple University at the time the work was going on.

Several previous authors are cited so frequently in this book that their contributions deserve special acknowledgment apart from simple listing in the bibliography. Students of broadcasting must be grateful to the *World Radio-TV Handbook*, edited by J. M. Frost and published annually by Billboard Publications. As the most comprehensive source of basic data about world broadcasting systems it has been indispensable to many of the contributors to this book as well as to the editor. Francis Bebey has made two landmark contributions to the literature of African broadcasting. First, *La radiodiffusion en Afrique noire,* published in 1963, gives the most comprehensive summary available of the early history of the medium and of its status at a critical turning point in that history. Second, his study of the training of African broadcasters, done as a UNESCO project with A. T. Quarmyne in 1967, gives us the most perceptive critique on the practice of broadcasting in Africa yet assembled. Unfortunately, UNESCO failed to give it the circulation it deserves. I have taken full advantage of the valuable insights provided by reports of the Zambian Broadcasting Services Research Project by Graham Mytton, Institute for African Studies research fellow at the University of Zambia. Those reports carry forward research interests first generated in the early 1950s at the Central African Broadcasting Service in Lusaka, about which Peter Fraenkel wrote so vividly in *Wayaleshi* (1959), also a much-cited source for the present study.

SYDNEY W. HEAD

Philadelphia

Broadcasting
in Africa

1   Introduction

1.1 Why This Book?

This survey may help somewhat to redress an imbalance. The study of broadcasting in Africa has been neglected, in the light of broadcasting's position of overwhelming dominance among the public media of the continent. Although a considerable literature on the mass media in Africa exists, it underplays the role of broadcasting. Whole books on news in Africa have been written without acknowledgment that most Africans get their news off the air, not off the page. To obtain a rough measure of the imbalance, consider Hachten's 1971 bibliography, *Mass Communication in Africa*—of the approximately 540 items listed, less than 13% deal explicitly with broadcasting—and consider the fact that, according to UNESCO's 1971 *Statistical Yearbook,* on the average every thousand Africans shared 45 radio receivers, but only 11 copies of daily newspapers, in 1969. Or consider that, according to estimates in a 1972 report of the University of Zambia's Institute for African Studies, over 77% of the Zambian population never read a daily newspaper, and over 74% never read even a nondaily news publication; in both urban and rural sampling areas, of those who had heard about a specific event then salient in the news, 67% learned of it from radio listening, 17% from newspaper reading (Mytton 1972a, pp. 38, 44, 52). And it costs the *East African Standard* over a dollar per copy to reach some rural areas of Kenya—a country whose per capita gross national product in 1972 was $137 (*African Journalist* 1972a, p. 1).

    Radio is the only medium in Africa able to scale the triple barrier of illiteracy, distance, and lack of transportation; broadcasting uses scores of local languages, most of which never appear in print; radio and television continue to grow, while daily newspapers decline; broadcasting stations generally have large staffs and modern equipment, while most newspapers are woefully understaffed and ill-equipped. One would expect, therefore, that scholars, observers, and commentators writing about the public media in Africa would have devoted a large part—if not the majority—of their attention to broadcasting. But they have not. How explain this curious neglect? Many reasons could be deduced, but let us consider three that seem particularly relevant to the present endeavor.

1. *Accessibility and convenience.* In part, print receives more attention simply because of its greater accessibility and convenience as a subject of study. A short-term visitor to a national capital can stuff enough newspapers into his baggage to give him materials for at least superficially assessing the performance of the press; if he wants to go deeper he can consult microfilms of even quite obscure news publications in major libraries. The output of broadcasting services, however, cannot be so conveniently anatomized. The study of broadcast performance requires either tedious, time-consuming monitoring of stations in the field or expensive arrangements for making and playing back recordings, which are equally tedious and time consuming to analyze.

2. *Government control.* Broadcasting in Africa is almost universally under direct government control, while a few news publications still retain some degree of freedom from official supervision. Newspapers, therefore, have attracted the attention and assistance of outside organizations hoping to nurture the Western ideology of an independent press in newly independent Africa; but they have written off broadcasting as a mere propaganda organ, beyond redemption. Yet on this score the steady advance of one-party states and nationalization of the press makes the line separating newspapers from broadcasting increasingly difficult to discern.

3. *Stereotyped expectations.* Westerners who all their adult lives have thought of the press as the Fourth Estate have tended automatically to expect the press to assume a similar role in developing countries. The press they know evolved gradually, acquiring in the course of time great power and assuming a historic role as defender of liberties. Broadcasting, which came only lately and only as a government-licensed medium, had no need to assume roles already adequately filled by the print medium; its primary role remained the peripheral one of satisfying the mass taste for light entertainment. These images may have been unconsciously projected onto developing countries, with the expectation that there the press and broadcasting would naturally assume their accustomed roles. But insofar as developing countries have a press tradition at all it is likely to be one of repression: "All colonial governments, without exception, maintained severe forms of censorship, either directly, as in Francophone countries, or indirectly through sedition and other laws" (Legum 1971a, pp. 28–29). In most of Africa modern media were introduced within a single lifespan, so that none lays claim to primacy by right of long-term seniority. Far from being a latter-day innovation imposed on a basically print-oriented culture, broadcasting is the only modern medium most Africans encounter in their daily lives—lives in which print plays no part at all.

When the International Press Institute set up a pioneer regional center for journalism training in Nairobi in 1961, its organizers planned exclusively in terms of print. They apparently did not feel that, looking realistically at African conditions, there might be as much need to train broadcasting journalists as to train print journalists. A member of the IPI teaching staff candidly confessed that "throughout our six years . . . we were to take more government and radio information personnel than we had envisaged, or perhaps—as an organization which at that time exclusively served the written press—IPI wished to" (Barton 1969, p. 33). Although the IPI's motives were pure, its outlook was parochial. We single out this example for its appositeness, not to imply that the IPI differed in this respect from other organizations. The fact is that the outside educational establishment in general exported to Africa its conventional print-oriented journalism curriculum. The first formal academic curricula for media education in Africa were designed almost as though broadcasting had not yet been invented.

These, then, may be some of the reasons—practical, ideological, and simply adventitious—which account for the fact that students of the media in Africa have allotted a disproportionate amount of their attention to print. In calling attention to this disproportion, and in attempting to contribute to its rectification, we in no way mean to denigrate the traditional libertarian role of the press in Western society. In Africa, however, conditions conspire to give broadcasting a different, more significant social and political role vis-à-vis the press than it has had in industrialized societies. This difference, we submit, justifies more intensive study of broadcasting in Africa than it has so far received.

1.2 Organizational Framework

The present study divides the subject into three major parts: description of individual broadcasting systems; description, as well as appraisal, of cross-system functions on a continental scale; and a critique leading to an inventory of subjects suggested for further study. A variety of contributing authors, including the editor, wrote the first two parts; the editor drew upon the work of the contributing authors as well as that of others in writing the concluding part.

1.2.1 Individual Systems

Since the medium of broadcasting takes no account of national boundaries, it seemed essential to consider all of Africa, not just Independent Africa or Africa South-of-the-Sahara. Our survey, therefore, considers the entire continent, from Cairo to the Cape, and includes the offshore islands as well as the mainland.

The broad scope of the survey involved the problem of dealing with the broadcasting systems of 58 different countries, territories, and dependencies. These 58 in turn embrace some 115 separate administrations under nearly as many different auspices. For although typically each country has one single monolithic government system, actually the range of administrative variations in Africa is still considerable. Nigeria has its federal Nigerian Broadcasting Corporation, but it also has regional services owned by the states and independent of the NBC. The Portuguese territory of Moçambique is alone in having no government station, with all official programming carried by one of several private stations. There were in 1972 more than 40 private, nongovernment radio stations in Africa, most of them owned by radio clubs in the Portuguese territories, but several in independent countries. This is not counting missionary-operated radio stations, of which there were at least seven. A dozen radio installations on African soil are owned by foreign governments—France, Germany, Great Britain, the Netherlands, and the United States. There is even a student-operated station, run by a high school in Moçambique; and a foreign television station, run by the American Forces Radio and Television Service in Ethiopia.

To describe in depth, with equal and uniform detail, each of these services would require an immense and highly repetitive catalog. We have attempted to avoid this outcome, in part by treating the individual systems in clusters, grouping them according to both geography and history. Some grouping is, of necessity, arbitrary: for example, the offshore islands have been treated as a group, though the only similarity between Madagascar and Tristan da Cunha is the fact of insularity. Within the more coherent groups we have encouraged varying emphases, partly as a matter of contributing authors' discretion, partly as a matter of accentuating features of special interest. Thus each of the three ex–British East African countries receives a different emphasis: the Kenya article devotes more than the usual space to broadcasting history because Nairobi had the first station in Tropical Africa; the analysis of Tanzania's system stresses politics because of the special role broadcasting plays in that country's unique political experiment; the treatment of Uganda's system leans on regionalism and polylingualism because these are especially significant problems there. The amount of space given to any one country relative to that given to another has no evaluative significance. The Gambia, for instance, receives more space than several of its near neighbors of much larger size simply because The Gambia was singled out to illustrate problems faced by a minimum-scale broadcasting system.

1.2.2 Cross-System Functions

Part 2 deals with broadcasting in Africa as a continent—that is, with subjects of common interest to individual systems, such as foreign aid, training, research, and educational uses of broadcasting. This organization of subject matter results in some repetition, especially because of multiple authorship. A conspicuous example of recurrence is Ghana's rural farm-forum experiment, first mentioned by Kugblenu in his description of the Ghanaian national broadcasting system (§ 5.2.2). The same subject crops up again as an example of Canadian foreign aid (§ 12.3.4), as an example of an educational application of radio (§ 15.2.1), and as an example of research (§ 16.3.3). This discontinuity may at times put the reader who wants to pursue all aspects of a particular subject to some trouble; hopefully liberal cross-referencing based on the decimal system of chapter, section, and subsection numbering will minimize this inconvenience. We feel it is outweighed, in any event, by the illumination that comes from having the same topic viewed from several different angles and by observers with alternative points of view. It is interesting, for example, to contrast Kolade's view of regional broadcasting in Nigeria, from his standpoint as the chief executive of the federal system (§ 5.1.12), with the view of Wilkinson, from his standpoint as an official of the BBC (§ 12.1.2). Even omissions can be revealing: compare, for example, the African writers' near-silence about foreign aid to their systems with the descriptions of aid projects by writers from donor countries.

1.3 Delimitations

We have tried to make this survey comprehensive within such delimitations as those imposed by feasible length, accessibility of information, and availability of contributing authors. Omissions and abbreviated treatments of specific subjects have been acknowledged at the appropriate points within the text. In particular we regret having had to omit entirely any systematic consideration of broadcasting law and of the economics of receiver manufacture, distribution, and sale; ideal balance would certainly have required more detailed treatment of foreign-aid activities of the Communist countries; and both qualitative and quantitative analyses of programming on a comparative basis would have been highly desirable.

Broadcasting in Africa is inextricably involved with politics. One-party states, military regimes, and other relatively authoritarian forms of government manipulate the media in general, but broadcasting in particular, as conscious instruments of both internal and external policy. Revolutionary movements seeking to free the remaining regions under foreign domination use broadcasting as a weapon of guerrilla warfare. Foreign governments broadcast huge amounts of propaganda into Africa from the outside and seek to influence Africa's own internal broadcasting systems from the inside. We have dealt with some, but certainly not all, of these political involvements. We have pointed out, for example, how and why North African freedom movements used broadcasting in ways that were not possible, in the past, in Tropical Africa; how differing colonial political concepts affected the development of broadcasting; how politics influences the choice of broadcast languages and the structuring of broadcasting systems in terms of local and regional versus national services; how and to what extent foreign governments seek to influence Africans by means of broadcasting; some of the political implications of foreign aid; and the role broadcasting plays in times of political crisis.

On the other hand, we have not in the main attempted to deal with the politics of individual African countries and of guerrilla movements. This omission was a consciously adopted delimitation. Admittedly it was a hard decision. As one critic of the manuscript observed, certain activities can hardly be treated as though they took place in a political vacuum. We agree, but believe that to provide the full political context for all the activities described would require a second volume as long as the present one. We must rely on the perceptive reader to fill in some of the material that belongs between the lines. We feel justified in hoping that the existence of the present book might in fact make it easier for someone to write the future book on broadcasting and politics in Africa.

1.4 African Broadcasting in Brief

1.4.1 Signal Propagation

Broadcasting in Africa is significantly affected by several physical factors unique to the tropical zone. These propagation problems are described in detail by Alfred Barghausen in Appendix 1. In brief, certain kinds of interference peculiar to the tropics affect radio signals using either the medium-wave (in the U.S., "standard broadcast") or the short-wave bands. This interference reduces the useful coverage area of given transmission facilities, relative to the coverage area possible with the same facilities in higher latitudes. Both ground-wave (local) signals and sky-wave (long-distance) signals are affected, the latter particularly in the east-west direction. Further loss of efficiency occurs because detailed information on the ground conductivity of most of the continent is lacking, so that engineers cannot plan medium-wave primary coverage areas scientifically. In any event, the number of medium-wave channels allotted to African countries by International Telecommunication Union agreements is insufficient to allow each country to plan ideal medium-wave radio coverage. In the long term, the solution to Africa's problems of radio broadcast coverage would be the adoption of frequency modulation (FM). Only South Africa has achieved full FM coverage, though over a score of systems incorporate experimental or small-scale FM components (app. 4).

For the present, African domestic broadcasting systems remain heavily dependent on secondary services obtained from sky-wave signals, which are much subject to fading, interference, and eccentric coverage patterns. This explains the stress that has been placed in Africa on extraordinarily high power (up to 15,000 kw.), and on the use of short-wave transmitters even for domestic services—both expedients for achieving distant sky-wave coverage from centralized facilities.

1.4.2 Parameters of Development

The conventional index used to estimate a broadcasting system's relative stage of development is a receiver-to-population ratio expressed as the average number of receivers available for every thousand persons in the population. UNESCO set 50 radio receivers per 1,000 inhabitants as a minimum target level for development in the 1960s (UNESCO 1961b, p. 35). In 1959, according to UNESCO, Africa averaged only 18 radio receivers per thousand inhabitants, as against a world average of 159. By 1969, Africa's index had risen to 45, but the world's index had risen to 232 (UNESCO, *Statistical Yearbook* 1971, p. 806).

However, the receiving facilities are but one of the two essential physical components of a broadcasting system. It is of interest to have some comparative measure of the stage of development reached by transmission facilities as well. UNESCO reports these facilities in terms of numbers of transmitters and their aggregate wattage. These data are significant, of course, but do not lend themselves to a meaningful index such as the receiver/population ratio. Moreover, these summations ignore the critically important factor of the geographical distribution of transmission facilities. Ideally transmitter sites would be so distributed throughout a large country as to supply equally reliable, high-quality *locally transmitted* signals in all parts of the country, with the *potentiality,* at least, for local or regional program origination, reflecting adequately all local interests and cultures.

A rough index of what we might call the "service distribution factor" can be obtained by dividing the area of a country by the number of different transmitter locations it uses. This yields an admittedly crude estimate, for population is not evenly distributed, nor do we have assurance that multiple transmitter sites are spaced for the best possible coverage of the total geographic area. On the other hand, the service distribution index does have the advantage of being based on fairly accurate facts to begin with, whereas the receivers/population ratio, when applied to developing countries, usually rests on highly unreliable estimates.

The mean land area served by each transmitter site on the continent as a whole in 1972, expressed in thousands of square miles, was 96; the range ran from the extremes of 5 for Malawi to 967 for The Sudan (see Appendixes 3 and 4 for sources of underlying data). By way of comparison, the corresponding service distribution index for Czechoslovakia was 2, and for the United States 1.6.

We have reported both the receivers/population ratio and the space/transmittter-site ratio as summarizing statistics at the head of each system description. More detailed demographic and systemic data are supplied in tabular form so as to permit easy comparative analysis in Appendixes 3, 4, and 5.

1.4.3 Descriptive Summary of Systems

Readers already familiar with broadcasting practice in Africa may wish to pass over this section, which is intended for those who have no personal experience of African broadcasting. It summarizes briefly the more obvious contrasts between the domestic systems described here and the systems most familiar in the industrialized west. These differences, be it noted, are more of degree than of kind. Politics, for example, may affect programming in Africa more conspicuously than in some regions, but politics determines the basic character of national broadcasting systems everywhere in the world. Africa's problems of polylingualism may be particularly acute, but such highly developed countries as Belgium, Canada, and Switzerland have these problems as well. What follows sketches generalized features of African systems, without describing any particular system. Moreover, exceptions can be found to nearly all the ensuing generalizations.

Governments own and directly operate stations in Africa, usually as part of a ministry of information or its equivalent. Broadcast employees therefore usually have the status of civil servants. Both transmission and studio facilities in Africa tend to be concentrated in the capital city. Three-quarters of the independent states have broadcast transmitters in four or fewer sites; 18 have only a single transmitter location each. Provincial transmitters, where they do exist, generally use medium waves and have moderate to low power, designed to serve immediate urban environs; rural areas depend on sky-wave service from more powerful medium-wave and short-wave transmitters located at the capital. Radio reception in less heavily populated rural areas is therefore likely to be poor, intermittent, or effectively non-existent. Usually provincial stations repeat the centrally-produced programming, originating little if any local or regional program-ming of their own. Centralization is, of course, even more characteristic of television because of limitations imposed by its line-of-sight propagation path.

Many radio services operate discontinuously, with periods of blackout between morning, midday, and evening program segments. Television usually goes on only in the evening, except for daytime schools television. Radio programming is fragmented still more by the need to divide time among several languages—sometimes as many as a score or more. Segments in minor languages tend to be very short and in some cases are scheduled for only a few minutes once a week.

Programming in general tends to be heavily colored by the concept of "nation building." This means a relatively high percentage of time devoted to educational and hortatory material, dealing with such subjects as literacy, civics, public health, agricultural improvement, cultural traditions, political commentary, and social guidance. Sometimes question-and-answer program series about personal social problems have remarkably high audience appeal because such problems are widespread and urgent in transitional societies. The lack of rural newspapers sometimes obliges radio to assume certain functions ideally more suited to print. For example, long lists of the results of school examinations may be announced over the radio.

Radio programming leans heavily on music, news, and talk formats. From 40% to 60% of television programming is likely to consist of imported syndicated entertainment series such as "Bonanza" and feature films—though African television services have in fact been more successful in developing local programming resources than was at first expected. Locally produced television programs tend toward news, public affairs, discussions, studio games, sports, and the traditional arts of dance, mime, and song.

Politics colors much of the programming. Explicit political material comes in the form of frequent public speeches by major government personalities, official statements and releases, and official commentaries on the news. The movements and ceremonial activities of the head of state or other important political figures receive extensive priority coverage. Some stations maintain special production units with the exclusive assignment of covering presidential appearances.

News copy usually comes to the station from the national news agency, which not only prepares official releases on local happenings but also receives, digests, and redistributes material from foreign news agencies to which it subscribes, such as Agence France Presse, New China News Agency, Reuters, Tass, and United Press International. This centralization of nearly all news sources automatically ensures compliance with government policies with regard to news handling. Some broadcasting stations are allowed to supplement the central news source with their own reporting, but many rely exclusively on the government information service for news copy. As to newsfilm, most television stations have their own film units to cover nearby events. The clientele of the chief foreign newsfilm service, the London-based Visnews Limited, included by mid-1972 all the African television stations with the exception of those in Liberia, Niger, and Upper Volta. Visnews is a worldwide nonprofit news agency, founded in 1957 at the instance of the BBC to forestall overdependence on American news sources (Curran 1972, p. 7). It is owned jointly by the BBC, Reuters, and the broadcasting organizations of Australia, Canada, and New Zealand.

Listeners and viewers usually have limited program choice. The national radio may broadcast two or three services which are simultaneously available in the chief cities, but usually not to the entire country. A good many of the smaller countries have facilities for only one radio service, and certainly a single television channel is the rule. Depending on location, alternative programming may come from spillover signals of transmitters in neighboring states; and listeners with short-wave radios have a choice of many international broadcasts from both African and non-African sources.

If 45 radio sets per thousand inhabitants seems low (§ 1.1), the figure for television is minuscule: only 3.2 sets per thousand (UNESCO, *Statistical Yearbook* 1971, pp. 806, 837). Though the average number of listeners per home radio set is probably high, public group listening seems less common than one might expect. Public group viewing of television, on the other hand, occurs frequently and justifies the assumption that the viewing audience is a good deal larger than the low number of sets at first suggests. Nevertheless, television remains an urban amenity to a much higher degree than radio.

1.5 Bibliographic Conventions

In order to make the book as useful to students of African broadcasting as possible, contributing authors were asked to provide full documentation. To avoid either cluttering the text itself with numerous footnotes or inconveniencing the reader by grouping citations by chapters, we have incorporated citations in the briefest possible form parenthetically at the appropriate points within the text. These shorthand citations refer to a single composite bibliography for the whole volume. Citations to articles in newspapers and journals for which there is no author are listed under the names of the publications themselves—again in order to keep citations within the text brief. Personal letters and ephemeral written material for which neither author nor title could be supplied have been noted within the text only, not listed in the bibliography.

Contributing authors have been credited at the heads of their contributions, which vary in length from whole chapters to short subsections. In each case the position of the credit line—whether at the head of a chapter, a section, or a subsection—indicates the extent of the authorship.

Part 1 National Systems

2   Egypt and the Maghreb

The North African states of Libya, Tunisia, Algeria, Morocco (the four states constituting the Maghreb), and Egypt have long been in continuous and intimate contact with European influences—in ancient times by means of war and merchant ships, now also by means of broadcasts. Major radio transmitters in Europe can reach the North African coast. European television can island-hop across the Inland Sea to bring live programming to North Africa. Maghreb countries even belong to the European Broadcasting Union (§ 13.2.4) and participate in its international program-exchange network, Eurovision. They also have a growing program-exchange service among themselves (Chakroun, 1972).

Constant and long-standing fringe exposure to European cultural and economic influences reinforced the division between the flourishing urban society of the littoral and traditional rural society of the interior. But the Arab nationalistic revival and broadcasting, which roughly coincided in time (Fanon 1965, p. 75), shattered the long isolation of the nomads, the oasis cultivators, and mountain dwellers of the remote interior. The North African countries suffer less from the isolating, balkanizing influences of tribalism than most of Sub-Saharan Africa. The great unifying influences of a common religion, Islam, and a common sacred language, Arabic, enable broadcasting to achieve a kind of universality impossible in countries with dozens of different languages, religions, and cultural traditions. Broadcasts in Arabic have common meaning and fascination, not only for the majority of the inhabitants of a single country, but for the peoples of the entire North African and Middle Eastern regions.

In a sense Islam and broadcasting seem made for each other. The taboos of Islamic social life, such as the segregation of women and the prohibition against alcohol, combined with poverty to render existence for the average citizen singularly monotonous. Broadcasting filled a social vacuum: "The physical and psychological isolation of the sexes, the scarcity of mixed social institutions, the rarity of clubs, theatres, dance halls, and so on, make listening to the radio the only relaxation" (Loya 1962, p. 100).

15

Arab leaders welcomed educational broadcasting as a noncontroversial way of overcoming the traditional insulation of women from the world. Women often form the majority audience for literacy and other adult-education broadcasts. For example, 70% of the participants in an Egyptian radio literacy course were women, "who can only be reached in their homes in this way" (Maddison 1971, p. 18).

These special advantages of radio in Arab societies enabled broadcasting to play a significant role in the independence struggles of North African countries:

> . . . radio ended Morocco's isolation from the outside world and allowed the poor and powerless to establish connections with Islamic reform and modernity in the Middle East . . . shortwave radio, especially, provided the external link which stirred up hopes that Morocco would win its struggle for independence. News broadcasts, United Nations debates, and statements issued by exiled nationalist leaders and broadcast over the Voice of the Arabs from Cairo, all turned the airwaves into a means of communion with popular heroes. [Schaar 1968, pp. 1–2]

In his classic study of traditional village life in Tunisia, *Change at Shebika,* Duvignaud constantly alludes to the transistor radio, an ever present influence in the lives of isolated, illiterate peasants who otherwise would have no way of gaining any concept of their membership in a modern nation-state: "With Independence and through such new technical devices as the radio (especially the transistor type which was indispensable to the wars of independence in both Tunisia and Algeria, particularly the latter) there came the factor of 'news,' of the 'word' which unified and indeed even created the nation" (Duvignaud 1970, p. 289).

Algeria, the last of the Maghreb countries to win independence, and the one which met the most violent colonial opposition, benefited in its independence struggle from the encouragement received by radio from its neighbors. "This Is the Voice of Algeria," a chapter in *Studies in a Dying Colonialism,* gives us a unique analysis of how the war transformed the radio receiver from an alien artifact into a prized symbol of freedom as valuable as a gun (Fanon 1965, pp. 69–97).

The Voice of the Arabs, Egypt's external service, dates back to 1953, and was in fact the voice of Gamal Abdel Nasser, the late Egyptian president. His David-and-Goliath performance against the great powers in the confrontation over control of the Suez Canal had somewhat the same inspirational symbolic meaning for all Africans as the performance of the nineteenth-century Ethiopian emperor Menelik in defeating the Italians at Adowa. The U.S. Central Intelligence Agency is said to have made a study of Radio Cairo's propaganda in 1956 and to have confirmed that Nasser was getting his message across with devastating success. So successful was he, in fact, that the United States is said to have considered strategems for countering Radio Cairo—even the drastic one of blowing it up; a milder proposal was to develop a competing radio service in the region, but "building a broadcasting capability to match that of Cairo would be like trying to transplant Hollywood to Des Moines, Iowa" (Copeland 1969, pp. 247–48). This last alludes to the reservoir of artistic talent available to broadcasting based upon well-established motion-picture and music industries centered in Cairo—another distinguishing feature which sets broadcasting in North Africa somewhat apart from broadcasting in Tropical Africa.

Cairo's propaganda is aimed not at the Arab world of the Maghreb and the Middle East alone. Its facilities have been made freely available to dissident groups from the rest of Africa to the south, some representing countries still under foreign domination, others representing revolutionary movements in the more conservative of the independent countries. Large Muslim populations all down the African coasts, east and west, and in the tier of states immediately south of the North African group provide further ready-made audience potentialities for Radio Cairo.

2.1 Egypt, by Timothy Green

Population: 34,200,000	Radio transmitter sites: 10
Receivers per thousand: 146	Area per site: 39,000 sq mi

2.1.1 Introduction

Traveling through Egypt, one never seems to be out of earshot of a radio; in shops, cafes, and bazaars transistor radios chatter constantly. The long-drawn-out struggle with Israel has made the Egyptians hypersensitive to any fresh nuance of crisis, always eager to hear what their president has been saying or doing. The gossip flies swiftly the moment an interesting item breaks. "We are a very political people," a leading Egyptian broadcaster remarked to me in Cairo, "we want to know all the time what America or Russia or Israel are up to. Radio is the key means of keeping in touch. Television still isn't a mass medium; the *fellahin* don't see it."

But radio reaches them all the time. Since about 1950, with the active encouragement of the late President Nasser, broadcasting in Egypt has developed not only into the most comprehensive and influential system in the Arab world, but into one of the most ambitious anywhere. The Egyptian Broadcasting Corporation operates no fewer than seven domestic radio services, together with the powerful Voice of the Arabs station cover-

Timothy Green is a free-lance writer, former head of the *Life* London Bureau, and author of *The Universal Eye: The World of Television,* a global survey published in 1972. Some portions of § 2.1.5 are reprinted, with the permission of Stein & Day, from the above volume, pp. 193–96.

ing the whole Arab world, and a wide range of other services in many languages.

Television, although not yet a mass medium, has not been neglected. Egypt has three television networks, one covering all the densely populated areas, a second within reach of about 90% of the population, and a third in English and French for foreigners living in Cairo and Alexandria. No other Arab or African nation offers such a comprehensive service. The limitations on television are that the cost of a set, about $250, is beyond the means of millions of Egyptians and that, even if they could afford sets, electrification does not yet extend beyond the main cities and towns. There are nearly 600,000 sets, or one for every 60 people, a far deeper penetration than in any other African country. However, both radio and television coverage are aided by the fact that, although Egypt sprawls over a vast 387,000 square miles of North Africa, 96% of that terrain is desert or marshland; most of the 35-million population is crammed into the Nile Valley and the Delta. Almost a third of the population lives in or around Cairo and Alexandria alone. Reaching it does not call for a highly sophisticated or costly network; reaching out to remote scattered villages in the desert does. For television the only answer may be some kind of satellite distribution, but that does not seem likely for the 1970s (see § 18.5.2). For the decade of the 1970s radio should retain its preeminence as the first line of communication.

2.1.2 History

Radio began in Egypt in 1926. At first a number of private commercial stations appeared in Cairo and Alexandria, bent mainly on making money quickly. But they gave way in the early 1930s to the Egyptian Broadcasting Corporation, under the control of the government. The new corporation, formally inaugurated in 1934, proceeded slowly with development of a nationwide network. Two services were operated: one in Arabic was on the air 14 hours a day, from 6:00 A.M. to 10:00 A.M., from noon to 3:00 P.M. and from 4:00 P.M. to 11:00 P.M. The second service, broadcast for four hours daily, was aimed entirely at foreigners living in Cairo and Alexandria; its programs were in French and English.

The real impetus for expansion came only after the overthrow of the monarchy in 1952. After the revolution, and particularly once young Colonel Nasser emerged as the undoubted leader of Egypt, broadcasting suddenly became a vital means of welding the new country together into a coherent nation and making its influence felt as a vital force throughout the Middle East. Radio networks grew; the number of broadcast hours jumped from 18 daily in 1952 to 49½ by 1955, and to 94 by 1960. As Mohamed Mahmoud Shaaban, the chairman of Egyptian radio, put it, "After the July revolution of 1952 the renaissance in broadcasting started" (Shaaban 1971).

A new broadcasting law was enacted that charged the Egyptian Broadcasting Corporation with achieving the following ends:

1. To enhance the standard of all kinds of arts.
2. To strengthen the national consciousness as well as the social cooperative feeling, to promote the sense of cooperation between individuals and groups; to encourage favourable habits and customs and to discourage improper ones.
3. To participate in the educational campaign among the people, and to follow up the intellectual and artistic activities among the cultivated circles.
4. To deal with social problems and to exhort adherence to moral and ethical values.
5. To revive the literary, scientific and artistical Arab Heritage.
6. To acquaint the people with the best products of human civilization.
7. To enlighten public opinion about internal and external news and to inform it of the various world trends.
8. To bring the Arab Republic of Egypt and the Arab world to the notice of foreign countries.
9. To promote talents in every field of intellect and inventiveness.
10. To promote relations between the residing compatriots and those who left the country.
11. To entertain the compatriots.

A rather long-winded and idealistic list of aims, but they show the new sense of purpose in broadcasting in Egypt and have been used to justify the great expansion in facilities.

The most tangible evidence of this development is the enormous radio and television center on the Corniche, on the banks of the Nile right in the heart of Cairo. There, a vast circular building of eleven television and 43 radio studios is crowned with a 28-story block of offices. Few countries can boast such elaborate facilities; indeed, only in North America, Britain, France, the Soviet Union, and Japan are there broadcasting headquarters on such a grand scale. Some 4,500 program staff and about 5,000 engineering personnel are employed—rather more people, as far as I can calculate, than are employed in broadcasting by all other Arab (or African) nations put together.

This veritable empire is formally under the wing of the Ministry of Information and Culture. The corporation is actually presided over by a president, who is appointed by, and is responsible to, the minister and a board of governors. This board includes the minister himself, the corporation president, and the four chairmen of the main broadcasting divisions—radio, television, engineering, and finance.

Government control is strong at all times. President Nasser, of course, was always shown by both radio and television in the best light. Broadcasting, Nasser realized long before most other Middle East leaders, is a powerful political weapon. Under Nasser a new set of directives was issued, replete with ringing phrases—"United efforts for the success of Arab nationalism and to resist imperialism . . . Throw light on the glories of our Arab history . . . heroic feats and the life of our heroes, leaders and pioneers who stood in the face of colonialist tyrants" (quoted in Dizard 1966, p. 148).

While he never used broadcasting personally to the same extent as Fidel Castro, whose television harangues in Cuba in the early 1960s are legendary, Nasser's daily round was closely attended by microphones and cameras (see Dizard 1966, pp. 132–54). Television was especially important in cultivating the Nasser image. As a senior Egyptian broadcaster put it to me in Cairo, "Nasser himself was not really known by our people until we had television. Before that they had only *heard* him on radio, but after 1960 everyone *saw* him. . . . Everything was done to give him dignity" (cp. § 10.6.6).

President Sadat has followed this tradition. And he has made sure that broadcasting has been firmly in the hands of his own personal supporters. After a political crisis in May 1971, when a potential coup by his vice-president, Aly Sabry, apparently got as far as surrounding the radio and television center with "friendly" policemen with orders to keep Sadat from entering, several leading executives, including the director of the main television channel, were hastily replaced. But these changes are detail; radio and television in Egypt remain in the image in which President Nasser created them. He was the architect.

2.1.3 Domestic Radio Services

In 1972 the Egyptian Broadcasting Corporation was operating 11 different radio services, seven of them for local audiences, the rest directed primarily at the world outside. In all, they were putting out a formidable 1,242 hours of programs each week—an average of 177 hours a day—a task that called for a program staff of over 2,000.

The cost of this extensive operation was met from three sources. First, a tax equal to a half a cent per kilowatt hour on everyone's electricity bill (a highly unusual way of raising broadcasting revenue); second, a government subsidy; and, finally, a limited number of commercials on three of the 11 radio services. The commercials yield about $450,000 a year. The total broadcast budget in 1971 was stated to be about $4.5 million, but the exact amount of government subsidy to radio for its overseas services is not clearly revealed. Radio was financed by license fees until 1960, but they were then replaced by the electricity tax. There is no accurate set count, but it is generally assumed to be about 5 million, or one radio among seven people. According to an Arab States Broadcasting Union survey, at least 80% of families even in rural areas had radios in 1970.

The mainstay of the radio services is the general program, broadcast on both medium and short wave, which is on the air for just over 20 hours daily—from 6:00 A.M. until shortly after 2:00 A.M. the following morning. This is the corporation's original program service, which started in 1935 and remains its flagship. Although directed primarily to the people of Egypt, it can be heard in several neighboring Arab countries. It is a reasonably lightweight service, with almost half its program time given over to entertainment. The Egyptians have always been alert to the fact that, while they may be using broadcasting as a means of propaganda, it must be also entertaining. As the chairman of radio told a broadcasting conference in Cairo, "Our social conditions require a lot of guidance; and the best form of guidance is the light one that goes straight to the heart and opens it to culture" (Shaaban 1971).

The composition of programs on the general service is: 46% entertainment, 20% news and information, 10% religious, 9% cultural (talks, seminars, literary lectures or discussions), 7% service (e.g., special broadcasts for farmers), 7% drama and 1% education. As this breakdown suggests, it is not a highbrow service.

Culture comes in more strongly in the "second" program, which is broadcast on medium wave only, for 3½ hours each evening. The aims of this service are, according to the chairman of radio: "To meet the taste of the cultured and at the same time enhance the cultural level of the ordinary listener, through presenting refined items covering scientific, literary and artistical fields" (Shaaban 1971). More than 75% of all the programs are described as "cultural," with drama constituting a further 20%. Although the emphasis is heavily on the Arab cultural heritage, the service does look at modern developments in art, music, and theater throughout the world.

The most direct domestic by-product of the resurgence of broadcasting after the 1952 revolution is the People's Program, which began on 25 July 1959. This service, on the air on medium wave for 9½ hours daily, is charged with serving the "development of the working class." Primarily, it puts out specialized programs for farmers, industrial workers, the police, the armed forces, and youth. Each evening at 7:00, for instance, there is a 15-minute rural magazine, "Our Countryside," which advises on everything from the marketing of crops to the establishing of farming cooperatives, from the treating of animal diseases to hygiene and family planning. The overall pattern for the People's Program, in percentages, is: information and news, 28; entertainment, 12; religion, 10; services, 10; culture, 10; drama, 10; education, 8; and unclassified, 12. This service does accept commercials, but there are very few of them, for the People's Program does not appeal to a mass audience with purchasing power. Advertising takes up only 0.11% of air time and in 1970 brought a mere $3,750 in revenue.

This new concern for the working people has not led to the neglect of the many foreigners who have always made Cairo and Alexandria extremely cosmopolitan cities. The first service created by the Egyptian Broadcasting Corporation in 1934 was in English and French for European expatriates; it continues, considerably expanded, today. It is on the air for 13 hours daily. But its character has changed since the revolution in 1952. Prior to that upheaval it was controlled by foreigners for foreigners. Nowadays, according to the chairman of radio, "Its main activity is presenting a true picture of Arab society and of the political, cultural, social, economic and industrial changes that have occurred" (Shaaban 1971). Programs are broadcast in six languages: English, French, German, Italian, Greek, and Armenian. Every morning between 7 and 8 the news is given in five languages and is often followed later in the day by multilingual commentaries. The news is heavily political and almost inevitably leads off with the president's activities that day and a full rundown of the latest moves in the confrontation with Israel. The editorials in the commentaries afterward do not mince words. Those I have heard are usually intent on cataloging how the Israelis in concert with the Americans and the British are intent on dividing the Arab world, which is fighting back gallantly against the crushing forces of imperialism.

Much more soothing is the newest radio service, which opened on medium wave on 9 March 1968, putting out Arabic music—both popular and classical—for 15 hours a day. Most of the time it is nonstop popular music, but about a quarter of the music is classical. This service carries no news.

A second highly specialized service broadcasts readings from the Qur'an or explanations of Qur'anic texts, nonstop for 13½ hours daily on both medium and short wave. This religious network started in 1964 and appeals mainly to the older generation. Initially, the program consisted almost entirely of Qur'an readings, but its scope has been expanded to include daily lectures from mosques and the answering of listeners' questions on interpretations of the Qur'anic text. The program is also aimed at "protecting the Qur'an from enemy distortionist campaigns" and "intellectually thwarting all devices of propaganda used by international Zionism" (Shaaban 1971).

Another offshoot of the postrevolution era is a local station in Alexandria. When it opened in July 1954 it was billed as the forerunner of a series of local radio stations, but up to 1972 there had been no others. The station is on the air for almost eight hours daily on medium wave and concentrates on entertainment (43%) and local news and views. It accepts commercials, mostly from local advertisers in the city, which bring in about $30,000 a year. The advertisements, however, hardly intrude, for they account for a mere 2.57% of air time, and program sponsorship is not permitted.

2.1.4 External Services

A local program of a rather different kind is Sudan Corner, which goes out for 6⅓ hours daily on medium wave and is directed both to the many Sudanese living in Egypt and to the Sudan itself. This program places considerable emphasis on news and information (26%), while the major part of the air time is given over to entertainment.

The Sudanese can, of course, also listen to Cairo's powerful Voice of the Arabs, the most energetic propaganda outlet in the Middle East. The service started in July 1953 with a modest one hour a day, but by 1972 it had expanded on both medium and short wave to 26 hours daily. It is the flagship station of the Arab renaissance. The chairman of Egyptian radio, outlining its aims in Cairo in 1971, listed them as: (1) The true representation of the pains and hopes of the masses throughout the Arab nation; (2) working for the union of the Arabs and mustering their forces against their enemies, in an attempt to bring about their ultimate unity; and (3) calling for the liberation of the Arab countries from imperialism and its lackeys (Shaaban 1971). The emphasis is on news and information (23%) and entertainment (53%). While the majority of programs are directed to the Arab masses at large, the Voice of the Arabs also puts out specialized programs for those Arabs living in Palestine (i.e., Israel), and for the peoples of the Arabian Peninsula and the Maghreb region of North Africa.

Voice of the Arabs has a companion service, Middle East Radio, also directed at the whole Arab world. It started in May 1964 and goes out on medium and short wave for 12½ hours daily. Its politics are much less strident, and it is conceived primarily for entertainment (63% of program time). The station is commercial and seeks to copy the brisk, peppy style of commercial radio in the United States. With a potential Arab audience of almost 100 million it is the prime medium used by international advertisers to sell their products throughout the Middle East. The commercials are for everything from Kent cigarettes to Sanyo radios and Danish poultry. Advertising rates range from $14.35 per spot for a series of 52 spots of 15 seconds to $24.25 for the same number of 60-second spots. The income from advertisements in 1970 was substantial— $420,000.

While Voice of the Arabs and Middle East Radio are directed at other Arab countries (together with a considerable audience within Egypt itself), the Egyptian Broadcasting Corporation also puts out extensive African and overseas services. These programs, started in 1953, are aimed at presenting the Arab cause to the world at large. In 1971 they went out on short wave in 33 languages in addition to Arabic, for a total of 46½ hours daily. Among the overseas specialist programs are regular lessons in Arabic, which were started in 1966.

Amidst this wide spectrum of radio programs the one topic that has been consistently neglected is education. Despite pressing problems of illiteracy and the need for widespread advice on simple health and hygiene, especially in rural areas, radio has not been fully harnessed to meet this challenge. Of all the radio services only the People's Program devotes time to education—about 8% of its total. At least this lack is now recognized, but it is primarily television that is attempting to fill the gap.

2.1.5 Television

The Egyptians have been the pacesetters for television in the Arab world. President Nasser realized the potential value of the medium in helping to build Egypt into a new nation in the late 1950s. And in one of the first agreements signed with the United States government after the clash over the building of the Aswan Dam, Egypt received a loan enabling a contract with the Radio Corporation of America to provide Egypt with a television network and the capacity to manufacture sets. Four-fifths of the sets sold in Egypt are now assembled there. Thus, the Americans, having surrendered to the Russians the opportunity to build the great dam on the Nile, came back to provide Egypt with television. Since the work went ahead at the time of Egypt's brief union with Syria, RCA also installed television in Damascus at the same time.

From the start the Egyptians did everything on a grand scale. Their immense radio and television center, completed in 1960, houses 11 television studios. The largest is 1,000 square meters and is equipped with a revolving stage and five black-and-white cameras. There are two other large studios, each 400 square meters. Two outside broadcast units are available. More than 2,500 program staff and over 1,000 engineers are exclusively employed in television. Almost half the program staff, incidentally, are women, who seem to enjoy complete equality with men. They direct, read the news, and even conduct sports interviews. A French-Egyptian agreement announced in 1971 looked toward introduction of the SECAM color-television system; if carried out this agreement would make Egypt the eighth country in the world to use SECAM and the first country in Africa to have color television.

Initially, television was financed by direct government grant, but in 1969 an annual license fee of $15 was introduced. In 1972 sets in use approached 600,000, yielding almost $9 million a year. Additional revenue of about $1.2 million came from commercials, which were confined to a limited number of spot positions, with no program sponsorship permitted. Program sales to other Arab countries brought in about $600,000 a year.

While most nations begin their television modestly with one channel on the air for a few hours each night, the Egyptians started out with three channels and were soon putting out a total of 24 hours of programs daily. This was later cut back to an average of 18 hours a day.

The first channel covers all the populated areas of the country and could be seen by an estimated 98% of the population if unlimited sets were available. The second channel reaches throughout the Nile Delta (where the majority of the set-owning population live), including Cairo and Alexandria. The third channel is just for Cairo and is given over entirely to programs in English and French for the diplomatic community and other foreigners living in Egypt. Many Egyptian broadcasters feel that this third channel is something of a luxury for a poor country; in fact, it was closed down for almost a year after the death of President Nasser, in 1970, but was revived in October 1971.

Both the Arabic channels are on the air for seven hours daily from Saturday through Thursday; they open at 5:00 P.M. and close about midnight. On Friday, the Muslim day of prayer, the first channel starts at 4:00 P.M. and continues until 1:00 A.M. The first channel concentrates on popular entertainment, news, and sports, while the second channel mainly carries minority programs and imported serials. Some 60% of the programs are locally produced. Unlike many other African or Arab countries, which have little theatrical or cinema talent to fall back on in seeking to create their own programs, Egypt has long had a lively film industry. At least 35 hours of filmed series are made each year. The budgets, compared with those possible in other African countries, are lavish. Between $7,000 and $10,000 is spent on a half-hour film, with three days devoted to shooting and a further two days to studio dubbing.

All the serials keep clear of overt political controversy. "We avoid politics," one director told me. "We try to do sentimental subjects or conflicts that are nothing to do with political ideas." One long-running saga was about the foibles of an aging Cairo schoolmaster and his family who had an endless succession of visits from relatives living in remote villages of the Nile Delta. Another popular serial in 10 half-hour episodes, presented in 1971, was "Ba'ad al 'Adhab" ("After Suffering"), which told of a young girl, married to an elderly rich businessman, who fell in love with a boy of her own age.

Such dramas have proved popular, not only in Egypt, but throughout the Arab world, so that Cairo has developed as a major source of syndicated television programs for smaller Arab nations. Egyptian entertainment can be seen nightly on screen from Kuwait to Khartoum, from Baghdad to Aden. For the Egyptians, of course, this is an ideal way of extending their influence by means of television throughout the Arab world. Although, as we have said, these sentimental and melodramatic serials are innocent of overt propaganda, they nevertheless have considerable implicit propaganda value, depicting as they do, in the background, an Egypt of ideal harmony, prosperity, and benevolence. Other Arab nations are fully aware of this. Some, like Saudi Arabia and little sheikdoms of the Arabian Gulf, prefer instead to pick up most of their programs from

Beirut, the other main production center of the Middle East, where they are made by a commercial station, Télé-Orient, which is out to make profit, not propaganda.

Along with the homemade dramas, Egyptian television also carries a limited selection of imported American and British series, including in 1972 "Nanny and the Professor," "The Addams Family," "The Avengers," "The Fugitive," and "Lancer"—all shown with Arabic subtitles because the cost of dubbing is too high. But once they have been subtitled, they are then bicycled on to other Arab countries. Egyptian television normally pays $150 an hour for the average imported series.

Egypt's military involvement with the Soviet Union was reflected in the screening of many programs from Communist countries. During May 1971, for instance, Egyptian television was offering a Bulgarian series about a resistance hero, a Czech documentary on industrial safety, and a Hungarian ballet.

News is given considerable emphasis. The first channel runs 15 minutes of news at 6:30 each evening, with the main bulletin following at 9:00 and a final five-minute summary at 11:30. The second channel carries a 30-minute "Twenty-Four Hours" news magazine at 8:00 each evening. Visnews and UPI-ITN services are taken. In 1972, however, there was no direct link either by satellite or landline to the Eurovision network of Western Europe, so that all news film had to come in by air freight and was therefore normally one day late. Despite the Soviet military presence and the admixture of Communist-produced television programs in the entertainment schedule, Egyptian news programming was not perceptibly influenced by Communist propaganda. There seemed to be no inclination to substitute the Soviet TASS for the British Visnews or other Western news agencies.

Sponsorship of television programs is not permitted, and spot commercials are limited to a total of 15 minutes before 9:00 P.M. and a further 15 minutes between then and midnight, averaging five minutes in any one hour. In 1972 the highest one-time rates for 60-second spots were $324 on Channel I, $268 on Channel II, and $72 on Channel III.

Since 1968, Egyptian television has put increased emphasis on educational television, especially on the second channel. They hoped by the mid-1970s to be able to turn this channel over entirely to education. These efforts have met with considerable opposition from the education authorities. As far back as 1961 Egyptian television tried to persuade the educators to use television in schools but met with little response. On their own initiative the broadcasters went ahead with their own schools programs for one hour a day, five days a week. These were later extended to three hours every day. They were mainly of an enrichment character in languages, mathematics, and physics and were aimed at the secondary level.

Gradually the education authorities have overcome their initial reserve about television; so the schools programs have been planned increasingly with the help and support of the Ministry of Education. A special five-week pilot project in 25 Cairo secondary schools early in 1970 was a forerunner of plans to start educational television on a national scale. The pilot scheme included lessons in physics, chemistry and biology, English grammar and usage, and five episodes of a simplified version of Dickens's *Tale of Two Cities*. The Ministry of Education was so impressed by this experiment that it immediately inaugurated a plan for regular TV lessons for schools for three hours a day. The ministry also bought 250 TV sets and installed them in secondary schools. To aid this development Britain's Overseas Development Agency contributed $200,000 for an educational-TV studio.

This initiative on schools television has also been matched by adult-education programs to combat illiteracy. A nationwide trial project in 1969 led to the formation of 300 viewing groups of 20 persons each. At the same time Egyptian television has persuaded some farming cooperatives to buy communal sets so that farmers can watch special programs on new agricultural techniques, family planning, and social development. As many as 1,000 communal sets are now in use, with cooperatives viewing a thrice-weekly farming program.

Although in 1972 it was still too early for many of these educational programs to have had any profound effect, their very existence showed how a television service can press ahead with educational television without much encouragement from other government departments. A UNESCO mission which visited Egypt in December 1970 to study the possible use of satellites for education and national development in the Arab states drew attention to these achievements in its report, which praised "the forward-looking and innovative role played by the national television service in taking upon itself the responsibility of proving in practical terms the opportunities provided by educational television" (Ploman, Berrada, and Clergerie 1971). This determination was underlined when I talked to the director of television a few months later. "In an underdeveloped country we must make the maximum use of television in all forms of education" he said. "We propose during the next two or three years to turn our second channel over completely to education for schools during the day and for adults during the evening."

Egypt is equally determined to maintain her leadership and influence in broadcasting throughout the Arab world. While some of her own broadcasting personnel are trained in such countries as Britain and East Germany, broadcasters from other Arab countries study at the Egyptian Broadcasting Corporation's own training center in Cairo. This center offers a general three-month course, either in radio or in television, for beginners.

Egypt's influence is also likely to be extended by means of the Arab States Broadcasting Union, which was created in Cairo in 1969. The Egyptians were most active in its establishment, and the very fact that its headquarters is in Cairo means that they remain the moving spirit behind it. The aims of the union include the interchange of programs among Arab countries, the creation of an Arab television news agency, and the coordination of the requirements of all Arab countries (just as the EBU does in Western Europe) for coverage of major news or sports events. In all these activities Egypt is well placed for the role of prime coordinator. The union is, of course, intergovernmental, and its aims are partly political (unlike the EBU or the Asian Broadcasting Union), but it makes no secret of this fact. "We are created within the framework of the Arab League," the managing director told me. "Of course we are under the influence of governments—but you show me broadcasters who are not in some way. We are a natural union sharing a common culture and language" (Green 1972, p. 202; for further discussion of the ASBU see § 13.2.3).

2.2 The Maghreb, by Ali Z. Elgabri

The Maghreb (Arabic, "land of the sunset," i.e., the west) comprises the four North African countries bordering the Mediterranean Sea to the west of Egypt—specifically, Libya, Tunisia, Algeria, and Morocco. Broadcasting in the Maghreb countries has to contend with far less ethnic and linguistic diversity than it does in most of Sub-Saharan Africa. Ethnically, the Maghreb consists basically of the remnants of the Berber stock which occupied the region in ancient times, and the descendants of Arab invaders from the east. Berber and Arabic dialects are spoken, with Arabic and Islamic culture providing a nearly universal common denominator.

2.2.1 Libya

Population: 1,900,000	Radio transmitter sites: 6
Receivers per thousand: 53	Area per site: 113,000 sq mi

The first country to the west of Egypt is Libya, which became an Italian colony in 1911. Italy gave up her claims in the aftermath of World War II, and Libya became fully independent in 1951. Libya started independent life as a kingdom, but the army deposed the king in September 1969, forming the Libyan Arab Republic. This event transformed Libya from one of the most conservative Arab countries into one of the most

Ali Z. Elgabri is Associate Professor, Departments of Speech-Communications and Cinema-Photography, Ohio State University, and was Cinema Instructor, Cairo College of Applied Arts, 1958–61. His Ph.D. dissertation (1967) was on mass media in national development.

militant. A characteristic expression of the way in which Arab militancy seeks to exploit the media is found in the following statement of broadcasting objectives published by the Libyan Ministry of Information:

1. To embody the Arab Revolutionary objectives of freedom, socialism, and unity and to permeate such objectives in the minds of the people;
2. To stress the fact that Libya is an integral part of the Arab homeland;
3. To tie up the Arab struggle to liberate the occupied Arab territories with the cause of freedom and liberation in the Third World. . . . [Libyan Arab Republic 1971, p. 81]

While the French had encouraged early development of broadcasting in the other Maghreb countries, Libya remained without radio even after independence. UNESCO gave substantial assistance in starting the service, conducting a preliminary survey in 1955 and helping to get it on the air in 1957. At first it broadcast three hours a day (Codding 1959, p. 56).

With the discovery of oil in 1959 Libya's economic outlook changed abruptly for the better, and this change was reflected in a great increase in broadcasting facilities and programming. The 1970–71 budget allocated almost $3.5 million to broadcasting (Libyan Arab Republic 1970, p. 243). In 1971 the domestic service, in Arabic, was on the air more than 18 hours a day, utilizing transmitters at Bayda, Benghazi, Derna, and Tobruk in addition to the main transmitter site at Tripoli. Programs originated at only two locations, Tripoli and Benghazi, the other stations acting as repeaters. Libya boasts two superpower medium-wave transmitters rated at 1,000 kw. each. In addition to the Arabic domestic service there is a "European" domestic service in English, French, and Italian.

Prior to construction of their own television service, Libyans in the vicinity of Tripoli could receive programs from the American Forces Radio and Television Service station at Wheelus Air Force Base, which the Americans evacuated in mid-1970. They could also pick up Italian television in the vicinity of Tripoli. Libya's own system was started in 1968 at Benghazi and Tripoli, toward the western and eastern ends of the coastal strip, respectively. The British Broadcasting Corporation gave substantial help, sending 26 staff members to assist with the launching of television and seconding 17 for a full year (*BBC Record* 1968, pp. 1–2). In 1972, six repeater stations were under construction (*Television Factbook* 1972–73, p. 1082b).

2.2.2 Tunisia

Population: 5,200,000	Radio transmitter sites: 2
Receivers per thousand: 77	Area per site: 32,000 sq mi

Tunisia, much the smallest of the Maghreb quartet, is wedged between Libya and Algeria, separating their common border for a short distance inland. It is also the most homogeneous of the Maghreb states, both ethnically and linguistically, which of course makes it the more easily served by a national broadcasting service (Reese et al. 1970, p. 57). The French assumed control in Tunisia in 1883. Agitation for independence started in the 1930s, but it was not granted until 1956. The French had introduced radio in 1930.

In 1971 Tunisia had radio stations at two locations—Tunis, the capital, and Sfax, a major coastal town in the southeast, which carried its own local program on one transmitter, the national program on another. The national and local services were scheduled from early morning to late night. No separate external service was programmed, but the national service, on short wave, was directed both to the rest of North Africa and to the Middle East. A domestic "international service," transmitted from Tunis, carried programs in French and Italian.

Tunisia's television service began in 1966 from Tunis. Between 1967 and 1971 eight repeater stations were installed, giving Tunisia one of the more elaborate television networks in Africa (*Television Factbook* 1972–73, pp. 1095b–96b). TV signals reach virtually all inhabited parts of the country, a rare achievement in African television. An automatic relay installed near Tunis enables picking up and rebroadcasting European television signals (*Middle East and North Africa, 1971–1972*, p. 624). The relay station receives signals from an Italian station on the small island of Pantelleria, about midway between Sicily and the Tunisian capital. The Italians installed the relay for the 1960 Olympic games and afterward gave it to Tunisia (NAEB 1968, p. 84).

When UNESCO published the results of a 1969 world survey of the uses of broadcasting in literacy training, a Tunisian project was selected as one of three which deserved extended treatment (Maddison 1971, pp. 61–68). The literacy project was carefully designed, with preexperimental and experimental phases running two years before the implementation phase began in 1969–70. An interesting aspect is its coordinated use of *both* radio and television. In the experimental year 30-minute television programs were scheduled five days a week, with 15-minute supplementary radio programs six days. Subjects covered were reading, arithmetic, history/geography, and civics/religion (see § 15.2.5 for further discussion of this project).

Radio from outside the country played an important role in fanning the revolutionary fires of the Tunisian independence movement, and broadcasting continued to have important political functions after independence. The director of the broadcasting corporation was made a member of the ruling party's Political Bureau to ensure that broadcasting would respond sensitively to political needs (Reese et al. 1970, p. 217). Later the government exempted television sets from customs duty—a strong indication of the value placed on the medium, for government treasuries rarely surrender sources of income once they have been established. In the early years of independence President Habib Bourgiba addressed the nation every week on the radio. The transistor set linked the remote nomad and oasis cultivator of the interior (60% of the population) to the citified Tunisian of the coast; it built up pride in being more than just a member of a village or of a tribe—the pride of being something new, a Tunisian: "Hasn't the radio said that more and more foreigners are coming to admire the country and to present their respects to Rais Habib? Everywhere in the world Tunis is admired, so the radio tells them. The radio says also that everyone must be agreeable to the visitors and let them go where they wish without being disturbed" (Duvignaud 1970, p. 192).

2.2.3 Algeria

Population: 13,800,000	Radio transmitter sites: 12
Receivers per thousand: 51	Area per site: 77,000 sq mi

For African countries where large numbers of Europeans settled, independence came, if at all, only with great difficulty, and often with bloodshed. Algeria shares this characteristic with such countries as Kenya, Rhodesia, and South Africa. Algeria's physical proximity to France, its mild climate, and its agricultural productivity naturally attracted French immigrants. More than a century of occupation began in 1830. Algeria became officially an integral part of France in 1898, with its own representatives in the metropolitan legislature. But the Algerians themselves were not allowed to share in the economic and political benefits of union. Their revolution started in 1954 and lasted through more than seven years of bitter armed conflict. Some of the French settlers ultimately formed the Organization de l'Armée Secrète (OAS), a terroristic third force which turned against France itself as well as against the Algerian revolutionaries when it became evident that France was preparing to relinquish control.

Radio played an important role in Algeria's bloody struggle for independence from France and French colonizers. Fanon described the tremendous impact of Arab broadcasts both from outside Algeria and from the clandestine Voice of Fighting Algeria. The latter, according to Fanon, "was to be of capital importance in consolidating and unifying the people";

writing in 1959, he predicted that "the radio will have an exceptional importance in the country's building phase." The French tacitly acknowledged radio's importance to the liberation movement by going to great lengths to jam its broadcasts: "A new form of struggle had come into being. . . . In the course of a single broadcast a second station, broadcasting over a different wavelength, would relay the first jammed station. The listener, enrolled in the battle of the waves, had to figure out the tactics of the enemy, and in an almost physical way circumvent the strategy of the adversary" (Fanon 1965, pp. 84, 85, 97).

To complicate matters still further, the intransigent French OAS also regularly used clandestine radio transmissions in its campaign (see app. 2 for a description of a dramatic incident in this radio warfare). Independence finally came in 1962, and on the order of a million settlers— mostly skilled workers and professionals—returned to France, leaving behind a crippled Algerian economy and infrastructure. But it is said that to this day Algerians still tend to follow radio programs with special attentiveness, a habit developed during the days when they secretly tuned in Radio Tunis, Cairo's Voice of the Arabs, and the Voice of Fighting Algeria to learn the latest news about the progress of their struggle.

The French had introduced both radio and television broadcasting very early into Algeria. Radio started in 1925 under private auspices but was taken over by the French government in 1957. Algeria became the first country in all of Africa to have a permanent television service when the French opened a station in Algiers in 1956.

In 1971 Algeria operated three domestic radio services, in Arabic, Kabyl, and French. The Arabic network was the most comprehensive, with transmitters in 11 locations and a daily uninterrupted schedule of 18 hours. The French network, also on the air 18 hours a day, had outlets in only three cities outside Algiers, the capital. Kabyl, the local Berber dialect, spoken by less than a quarter of the population, was broadcast about 12 hours a day from Algiers and only one other town. Algiers alone broadcast all three language services. Algeria's medium-wave services have grown with extraordinary rapidity, such that by 1972 it had the highest aggregate wattage in the whole of Africa (app. 4).

Algeria at first had no external service as such, but directed its regular domestic services abroad for a short period in the mornings and from noon until midnight on the same transmitters used for the domestic services. Arabic programs were beamed westward toward Morocco and eastward toward the other North African countries and the Middle East, French toward Europe, and Kabyl toward the other Maghreb countries. In mid-1971, however, the inauguration of eight powerful new short-wave transmitters designed to beam signals to North Africa and the Middle East was announced by the Ministry of Information and Culture. The five 100-kw. and three 50-kw. transmitters were installed on the outskirts of Algiers, where new studios designed especially for the external service were expected to be completed by 1973 (*EBU Review* 1971, p. 219). In mid-1972, moreover, the government announced the inauguration of two long-wave transmitters of 750 kw. each, capable of operating in tandem to produce 1,500 kw. Installed at Tipaza, a town on the Mediterranean coast near Algiers, with Czechoslovak aid, this superpowered installation was intended to serve countries bordering the western Mediterranean (*EBU Review* 1973). Algeria and Morocco are the only African countries broadcasting in the long wave band, which is used primarily in Europe (see § A1.2).

A few years after the opening of its first television station in 1956, Algeria began supplementing its own programming with live programs direct from Europe via a relay station on the Balearic Islands. This facility brought programming from the French domestic television network and from the European Broadcasting Union's international network, Eurovision (see §13.2.4). Many of Algeria's television installations were destroyed during the independence struggle but were reactivated by 1964. In 1972 the Algerian television network broadcast 65 hours a week. Programs originated from three of the seven main transmitter sites— Algiers, Oran, and Constantine. With the help of 13 additional low-power repeaters, the network was estimated to be able to cover an area occupied by 80% of the population. Half the programming was imported, mostly from France, but the aim was to reduce programs from foreign sources to 30% of the total (Ploman, Berrada, and Clergerie 1971, p. 50).

Even before 1950 the French had introduced educational applications of radio: an adult-education program in French was transmitted daily, Arabic was used in the presentation of courses on both the French and Arabic languages, and a program in Kabyl dealt with general information (Williams 1950, p. 21). In the postindependence period the need for educational exploitation of broadcasting became urgent because of the withdrawal of French teaching personnel and the deep social division left by the French between the developed and undeveloped sectors, represented by the Europeanized coastal cities and the isolated villages of the interior. UNESCO started the televised Arabic Literacy Pilot Project in Algeria in 1969; lessons were published in advance in the Arabic newspapers as an efficient means of getting written material into the hands of participants. Four lessons a week were broadcast, each devoting part of its time to language, to reading, and to writing. Each lesson grew out of a "theme linked to the interests and activities of the daily life of the majority of viewers" (Maddison 1971, pp. 6, 16, 24). By 1971 the ETV schedule had been expanded to include series on teacher training, mathematics and science, and the English language. At that time studies were being made, with UNESCO help, on establishing a radio-TV educational center to help achieve the sweeping new Algerian educational goals announced in its 1970–73 development plan. The center would work with the national broadcasting system, assuming responsibility for production, training, and research and evaluation in connection with educational programming (Ploman, Berrada, and Clergerie 1971, pp. 58–59).

2.2.4 Morocco

Population: 15,800,000	Radio transmitter sites: 12
Receivers per thousand: 95	Area per site: 14,000 sq mi

As we move westward through the Maghreb, we find the level of broadcasting development steadily rising. Morocco, the westernmost of the Maghreb quartet, has much the largest broadcasting audience of the four, whether measured in terms of absolute numbers of receivers or in terms of the ratio of receivers to population. By the same token, it has the most elaborate radio and television systems of the four countries. Contrary to the tendency elsewhere in Africa to centralize production facilities, as of 1971 Morocco had five radio-production centers in addition to the main one at Rabat. The transmission center at Sebaa-Aioun, near Meknes, has been described as one of the largest and most modern in Africa—and it is just one of a number of transmitter sites (*Interstages* 1971, p. 5).

France's interest in Morocco, like its interest in Algeria, dates back to 1830. Spain, separated from Africa by no more than the few miles of the Straits of Gibraltar, also took a strong interest in Morocco. From 1906 until Morocco won independence in 1956 the country was divided as a protectorate between France and Spain. After independence Morocco reabsorbed the previously internationalized city of Tangier, but Spain continued to control certain enclaves, such as the Mediterranean coastal town of Ceuta, at the point of land nearest the Spanish coast, approximately opposite Algeciras. As a result of the double occupancy, both French and Spanish are used in Morocco as well as the official language, Arabic, but Spanish is on the decline.

Interest in broadcast news, already mentioned as a characteristic of Maghrebian audiences generally, seems even to be intensified here. The visitor cannot fail to be struck by the universal appetite for the latest word:

As one walks down the narrow alleys of Fez or along the main street
in the old *medina* of Rabat it is easy to follow a news broadcast or
a tune while shopping around. Nearly every merchant has his radio
switched on, and the cities buzz with a cacophony of live and
recorded sounds. In private houses, short-wave sets occupy choice
spots in master bedrooms and, if the owner is wealthy, a television set
sits in the center of the reception room. . . . All sounds in the *medina*
seem to stop for the news . . . and from every corner one hears the
voice of the Moroccan broadcaster ringing forth from open windows
and courtyards. . . . Everyone seems to tune to the same station at the

same time . . . listening to the radio, and, more recently, television-viewing, have become Morocco's most popular national pastimes.
[Schaar 1968, p. 1]

An unusual feature of radio history in Morocco is that even after independence stations continued to be for a time operated by private commercial companies. Not until 1959, three years after Morocco became independent, did the Moroccan government outlaw private ownership. The government then purchased two private stations in Tangier and another in nearby Tetouan. Television, too, first started as a private venture, as early as 1954. Morocco would have been counted the first African country with television, ahead of Algeria, had not the company failed after two years. The government bought its equipment but did not itself reintroduce television until 1962, by which time much of the old equipment was outmoded (Eisele et al. 1965, p. 284).

In 1971 Morocco's radio system provided three medium-wave domestic services—the national service in Arabic; a domestic "international service" in French, English, and Spanish; and a vernacular service in Berber. The national service was fed to medium-wave transmitters in 10 cities, and also to FM transmitters in three of those cities. The service in European languages went to other medium-wave transmitters in seven of the same cities, and also to other FM transmitters in three of them. Finally, the vernacular service in three Berber dialects went to six cities. Five of the cities have three medium-wave transmitters each, enabling simultaneous local broadcast of all three domestic services.

The Atlas Mountain chain divides coastal Morocco from the interior, effectively screening out daytime transmissions from the main population centers, which are all on the coast. In order to serve the remote, widely scattered villages of the interior, the government installed a 400-kw. long-wave transmitter near Azilal, in the heart of the mountains, in 1971. It was reportedly carrying the home service to the Moroccan hinterland, which shades off into the Algerian Sahara (*Interstages* 1971, pp. 7–8). The following year, according to plan, the Azilal site acquired a second 400-kw. transmitter. Operating in tandem, the two transmitters produce 800 kw. The station's use of long waves suggests that the Azilal installation may also be intended for European audiences. One source refers to it specifically in connection with external broadcasting (Nyrop et al., 1972, p. 152).

The external service aims short-wave transmitters toward five target areas: Spanish Sahara (immediately south of Morocco), West Africa, Equatorial Africa, the Middle East, and South America. This service originates from the capital, Rabat. A secondary external service, the Voice of Morocco, originates in Tangier, using a short-wave transmitter installed in 1971, broadcasting in Arabic, Spanish, and French.

In 1972 the television system had major outlets in eight cities, plus secondary outlets in eight others. When reintroduced in 1962, television was an immediate success, with more than 9,000 sets sold in the first year and a half. Few African television systems can boast that many receivers in use after a decade of operation. Late in 1962, TV was used systematically by the government to drum up support for a referendum by which Moroccans approved the constitution proffered by the monarch. The government set up 1,000 reeceivers in public places in the Rabat area and lent many transistor radios to government officials in the country-side, beyond the reach of television (Schaar 1968, p. 3). In 1965 a relay tower was erected near Tangier to enable pickup of European television signals for rebroadcast.

The Voice of America has a relay station in Tangier, equipped with 10 short-wave transmitters. When Morocco outlawed nongovernment broadcast installations in 1959 it made an exception for the American installation, in return for which the VOA allowed Morocco to use some of its high-powered transmission facilities for external broadcasting (Nyrop et al. 1972, p. 153).

3   The Horn

The northeastern tip of Somalia thrusts a pointed, hornlike projection into the Arabian Sea. Imagining this as a rhinoceros horn, one can picture Ethiopia and, optionally, the Sudan as forming the head of the beast. Thus the whole area is sometimes called the "Horn of Africa." Under this rubric we treat Ethiopia, the Sudan, and Somalia. The French Territory of the Afars and Issas also lies within this region, forming a small enclave around the port of Djibouti, at the mouth of the Red Sea, but discussion of it is reserved for the chapter on dependencies (§ 9.4.1).

3.1 Ethiopia, *by Sydney W. Head*

Population: 25,300,000	Radio transmitter sites: 3
Receivers per thousand: 7	Area per site: 157,000 sq mi

Ethiopia presents an especially difficult terrain configuration for broadcast coverage. The heart of the empire consists of high, cool plateaus—"a vast mountain massif with a mean height of between 7,000 and 8,000 feet. It rises from the torrid plains abruptly and almost perpendicularly, and this steep escarpment has had a profound influence on the course of Ethiopian history in its deterrence of the would-be conqueror. It has also for many centuries enabled the people to live in isolation from the outside world and to stem the flood of advancing Islam" (Ullendorf 1960, pp. 23–24). Within this fastness the highlands are broken by deep river gorges and geological rifts. The great rift that forms the lakes of central Africa continues through Ethiopia, creating smaller lakes on its way to the Red Sea. The gorge of the Blue Nile winds its way down from northern

Sydney W. Head was adviser to Ethiopia's Ministry of Information, 1962–69, first under the auspices of the African-American Institute, later as Chief of Party for an AID-financed contract between the ministry and RTV International. Recent information was supplied by Negash Gebre Mariam, Deputy General Manager of the Ethiopian Broadcasting Service.

Ethiopia, eventually to debouch in the deserts of the Sudan. These terrain features have served as natural barriers, not only to invasion from the outside, but also to internal communication. Ethiopia now uses broadcasting as an instrument of unification, to help overcome the internal linguistic and ethnic divisions which geography has perpetuated over Ethiopia's long history of independence.

3.1.1 Development of Radio

Ethiopian radio appears to be unique in Africa in not having been established by a colonial power. Foreigners from many countries have taken a hand in its development, but it cannot be said to represent the philosophy of any one outside system. Radio broadcasting in Ethiopia dates essentially from the restoration of Emperor Haile Selassie I in 1941. Briefly in September 1935, under the pressure of the Italian invasion, which had already begun in the north, the emperor used a broadcasting station in Addis Ababa. It had been hastily assembled from radiotelephonic equipment so that the emperor could try to win support and sympathy from the outside world (Ethiopia 1963, pp. 22–23). Soon after, however, the Ethiopian army withdrew from the capital, destroying this facility so that it would not fall into the hands of the invaders. Five years later, in 1941, the British escorted the emperor back into the city after the defeat of the Italians. Short-wave communications equipment was once more pressed into service for broadcasting purposes.

Radio began in 1941 with a staff of seven, broadcasting four hours a day in the official language, Amharic, and in Arabic and English (Ethiopia 1966, p. 2). In 1942 the Press and Information Department in the Ministry of Pen assumed responsibility for broadcasting. During the 1950s the Imperial Bodyguard also operated its own broadcasting station, using a 1-kw. short-wave transmitter.

Not until 1959, when the present Ministry of Information was first formally budgeted, did the modernization and expansion of Ethiopian broadcasting begin. In 1960 two 10-kw. short-wave transmitters were installed. These came as part of a $2.5-million United States technical-assistance agreement made in 1957 (§ 12.2.1). The original plan as recommended by an American engineering consultant called for a series of moderate-power medium-wave transmitters, strategically placed geographically throughout the empire. This dispersal was designed to cope with the extraordinarily difficult terrain. However, the Ethiopian government demurred, apparently reluctant to assume responsibility for so many outlying stations; after much delay, a compromise plan was adopted, involving high-power transmitters and only two locations outside Addis Ababa.

The Ethiopian government meanwhile installed its first medium-wave facility, a 1-kw. transmitter, in 1961, followed by its first high-power short-wave facility in 1964. Two years later, in 1966, the American-

supplied high-power, medium-wave transmitters, which had been purchased with funds accumulated from the sale of surplus foods shipped by
the United States to Ethiopia, finally went on the air. A 100-kw. transmitter is located on the outskirts of Addis Ababa, which is near the
geographical center of the country; a second 100-kw. transmitter is at
Harrar, a major town in the eastern part of the country, important as the
first stop on the Franco-Ethiopian Railway, which connects Addis Ababa
to the French-controlled port of Djibouti; and the third transmitter, only
50 kw., is located about 40 miles south of Asmara, capital of the northern
province of Eritrea and railhead for a short rail line that runs up from the
Red Sea port of Massawa. The Asmara transmitter has lower power and
an inconvenient location beyond reach of the city power supply in order
to avoid interfering with Kagnew Station, the American military communication base located at Asmara. The American Forces Radio and Television Service operates low-power radio and television transmitters within
Kagnew Station, and these also serve the local community of Asmara.

3.1.2 Radio Programming

About 70 languages are spoken in Ethiopia, eight by substantial numbers (Lipsky 1962, p. 52). Amharic, a Semitic language unique to
Ethiopia and written by means of a syllabary rather than an alphabet, is
the language of the Amharas, the dominant ethnic group. No complete
national census has been made, but informed observers estimate that
Amharic is the native tongue of probably somewhat less than half the
population. Gallinya, a Cushitic (i.e., non-Semitic) language, is believed
to be spoken by a majority of the population. Tigrinya, another Semitic
tongue, is considered important because it is the dominant language of the
northern province of Eritrea, where there is a troublesome separatist
movement. Arabic is also widely used in Eritrea.

Radio Ethiopa's main transmissions are on the air simultaneously on
short and medium waves, for about 15 hours per day, using nine languages.
Amharic, the official language, occupies about half the schedule, which
is interrupted each weekday by a four-hour closedown in the morning and
a 1½-hour closedown in the afternoon. In 1973 the 6½-hour weekday
national Amharic service broke down nominally (i.e., without taking into
account advertising and variations in program timing) in percentages as
follows: music, 57; information/guidance, 22; news and commentary,
15; religion, 4; miscellaneous, 2.

English, the second language of Ethiopia, occupies two hours; Somali,
four hours; Arabic, one hour; and French and Afar, a half-hour each.
The transmitters are split for an hour in the early evening between Afar/
French and English. The Afar service is aimed at the French Territory of
Afars and Issas, that is, the port of Djibouti, which is important to
Ethiopia's external trade. The short French segment is a holdover

from an international service in English, French, Swahili, and Arabic which was tried in 1961 but discontinued after a year. There are two motives for retaining at least a token service in French: to serve the large diplomatic community in Addis Ababa, which is the seat of the Organization of African Unity and the U.N. Economic Commission for Africa, whose staffs include many Francophone Africans; and to reach the French-speaking community at the port of Djibouti, as noted above. The Somali and Arabic segments also function simultaneously as domestic and external services, in the sense that Ethiopa has substantial Arabic- and Somali-speaking populations and has borders on both Somalia and Arabic-speaking Sudan.

The regional transmitters at Asmara and Harrar cut away from the national service in the evenings for local vernacular segments. In 1972, the Asmara transmitter carried 1¼ hours of Tigrinya and 45 minutes of Tigre programs daily, while the Harrar transmitter carried 1½ hours a day in Gallinya. These local programs featured music, news, commentary, sports, and a small amount of informational programming concerning farming, homemaking, education, and the like.

3.1.3 Television

Ethiopia first glimpsed television in 1963, on the occasion of the founding meeting of the Organization of African Unity in Addis Ababa. An alert manufacturer realized that even the large amphitheater of Africa Hall, the U.N. style of building where the meeting took place, would not be able to accommodate all who wished to observe the historic events. The company therefore installed a temporary closed-circuit television system to enable crowds to follow the action on monitors in the lobby. Broadcast television started the next year, in November 1964. Several companies had submitted package proposals. That of Thomson Television International, a British company (see § 17.3) won the contract. On very short notice, TTI undertook to put Ethiopian television on the air in time for Emperor Haile Selassie's coronation day, 2 November. TTI provided three expatriate officers, but otherwise the station went on the air with an all-Ethiopian staff trained on the spot (Ethiopia 1966, p. 3). The original studio and the main transmitter were located in Addis Ababa's City Hall, a suitably elevated and central location for coverage of the capital, which has a population of nearly a million. Later, two translators were added, one south and one north of the city, as well as two additional studios.

In 1972 the general television schedule ran on weekdays from 8:00 P.M. to about 10:30 P.M., preceded by an hour of educational programming for young people. Examples of the content of the latter are "Watch Mr. Wizard," programs on geography and science, and a BBC English-language series, "Walter and Connie." Regular in-school broadcasts ran from 9:00 A.M. to 11:30 A.M. They were produced by the Ministry of Education's Mass Media Center, which is described in detail in § 15.4.

The general evening television service included the usual run of imported syndicated shows in English—"Star Trek," "Here's Lucy," "Mod Squad," and a weekly feature film. These occupied only about a third of the time, however, the rest being devoted to news in Amharic, English, and French, and to locally produced Amharic programming, mostly of an informational character.

3.1.4 Autonomous Status

In 1952 the Ethiopian government set up the Imperial Board of Tele-communications to take charge of the empire's telegraph, telephone, and radio communication services. The IBTE is an autonomous chartered corporation, wholly owned by the government but empowered to earn a profit. It was created as a result of a survey conducted at the request of the World Bank, to which Ethiopia had applied for reconstruction aid after the ravages of the Italian occupation (Ethiopia 1963, p. 24). Several such quasi-independent corporations have been set up in Ethiopia to take over specific technical functions from the archaic bureaucracy of the regular government ministries.

The programming of broadcasting stations is a function of the Ministry of Information, which is to "own, manage, and operate Government-owned radio and television [broadcast] stations" (*Negarit Gazeta* 1966, p. 135). From its outset the IBTE assumed responsibility for installation, technical operation, and maintenance of both radio broadcasting transmitters and studios. Not having engineering capability of its own, the Ministry of Information, when it took over broadcast programming, continued the dependence on IBTE. This dependence was formalized in 1961 with a contract between IBTE and the ministry. The resulting division of opera-tional responsibility between two quite different types of organizations has had unfortunate results for broadcasting. For one thing, it is expensive— since IBTE expects to make a profit. Payment to IBTE for technical services in 1971–72 amounted to $600,000, well over half the total government subvention to the broadcasting service.

More important, perhaps, is the fact that the IBTE's common-carrier orientation, which places emphasis on message carriage, not on messages themselves, is fundamentally out of sympathy with broadcasting's concern with message content and quality. For example, IBTE's broadcast control-room operators were trained at the board's Training Institute, which was established with the help of the International Telecommunication Union in 1953; though doubtless well grounded in technical aspects of their job, they received no instruction in the aesthetic aspects of broadcast produc-tion. As two expert observers, themselves Africans, remarked, "Courses planned specifically to meet the requirements of broadcasting rather than a telecommunications service would have been more beneficial" (Quar-myne and Bebey 1967, p. 9).

IBTE is probably not averse to being relieved of the headaches associated with its broadcasting responsibilities. One reason this has been impossible, however, is that IBTE's specialized broadcasting engineers and technicians would not have been willing to exchange the salary scales and attractive fringe benefits of the board for the regular conditions of civil service employment governing EBS personnel. One of the advantages of corporate status is the possibility of being exempted from the detailed supervision of the civil service commission, known in Ethiopia as the Central Personnel Agency, the law of which provides for optional exclusion of "designated Public Authorities" from its regulations (*Negarit Gazeta* 1962, p. 34).

For much the same reasons that IBTE itself was organized, then, consideration was given to conferring autonomous status on broadcasting. Such status would, potentially at least, allow it to plow back its earnings, which otherwise would go directly to the central treasury; to make special provision for remuneration of talent, apart from regular civil service salary scales; and generally to conduct its affairs in accordance with accepted business methods. As an example of the advantage of being able to use earnings, take the hypothetical case of a major commercial client who expresses a willingness to enter into a large commercial contract provided certain special program materials and talent can be provided. Working within the confines of a fixed annual budget, station management could not buy unbudgeted extra program materials or hire unbudgeted additional talent and so would have to turn down the proffered business. If, on the other hand, management were free to use income to defray current expenses, the unexpected additional expense could be met out of the equally unexpected additional income.

A plan for setting up broadcasting as an autonomous service shuttled back and forth within the government for several years before being promulgated in 1968 as an Imperial Order. The order provided for the Ethiopian Broadcasting Service as "an autonomous public Authority within the Imperial Ethiopian Government" which will "operate under the direction, control and supervision of the Minister of Information." It is subject to the IBTE's "licensing and authorization powers." Among its own powers are: buying, owning, and disposing of property; entering into contracts; borrowing "when authorized by law"; establishing branch offices; erecting transmission, relay, and other facilities; and selling time. It is to be financed from the sale of time and other earned income, from gifts, and from government subsidies and appropriations (*Negarit Gazeta* 1968, pp. 90–93).

The last point, the fiscal arrangement, seems to differentiate the EBS status from that of an organization like the IBTE, which not only defrays expenses out of income but also realizes a net profit. Clearly EBS, with its obligation to carry much material which is in the national interest but which is unviable commercially cannot be expected to earn its own way. However, the difference is more apparent than real. The IBTE's biggest customer for telephone and telegraph services is in fact the government; it could not possibly pay its way if it relied exclusively on income from customers in the private sector. If the government paid EBS for providing broadcasting services in the same way that it pays IBTE for telephone and telegraph services, EBS too would be able to show a net "profit." This view has not been adopted, however, and EBS continues to be regarded as subsidized by government. In the 1971–72 budget year, its broadcast advertising realized about $600,000, and it received a government subsidy of $1,136,000 (*Negarit Gazeta* 1971, p. 204). EBS's new autonomous status has resulted in the retention of advertising revenue for defrayal of operating expenses other than salaries, but apparently other potential benefits of autonomy had not yet been realized in 1972.

3.1.5 The Audience

No national audience survey of both rural and urban areas has been attempted in Ethiopia, and estimates of total radio-receiver circulation must be taken as very rough indeed. Two radio surveys of self-selected respondents, mostly students, were conducted in 1966 and 1967 (Head 1968). The earlier survey, representing nearly 8,000 students, was made by an electrical appliance firm; the second, conducted by the station itself, represented a few more than 2,000 respondents to a letter-writing contest in which radios were given as prizes. An open-end question asking for suggestions for improving Radio Ethiopia produced some 70 useful ideas that were taken under consideration by management.

In 1969 a Swiss research firm, conducting a survey for Ethiopia's Ministry of Information as well as the United States Information Agency, followed a scientific sampling design but still confined the survey population to urban literates (SCOPE 1969). The sample consisted of nearly 1,200 students, business men, civil servants, and professionals in five major towns. Less than 1% of the sample reported not listening to radio at all, and 83% said they listened daily.

In reply to a question about listening in the past week, 92% of the sample reported listening to Radio Ethiopia, 65% to the BBC, 41% to the VOA, 13% to Moscow, 13% to Germany, 12% to the Sudan, and smaller percentages to Peking, Cairo, Somalia, and Italy. The 8,000 students who responded to the earlier of the two surveys mentioned above agreed in putting the BBC first among foreign stations listened to "regularly" or "occasionally" but put the Sudan second (43%), followed by Egypt (39%), VOA (26%), Russia (17%), Somalia (15%), and West Germany (10%). The variation reflects differences between student interests and those of more mature listeners, as well as differences between the geographical distributions of respondents and between economic conditions in 1966 and 1969. However, both surveys make an important point about the extent of foreign listening by educated Ethiopians. The significance of these data is enhanced by answers in the 1969 survey to a question about the *reasons* for listening to foreign stations. Answers clearly indicated purposeful choice. Ninety percent of those who listened to Radio Omdurman in the Sudan, for example, said they did so for its music (Sudanese music is very popular among Ethiopian urban listeners), whereas 86% said they listened to the BBC for its news. The characteristics, in terms of broadcasting, of the great mass of the Ethiopian population—rural dwellers without formal education—remain to be tested, but it is safe to assume they differ considerably from those of the educated, urban elite. Foreign listening is probably confined to the latter group—an assumption on which some of the station's program policies seem clearly to be based.

3.1.6 Technical Aid

As we pointed out at the beginning of § 3.1.1, Ethiopian radio is unique in not having been a colonial by-product. The Italian occupation of five years was essentially that—a military occupation, with much of the country still in the hands of Ethiopian patriots and the occupiers confined to major cities and garrisoned strong points. Though the Italians used broadcasting during the occupation, their facilities were destroyed and Ethiopia had to start over in 1941. The lack of a colonial connection meant that neither Britain nor France felt the special obligation to assist the development of broadcasting in Ethiopia that they did in the countries for which they had responsibility as former colonial powers. The Ethiopian Ministry of Information has therefore had a great variety of advisers, from both East and West. The British, however, do occupy a special historical niche: they supported the emperor's return to power, provided most of the military force to accomplish it, and retained thereafter a certain sense of commitment; on his side, the emperor spent most of his exile in Britain, where his cause was vigorously supported, and so he had good reason to feel warmly toward the power which restored him to his throne. British broadcasting aid has been mostly committed to educational uses; the main project, the Mass Media Center, is described in § 15.4.

The West Germans have had a major aid input, not all of it actually realized. A training center the Germans operated at Radio Ethiopia from 1964 to 1970 was a unique undertaking of its kind (see § 14.4). The Germans also offered to provide the technical equipment to furnish a complete radio studio complex. This was an important offer because Radio Ethiopia still depends on production facilities crudely improvised by IBTE in an existing administration building. They lack sufficient space, acoustical isolation, and up-to-date audio equipment. The German offer of equipment was contingent upon the Ethiopian government's erecting the necessary building. Plans were drawn up for a complete broadcasting house, combining offices and both radio and television production facilities (the old radio studios are located at the Ministry of Information, while the original television studio is in the City Hall, several blocks away). Excavation for the new building's foundation was begun at an ideal site, near the national university and other cultural resources of the capital. However, a shortage of government funds forced the shutdown of construction in 1968. By 1972 there had been no move to reactivate this vitally important project.

Because of a mutual defense agreement dating back to 1953, the United States had a strong political incentive to aid Ethiopia. Under that agreement, Ethiopia received military equipment and advice, and the United States obtained the right to operate Kagnew Station, a military communications installation in Asmara, Eritrea (SIPRI 1971, p. 17). The AID broadcasting assistance initiated in 1957 (see § 3.1.1) eventuated in the addition of 270 kw. of broadcasting power to Ethiopia's aggregate wattage, as well as in providing a comprehensive program of on-the-job training and expert advisory services. These projects are described in more detail in § 12.2.1.

3.1.7 Radio Voice of the Gospel

Though not in the formal category of technical aid, the usefulness of the Lutheran World Broadcasting Service's international broadcasting station, ETLF, located on the outskirts of Addis Ababa, must be mentioned. The station aids Radio Ethiopia in two ways: it supplies training to Ethiopian broadcasters, and it acts as a healthy element of competition. The Lutheran station—generally referred to as RVOG, or Radio Voice of the Gospel— demonstrates vividly that a high level of technical efficiency and production quality can be achieved on a restricted budget and within limitations imposed by local conditions most of which are shared by Radio Ethiopia. EBS officials regard the object lesson as valuable—indeed, they have even invited RVOG to set up a television station in Addis Ababa.

The contract permitting erection of RVOG, signed with the Ethiopian government in 1959, provides for the eventual turnover of the facilities to the government. The original capital investment amounted to over $1.8 million, most of it contributed by some two dozen countries, with the United States and Germany giving the largest shares (LWF 1970, p. 99). Legally the Lutheran station comes under the jurisdiction of the Ethiopian Ministry of Information, and one of the duties of the minister is to "issue licenses for the private ownership, management and operation of radio and television stations" (*Negarit Gazeta* 1966, p. 135). In practice the Ethiopian Broadcasting Service maintains a "liaison officer" to keep the station informed of government policy concerning broadcast coverage of current events. The ETLF studios, dedicated in 1963, are located on the outskirts of Addis Ababa in a spacious compound large enough to accommodate staff housing as well. The transmitter site is farther out of town, near the one used for the Ethiopian Broadcasting Service transmitters.

RVOG's principal business is broadcasting internationally; it uses two 100-kw. short-wave transmitters beamed to other parts of Africa, Ceylon, China, India, and the Middle East. Short segments of English and Amharic are also radiated by one of these transmitters, using a nondirectional antenna, for Ethiopian audiences in the more distant parts of the empire. RVOG also uses a 1-kw. medium-wave transmitter to serve local Ethiopian audiences in Amharic, English, and French. However, RVOG does not itself produce programming for local consumption, except for news bulletins and certain other special materials. As in other areas served by RVOG, programming intended for Ethiopian audiences originates at local production studios independent of the station itself—in this case at the Mekane Yesus Lutheran Mission in Addis Ababa. The Ethiopian Orthodox church also produces programs of its own, in its own studios, as part of RVOG's local schedule. According to the 1969 SCOPE survey previously mentioned, RVOG has a good following in Ethiopia: 67% of the sample members who said they listened at least once a week to any broadcasts said they had listened to RVOG "in the past week" (SCOPE 1969, p. 171). RVOG's programming in general and its broadcasting philosophy are discussed in detail in §§ 11.2.3 and 11.3.

3.2 The Sudan, by Ali M. Shummo

Population: 15,800,000	Radio transmitter sites: 1
Receivers per thousand: 6	Area per site: 967,000 sq mi

[EDITOR'S NOTE. The Sudan occupies a transitional geographical and ethnic position between the Sahara desert on the north and the tropical rain forest on the south, between Arabs and Nilotic Blacks, between Islam and Christianity. The capital, Khartoum, is located at the junction of the two Niles, the White flowing north from central Africa, the Blue flowing northwest from the Ethiopian highlands. The rivers divide the capital into three cities: Khartoum proper, the location of government offices and Westernized residential areas, lies between the prongs of the Y; Khartoum North, an industrial suburb, lies across the Blue Nile from Khartoum; and Omdurman, the less Westernized residential and business sector, lies along

Ali M. Shummo is Under Secretary, Sudan Ministry of Information and Culture; former Director General of Sudan Television; former President, Arab States Broadcasting Union; and member, International Broadcasting Institute Board of Trustees and OIRT executive council.

the west bank of the White Nile. Here the broadcast studios are located, and for that reason the signature "Radio Omdurman" is used.

During the colonial period the British insulated the Pagan and Christian Nilotic tribesmen of the tropical south from the Arabic-speaking Muslims of the north, who are in the majority. Since independence in 1956 the north and the south have been at odds, most of the time engaged in what has amounted to outright civil war. Early in 1972, with the granting of self-governing status to the southern region, there seemed at last to be prospects of a settlement of the long-drawn-out strife. It was presumed that self-government would, in time, include control by the south of its own broadcasting facilities and programming—an important development, since the broadcasting needs of the south differ from those of the north. This devolution had not taken place, however, at the time the following section was written.]

3.2.1 Radio

The Sudan has always been in contact with the civilizations of the Middle East through the Nile Corridor. As a result it has played a significant role in the dissemination of political, cultural, and economic ideas to the rest of the African continent. However, the sheer size of the Sudan poses special problems for broadcast coverage. It occupies 8.3% of the African continent, reaching north to south about 1,275 miles and east to west about 1,000 miles. The land is thinly populated, averaging a density of only 16 persons per square mile; in contrast, Egypt's density is 88 per square mile. The most heavily populated provinces are Khartoum and Blue Nile. More than 60% of the population is concentrated in the central area, where the water resources and, consequently, most of the development schemes are located.

Radio broadcasting in the Sudan started in 1940, a relatively early date for African systems. Transmission capacity was greatly enlarged in the early 1960s with the addition of two 50-kw. short-wave and two 100-kw. medium-wave transmitters, partly as a result of an agreement with the United States Agency for International Development (see § 12.2.1). Even with these high-power transmitters at its disposal, however, by 1972 Radio Omdurman had still not been able to cover the whole country effectively because all radio transmitters had been concentrated in the vicinity of the capital, with the minor exception of a small transmitter operated in the south for a short period of time in the 1960s. The government planned to remedy deficiencies in coverage by the end of 1973 by installing provincial medium-wave transmitters at strategic points distant from the capital—in the south at Juba, in the east at Port Sudan, in the west at Nyala, and in the southeast at Sennar. The last was to be the main transmitter for the network, with the extremely high power of 1,500 kw. These facilities were planned on the basis of a Czechoslovak loan.

As in most countries where broadcasting started relatively early, the Posts and Telegraphs Department first assumed responsibility for broadcast technical installations and operations. Usually, P&T withdrew, once the national broadcasting organization became a going concern. In the Sudan, however, the present Ministry of Communication has retained the original P&T technical responsibility for broadcasting, even down to such details as control-room operations and the purchase of recording tapes. The Ministry of Information and Culture, which is responsible for programming, paid the Ministry of Communication about half a million dollars for technical radio services in 1971. Divided authority between technical and programming operations created friction and inefficiency. The Ministry of Information and Culture had planned for a number of years to take over its own technical operations but had not yet done so by 1972 as far as radio was concerned, although it had from the outset assumed engineering responsibility for television.

Radio Omdurman is financed by government subvention. Its budget, which amounted to nearly $1.5 million in 1971, is not affected by monies collected for receiver license fees and advertising revenues, which go directly to the central treasury. The collection of fees is the responsibility of Posts and Telegraphs, but the license law, which dates back to colonial times, has never been vigorously enforced. About a quarter of a million dollars a year is realized from radio and television advertising combined.

Radio Omdurman broadcasts domestically, basically in Arabic, but with an additional special service designed for the southern regions where Arabic is not the mother tongue. Of the total of approximately 150 hours' radio programming a week in 1972, about 25 hours, or 17%, were intended for the south. Six African languages, English, and simplified Arabic were used. An external service has been discussed from time to time, but in 1972 only a half-hour a week in Somali could be classified formally as programmed for external consumption. There was no systematic radio schools broadcasting, although the Ministry of Education offered special programs to assist students toward the end of each academic year.

Technical training in broadcasting can be obtained locally at the Khartoum Technical Institute, the Senior Trades School, and the Khartoum Vocational Training Center. By 1972, however, none of these schools had ventured into the training of program personnel, nor had Khartoum University established a curriculum for students interested in the mass media. Relatively large numbers of Sudanese broadcast personnel have therefore been trained abroad. Up to 1972 nearly a hundred had studied in other countries, over half of them in Egypt and Lebanon. Others had had gone to America, Britain, France, Hungary, Kenya, and West Germany.

3.2.2 Television

Sudanese television began experimentally in 1962, with West Germany assisting in supplying equipment and training personnel. German television technicians remained in the Sudan for five years after making the initial installation. Forty-one Sudanese television trainees went to Germany for study, and another nine received training in Egypt, Czechoslovakia, Japan, and Britain. Regular transmissions of five hours an evening started in 1963. The station is in Omdurman, near the site of the radio studios, where its signal can reach the two-million population of Khartoum Province.

In 1972 a second station was opened in Wad Medani, a town on the Blue Nile, 180 km. southeast of Khartoum, again with West German aid. The Wad Medani transmitter serves the Gezira, a huge irrigated cotton-growing project of nearly two million acres. There are some 1,500 villages in the Gezira, with a total population of two million. Programs reach Wad Medani from Omdurman by means of a microwave relay system. According to the plans, each of the Gezira's villages will have at least two public receiving sets—one for men and one for women. The Gezira Board, the government agency responsible for administering the agricultural project, will pay half the cost of the sets, the villages themselves the other half. However, most of the villages are without electricity; therefore, the means for generating power locally will have to be provided before the scheme can be fully realized.

As we have said, the Ministry of Information and Culture assumed responsibility for the technical aspects of television from the outset, thereby avoiding the dilemma of split responsibility which plagues radio broadcasting. About 60% of Sudanese television programming is locally produced. In the first quarter of 1972, the station categorized its 34 weekly hours of regular programming approximately as follows: films and film series, 33%; other entertainment, 18%; news and politics, 18%; cultural and religious programs, 15%; other, 16%. The largest segment of imported entertainment programming came from America, an almost equal amount from Arab countries, and the rest from England. Among the familiar English-language titles in the entertainment schedule were "Alfred Hitchcock Presents," "The Saint," "The Bold Ones," "Mod Squad," and "Peyton Place." Local programming is in Arabic, with Arabic subtitles for English-language films. The station depends on the ministry's Cinema Production Section for local newsfilm but plans eventually to set up its own film unit. In 1972 about three-quarters of the station's newsfilm came from VisNews (§ 1.4.3), a third from the ministry, and the rest from the Middle East News Agency.

The Ministry of Information and Culture puts the facilities of Sudan Television at the disposal of the Ministry of Education for schools television. The initial effort was in the field of English-language teaching, with the help of the British Council. Instructional programs at the secondary level in such subjects as science, mathematics, and geography at the secondary level were broadcast three times a week during the 1972 academic year.

3.3 Somalia, *by Sydney W. Head*

Population: 2,790,000	Radio transmitter sites: 2
Receivers per thousand: 22	Area per site: 123,000 sq mi

The Democratic Republic of Somalia occupies the tip of the Horn of Africa, pointing toward the northeast. The shape of its actual land mass is like a figure "7," with the horizontal stroke on the Gulf of Aden and the vertical stroke on the Indian Ocean. Like Cameroon (§ 5.4.3), Somalia is made up of two former colonial territories with different linguistic ties, in this case English and Italian. Arabic is also influential because virtually all Somalis are Muslim. The indigenous Cushitic Somali language is spoken universally, making Somalia one of the three mainland African nations without internal linguistic rivalries, aside from those inherited from colonial influences. However, Somalia was not so fortunate with regard to a written language, the advent of which was long delayed by the inability of the Somalis to agree on whether to use the Arabic, the European (Latin), or an invented alphabet. This argument was not resolved until the fall of 1972, when the Latin alphabet was chosen as economically the most practical (*Africa Research Bulletin* 1972c). Up to that point Arabic, English, and Italian had all been recognized as official written languages.

Somalia's binational colonial inheritance is reflected in the placement of its two radio transmitting sites: Mogadishu, the present capital and chief city of the former Italian Somaliland; and Hargeisa, chief city of the northern region, the former British Somaliland Protectorate. The main government radio service, Radio Mogadishu, broadcasts in Somali, English, Italian, Arabic, Amharic, and Galla. Service from the Hargeisa station is known as Radio Somali and rebroadcasts Somali and Amharic transmissions from Mogadishu as well as originating regional Somali programs (*Africa South of the Sahara* 1971, p. 684). Both services come under the jurisdiction of the Ministry of Information and National Guidance.

The Somalis are mostly nomadic pastoralists who shift with the seasons to find water and fodder. Precise geographic boundaries have no meaning in this way of life, so that substantial numbers of Somalis live either part of the year or permanently in territory technically belonging to neighboring Kenya to the southwest and Ethiopia to the east. This has led to irredentism and recurrent border disputes. Also politically sensitive are relations with the French Territory of Afars and Issas, that small colonial enclave surrounded mostly by Ethiopian territory, but also abutting on the extreme northwest tip of Somalia (§ 9.4.1). Radio propaganda has played a conspicuous part in border confrontations between Somalia and her neighbors. Somalia's relations with Kenya and Ethiopia reached the point of violence in the mid-1960s, but following a 1967 détente tensions relaxed somewhat. Although the propaganda barrage back and forth became less virulent, Somalia continued to aim broadcasts at the border areas—in Swahili for Kenya, in Amharic and Galla for Ethiopia, and in Afar for the F.T.A.I.

Ethiopia and Kenya were already receiving substantial military aid from the United States and Britain respectively when Somalia became independent in 1960. Frustrated in attempts to get arms from the West, she turned to the Communist countries for assistance, while keeping the lines open for Western assistance in other spheres such as agriculture. Somalia has received some $35 million in military aid from the USSR (Diamond and Fouquet 1972, p. 40), and media development assistance from several Bloc countries. In 1962, for example, it was announced that Somalia had accepted a USSR offer of a 50-kw. radio transmitter (USIA 1962, p. 20). The following year the West German government provided new studio facilities. The new transmitter was intended for the external service, which had ambitions for reaching audiences as far away as Ghana and India (Kaplan et al. 1969b, p. 244).

Obscure though Somali broadcasting may be in the wide spectrum of African broadcasting, its early history is one of the few that have been documented by indigenous scholars. Suleiman Muhammed Adam, a Somali historian, has written an excellent short history of broadcasting in his country which, according to Somalia's minister of information, is "significant not only in that it gives us our first documentation on Somali broadcasting, but also that it is one of the first documentations on any sphere of activity in our national life" (Somalia 1968, p. 1).

Of the two radio stations in present-day Somalia, the one in Hargeisa started first, in 1943, as an experimental British Army installation called Radio Kudu. From its original 100 w. of power it eventually reached 10 kw. in 1961. The British were willing to invest this much to combat the growing influence of Communism, according to the Somali historian (Somalia 1968, p. 7). The Italians did not start radio in their sector until 1951. In the following 15 years, Mogadishu Radio had 14 different directors. Little wonder that the Somali government felt it necessary to appoint a commission to find out what was wrong with its broadcasting setup! In 1965, the commission, with the help of a UNESCO adviser, recommended a complete reorganization of the radio system (Somalia 1968, p. 21).

In 1973 Mogadishu was listed as originating morning, midday, and evening segments in Somali, with a half-hour in each of the languages English and Italian. The Hargeisa transmitter offered short home-service segments in Somali in the afternoon and evening, amounting to only three hours per day. Presumably the Hargeisa station was assigned at other times to external broadcasts aimed at Ethiopia and the F.T.A.I., since it is much more favorably located for propagation to those areas than the main station at Mogadishu. Radio Somali at Hargeisa, but not the main station at Mogadishu, was listed as selling commercial time (German Africa Society 1970, p. 228). However, since the per capita income of its mostly pastoral population is one of the lowest in Africa (app. 3), commercial sales cannot be expected to contribute significantly to the broadcasting budget.

4　　East Africa

The regional name "East Africa" goes back to that of the Imperial East Africa Company, which opened the area to British commerce in the late nineteenth century. In 1895 the British government took over from the company, creating the East Africa Protectorate, which in 1920 became the colony of Kenya. The jumping-off place for these developments was the island of Zanzibar, just off the coast near where Kenya's and present-day Tanzania's borders meet. This was the ancient entrepôt for African trade routes that wound their way into the interior to Lake Victoria, and for Indian Ocean sea routes to the East. Zanzibar became a British protectorate in 1890, and Uganda, at the other end of the overland trade route, became one in the period 1894–96. Tanganyika, before World War I a German colony, eventually became a British trust territory.

As in the group of territories constituting British Central Africa (chap. 7), economic considerations suggested federation—with one partner, in this case Kenya, having the largest European settler population and the most to gain. Although federation was never achieved in East Africa, the four territories did share a number of essential common services, such as rail and air transportation, currency, postal service, telecommunications, customs, and a regional university. After independence, nationalistic rivalries caused the fragmentation of some of these common services, but in 1947 the independent countries formed their own East African Economic Community to preserve and enlarge others. Consideration was given during colonial times to the idea of a regional broadcasting system as one of the East African common services, but the linguistic and cultural differences among the four territories made the idea impracticable. Moreover, Kenya's head start, as the first territory in Sub-Saharan Africa to initiate broadcasting, would have given the colony a dominant position vis-à-vis the other three territories.

The railroad, which started in Mombasa, went through Kenya to Nairobi, then on to Uganda and Lake Victoria, introduced one of British East Africa's most intractable socioeconomic problems, one which affected broadcast practices in the region both during the colonial period and after.

Laborers imported from India to work on the railroad settled in the region and ultimately prospered as its ubiquitous shopkeepers and commercial entrepreneurs. The Asians (as the Indians are called) kept themselves apart from the Africans, and the British encouraged the distinction by small kinds of preferential treatment for the Indians. The Africans came to resent their preferred position and their prosperity. When independence came to the East African territories the Indians found themselves in limbo—rejected alike by their African neighbors, their ancestral homelands, and their one-time colonial masters.

Their segregated way of life and their prosperity had made the Asians especially prone to become heavy consumers of broadcasting. They were a good market for sets and good advertising targets. The migration of large numbers of Asians from Kenya beginning in late 1967 was immediately reflected in a decline in Kenya's radio commercial revenue. Africans, though much more numerous, could afford to buy few sets and offered little attraction to advertisers. For these reasons broadcasting services tended to cater disproportionately to the Indians. The demand for Asian languages added to their existing problem of having too many indigenous language groups to serve adequately on the air.

This chapter concludes with Burundi and Rwanda, which occupy small neighboring enclavelike areas in the northwest corner of Tanzania next to the Uganda border. They have little in common with British East Africa, other than the fact that they were once part of German East Africa, along with Tanganyika. Their much longer association with Belgium after World War I gave them French as their international language. Geographically, however, there is some justification for regarding Burundi and Rwanda as belonging to the East African region (de Blij 1971, p. 354), and for the purpose of describing their broadcast systems it is more convenient to treat them here than to classify them with the Francophone countries to the west.

4.1 Kenya, *by John Stewart Roberts*

Population: 11,200,000	Radio transmitter sites: 3
Receivers per thousand: 45	Area per site: 75,000 sq mi

Of the three British East African territories, Kenya Colony had the most attraction for British settlers. Although bisected by the equator, Kenya affords a temperate climate in the highlands above 5,000 feet, well suited to Europeans and to plantation agriculture. European settlement and personal investment dating back to the early years of the century helped

John Stewart Roberts is a news writer for the Voice of America. He spent nearly five years in Ethiopia, Kenya, and Zambia as broadcasting adviser and instructor and served on the RTV International advisory team discussed in this section.

Kenya advance more rapidly economically than its neighbors. But it also experienced a more traumatic upheaval when the independence movement brought the interests of settlers and of Africans into direct confrontation.

4.1.1 Broadcasting History

No doubt because of the size and seeming permanence of the European settler population, Kenya led in the development of broadcasting. That it was the first territory in tropical Africa to offer a regular broadcasting service lends particular interest to this aspect of Kenya's development. A 1927 agreement between the colony's government and a private concern, British East African Broadcasting Company, led to establishment of the first regular radio service in 1928 (Bebey 1963, p. 21).

In 1931 the service was taken over on a 25-year contract by the British East Africa Cable and Wireless Company, which undertook to operate it and bear the costs in return for a monopoly on the colony's international telegraphic traffic (Codding 1959, p. 51). Cable and Wireless assumed responsibility only for English and Asian programs; the colony's Department of Information rented transmitter time from the company to broadcast afternoon programs for Africans. By 1954 the department was scheduling 41 hours a week, divided among the Kamba, Kikuyu, Luo, and Swahili languages. Meanwhile Cable and Wireless supplied 44½ hours in English and 29¼ hours in Asian languages. Additional services came from a station which the British Forces Broadcasting Service set up near Nairobi in 1948; it provided 91 hours a week, of which 2¼ hours were for Africans (Kenya Colony and Protectorate 1954, pp. 4–5). These examples of time allotments to the several language services tell something about the colonial outlook of the times. Further evidence of that outlook is found in the recommendation of the Kenya Broadcasting Commission, which said in its 1954 report, "In order that the Broadcasting Service shall have the benefit of advice and direction from the three major groups of the community, we suggest that, for the first period at least, the Board of Governors . . . should have, say, four Europeans, two Asians, and two African members" (Kenya Colony and Protectorate 1954, p. 7).

When the Cable and Wireless contract expired in 1956, the Kenya Broadcasting Service was set up as a government function, as recommended by the commission. Anticipating independence and apparently foreseeing a need to insulate the broadcasting system from future direct government control, however, the colonial authorities transformed the KBS in 1961 into the Kenya Broadcasting Corporation, to be operated by a private contractor. A consortium of British, Canadian, American, and East African commercial interests obtained the operating contract. The corporation's board consisted of three government representatives, three representatives of the general public, and three members representing the interests of the contractors. Funds were to come from government subsidies, receiver license fees, and advertising (Kenya Colony and Protectorate 1961, pp. 108, 122–23). Though short-lived, this interesting arrangement was hailed at the time as a "unique development in the field of broadcasting as a joint cooperative effort between the public, private enterprise, and the government with no group having a majority voice" (Dean 1962). The provision for government subsidization was providential, for KBC lost over $280,000 in its first year of operation (Hachten 1971a, p. 207).

The KBC consortium's primary interest lay in television. The 1954 commission had dismissed that subject with the remark that "television using present techniques at present costs appears, for the time being, to be economically impracticable in Kenya" (Kenya Colony and Protectorate 1954, p. 39). However, a special commission appointed in 1959 recommended that television be started soon (USIA 1960a, p. 19). Accordingly, in 1962, a little more than a year before Kenya's independence, which came on 12 December 1963, KBC inaugurated television. It soon made KBC's previous operating losses seem small.

As frequently happened in those heady days of African television pioneering, anticipated advertising revenues had been grossly overestimated. The National Broadcasting Company of New York, a silent partner in the KBC consortium, seconded an experienced commercial television manager to Nairobi for six months to pull the corporation out of the red. He stayed 18 months. He was in charge when independence came, and television won praise for its coverage of the historic ceremonies (letter from NBC International, 30 March 1972). The station manager received a personal letter of thanks from President Jomo Kenyatta for the five outside broadcasts, the 23 filmed public events, and other special coverage; 500 viewing centers had been set up and an estimated 1.5 million Kenyans saw the history-making spectacle (Awori 1964, p. 20).

But the American manager could not work miracles. A TV circulation that began to level off at only a few thousand sets—mostly owned by expatriate Europeans and Asian shopkeepers of somewhat doubtful tenure—could not provide sufficient commercial support for an operation of the scope the country demanded. The corporation kept returning to the government for more money. A commission of enquiry was appointed to study the new nation's future broadcasting needs, and it decided that the KBC consortium was not among them. Effective 1 July 1964, the Ministry of Information and Broadcasting took over responsibility, renaming the service the Voice of Kenya, which since then has been a direct government function (*EBU Review* 1964, p. 45). The government continued to glean what revenue it could from advertising but in 1969 gave up trying to collect annual receiver license fees. Kenyans thereafter payed a single fee upon purchase of a set—about $2.80 for radio and $8.40 for television. But the import duty on receivers remained at 50%.

4.1.2 Radio

The Voice of Kenya has 19 radio studios which feed transmitters located at the capital, Nairobi, in the south-central part of the country; at Nandi Hills, near Kisumu, in the southwest, near Lake Victoria; and at Kenya's second city, Mombasa, on the coast in the southeast corner. This confinement to southerly locations is dictated by the fact that most of the northern part of the country consists of sparsely populated dry savannah and desert. Thus, although medium-wave transmission facilities in 1972 covered on the average only about 10% of the land area, they reached 45% of the population of some 11 million (Swedish Telecommunication Consulting AB 1972, 1:22).

In 1972 VOK radio was offering three domestic services: the national service, in Swahili; the general service, in English; and the vernacular service, in 14 local languages other than Swahili. The regional coastal station at Mombasa originated 2½ hours of Swahili local programming as well as rebroadcast programs from the national service. The national service was on the air about 123 hours per week, the general service, 87 hours; and the vernacular service, 184. The vernacular service offers a larger number of hours than the others because it is regionalized, so that languages of one region can be transmitted simultaneously with those of another region. In a sample week, the national and general services had approximately the same distribution of content by categories, with the general service a little higher on entertainment and music (60% vs. 54%) and news and current affairs (20% vs. 17%). Vernacular programming consisted mostly of news and traditional music.

The Ministry of Education Schools Broadcasting Unit produces radio lessons in a VOK studio especially designated for its use. They go out on medium wave, with supplemental coverage on short wave for schools not otherwise reached. In 1972 VOK scheduled schools broadcasts from 9:40 A.M. to 12:00 noon five days a week and from 2:10 P.M. to 4:45 P.M. three days a week. Radio lessons were aimed at students and teachers of primary and secondary schools and at training colleges. Lessons varied from 20 to 30 minutes in length and dealt with such subjects as English, Swahili, French, history, geography, civics, science, health, mathematics, agriculture, and teaching. Schools registered voluntarily and received teachers' guides and course pamphlets for students free of charge. A long-term project to use radio teaching in combination with correspondence study for the upgrading of teaching in Kenya was launched in 1966 with help from Canada (see § 12.3.3) and the United States (University of Wisconsin 1969).

4.1.3 Television

As noted earlier, Kenya television began in 1962. To supplement the national station in Nairobi, VOK opened a regional station in Mombasa in

1970. It originated local news but otherwise repeated Nairobi programs on a delayed basis; the programs were shipped on film or tape by bus from the capital. A repeater station at Timboroa, near the Nandi Hills regional radio station, serves a group of towns in the southwest, and a smaller repeater at Nyeri serves an area about 65 miles north of Nairobi. Though these four outlets covered only 8% of the land area, they reached about 45% of the population (Swedish Telecommunication Consulting AB 1972, 2:24).

VOK television had one large studio and a talk studio in 1972, but it also made extensive use of a mobile unit equipped with a portable microwave link for live pickups in the Nairobi area. A new repeater link enabling pickups anywhere in Nairobi was inaugurated during the first All African Trade Fair in 1972; also, plans were announced for adding another mobile van, equipped for video recording (Amira 1972, p. 53). Much of the studio equipment, however, had served well beyond its normal life expectancy, since the original installation was made in 1962.

In 1972 VOK produced about 60% of its programming locally—a high proportion, especially considering the small size of its production staff, about 20 people in all. VOK actively encourages Kenyan artists to use the broadcast media. For example, young Kenyan actors regularly present plays on television in both English and Swahili.

The television service was on the air about 30 hours per week in 1972. News, current affairs, and talks occupied 39% of total program time, an unusually high proportion. The government shows marked concern about the influence TV may have. For example, an experienced observer remarked that VOK "has quite the strictest rules I have encountered anywhere regarding violence on TV—no killing, no shooting, no fighting, no poisoning, no stealing may be shown" (Green 1972, p. 252).

Nairobi is a lively, modern commercial center, and advertising is relatively highly developed there. A number of advertising agencies offer full-scale services to their clients, including production of television programs. For example, an agency produced the series "Kenya Kitchen," taping it in the demonstration kitchens of the East African Power and Lighting Company.

4.1.4 Audience Data

In 1969, VOK commissioned a national audience survey from a commercial research organization (Associated Business Consultants 1969). The surveyors, using methods of selection designed to yield a probability sample projectable to the entire population, interviewed a sample of more than 5,000 adults, 60% in rural and 40% in urban areas (see § 16.3.1 for more details on sampling procedures).

According to the survey, the size of VOK's radio audience had previously been seriously underestimated. The surveyors estimated the number of radio receivers in homes to be 774,000; in public places, 6,000. This meant that about half the homes in Kenya either owned or rented radio receivers, a relatively high percentage for Africa, but not unexpected considering the long years the country had been served by radio. The average audience size for home receivers was 3.7 persons; for receivers in public places, 9.9.

About three-quarters of the respondents said they "usually" listened to the radio, although only a little more than half claimed to have listened "yesterday." The national service (in Swahili) was by far the most popular of the three VOK services—half the sample said they had listened to it "yesterday"; 14% said they listened to the general service (in English). The vernacular service, of course, appeals to much smaller groups and has much less time in which to reach each language group; the largest vernacular audience, only 8% of the total sample, represented those who said they had listened "yesterday" to the Kikuyu service. This relatively low listenership for the language of the largest tribal group illustrates the problem of serving linguistic minorities with a mass medium like radio. More than twice as many in the sample (18%) said they listened to neighboring Tanzanian radio, presumably in Swahili, as listened to any local Kenyan language. Other foreign services with significant listenership were originated by Uganda (5%), Ethiopia (3%), the BBC (2%), and the VOA and Somalia (1% each). These findings are borne out roughly by a BBC and Deutsche Welle survey of 1971, in which preferences for foreign stations were said to have been expressed in the following order of descending frequency of mention: Tanzania, BBC, VOA, Ethiopia, Germany, Moscow, Cairo, Peking (*Rundfunk und Fernsehen* 1971a, p. 224).

As for television, the 1969 survey indicated the number of sets in use to be 20,000 ± 1,000. The study was made before the regional station opened in Mombasa, for which the surveyors projected an eventual circulation in several years of about 3,800. According to the sample, home receivers averaged seven viewers per set, while public receivers averaged 74.5 per set. The surveyors estimated that there were about 850 public sets including those in bars and other places of business. In 1972 the ministry claimed more than 800 community "viewing halls" (letter from acting director of broadcasting, June 1972). Adding these community viewing facilities to places of business with sets makes for a sizable out-of-home television audience. An interesting sidelight on the measurement of sets-in-use was the comparison made by the researchers between estimated sets and the official customs records on importations. According to the latter, in the period July 1962–June 1969, 18,600 television receivers entered Kenya through normal channels. If the survey's estimate of 22,000 sets in use was correct, some 6% had evaded customs.

4.1.5 Training and Development

The VOK has been particularly fortunate in the scope and variety of the training opportunities available to its staff. In addition to the BBC, the Centre for Development Overseas, and other such resources (§ 14.2),

VOK has access to the Kenya Institute of Mass Communication, construction of which started in Nairobi in 1965. The institute opened in 1970 as probably the most complete broadcast training center in Africa (Mumanyi 1971). In addition, a new school of journalism at the University of Nairobi started at the same time (§ 14.3.2).

Kenya's media have also received extensive bilateral aid from a number of countries, such as the German film-production project mentioned in § 12.4.3. The major bilateral-assistance project was a $1.5-million contract financed by the United States Agency for International Development during the period 1966–70. It supplied five advisers to VOK for two years, seven for an additional two years, in the fields of management, engineering, production, news, and commercial operations. This was one of AID's most extensive undertakings in support of a government-commercial broadcasting system in Africa (see § 12.2.1). The goals of the project as defined by the Kenya government were to advise and assist in modernizing and streamlining the VOK's organization, to help complete staff Africanization (VOK still had 82 expatriates on its staff when the project began), and to build up commercial revenue. A contract for these services was awarded to RTV International of New York, a consulting firm specializing in this type of work (see § 12.2.1 regarding other such contracts). The following description and analysis are based on the company's report to AID (RTV International 1970), correspondence with other members of the advisory team, and this writer's personal observations.

The project got under way in 1966, and its accomplishments by the time of its expiration in 1970 were as follows: (1) The contractor had conducted or arranged training of several kinds—on-the-job training, in-house classroom instruction, and overseas scholarships—for some 500 of VOK's 700 staff members. Thirty went to the United States for advanced study for periods ranging from six months to two years. (2) The VOK staff had been completely Africanized. (3) The station's organizational plan had been streamlined and modernized. (4) VOK's commercial operations had been overhauled, a modern rate card had been published, and its gross commercial revenues had increased from annual billings of £180,000 at the start of the project to over £600,000 at its close. Increased commercial income was of no direct benefit to VOK, however. It could not be used as an incentive for greater staff efforts, inasmuch as advertising revenue went directly to the Kenya central treasury.

Although the RTV International project attained some of its objectives fully, it fell short of ideal fulfillment in others, particularly those concerning organization and staff. The benefits of training were nullified to a large extent by low staff morale and rapid personnel turnover. These adverse conditions were traceable to the methods used for the recruitment of staff and for the setting of salary scales, promotion policies, job assignments, and the like. VOK, as a government entity, is naturally subject to the civil service code that controls government employment generally. The civil service, however, takes little account of the special requirements of broadcasting. RTV International in presenting its organizational plan for VOK pointed out that existing personnel policies and practices "had a tendency to discourage individual initiative and effort, while condoning mediocrity and inefficiency." The plan indicated that the jobs of well over 200 superfluous employees were being protected by their civil service status, while much-needed, highly trained employees were resigning because of inequities, inadequate pay, or lack of promotion and were seeking more lucrative and satisfying work in private industry.

The advisory group recommended recognition of the special personnel requirements of broadcasting by the setting up of a broadcasting commission which would perform the functions of the civil service in that field. This recommendation proved unacceptable, however, and so the advisers could not fully realize all the improvements envisioned in the organizational plan. As if in justification of the advisory group's findings, about a year after the project ended the Kenya government suddenly replaced much of VOK's upper-echelon staff with junior officers (*Rundfunk und Fernsehen* 1972c). The official reason cited was that lax management had led to poor staff discipline and deterioration of the service—precisely the kinds of problems the RTV International group had sought to correct.

Discouraging though such setbacks are—especially when they stem from a built-in "failure factor" such as the inflexible personnel policies previously described—on balance one must say that the VOK made the transition from a foreign-owned, foreign-managed operation to an independent one with minimum disruption. In a newspaper interview shortly before leaving Kenya, the head of the RTV International team said, "We are going away feeling that we leave behind a nucleus of very capable, very ambitious, very knowledgeable broadcasters at the Voice of Kenya. We are frustrated because we have not been able to overcome the difficulties that are inherent . . . in a developing country. . . . What is in fault is not the fault of the staff; it is the fault of the circumstances and the system under which it is operating" (Darling 1970, p. 15).

4.2 United Republic of Tanzania, *by Graham L. Mytton*

Population: 13,300,000	Radio transmitter sites: 2
Receivers per thousand: 17	Area per site: 182,000 sq mi

4.2.1 Historical and Political Background

The union of Tanganyika with the island of Zanzibar brought into being the United Republic of Tanzania in 1964. The former Tanganyika, the mainland part of the republic, had become independent in 1961 and was the first of Britain's East African territories to do so. Many areas of government on the mainland and on the island, including broadcasting, continued separate existences after the union. The two entirely independent broadcasting systems are known as Radio Tanzania Dar es Salaam (RTD) and Radio Tanzania Zanzibar (RTZ).

Unlike its neighbor Kenya, Tanganyika did not absorb large numbers of European settlers, which helped to promote a more speedy and peaceful transition to independent majority rule. It also meant that such facilities as were developed in the country were for the indigenous people. When the first broadcast transmitter was inaugurated in 1951 in the capital, Dar es Salaam, its target audience was mainly African. In Kenya, on the other hand, where broadcasting had started in 1927, the settler community was long the primary target audience (§ 4.1).

Tanzania is about the same size as Nigeria, but with less than one-quarter of that country's population. Its population in 1972 was about 13 million. With only about 6% living in towns, the country was one of the least urbanized in the world. This, together with the uneven distribution of the people, has hampered the development of the mass media. The population is concentrated mostly around the periphery of the country, including the coastal area near Dar es Salaam in the east (Svendsen and Teisen 1969, p. 22).

Tanzania's economy remains predominantly agricultural, with about 95% of the agricultural output from the "traditional" sector (Legum 1971b, p. B177). The gross national product for 1969 was only $85 a person (*Africa South of the Sahara* 1972, p. 824); by this measure, Tanzania is among the poorest countries in the world. Most of the people live lives of extreme simplicity, and of downright hardship during periods of shortage caused by droughts or crop failure.

The main feature of the government's strategy for solving Tanzania's problems is a form of socialism originally outlined in a highly original and authoritative document, the "Arusha Declaration" (TANU 1967). Since

Graham L. Mytton was Zambian Broadcasting Services Research Fellow at the Institute for African Studies, University of Zambia, 1970–73; he studied the political role of mass media in Tanzania for his Ph.D. dissertation at Manchester University; and he has worked for BBC as studio manager.

its promulgation in early 1967, the economic, social, and political direction of mainland Tanzania has changed considerably. The Arusha Declaration asserts that development which benefits all the people can be achieved only through hard work, self-reliance, and socialist agriculture. The latter is of prime importance to the success of the policy, and Tanzanians are encouraged to live together in *ujamaa* villages (*ujamaa* is the Swahili word for "brotherhood" or "familyhood"), where they work together for the common good, sharing both prosperity and hardship.

Before the British left Tanganyika in 1961 they set up a broadcasting corporation similar to the BBC, as they had in other colonial territories. This arrangement proved unpopular with the local political leaders after independence, especially when members of the Tanganyika Parliament found they could not exercise much control over the operations of the Tanganyika Broadcasting Corporation. Though asked each year to vote for a government subvention, they could not make their views and demands felt, since the TBC was outside the direct control of any minister. Some politicians also questioned the right of the TBC to speak independently and impartially about the nation's situation. Under its charter, the TBC had freedom of expression, but many political leaders felt that once the government had decided on a policy the matter should not be discussed further—especially not on the radio. Such discussion, they thought, would only confuse the people. These arguments won, as they did also in Zambia and in Kenya, whose broadcasting corporations also had short lives. The TBC was dissolved in 1965, the year Tanzania became a one-party state. In his speech to Parliament announcing the take-over of broadcasting, the minister responsible for the medium said that radio should be tied in with the government's attempts to "mobilize the masses" in all fields (Tanzania, *Parliamentary Debates,* March 1965, col. 40). In the years following, the movement toward socialism made it even more inevitable that radio should assume this supportive role.

Any discussion of mainland Tanzania must include a mention of the ruling party, TANU (Tanganyika African National Union), which is at the center of political life at all levels in the country. Tanzania became a one-party state by law in 1965, but even before this the TANU party had encountered no serious rivals. In spite of the law forbidding the formation of other parties, mainland Tanzanians enjoy a remarkable degree of political freedom. At elections they choose between candidates with bona fide differences in viewpoint. The party is a mass party, not a vanguard movement on the lines of ruling Communist parties. President Nyerere maintains an independent socialist policy, free from Marxist dogma, which he regards as irrelevant to Tanzania's needs (Nyerere 1969).

The pervasive influence of TANU has made its mark on broadcasting, particularly since the Arusha Declaration of 1967. Radio is now seen as playing an important role in political education. In particular it supplements the activities of TANU in the encouragement of hard work and self-reliance, and in teaching people about their role in the developing economy. Tanzania's broadcasting system is entirely under the control of the government as a department of the Ministry of Information and Broadcasting. Between 1967 and 1971, the annual amount budgeted for broadcasting was between $600,000 and $700,000 (Tanzania, *Estimates of Revenue and Expenditure,* 1967–71). The radio budget for the year 1971–72 was about $653,000 (letter from Stephen Mlatie, RTD assistant director, 6 May 1972). With these modest allocations, Radio Tanzania Dar es Salaam operated three main networks.

4.2.2 Facilities

One of the problems of radio transmission in Tanzania is the geographical position of the capital, Dar es Salaam, on the coast. Better coverage could be achieved from a more central position. In 1972, all networks were beamed from Dar es Salaam. But the main reliance for nationwide coverage was placed on short-wave transmitters, which used ten frequencies, changed during the day to suit propagation conditions.

New medium- and short-wave transmitters were being installed as funds became available. Meanwhile, reception in 1972 was particularly poor in some densely populated areas on the periphery of the country. The 1969–74 Five-Year Plan recognizes that people in these areas can listen more easily to foreign radio stations (Tanzania 1969, 2:111). Two regional transmitters came into service in 1972, in Mbeya in the south, and in Mwanza in the northwest. A third one, at Arusha in the north, was expected to come into service in 1973 (letter from Stephen Mlatie, RTD assistant director, 6 May 1972). A further transmitter was planned for Tabora to improve transmission in the west of the country. Antiquated transmitters in Dar es Salaam were to be replaced (Tanzania 1969, 2:111).

The general poverty of mainland Tanzania also put a brake on the growth of set ownership in the rural areas. While most Tanzanians listen to the radio at least some of the time, there was only about one set for 26 people (Mytton 1970, p. 13). This, coupled with the concentration of set ownership in the towns, led the government to plan the setting up of community receivers: "Radio is the major mass media [sic] for effective communication with the people. It is planned to set up listening points so as to reach a larger number of people who cannot afford to buy their own radio sets" (Tanzania 1969, 2:111). These community listening centers will probably go mainly to *ujamaa* villages and be a further encouragement to settlement in these new schemes. One of the most frequent suggestions people in remote areas made to me in the course of my research in 1967–68 was that the government should provide this service. At that time public sets were found only at the markets in some of the major towns, notably in the main market in Dar es Salaam (Condon 1968, p. 142).

A radio factory started production in Arusha in 1967. A serviceable three-band set could be obtained in 1972 for about $42. The government encouraged the manufacture of even cheaper sets (Tanzania 1969, 2:111).

4.2.3 Programming

RTD broadcast three main services in 1972: the national, commercial, and external services, with an additional service for schools during term time. The national service, on the air weekdays for thirteen hours, and Sundays for seventeen hours, is entirely in Swahili. A "Third Program" broadcasting educational material for adults, previously a separate service with limited coverage, was incorporated into the national service in 1971 (Maro 1971, p. 33).

The commercial service, also entirely in Swahili, broadcasts on 100-kw. medium-wave and 50-kw. short-wave transmitters at peak listening times daily for 9½ hours. This service, introduced before the Arusha Declaration and Tanzania's commitment to socialism, is a purely commercial venture aimed at the large Swahili-speaking population of the entire East African area. In 1972 it remained a medium of light entertainment, mostly popular music and sponsored commercial features and competitions. Its future seemed doubtful in the changed political climate, especially since it used the most powerful transmitter and enjoyed better reception in many parts of the country than the national service (Mytton 1968, p. 97). With the gradual take-over of private business by the state, fewer and fewer local advertisers used the commercial service.

The third program, the external service, is quite unlike the external services of most other countries. It was started in 1966 mainly to broadcast news and commentaries to central and southern Africa and the Comoro Islands, that is, to areas still under colonial or minority rule. Similar external broadcasting had earlier been carried on a smaller scale over the national network, when time was made available to UNIP, the leading political movement in Northern Rhodesia before that country became independent as Zambia in 1964. The unusual feature of the external service is that it carries programs specifically aimed at aliens and others living in Tanzania itself who do not speak Swahili (RTD 1972b). Until 1970 a separate English service for this category of listeners was also provided, but the government decided that this was an anomaly, and all English-language broadcasting was incorporated into the external service. In 1972 it offered 7½ hours per day, four of them aimed at Central and Southern Africa.

The languages used on the external service vary but usually include (besides English) Portuguese, Afrikaans, and the main African languages of Rhodesia, South Africa, South West Africa (Namibia), and Moçambique. The major liberation movements of these territories receive free time from RTD. They include the PAC and ANC of South Africa, FRELIMO of Moçambique, SWAPO of South West Africa, and ZANU and ZAPU of Rhodesia. These organizations receive support for their broadcasting activities from the Organization of African Unity's Liberation Committee, whose headquarters are in Dar es Salaam.

With the addition of schools broadcasts during terms six days a week, RTD's total broadcast time amounted in 1972 to 232 hours per week, which represented more than double the output of a decade earlier (Tanzania, *Parliamentary Debates,* no. 4, 1961, col. 120).

The widespread use of Swahili is an important factor in offsetting some of Tanzania's other mass-media problems. Originally a traders' lingua franca combining elements of Arabic and indigenous languages of the area, Swahili has been adopted as the official language, thus making Tanzania one of the few African states (other than the Arabic-speaking north) which has been able to choose an indigenous national language and to loosen the hold of English or French. Most people already understood Swahili as a second language, though their mother tongue might have been any one of those spoken by some 120 different tribes. Swahili offered an ideal choice. It is related to the major local African language group but is not explicitly associated with any particular ethnic group, although it does have links with the Muslim culture of the coast (Condon 1968, p. 146).

TANU, the ruling party, has its own radio programs. A full-time TANU radio officer produces features both for the general public and for special audiences such as the police, the national service, and the army. A TANU officer told me in 1968 that he saw a special role for these programs in reaching across the party bureaucracy directly to the rank-and-file member, who could be told what he should expect from his local leader. As the TANU officer put it, "The people have to be advised about what their local leaders are supposed to do. We want people to be able to say, 'You are misleading us' to corrupt or weak local leaders."

Despite a trend toward such instrumental use of radio in the other services, most of the output of the commercial service has continued to be light entertainment. Some of the more doctrinaire political leaders have urged less frivolity, but RTD recognizes the legitimate role of entertainment: "The radio can bring variety and stimulus to the monotony of a peasant's or worker's life, to augment *but not replace* such forms of local participatory entertainment as dances, ceremonies, or story-telling. The benefits of such forms of relaxation, attacked though they may often be by some, are undoubted. Man cannot live by work alone, and a refreshed spirit has more to contribute in field and workshop than that of a man who sees the days ahead as nothing but toil and effort" (RTD 1968, p. 3).

In the national service, however, the distinction between programs of different types—entertainment, political, educational, and so on—has become blurred. Many of the most popular songs, for example, convey political messages, as illustrated by the 1967 "Azimio Song" ("Declaration

Song"), about the Arusha Declaration; and many drama and poetry programs incorporate political or educative content. One should keep this caveat in mind in noting how the output of the national service was allocated in 1972: music, 50%; politics and education, 14%; news commentaries, 12%; magazines, features, discussions, and talks, 9%; variety and other light entertainment, 5%; religion, 4%; education (systematic instruction), 2%; drama and poetry, 2%; children's programs, 1%; and other, 1%. The commercial service devoted about 80% of its time to general entertainment (mostly music), 13% to news, and the rest to features, discussions, and talks (based on RTD 1972b).

In 1972 RTD had a staff of about 350 which produced all the programs of the service, other than those previously mentioned that were produced cooperatively by ministries and educational interests, plus a few received in Swahili, such as the weekly U.N. program. There have even been some attempts to limit the amount of recorded foreign (in particular, Western) popular music programmed by RTD. The national service has cut back on such music, but no restrictions were imposed on the commercial service, which played a mixture of popular recorded music from East Africa, Zaïre, and Western countries.

One of the weaker features of Tanzanian broadcasting has been news. While there is no formal censorship, the tendency is to "play it safe." The newsroom at RTD gets news from information officers posted around the country, but it has never had a full team of its own reporters. Consequently, it tends to rely on official statements rather than on independent reporting. This is not just because the radio is government owned. Newspapers also belong to the state, yet maintain their own teams of reporters. Often an important news item reported in the press is ignored by the radio, simply because no official statement has been released by a government source: "Thus when Oscar Kambona, former Tanzanian Minister and TANU Secretary General made a strong attack on the President from London, three of the papers gave extensive coverage, the TANU papers predictably making fierce attacks on what he said. It was not until three days after Mr. Kambona's statement that the radio mentioned the event or what he had said." (Mytton 1968, p. 99).

There has also in the past been a tendency toward repetitive exhortation in news bulletins. When the president made a speech anywhere in the country, everything he said was dutifully reported—even when he had been reported as saying exactly the same things elsewhere the day before. The activities and speeches of ministers were reported in full, irrespective of their news value. Recognizing the self-defeating tendency of such reporting, the government ordered information officers to report less on the routine activities of leaders, more on the activities of the ordinary population. The coverage of news, both domestic and foreign, improved considerably following this directive, and the appointment in early 1972 of the former editor of the *Standard*, Tanzania's leading daily newspaper, to head the RTD newsroom was an indicator of the importance attached by the government to further improvement of radio news.

4.2.4 Audiences

In 1960 it was estimated that Tanganyika had 72,000 radio sets and an African listenership of 377,000 (Tanganyika Broadcasting Corp. 1960, p. 2). A Dar es Salaam survey in 1966 indicated that half the respondents had radio sets (Marco Surveys 1966); and in 1967 two Dar es Salaam studies found that nearly two-thirds of the sampled urban residents had radio sets in their houses (Condon 1968, p. 147; Mytton 1970, p. 14). About 90% of the city residents were classified as "listeners," with 72% listening every day.

Upcountry, and especially in the rural areas, the situation is somewhat different. Research in four separate rural areas in 1968 found that on the average one in four or five households had a radio set. But there was great variation from place to place. Many more households had sets in the relatively prosperous coffee-growing area on the slopes of Mount Kilimanjaro than in the poorer parts of the coast region around Dar es Salaam. The area with the lowest rate of set ownership was found to be the "shanty" settlements just outside the city limits (Mytton 1970).

Radio licenses were abolished in 1969. In the last year of collection, about $318,000 was received from licenses. Since they cost about $2.80, only about 115,000 sets were licensed (Tanzania, *Estimates of Revenue and Expenditures*, 1969). The government realized that most set owners were not paying, and yet enforcement was impossible. Moreover, it regarded radio (apart from the commercial service) as an essential public service fully entitled to support from the annual budget.

No nationwide audience survey has been carried out since 1960, but if my partial survey of 1967–68 can be regarded as accurate, and Condon's survey confirms it in most respects (Condon 1968), there are at least 500,000 sets in the country, and about 8 million listeners, of whom 3 million have access to radio sets daily (Mytton 1970, pp. 13–14). Whatever the true figures, they are certain to be nearer to these than to those given in the standard reference books (UNESCO, *Statistical Yearbook*, 1970, pp. 732–33; *WRTH* 1972, p. 299).

4.2.5 Educational Broadcasting

RTD's Schools Broadcasting Section works with the Ministry of Education, producing not only schools programs, but also pamphlets, posters, and books to go with the broadcasts (Welsh 1968, pp. 123–24 et passim). But radio in Tanzania has also been given important tasks in making education available to the general public. Adult education is defined in Tanzania in the broadest sense, and little or no distinction is made between educational broadcasts and political broadcasts. Increasingly, the educational programs have incorporated political content reflecting the philosophy of socialism and self-reliance.

Adult-education broadcasting at RTD was not well coordinated at first. Different departments of the government had their own radio programs, often on similar subjects, with some confusion about the aims of the broadcasts. In addition, the production of these programs was of poor quality. In the 1970s broadcasters responsible for adult-education programs were encouraged to move away from straight lectures (Remtulla and Barrett 1971, p. 2). Special training for educational broadcasters at the University of Dar es Salaam Adult Education Institute and handbooks on adult-education broadcasting methods relevant to Tanzania helped to improve the output (Welsh 1969, 1970). Broadcasters were trained to exploit the versatility of radio—to use plays, features, songs, and even poetry in all types of educational programs (RTD 1968, pp. 3–4). The Adult Education Institute developed a radio department, one of whose roles was to coordinate the work of government departments involved in broadcasting.

The Cooperative Education Centre in Moshi pioneered in the development of radio forums in Tanzania. It produced a series, "Jifunze Ushirika" ("Learn to Cooperate"), for weekly transmission by RTD (Cooperative Education Centre 1968, p. 11). The programs consisted of dialogue between members of a cooperative producers' society. Each of the 51 programs was supplemented by a discussion manual covering the main points of the subject broadcast, and the programs were followed by group discussions, or forums. An estimated 300–400 groups participated in these programs (Sarikoki 1967, p. 7).

The University of Dar es Salaam's Adult Education Institute started a series in 1971 known as "Wakati wa Furaha" ("A Time for Rejoicing") to mark the celebration of mainland Tanzania's first ten years of independence. Textbooks and study guides in Swahili were produced for the study groups taking part. An evaluation showed that the program got across effectively to a wide national audience (University of Dar es Salaam 1972, pp. 7–8).

The University's Adult Education Institute ran a similar program on Tanzania's Second Five-Year Plan, putting strong emphasis on the active participation of the rural peasant. In his speech of introduction, President Nyerere ended with the words *kupanga ni kuchagua* ("to plan is to choose"), which became the title of the new series (Bancolle and Chande 1970, p. 3). Thus, radio is used to bring the people, especially those in rural areas, information about Tanzania's problems and how they must be faced. The government is concerned that radio should not lead listeners to expect too much, lest they be caught in the so-called revolution of rising expectations. The emphasis is increasingly on self-reliance. In particular, RTD has tried to promote the *ujamaa* villages:

Radio is playing a big role. . . . At the moment we have a radio man visiting the villages to record material for broadcasts. The Ministry of Agriculture has trained their own staff and are [sic] stationed in every region as a correspondent to report the activities and achievements of the villages. From these reports, a radio programme is made. The Ministry of Information has information officers in every region. They know how to use recording machines and make reports in the form of Regional News Reels after every two weeks or so. The emphasis on this is to make the peasants in the villages speak themselves, giving their views and experience they have in the villages. [Mlatie 1969, p. 3]

4.2.6 Training

Broadcasters in Tanzania have been made aware, through seminars and meetings, of their role in the government's plans. The training of broadcast personnel has been localized to some extent; previously many officers went to the BBC and elsewhere. The decline in reliance on BBC training has come about partly because its value has been questioned by some in government, partly because strained relations have developed between Tanzania and Britain. In 1971, a three month in-service course in Dar es Salaam on broadcast techniques for studio operators (an area of training previously much neglected) was conducted by Radio Sweden in cooperation with the Canadian International Development Agency (*COMBROAD* 1972b, p. 54).

4.2.7 Zanzibar Broadcasting

As was indicated at the outset, mainland Tanzania's broadcasting system has no connection with that of Zanzibar. Little direct information is obtainable about the island system. It is said to use a medium-wave transmitter of 2 kw. and two short-wave transmitters of 10 kw. and to broadcast entirely in Swahili 13½ hours a day (*WRTH* 1972, p. 129). Broadcasting comes under the direct control of the Revolutionary Council and reflects in many ways that council's arbitrary policies.

In 1972 mainland Tanzania had no television service, and no plans to introduce one. The view held in government and party circles was that television would mainly benefit the urban areas, whereas Tanzania's commitment is to rural development. Radio reaches the majority of the population, and the primary goal of the Ministry of Information and Broadcasting is to obtain satisfactory reception in every part of the country, to help rural development. Zanzibar, however, announced plans to introduce television in the islands by 1973 with the letting of a contract for nearly a million pounds to British firms which were to start installation in mid-1972 (*Africa Research Bulletin* 1972a). This decision provides a further example of the independence of the island from the Union government. Zanzibar town lies only 45 miles from Dar es Salaam; the mainland capital will thus be within receiving range of a moderately powerful television transmitter. It would indeed be ironic if the Union government, after having made the heroic decision to deny itself television on logical economic and social grounds, found TV nevertheless introduced by Zanzibar through the back door, so to speak.

4.3 Uganda, by Edward M. Moyo

Population: 9,800,000	Radio transmitter sites: 6
Receivers per thousand: 28	Area per site: 15,000 sq mi

4.3.1 Regionalization of Services

Broadcasting in Uganda must try to cover a country remarkable for the variety of both its terrain features and its ethnic makeup. Uganda has no fewer than 36 major mountain peaks within its borders. The terrain varies from the arid savanna of Karamoja in the northeast, to the snow-capped Mountains of the Moon in the west, to the swampy shores of Lake Victoria in the southeast. It occupies an "ethnic transitional zone," comprising Bantu, Nilotic, and Nilo-Hamitic elements (de Blij 1971, pp. 357–58). Intense loyalties to several long-established kingdoms helped keep alive linguistic and cultural differences among the many ethnic groups that make up the population of about ten million. The last ruler of Buganda, one of the traditional kingdoms, was deposed as recently as 1966. The British had favored the Baganda over others because they were both numerous and politically well organized. One of the complications of independent Uganda's political life has been the reluctance of the Baganda to give up their preferred status. Uganda has thus been obliged to devise a radio service responsive to wide ethnic differences within its borders. That response can be seen in terms both of the languages used in broadcasting and of the regionalization of programming.

Uganda's Second Five-Year Plan, for the period 1966–71, foresaw a flexible combination of regional and national radio services (Uganda 1966, pp. 124–26). In 1972 this plan was refined by a Ministry of Information and Broadcasting Subcommittee, which recommended a general service, physically available via short waves to the entire country, though not necessarily always national in appeal (Uganda 1972, par. 3.1). This nationally distributed programming would interlock with regionally oriented programming released through four 100-kw. medium-wave transmitters, one each in the Eastern, Northern, Western, and Midland regions. At times the regional transmitters would carry programs of broad national concern simultaneously with the national service—for example, "broadcasts to the

Edward M. Moyo is a production staff member at station WSYR-TV, Syracuse, New York. He has worked in radio in Rhodesia and Zambia and was a lecturer at Makerere University, Uganda, 1970–72.

nation" by the president or any one of the ministers, schools broadcasts, and news—in international languages, rather than in local vernaculars (Uganda 1972, par. 3.3). At other times one particular regional program might be of sufficiently wide interest to be carried by one or more of the other three regional stations, or even by the national service. In its second phase, this regionalization scheme would provide six more transmitters of lower power to fill in gaps in regional coverage, particularly along the borders of the country. The expansion program was financed by a $2.5-million loan from a British electronics manufacturing firm.

Regionalization would not, however, be carried to the point of decentralizing the production of programs, which would continue to originate at studios in the capital, Kampala. Thus the 100-kw. medium-wave transmitter at Mbale in the Eastern Region, the first of the four to be put into service, has no studio facilities for local originations. Instead, Kampala makes liberal use of mobile recording units for gathering program materials throughout the country. No official rationalization has been put forward, but it seems clear that the decision to regionalize transmission while at the same time continuing to centralize program production at Kampala was motivated by considerations of political security. The lesson of such episodes as Moise Tshombe's seizure of the provincial radio station at Lubumbashi in Katanga has not been ignored (see app. 2).

By 1974 Uganda expects to have a full-scale external service in operation. The government has entered into a contract with a Dutch firm for two 300-kw. short-wave transmitters and associated equipment, including sophisticated directional-antenna arrays and switching gear. Initially, programs will be beamed to North Africa, but eventually to all parts of the world. In the meantime, in 1972 the national service carried short-wave Arabic, French, and Swahili news programs intended essentially for external consumption.

4.3.2 Language Problems

The multiplicity of languages and the intensity of ethnocentric loyalties in Uganda made it impossible politically to designate a single national language, other than English, when independence came in 1962. Luganda, the language of the Baganda, the largest and most powerful tribe, was then in widespread use, but during the regime of President Milton Obote, the Baganda fell from political favor. Moreover, other tribal groups would much rather learn Swahili than the language of a rival group. As long as the Baganda feel no compulsion to learn Swahili and the other tribes feel no compulsion to learn Luganda, the problem of a national language for Uganda seems likely to remain unresolved. When the army came to power in 1971, many people assumed Uganda would designate Swahili as the official language of the country, since it had been made the official language of the army. However, General Idi Amin rejected Swahili because it was an international language rather than one indigenous to Uganda.

From the outset, Radio Uganda featured local languages. When radio was introduced by the British in 1958, Luganda occupied seven hours a week, English only 3½. Four years later the number of hours per week had increased to 54 and the number of vernaculars to six (Uganda 1959, p. 8). By 1972, the following local languages, categorized by regions, were used: Eastern Region: Ateso, Lusoga, Kupsbiny, Lusamia/Lunyole/Lugwe, and Lumasaba; Northern Region: Alur, Kakwa, Karamojong, Kuman, Lugbara, and Luwo; Western Region: Rukonjo, Runyakole/Rugiga, and Runyoro/Rutoro; Midland Region: Luganda. The slashes link related dialects combined for purposes of broadcasting as a single-language service; even this device has its complications, however, for native speakers of each dialect must alternate as readers (cf. § 7.1.2). In addition to these 19 local languages, in 1972 Radio Uganda used English for its national service and Arabic, French, and Swahili for its developing external service—23 languages all told.

Using so many language services is expensive. The additional cost in base salaries for production personnel alone to broadcast in local languages in Uganda was estimated at over $100,000 a year (Nsibambi 1971, p. 64). Such multilingualism also divided the available air time into small parcels and limited vernacular programming essentially to news (which is translated from a common newsfile prepared in English). A single-language service might broadcast on the order of an hour's news per day (say, 15-minute summaries morning, noon, evening, and night), but each Radio Uganda channel carries about *five* hours of straight news a day. Thus, no special language group receives a continuous service, and much of the time broadcasts are unintelligible to a large portion of the national audience. This tends to drive listeners to foreign stations. For example, on the border in the far northwest of Uganda, people of Arua listen to Swahili programs from Radio Bukavu, a regional transmitter in Zaïre, when Radio Uganda is broadcasting in vernaculars they do not understand. Uganda listeners can also pick up Swahili from nearby Tanzania, Kenya, and Rwanda—not to mention the many Swahili programs beamed toward them by overseas stations.

A 1971 survey indicated that, of a sample of Ugandans who "listened yesterday," 13% tuned to the Voice of Kenya, 11% to Zaïre, 10% to Radio Tanzania, and 5% to Burundi. Of services from outside Africa, only the BBC, with 5%, and the VOA and India, with 1% each, drew enough sample listeners to report in percentages, but smaller numbers said they listened to Peking, Moscow, and Pakistan (Associated Business Consultants 1972, table R-7).

An unexpected aspect of the language problem in broadcasting came to attention only after the government had decided to provide medium-wave regional services as previously described. The Ministry of Information and Broadcasting appointed a subcommittee to study the plights of (1) citizens who could not pick up the new medium-wave service in their own regions because in the past they had depended entirely on short-wave service and had invested in receivers capable of receiving short wave only; and (2) citizens who had migrated from their original tribal areas to other regions of the country and so could not pick up the special regional programs prepared for their benefit (Uganda 1972, par. 1.1). The subcommittee recommended that a national short-wave service continue after the regional medium-wave services had been established, to serve listeners with short-wave-only receivers (Uganda 1972, pars. 3.1–3.5).

Politics obviously had a lot to do with the number and the choice of vernacular languages used on Uganda radio. There can be little doubt, for example, that the timing of the introduction of programs in Swahili was prompted at least in part by the fact that Swahili was the official language of the Uganda Army, which assumed power on 25 January 1971. Rukonjo, spoken by only a few thousand people in western Uganda, was introduced in March 1972, apparently as a political concession to the Bwamba/Bakonjo group. Hindustani, on the other hand, quietly disappeared from both radio and television in 1971 with no public announcement. This language had served the Asian community of some 60,000, which at the time was being accused of having "failed to integrate with the indigenous people" of Uganda.

4.3.3 Television

Uganda television started in 1963 when an American company undertook to install equipment and provide on-the-job training. Studios were set up in a disused hospital building in Kampala—for once a low-budget station started with enough floor space! This type of rather unconventional improvisation characterized the first years of Uganda television, which from the start made extensive use of outside broadcasts, rapidly trained Uganda crews to assume full production responsibility for local programming, and introduced schools television (see Nugent 1967, p. 20). Uganda television also made more rapid progress than most Tropical African countries in extending the service beyond the capital. The 1966–71 Five-Year Plan envisioned television service wherever electricity was available; it looked forward to "comprehensive mobile recording facilities to enable the many historic, cultural, and exciting events . . . to be brought to the viewing audience" (Uganda 1966, p. 126). By 1972 the television system had six origination points, and plans existed for additional facilities to enable 90% coverage of the entire population within a few years. These plans were based upon a survey made by a Japanese company, in accordance with a 1970 agreement. Uganda's Third Five-Year Plan, for

1971–76, called for a completely new center for television production in Kampala, and a receiver located at every community center equipped with electricity (Uganda 1971, pp. 374–78).

4.4 Burundi and Rwanda, *by James M. Kushner*

Burundi and Rwanda are small, densely populated, landlocked nations, once part of German East Africa, later (after World War I) mandated to Belgium as Ruanda-Urundi. They became independent as separate states simultaneously in 1962. Both have precarious economies, heavily dependent on coffee, most of which is bought by the United States. Literacy is low, and daily papers are nonexistent, so that radio broadcasting plays the major role in government contacts with the populations of both countries. Yet national budgets are too cramped to allow for adequate development of a full range of broadcasting services based on their own resources. Therefore both countries, in different ways, depend partly on supplementation of their national broadcast services by foreign organizations.

4.4.1 Burundi

Population: 3,600,000	Radio transmitter sites: 1
Receivers per thousand: 28	Area per site: 11,000 sq mi

With 3.5 million persons living in a highland area about the size of Belgium, Burundi has the distinction of being the most densely populated country on mainland Africa. Radio stations operating in this small republic include the government-run Voice of the Revolution and Radio CORDAC, a Protestant missionary radio service directed to listeners throughout Central Africa. Burundi has no television service.

Established in 1960, Voice of the Revolution programs locally produced entertainment, news, commentary, and weather reports in Kirundi, French, and Swahili for domestic use on one medium-wave and two short-wave stations (McDonald et al. 1969, p. 33). The weekday schedule calls for 11½ hours of programming, from 5:30 A.M. to 8:00 A.M., 12:00 M. to 3:00 P.M., and 5:00 P.M. to 11:00 P.M. There are no license fees on receivers and no commercials on the VOR, which is financed entirely by direct government appropriation.

Although Burundi was a Belgian colony, the French have had a pronounced influence on the government broadcasting system. VOR sub-

James M. Kushner is Social Science Analyst, Near East and Africa, Research and Assessment Office, United States Information Agency. He served as a Peace Corps volunteer in Kenya, 1967–69, and Broadcasting Instructor, University of North Dakota, 1970–71. The opinions expressed are those of the author and not necessarily those of the United States Information Agency.

scribes only to the news file of Agence France Presse, having dropped TASS early in 1971 (USIS Bujumbura Field Message, 8 February 1971). French technical advisers work in the modern, Burundi-built but French-equipped administrative and technical headquarters of the National Broadcasing Organization, dedicated in June 1971 by the minister of information (*Bulletin quotidien de l'ACI,* Brazzaville, 3 July 1971, p. 10).

Burundi's second radio service is Radio CORDAC, an interdenominational Protestant radio station broadcasting since 1963 from the capital, Bujumbura, and from nearby Nyakarago, on the mountainous Continental Divide. CORDAC stands for Corporation Radiodiffusion de l'Afrique Centrale. I am indebted to its director, James E. Morris, for information on the service. CORDAC obtained a franchise from the Burundi government in 1963. Under the terms of the agreement the station may not broadcast any political or sectarian (denominational) material; new transmitters and frequencies must be approved by the Burundi Department of Telecommunications; and any program changes must have the approval of the Ministry of Information.

In early 1972 four transmitters radiated programs in French, Kirundi, English, Swahili, and Ebembe (a dialect of eastern Zaïre) for a total of 45¾ hours weekly. The programs, 70% religious and 30% educational and informative, were produced both locally and by arrangement with studios elsewhere in Africa and the rest of the world. CORDAC acquired a 17-acre site for its antennas and transmitters at Nyakarago, upon which six directional antennas, a single omnidirectional multiband antenna, and transmitters ranging up to 10 kw. were to be installed in 1972 or soon thereafter. These hopeful construction plans were contingent on the cooperation of missions and African churches in the area, on finances, and on local political conditions (letter from Robert D. Kellum at CORDAC's North American Headquarters, 10 March 1972).

The Radio CORDAC staff included 13 missionaries (from the United States, Switzerland, and Sweden), and 17 Africans representing Protestant churches in Zaïre and Burundi. The Africans received on-the-job training and carried on the bulk of station operations. An executive board on which Africans were a majority administered overall station affairs.

In 1964 CORDAC started a secondary-level, four-year radio training institute. The first three years are devoted to academic study (including mathematics, science, English, and French as well as broadcasting subjects), the fourth year to practical work at the CORDAC station. Of its first intake of ten students, four were graduated in 1968. Two of these were working in radio for the Burundi government in 1971, one for a local commercial radio firm. After a hiatus, during which problems of official accreditation were solved, the school took in a second class in 1971. One class goes through the entire four-year cycle before another class is admitted.

The optimistic plans of Radio CORDAC were halted, at least temporarily, in mid-1972, however, when Burundi experienced political turmoil which forced the closing down of the station. In September, after three months' blackout, the station returned to the air, but only three of the African staff were able to resume their duties (*ICB Bulletin* 1973).

4.4.2 Rwanda

Population: 3,600,000	Radio transmitter sites: 1
Receivers per thousand: 14	Area per site: 10,000 sq mi

The Republic of Rwanda is a small, densely populated country dotted with alpine lakes and active volcanoes. The literacy level is about 10%, primarily in Kinyarwanda and French. Rwanda has no television. Radiodiffusion de la Republique Rwandaise, the noncommercial, government-owned and -operated radio service, includes a domestic service—popularly called "Radio Kigali," after the capital city—and a limited external service operated under unique circumstances.

For domestic use, Radio Rwanda has one 50-kw. short-wave transmitter (Nyrop et al. 1969, p. 93), broadcasting 94 hours weekly. The station was built and equipped for Rwanda in 1965 by the West German government, in return for the right to establish a Deutsche Welle relay station at Kigali (§ 12.4.2). A daily, hour-long external-service program "Publicity in Africa" is relayed in French, English, and Swahili by Deutsche Welle facilities, on behalf of Radio Rwanda, to the East African region. In 1972, Deutsche Welle's own two 250-kw. short-wave transmitters rebroadcast sixteen hours a week of Germany's external service in Amharic, English, French, German, and Hausa to target audiences throughout Africa.

Radio Rwanda is financed largely by an annual license fee on receivers of about $1. West German and French advisers have had a predominant influence at the station, which broadcasts domestically in French, Kinyarwanda, and Swahili.

An innovative educational experiment in Rwanda is the Radio University of Gitarama, named for a town about 40 miles southeast of Kigali. Starting in 1962, Dominican primary teachers, assisted by other teachers and technicians, developed rural audiovisual centers for children and adults whose formal educational opportunities were limited. Equipping each center with projectors and radio receivers, the university geared its teaching to slides synchronized with educational broadcasts—all developed, written, and performed at the Gitarama center (*Marchés tropicaux* [Paris], 21 October 1967, p. 2753; Adjangba 1968).

Anglophone West Africa

Two of the countries treated in this chapter, Nigeria and Ghana, hold a special interest for students of broadcasting. Nigeria, whose population of over 55 million is much the largest in Africa, has a unique combination of both a fully developed federal broadcasting system and independent regional systems operated by the states within the federation. This degree of decentralization of government-controlled facilities is unique in Africa. One of the state systems, that of Western Nigeria, has the oldest television service in Tropical Africa. It has been in operation since 1959.

Ghana's radio system, which dates back to 1935, has the longest history of independent operation in West Africa—since 1956, when Ghana became the first West African colony to achieve independence. One reason radio developed rapidly in the independent state of Ghana was that its first president, Kwame Nkrumah, recognized it as a means of furthering his dream of Pan-Africanism.

5.1 Nigeria, *by Christopher Kolade*

Population: 55,100,000	Radio transmitter sites: 18
Receivers per thousand: 28	Area per site: 20,000 sq mi

As a target for broadcasting, Nigeria's large population is extremely diverse. More than 250 ethnic groups have been identified, some with as few as 10,000 members (*Africa South of the Sahara* 1971, p. 552). Indigenous languages number in the hundreds (Crowder 1966, p. 24). English, though it must be regarded as distinctly a minority language, is the only one understood nationally; it thus forms a bond among the elites of the various ethnic groups as well as a lingua franca for broadcasting. The broadcasting

Christopher Kolade is Director-General, Nigerian Broadcasting Corporation. He was previously Director of Television and then Director of Programs for the Corporation; Vice-Chairman, International Broadcast Institute; and member, Ecumenical Satellite Commission, World Association for Christian Communication.

system of the country faces two major challenges: how to reach the whole land area with an acceptable broadcast signal, and how to satisfy the program needs and desires of a very wide variety of subaudiences.

Nigeria's political organization reflects its ethnic diversity, for it consists of a federation of 12 states. Prior to 1967 it was subdivided into four regions, and the broadcasting system is gradually adjusting to this change in political organization. The prolific broadcasting activity which is characteristic of Nigeria indicates that both the federal government and the state governments have assigned broadcasting an important role in the tasks of national development.

Under the Nigerian constitution, both the federal government and the state governments are free to set up broadcasting services. Although only five of the 12 state governments have actually done so (a sixth had plans on the drawing boards in 1972), it is quite possible that Nigeria may eventually have as many broadcasting services as there are states in the federation, in addition to the federal system itself.

5.1.1 Federal and Regional Services

The principal broadcasting organization in Nigeria is the Nigerian Broadcasting Corporation, usually referred to as NBC. It operates a nationwide network of 18 stations, with its main originating site in the federal capital, Lagos, from which the National Program goes out to the whole country. This service is also known as "Radio Nigeria"—that is, a service designed to serve common national rather than local or regional interests. The latter are served in two ways: (1) Stations of the NBC located away from the center, at the capital cities of the several states, carry the National Program only part of the time; the rest of the time each carries programs tailored especially for the peoples of its particular coverage area. (2) Some of the states also have their own broadcasting systems, entirely independent of the NBC and oriented toward serving local needs. There is also an external service, Voice of Nigeria, which is operated by NBC on behalf of the nation as a whole.

Broadcasting in Nigeria thus presents a picture of multiplicity. There are multiple stations, multiple owners, and multiple services. However, the great majority of the domestic stations belong to the federal government, which also owns and operates NBC-TV, the Lagos television station, and Voice of Nigeria, the external service. Nigerian television does not yet operate television on a network basis; the video services are essentially confined to their cities of origin.

The Western Nigeria Government Broadcasting Corporation operates localized radio and television stations with the call signs WNBS and WNTV. Based in Ibadan, these stations broadcast principally to the Western State of Nigeria. The northern part of Nigeria is covered by Radio-Television Kaduna (RKTV), operated by the Broadcasting Company of Northern Nigeria as an agent of six states: North Central, North-Western, North-Eastern, Kano, Kwara, and Benue-Plateau. These states once formed a single entity, the Northern Region, in the days when Nigeria consisted of only four political regions instead of the present 12 states.

ECBS is the call sign of the Enugu radio station owned by the government of the East Central State and operated on its behalf by the East Central State Broadcasting Corporation. In 1972 the Midwest State government set up a television station in Benin, and the Rivers State, with its capital in Port Harcourt, announced plans for starting a radio station.

5.1.2 Control and Structure

The federal government is the licensing authority. All state governments wishing to start broadcasting services must first obtain licenses from the federal Ministry of Communications. This ministry allocates broadcasting frequencies and regulates the design and power of technical equipment.

Early in the history of broadcasting in Nigeria, it was felt that radio and television should be free from direct political control. Accordingly, in 1957 the Nigerian Broadcasting Service, originally a department of government, was turned into a public corporation, the Nigerian Broadcasting Corporation. All other broadcasting services in Nigeria have followed this pattern, and each corporation is entrusted with considerable freedom and initiative to run its day-to-day affairs. Each has a board of governors whose chairman and members are appointed by the appropriate government. The board makes general policy, and its members are appointed for a fixed term, usually three years in the first instance. They may be reappointed for subsequent terms, without limitation. Next below the governors is, usually, a board of directors, at the head of which is the chief executive officer, known as director-general at NBC and the East Central State Broadcasting Service, or managing director at the Western Nigeria Broadcasting Service. Directors take responsibility for the usual operational areas such as programming, news, technical services, and administration.

5.1.3 Finance

A Nigerian pays an annual license fee of about $1.50 for the use of a radio receiver. The annual license fee for a television set is about $7.50. With an estimated 2.5 million radio sets and fewer than 100,000 television receivers in the country, the maximum revenue receivable from licenses is less than $5 million annually. Since the recurrent budgets of all the broadcasting stations in the country run to a yearly figure of $12 million or more, broadcasting clearly cannot be financed from license revenue alone. In fact, the amount actually collected by the Ministry of Communications for broadcast licenses has never exceeded $2 million in any one year. License revenue goes directly to the Treasury, so that neither the federal government nor any state government draws directly upon this income to finance any part of its broadcasting operations.

As for advertising revenue, it covers less than 15% of the budgeted expenditures of NBC. The broadcasting corporations are allowed to keep their commercial earnings, and the responsible government makes up the difference between this income and the total budgeted running costs of the organization. Broadcasting in Nigeria thus depends mainly on annual subventions from government. In setting up its broadcasting service, each government has accepted this fiscal responsibility. For the federal external service, operated noncommercially by the NBC, the federal government of course pays all bills.

5.1.4 Technical Facilities

The NBC's National Program, operating from Lagos, broadcasts material designed for countrywide listenership. The NBC also has state studios and transmitters in Ibadan, Kaduna, Sokoto, Kano, Maiduguri, Jos, Enugu, Calabar, Port Harcourt, and Benin. These provincial stations broadcast the national programs which they judge to be of interest to their respective states. Finally, NBC also has provincial broadcasting houses in Ijebu Ode, Zaria, Katsina, Onitsha, and Warri. These cater for even smaller audiences in specific cultural areas. In all, the NBC operates 21 transmitters in Lagos and at state capitals ranging in power from 250 w. to 100 kw. These are designed to cover the entire federation. For example, every hour a national news bulletin or news summary is broadcast by the entire network.

In theory, these transmitting facilities should make it possible for anyone in any part of Nigeria to listen comfortably to the National Program, either on his nearest NBC station via medium wave, or else via short wave, usually from Lagos. In practice, however, radio reception is often poor in quality in some parts of the country. This unsatisfactory coverage has been attributed, among other things, to faulty planning of the original transmitter network layout. A survey conducted in 1969 found that "the domestic medium wave transmitting facilities were installed with limited funds . . . located on poor ground . . . (and) operated at low efficiency. . . . Nearly all the transmitters are using the upper medium wave frequencies. This combined with low ground conductivity, characteristic of Nigeria, results in a further reduction of radio service" (Marshall 1969, p. 8). A new national network has therefore been planned and is expected to replace the present facilities completely by the end of 1974. There will be a 50-kw. medium-wave transmitter in every state of Nigeria, backed by a supplementary network of strategically sited short-wave transmitters varying in power from 10 kw. to 20 kw. each. Hand-in-hand with the development of these transmitting facilities, studios will also be improved. The local NBC studio in every state will be enlarged and re-equipped, and an increased level of local programming responsibility will be assigned to these stations.

In addition to the federal facilities just described, six other transmitter installations carry the programs of the state corporations, while five more 100-kw. transmitters carry the external service of Radio Nigeria.

It is difficult to estimate the number of radio and television receivers in Nigeria. Those concerned with such matters have, for many years, contented themselves with intelligent guesses. Current thinking puts the number of radio receivers at about 2.5 million and that of television receivers at 80,000. These figures are the lowest agreed to by most market researchers in the country. There are also about 45,000 wired receivers in four states—Lagos, West, Kwara, and Midwest—all designed for single-channel reception and fed only programs broadcast by the Nigerian Broadcasting Corporation. It has been estimated that roughly 60% of the radio receivers in the country are concentrated in the centers of high-density population. Cities like Lagos, Ibadan, Kano, Enugu, and Benin show the highest concentrations and so tend to be the first targets of radio advertisers. The story in respect to television is similar; here again, nearly all the receivers are to be found in Lagos, Ibadan, Kano, and Benin.

Community listening was apparently once common in Nigeria. Some native authorities, notably in Sokoto Province, were recorded as "installing community listening kiosks with dry battery receivers" in the mid-1950s, and the Nigerian Broadcasting Service at that time proceeded "cautiously with experiments in community listening" (Great Britain 1956, p. 76). Little progress has been made in recent times, however; there are only a few experimental community-listening projects left in the North-Western, North-Central, and Western states.

5.1.5 Programs

Each station of the Radio Nigeria network broadcasts for 18½ hours daily, beginning at 5:30 A.M. local time and closing at midnight. The weekly content of the National Program breaks down in round numbers as follows: music, 43%; news, 13%; education, 11%; indigenous-language magazines, 8%; religion, 8%; current affairs, 4%; programs for women and children, 3%; sports, 3%; and miscellaneous, 7%.

As English is the language of official business in Nigeria, it is also the principal language of broadcasting on the Radio Nigeria network. All national programs are broadcast in English, but in addition the national news is translated into nine indigenous languages and broadcast over the National Program originating from Lagos. These nine languages—Hausa, Yoruba, Ibo, Fulani, Kanuri, Tiv, Ijaw, Edo, and Efik—are mother tongues of more than 45 million Nigerians. One or another of them is understood by the minority groups who make up the rest of the population. However, no fewer than 27 indigenous languages are actually used on the network of Radio Nigeria at various times.

The NBC no longer rebroadcasts foreign programs directly, but the corporation has program-exchange arrangements with many stations and organizations in Africa and Europe, as a result of which special programs, such as "Music of Other Lands," are devised to carry material produced by foreign sources. The NBC is an active member of the Union of African Radio and Television Organizations and the Commonwealth Broadcasting Conference. Most of its program-exchange agreements are concluded with organizations belonging to these two bodies. The corporation is also associated with both the Asian Broadcasting Union and the European Broadcasting Union.

Stations of the national network are interconnected by microwave relays operated by Posts and Telegraphs. The national news, in English and in the nine main Nigerian languages, is broadcast on the entire Radio Nigeria network, carried simultaneously by all NBC stations. Special-events broadcasts, such as an address by the head of state, must also be carried simultaneously on all stations. Besides these, other national network programs are usually scheduled by mutual agreement among all stations. Twice a year, the program chiefs of all NBC stations attend a National Program Planning Conference for this purpose. Basically, national network broadcasts cover the following fields in addition to news: education, current affairs, religion, sports, and children's programs.

Approximately 22% of the entire NBC program schedule is carried by the full network. Beyond this, each NBC regional station individually either produces its own local programs or carries more broadcasts from the National Program, in accordance with its estimate of the local or state audience's interests and its own production capacity. The percentage of programming originated by the local stations of the federal network therefore varies, ranging from 80% local in the larger stations (e.g., Kaduna) to less than 10% local in the smaller ones (e.g., Warri).

5.1.6 Educational Broadcasting

Educational broadcasting is one of the major activities of the Nigerian Broadcasting Corporation, taking up 11% of the total radio air time of the federal service each week. All of it is directed to in-school audiences, ranging from the primary to the secondary and even postsecondary levels of education. There is no formal adult education by radio or television.

One of the interesting features of educational broadcasting in Nigeria is the element of joint production which characterizes it. Several state government ministries of education have their own school broadcasting units which produce a few program series every school term. All such programs are broadcast nationally by Radio Nigeria. In addition, the School Broadcasting Department of the NBC produces its own programs, which are also broadcast to schools all over the federation. The notes issued by the NBC Schools Unit point out that "School Broadcasting in Nigeria is a shared responsibility between two bodies—the Nigerian Ministries of Education which control the content of the syllabuses on the one hand, and the Nigerian Broadcasting Corporation which operates the national radio network. The foundation of educational broadcasting has been laid . . . on this partnership principle" (Nigerian Broadcasting Corporation 1972, p. 2).

Educational broadcasts cover the following subjects: English, history, and science for primary schools; English, French, science, geography, history, and home economics for secondary schools and teachers' colleges; general studies for postsecondary institutions. Topics discussed under the general title "Talks for Advanced Students" have included: "Pre-Colonial Political Institutions," "The Rule of Law," "The Organization of African Unity," "The Study of African Languages," "The Nature of Science," and "The Contribution of Islam to Civilization."

The educational broadcasts of the NBC are mostly aimed at the enrichment of normal classroom lessons. Very little direct teaching is done. NBC's educational programs were used by 4,628 schools in 1971. All the broadcast lessons are supplemented with notes for the classroom teacher, sent out well in advance of the broadcasts so that teachers can prepare their classes for them. Students' pamphlets are also provided for the broadcasts in French and science.

5.1.7 Commercial Broadcasting

Advertising on radio and television in Nigeria was begun by the stations owned by the (then) regional governments. For many years, the NBC set its face firmly against the commercialization of broadcasting. The original NBC Ordinance explicitly forbade advertising on the air: "The Corporation shall not . . . receive money or any valuable consideration from any person in respect of the sending or emitting . . . any matter whatsoever and shall not send or emit any commercial advertisement or sponsored programme" (NBC Ordinance, pt. 3, clause 14). However, attitudes changed over the years, and by 1963, the NBC had decided to "go commercial." The federal government made the necessary legislative change to legalize advertising by the corporation. Even so, certain significant conditions were laid down, including the stipulations that "the general character of NBC programmes was not to be altered . . . and that the balance between entertainment, information and education was to remain unchanged" (Nigerian Broadcasting Corporation 1967, p. 11).

The corporation now has a full-scale Sales Department, which sells air time for spot advertisements and also offers programs for sponsorship to advertising agencies both in Nigeria and overseas. However, commercial broadcasts on the NBC are restricted to certain times of the day:

early morning, midday, and early evening. Not more than nine hours of programming may carry advertisements on any one day, and the advertisements themselves may not exceed 25% of the total air time for the programs which carry them.

Because of the three-tier system of broadcasting practiced by the NBC (national, state, and local) its commercial broadcasts provide flexible coverage of the market at three levels. This offers the advertiser the opportunity to select his audience in terms of both geographical and language considerations. A full range of commercial products is advertised throughout the country, but the NBC refrains from advertising alcoholic beverages in the predominantly Muslim areas of northern Nigeria. In 1972 the major products advertised on radio included: analgesics, 24% of gross revenue; baby foods, 16%; beverages (nonalcoholic), 14%; cosmetics, 8%; tobacco, 7%; alcoholic beverages, 7%. On television, the top places were taken by the airlines and cigarette manufacturers.

5.1.8 External Service

The NBC began external broadcasting in 1962. From the start it was agreed that the federal government would bear the total cost of this service. In 1972 the Voice of Nigeria transmitted 8½ hours of programs every day, in four languages: English, French, Hausa, and Arabic. Three main types of programs were broadcast in each language service: news and current affairs, cultural programs, features, and documentaries. Although most of these programs are about Nigeria ("Nigeria Sings," "Nigerian Newsletter," "Music from Our States," "Nigerian Scene"), some broadcasts, notably those dealing with current affairs, look further afield ("The World in Perspective," "Window on the World," "African Development"). See § 10.6.2 for more details on the external service.

5.1.9 Television

The Federation of Nigeria has seen a great deal of activity in television since the first station, WNTV, Ibadan, pioneered television in Tropical Africa in October 1959. Two other television stations (RKTV, Kaduna; and NBC-TV, Lagos) began their operations three years later, and a fourth was scheduled to open at Benin in 1972. Before 1967, television station ENTV operated in Enugu, Eastern Nigeria, but it was put out of action during the civil war (1967–70). It was due to reopen in 1973.

A relatively high percentage of programming on Nigeria's television stations is indigenous and locally produced. On NBC-TV for example there is about a 50–50 division between local and foreign programs. Forty hours of programs are transmitted every week, and 19 of these hours feature locally produced material. Most foreign programs are the well-known drama series produced in the United States and Europe. The foreign drama slot at 8:00 each evening was filled in 1972 by: "Mission

Impossible," "Mod Squad," "Mannix," "Danger Man," "Dan August," "Bonanza," and "The FBI." Altogether, of the 20 hours of foreign programming, drama accounts for 13, and children's entertainment for four. The rest is taken up by music, comedy, and documentaries.

5.1.10 Audience Relations

There is as yet no regular audience research in Nigeria. Although broadcasting organizations make efforts from time to time to discover basic information about their listenership, such efforts are sporadic and have hardly produced the kind of far-reaching and enduring results desired by advertisers and communication scholars alike.

One project, however, deserves mention because it stands out from all others. This was a television research project, conducted in 1961, about which a report was issued under the title "1961 Lalupon Omi Adio Communications Project: Case Study of the Impact of TV on a Nigerian Village" (Rimmerman and Olusola 1961). Referring to this report recently, one of its writers observed,

A relatively unfamiliar product whose identity was guessed by 4% of the audience (200 villagers) received such a boost after it appeared for only 40 seconds on a television programme. The figure 4% rose to a flighty 77%! A brains trust programme discussed the question: If you could grant one gift to each Nigerian baby born today, would you choose Wisdom, Wealth or Good Health? Before the programme, the villagers responded as follows: Wisdom—35%, Wealth—17%, Good Health—48%. The concensus of the TV panel was that Good Health was the wisest choice and . . . wealth was not worth anything on its own. [After the programme] 76% of the villagers decided in favour of Good Health, and none would offer wealth. [Olusola 1971, p. 5]

Other research projects in Nigeria since that experiment have been multimedia market-research efforts, sponsored by a combination of media operators and designed to discover the relative popularity of radio, television, and the newspaper with specific types of audiences.

5.1.11 Training

The Nigerian Broadcasting Corporation has extensive facilities for the training of staff. The corporation uses on-the-job training; its own Staff Training School; relevant courses in Nigerian universities, colleges, and trade schools; and advanced overseas courses and working attachments.

The NBC Staff Training School offers courses to producers, operators, and technical staff. Within six months of recruitment, a new member of the staff attends an induction course lasting from two to three weeks, in order to become familiar with the organization and operations of the corporation. During the next six years, the technical staff and the operators must attend a junior course, an intermediate course, and a senior course. There is an interval of two years between courses, and success in a course means immediate advancement up the worker's career ladder. Production courses are organized differently, in that they may be taken at any time during the producer's career, whenever he is considered fit for the appropriate course.

Outside the NBC, several institutions in Nigeria offer training courses relevant to broadcasting. Notable among these are: the Institute of Mass Communication, University of Lagos, which prepares students for degrees and diplomas in mass communication (see § 14.3.2); the Institute of Administration, University of Ife, for courses leading to the Diploma in Public Administration; Yaba College of Technology, for technical courses; and the Federal Training Centre, Lagos, for training in secretarial duties.

Overseas training is reserved for members of staff who, having reached a high level of maturity and performance, require a broadening of their outlook at an advanced level. Most such trainees go to the training institutions of overseas broadcasting organizations such as the British Broadcasting Corporation, Australian Broadcasting Commission, Canadian Broadcasting Corporation, and Radio Nederland. Television training is obtained at the Thomson Foundation College in Glasgow and the Centre for Educational Development Overseas in London (see § 14.2.2). NBC staff have also had working attachments in many countries, including Egypt, Japan, the United States, and Western Germany.

5.1.12 The Past and the Future

Broadcasting came to Nigeria by stages. In pursuit of its colonial interests, Britain found it convenient to set up an experimental radio-receiving station in Lagos in December 1932, to pick up the short-wave transmissions of the BBC Empire Service. Three years later, the receiving station became a "radio distribution station," that is, a rediffusion center, extending beyond Lagos to Ibadan and Kano. Gradually, the wired service was taken to other population centers in the country. Broadcasting as such began in 1949 and became a fluorishing activity deserving its own status as a government department under the title "Nigerian Broadcasting Service." The NBS was inaugurated in 1951, as a result of the decision of the Nigerian government to modernize the service. Independent status was envisioned from the outset—"the BBC was asked to lend sufficient staff to enable the service to be developed—first as a Department of Government, but with the ultimate object of turning it into a Corporation staffed by Nigerians" (Great Britain 1956, p. 75). The Nigerian Broadcasting Service took the predestined step within six years, becoming the Nigerian Broadcasting Corporation in April 1957. Its ordinance enjoined it to provide impartial broadcasting services, reflecting the cultures of all parts of Nigeria and covering the entire country with its signals. It was also expected, in due course, to produce broadcasts for external transmission.

The infant corporation instituted a three-year program of action aimed at (1) improving program standards and the diversity of programs; (2) substantially increasing the amount of program material originating in Nigeria, with corresponding decreases in material imported from abroad; (3) improving technical coverage by the introduction of additional and more modern transmitters and allied equipment; and (4) hastening the process of Nigerianization (Nigerian Broadcasting Corp. 1967, pp. 4–5).

It was quite clear from the Ordinance of Incorporation that the NBC was to be a national organization with regional branches. However, no one seemed to foresee the rise of other broadcasting stations independent of the NBC. But then, the political development of the country evolved in such a manner that the three regions originally making up the federation became progressively stronger and more autonomous. Indeed, all the regions achieved a large measure of internal self-government—the West and the East in 1957, the North in 1959—before the federation itself became independent, in October 1960.

Given this political atmosphere, and the fact that broadcasting was not an exclusive federal subject in the constitution, the regions soon became impatient with the NBC, which, in spite of its three-tier system of broadcasting, operated on a centralized policy made in the federal capital. To the regions, this was unsatisfactory, and they longed for broadcasting resources which they themselves could control. First the West (1959), then the East (1960), and finally the North (1962) set up their own government broadcasting corporations and began transmitting their own programs on both radio and television. Perhaps because of the tremendous size of the country, all these broadcasting stations have operated without the kind of cutthroat competition which might otherwise be expected. Indeed, there has been a great deal of cooperation, with one station sharing facilities with another whenever the occasion has demanded it. As the historian of Nigerian broadcasting, Ian Mackay, observes,

These stations did not arise through any desire of competition—unless it be in a commercial sense for a mass audience—for they do not increase the range of programmes. Rather they provide a changed emphasis when required. The dice [are] loaded against the NBC which, as a federal system, must cater for both nation-wide and regional interests—on one network—while the Regional Government-owned stations operate in the more limited franchise of a regional image only. [Mackay 1964, p. 63]

As to the future—insofar as it can be seen—it may witness a voluntary coordination of broadcasting effort. More stations will be built, but policy will become a subject of central discussion and consultation. Since 1969 there has been talk of a national broadcasting authority which would regulate the practice of broadcasting in all of Nigeria, and indications in 1972 were that such an authority would come into being in two or three years. This confirms Mackay's views that there is room, "if not for amalgamation, then at least for a degree of coordination. A united broadcasting and television authority in which control could be shared by the Federal and [State] Governments would be a force of incalculable strength and would make for maximum stability of purpose" (Mackay 1964, p. 64).

5.2 Ghana, *by John Kugblenu*

Population: 9,000,000	Radio transmitter sites: 3
Receivers per thousand: 86	Area per site: 31,000 sq mi

Ghanaian broadcasting comes under the jurisdiction of a statutory corporation. The instrument of incorporation in effect in 1972 was promulgated in 1968, as Decree 226 of the National Liberation Council. It states in part: "The objects of the Corporation shall be to undertake sound, commercial and television broadcasts, to prepare in the field of culture, education, information and entertainment programmes reflecting national progress, aspirations and to carry on an external service of sound broadcasting." The Ghanaian Broadcasting Corporation introduced commercials for both the radio and the television services in 1967 and by 1971 was grossing about half a million dollars from this source annually. Additional revenue comes from advertising in the weekly *Radio and TV Times,* from the monthly rental of rediffusion boxes at 39¢ each, and from license fees on television sets. A set buyer pays $7.80 upon purchase (or less, on a descending scale as the license year runs out), thereafter $7.80 annually. If no outside antenna is obvious, however, evasion of payment is easy. In 1972 the GBC began tracking down delinquent set owners, using the sales records of retailers as a source of names. Threats to publish the names of defaulters produced a rush to pay up. Nevertheless, the government subvention necessary for fiscal 1971–72 to supplement earned revenue amounted to over $3.5 million (Ghana 1971, p. 136).

5.2.1 Broadcast Services

Radio. To carry out its mission, in 1972 the corporation was operating three short-wave domestic radio networks, known as GBC-1, GBC-2, and GBC-3; and an external service. GBC-1 is mainly a Ghanaian language service, utilizing the six main indigenous tongues: Akan (Twi or Fante), Ga, Ewe, Nzema, Dagbani, and Hausa. As an exception, GBC-1 also

John Kugblenu is a graduate of the Ghana Institute of Journalism. He worked in Ghana for the *Daily Graphic* and the *Evening News* before joining the GBC as editor of *Radio and TV Times* in 1968, following a State Department tour of the United States, where he worked briefly for the *Hartford Courant,* Connecticut.

carries daily news bulletins in English. On weekends the service is continuous from early morning to late night, but on weekdays a four-hour break occurs in the mornings. GBC-1 is designed especially for reception by the wired relay (rediffusion) system. In December 1972, more than 56,000 rediffusion speakerboxes were in use in 46 towns. The government was looking into the possibility of eventually substituting low-cost transistor radios for the wired boxes (*Weekly Spectator* 1972).

GBC-2 is the commercial radio service, which uses English as its medium except for occasional advertisements in Ghanaian languages. This service relies heavily on popular music, including both imported soul music and indigenous highlife. Like GBC-1, the commercial service runs continuously throughout the day only on weekends.

The third sound service, GBC-3, operates only in the late afternoon and evening. It carries sophisticated discussion and interview programs, classical music, drama, book reviews, and the like, all in English.

The external service, inaugurated in June 1961, beams programs in Portuguese to Angola and Moçambique; in Arabic to the Middle East; in Swahili to East Africa; in Hausa to West Africa; in French to Central Africa, Malagasy, and Europe; and in English to Ethiopia, Somalia, the Sudan, North America, the Caribbean, Europe, and other parts of Africa (see §§ 10.2, 10.6.1).

Television. In 1965, the thirtieth anniversary of Ghanaian sound broadcasting, Ghana's television service opened, after perhaps the longest and most carefully planned preparatory exercise undergone by any African television system (Ghana n.d., p. 9; see also § 12.3.5). The service started with the avowed intention of completely dedicating itself to education, information, and nation building. Inaugurating the system, the then president, the late Kwame Nkrumah said, "Ghana's television . . . will not cater for cheap entertainment nor commercialism. Its paramount object will be education in the . . . purest sense. Television must assist in the socialist transformation of Ghana" (Ghana Information Services 1965, p. 76). Though the aim was worthy, it proved impracticable in the long run. During the year following Nkrumah's deposition, Ghana TV went commercial. In 1972 GBC-TV devoted about 11% of its time to news, 12% to music, 8% to sports, 6% to drama, and 5% to religion. However, the biggest chunk of time, over 24%, went to syndicated entertainment shows from Britain and the United States, including such mass-appeal series as "I Love Lucy," "Mod Squad," and "Julia." The service opened at 6:00 P.M. (4:00 P.M. on Sundays) and telecast a total of about 31 hours a week.

5.2.2 Specialized Units of the GBC

Engineering. The responsibilities of the GBC's highly developed Engineering Division extend to the operation of studio-transmitter links, a monitoring service, and the wired rediffusion service; the maintenance of vehicles and buildings of the corporation; the purchasing and control of stores; and the provision of simultaneous-interpretation equipment for international conferences and of public address systems for public events. As noted in § 5.2.3 the division also operates its own training school, which is capable of turning out 100 junior technical assistants annually. It maintains and operates 20 radio studios (14 for domestic services, six for the external service), two television studios, and a mobile TV pickup unit, as well as the transmission facilities summarized at the head of this section. More than half of the corporation's 3,000 employees work for the Engineering Division. The main transmitter at Accra is supplemented by a small transmitter at Tamale, some 250 miles to the north. Programs are flown up from Accra daily. In late 1972 a Japanese team made a survey, which included study of the possibility of linking a station as far north as Bolgatanga, 500 miles from Accra, by microwave.

All Radio Ghana transmissions are monitored at a receiving station some 13 miles outside Accra. This station also monitors the output of other broadcasting organizations as required. The Engineering Division maintains and modernizes the transmission lines and receiving-amplifying equipment of the rediffusion system, which serves, as noted above, more than 56,000 subscribers.

Programs and audiences. News and sports rank near the top in popularity among both radio and television programs in Ghana. Live play-by-play coverage of soccer in both media on Sunday afternoons pulls maximum audiences. Originally, sports news commentaries were given in English alone, but more recently live commentary in local languages on GBC-1 has greatly increased the number of knowledgeable sports fans.

The GBC has a Religion Department, and each service carries religious programming, which includes readings from the Qur'an on Friday mornings, as a public service. In addition, the commercial radio network carries several internationally syndicated, sponsored religious series such as Billy Graham's "Hour of Decision," Christian Science's "Truth That Heals," and Seventh Day Adventists' "Voice of Prophecy."

Live music of quality is assured by the GBC Variety Orchestra, a 32-member unit of musicians with formal training. They prepare both classical and popular music for both radio and television. In addition, musical features come from choral societies, local dance bands, traditional musicians and drummers, and students of classical music.

Feedback on audience reactions comes from regular quarterly returns of mail questionnaires sent in by three separate audience panels: one of 380 members for domestic radio, one of 250 members for television, and one of 70 members for external radio. Each panelist receives a free annual subscription to the *Radio and TV Times,* whose normal price is $3.24, and remission of rediffusion rentals and TV license fees. It was planned to more than double the panel sizes in 1972.

This research is conducted by the GBC Audience Research Unit, headed by an official with a master's degree in social psychology. The unit planned its most ambitious survey to date in 1971, in cooperation with the University of Ghana. This was to be the first study attempted by the GBC using field interviews of a sample representative of the entire nation. Interviews were to be conducted by university students and the data analyzed by computer. Results of the analysis were expected by the end of 1972.

Schools broadcasting. The GBC offers both radio and television schools broadcasts, the former from 10:45 A.M. to 11:55 A.M., the latter from 9:30 A.M. to 12:55 P.M. As early as 1957, when Ghana launched her Accelerated Development Plan for Education, the GBC played it part by establishing a Schools Radio Section. In 1972, this section offered eleven subjects, including English, French, African history, science, and teaching methods, to primary and secondary Schools and training colleges. The broadcasts serve as supplementary enrichment. Television teaching started in 1965. In 1972 the Television Schools Section offered material for seven courses, including English literature, geography, general science, mathematics, and teaching methods, to secondary schools and training colleges.

The Schools Broadcasts Advisory Board, composed of eminent educators as well as specialists from such organizations as the Ghanaian Historical Association, assists in the guidance of the GBC Schools Section. Illustrated handbooks containing summaries of program content and suggested exercises for program follow-up are sent to each participating institution before the start of each series. Two liaison officers follow through by visiting the schools and bringing back advice on how to improve the usefulness of the programs. In addition, those who utilize the programs fill out questionnaires, and headmasters and tutors are occasionally invited to attend seminars at GBC.

Initially, GBC undertook the responsibility of supplying and maintaining wired speakers to the schools, but the Ministry of Education plans to replace the rediffusion boxes with radio receivers. In the initial stages of the Schools Television Program the GBC again supplied receivers.

Among future plans of the Schools Radio Section of the GBC in 1972 were the introduction of radio programs on the reading of Twi, Fante, Ga, and Ewe; and a primary school program to be called "Listen and Do." For its part, the Television Section planned to extend its service to the primary schools and eventually to all secondary schools.

Rural broadcasting. In 1971 about 60% of Ghana's adult population was engaged in agriculture, and 85% of her people lived in rural areas. The Rural Broadcasting Section of the GBC thus plays a vital role, serving the farmer, the fisherman, and the rural dweller generally. The first rural broadcasts started in 1961 with a magazine program in Akan called "Adwuma Adwuma O" (Akan for "Well done!", an idiomatic greeting to a worker busy at his job). The section next introduced a 30-minute daily program especially for rural women, translated into all six major indigenous languages.

Members of the unit have had training in rural broadcasting in Australia and Canada. They work closely with the Ministries of Agriculture and Health and the Department of Social Welfare and Community Development.

In 1964–65 Ghana was selected as the site for a major UNESCO experiment in the application of the concept of the rural-development radio forum to African conditions (see § 15.2.1 and Coleman, Popku, and Abell 1968). As a result the GBC became something of an expert on the subject of forums and has trained rural broadcasting personnel from a number of nearby African countries. In 1970 the GBC organized a six-day seminar on the subject for Anglophone countries of West Africa, with help from the German Foundation for Developing Countries and the U.N. Food and Agricultural Organization. Fifty participants attended from six countries.

Some of the busy 13-member staff of the Rural Broadcasting Section serve as hosts on a vernacular, rural, half-hour television program, scheduled in Akan on Mondays, in Ga on Wednesdays, and in Ewe on Fridays. The work of the section was still, in 1972, concentrated mainly in the Eastern and Volta regions of Ghana.

5.2.3 Training

In-house programs. The corporation itself runs three training programs for which it maintains its own teaching staff, supplemented by senior operating-staff members who lecture in their fields of specialization. The Engineering Training School dates back to 1955. It was followed by the Program Training School (sound), and, in the 1960s, by the Television Production School.

The Program Training School (sound) offers a general course for new employees. To qualify for appointment, candidates must have a General Certificate of Education. The course lasts six to eight weeks. This school also runs special workshops for existing staff, on such topics as voice production, English pronunciation, and mastery of Ghanaian languages.

Television training actually began well before television itself in Ghana, as a result of a technical-assistance agreement between Ghana and Canada (see § 12.3.5). Before the inauguration of television, Ghanaian specialists in all the main TV job categories had received on-the-job training in Canada as well as closed-circuit training at home. Some of the initial group of producers also took courses in Italy and East Germany at this time. A lull in the training program followed the opening of the television service in 1965, but the Television Production School was revived in 1968 and has since continued to train newly recruited personnel as cameramen, producers, newsmen, and the like. In 1972 the school's plans included conversion of a former sound drama studio into a closed-circuit television training studio for technical program staff and schools television teachers. This project was to be financed by the British government under its Technical Assistance Program.

An intensive course in educational and documentary film making for GBC staff members was launched in late 1970, under the direction of a four-man team from the Friedrich-Ebert Foundation of West Germany (see § 12.4.3). Among the subjects taught were scriptwriting, camera operation, production, and editing. By 1972, it was understood that the team would conclude that aspect of the training program to concentrate on mobile cinema van operations. Apart from the training benefits of this program, the GBC gained valuable equipment, including such items as a sound-on-film camera, film-editing equipment, and minivans.

The GBC was selected as host for a pilot training project of the Commonwealth Broadcasting Conference in 1970. This was an eight-week course for radio program operators, conducted by experts from the Canadian Broadcasting Corporation and the GBC. Radio men from Ghana, Uganda, Sierra Leone, and The Gambia attended (*Radio and TV Times* 1970).

Ghanaian training outside GBC. An important training resource outside the GBC is the Ghana Institute of Journalism, which is run by the Ministry of Information. It offers a curriculum covering current affairs, African history, economics, English literature, French, shorthand, typing, and theory and practice of journalism. This is an 18-month course, divided between academic and practical work. The latter involves secondment of students for on-the-job training to the national daily newspapers, the GBC, the Ghana News Agency, or the Public Relations Secretariat.

In January 1972, the vice-chancellor of the University of Ghana announced the establishment of the Institute of Journalism and Communications Study under the Faculty of Social Studies, starting in the 1972–73 academic year (*Ghanaian Times* 1972, p. 1). It was planned that the institute would offer a two-year graduate course for degree holders and also an in-service training course for working journalists. In announcing the institute, the vice-chancellor stressed Ghana's need for specialized journalists "in such fields as science and economics to be able to interpret the country's social and economic development" (*Ghanaian Times* 1972, p. 1).

Valuable as such training would undoubtedly be, the present writer cannot refrain from pointing out the danger of overproduction. Traditional British skepticism about the formal training of journalists is based in part upon concern that a diploma carries no guarantee of employment. In the words of Sir Linton Andrews, speaking of the diploma course at the University of London, "There must have been bitter hearts among those who spent two hard years on learning to be journalists without ever getting even the humblest job in a newspaper office. How much better it would be if this kind of training could be given to those about to make ready use of it" (Andrews 1963, p. 72). Many graduates of Ghana's Institute of Journalism were unemployed in 1972. Initially, the Légon graduate journalist may have a chance, but after a decade, what will happen to the accumulation of graduates, with so few daily papers and only a single broadcasting organization in Ghana to offer employment? It may be symptomatic that a 1971 help-wanted advertisement for reporters in Accra attracted more than 600 applicants.

Overseas training. In addition to training in Ghana, many GBC employees have benefited from overseas training opportunities. In 1971 alone, for example, 16 officials, including the director general, studied in Britain. Eleven officials were attached to the BBC for periods ranging from three to six months each, while three others attended the Thomson Foundation College in Glasgow. In the same year, six staff members were attached to the ORTF in France, two went to West Germany, two to Holland, one to Nigeria, and one to the United States.

5.2.4 Receiver Assembly

Ghana has two electronic assembly factories—Ghana Sanyo, and the Electronics Division of the Ghana Industrial Holding Corporation. Fifty-one percent of the former is owned by the government, with a consortium of three major Japanese firms, including Sanyo, holding the rest. The Industrial Holding Corporation is a wholly state-owned enterprise, but it gets all its component parts from Philips Company of Holland, selling assembled sets under the brand name "Akasanoma" (the Akan word for "sparrow").

Except for the wooden cabinets of television sets, all the component parts for both radio and television sets are imported from Japan and Holland. The two factories are located at Tema, the seaport 18 miles from Accra. A 75% ad valorem tax is imposed on imported parts, and factories pay a 10% excise duty and a 7½% sales tax. The last two taxes were abolished for single-band battery radios in 1973. The factories benefited from the five-year tax holiday awarded infant industries under the Capital Investments Act. The cheapest television set, with only a nine-inch screen, retailed at $113 in 1972. One with a 20-inch screen cost $364. An external antenna plus installation fee amounted to $40–$50 more. Even the one-third down payment required for hire purchase obviously freezes out the great majority of a population whose per capita income is only $120. As for transistor radios, the locally assembled sets ranged in price from about $23 to $47 in 1972. Fortunately, batteries, locally manufactured at Tema by a branch of Union Carbide, cost only 15¢ each.

5.3 The Gambia, *by Swaebou J. S. Conateh*

Population: 360,000	Radio transmitter sites: 1
Receivers per thousand: 166	Area per site: 4,000 sq mi

[EDITOR'S NOTE. With only about a third of a million population in an area of about 4,000 square miles, The Gambia is the second-smallest independent country of mainland Africa. Geographically, it is one of the most curious legacies of colonialism—a narrow strip of land on either side of the Gambia River, extending inland for 200 miles, never more than 20 miles wide, sometimes as narrow as seven. Obviously, this long, vermiform shape is impossible to cover efficiently with a broadcast signal. The broadcasting system of this ministate was selected for rather full treatment because it serves as a classic example of those systems which chafe under all the excruciating problem imposed by chronically inadequate budgets and built-in limitations on resources, yet which still manage to perform respectably. Credit for this performance must go in large part to a few highly professional, dedicated broadcasters, both expatriate and African, who have refused to be daunted by circumstances. One of those deserving of this praise is the author of the following article on broadcasting in The Gambia.]

5.3.1 General Description

The Gambia's broadcasting system, which until May 1970 meant Radio Gambia only, is the youngest in English-speaking West Africa, for it was ten years old in May 1972 (for details on radio history in The Gambia, see Thomasi 1970). Radio Gambia itself was a development project under the wing of the then Information Office. In 1969, the two were made into one government department with a director of information and broadcasting at the head. For day-to-day administration—including the content and quality of broadcasts, program planning, personnel, contracts and budget control—there is a broadcasting officer responsible to the director. The director is finally responsible for all budgetary, financial, development, and policy questions.

As a noncommercial station and a government department, Radio Gambia's finances are provided by parliamentary appropriations. These appropriations stood at a little under £35,000 in the 1971–72 budget (Gambia 1971, p. 20). The largest single budget item is personal emoluments, 50% of the total; the second largest, the fees to Cable and Wireless

Swaebou J. S. Conateh is Broadcasting Officer, Radio Gambia, where he served as News Editor prior to his present appointment. He was a 1968 graduate of the William Allen White Journalism School, University of Kansas; and he has had newspaper experience with the *Kansas City Star,* the UPI, and the *Hutchinson News.* As a hobby, he edits The Gambia's only literary journal, *Ndaanan.*

for technical services, 28%. The station's established staff is appointed by the Public Service Commission. There is, in the president's office, a minister of state responsible for information and broadcasting. This officer is also responsible for other portfolios in the president's office, and his full title is "Minister of State for Information, Broadcasting, and Tourism."

In the absence of legislation on broadcasting, Radio Gambia is generally governed by civil service regulations and ministerial directives. Since The Gambia is a multiparty state, the station has tried to be nonpartisan in its broadcasts without being antigovernment; it has been especially successful in making the daily news broadcasts free from partisan bias. A 1972 report in the London *Times* said the station has "British style rules about election broadcasting with political broadcasting time allotted to the parties. During the campaign, election meetings are covered on their news merit" (Wolfers 1972).

The financial year ending July 1972 formally saw the end of a longstanding administrative arrangement between Radio Gambia and the Posts and Telecommunications Department. Under this arrangement, Radio Gambia was dependent on the Post Office for all engineering and technical operations and advice. Radio Gambia now has its own engineering branch, though it still depends on the Post Office for the hire of telephone lines and consults it on important questions of engineering policy and practice. By 1972, with the sole exception of the chief engineer, all members of Radio Gambia's administrative, technical, and program staffs were Gambians.

5.3.2 Radio Syd

In May 1970, a Swedish entrepreneur, Mrs. Britt Wardner, opened a privately owned commercial broadcasting station on the outskirts of Bathurst. Known as Radio Syd ("Radio South"), this station is a lineal descendent of Radio Caroline, the pirate station which once operated off the coast of Sweden. When the Swedish authorities forced it to close down, the owner moved to the Canary Islands, where she obtained a license to operate for one year in 1964. The license was not renewed, and the owner finally beached her floating station in The Gambia.

Radio Syd, using a 5-kw. medium-wave transmitter, broadcast in 1972 in English, French, Swedish, Wolof, and Mandinka. It took advantage of the fact that the national system, Radio Gambia, operates noncommercially and tries to offer a balanced program of information and education as well as entertainment. Under the terms of the agreement signed with The Gambia government, the management of Radio Syd undertook to broadcast not more than 20 hours of music and commercials daily, to relay news and programs of national importance from Radio Gambia, and to have the license renewed annually.

The station's main attraction for advertisers is the fact that it puts a strong signal not only into Bathurst, but also into Serekunda, Kaolack, and Dakar—all major urban centers of Senegal and The Gambia. Because the station drew a sizable number of youthful listeners away from Radio Dakar, the Senegalese authorities were not happy with the competition; however, their appeal to the authorities in The Gambia to withdraw the station's license was unsuccessful. Senegal thereupon adopted a law requiring that "anyone in Senegal directing a commercial at the country from a foreign radio or television station would need prior permission of the authorities" (*West Africa* 1970). This move apparently seriously affected the station's revenue. Mrs. Wardner herself has entered into the more promising tourist-based hotel industry in Bathurst and in 1972 was reportedly running Radio Syd at a loss. None of the station's local staff members were formally trained in radio work, and frequent technical breakdowns occur; so in 1972 there was some doubt that Radio Syd would long survive as an independent, private, commercial venture. Were it to fail, the government itself might find it politic to start its own revenue-earning commercial radio service, as an adjunct to the noncommercial service of Radio Gambia. The question of going commercial has been raised in the past more than once, but the example of Radio Syd may have served to overcome some of the traditional resistance to broadcast commercialism, just as the example of the pirate stations did in Europe.

5.3.3 Radio Gambia

In contrast to Radio Syd, Radio Gambia follows a comprehensive public-service-oriented programming policy. It tries to emulate the BBC, in the sense of catering to the tastes of all interest groups and of facilitating communication between the governors and the governed. As the national station, Radio Gambia is conscious of its role as a national unifying force.

It is all the more unfortunate, therefore, that Radio Gambia does not even own its transmission facilities, but must rent them from a private communications company, Cable and Wireless. Moreover, the single 3.5-kw. short-wave transmitter was not even designed for broadcasting, and at no time can it adequately cover the whole 200-mile length of The Gambia. The very shape of the country itself presents special problems in the design and location of a transmitter system capable of covering the whole with a satisfactory signal efficiently.

In short, the constraints of limited resources and the endless competition for priority have always held back the growth of broadcasting in The Gambia. The station has perhaps the smallest staff and the smallest budget of any radio service of its size and scope of responsibility. It is all the more remarkable, then, that the station successfully broadcasts more than 70 hours a week, carefully hoarding the morning and early evening hours (when reception conditions are optimal throughout the country, within the severe limitations of the present transmission facilities) for those programs designed to cater to the interests and needs of the total population.

On the brighter side, in 1970 Radio Gambia at last was able to move into a well-equipped, modern building containing four studios, built with the aid of a British loan of £120,000. A 100-w. FM transmitter links the studios to the short-wave transmitter site seven miles away. Meanwhile the government is actively working on acquiring transmitters capable of covering the whole country and enabling simultaneous multilanguage broadcasts. One of the station's most intractable problems has been the fact that it must broadcast in English and five local languages daily—all over a single channel. In 1972, time was distributed among the six languages as follows (in percentages): English, 42; Wolof, 25; Mandinka, 25; Fula, 4; Jola, 2; and Sarahuleh, 2. It is proposed that when facilities permit multichannel broadcasting, one channel will serve local languages, while another will be devoted exclusively to English, which remains the official national language (see Conateh 1972a, 1972b).

5.3.4 Programming

Programming remains highly speculative at Radio Gambia in the absence of systematic audience surveys. The quarterly changes in the program schedule have largely been influenced by the number and nature of listener letters received and the desire to avoid duplication and monotony. On the basis of informal feedback, one can safely say that the national-news, audience-request, cultural, advisory, sports, music, and oral-history programs have proved the most successful.

The bulk of Radio Gambia's programs is produced locally by a small production staff working under the direction of the broadcasting officer and two producers. The programming policies of the service may be summarized in the following statement of goals for Radio Gambia:

1. To make a serious effort to maintain credibility and to use fully and responsibly the position of the broadcasting service as the most accessible source of information and instruction in the country.
2. To engage a sizable group of free-lance performers on either a regular or an irregular basis. The aim here is to make full use of a most natural and valuable source of local material for local programs.
3. To use outside broadcasting regularly to cover such events as prayers from the mosque (The Gambia is 85% Muslim) and weekly sports competitions, as well as special events such as independence celebrations, religious festivals, state visits, and chiefs' conferences.
4. To extend the use of recordings of local music, oral history, and culture-oriented programs. These are designed to cater to the taste of the bulk of the station's listeners, especially in the provinces, where the majority of the population lives, and also to instill in Gambians a greater awareness of the rich diversity of their cultural heritage. The station works with the archivist at the national Records Office to transcribe for permanent retention some of this material for future use by research students.
5. To foster multilingual broadcasting and programs broadcast for special

minority groups—Christians, language groups, youths, children, and motorists. The news is broadcast daily in six languages—three times a day in English, Wolof, and Mandinka and once a day in the less widely spoken Fula, Jola, and Sarahuleh.

6. To be constantly aware of its public-service role and the need for advisory or instructive programs on self-help, community development, improved farming methods, better health practices, cooperatives, rural transformation, and national development. The Ministries of Health, Agriculture, and Police provide material for, and participate in, programs designed to complement and foster their efforts in the field. Among mass-education campaigns in which the station successfully assisted the government were the change to decimal currency, the switch to right-hand driving, the adoption of a republican constitution, and measures to combat smallpox and rinderpest (see Conateh 1971). Overall, Radio Gambia offers an unusually high percentage of news and current-events programming—over 29%, about the same percentage as music.

One of the noteworthy features of programming at Radio Gambia is the fact that cognizance is given to the late entry of the station into the highly competitive broadcasting field. One of the natural consequences of its late entry was that it had to win back its audience from Dakar, from other West African stations, and from the BBC and the VOA. Radio Gambia's stratagem was to co-opt competitive programs and present them over its own facilities. Thus the station rebroadcasts without delay the BBC's "World News" three times a day, "Commentary" once a day, "News of the African World" once a day, and "BBC Sports Review" once a week. Many other programs are carried on a delayed basis from a variety of national and international organizations, among them: Deutsche Welle, Voice of America, Radio Canada International, Radio Vatican, Radio Moscow, Radio Nederland, the ORTF (France), the Union of National Radio and Television Stations of Africa (URTNA), the United Nations, the BBC, Commonwealth West African countries, and Radio Dakar. Some of the programs from these sources have regular slots in the published schedules, others are used as inserts in current events and magazine programs. Radio Gambia has a cooperative agreement with Radio Dakar, Senegal's broadcasting service, for the exchange of programs and for mutual assistance. The first of a number of planned cooperative ventures to be realized was the inclusion of special programs in the schedules of each country's service on the occasions of the national holidays of the two countries.

Like most African stations, Radio Gambia depends on outside contributors, or free-lance artists and experts, for local specialized materials and performances. The station issues a standardized rate card, which provides for payment by the minute. For example, in 1972, a straight talk earned

20¢ per minute; music from 10¢ to 24¢ per minute; a musical group (five or more performers), 48¢ per minute. Special free-lancers employed on a regular basis—for example, those with ability in one of the minority languages—may be paid a flat monthly rate.

Among the most popular outside contributors to Radio Gambia programming are the *griots*. Here, as in Senegal and much of Guinea and Mali, the *griots* are a professional caste of traditional entertainers, something like the wandering minstrels of the Middle Ages in Europe. Formerly, the chiefs and big traders acted as their patrons. In modern times it is the radio. They maintain the musical and oral traditions of the people, usually singing to the accompaniment of musical instruments, which may be an African xylophone, a 21-string harp (the *kora*), a violinlike instrument (the *halam*), or others, depending on the tribe. The *griot's* art is thus well suited to radio, and Radio Gambia makes use of him, not only as musician and as storyteller, but also in a sense as teacher. Since *griots* have cultivated the art of oral delivery to a high degree, they are very effective speakers in the vernacular and are used to relay information on such topics as public health, farming methods, and national unity and development to non-English-speaking audiences.

5.3.5 Future Plans

As to possible future developments in broadcasting as a whole, it should be noted that there are no plans in The Gambia for television. The authorities are taking more interest in the Information Office Film Unit, which has had a marked success in the production and presentation throughout the country of adult-education films on agriculture, community development, and health, both in English and in the local languages. Under the terms of an agreement between the Gambian and Senegalese Information Services, the two countries' film units will exchange film productions. The agreement includes the use of Gambian productions by the UNESCO-assisted educational-television service in Dakar—a recognition of the educational value of the products of the Gambian film unit. Of course, when Senegal's TV service is established, Gambians may benefit from spillover coverage. In The Gambia, however, where the development of radio broadcasting itself has been slowed down by lack of funds, both television and external broadcasting fall in the same category—beyond the financial means of the country because of the competition from other projects of higher priority.

Other questions for the future include schools broadcasting; the expansion of the farm-rural broadcasting wing (in 1972 still a pilot project); the organization of scientific audience surveys; and, through the systematic training of staff, qualitative improvements in the standards of the programs broadcast. The management has consulted both the Ministry and the Department of Education about educational broadcasting, but no definite proposals had taken shape by 1972. Nevertheless, Radio Gambia was starting preliminary training of staff in educational-broadcasting techniques so that if the educational authorities should request such services the station would be ready to respond.

5.4 Liberia, Sierra Leone, and Cameroon, *by Sydney W. Head*

5.4.1 Liberia

Population: 1,500,000	Radio transmitter sites: 1
Receivers per thousand: 166	Area per site: 43,000 sq mi

In 1822 repatriated slaves from America settled on the coast of what is now Liberia. It became an independent republic in 1847 and so has the longest history of independent existence of any state in Africa except for Ethiopia. As one might expect, American influence has always been strong, but it has not always been an easy relationship. The United States refused to recognize the republic at all until 15 years after its founding and, during the 1930s, severed diplomatic relations for several years. Radio was started by an American, but Liberia chose a British company to modernize the station and to introduce television.

Liberia houses the largest concentration of radio-transmitter power relative to its size of any country in Africa. Its own national service has only two 10-kw. transmitters, but it provides transmitter sites for ELWA, the pioneer Christian missionary station of Africa; for the Voice of America's main African relay station; and for two small private stations serving a mining community. For a short time Liberia also housed a second missionary station, and from 1966 to 1968 a BBC relay station, pending completion of the BBC's major facility on Ascension Island (§ 9.3.2).

Liberian radio started in 1949 as the hobby of an American medical doctor who had come to Liberia on a public health project sponsored by the United States and had decided to stay on. He received a Liberian government subsidy to keep the station on the air, which he did from his own residence in Monrovia, the capital (Reed 1970, p. 91). In 1959 the government set up the Liberian Broadcasting Corporation, which arranged a contract with the British firm Rediffusion to build, own, and operate a new radio station. The station went on the air in 1960. Four years later its ownership reverted to the government. Rediffusion received a 25-year management contract and advanced the government a quarter-million dollars on long-term loan (Checchi & Co. 1965). Still later, in 1968, the government resumed management of the station through the Liberian Broadcasting Corporation. In 1971, under the call letters ELBC, it operated 17½ hours per day, transmitting simultaneously on medium and short wave. Most of the programming was in English, with news three times a day in local languages.

In 1964 the corporation launched television in Monrovia, the capital, with help from Rediffusion and a British equipment manufacturer; at that time Rediffusion increased its loan to a million dollars (Checchi & Co. 1965). The installers seem to have established a record by putting the TV station together, from crates to cue lights, in "12 days, 6 hours, and six minutes" (Grant 1965, p. 22). In 1972 ELTV broadcast about 30 hours per week, one-third of them live. Three repeater stations enlarged the area of coverage, one inland at Bomi Hills, an industrial site about 40 miles north of Monrovia; one at Mano River, on the Sierra Leone border; and one at Harbel, site of the Firestone rubber plantation southeast of the capital. Rediffusion claimed to offer a television-receiver maintenance service "unique in Africa"—repair or replacement within one day in Monrovia, within two days outside the capital (information from Intercontinental Services, ELTV's New York sales representative).

Radio station ELWA, licensed to the Sudan Interior Mission, opened in 1954 near Monrovia with a single 1-kw. medium-wave transmitter. Later the mission increased its medium-wave power to 10-kw. and added two 10-kw. and two 50-kw. short-wave transmitters. ELWA programs both domestic and international services. Its programming is described in § 11.2.3.

By 1970 the Voice of America had invested over $15 million in its relay transmitter complex near Monrovia (Reed 1970, p. 98). VOA had previously depended for its African coverage on relay transmitters in the Mediterranean area, but as United States interests in Africa south of the Sahara developed it became evident that the Mediterranean-based stations could not lay down an adequate signal in the central and southern sectors of the continent. Monrovia provided the solution, located as it is about a third of the way down the west coast, in a good position to receive short-wave transmissions across the Atlantic from VOA transmitters on the American mainland, and with an unimpeded propagation path over water for rebroadcasting to the southern third of the African continent. The station opened in 1964. At first it originated part of VOA's African programming from its own studios, as well as rebroadcasting material relayed from Washington. These originations were discontinued in 1968 as an economy measure, however, and the Monrovia complex became strictly a rebroadcast facility for material originated in VOA's Washington studios. It uses two 50-kw. and six 250-kw. short-wave transmitters which can be fed to a choice of more than a score of directional antennas.

The Liberian-American-Swedish Mining Company extracts iron ore from the remote mountains of the interior at Nimba, about 180 miles inland from Monrovia. The company operates two small medium-wave stations of 100 w. for the benefit of its employees. One serves Nimba, at the railhead; the second serves Buchanan, the seaport at the other end of the rail line. In 1971 the stations depended primarily upon rebroadcasts of ELBC and BBC programs, with some local origination of news and information of interest to the mining community.

5.4.2 Sierra Leone

Population: 2,600,000	Radio transmitter sites: 1
Receivers per thousand: 19	Area per site: 28,000 sq mi

Like its neighbor Liberia, Sierra Leone came under systematic European influence as a result of serving as a new African homeland for freed slaves, starting in 1787. In 1808 the coastal strip became a British colony, though the interior did not come under formal British control until 1896. Sierra Leone became independent in 1961.

Radio in Sierra Leone in one sense dates back to 1934, for in that year it acquired a rediffusion system, the first of the British West African territories so equipped. The wire system was flourishing in 1952, when it had 2,300 subscribers (Hailey 1957, p. 1247). In 1961 a rediffusion subscription cost £4 a year. The government began phasing out the system in 1964.

Broadcasting as such started in 1955, when Britain made a £23,000-grant to establish a studio and a 5-kw. transmitter in Freetown, the capital (Bebey 1963, pp. 22, 144). Sierra Leone Broadcasting Service, a government department, was created in 1958. In 1972 it offered about 16 hours of radio programming a day, with a period of closedown from 10:00 A.M. to 12:30 P.M. English, the official language of Sierra Leone, occupied 60%–70% of broadcast time; Krio (a pidgin lingua franca), Mende, Temne, and Limba occupied most of the rest, though weekly news summaries in nine other local languages were also scheduled. A weekly 45-minute magazine program in French was also broadcast, an incipient external service intended for reception in neighboring Francophone countries (Findlay, 1973, p. 2). An unusual feature of Sierra Leone radio news programming is the fact that it rebroadcasts news daily not only from the BBC, but also from the VOA and Radio Moscow. Four 20-minute schools broadcasts are scheduled on weekdays during the school term.

Television went on the air in 1963, at first administered separately from radio by a consortium of commercial interests led by Thomson Television International (§ 17.3). In 1971 television was opening at 6:30 P.M. and signing off at 11:00 P.M., with an extra hour on Sundays.

In 1969 Sierra Leone asked the Commonwealth Broadcasting Conference (§ 13.3) to advise on the future development of its broadcasting services. The conference arranged for a three-man committee made up of experts from Ghana, Canada, and Britain to make a survey. Its report, published by the Sierra Leone government in 1970, was "very critical of the existing radio and television services" (Millar 1972, p. 35). Among other things, the committee recommended (1) setting up an independent public corporation in place of the existing government broadcasting department; (2) merging the radio and television services; (3) inaugurating a training program; (4) constructing a new broadcasting center and replacing superannuated equipment; (5) expanding television to cover the country as a whole instead of just the capital, Freetown; and (6) developing a broadcasting news service separate from the Information Department. The government accepted the main recommendations, with one exception—the idea of vesting control in an independent public corporation was rejected.

The next step was an engineering survey, carried out by a BBC expert. His recommendations included using FM radio to cover Freetown, resiting the main television transmitter, and adding four small TV repeater stations. The package was put out to bid and came in at over $8 million. This amount was considered beyond the resources of the government, which shelved the whole scheme. In mid-1972, nevertheless, it announced that a contract had been let for installation of a 250-kw. short-wave transmitter.

Meanwhile, in 1969 a BBC veteran had been employed on a three-year contract as director general to carry out the recommended developmental steps. The cancellation of the plan prevented full utilization of his expertise, but he reported progress at least on aspects of the plan not requiring major new equipment, such as staff training and the combining of the radio and television organizations (Miller 1972).

5.4.3 Cameroon

Population: 5,800,000	Radio transmitter sites: 4
Receivers per thousand: 37	Area per site: 46,000 sq mi

Since it is a federation of two territories, one that had been part of Anglophone, the other of Francophone West Africa, Cameroon might have been included in either group. The Francophone group would have been the more logical perhaps, because the former French Cameroun is much the larger of the two parts; but we have have grouped it with the Anglophone countries because of the large number of states in the Francophone group.

Cameroon occupies the point on the West African coast where it turns southward after running east-west beneath the western bulge—a turning point sometimes called the "hinge" of Africa. It is unusual in that it is a federation of two states having different official languages. At one time the German protectorate of Kamerun, the region was divided between the French and English following World War I. East Cameroon, comprising the great bulk of the land area and four-fifths of the population, went to the French and became fully independent in 1960. The next year West Cameroon, the British sector, was offered the choice of joining Nigeria or Cameroon; the territory split into north-south factions, the north electing to become part of Northern Nigeria, the south to federate with the former French Cameroon. The two states of the federation officially retained their colonial languages, French and English, with federal functions carried out on a bilingual basis. An observer in the early 1960s remarked that "the gap between the communities using the official languages is left largely unfilled by the radio and newspaper services. . . . Radio broadcasts are made in both languages . . . but only the major news items are translated into both. English language broadcasts . . . tend to carry only items about West Cameroun or the English-speaking world, and the reverse is true for the French-language broadcasts" (Johnson 1965 p. 211). The language dilemma of Cameroon is compounded by the fact that it has some 200 tribes speaking 24 major African languages and many times that number of dialect variations.

Radio started in the French sector, at Douala, the main seaport, in 1941. The station had only 150 w. and went off the air in 1944, to be revived again in 1946. It remained a distinctly amateur operation, with the listeners themselves often providing phonograph records and other program material until 1955, when SORAFOM (see § 6.1.3) brought French aid and professionalization (Bebey 1963, pp. 36–37). Radio did not come to Yaoundé, the present capital and location of the chief national station, until 1955, again with the help of SORAFOM. The smallest station in East (Francophone) Cameroon, at Garoua in the far north of the country, was established by SORAFOM in 1958 (Bebey 1963, p. 38). Bebey describes an interesting local program of the early 1960s at Garoua for which listeners hire *griots* to sing their praises on the radio (Bebey 1963, p. 87; for a discussion of *griots,* see § 5.3.4). West (Anglophone) Cameroon had previously depended on the Nigerian Broadcasting Corporation for its radio services, using a recording studio for preparing programs for release over the NBC. Not until 1967 did it acquire its own station, in Buea, located on the coast (LeVine 1971, p. 80). The Buea station originates its own news in English but also rebroadcasts both French and English news relayed from the national station at Yaoundé. Of the four Cameroon stations, the one at Garoua was the only one not broadcasting in English in 1971. Otherwise, all use both English and French, with a relatively small amount of time allotted to a few local languages.

6   Francophone West and Equatorial Africa

R. Arnold Gibbons

[EDITOR'S NOTE. This chapter groups together the 14 independent states which emerged from colonial French West Africa, French Equatorial Africa, and the Belgian Congo. This may seem an unwieldy number of systems to discuss in a single chapter, but in fact many of them can be discussed on a group basis. France set up broadcasting in most of her African colonies relatively late, in accordance with uniform plans, and under highly centralized metropolitan control. Even after independence, broadcasting in most Francophone states continued under similar conformist influences.]

6.1 The Francophone Colonial Legacy

6.1.1 Geography

The French colonial empire in Tropical West Africa consisted of two groups of territories, French West Africa and French Equatorial Africa. The former was the larger group, occupying much of the Atlantic seacoast along the great westerly bulge of the upper half of the continent. Dakar in Senegal, the most western point in Africa, has obvious special strategic importance in terms of its geographical relationships to the Americas and to Europe. It served as the colonial administrative center for France's West African territories. Although called "West Africa," parts extended far into the interior, halfway across the continent at its widest point. These inland territories, transitional areas between the Sahara and Tropical Africa, became the modern landlocked states of Mali, Niger, and Upper Volta.

    The smaller French Equatorial group had its headquarters at Brazzaville, Congo, below the corner formed by the southward turn of the coastline

R. Arnold Gibbons is Assistant Professor of Communications, Ithaca College, and Research Associate, Cornell University Africana Studies and Research Center. He has worked for the BBC and Deutsche Welle.

from the continental bulge. This group became the modern coastal states of the Congo and Gabon and the landlocked states of the Central African Republic and Chad. Chad reaches up into the interior to border on Niger, thus linking the two French groups. One could in fact have started at the mouth of the Congo River and have traveled in a great curve northeast through the French Congo, the Central African Republic, Chad, Niger, and Algeria, over 2,000 miles to the shores of the Mediterranean without leaving French territory. Inland to the east of the French Congo lay the huge bulk of the Belgian Congo, now Zaïre. On the eastern border of the Belgian Congo, intruding into Tanzania as a sort of enclave, are the two ministates of Burundi and Rwanda, once also Belgian dependencies. They were treated as part of the East African group of countries in chapter 4.

The French West African coastal territories alternated, roughly, with Britain's coastal possessions. Often arbitrary colonial boundaries divided tribes and cut up ancient kingdoms. Despite these overlaps and the cheek-by-jowl proximity of the colonies, the Francophone and Anglophone states, as groups, developed distinct personalities which are adumbrated in their present-day broadcasting systems.

6.1.2 Broadcasting Policies

The broadcasting systems introduced into colonial territories clearly reflected the national characters and colonial policies of the metropolitan countries (Kucera 1968). It comes as no surprise, therefore, to find that broadcasting in French-speaking Africa differs markedly from broadcasting in former British colonies. France tended to use radio primarily as a means of disseminating French culture—"radio under French colonial rule was always *French* radio" (Hachten 1971a, p. 18). Britain was more inclined toward localizing the medium and encouraging it to help preserve local culture; she used it to inform, to train, and at times to distract her African subjects: "Boredom leads to discontent, and there is a very real need for some means of bringing wholesome amusement to the African" (Twining, Brashern, and Richards 1939, p. 9). Rather than Whitehall, it was the white British settlers in territories like Rhodesia who opposed the development of broadcasting policies designed genuinely to serve indigenous populations (see Fraenkel 1959).

While British colonial stations pioneered in the extensive use of vernaculars and the cultivation of African arts for their own sake, their French counterparts stressed the use of the French language and the evolution of Africans into Frenchmen with black skins—into *évolués,* as they were frankly called. The highest qualification an African broadcaster could earn was perfect mastery of classical French—a qualification still of primary significance in most Francophone African systems. By the same token the French discouraged the development of local print journalism, favoring instead official bulletins and the importation of more formal publications from France. By contrast, local newspapers flourished in British West Africa, which has a long history of private African journalism.

Administratively, France preferred strong centralization, while Britain favored "indirect rule" by giving considerable autonomous authority to local commissioners and "native administrations." The French tried to submerge local differences of language, culture, politics, and economics by superimposing one unified system on all areas, in keeping with her two theoretical guidelines to colonial rule: *la pacte impériale* and *la mission civilisatrice*. While the British created territorial governments within their colonies early in their rule, the French did not begin the devolution of authority to territorial regimes until 1956 with the passage of the Loi Cadre.

This Gallic urge to centralize control affected colonial broadcasting in many ways. For example, it created dependence on rebroadcasts of material produced originally in France and for France; it placed reliance on a few powerful stations covering whole regions, rather than on smaller independent local stations for each separate territory. Francophone broadcasting in Africa was also strongly influenced by the exigencies of war. When the Nazis occupied the French homeland and the North African littoral in World War II, Brazzaville in French Equatorial Africa became an important headquarters for the Free French resistance movement. The other principal French urban center on the African coast, Dakar in Senegal, though closer to Europe, at first came under the influence of Vichy, the French puppet government, though it was later neutralized. Brazzaville remained free of German encroachments and so developed into an important, and early, international broadcasting center. Radio Brazzaville "played an outstanding role as a medium of propaganda not only on behalf of Free France but for the whole Allied cause" (Thompson and Adloff 1960, p. 315). Similarly, the Belgians relied on a propaganda station in Leopoldville, now Kinshasa.

These internationally oriented stations used Africa simply as a pied-à-terre, aiming their broadcasts at North Africa, Europe, and America, rather than at local audiences. After the war such bypassing of local needs caused resentment among Africans (Thompson and Adloff 1960, p. 316). Radio Brazzaville continued to operate as a part of the French government broadcasting system, side by side with independent Congo's own national system, also centered in Brazzaville, until 1972. In September of that year Radio Brazzaville was finally nationalized.

World War II also affected the political climate in Francophone Africa. In opting to support the Free French against Vichy and the Germans, the Francophone Africans in effect opted for their own ultimate freedom. Although this did not come at once, when independence did arrive it came wholesale. Previously, the French colonies had been regarded as integrally united with metropolitan France. In accordance with a revised French constitution of 1956, however, de Gaulle offered the colonies the option of either internal self-government under a "French Community" concept, or complete severance of French ties. Considering the utter dependence of the colonies on French expertise and investments, the choice was perhaps less generous than it sounds. Only Guinea chose to go it alone, for which she paid dearly, suffering "a series of punitive reprisals on the part of the outgoing French authorities. Files and equipment [were] destroyed, while personnel, technical assistance, and financial aid were abruptly withdrawn" (*Africa South of the Sahara* 1971, p. 372). Radio, of course, was particularly susceptible to such forms of sabotage.

6.1.3 French Aid

In preparation for the 1958 referendum, France began to strengthen hitherto-weak local radio facilities in her colonies, as well as to train more African personnel. The French, perhaps more than any other major power, seem to have foreseen the international political potentialities of television as well as radio. This was perhaps due to General de Gaulle's intensive personal exploitation of television. He had learned to appreciate the political values of broadcasting during the war years, when the Brazzaville propaganda station went on the air. In fact, he himself spoke over the predecessor, smaller station there, to stiffen the morale of the Equatorial colonies in 1940 (Thompson and Adloff 1960, p. 315).

In any event, as early as 1950 a French government commission advised a major increase in technical assistance to colonial broadcasting services (Dizard 1966, p. 242). In the postindependence period the doctrine of cooperation between France and French-speaking Tropical Africa was formalized in a series of bilateral agreements dated 1960–64 (Ginesy 1968, p. 33). These protocols included the former Belgian colonies of Zaïre, Rwanda, and Burundi as well as the island of Madagascar. The agreements covered a variety of economic and cultural areas, but they singled out the mass media for special attention. Radio, television, newsfilm laboratories, and production studios were specifically mentioned, along with the more traditional media, as appropriate activities for special assistance.

In 1956 France created a specialized agency to implement broadcasting aid projects, the Société de Radiodiffusion de la France d'Outre-Mer, which became universally known as SORAFOM. Its initial budget was $4 million, and it at once assumed a pivotal role in broadcasting developments in Francophone Tropical Africa (Amande 1963, p. 4). SORAFOM's activities were all-encompassing—it built and managed radio stations, trained over 300 Africans in the first year of its Studio-École de Maisons-Laffitte near Paris (Dizard 1966, p. 242), organized station staffs, acted as purchasing agent for technical equipment and supplies, produced program materials for overseas use, and set up guidelines for future developments. The unusual training approach used at Studio-École is described by

Quarmyne and Bebey (1967 pp. 19–21). At first SORAFOM paid all costs of its broadcasting development projects from French government funds; later 30%–40% of the costs were absorbed by the recipient governments. At the time of the.1958 referendum, SORAFOM controlled 21 stations (*Africa Report* 1960, p. 8).

Within a few years "la France d'Outre-Mer" became a misnomer, and SORAFOM was replaced by OCORA (l'Office de Cooperation Radiophonique), which came on the scene in 1962 in .time to implement SORAFOM's television plans, bringing with it a "new emphasis on the role television would play as both a political and a cultural force in France's relations with its former African territories" (Dizard 1966, p. 242). OCORA launched the first television station in French-speaking Tropical Africa in 1962, at Brazzaville; others followed the next year at Dakar (Senegal), Libreville (Gabon), and Abidjan (Ivory Coast). Funds for these installations came from both French aid and, to the extent possible, the local African governments concerned.

In 1969 OCORA in turn was replaced by yet another agency, ORTF— l'Organization Radiodiffusion-Television Française. This represented the ultimate in centralization, since it really involved a merger of all the OCORA overseas-aid functions in broadcasting with all the domestic and external broadcasting services of France itself.

6.1.4 Postcolonial French Influence

France's economic and cultural domination of her former colonies continued after independence to such a degree that it often seemed as though independence were hardly more than a facade of nationalistic perquisites. The first American ambassador to newly independent Gabon describes in detail the bitter resentment of the private expatriate French toward this "foreign" intrusion into "their" domain. They sabotaged all efforts at American aid and even went so far as to bomb the American embassy (Darlington and Darlington 1968, p. 159 et passim). Telecommunications still served as umbilicals to keep the Francophone countries dependent on Paris and isolated from their African neighbors: ". . . development of a Pan-African telecommunications network has been rather slow. This had been caused by the continuing interest of some of the colonial powers in the external telecommunications services of the newly independent states . . . particularly in all the Francophone countries in which the French-controlled company, France Cables et Radio, still holds an exclusive franchise" (Elias 1971, p. 71). Radio and television programming in the Francophone countries of Tropical Africa remained heavily dependent on French sources. According to one report, "what in practice amounted to a closed system was established between the metropolitan power and most of the sub-Saharan French-speaking broadcasting stations. Between 1960 and 1970 France participated in the establishment of 28 radio stations in Africa, and approximately eighteen thousand hours of radio programmes a year were sent from France to Africa" (Stokke 1971, p. 100). In 1970 ORTF sent thousands of news items to Africa by short-wave, as well as materials for reference libraries, and packaged programs; 200 trainees studied in France; 90 hours of TV "film magazine" material were supplied; and France coproduced 13 documentaries and made available about 500 hours of French TV programs for use by African stations, six of which were built by French aid" (Stokke 1971, p. 113).

As another example of the uniformity among the Francophone systems, one might cite the fact that all the stations that sell time appointed the same sales-representative organization, Informations et Publicité, a subsidiary of the Havas advertising agency. Of the 14 countries under consideration, all but three—Guinea, Mali, and Togo—sell radio time. All restrict commercials either to fixed times in the day or to limited day-parts; sometimes special rules are made for holidays, Sundays, or, where Islam is dominant, Fridays (German Africa Society 1970). Television is less commercialized, with only four of the seven countries which had television in 1972 offering it to advertisers—Congo, Ivory Coast, Gabon, and Zaïre (*Television Factbook* 1972–73).

In fairness it should be added that the intricacies of French relations with her former colonies lend themselves to varied interpretations. French "cooperation"—a term preferred to "aid"—has been characterized as having "a vague almost mystical air of fraternity, and yet there is an undertone of hard work and getting down to business. It also implies a footing of equality absent from 'aid' and 'assistance,' which perhaps blurs over the difference between developed and developing" (*West Africa*, 27 August 1971, p. 947). Increasingly, too, France seems to have accepted participation in multilateral assistance projects. The educational television project in the Ivory Coast might be cited as an example (§ 15.5). In 1971 the French secretary of state for foreign affairs was quoted as saying that "the French government is more and more conscious of the fact that the completion of certain projects can be effected less and less by a single financial source" (*Fraternité-Matin*, Abidjan, 30 December 1971).

6.1.5 Belgian Colonial Policy

Zaïre's colonial background differs completely from that of French Equatorial Africa. An immense territory, the second-largest country south of the Sahara, Zaïre occupies much of the Congo River basin; but it is nearly landlocked, being cut off from the sea by Angola to the south and Congo (Brazzaville) to the north and left with only a small corridor to the Atlantic at the mouth of the Congo River. Zaïre originally came under Belgian domination as an independent state, the private property of Leopold II, king of the Belgians. In 1908, as a result of scandals concerning the mistreatment of African workers in Leopold's great private fief, world public opinion forced him to turn it over to Belgium as a colony. The chief city of the Belgian Congo was first called Leopoldville; later, Kinshasa—one of the many shifts in nomenclature which will doubtless tantalize beginning students of African history and geography for generations. Brazzaville and Kinshasa, the capitals of the two Congos, the French and the Belgian, face each other across the Congo River. For a time the independent Congos were identified by linking each country's name with its capital's name—Congo-Brazzaville and Congo-Kinshasa. In 1971 the latter officially became Zaïre, and subsequently a wholesale conversion from European to Congolese place names and personal names took place.

Under Belgian rule, administration of the Congo was left largely to commercial concessionaires, the Catholic church, and appointed native chiefs. The Belgian Congo thus lacked entirely the tight centralized metropolitan administrative control so characteristic of the French colonial experience. Confronted with the example of the 1958 French referendum, along with the imminent breakup of the British colonial empire in Africa (signaled by the independence of Ghana in 1957) and the growth of an independence movement within the colony itself, Belgium abruptly announced, in January 1960, its decision to grant Congo independence. Within six months Congo-Leopoldville was launched as an independent state, and within a week internal disorders began. The Belgians had done little to prepare the new nation to cope with the immediate problems of independence. The devastating civil disorders the country underwent in the following decade were perhaps inevitable, given the history of the colony and Belgium's lack of long-term preindependence planning.

6.2 French West Africa

The nine countries of French West Africa will be discussed briefly, individually, according to the order in which they first started broadcasting: Senegal, Ivory Coast, Guinea, Togo, Dahomey, Mali, Mauritania, Niger, and Upper Volta.

6.2.1 Senegal

Population: 3,900,000	Radio transmitter sites: 8
Receivers per thousand: 71	Area per site: 9,000 sq mi

Radio Dakar, established in 1939, was the pioneer station in the French territories of western Africa. Its mission was to provide regional coverage for the Francophone countries. Accordingly, it became known as Radio-Inter-Afrique Occidentale Française, or "Radio Inter" for short, after SORAFOM took over in 1955. SORAFOM set up a separate Radio

Senegal in Saint Louis (then the capital of Senegal but now the site of a regional station) to provide a more localized service for Senegalese and Mauritanian listeners. After independence Radio Senegal was moved from Saint Louis to Dakar, and ultimately the facilities of the two stations were combined into one (Bebey 1963, pp. 34–36).

The modern Senegalese radio system, Radiodiffusion du Sénégal, operates four regional stations and offers two domestic services, national and regional. French and seven local languages are used. It has by far the largest audience of the 14 states under consideration. The external service, called Sénégal-Inter, broadcasts in Arabic, English, French, and Portuguese.

Senegal's small television installation in Dakar is unusual in that it was built exclusively for educational purposes. Set up with the help of UNESCO, the station was used for a controlled long-term experiment, starting in 1965, on the use of television in adult education (Fougeyrollas 1967). This project is discussed in more detail in § 15.2.4.

6.2.2 Ivory Coast

Population: 4,200,000	Radio transmitter sites: 4
Receivers per thousand: 51	Area per site: 31,000 sq mi

Although Ivory Coast's prosperity after independence permitted her capital, Abidjan, to rival Dakar in economic activity and urban glamor, Senegal's earlier primacy as the broadcasting center of the region continued to be reflected in a much higher ratio of radio receivers per thousand population—17 for Ivory Coast versus 69 for Senegal (UNESCO, *Statistical Yearbook* 1971, pp. 815, 817). Radio Abidjan started in 1949 with power of only 200 w. More than a decade was to pass before the installation of a modern, high-powered transmitter of 100 kw. (Bebey 1963, pp. 38–39).

An experienced observer on a visit to the Ivory Coast in 1965 was impressed by the pervasiveness of French influence, still observable in Radio Abidjan's service after five years of independence:

The French style of broadcasting pervaded Radio Abidjan; a listener could easily imagine he was tuned to a Parisian station. Music was mostly French or French versions of American popular music. There was little indigenous music or even the popular West African "high life" music. . . . Announcers were both French and Ivoirien and spoke in excellent French. In fact all but 6 of 175 hours a week of broadcasting were in French. There was a very limited amount of news broadcast in nine of the vernacular tongues. [Hachten 1971a, p. 191]

In 1972, Radiodiffusion-Télévision Ivoirienne offered national and external radio services from Abidjan. A regional transmitter at Bouaké, located in the center of the squarish-shaped country, started operations in

1966. It rebroadcasts programs from Abidjan and also originates some local programming. Since the Ivory Coast's population is fragmented into six major ethnic groups and more than 60 tribes, it has an urgent need for a less centralized broadcasting system. Apparently as a step in the direction of decentralization, RTI has installed four experimental FM stations at widely separated centers. In 1971 RTI used French, English, and seven vernacular languages.

In early 1972 Radio Abidjan averaged 251 hours of air time a week. In percentages, the content of the service broke down as follows: information, 41; variety, 35; education, 12; advertising, 5; arts and science, 4; and miscellaneous, 3 (unpublished data, UNESCO Statistical Office, January 1971). By 1975, however, it was planned to double the number of services from two to four and to increase aggregate broadcast hours to 441 a week (interview with director-general of RTI, January 1972).

Television went on the air from Abidjan in 1963, in studios improvised in an abandoned villa and with a program service of 1½ hours a day. In 1966, however, the television service moved to new quarters, with six large studios, first-class equipment, and a staff of 250, and its schedule was expanded to five hours daily in two segments, noon to 1:30 P.M. and 7:00 P.M. to 10:30 P.M. In 1972, there were also four provincial stations, which gave Ivory Coast the most sophisticated television network in the Francophone group. Understandably, Ivory Coast has by far the largest number of television receivers in circulation of all the Francophone countries under consideration.

One of the regional television stations, located at Bouaké (also the site of a previously mentioned regional radio transmitter), has assumed importance as the home base of the most ambitious educational television project in Africa. This project is described in detail in § 15.5.

6.2.3 Guinea

Population: 3,900,000	Radio transmitter sites: 1
Receivers per thousand: 26	Area per site: 95,000 sq mi

A 1953 experimental French station in Conakry made Guinea one of the early broadcast-origination points in French West Africa. The Conakry station began a regularly scheduled service in 1956. However, Guinea was the one territory among France's West African colonies which in 1958 had the temerity to decline de Galle's offer of independence as a member of the French Community (§ 6.1.2). As retribution for this lèse-majesté, Radio Conakry lost not only its expert French personnel but also its equipment (Browne 1963, p. 114). Nevertheless, Guinea managed to get back on the air in 1959 with five hours of programming a day.

After the rupture with France and the consequent cancellation of all

French aid, Guinea turned to the Communist Bloc for assistance. In 1961 East Germany gave a 100-kw. transmitter and installed more than 100 public speakers in Conakry; the next year Czechoslovakia installed a repeater station, the first of a planned chain of regional outlets (USIA 1962, pp. 19–20). At the dedication of the East German transmitter, Radio Conakry was renamed "Voice of the Revolution." Relations with the Communists have fluctuated from warm to cold, as have those with the United States. For example, Guinea expelled the U.S. Peace Corps in 1966 but invited it back in 1969.

Guinea's militant Africanism has frequently brought her into conflict with neighboring African countries as well as with Portugal, whose "overseas state" of Guinea adjoins the Republic of Guinea's territory on the north. This militant outlook was reflected in broadcasting in several ways. An example is the very name, "Voice of the Revolution." At one point the station tried to eliminate all foreign music and rely entirely on African music (Browne 1963, p. 117). This premature effort at Africanization failed, somewhat like Nkrumah's effort to Africanize television in Ghana (§ 5.2.1). As another example of its militancy, Guinea began provocative broadcasts in the languages of neighboring countries such as the English Creole of Sierra Leone, Portuguese Creole, and the Manding of Mali and Senegal (Browne 1963, p. 116).

6.2.4 Togo

| Population: 1,900,000 | Radio transmitter sites: 1 |
| Receivers per thousand: 24 | Area per site: 22,000 sq mi |

Togo, the smallest of the West African Francophone countries, was part of the German colony of Togoland from 1884 until World War I, when the French and British captured the territory with troops from their neighboring colonies. After the war Britain and France divided Togoland, the British part ultimately opting for union with Ghana, the French part becoming the independent state of Togo in 1960. Togo acquired its first broadcast transmitter in 1954, which went on the air 10 hours a week with 200 w. of power. By 1961, the year following independence, Togo's strongest transmitter had a power of 4 kw., but it could still reach only a fifth of the population. A license fee of about $4 a year imposed in 1961 did nothing to encourage set buying, and an attempt to develop a wired rediffusion system in Lomé, the capital, attracted only 150 customers at a subscription rate of over $16 a year (Bebey 1963, pp. 148–49). Later, West Germany donated a 100-kw. medium-wave transmitter, in keeping with its policy of assisting former colonies (see § 4.4.2). It went on the air in 1964.

Coverage still remained incomplete because of the unusual distribution pattern required by Togo's geography and the location of its capital. The country is a narrow, 360-mile-long strip of land. Lomé is located at the extreme southwestern corner, on the 31-mile Atlantic coastal frontage. Thus radio transmitters situated in the capital radiate southward out to sea and eastward into neighboring Dahomey, but in the northerly direction they need to send signals more than 300 miles to reach the border with Upper Volta.

Togo's service in 1971 was typically intermittent, going off the air weekdays at 9.00 A.M., back on from noon until 2:00 P.M., then off until the evening segment, 4:40–11:00.

6.2.5 Dahomey

Population: 2,500,000	Radio transmitter sites: 3
Receivers per thousand: 29	Area per site: 14,000 sq mi

Dahomey offers much the same signal-distribution problem as Togo, its neighbor to the west. It, too, has an elongated shape, with the chief city, Cotonou, located on the coast at the extreme southern end. Dahomey had one of the least adequate radio systems of all the western Francophone countries; its most powerful transmitter was a 30-kw. short-wave facility apparently installed in 1961 (Bebey 1963, p. 41). However, the Broadcasting House built on the Atlantic shore at Cotonou in 1957 was said to have been the only one in Africa at the time "designed and constructed on professional lines" (da Piedade 1963, p. 6); and Bebey described it as one of the "plus belles maisons de la radio de l'ouest africain" (Bebey 1963, p. 97).

In 1971 Dahomey had three low-power transmitters in Cotonou in addition to the 30-kw. one, and a small regional transmitter of 100 w. in Parakou, a town midway between the northern and southern borders. In a move to improve the signal coverage of the heavily populated south, the first of two new 50-kw. transmitters provided by West Germany was opened in 1972 in Abomey, a major provincial town about 70 miles north and slightly west of Cotonou (*Africa Research Bulletin* 1972a; and § 12.4.2). Radio Dahomey broadcasts mostly in French, with supplementation in five African languages (Thomas 1969, p. 5). According to 1972 reports, France had agreed to supply Dahomey with television by the end of that year.

6.2.6 Mali

Population: 5,100,000	Radio transmitter sites: 2
Receivers per thousand: 15	Area per site: 140,000 sq mi

Unlike the states so far discussed, Mali is completely landlocked, although the navigable headwaters of the Niger River flow from the southwestern region, where the capital, Bamako, is located. For a short time after independence Mali and Senegal formed a federation, with Senegal providing Mali the most direct access to the sea. Although the federation lasted less than two years, it had the effect of delaying the development of Mali's broadcasting facilities, since the federal radio installation was at Dakar. Mali temporarily acquired a colonial experimental station in 1957 while it was still known as the French Soudan. At that time it was conceived that Bamako's hublike location in the interior, with the coastal Francophone territories radiating out toward the sea like spokes, might justify its development as a major regional broadcasting facility (see *Africa Report* 1960). Perhaps for the same reason URTNA, the union of African broadcasting systems, chose Bamako as the site for its monitoring service (§ 13.2.2).

In 1971, the Mali domestic service, in French and five local languages, originated from Bamako and was relayed by a repeater regional transmitter at Mopti, about 300 miles northeast of the capital. Transmitters supplied by China enabled Mali to offer an external service, for which it claimed an impressive list of target areas in Africa, Asia, and the Americas. It was uncertain how effective this service would be, inasmuch as each target area received programming for only one hour on one day a week.

6.2.7 Mauritania

Population: 1,200,000	Radio transmitter sites: 1
Receivers per thousand: 67	Area per site: 398,000 sq mi

When Mauritanian radio started in 1957, the colony did not yet have a capital city, and the original broadcasting installation was made temporarily near Dakar, in neighboring Senegal to the south (Bebey 1963, pp. 43–44). The Mauritanian capital, Nouakchott, was built, starting in 1958, on the coast about 150 miles north of Dakar. Mauritania took over control of its broadcasting there in 1962. Although the service uses five languages, it is on the air for only eight hours a day, in the usual morning, midday, and evening segments.

6.2.8 Niger

Population: 3,800,000	Radio transmitter sites: 10
Receivers per thousand: 26	Area per site: 49,000 sq mi

Niger lies to the east of Mali and is therefore even farther inland, close to the heart of Africa's northern mass. Niger's broadcasting started with the standard SORAFOM installation in 1958. But Niger has developed a more varied regional distribution system and range of domestic services than most of the Francophone countries of the area. In addition to the main transmitters at Niamey, the capital, low-power medium-wave repeater stations relay programs to audiences in eight local areas, well distributed throughout the populated southern region of the country. Three different services were offered in 1971, and each local transmitter relayed the appropriate service or service combination to its area. Niger has had television since 1965 and has had some success with experimental educational programming (§ 15.2.3).

6.2.9 Upper Volta

Population: 5,100,000	Radio transmitter sites: 2
Receivers per thousand: ·18	Area per site: 53,000 sq mi

As the name implies, Upper Volta is an inland state, located at the headwaters of the Volta River. It is cut off from the sea by Ivory Coast, Togo, Dahomey, and Ghana. The capital, Ouagadougou, is well placed for radio transmission, near the geographic center of the country. A regional repeater station is located in the southwest. Radio broadcasting started in 1959, the year before independence. Television was introduced early, in 1963, but went off the air temporarily in 1966 (*Television Factbook* 1972–73, p. 1099b). In 1972 it listed programs only three days a week, from 7:00 P.M. to 10:00 P.M.; nevertheless, plans were afoot to introduce two additional stations.

6.3 Francophone Equatorial Africa

The equator intersects the African continent about five degrees south of the corner formed where the east-west-oriented coast of the great bulge turns south, near the point where the Nigerian coastline meets the Cameroonian. The equator actually cuts through Gabon and the Congo, but the Central African Republic and Chad lie well to the north, so that for them "equatorial" is a misnomer. Nevertheless, France combined these territories into a federation called Afrique Equatoriale Française, or AEF. De Gaulle, in the referendum of 1958, extended the offer of autonomy within the French Community to these colonies as well as to those of French West Africa.

6.3.1 The Congo

Population: 940,000	Radio transmitter sites: 2
Receivers per thousand: 74	Area per site: 66,000 sq mi

The Congo capital, Brazzaville, served as administrative headquarters for the AEF and grew into the biggest city of the federation. It lies on the right bank of the Congo, some 250 miles inland, but is connected by rail to Pointe Noire, the major port for the region; it also connects by means of the Ubangui River far into the interior, all the way to the Central African Republic.

In 1935 Europeans living in Brazzaville started a small private broadcasting station which the Free French commandeered in 1940. They purchased a 50-kw. transmitter from the United States and put it on the air as an allied propaganda organ in 1943, as described in § 6.1. The successor to this station, Radio Brazzaville, was still operated as part of the French government system in 1972, broadcasting three international services, all relayed from Paris and aimed at Africa, Madagascar, and the Far East. In the fall of that year, however, the Congo nationalized Radio Brazzaville and took over control.

Meanwhile, in 1946 the Congo colony had acquired its own station, which was called Radio-AEF, reflecting the fact that it was supposed to serve all four territories in the federation, though in fact it was far too weak to do so. A second federation station was set up in Chad (whose nearest border was over 800 miles to the north), but this operation was soon suspended. The federation paid a subsidy to Radiodiffusion Française, as the broadcasting system of metropolitan France was then called, to operate these federal stations. Although Radio AEF-Brazzaville used five local languages as well as French, they could have had little impact, for Europeans and African *évolués* had nearly all the receivers (Thompson and Adloff 1960, p. 317).

With the coming of independence in 1958, each of the four newly independent countries chose to operate its own radio service, but Radio-AEF continued its regional role for a time as "Radio Inter-Equatorial." In 1960 this role was finally abandoned for good. The next year Radio Congo opened a new building in Brazzaville, launched a second service in local languages, introduced new informational programs, and set up a local facility for accelerated basic training in radio—without, of course, foregoing the customary polishing of more advanced trainees at SORAFOM's Studio-École in Paris (Bebey 1963, p. 92). New facilities, including two 50-kw. transmitters, provided by China at a cost of over $600,000, were put into use in 1967 (McDonald et al. 1971a, p. 121). In 1971 Radio Congo used, in addition to its Brazzaville transmitters, two repeater transmitters on short and medium waves at Pointe Noire, Brazzaville's seaport.

As previously related (§ 6.1.3), in 1962 OCORA chose the Congo as the first Francophone country in which to install a television service. This appears to have been more in deference to Brazzaville's historic position as a bastion of French influence than to the Congo's readiness to sustain television, for the service made slow progress. Estimated circulation in 1972 was still under 2,000, and programming amounted to only about 25 hours a week.

6.3.2 Chad

Population: 3,700,000	Radio transmitter sites: 1
Receivers per thousand: 74	Area per site: 496,000 sq mi

France revived a discontinued AEF federal station in Chad in 1955, in part because of alarm at the propaganda inroads of Radio Cairo's "Voix des Arabes." Radio Fort Lamy continued to have a regional mission, half its running costs being defrayed by the metropolitan government and a quarter each by the AEF and Chad itself. Chad agreed to pay its share only when assured of representation in the station's management. Broadcasts were mainly in French, Arabic, and Sara, the language of a leading tribe in the southern region (Thompson and Adloff 1960, pp. 316–17).

Chad's facilities in 1972 comprised a 4-kw. and two 30-kw. short-wave transmitters, and a 1-kw. medium-wave transmitter. They are located at the capital, Fort Lamy, which is on the western border, so that signals radiated in a westerly direction serve Nigeria rather than Chad. The farthermost northern border of Chad is 750 miles distant from Fort Lamy, its eastern border, 450 miles. Apparently with a view to overcoming to some extent the physical isolation of the transmission center at Fort Lamy, the system operates a series of six production centers in towns 150–400 miles distant from Fort Lamy (Chad 1966).

Chad had no television in 1972, though it had earlier been reported that the Soviet Union had agreed to assist in the establishment of a station (Nelson et al. 1972, p. 99).

6.3.3 Central African Republic

Population: 1,500,000	Radio transmitter sites: 1
Receivers per thousand: 40	Area per site: 241,000 sq mi

The Central African Republic (CAR) intervenes between the Congo and Chad. Although landlocked like Chad, it has the advantage of a navigable river, the Bangui, which reaches all the way to Brazzaville, whence goods may be shipped on by rail to the Atlantic port of Pointe Noire.

Prior to independence the territory had no radio service of its own; theoretically, it was served by the federal stations in Brazzaville and Fort Lamy. A temporary national radio station went on the air from the capital, Bangui, in 1958, the year of the CAR's independence. SORAFOM had designed a special portable 250-w. transmitter-recording studio combination mounted on a truck for just such emergency uses (Bebey 1963, p. 45). CAR's permanent Radio House was completed in 1962.

6.3.4 Gabon

| Population: 490,000 | Radio transmitter sites: 2 |
| Receivers per thousand: 184 | Area per site: 52,000 sq mi |

Gabon, the last of the Equatorial Francophone group to obtain its own service, started broadcasting in 1959. By 1961 the system was equipped by SORAFOM with its standard sending complement—1-kw., 4-kw., and 30-kw. transmitters (Guillard 1963, p. 14). In 1961 all programs, 60% of which were devoted to music, were in French (Bebey 1963, p. 104).

By 1971 the Gabonese system had, with French help, undergone considerable expansion. The main station at the capital, Libreville, was supplemented by three medium-wave regional repeater stations, well disposed in relation to the capital, which is situated on the coast near the northern border. One of the repeater points, Franceville, at the extreme opposite corner of the country toward the southeast, also has a short-wave transmitter. The service still uses French exclusively.

Gabonese television opened in Libreville as early as 1963, and a repeater station was activated in 1965 at Port Gentil, another coastal town, about a hundred miles south of the capital. Both transmitters have the very low power of 50 w. and are planned primarily for educational use (*Television Factbook* 1972–73, p. 1072b). Apparently for this reason the number of sets in use remained low, even after nearly a decade of operation.

6.4 Zaïre

| Population: 17,800,000 | Radio transmitter sites: 8 |
| Receivers per thousand: 6 | Area per site: 183,000 sq mi |

The equator also intersects Zaïre, the former Belgian Congo, which we are treating in this section because of its geographic contiguity with the AEF and the fact that after they became independent France extended aid to the former Belgian colonies as well as to her own.

The colonial history of Zaïre was reviewed briefly in § 6.1.5. Radio developed quite differently there from the way it did in the AEF because of the difference in colonial policies between France and Belgium. The Belgian colonial government permitted, and even encouraged, private stations, which pioneered as early as 1936 in the use of radio for educational and religious purposes (McDonald et al. 1971a, p. 270). It also encouraged the development of programming designed especially for Africans and the use of vernaculars in broadcasting.

During World War II private stations gave time to the government for daily talks in French addressed to African *évolués* (Williams 1950, p. 28). In 1942 a private station, Radio Congolia, started programs in African languages which were later subsidized by the colonial government (McDonald et al. 1971a, p. 270).

In 1940 the metropolitan Belgian government set up Radio Congo-Belge with a 50-kw. transmitter in Leopoldville as an international propaganda station, along the lines of France's Radio Brazzaville just across the Congo River from Leopoldville, also organized at this time (§ 6.3.1). In 1944 this facility was turned over to the colonial government, which at first broadcast mostly in European languages (McDonald et al. 1971a, p. 270). Radio Congo-Belge took over "native" broadcasting in 1949 and, using four African languages as well as French, began offering an hour a day in programs prepared by the Native Affairs Department. The authorities set up some 40 public loudspeakers in the provinces and encouraged the sale of the low-cost "Saucepan Special" receivers that had been developed in Rhodesia (§ 7.1.1). At this time the Belgian Ministry for the Colonies made public an ambitious ten-year developmental program looking toward providing continuous services, both national and local; local origination of regional programming; introduction of a wired wireless service; and widespread use of public loudspeakers (Williams 1950, pp. 28–30). By 1959 RCB offered a special service, Radio Congo-Belge Africain, featuring programs in local languages. By this time "a high percentage of programming was directed to African listeners" (McDonald et al. 1971a, p. 270). Meanwhile, the Belgians had developed stations in the five regional capitals, and these originated local programming as well as rebroadcasting material from the main station at Leopoldville.

Independent Zaïre thus inherited a strong radio broadcasting system, already largely Africanized. In 1971 it operated six regional stations with a minimum transmitter power of 10 kw. and a maximum of 100 kw. These stations originated their own regional programming and also carried material from the national service originated in Kinshasa. Radio Lubumbashi, in the capital of Katanga province, broadcast an external service, La Voix de la Fraternité Africaine, using a 100-kw. transmitter, in Swahili, French, Portuguese, and English. Possibly Lubumbashi was chosen for the external-service site rather than the national capital, Kinshasa, because the location of the former on the southern border and about midway in the continent between the east and west coasts is ideal for reaching Rhodesia and Portuguese Angola and Moçambique.

In 1966, with the help of OCORA, Zaïre inaugurated television at Kinshasa. The next year all private broadcasting stations still in operation were suspended, with one partial exception—the College of Saint Francis de Sales in Lubumbashi. Its Radio Collège had been using medium-wave, short-wave, and FM transmitters, and in 1966 it had added television. The government allowed the college to continue television operations even after the 1967 ban on private broadcasting. It operated in close collaboration with the Radiodiffusion-Télévision Nationale Congolaise, the government system. This was because of a remarkable production center which had been started in 1963 at the college in Lubumbashi, dedicated to turning out educational and cultural programming. Known first as STAR (Service Technique Africain de Radio-Télévision), later as TELE-STAR, the production center was supported initially by Catholic and Protestant missions. Later it received assistance, not only from the Zaïre government, but also from Belgium, Germany, and the United States—striking testimony to the quality of its product. TELE-STAR's programs center on health, education, emancipation of women, problems of youth, general science, and world problems (Volz 1972, p. 9). In 1970 TELE-STAR was reconstituted as a nonprofit corporation, and was thereby removed from the exclusive control of religious authorities (for details on the organization and operation of TELE-STAR see Davis 1970). In 1972 a Kinshasa TELE-STAR production center, built with American and German assistance, was completed (*Rundfunk und Fernsehen* 1972d, p. 102). Other aspects of TELE-STAR are discussed in § 11.2.2.

South-Central Africa

When the British federated their two protectorates of Nyasaland and Northern Rhodesia with the colony of Southern Rhodesia in 1953, they called the new group the Central African Federation. This may seem a misnomer, for the Central African Republic, a thousand miles to the north, is much closer to the real geographical center of Africa. Looked at parochially, however, the Rhodesias and Nyasaland can be considered "central" in the sense that they lie inland and between British East Africa and South Africa.

7.1 Zambia and Southern Rhodesia, *by Jon Powell*

The Rhodesias, whose north-south demarcation line is the Zambesi River, evolved as a result of the northward thrust of the British South Africa Company. When the company lost its charter early in the 1920s, Southern Rhodesia, which had already acquired a substantial European population, was annexed as a colony by the British Crown and given internal self-government. Northern Rhodesia became a protectorate administered by the Colonial Office. Nyasaland had been a British protectorate since 1891.

7.1.1 Pre-Independence Radio

Southern Rhodesia acquired a rudimentary radio service as early as 1932, with improvised transmitters at both Salisbury and Bulawayo (Huth 1937, pp. 239–40). Northern Rhodesia, with its much smaller European population, lagged behind. World War II finally provided the incentive for setting up a station in Lusaka, the northern capital. The government's Information Department installed a 300-w. transmitter in 1941 for the

Jon Powell is Associate Professor and Coordinator of the Radio-Television-Film Area, Department of Speech Communication, Northern Illinois University. His teaching specialization is comparative and international broadcasting. His Ph.D. dissertation (1963) was on international broadcasting by the United States.

purpose of disseminating war-related information (Franklin 1949, p. 3). From the outset the Lusaka station addressed programs to Africans in their own languages, becoming the African pioneer in the field of local vernacular broadcasting.

The story of the Lusaka station's pioneer achievements is fortunately preserved in a book of reminiscences by one of its original staff members, Peter Fraenkel, in *Wayaleshi* (Fraenkel 1959), as well as in official reports by Harry Franklin, Lusaka's far-sighted information officer (Franklin 1949, 1950). In 1945 Franklin proposed that Radio Lusaka concentrate on developing programming for Africans. Since Northern Rhodesia could not afford such a specialized service on its own, the administrations of Southern Rhodesia and Nyasaland were persuaded to share in the operating costs, while the British government agreed to provide capital funds. Thus the Central African Broadcasting Station came into being—the first "fully-fledged station broadcasting exclusively to Africans" (Fraenkel 1959, p. 17). When Hortense Powdermaker visited in Lusaka in 1953 she found the CABS broadcasting in a different language each day of the week on a 2 P.M.–9 P.M. schedule—six days of African vernaculars, one day of English. "Broadcasting House was the one example I found," she wrote, "of an actual partnership between Europeans and Africans" (Powdermaker 1962, pp. 233–34).

The CABS specialization focused attention on the particular urgency of audience building among African listeners. Among the by-products of this effort were the world's most extensive collection of indigenous African music; first attempts at systematic audience research among African audiences; and a breakthrough in that most formidable barrier to audience growth—the lack of a receiver which Africans could afford to buy.

Franklin tried for three years in the late 1940s to persuade British manufacturers that a potential mass market existed among Africans for a very simple, inexpensive, battery-operated short-wave radio receiver. One must bear in mind that this was before transistors made small, low-cost receivers commonplace. He finally persuaded a battery company to invest in the research and development of the idea. One of the early models was mounted experimentally in a nine-inch-round aluminum housing originally intended as a saucepan. Thus was born in 1949 the famous "saucepan special," a four-tube tropicalized short-wave receiver, which succeeded even beyond Franklin's expectations. It cost £5, and its battery, which lasted 300 hours, cost an additional £1 5s. (Franklin 1950, p. 17). In 1972 a comparable set, locally produced, cost about £9 (Mytton 1972b, p. 25). According to Franklin no more than 20 or 30 Africans had radios in the whole of Northern Rhodesia prior to the appearance of the saucepan special, which, he called "the poor man's radio"; within three months 1,500 of the saucepan specials had been sold. Sales continued so briskly that in the next few years more than 50,000 sets were imported (Codding 1959, p. 52). Interest was shown in other colonies; for example, the British bought 3,000 of the specials to distribute to district officers, police posts, and village headmen in the Somali Protectorate (Somalia 1968, p. 9). Franklin had hopes of capitalizing on a world market for the inexpensive receivers, but technology overtook the saucepan special; soon the transistor radio came into mass production and turned Franklin's brainchild into a mere historical curiosity.

As time went on, the easy, fruitful working relationship between the few dedicated Europeans like Fraenkel and the African staff which Powdermaker had observed at Lusaka's Central African Broadcasting Station began to erode. Along with it went the goodwill and confidence of its listeners. The political maneuvers leading up to federation, which the Africans generally regarded as a device for perpetuating European domination, embittered relationships and aroused suspicions about the motives of the station. By the time the federation issue was settled, "the faith that our audience had once had in our broadcasting station," Fraenkel sadly wrote, "had collapsed completely" (1959, p. 207).

The Central African Federation formed in 1953 from these three territories had some economic justification, especially from Southern Rhodesia's viewpoint, but it generated strong political opposition among important groups in all three member territories. As a consequence of federation came a new broadcasting organization. The Federal Broadcasting Corporation, with headquarters in Salisbury, was set up in 1958. The corporation had radio studios in two other Southern Rhodesia towns, Gwelo and Bulawayo; in Northern Rhodesia at Lusaka as well as the chief town of the Copperbelt, Kitwe; and in Nyasaland's largest town, Blantyre (Bebey 1963, pp. 134–35). Lusaka continued to use African languages as well as English, but the spirit which had animated the original station had long since been drowned by the rising tide of animosity between the races.

The federation lasted just a decade. With its dissolution came independence in 1964 for Nyasaland, as Malawi, and for Northern Rhodesia, as Zambia. Southern Rhodesia reverted to her prior status as a self-governing colony. With the example of their erstwhile federal partners before them, the white Southern Rhodesians foresaw a similar devolution of power to the African majority in the colony if Britain continued to insist on eventual proportional representation. Extended negotiations to obtain complete independence began. Britain, however, refused to surrender her legal obligations in the colony without some guarantee that the rights of the African majority would be protected. In 1965, after two years of fruitless negotiation, the European-dominated government of Southern Rhodesia issued a "unilateral declaration of independence."

The centralization of the federal system in Salisbury under the corporation had given Southern Rhodesia the lion's share of broadcasting facilities. When the federation dissolved in 1963, each member's radio system suffered. Zambia and Malawi, in particular, started with less than adequate resources for independent operation, so that the first task of their newly independent broadcasting organizations was to repair the damage of the separation.

7.1.2 Zambia

Population: 4,200,000	Radio transmitter sites: 4
Receivers per thousand: 24	Area per site: 73,000 sq mi

The original Radio Lusaka of 1941 was to go through two more name changes. Already it had been, successively, the Central African Broadcasting Station and part of the Federal Broadcasting Corporation of Rhodesia and Nyasaland. With the independence of Northern Rhodesia as Zambia in 1964 it became, first, the Zambian Broadcasting Corporation, and finally, in 1966, the Zambian Broadcasting Services, or ZBS.

ZBS falls under the Ministry of Information, Broadcasting and Tourism, and is financed by government budgetary appropriation. Receiver license fees and advertising generate revenue, but these moneys go directly to the central treasury and have little bearing on the amount appropriated to run ZBS. Its operating budget in 1972 amounted to about $1.7 million —about twice the system's gross revenue, which amounted to $266,000 from license fees and $609,000 from advertising (Zambia 1972, pp. 10, 47). The minimum radio license fee was $1.40 a year for the very poor, twice that for others. A combined radio-television license cost $14.00.

Radio. In 1971 Zambia's short-wave facilities were still concentrated at Lusaka, but there were also three regional medium-wave stations. These, however, were confined to towns on the "line-of-rail," which runs approximately north and south through the middle of the country, leaving the eastern and western extremities without local service. This centralization of facilities was maintained when China gave Zambia a 200-kw. medium-wave and two 50-kw. short-wave transmitters. These were to be installed at Lusaka by Chinese technicians, working with Zambian trainee counterparts. The installation was scheduled for completion in 1972, when it was expected that the new facilities would improve service to the remoter areas of the country (Carpenter 1971b).

Transmitter facilities were so deployed that each of two services, the home and the general, could be aired simultaneously. In 1971 the general service carried 98 hours weekly in English and 11 hours each in Bemba and Nyanja, the two most widely used local languages. The home service divided its time among seven vernacular languages, the number of hours devoted to each varying in accordance with the number of speakers who use them. Together the two services broadcast some 240 hours a week. This appears an impressive total, but in fact the necessity of broadcasting news along with literacy, agriculture, health, and other specialized information programs in eight different languages drastically limited the program time available for listeners in any one language group (Mytton 1971b, p. 5).

In order to give each language fair access to available time, the Bemba and Nyanja segments of the general service alternated in two-hour blocks during off-peak hours. Similarly, the home service scheduled each of the seven local languages in rotating two-hour blocks so as to give some peak-listening time to each (Kaplan et al. 1969a, p. 253). These expedients are necessary because, though many listeners actually understand more than one language, the use of one's own language on the radio is a recognized status symbol. By the same token, devoting a disproportionate amount of radio time to one language causes resentment among speakers of other languages (Mytton 1971b, pp. 5–6).

In a 1971 sample week the content of the Home Service, in percentages, was as follows: talks, 41; education, 19; music, 19; news and current affairs, 12; sports, 4; religion and drama, 2 each; and children's programs, 1; unclassified, 2. This analysis suggests an unusually high percentage of serious informational programming; however, the duplication of some program elements in all seven vernaculars inflates the percentages.

The Zambian government emphasizes the value of radio as a means of adult education. For example, a radio farm-forum project of the type first used in Ghana (§ 5.2.2) was introduced in 1966. By 1970 it had developed some 600 participating forum groups in all seven major language areas of the country (Natesh 1971). Another example is a literacy training project, begun in 1969, which again used all seven major languages (Natesh 1971 and 1972). Radio is also used systematically for in-school broadcasting and adult education in English. In 1970, 17 hours a week were devoted to the former, six to the latter during school terms (Mytton 1971b, p. 5).

Zambia has been hospitable to religious organizations seeking program time on government broadcasting facilities. An unusually successful ecumenical approach to this type of broadcasting is Multimedia Zambia, a nonprofit organization representing 18 Protestant church groups and nine Roman Catholic dioceses. Multimedia Zambia was responsible for 2,400 programs on ZBS in 1971 (Carpenter 1971a, p. 36). Participating churches pay the salaries of personnel to staff the Religion Department of the station (§ 11.2.1 has other details on Multimedia Zambia).

Zambia has no formally constituted external service. However, it made its broadcasting facilities available to the Movimento Popular de Libertaçao de Angola, a liberation group which in 1972 aimed more than five hours of programming a week at Angola (Mytton 1972a, p. 12).

Television. Zambia's television service began as part of the federal system in 1961. The original station was a commercial, advertising-supported undertaking run by a concessionaire, Rhodesian Television Limited, which chose to locate the station at Kitwe, the chief town of the prosperous Copperbelt, where many Europeans work, rather than at the capital, Lusaka. After independence, Zambia continued similar commercial arrangements initially, but in 1966 it amalgamated both radio and television in the Zambian Broadcasting Services, under full government control (Kaplan et al. 1969a, pp. 255–56). ZBS continued to sell both television and radio advertising. Meanwhile a second station had been opened in Lusaka in 1965, and in 1968 ZBS set up a repeater station in Kabwe, a town midway between Kitwe and Lusaka. The three stations are programmed as a network, with microwave interconnection. Lusaka became the principal production center, but educational broadcasting production continued to originate from Kitwe.

Originally, most of the television programming was imported, but the official policy has been to replace foreign programming with local production to the extent possible (ZBS 1969, p. 2). In 1971 locally produced shows, including news, public affairs, educational, and variety programs, still constituted only a third of the ZBS schedule of about 48 hours a week, exclusive of schools broadcasts, all in English. The breakdown by program type for a sample week, in percentages, was: drama, 33; general entertainment, 16; children's programs, 14; news and current affairs, 11; talks, 11; sports, 7; education, 5; religion, 1; and unclassified, 2. Among the syndicated imports were "The Flintstones," "The Flip Wilson Show," "Steptoe and Son," "The Untouchables," and "Wagon Train" (*Sunday Times of Zambia,* 26 September 1971, p. 8).

The Educational Television Service based at Kitwe is operated by the Ministry of Education. In the 1970 school-term TV subjects included English language and literature, geography, history, and French, for a total of about 26 hours of ETV programming per week (*Telecommunication Journal* 1970, pp. 67–68). The Ministry of Education had an eight-man ETV staff and its own production studios and videotape recorders (Chilangwa 1970).

Audience studies. In 1970 ZBS and the University of Zambia began an ambitious three-year audience-research project to include a national survey of people in all parts of Zambia, both rural and urban. This represented an interesting carry-over from the pioneer research work of the CABS, mentioned in § 7.1.1. In fact the University of Zambia studies actually followed the research recommendations of Michael Kittermaster, the original director of the CABS. Kittermaster had left Lusaka after federation, but he returned when Zambia became independent and was director of broadcasting until 1967 (Mytton 1972a, app. 1).

Special attention was paid to the problems of broadcasting in local vernaculars. Although only seven local languages are officially recognized and used in the primary schools, some 70 languages and dialects are in actual use in Zambia (Mytton 1971b, pp. 5–6). In one of the early reports of this research project, it was shown that in nine towns investigated the mother tongues of about half the sample members were languages other than those used on the radio; many of the rest spoke "relatively closely related" languages, but 17% of the sample spoke languages not closely related to those broadcast (Mytton 1971a, p. 9).

Some key findings of the countrywide study were that about a third of the sample owned radio sets and over half listened to ZBS; that, though television viewers were confined to urban areas, the TV audience was not "almost exclusively expatriate and wealthy Zambian" as had been previously supposed; that over half the sample thought the radio did not program enough Zambian music; that the most popular programs, all in African languages, were a storytelling program, a question-and-answer program dealing with personal problems, and record-request programs; and that nearly a quarter of the sample reported listening to foreign radio stations (Mytton 1972a). Technical details about the Zambia research project are discussed in § 16.4.

7.1.3 Southern Rhodesia

Population: 5,300,000	Radio transmitter sites: 7
Receivers per thousand: 40	Area per site: 21,000 sq mi

By 1972 Rhodesia's independence from Britain had still not been legitimized, so that technically its name remained "Southern Rhodesia." A series of United Nations resolutions called for sanctions against Rhodesia following the unilateral declaration of independence, or UDI, in 1965. These resolutions resulted in boycotts which apparently had only limited impact because of evasions and the sympathetic help Rhodesia received from South Africa and Portugal.

The president of Rhodesia appoints the board of governors for the statutory body responsible for radio and television, the Rhodesian Broadcasting Corporation. RBC owns and operates all radio services; in the case of television it owns the transmission facilities but contracts for programming with a private commercial company, Rhodesia Television Limited. RBC's ultimate control is assured, however, by the fact that it owns 51% of the stock of the program company (RBC 1970, pp. 1, 16).

RBC's financial support comes from receiver license fees and advertising revenue. Two classes of radio-receiver licenses are issued: "concessionary" licenses for Africans at about $3, and ordinary licenses at $6; combined radio-television licenses cost $18. In the fiscal year 1970–71 the corporation netted about $1.2 million from license fees and realized net advertising revenue of about $1.1 million. Despite the U.N. sanctions, all categories of income showed an increase from the preceding year (RBC 1971, p. 7).

RBC offers two domestic services: the general service, which uses only English and serves the European minority; and the African service, which uses three principal local languages—Shona, Ndebele, and Nyanja—as well as English. It is not a completely independent service, however, since part of the time it repeats the general service (*WRTH* 1972, p. 123). RBC does not go off the air midmorning and midafternoon as do many African broadcasting services. Continuous operation from early morning to late evening was introduced in 1965 (RBC 1970, p. 4).

Transmitters are located in seven towns, five of them along the rail line which runs roughly southwest from Salisbury through Gatooma, Que Que, Gwelo, and Bulawayo. All seven towns offer the general service on medium waves, but only three—Salisbury, Gwelo, and Bulawayo—offer the African service on medium waves. All medium-wave transmitters are low power except for a 100-kw. transmitter used for the general service in Gwelo. There are also three short-wave transmitters at Salisbury, a 10-kw. used for the African service, a 20-kw. used for the general service, and a 100-kw. shared by both. In 1972 the government was contemplating establishing an FM network as a high-priority goal for future radio development.

A local commercial service using 1-kw. medium-wave transmitters operates in the three main industrial cities of Salisbury ("Radio Jacaranda"), Bulawayo ("Radio Matopos"), and Umtali ("Radio Manica"). The Umtali commercial service shares a single transmitter with the general service. The African service also accepts advertising.

Rhodesia Television Limited leases transmission facilities from RBC under a contract running through 1979. Facilities at the outset of 1972 included transmitters at Salisbury and at Bulawayo, in the southwest, with a third transmitter planned for Umtali, in the east, by the end of the year. The contractor handles television sales through a subsidiary company and turns over a portion of the receipts to RBC (RBC 1970, p. 6). The programs are all in English.

In response to the sanctions invoked by the United Nations following UDI, the United States government banned the export of television programming to Rhodesia, except for news and documentaries (see Powell 1969). However, foreign distributors who market American programs evaded the ban. Thus the 1971 program schedule listed such American feature films as *Valley of the Dolls* and such syndicated series as "Mission Impossible," "Mannix," and "Halls of Montezuma." The TV program content for a sample week broke down as follows in percentages: feature films, 25; drama, 23; education, 14; news and current affairs, 12; general entertainment, 10; talks, 8; children's programs, 6; and religion and sports, 1 each.

Although Rhodesian television realized a net profit for the corporation of about $237,000 in 1970–71, the commercial contractor nevertheless expressed concern that the ban on program exports might eventually have an adverse effect (Rhodesian Television Limited 1971, p. 2). Meanwhile the United Nations sanctions seemed already to have inhibited any extensive physical improvement of the television facilities. The equipment is of British origin, so that it is difficult to obtain replacements and to expand upon the existing facilities. The press once discussed the desirability of introducing color television but dismissed it as something to be considered only if sanctions were lifted (letter from Lewis R. McFarlane, U. S. State Department South African Affairs officer, 3 February 1972).

Educational TV programming prepared by the African Education Department was addressed to the primary grades daily, from 11:10 A.M. to noon, in 1971. The programs dealt with English, music, history, "story time," and "question time." A special 45-minute program for teachers, "Teachers' Magazine," was scheduled once a week. On Sundays from noon to 1:00 P.M. a general adult-education program, "Learning Does Not End," was provided (letter from Peter Lockitch, Rhodesian Television Limited, 1 November 1971).

7.2 Malawi, by William E. Mackie

| Population: 4,400,000 | Radio transmitter sites: 10 |
| Receivers per thousand: 25 | Area per site: 5,000 sq mi |

Malawi, formerly the British Protectorate of Nyasaland and later the reluctant junior partner in the Federation of Rhodesia and Nyasaland, became an independent nation in 1964. Even before full independence, plans had been made for a national radio service, the Malawi Broadcasting Corporation, which began operation on 1 January 1964 (Chalmers 1962, p. 1). When Nyasaland became a part of the Central African Federation the Central African Broadcasting Station at Lusaka (see § 7.1.1) was transformed into the African service of the Federal Broadcasting Corporation. After complaints that the Lusaka transmitters were not providing adequate service in Nyasaland, a relay transmitter was installed in 1960 near Zomba, Nyasaland's capital. Federal broadcasting in Nyasaland ended in 1963 when the country seceded from the federation. The federal facilities in Nyasaland consisted of a studio center in Blantyre, Nyasaland's major city, a 20-kw. short-wave transmitter, and a 250-w. medium-wave transmitter. These properties were transferred to the new government. One effect of the breakoff from the federal network was cancellation of all advertising

William E. Mackie is Writer-Producer, Coronet Films, Chicago. He was formerly assistant professor of speech and dramatic art, University of Missouri, and he served as Chief of Party, University of Missouri Mass Communication Project in Malawi, 1965–68.

contracts in the fall of 1953, which left Nyasaland with neither commercial income nor a commercial department (Headland 1965, p. 24).

7.2.1 Facilities

Primary coverage in Malawi is provided by a seven-station medium-wave network. Additional internal as well as external coverage is provided by short-wave transmitters which generally broadcast the same programs carried on the medium-wave service. All programs are fed to the network from Broadcasting House, MBC's program, control, and administrative headquarters in Blantyre. The National Transmitting Station, ten miles from Blantyre, houses a 10-kw. medium-wave transmitter and three short-wave transmitters and feeds programs to other transmitters by a combination of land lines and low-power FM broadcast transmitters.

Small recording studios are located at Fort Johnston (on the southern shore of Lake Nyasa), Karonga (on the northern shore of Lake Nyasa), Mzimba (in north central Malawi), and Zomba (in south central Malawi). Tapes made in these studios are sent to Blantyre for transmission on the network. Only the studio in Zomba, Malawi's capital, is directly connected to Broadcasting House in Blantyre by land lines. It is used for live reports on the proceedings of Parliament; also, most agricultural programs are recorded at the Zomba facility.

The Blantyre production complex consists of eight studios, each with its own control room. MBC's studios are all in almost constant use in order to supply the more than 18 hours of programming required daily. All programs except newscasts and listener-request record programs are prerecorded.

A short-wave monitoring facility located at Broadcasting House in Blantyre provides information for political analysis by the government. Recorded excerpts from foreign broadcasts, especially from the BBC World Service, are frequently incorporated into news and feature programs (interview with Hans von Goertzke, head of Current Affairs Section, 1970).

The MBC Commercial Department estimated that in 1971 Malawians owned 100,000 radio receivers, or one receiver for every 40 persons. Nearly 70% of these receivers were multiband short-wave and medium-wave sets. In an effort to multiply the effectiveness of the few radios available in rural Malawi, where an estimated 97% of the country's people live, farm-forum listening groups have been organized by Malawi's agricultural extension service. All secondary schools and most primary schools have also been given radios by the government (MBC 1967, p. 9).

Several models of battery-operated transistorized receivers are manufactured in Malawi by the Nzeru Company (*nzeru* means "wisdom" in Chichewa, Malawi's major language). The firm, organized with government help, started production in 1966. At that time, the least expensive model cost $13.20. Nzeru radios are assembled from imported basic components, but circuit boards and cabinets are fabricated locally. The company is protected by a 20% import duty on radios manufactured abroad.

In 1972, there were no plans to develop a television service in Malawi. The government felt that the country's limited resources should be invested in making radio a more effective nation-building tool.

7.2.2 Governance

The Malawi Broadcasting Corporation is a public corporation controlled by a board of directors consisting of a chairman and from four to seven other members. The chief administrative officer is the director general. The board members and the director general are appointed by the president through the minister responsible for broadcasting affairs (Malawi 1964, pp. 5–7). In May 1972, the first Malawian director general was appointed, to replace a BBC officer on secondment (COMBROAD 1972d, p. 44).

While general policy and operational responsibilities rest with the board and the senior staff, the government is empowered to exercise final control over policy and output. Responsibility for broadcasting has generally rested with the minister of information, although the president is free to assign broadcasting to any minister he chooses.

The MBC is financed by government subvention and advertising revenue; listener licenses were abolished in 1966 in an effort to encourage Malawians to purchase receivers. The corporation operates on an annual budget of approximately $500,000, of which about 35% comes from advertising revenue (MBC 1970b, p. 21). Its Commercial Department contracts for most advertising through agencies in Salisbury, Rhodesia, and drug and soap products account for approximately 50% of the advertising revenue (interview with the MBC's commercial manager, 1969). Additional revenue comes from the operation of the Production Services Department, which records commercial materials for use on MBC and in other countries; and from the Commercial Department's fees for acting as sales agent for the mobile-cinema service operated by the Malawi government.

The MBC's broadcast day is divided into three time categories. In 1971 a "Class A" run-of-schedule sixty-second one-time announcement cost approximately $20, reduced (for example) to $18 for an order of 30 spots within a 30-day period. Fixed-time spots and spots adjacent to news programs were surcharged 12% and 25% respectively (MBC 1970a). The sponsorship of programs, including newscasts, is allowed. A unique feature of MBC's commercial operation is the availability of public-service programs for sponsorship on an identification-only basis at 50% of normal rates. Sponsors of such programs may mention their sponsorship at the beginning and end of the programs but may not run commercials as such.

Agricultural and adult-education features have been sponsored on this basis.

In 1970, a local rate card was introduced to encourage advertising by small businesses in Malawi. At that time the local rates were approximately a third less than the rates charged national and international advertisers. All advertising purchased through advertising agencies was billed at the national rates.

7.2.3 Programming

Because only a single national service is broadcast, MBC has evolved a block programming format to serve its several audiences. As in most developing nations, programming is made more difficult by the great differences between the needs and tastes of two major audiences, the urban-modern and the rural-traditional. One advantage enjoyed by MBC is that almost 95% of its listeners understand a single language, Chichewa. The only other language used in broadcasting is English.

The major programming blocks in 1970, according to the published program schedule, were: sign-on to 8:00 A.M., commercial programs for general audiences; 9:00 A.M. to 12:00 M., schools broadcasting; 12:00 M. to 1:30 P.M., commercial; 1:30 P.M. to 4:15 P.M., village programs; 4:15 P.M. to 6:00 P.M., adult-education and current-affairs programs for urban Africans; 6:00 P.M. to 7:30 P.M., news, public-service, and commercial programs for general audiences; and 7:30 P.M. to 10:00 P.M., music, drama, and variety programs for Europeans and English-speaking Africans. The time chosen for village programs is based on Malawi's traditional work pattern during the growing season. Farmers work in their fields from very early in the morning until midday, then return to their homes to eat and relax during the heat of the day.

The MBC's 127 hours of programming a week in 1970 broke down into broad categories approximately as follows (in percentages): music (both popular and traditional), 49; educational (classroom, adult, and agricultural), 20; news and current affairs, 17; drama and variety, 9; religious, 3; promotional, 1; and miscellaneous, 1. A 1970–71 listenership survey indicated that the most popular MBC program was "Zimene Mwatifunsa" ("Listeners' Requests") (Malawi 1971, p. 53).

Remote broadcasts are a major means of reporting political events to Malawi's citizens, and the MBC produces approximately 50 outside broadcasts each year (MBC 1970b, p. 10). A remote-broadcast vehicle supplied by the Federal Republic of Germany is used for most outside originations. Presidential speeches are broadcast live if local facilities permit. If the distance is not too great, remotes are fed to Broadcasting House in Blantyre by VHF mobile transmitter. Because many news events in a country like Malawi take place at the nation's single international airport, an interview studio has been installed there and permanently connected to Broadcasting

House by land line. Programs from remote areas without telephone service are recorded and broadcast at the earliest opportunity.

Most MBC programs are produced by the corporation's own staff, but transcribed programs from foreign sources are also used—in 1969 from as many as 17 countries (MBC 1970b, p. 15). Most externally produced programs came from the BBC Transcription Service.

In 1970, according to its published schedule, MBC's News Department produced approximately 11 newscasts daily. The station subscribes to Reuters and the Malawi News Agency (a government service) and also obtains news items from foreign stations via its own monitoring service. In 1970, the Current Affairs Section of the News Department produced more than seven hours of programs a week featuring nation building and African and international affairs (MBC 1970b, pp. 14–15).

Several government ministries cooperate in producing special programs. One of the most popular and unusual is "Radio Doctor," a commercially sponsored weekly series jointly produced by MBC and the Ministry of Health. Listeners are invited to write the "Radio Doctor" for advice on the treatment of common illnesses. This format enables motivated introduction of personal hygiene and public-health information into the program.

7.2.4 Special Services

About a quarter of a million Malawians temporarily leave their country each year to work in neighboring countries. For both political and security reasons the government would like to maintain contact with this large body of migrant citizens. Early in 1971 MBC began an international service on its 100-kw. transmitter aimed at this audience as well as at other external listeners. Listener mail from other countries indicated that MBC already had a sizable external listenership, especially in Rhodesia and Zambia. For example, in 1970 MBC received more than 7,000 pieces of foreign mail, according to the corporation's annual report (MBC 1971, p. 25). The new service was expected to increase the size of this audience.

Since agriculture is Malawi's major source of income, broadcasting aimed at improving farming practices has high priority. The Extension Aids Branch of the Ministry of Agriculture produces agricultural programs with the help of MBC personnel and facilities. More than 500 listening groups had been organized by the extension service by 1969, principally in the Central and Southern regions of Malawi, where agriculture is most concentrated. The farm-forum programs reached an estimated weekly audience of 115,000 listening-group members (MBC 1970b, p. 19). Other agricultural programs included "O Phiri" ("The Phiri Family"), a weekly serial drama in Chichewa, and "The World of Agriculture," a weekly magazine program in English.

The Malawi Committee for Education by Radio, composed of representatives from the Ministry of Education, the Malawi Correspondence College, and the MBC, was organized in 1965 to advise on the use of radio to help solve some of the country's educational problems. Radio is used for direct teaching, enrichment, and teacher training, with the programs designed for primary schools, secondary schools, and the national correspondence college. More than 15 hours of formal educational programs are broadcast each week during school terms (MBC 1970b, p. 17). The Schools Broadcasting Unit, operated jointly by the Ministry of Education and MBC, produces most of these educational materials. Programs produced by the unit won three successive special awards in the Japan Prize International Educational Program Contest. The Schools Broadcasting Unit conducts regular teacher-training sessions in the utilization of educational broadcasts.

When some of the secondary schools complained that they found educational broadcasts difficult to fit into their school timetables, Schools Broadcasting instituted a tape service starting in 1968. This service supplies recordings of educational programs on request. In 1970 almost 300 programs were duplicated and distributed to secondary schools (MBC 1971, p. 23).

7.2.5 Finances

Substantial support for MBC in the areas of equipment, operational personnel, and training have come from Great Britain, the United States, the Federal Republic of Germany, South Africa, Israel, and the United Nations. MBC's medium-wave transmitters were all provided by the United States. Its 100-kw. short-wave transmitter was a gift of the Federal Republic of Germany. According to MBC annual reports, MBC received foreign-aid grants amounting to about $900,000 in the years 1964–70.

Overseas training for more than 50 of MBC's approximately 100 program and engineering staff members has also been arranged through aid programs. Personnel have trained in London with the BBC; in Germany at government broadcasting installations; and at American universities, technical schools, broadcasting stations, and advertising agencies. In-country on-the-job training has been conducted by expatriate advisers and senior MBC staff members. Local technical training is available through the Malawi Polytechnic College in Blantyre. More than 20 Peace Corps and British Volunteer Service Overseas specialists assisted with schools broadcasting and staff training between 1965 and 1970.

MBC has explored a number of means for earning additional revenue to reduce the level of government financial support. These include the sale of production services to agencies and to other broadcast services, commercial representation for Malawi's mobile cinema circuit, production of advertising films, selling space in MBC publications, and even the unusual expedient of leasing transmitter facilities during certain time periods to outside contractors. In July 1972, an American firm began an international commercial service using MBC's 100-kw. short-wave transmitter. The service, called Lakeland Radio, broadcast daily musical programs pre-recorded in the United States for one hour in the morning and one hour in the evening (interview with Mark Wodlinger, 1972; see also § 8.4.1).

8   Southern Africa

Peter B. Orlik

Any examination of the broadcasting systems of Southern Africa (Botswana, Lesotho, the Republic of South Africa, and Swaziland) must be largely shaped by the area's two pervasive conditions: (1) South Africa's political, economic, and geographic dominance of the region; and (2) the absence into the 1970s of broadcast television, itself a by-product of this same dominance. Thus, the following analysis will both begin with, and place primary focus on, broadcasting within the Republic of South Africa, with special attention on the television impasse.

8.1 Radio in the Republic of South Africa

Population: 21,500,000	Radio transmitter sites: 86
Receivers per thousand: 109	Area per site: 9,000 sq mi

8.1.1 Afrikaner Hegemony

Antagonism between South Africans of British stock and those primarily of Dutch descent ("Afrikaners," or—a more history-laden term—"Boers") has affected South African broadcasting from its inception when the Boers imported German wireless telegraphy sets for use in their turn-of-the-century war against the British. Her Majesty's forces captured these primitive devices, however, which "did not prove of practical value" to either side. This abortive attempt at military use of wireless seemingly overshadowed an even earlier start, for in 1897 a Port Elizabeth post office engineer named Edward Jennings allegedly "invented wireless telegraphy independently of Marconi, but received no encouragement" (Rosenthal 1961, p. 583).

Peter B. Orlik is Associate Professor of Speech and Head, Broadcast and Cinematic Arts Area, Central Michigan University. He is the author of many articles on broadcasting; and his Ph.D. dissertation at Wayne State University was a study of the South African Broadcasting Corporation.

Primarily because of South Africa's strategic location on one of the world's main shipping lanes, the next two decades brought substantial advances in wireless telegraphy and wireless telephony. By the early 1920s, enough amateurs were engaged in the latter for the government to issue regulations, which it did in August 1923. Most of the regulatory power— such as providing for the licensing of radio transmitters and receiving sets as well as stipulating the advertising limit (six minutes an hour)—rested with the postmaster general (Patrick 1962, p. 13). Though a handful of stations were subsequently started, the small number of receivers, the low power of the stations, and the refusal of many to pay their listeners' fees threatened to halt all broadcasting activity by early 1927. Then, I. W. Schlesinger, the founding father of the South African film industry, saw commercial potential in broadcasting and secured a 10-year license from the government for his new African Broadcasting Company, which became the sole radio broadcaster in the region save for an occasional amateur.

Having survived a financially troubled childhood, by 1934 the ABC had achieved both popularity and fiscal stability. Nevertheless, diverse interests and cross-pressures were soon to cause its demise. The success of the British Broadcasting Corporation as an archetype for the "public broad-casting" ideal appealed to a South African administration which had allowed commercial radio only as an alternative to no radio at all. Further, the ABC's reliance on entertainment and its studied avoidance of Afrikaans-language programming offended many white South Africans.

8.1.2 SABC Founded

After a visit and report by Sir John Reith, BBC director-general, the South African Parliament passed the Broadcast Act of 1936. It established the South African Broadcasting Corporation as a monopoly and simul-taneously dissolved the ABC. On 1 August 1936 the changeover officially took place. The same facilities and staffs were engaged but were man-aged now by a governmental board of governors, whose most pressing immediate task was to bring Afrikaans programming up to quantitative parity with English programming. Simultaneous bilingual announcements soon proved too cumbersome, however, and facilities too limited, to permit the establishment of two separate language services. It was decided instead that Afrikaans programming would be aired via two rented short-wave transmitters until additional funds and facilities could be secured. Though this plan did not escape Afrikaner criticism, the bulk of the Afrikaans-speaking citizens lived outside the range of the city-based medium-wave transmitters and thus already depended on short-wave ser-vice (Roos 1954, p. 42). Still, the Afrikaans service remained in limbo even into the World War II period. The war accelerated the movement of Afrikaners to the cities in search of industrial jobs, thereby increasing the demand for an adequate medium-wave Afrikaans service. Wartime priorities did not include domestic broadcasting, however, and the demand remained unmet.

Afrikaner opposition to fighting a war alongside the British prevented the passage of a conscription act. It also brought a subtle but continuous transformation in SABC personnel as more and more English-stock employees volunteered for military service and their places were taken by Afrikaners set on rectifying the imbalance between the English and Afrikaans services. An English-stock radio actor long affiliated with the SABC recalls the corporation's internal climate of that time:

Although no one liked to admit or talk about it, there was very close to the surface an antagonism between Afrikaans and English and a definite belligerence on the part of an Afrikaans speaking group, engendered by a so-called inferiority complex. The English speaking section—rather stupidly condescending at times—blandly ignored the situation but gradually key administrative posts were filled by Afrikaans speaking and/or sympathetic individuals. It should be remembered that the Smuts Government during the war contained many Afrikaners and that there was a strong dedicated anti-British group. . . . So that while almost all English-speaking people innocently stood by, the ground was thoroughly prepared for an Afrikaner take-over in Broadcasting. [Personal letter, 25 June 1968]

For their part, English-speaking staff members, especially those with friends or relatives in the military, resented the refusal of Afrikaners to suport the Allied cause. Some of this ill-feeling found an outlet in Freedom Radio, a pirate station whose one-hour evening transmissions attacked the Nationalist opponents of the war. It opened with the sign-on "Wherever the enemies of freedom may be, there are watching eyes and listening ears to guard our cause." These broadcasts were much more vitriolic than anything ever heard on the English-dominated, prewar SABC. Many claimed, in fact, that Freedom Radio was run clandestinely by some of the corporation's key English-speaking staff. The numerous quick shutdowns, supposedly accomplished to avoid SABC detection, seemed a little too neatly timed to be merely coincidental (interview with Father Robert Barrett, 1 May 1968).

In the postwar period, the movement to upgrade the Afrikaans service gained impetus from the Afrikaner-backed Nationalist party's victory in the 1948 election. This party has dominated South African politics ever since. It enabled the Afrikaners increasingly to control the SABC's board of governors. At the same time, approval of a new commercial service promised funds needed for facility parity among all three services.

The sociopolitical shift within the corporation and the country as a whole clearly manifested itself as the 1950s began. First, the SABC governors established the corporation's own news-gathering service and, as of 16 July 1950, ended the practice of carrying BBC news over corporation facilities

(*Times* [London], 14 July 1950, p. 5). Second, the promised new commercial service, Springbok Radio, was born on 1 May 1950. Springbok secured the great bulk of its advertising from the established business sector. Since that sector was overwhelmingly controlled by English-stock interests, Springbok became more and more English in character. This prompted the leading Afrikaans daily, *Die Transvaler,* to complain that the service was exposing Afrikaner homes to a blast of "foreign" influences (Patterson 1957, p. 256).

Radio's popular and financial success, however, was not affected by such controversies. In 1957, each of the three services received an equal share of the 70 hours a day being broadcast over 52 transmitters. In addition, a rediffusion system for the black Africans—officially termed "Bantu"—had been initiated in 1952 for Orlando Township, outside Johannesburg. This single-channel wired loudspeaker system was operated by a British firm and had extended to 11,910 African subscribers by 1957, when the SABC organized a new program service to provide 16 hours daily especially for the closed circuit distribution system. It served only the area adjacent to Johannesburg, however, and there was little prospect of its extension to other African locations. Nor was there sufficient medium- or short-wave spectrum space available to permit converting the Bantu Service to open circuit status. This circumstance added impetus to the idea of resorting to FM, in the VHF band where there was plenty of room. FM could bring high quality signals to Bantu locations as well as to many underserved rural White-occupied areas.

8.1.3 Development of FM

The opportunity to embark on FM came sooner than expected. SABC engineers realized as early as 1959 that the development of transistors would soon put low-cost portable receivers within reach not only of rural Whites but also of Blacks in the nonelectrified reserves, where rediffusion could not easily be used. A nationwide FM system, able to provide a variety of regional listeners simultaneously with a variety of program services without mutual interference, thus seemed feasible.

An SABC analysis of "programme and quasi-political requirements" indicated that each FM location should have enough transmitters to radiate simultaneously the three "European" services (i.e., Afrikaans, English, and Springbok), as well as one or two "Bantu" services, depending on the indigenous language or languages spoken in each station's locale. Some urban stations would also have yet another transmitter to provide for simultaneous European regional programming (Collett 1964, pp. 56–57). Technical data relating to FM propagation characteristics and schemes for interconnection were gathered from broadcasting organizations in West Germany, Italy, the Netherlands, Switzerland, and the United Kingdom. At the same time, the International Telecommunication Union allocated the band 87.5 mHz.–108 mHz. for FM sound broadcasting in South Africa and in the mandated territory, South-West Africa (Stevens 1964, p. 58).

The SABC's dependence on rebroadcasting rather than on relays for its FM network interconnection limited the maximum spacing between stations. Tests conducted by SABC engineers indicated that, at what they considered the optimum maximum power of 40 kw., an FM station could radiate a signal a distance of 110 km. A network grid of equilateral triangles having side lengths of 110 km. was laid out on a topographical map, with slight distortions of the triangles so that their corners could be superimposed on suitable high points of the terrain (Stevens 1964, pp. 59–61). After a number of primary sites had been field checked, the corporation allocated funds for construction of the first FM stations in December 1960. In 1961 the mass of technical data for the projected FM system was sent to Hamburg's Institut für Rundfunktechnik, where experts programmed the information for feeding into Stockholm's BESK computer; the final printout called for 485 FM transmitters located at 123 station sites. By the end of 1961, the prior capital expenditures for all the corporation's studios, transmitting stations, and general equipment totaled just over $11.2 million. The projected FM network *alone* was expected to cost at least three times this figure (Patrick 1962, p. 13).

Also by the end of 1961, the "mother mast" for the entire FM system had been erected on Brixton Ridge, Johannesburg. Christened the Albert Hertzog Tower, in honor of the then minister of posts and telegraphs, the 771-foot concrete and steel structure includes an observation turret, complete with restaurant; and six 10-kw. transmitters, the outputs of which are fed to a single wide-band aerial (SABC 1962).

The subsequent expansion of the FM network had its greatest impact on African programming. By 1964, this encompassed seven separate services under the collective designation "Radio Bantu": the Xhosa service in Cape Province; the South Sotho service in the Orange Free State; the Tswana service in the Northern Cape and Western Transvaal; the North Sotho service in central Transvaal; the Zulu service in Natal and the southeastern portion of the Transvaal; and the Tsonga and Venda services in northeastern Transvaal. Radio Bantu thus provides South Africa's Black population with multicultural and pervasive programming via low-cost transistorized FM portables.

8.1.4 Commercial Services

The first of the commercial, White-oriented regional FM services, Radio Highveld, went on the air in 1964 to cover the Transvaal High Veld area, the Orange Free State, and part of the Northwestern Cape region. The next year, a counterpart FM service, also commercial, began serving the Western Cape as Radio Good Hope. Finally, in 1967, the third of the

White regional services, Radio Port Natal, began serving the midlands and the Natal coastal region with commercial programming. In dedicating this service, the chairman of the SABC's board of governors indicated that Radio Port Natal, like its two older sisters, "is a service that will not be too high-minded. Its appeal will be broad in a particular way. We are going to try to give those listeners who dislike too much of the spoken word, or who may not be in the mood to listen to plays or discussion programmes or talks . . . middle of the road music . . . plus news on the hour every hour" (*SAUK/SABC Bulletin* 1967).

The popularity of the regional commercial services, each on the air for 133 hours a week, has been high. Their broad-appeal programming is continued by Radio South Africa, a domestic all-night service which takes over the transmitters of the three regional services and of Springbok Radio when they all shut down at midnight. It provides entertainment and talk participation for all of South Africa from midnight until 5:00 A.M. Each night as many as 100 telephone messages, from as far away as South-West Africa and Rhodesia, are broadcast in a modified two-way "talk radio" format. The resulting conversations may be in French, German, Italian, or Greek.

This all-night use of the FM facilities has contributed to a healthy growth in advertising revenue. In 1971, the net commercial revenue from all services amounted to $16,240,000, while license fees brought in slightly less than $14,000,000 (letter from N. J. Naudé, SABC public relations head, 18 February 1972). Advertisements are sold primarily as 15- and 30-second spots. Instead of being clustered, they are trafficked in much the same manner as those on commercial stations in the United States. In 1972, rate cards offered 30-second spots at $14–$84 on Springbok, $49–$168 on Radio Bantu, $7 to almost $15 on Radio Good Hope, $7 to over $43 on Radio Highveld, and approximately $4–$6 on Radio South Africa. A variety of package plans, called "snap campaigns," were also available, as were program-sponsorship opportunities, mainly on Springbok.

The rates seem to depend on signal coverage instead of on measured circulation. Though the Post Office issues licenses, and postal inspectors detect and prosecute evaders, official data are not made available on either the extent of evasion or the actual number of receivers in the republic. In 1972, medium- or short-wave service was said to be available to the entire republic, and FM service to 97.5% of the population. Beyond this, the Post Office and the SABC state that, as of the beginning of 1971, there were 1,856,119 license holders in the republic, plus about 40,000 in South-West Africa. Each license is assumed to cover from two to three receivers. No attempt is made to break down receiver ownership by racial group except to state that, "as far as the Coloureds, Asian and Bantu homes are concerned, very few of them tune in to any transmissions other than FM" (letter from N. J. Naudé, SABC Public Relations Head, 18 February 1972).

8.1.5 External Service

In addition to its FM explosion, the SABC's building program in the 1960s included the initiation of a worldwide external service, called Radio RSA, the Voice of South Africa. Broadcasting on a small scale to the rest of the continent had begun in the 1950s from a single short-wave transmitter near Pretoria, as well as from the Paradys station near Bloemfontein, erected in the years 1956–57 to provide service for South-West Africa; significant external and transcontinental broadcasting, however, was really started with the completion of the huge H. F. Verwoerd Station at Bloemendal near Johannesburg. Dedicated on 27 October 1965, this facility utilizes four 250-kw. transmitters within a unique 23-sided switchhouse. From this building, all four transmitters can be coupled to any of the station's 38 aerial arrays by pressing a switch on the control-room console, which can also preset a transmitter to select automatically a new frequency and aerial with appropriate orientation for each target region.

Despite South Africa's precarious diplomatic position in the world's forums, and despite vitriolic broadcasts to and about South Africa by other states, Radio RSA's offerings remain largely apolitical save for the clearly labeled "Comment," and a tendency to give priority to news stories favorable to the United States, other Western countries, and Rhodesia, and unfavorable to the Eastern Bloc. Still, this formula for selecting news does not seem to be applied at the expense of the integrity of the individual stories themselves. Once an item has been earmarked for airing to a given region, its hallmark appears to be studied accuracy (see § 10.6.5 for more on Radio RSA).

8.1.6 Domestic Programming

The alleged prevalence of propaganda in the *internal* English and Afrikaans services, however, has been the subject of vigorous controversy within South Africa. This has been especially true of an increasing number of short opinion programs such as the daily feature "Current Affairs," which one South African characterized as "thick with pro-Government commentary" (interview with a South African law lecturer, 25 April 1966). An SABC actress considered it and a sister-program, "News at Nine," "so biased that my husband and I no longer switch it on but rely upon the less 'slanted' Springbok radio news at 10:30 P.M. We have noticed that any news discreditable to other African states, or dealing with race problems in other countries has pride of place in the news, even if relatively unimportant" (personal letter, 30 June 1968). Helen Suzman, the lone Progressive party member of Parliament, maintained that "the notorious 'Current Affairs' programme is without doubt pure Nationalist propaganda" (personal letter, 11 June 1968). In answer to such charges, an SABC official told an American author, "We feel that the SABC has an absolute right . . . to present its side of things, an absolute right. Are we not always under attack by the English-language press? Aren't they always charging us with all sorts of things? Then why are we not perfectly justified in having an editorial voice, too, and in responding to criticism?" (Drury 1967, p. 130).

The Afrikaans service features many more dramatizations and discussions of South Africa's history, religious broadcasts, recitals, lectures, and *boeremusiek* ("Afrikaner folksongs") than the English-language service. The latter has meanwhile become progressively more entertainment-minded as first Springbok and then the three commercial FM regional services have begun to vie for audience. Humor programs, light drama, and pop music thus are more prominent on the English-language than on the Afrikaans-language broadcasts. As one of the SABC governors took pains to point out, however, this does not make the English service a noncommercial copy of Springbok. "It is more conservative and offers its listeners, particularly the older group, a variety of interesting programmes" (Williams 1967).

Springbok, on the other hand, is dynamic, varied, and unabashedly commercial, mixing quiz programs like "Bingo at Home" and "The Surf Pick-a-Box Show" with a seemingly endless number of mysteries, serials, and spoofs, plus up-tempo music. A serial, "The Reverend Matthew," was reminiscent of certain American TV offerings; it featured a young and dynamic clergyman in a small country parish who finds that "amongst the many events which cause consternation in the town are dishonest business deals, robberies, mischief-making by unscrupulous women, the usual conflict between parents and children, and people seeking sanctuary in Victory Hill from the unhappiness of their pasts" (*SAUK/SABC Bulletin* 1968). Summing up Springbok's impact and character, a South African radio actress mirrored the opinion of many older listeners: "I suppose Springbok Radio performs a service by providing healthy competition for the standard English and Afrikaans channels. Many more people listen to Springbok than to the other two, I think. They sponsor some good overseas programmes and certainly produce some much better-type plays, as well as some horrible ones. I think much of it is vulgar, idiotic and puerile" (personal letter, 30 June 1968).

8.2 South African Television

South Africa entered the 1970s with the distinction of being the world's only country among those of comparable economic development without a broadcast television service. Television had been demonstrated there as early as the Empire Exhibition of 1936. Though broadcast television was prohibited, closed-circuit video systems eventually came into widespread use. By June 1971, the postmaster general had authorized 1,226 CCTV systems for medical, educational, and industrial applications, as well as 192 demonstration systems (letter from J. N. Naudé, SABC public relations head, 28 June 1971). That broadcast use of television in South Africa was still prohibited in 1972 is evidence of a unique complex of attitudes and conditions peculiar to the country. Protelevision forces were not wanting, however, as the following analysis will show. Indeed, one might say that television was inevitable—ultimately, all the antitelevision forces could do was to postpone the day of its arrival, and perhaps to restrict the scope of its development.

8.2.1 Political Maneuvers

During the mid-1950s, the Nationalist government flatly declared that broadcast television for South Africa was not even to be considered. The government argued (1) that reliance on American- and British-produced features would be unavoidable and highly detrimental to the recently achieved broadcast equality of the English and Afrikaans languages, (2) that the potential political impact of television was unknown, and (3) that the psychological impact of the medium on the urbanized Bantu might be dangerous in a country where Caucasians alone possess the vote but constitute only one-fifth of the population.

Prophesying cultural suicide, Minister of Posts and Telegraphs Albert Hertzog had long denounced "that evil black box." In 1960 Prime Minister Verwoerd added his voice, but he stressed economics—the high cost of television and the number of competing systems still under development. Commercial interests, both within and without South Africa, offered financial inducements to the government throughout the 1960s, but the Nationalists stood firm behind the negativism of Hertzog. The political friends of television had no better luck in 1966 when the largely English-stock United party went down to its usual defeat, taking with it the slogan Want TV? Vote U.P.

In 1968 Hertzog, leader of the Nationalists' extreme right, or *verkrampte,* wing, engaged in an undeclared war with his own prime minister and party chief, Johannes Vorster. When Hertzog's rightist infiltration of Afrikaner student groups and the SABC became apparent in 1968, the prime minister relieved Hertzog of his Ministry of Posts and Telegraphs portfolio. Hertzog then formed his own Reconstituted Nationalist party, which lost its entire parliamentary contingent in the 1970 general election. A real as well as a symbolic obstacle to at least the *discussion* of television was thus neutralized, leaving greater maneuvering room for the prime minister and the provideo interests in the public and business community.

Soon after assuming the office, the new P&T minister, Basie Van Rensburg, agreed to sanction increased utilization of closed-circuit TV systems while broadcast television's alleged "damaging influence" on young people and its high cost were analyzed (*News/Check* [Johannesburg], 8 March 1968, p. 3). Thus the television debate began to change from the videophobia of Hertzog to the pragmatism of Van Rensburg and Vorster.

Van Rensburg's loosening of restrictions on closed-circuit systems made possible a number of CCTV exhibits at the 1968 Rand Easter Show, where the equipment displayed by Gallo, Philips, General Electric, and Decca emphasized classroom uses, traffic control, bank security, and medical applications of television (*South Africa Financial Gazette* [Johannesburg], 5 April 1968, p. 9). That same month, a Johannesburg newspaper whipped video speculation to new peaks by reporting that the SABC had drawn up architectural plans for television studios as the second stage in the construction of its vast Auckland Park complex near Johannesburg (*Star* [Johannesburg], 4 April 1968).

8.2.2 TV Plans Announced

In July 1969 the first "moon-walk" set off severe political repercussions in South Africa as the citizens came to realize that they were virtually the only people in the entire developed world unable to watch the historic event on television. A movie of the landing shown at the Johannesburg Planetarium drew 6,000 people to vie for 500 seats, and they had to be dispersed by the police. The United party promptly called for a referendum on television. In December 1969, the Nationalist government responded by naming a 12-man commission to investigate and make recommendations concerning a national television system.

Finally, in March 1971, the report of the commission went to the Cabinet. In late April, the minister of national education announced to Parliament that the government had accepted the concept of introducing television in no less than four years' time. Strict control of the medium was to be vested in his own ministry; all transmissions were to be in color; and two separate services were envisioned: a "White" channel for English- and Afrikaans-speaking Europeans, Asians, and Coloureds; and a separate "TV-Bantu" channel (*Financial Mail* [Johannesburg], 3 September 1971).

On 28 October 1971, the government suddenly announced it had decided to support the recommendation of the Commission of Inquiry and to adopt the Telefunken PAL system as South Africa's television standard. The French were infuriated by South Africa's rejection of their SECAM system, and it was feared that French arms sales to the republic, in defiance of a United Nations embargo, might be affected (Hobbs 1971). Thus one issue was resolved even as another was being raised. If television were no closer, manufacturers were at least made aware of the electronic standards upon which to draft plans.

At the start of 1972, then, it appeared that the republic's TV system would ultimately be dual channel, with Whites, Asians, and Coloureds

sharing one channel and Africans being served by the other. All transmissions would probably be in color. The Commission of Inquiry had
endorsed specifications for all receivers—a 26-inch picture tube, color, a
$1,000-retail price—and this endorsement received at least tacit approval
from the government. It appeared that South Africa's PAL color system
would probably not be operable before 1975 at the very earliest, with
the combined English/Afrikaans service to be radiated from 16 high-
power transmitters and six low-power transmitters. This, it was estimated,
would bring television to 75% of the White population, 60% of the
Coloureds, and 84% of residents of Asiatic origin. Five years after the
initiation of service, perhaps five more stations would be erected, raising
total coverage to 78% of the Whites, 64% of the Coloureds, and 86%
of the Asians. Only when these percentages were achieved was it expected
that Bantu-TV would be attempted (*Financial Mail* [Johannesburg], 3
September 1971).

The SABC also explored the possibility of using CATV to serve out-
lying areas as well as to provide a less expensive alternative for citizens
unable to purchase their own color sets. Through this scheme, a subscriber
would probably rent a black-and-white set as part of his monthly cable-
service fee (*Rand Daily Mail* [Johannesburg], 2 November 1971, p. 3).
Last, it was envisioned that the already prevalent use of closed-circuit
television would become even more widespread.

8.3 Conclusion

South Africa has developed the most sophisticated radio-broadcasting
system on the continent, whether viewed in terms of technology, economics,
or organizational ingenuity. The boldly conceived FM networks; the provisions for regional and local services; the efficient deployment of facilities
even during the hours from midnight to 5:00 A.M. by Radio South Africa;
the sprightly international commercialism of Springbok Radio; the flexibility provided by options for alternative regional commercial coverage via
Radio Bantu, Radio Port Natal, Radio Good Hope, and Radio Highveld;
and the effectiveness of the external service, Radio RSA, in dealing with
the handicap of a virulently unfavorable national image—all testify to the
skill with which South Africa has adapted conventional broadcasting to
suit its own peculiar socioeconomic, geographical, and political needs.

One can guess that South African television will likewise eventually
offer an instructive model of adaptation to local conditions. After all, it
can learn from the mistakes and successes of all the rest of the world
without undergoing expensive trial-and-error experiments. It can start
with a highly developed technology, already stabilized by years of practical
application. As the last economically developed country to open itself up
to the influence of television broadcasting, South Africa will provide com-

munications researchers with a unique real-life laboratory. Students of
media from all over the world can be expected to converge on Capetown,
Durban, and Johannesburg when the time comes. South African television
may well become the world's most-analyzed video system.

8.4 Swaziland, Lesotho, and Botswana

As was mentioned at the beginning of this chapter, the Republic of South
Africa exercises a profound geopolitical influence on its three newly
independent neighbors. Lesotho and, for all practical purposes, Swaziland
and Botswana are surrounded by the republic's land mass and are dependent on its good offices for what little external trade and commerce they
enjoy. Nevertheless, at least for Swaziland, a geographic debit may have
been turned into an economic asset via broadcasting.

8.4.1 Swaziland

Population: 420,000	Radio transmitter sites: 1
Receivers per thousand: 119	Area per site: 7,000 sq mi

Swaziland's modest domestic service originates from its capital, Mbabane,
and relies on one 10-kw. medium-wave transmitter and a small FM transmitter. Before its independence in 1968 the country was also served by a
750-w. medium-wave British Forces station known as "Tiger Radio." In
1972 the Swaziland Broadcasting Service continued to rebroadcast BBC
news, and about half its transmissions were in English, the rest in siSwati.
The general service was broken into three segments—early morning,
midday, and evening. During the school term, however, schools radio
fully occupied the morning and early afternoon hours.

In 1971 an American firm, Intermedia, secured an "external authorization" from the government of Swaziland permitting the company to erect
a station on Swazi soil for the purpose of beaming medium- and short-wave
commercial broadcasts to South Africa and Moçambique (see § 7.2.5 for
an associated project in Malawi). The station was to accommodate two
American-built transmitters, a 50-kw. medium-wave and a 50-kw. short-
wave, to be located just inside the Swazi border opposite the South African
town of Amsterdam. It was scheduled for full operation early in 1972,
broadcasting a commercial format of American contemporary music. A
Johannesburg sales office had already been set up.

For its part, the Swaziland government received title to 20% of the
station's stock. Understandably, neither the South African nor the Portuguese government was as pleased with this plan as the Swazis. According
to Mark Wodlinger, president of Intermedia, the three top officials in the
SABC warned him they would do "everything possible" to prevent the

Intermedia station from operating. On the other hand, certain South African cabinet ministers and M.P.'s gave assurances that, as long as the station avoided broadcasting news or "propaganda," it would be left largely alone (letter from Mark L. Wodlinger, 28 September 1971). Intermedia appointed to its board of directors the just-retired South African commissioner of police, General Gous, formerly in charge of all the republic's internal security matters. The General, along with Inspector Gomes Lopez, head of internal security for Moçambique's Police Intelligence Department, would apparently serve to reassure their governments that Intermedia would not digress from a strictly neutral musical format.

Intermedia planned to offer commercial rates comparable to those of South Africa's regional FM services, Radio Highveld, Radio Good Hope, and Radio Port Natal. Nonetheless, Wodlinger felt his company would not offer undue commercial competition: "Since South Africa has an announced policy of helping their underdeveloped neighbors and Swaziland is part of their common market, it appears that they would not be likely to alienate this little country over a few dollars. This would seem to be even more true since South Africa is attempting to show other black nations of Africa their friendly spirit and attitude toward them" (letter from Mark Wodlinger, 28 September 1971). Intermedia also planned to enter television by means of a closed-circuit system within Swaziland.

8.4.2 Lesotho

Population: 1,000,000	Radio transmitter sites: 1
Receivers per thousand: 101	Area per site: 12,000 sq mi

Lesotho, Swaziland's sister enclave to the southwest, began its broadcasting under nongovernmental auspices in 1964, from the Catholic Community Centre in Maseru, the capital. The following year, as the preindependence election approached, the center began to incorporate news bulletins compiled by the government Department of Information in its broadcasts. Two months after independence, in December 1965, radio in Lesotho came more formally under government control when the prime minister, Chief Leabua Jonathan, set up an advisory board for the establishment of the Lesotho National Broadcasting Service (LNBS). Some $300,000 was provided as capital, and the BBC sent an engineer in April 1966 to supervise the installation of the transmitters and studios. Radio Lesotho officially came on the air on the anniversary of Independence Day, 4 October 1966, with a 660-w. medium-wave transmitter. Two 10-kw. transmitters were subsequently obtained to broadcast from a tower at Lancers Gap, located on a 1,000-foot plateau some four miles from the studio site in Maseru.

According to the former head of LNBS, J. J. Niemandt, who supplied much of the above information, in 1972 the production center consisted of a single-level cement-block structure containing staff offices, a record library, and two studios. Plans had been drawn up for an additional studio block to be built during the 1970–75 Development Plan, which anticipates a capital and recurrent broadcast expenditure of about $165,000 during the plan. The newest 10-kw. transmitter fills in coverage gaps so that all the inhabitants of Lesotho can receive their national service in Sesotho and English. The schedule includes a morning relay from the BBC.

In 1972, six members of the Broadcasting Service studied abroad, in Britain, Germany, and Holland. Schools broadcasting was introduced that year, and in April commercial operations began (*COMBROAD* 1973).

The original small Catholic station has since shut down, leaving all broadcasting in the country in the hands of the LNBS, which falls directly under the jurisdiction of the prime minister. He must insure that the system provides "an effective, technically efficient and nationally available channel of communication to disseminate knowledge, information, news and advice of importance and concern to the people of Lesotho in an impartial and attractive format governed by the country's cultural traditions" (letter from J. J. Niemandt, 28 July 1971).

8.4.3 Botswana

Population: 620,000	Area per site: 232,000 sq mi
Receivers per thousand: 48	Radio transmitter sites: 1

Radio Botswana began in what was known as the British Bechuanaland Protectorate, starting with a disused police transmitter as a power plant and a prison cell as a studio. In 1972 it was housed in what had been the residence of the former protectorate's prime minister (Donald 1971, p. 39). The system's two 10-kw. short-wave transmitters and a 1-kw. medium-wave transmitter, located in the capital, Gaberone, are not powerful enough to reach all portions of this sparsely populated land, but a new 50-kw. medium-wave transmitter was planned for installation in 1972.

According to P. Molefhe, broadcasting officer, many problems of program and facility expansion were mitigated with BBC help. Almost all overseas-trained staff of Radio Botswana received instruction at the BBC in London (see § 14.2.1). In 1972 Radio Botswana rebroadcast news programs as well as several other information programs of the BBC World, African, and Home services. In fact, a Botswanan government policy directive dated 7 January 1969 stipulated that "the BBC should continue to be the main source of news, but arrangements should be made to repeat it in Tswana" (Botswana 1969).

Nevertheless, locally produced programming was on the increase in 1972, with efforts made to strike a balance between the main indigenous language, Tswana, and the official language, English. This was apparent from the monthly 16-page program guide which was completely bilingual. Most local features described in the guide were independently prepared by government departments, each of which had its own broadcast unit. The Extension Division of the Ministry of Agriculture, for example, was responsible for two 20-minute programs for farmers, "Pitso ya Balemi" (a farming lesson) and "Sethitho le Boitumelo" (an agricultural serial play). The Department of Community Development supplied two 25-minute features, and the broadcast unit of the Ministry of Education produced some 15 hours of school programs weekly, including six levels of English as well as series on history, science, French, and Tswana literature. Such diffusion of production responsibility creates quality-control problems, and Broadcasting Officer Molefhe indicated that one objective of RB is "to take programme production out of the hands of individuals and establish groups composed of one programme producer and several assistants, making the producer responsible for supervision and quality" (letter from P. Molefhe, 26 October 1971). Accordingly, by 1973 a schools broadcasting unit had been formed which was producing 34 quarter-hour programs per week, covering both formal school subjects in English and adult education subjects in Tswana (Salisbury 1973).

Administratively, Radio Botswana is a government agency managed by the broadcasting officer, who reports to the permanent secretary to the president. According to a directive issued by the Ministry of Home Affairs, "reasonable criticism of Government is permitted but Government's reply must be broadcast at the first opportunity if it cannot be given at the time the criticism is uttered" (Botswana 1969). If such criticism were contained in domestic news, it would in fact probably have come from the government's own Botswana Information Services, which compiles the national news read over Radio Botswana. As Molefhe discreetly pointed out in his letter to the author (26 October 1971), "Radio Botswana as a Government instrument is naturally controlled by it and I would hesitate to say the actual practice can be divorced from its official relationship."

9   Islands and Territories

This chapter deals with three independent island states off the shores of Africa, with the large continental and insular Portuguese dependencies, and with the remnants of British, French, and Spanish colonial empires, mostly in the form of islands.

9.1 Independent Islands, *by Sydney W. Head*

The independent Indian Ocean islands of the Malagasy Republic and Mauritius lie several hundred miles off the southeast coast of Africa. Only minorities of their populations claim African descent, but the islands are nevertheless identified with Africa geographically and politically.

9.1.1 Malagasy Republic

Population: 7,300,000	Radio transmitter sites: 1
Receivers per thousand: 69	Area per site: 227,000 sq mi

Across the Moçambique Channel, 250 miles offshore, lies the fourth-largest island in the world—Madagascar, or the Malagasy Republic. The island became a French protectorate in 1885 and achieved full independence in 1960, under the same circumstances as the Francophone territories of the West Coast (§ 6.1). The indigenous language, Malagasy, is non-African and is universally understood on the island.

The French introduced radio in 1931, in Tananarive, the capital, which is located centrally on the interior plateau. Madagascar thus became the first French dependency in Africa to have a radio service. The first station had about 500 w. of power and broadcast only two hours a day. SORAFOM assisted in the development of the system, as it did in the West African Francophone countries (§ 6.1.3). Shortly after independence, the government mounted a campaign called "Operation Transistor" to increase the number of receivers in use. Encouraged by duty-free imports and sales on credit, the public bought 42,000 sets in less than a year (Bebey 1963, pp. 33, 116).

The government radio system provides two domestic services and an external service. A home service in Malagasy and a French service are offered on paired medium-wave and short-wave transmitters of equal power. An international service beams French and English toward the mainland on a 100-kw. transmitter. Radio Université, apparently using one of the regular government short-wave transmitters during off-hours, broadcasts programs concerning the national university's activities during school term (German Africa Society 1970, p. 122). There is said to be a rediffusion system in operation at Fenoarivo, about 75 miles northwest of the capital (*Africa South of the Sahara* 1971, p. 468). In 1971 Radio Nederland began the installation of a relay station on the island (*Rundfunk und Fernsehen* 1972b, p. 103). The Dutch station went into full operation in mid-1972, using two 300-kw. short-wave transmitters. The Malagasy government also has an agreement with the United States to provide a base for a satellite-tracking station at a site 28 km. outside the capital.

Television was first introduced in 1965, but it soon went off the air. Although it was reintroduced in December 1967, with the assistance of the French OCORA (*Interstages* 1968), it has continued to make only slow progress, judging by the reported small numbers of receiving sets in use.

9.1.2 Mauritius

Population: 840,000	Radio transmitter sites: 1
Receivers per thousand: 67	Area per site: 7,200 sq mi

Still farther from Africa, 500 miles east of Madagascar, lie tiny Mauritius and three groups of still smaller, widely scattered islands, all of which France held for nearly a century; the British took over in 1810. When Britain abolished slavery in the colony in 1833, the majority of the Mauritians were Africans; however, Indians who were brought in as plantation laborers thereafter eventually assumed dominance. It is estimated that a quarter to a third of the present population are Creoles, descendants of Africans and other races. Although the Creole language, a mixture of African languages and French, is widely spoken, broadcasting is in French, English, Hindustani, and Chinese.

The British started radio in Mauritius in 1944. Four years before independence, which came in 1968, the Mauritius Broadcasting Corporation was set up. In 1971 an afternoon and evening schedule of about seven hours, on one short-wave and one medium-wave transmitter, served the whole group of islands. The service operates commercially and claims to cover, also, Réunion, Madagascar, Zanzibar, and the Moçambique coast (German Africa Society 1970, p. 133).

Television, which started in 1965, seems to be relatively well developed, with three repeater stations and programs scheduled in two day-parts. It, too, is operated commercially and claims viewers in Réunion, an island about 80 miles to the west.

9.1.3 Equatorial Guinea

Population: 280,000	Radio transmitter sites: 2
Receivers per thousand: 267	Area per site: 6,000 sq mi

Unique among African nations in that it consists of both an island and a mainland component, Equatorial Guinea is classified in the insular group because its island component, Fernando Póo, is economically dominant. Fernando Póo is the chief of a group of small islands located only 20 miles off the Cameroon coast; it is united politically with Rio Muni, an enclave-like corner of Gabon, 100 miles down the West African coast. The two territories had previously been called Spanish Guinea and Equatorial Guinea. Prior to independence in 1968 they had constituted Spanish provinces, and Spanish is still the official language. While the majority of the Rio Muni population belongs to one ethnic group, the Fangs, the much smaller Fernando Póo population, are a mixture of immigrants and migrant laborers from neighboring African states, particularly Nigeria and Cameroon. The original inhabitants, the Bubi, are in the minority. Broadcasting is mostly in Spanish, with limited services in English, Fang, Bubi, and other African vernaculars. There are stations, each with one transmitter, at both the capital, Santa Isabel, on Fernando Póo; and Bata, the provincial capital of Rio Muni. The Bata station is listed as "government-commercial" in *WRTH*, but it failed to supply data for the German Africa Society commercial directory. Television was started on Fernando Póo in 1968.

9.2 Portuguese Dependencies, *by Alexander F. Toogood*

Many of Portugal's half-dozen African territories are no more than coastal islands, but the two biggest constitute the largest land mass under one flag in Sub-Saharan Africa; its area is greater than that of all Western Europe. Angola and Moçambique are vestiges of Portugal's plan to control a broad strip across Southern Africa, from the Atlantic to the Indian Ocean. Cecil Rhodes's plan for a Cape-to-Cairo route ended that dream, but Portugal retained the two ends of the strip—Angola in the west and Moçambique in the east. Broadcasting in these vast territories assumes a

Alexander F. Toogood is Associate Professor of Communications, Temple University. He has written extensively on colonial and British Commonwealth broadcasting, including a book on Canadian broadcasting based on his Ph.D. dissertation at Ohio State University.

pattern which is distinctive in the continent. It constitutes Africa's most diversified system of control, leaving room for private enterprise and advertising support as well as direct government operation. In *Muffled Drums,* Hachten (1971a, p. 19) lists the African countries with the greatest number of separate broadcast services; Angola places first and Moçambique fourth.

Portugal was the first European nation to become firmly entrenched in Africa, and it retains the world's oldest established empire. A 1972 constitutional amendment designates the African territories as "states," integrally part of Portugal, and all their inhabitants are regarded as "Portuguese" without distinction. Portugal's five African states elect 23 of the 130 deputies in the National Assembly in Lisbon. More than 5% of Portugal's European-born population live in Africa. Not even at the height of colonialism could any other nation claim such a high personal investment in the continent. In terms of absolute size of its white population, Angola ranks second, after South Africa, and Moçambique fourth, after Rhodesia (Abshire and Samuels 1969, p. 205).

Despite the designation of the African territories as "states," the lives of their citizens are regulated by the all-powerful Overseas Ministry in Lisbon, which subsumes such ministerial functions as justice, education, health, public works, and customs. Within this framework, however, Portugal minimizes racial prejudice, whether de jure or de facto. Intermarriage is encouraged, and antisegregation laws are strongly enforced (Abshire and Samuels, 1969, pp. xi, 91 et passim). In the small insular states of Cape Verde and São Tomé and Principe as much as 80% of the population are mixed-blood *mesticos* descended from Africans brought over from the mainland and from southern European settlers.

To impose a semblance of unity over such diverse lands of mutually unintelligible tongues, the government accepts Portuguese alone as the official language. Therefore, Portuguese is overwhelmingly the language of broadcasting, though vernacular broadcasting seems to be on the increase. Portugal seems increasingly to realize that its monolingual policy, however logical it may appear as a long-term strategy for furthering national integration, renders its African broadcasting systems incapable of counter-propaganda. The growing barrage of revolutionary messages from freedom-fighter groups using broadcast facilities in neighboring countries can be answered only in the languages of the people.

9.2.1 Ownership and Control

This section and the ones that follow draw extensively from correspondence with three broadcasting organizations that responded to enquiries: Radio Clube de Moçambique and Radio Mocidade of Moçambique; and A Voz de Angola. Additional information was supplied by the Embassy of Portugal in Washington, D.C.

In 1972, broadcasting in the Portuguese African provinces was limited to radio. Television had been investigated, and there were initial experiments in Moçambique in 1967, but the economic conditions of the territories do not encourage any hope for television in the immediate future. FM radio, however, has been extensively developed, to the point where Portuguese Africa ranks second in its use, after South Africa.

The Portuguese territories provide a major exception to the rule of predominant government ownership and operation in Africa. Most of the private stations are called *radio clubes,* a holdover from earlier broadcasting, which relied on amateur transmissions, with club members subscribing to cover the costs of station equipment and operation. Later, these amateur services developed into commercial stations, but still as private clubs. With their subscriptions and their commercial sales they preserve a mixed broadcasting economy, and independence from direct government control.

Radio has thus not become exclusively the prerogative of the traditional power structure in Portuguese Africa—the church, the financial institutions, the law-and-order agencies. While all the daily newspapers in Moçambique are owned by either the Catholic church or the metropolitan government's overseas bank, such interests in broadcasting remain minimal. The church has stations in Moçambique and Angola, but their role is minor. The government broadcasts over its own stations in all territories, except in Moçambique, where it has access to the facilities of the main radio club. Though government broadcasts were strongly propagandistic in the 1950s, they later became relatively objective (Herrick et al. 1967, p. 253). In any event, government services have little influence in the total broadcasting pattern.

Mainland Portugal has always permitted a large degree of private investment in the media, even while imposing close political supervision. As a result, European Portugal itself has a mixed public and private broadcasting system in both radio and television. Emery (1971, p. 261) reported that in the 1970s broadcasting in mainland Portugal was still officially censored and strictly supervised by government, but such direct control is not imposed in the African territories. There one finds considerably more leeway regarding editorial policy and news coverage (Herrick et al. 1969, p. 178). True, these broadcasters tend to avoid controversies and to minimize comment, but self-censorship arises out of the prevailing climate in which broadcasting operates rather than from political fiat.

A lack of sustained political supervision can be seen in the fact that the governors general grant licenses for transmission without fees and for indefinite terms. The actual licensing and regulating of stations are handled by each provincial Department of Post, Telegraph, and Telephone. This localization of responsibility in a technical department points to the predominant concern with technical rather than political control. Existing regulations deal solely with technical matters; there are no explicit regulations pertaining to program content or advertising practices.

Article 22 of Portugal's constitution of 1933 provides for the state to "safeguard the country against influences which distort truth, justice and the commonweal." This article prohibits direct criticism of government policies but does not prevent criticism of the methods used to implement such policies or of the officials involved. When prefixed with suitable expressions of loyalty to the system in general, differences of opinion may be quite freely expressed (Herrick et al. 1967, p. 243).

Article 23 requires that radio must disseminate news of national importance at the request of the government, which in practice amounts to broadcasting all government handouts. The principal source for such material is each African state's Center of Information and Tourism, whose deceptively mild title conceals a potent political force. Founded in 1959 to improve security in some of the territories, the information centers were entrusted with official government propaganda. Apart from issuing their own news items, the centers act as the chief gatherers and distributors of news received from the two private, though officially supervised, Portuguese news agencies, as well as from the major international news services such as Reuters and UPI. Of all the media, radio is the most dependent on news from the information centers (Herrick et al. 1967, p. 244). In fact, most stations rely on their local centers as their only news sources. Aside from the requirement of carrying news of national importance, however, the government imposes no further direct controls on program content.

9.2.2 Programming and Finance

Two major private broadcasting organizations cover the entire territory of Moçambique, and the government service covers most of Angola. The remaining stations usually have low power and serve only their immediate vicinities. Radio Clube de Moçambique has an interconnected network; otherwise there are neither network programming services nor frequent program exchanges. Stations use some material from independent producers in Portugal, but most of the programming originates locally at each station. Undisturbed by television, some stations use older radio formats such as dramas, serials, and game shows. However, most of the fare is more contemporary, consisting principally of modern popular music, news and sports coverage.

Advertising on stations which accept commercials usually consists of spot announcements, although most stations also permit the sponsorship of programs (German Africa Society 1970). Despite the income from advertising and from radio-club subscriptions, radio is not actually a profit-making venture. Indeed, since 1964, the government has allocated subsidies to private radio stations.

Until 1966, when Angola started the local manufacture of transistor radios, imported receivers were extremely costly. In addition, a purchase tax is imposed on new receivers. This is scaled according to the set's value and reception capabilities. A simple AM receiver's purchase tax can range as high as $38. Short-wave receivers have an even higher tax—a calculated move to keep such receivers out of the hands of the poor, to whom international broadcasters beam anti-Portuguese propaganda (Herrick et al. 1969, p. 183).

The annual receiver license fee of about $4.50 helps support the government's metropolitan broadcasting system, Emissora Nacional de Radiodifusão, or ENR, which is based in Lisbon. ENR's Regional Division operates in all the African states except Moçambique through the Centers of Information and Tourism. ENR's external service also broadcasts directly from Portugal to the overseas territories. These metropolitan broadcasts include music, dramas, short stories, serials, live sports coverage, general information, and news (da Silva 1968, p. 16).

9.2.3 Angola

Population: 5,700,000	Radio transmitter sites : 12
Receivers per thousand: 19	Area per site: 40,000 sq mi

The western anchor of Portugal's projected cross-Africa empire, Angola, has a population of 5.7 million, of which whites total only a quarter-million. Five separate broadcasting services originate from Angola's capital and largest city, Luanda. Its quarter-million inhabitants have a wider choice of domestic programming than those in any other city in Sub-Saharan Africa. But Luanda's situation on the coast in the northwestern corner of the vast country is far from ideal from the point of view of disseminating a national broadcasting service. It is nearly 1,000 miles to the extreme southeast corner of the country; moreover, the main land mass is a plateau which rises sharply from the narrow coastal plain where Luanda is located.

Radio Angola, the government radio service, has attempted to compensate for its unfavorable position at Luanda by increasing its short-wave power to 100 kw., and by situating repeater stations in the two most distant regions, at Lunda in the northeast and at Cuanda Cubango in the southeast. Future plans call for additional regional stations, but until they are installed, coverage will continue to be spotty. Nonetheless, Radio Angola has by far the largest audience in the state. It offers three program services, but since Programs B and C use the same transmission facilities at different hours, only two services are available simultaneously. Program A runs a broad-based popular-appeal service in Portuguese from 5:00 A.M. to midnight. Program B offers a more diverse service from 6:20 A.M. to 5:00 P.M., which includes broadcasts in French, aimed at Zaïre, and in English aimed at southwest Africa. Program C is limited to evenings; it takes over the daytime transmission facilities used for Program B and offers more highbrow programming than that on Program A. Although only 25% of Angola's population speak Portuguese, the government service does not cater to the other 75% in terms of language, consistent with the policy of trying to achieve unity through Portuguese cultural domination.

The dominance of Portuguese is counterbalanced to some extent by a relative newcomer to Luanda-based broadcasting, A Voz de Angola, which went on the air in 1968. This is a private, noncommercial venture, independent of government. Established as a nonprofit syndicate, it first relied on private support and listener contributions. This proved an insecure financial foundation, and in 1972 attempts were being made to change the structure into a radio club which could use advertising revenue to help cover costs. A Voz de Angola is on the air 15½ hours on weekdays and up to 18½ hours on Sunday. Its two 100-kw. transmitters, along with short-wave and FM outlets, enable it to reach 80% of the state. More than the other services in Angola, this station aligns itself specifically with the local Africans. In addition to broadcasts in Portuguese it offers programs in nine local languages. Many of the latter are built around African music and folk stories. Music is the programming mainstay, but there is a large amount of general education, mostly aimed at the rural audience. A full 30% of on-air time is devoted to such subjects as health, agriculture, home economics, nutrition, cooking, and child care. A considerable degree of station control is in the hands of Portuguese Africans who hold senior managerial and programming responsibilities.

In 1972 the leading private radio service with commercial programming in Luanda was the Radio Clube de Angola. It programs daily from 5:30 A.M. to 11:00 P.M. in Portuguese. Although basically a popular-music service, its schedule includes some classical music, news, public-service programming, and programs for women. It joins with a local newspaper in publishing its own Sunday supplement and acts as a concert entrepreneur in bringing live talent to the area. Another private station in the capital, A Voz de Luanda, offers Portuguese programming in the evening hours.

The Roman Catholic church operates the fifth Luanda-based service, the 24-hour-a-day Radio Eclesia. Unlike the church's broadcasting operations in many neighboring countries, this station has no missionary or educational function; it accepts advertising and aims its popular programming in Portuguese to a general audience.

Each of the 12 major provincial communities in Angola is served by its own local station, and all but one have power of 1 kw. or less. Most, capitalizing on the peak listening hours of early morning, noon, and evening, offer limited services. The exception among these provincial stations is Radio Clube do Huambo, at Nova Lisboã, the major city of the central plateau and the center of the country's most densely populated area. Using a medium-wave and three short-wave facilities at 10 kw., and also an FM transmitter, it reaches a wide audience. It offers two services. The major one, in Portuguese, is on the air continuously with popular programming from 5:00 A.M. to 11:00 P.M. The second is an evening service, with local-language programs, particularly the most widely used vernacular, Umbundo, from 4:00 to 7:00, and with Portuguese programs from 7:00 to 10:00.

Radio Clube do Huambo joins three other nearby commercial stations in this southeast central region to offer a combined advertising rate for all four stations. A similar sales organization, Radio Commercial de Angola, with a head office in Luanda, sells time for four other broadcasting stations scattered throughout Angola—Radio Clube de Cabinda in the extreme north (in Portuguese Congo, separated from the main part of Angola by Zaïre's access corridor to the sea); Radio Clube do Bié near the country's center; and two stations in the south, Radio Clube de Moçamedes and Radio Commercial de Angola in Sa da Bandeirs. In other parts of the territory, four additional radio clubs similarly serve local needs.

Angola has still one more radio service, a noncommercial short-wave station, Radio Diamang. The Angola Diamond Company operates it for the benefit of its mining employees in Dundo, on the northeastern border with Zaïre, one of the remotest areas in Angola. This northeastern area has been one of the most politically troubled. It saw major disturbances in the 1960s. The Black Nationalism movement had split into two warring factions: the Governo Revolucionario de Angola no Exilio (GRAE) and the Movimento Popular de Libertação de Angola (MPLA). Both organizations broadcast directly into Angola from radio stations in neighboring countries, GRAE from Zaïre and MPLA from Congo and Zambia (Abshire and Samuels 1969, p. 395; and § 7.1.2). Considering that in 1971 there were only about 95,000 receivers in the country, one-third concentrated in the Luanda district and mostly in the hands of Europeans, it seems doubtful that broadcasts by the nationalist movements could have had widespread impact. In any event, GRAE and MPLA appeared to spend more time attacking each other than in furthering Angolan freedom (USDOS 1971, p. 4). It may be a measure of Portugal's insecurity that it nevertheless tried strenuously to counter the propaganda broadcasts by increasing Radio Angola's provincial coverage and by giving financial support to private stations.

9.2.4 Moçambique

Population: 7,700,000	Radio transmitter sites: 5
Receivers per thousand: 14	Area per site: 60,000 sq mi

Moçambique occupies a long, narrow strip of Africa's east coast stretching from South Africa to Tanzania. Although smaller in area than her sister territory to the west, Moçambique in 1966 supported a larger population: 7.7 million people, of whom 100,000 were whites, 35,000 *mesticos,* and

20,000 Asians. It has the most diverse background of all the Portuguese overseas territories. This, together with its distance from Lisbon, has enabled the radio stations to join with other local economic interests in breaking away from strict government control. In the nearby models provided by Cecil Rhodes, Moçambique saw large foreign-financed companies and a business community geared toward managerial efficiency rather than toward the individualism found in Angola. In broadcasting, the result has been a strongly centralized system, shared by two radio organizations heard throughout the state: the large nonprofit Radio Clube de Moçambique and the more commercial Emissora do Aero Clube da Beira.

The Moçambique radio club has headquarters in the capital, Lourenço Marques, a seaport located at the south end of the long coastline, near the South African border. It has five subsidiary stations, spaced northward along the coast, such as to blanket the entire territory and to reach into neighboring Central Africa and Tanzania as well. The regional subsidiary stations vary in the amount of the Lourenço Marques programming they carry and the amount of provincial programming they originate on their own. At Lourenço Marques the club originates five different program services:

Program A, the major domestic service, runs from 4:00 A.M. to 10:00 P.M. on six medium- and short-wave transmitters of power up to 50 kw. It offers popular programming in Portuguese: music, interviews, dramas, and women's features.

Program B is a 24-hour international commercial service, in English and Afrikaans, called Lourenço Marques Radio. It uses Top-40 commercial programming and is aimed solely at the young-adult South African audience. Operating a 100-kw. transmitter, it covers most of South Africa. Lourenço Marques Radio, which dates back to 1935, sells its time to South African advertisers and claims to be the first commercial operation available to them. In 1946 an "associate company" was set up in Johannesburg to promote the station and to sell air time; these functions were taken over by the South African Broadcasting Company in mid-1972 (letter from L. C. Bonell, administration organizer, Lourenço Marques Radio, June 1972). This assumption by SABC of the sales and promotion functions apparently was a move to ensure that the South African government would prevail, should any dispute over programming policies arise (see § 10.6.4 for further comment on Lourenço Marques Radio).

Program C is an evening service, using low-wattage medium-wave and FM transmitters. Completely free of commercials, this service features classical music, Portuguese folk music, and religion. It also carries Radio Universidade, which offers instructional programs on Saturday evening and Sunday morning.

Program D provides an alternative light Portuguese program on separate facilities during peak listening hours.

The fifth program service from the club in Lourenço Marques is called A Voz de Moçambique. Although the facilities belong to the private club, the entire service is produced by Moçambique's government Information and Tourist Center and is designed specifically for the African population. The government has no separately run facilities of its own. On weekdays it provides service from 5:00 P.M. to 8:00 P.M., but on weekends it also broadcasts in the morning. The programming usually alternates between the two major local languages, Shangana and Ronga; however, there are occasional broadcasts in eight other languages. A Voz de Moçambique also offers formal instruction in the Portuguese language. Initially, this vernacular service was restricted to low-power transmitters, but in 1970 the power was increased to 100 kw. With this high power, A Voz de Moçambique is considered part of the territory's international service, for it is widely heard in neighboring Malawi and Tanzania. The government uses the service extensively to counter propaganda from external sources (Abshire and Samuels 1969, p. 212).

Moçambique's second radio service originates in its second largest city, Beira, another seaport, located about a third of the way up the coast from Lourenço Marques. Emissora do Aero de Beira, owned and operated by the Beira Flying Club, schedules a full day of popular commercial programming with music, news, and live sports coverage on Sundays. It also offers a subsidiary service, Hora Africano, 2¼ hours of programming in local African languages.

Two noncommercial radio stations also serve Moçambique, each limited in coverage and oriented toward special audiences. Radio Pax da Beira, a missionary station operated by the Franciscan order, provides morning and evening programming on weekdays and a full weekend service. It broadcasts mostly in Portuguese but also uses two local languages, Sena and Shangana. Radio Mocidade is owned and operated by a high school, Liceu Salazar, in Lourenço Marques. It aims three hours of programming a day specifically at its students, but the goal is entertainment rather than instruction. Students produce all the programs and handle all station operations themselves under a teacher's supervision. The station is financed by the government and by private donations.

9.2.5 Other Territories

Portugal has four smaller African territories. Portuguese Guinea consists of a wedge of land on the sea coast between Senegal and the independent republic of Guinea, along with a nearby off-shore archipelago. Three other Atlantic Ocean archipelagos are ruled by Portugal: Cape Verde Islands, São Tomé and Principe, and Madeira. Each consists of a group of mountainous, volcanic islands the majority of whose inhabitants are descended from African slaves and early Portuguese and other South European settlers. They depend on a plantation economy.

Cape Verde Islands. The Cape Verde Islands consist of 25 islands and islets 250 miles off the coast of Senegal that form an overseas Portuguese state. They have a population of about a quarter-million. Two radio clubs operate commercially in addition to the government's Radio Barlovento. The Cape Verde Radio Club broadcasts over a 5-kw. short-wave transmitter and also an FM transmitter, located at Praia, the administrative center of the islands. Both the Mindelo Radio Club and the government station are located on Saint Vincente Island in the main population center of Mindelo. They have a 250-w. and a 1-kw. transmitter, respectively. Both operate commercially, program in Portuguese, and are on the air for only relatively brief time segments.

São Tomé and Principe. The territory of São Tomé and Principe is located in the Gulf of Guinea. São Tomé, the main island, lies about 175 miles offshore, almost on the equator. With its associated islands it constitutes the smallest of Portugal's overseas states, with a population of about 75,000. A commercial radio club operated the only station in the islands until 1972, when the service was taken over by the regional office of ENR, the state radio service in Portugal. Its facilities consist of two short-wave transmitters of 1 kw. and 5 kw. and an FM transmitter, which provide a continuous service in Portuguese. Portugal is said to have plans for using São Tomé as the base for rebroadcasting its mainland state radio service to Africa (*WRTH* 1972, p. 124).

Madeira. The third Portuguese territory in the Atlantic, Madeira, consists of two thickly populated islands and a number of rocks situated about 500 miles west of Casablanca. The population of about a third of a million is served by three stations, all in Funchal, the capital. Two are private commercial stations, one government. All three use 1-kw. medium-wave transmitters; in addition, the government station has an FM transmitter.

Portuguese Guinea. Also known as Bissau, the name of its chief port, Portuguese Guinea is the least developed of Portugal's African territories. In 1971 it was largely in the hands of African nationalists and merely garrisoned by the Portuguese under a state of siege (*Africa South of the Sahara* 1972, p. 148). According to news reports in mid-1972, a group fighting for freedom claimed to have destroyed a 100-kw. transmitter which had just been installed near Bissau. The government station had been offering a full 19-hour service on a 1-kw. medium-wave and a 10-kw. short-wave transmitter; yet as of 1972 they served fewer than 9,000 receivers distributed among a population of over half a million.

9.3 British Insular Dependencies, *by Sydney W. Head*

The British African Empire has dwindled down to four small island possessions, the Seychelles in the Indian ocean, and St. Helena, Ascension Island, and Tristan da Cunha in the South Atlantic.

9.3.1 Seychelles

Far out on the Indian Ocean, more than a thousand miles east of Africa— yet still closer to Africa than to any other continent—lies the Seychelles archipelago. It consists of some 95 islands and islets, originally colonized by France but ceded to Britain in 1814. Though English is the official language, French still retains more prestige among the Seychellois, even after over a century and a half of British rule (Stoddard et al. 1971, p. 59). The Creoles provide an ethnic link with Africa. Descended from French settlers and African slaves brought in to work the islands' plantations, they are in the majority. The Creole language, a mixture of African tongues and French, serves as a lingua franca.

The Department of Tourism, Information, and Broadcasting started radio in 1965 on Mahé, the principal island. In 1971 the broadcast schedule ran about five hours a day in English, French, and Creole. Using a 1-kw. medium-wave station, the service was estimated to reach 80% of the population, which stood at about 50,000 (Stoddard et al. 1971, p. 68). The Far East Broadcasting Association operates a 50-kw. short-wave station in Mahé, the "first and only" British missionary radio station (Winter 1971, p. 2). The United States maintains a space-tracking station on Mahé.

9.3.2 South Atlantic Islands

Saint Helena, 1,200 miles west of South Africa, is the chief of Britain's three widely scattered volcanic dots on the chart of the South Atlantic. The others are Ascension Island, 700 miles southwest of Saint Helena, and Tristan da Cunha, 1,500 miles south.

Saint Helena. Britain has possessed Saint Helena since 1659. Once a victualing port for sailing vessels rounding the Cape, Saint Helena lost its usefulness when the Suez Canal altered shipping routes. The government runs a 1-kw. medium-wave station a few hours a day to serve the population of about 5,000.

Ascension Island. Britain occupied Ascension Island in 1815, but not until 1966 did she find much use for it. In that year the BBC opened its Atlantic Relay Station on the tiny rock, only 34 square miles in area, but ideally located for the purpose of retransmitting the BBC's external broadcasts. Its four 250-kw. short-wave transmitters pass on BBC World Service programs to Africa, New Zealand, the Middle East and Eastern Europe, the West Indies, and the Americas. The BBC also provides a local service on a 200-watt medium-wave transmitter to the island's population of about 2,000. The United States maintains a space-tracking installation on Ascension, which provides AFRTS material for American technicians on duty there.

Tristan da Cunha. Halfway between South America and the tip of South Africa, lonely Tristan da Cunha is a 40-square-mile island with four smaller satellite islands. The British took possession in 1816, and the first male settlers sent to Saint Helena for wives. During the days of sail it had some value as a supply base for Atlantic shipping, but steam passed it by until World War II when it gained new importance as a British naval base. The population numbers only a few hundred, who are served by a government 40-watt short-wave station.

9.4 French Dependencies

9.4.1 French Territory of Afars and Issas, *by James M. Kushner*

Population: 130,000	Radio transmitter sites: 1
Receivers per thousand: 77	Area per site: 9,000 sq mi

The French Territory of Afars and Issas, a hot, dry, and generally barren colony about half the size of Denmark, is an enclave on the Red Sea coast between Ethiopia and Somalia. Half of its estimated 125,000 persons are nomadic herdsmen, and half live in Djibouti, the capital and a potentially important port city near the southern entrance to the Red Sea. The French contingent in Djibouti accounts for most of the literate population. The FTAI has both radio and television service, but even though every nomad group in the territory is said to own a transistor radio (Thompson and Adloff 1968, p. 157), mass communication scarcely exists outside the capital. In 1972 there were believed to be approximately 12,000 radio receivers and 2,000 television sets in the FTAI.

Radio Djibouti, the noncommercial government station, is operated by the Posts and Telegraph Department with funds from the state budget (*Industries et travaux d'Outre-mer* 1968, p. 16) as an overseas facility of the Office de Radiodiffusion-Télévision Française, Department of Regional and Overseas Stations. The radio service broadcasts on one short-wave and one medium-wave frequency to East Africa and the Arabian peninsula in Afar, Issa (Somali), and Arabic. It also supplies French-language programming on medium wave. Most of the French and Arabic material comes from Paris. "Afrique-Inter," a variety program in French featuring African arts, sports, and fashions, is an example of one of the overseas services broadcast directly from France by the ORTF. The local staff—trained in Paris or the French provinces—produces programs in both Afar and Issa. The French schedule is varied and sophisticated and includes many amenities of the French domestic France-Inter service. Arabic and local-vernacular broadcasts consist primarily of news, commentary, music, and cultural affairs. Approximately five hours each of Afar and Issa, four hours of Arabic, and nine hours of French were scheduled in 1972. Television came to Djibouti in 1967 in the form of a low-budget mini-station of a type packaged by France especially for her overseas territories. The station, which is described in detail in an EBU monograph, has a 50-watt transmitter and a single studio with one vidicon camera (EBU Technical Committee 1972, pp. 88–92). As of 1972 circulation remained small, on the order of 2,000 receivers, whose cost averaged $240 (Thompson and Adloff 1968, p. 158). The daily program schedule of about three hours consisted of 35 minutes of news in Afar, Arabic, and Somali, followed by news in French and a lineup of French-produced films, serials, variety shows, and documentaries. The station went dark on Mondays, but on Fridays increased the use of local languages with live presentations of folk groups and commentaries on Parisian news films. *Le reveil de Djibouti,* FTAI's official newspaper, published detailed weekly radio and television listings for French-language broadcasts, but no program details for broadcasts in the other three languages.

The development of broadcasting in the FTAI can be attributed, or at least traced to the territory's strategic geographical situation. In 1966 French authorities announced that Radio Djibouti would expand its operations in order to "spread French culture throughout East Africa and the Near and Middle East," although the deteriorating Middle Eastern political situation and a consequent increase in propaganda broadcasts from neighboring stations were surely not overlooked (Thompson and Adloff 1968, p. 158).

An ORTF spokesman, François de Sainte Marie, while conceding that, formerly, only officials and the small privileged class of Gallicized Africans listened to the overseas newscasts and features on the radio, claimed the appeal was now being broadened: "Our objective is to go beyond the most educated classes and to reach the middle social layer. . . . African reaction and the continuous mail we receive prove that we are reaching a large number of listeners" (*Le Figaro* 1972, p. 21). He attributed this success, among other reasons, to the integration of programs with purely African content into French network programs.

9.4.2 Indian Ocean Islands, *by Sydney W. Head*

All that remains of France's once widespread insular possessions in the Indian Ocean are Réunion and the Comoro Island group.

Réunion. The small island of Réunion, which lies somewhat over 400 miles east of Madagascar, was claimed originally by the French, in 1649. The French brought Africans over from Madagascar and Moçambique prior to the abolition of slavery in 1848, when some 60,000 Africans were freed. At a later time Indians were brought in to work the plantations. French is the official language, of course, but the common language is Creole. The island is heavily populated, with nearly half a million persons crowded into an area of only a thousand square miles. ORTF, the official French broadcasting service, operates radio and television. In 1972, radio was operated 16 hours a day and television four, with 86,000 radio and 26,000 television receivers in use. ORTF operates an 8-kw. medium-wave transmitter and a 4-kw. short-wave transmitter for local programming, as well as a second 4-kw. medium-wave transmitter to rebroadcast the French overseas service. Réunion radio also serves Mauritius (120 miles away), Seychelles (1,200 miles), and Madagscar. The island is almost round, with a very high central mountain; since the populated areas are confined to the coast, the main television transmitter is supplemented by eleven repeater stations (*Television Factbook* 1972–73, p. 1090b).

Comoro Islands. The Comoros are an archipelago of 41 volcanic islands between the Moçambique-Tanzania border and the northern tip of Madagascar. The French colonized the islands in 1841. Their population of a little over a quarter-million is a mixture of Africans, Arabs, Malays, Portuguese, Dutch, French, and Indians. Arabic and Swahili are widely spoken. The ORTF operates the radio service, a 4-kw. short-wave transmitter, for about four hours a day in French and Comorian, the lingua franca.

9.5 Spanish Dependencies, *by Sydney W. Head*

Spanish Sahara. Spain has retained a rather large chunk of territory on the west coast of Africa between Morocco and Mauritania which it annexed in 1884. However, as the name implies, it consists entirely of desert—"a destitute and entirely artificial political unit," possibly of some value because of phosphate deposits and as a protective shield for Spain's Canary Islands (*Africa South of the Sahara* 1971, p. 768). Spain apparently uses the territory as a base for propaganda broadcasts, since there is a 50-kw. medium-wave transmitter at El Aioun, one of the two coastal towns. The other town, Villa Cisneros, serves as a military penal stockade, where Spain operates a 10-kw medium-wave station.

Canary Islands. The beautiful and productive Canaries contrast sharply with Spanish Sahara. They consist of a 13-island archipelago only 70 miles offshore at its nearest point. The islands have been Spanish possessions since the fifteenth century. The original inhabitants may have been Berbers, but if so they have long since been completely assimilated with the Spanish colonists. The islands are divided into two provinces, integral with Spain: Las Palmas and Santa Cruz de Tenerife. The population of about a million is served by nine different radio organizations, five in Las Palmas and four in Tenerife. The Spanish government operates a high-powered station at

Tenerife which serves as a relay for programs originated in Madrid and aimed at South America. The others are private stations, unusual in that each has an FM transmitter as well as a low- or medium-power medium-wave transmitter. Television started in 1964, with stations on both Las Palmas and Tenerife. The Las Palmas station is listed, along with those at Madrid and Barcelona, as one of the main Spanish television-production centers (*Television Factbook* 1972–73, p. 1091b).

Spain also has a small medium-wave radio station and a television station in each of two enclaves, Ceuta and Melilla, on the Mediterranean coast of Morocco, as well as a television station in a third enclave, Sidi Ifni, on the Atlantic coast.

Part 2   Cross-System Functions

10 International Broadcasts to African Audiences

Donald R. Browne

[EDITOR'S NOTE. In 1972 some 40 nations outside of Africa and 19 within Africa were pumping propaganda by radio into and around the continent. In addition, several religious stations operating outside and three major religious stations operating within the continent, as well as the United Nations in New York, added their perhaps less self-serving share of traffic to the overcrowded short-wave spectrum. As African colonies won independence and as colonial hegemonies faded, rival European and Asian powers began to compete for markets, ideological converts, and third-world leadership. At the same time, the operation of an external service became a status symbol among the new nations themselves—alongside such luxuries as television, jet airlines, and embassies abroad. The result is a stunning babel of voices issuing from the short-wave receivers of Africa. Many of these would-be international voices are drowned out in the general hubbub, overwhelmed by the signals of major international broadcasters who, using immensely powerful transmitters equipped with sophisticated directional-antenna arrays, occupy six or eight different frequencies simultaneously. Some, like the Voice of America's relay complex at Monrovia, Liberia, are even located on African soil, where their massive wattage can be even more effectly deployed. In this chapter Browne identifies the principal international radio voices heard in Africa, discusses their characteristics and objectives, and analyzes factors which make for success or failure in this intense and expensive war of words.]

10.1 Colonial Period

Great Britain, France, Portugal, Belgium, and Spain were broadcasting to their African colonies as early as 1931. The colonial broadcast services, intended to provide European settlers and administrators with a touch of

Donald R. Browne is Professor of Speech-Communication, University of Minnesota. He served with the USIA in Africa, 1960–63, and has conducted field research on international broadcasting in Africa, Asia, Europe, and the Pacific.

"home away from home," concentrated almost solely on political, economic, social, and cultural life in the home country; furthermore, these services used the languages of the motherlands, never the vernaculars of African peoples.

A brief variant of the prevailing European orientation occurred just before and during World War II, when the Italian and German governments laid assaults on "native" African listeners. The chief targets for these broadcasts were the Arab and Berber populations of North Africa and the Afrikaners in the Union of South Africa. Arabs and Berbers were urged to "cast off the colonial yoke" and, as the military struggle for North Africa intensified, to commit acts of sabotage (see Schnaible 1967, pp. 258–313; Ettlinger 1943, pp. 110–11, 167–72; Pohle 1955, pp. 418–61). Afrikaners were urged to keep South Africa neutral; they failed to do so, and the broadcasts thereafter suggested minimizing cooperation with Great Britain.

Axis radio propaganda provoked the BBC into starting broadcasting in Arabic in 1938 and in Afrikaans in 1939. As to the other major colonial powers in Africa, Spain and Portugal remained more or less neutral during World War II, and Belgium and France fell under German rule. France bore the additional burden of the Vichy government in the southern portion of France. The Free French used one of France's African locations, Brazzaville in the Congo, to reach supporters of the Free French and to attack the Nazis (see § 6.1). These broadcasts, however, were directed chiefly to listeners in Europe and North America and to French settlers in overseas locations, and they used European languages exclusively (see Gaskill 1942, pp. 35 ff.).

The BBC intensified its efforts during World War II, formally designating its African Service in 1941. It included broadcasts in English, Afrikaans, French, German, Portuguese, and (enigmatically) Serbo-Croatian. By late 1943 the BBC offered a brief daily service in "Moroccan Arabic." Unless Afrikaans and Arabic are regarded as exceptions, at that time there appear to have been no regularly scheduled broadcasts, from any source, using indigenous African languages.

After World War II, most international broadcasting to Africa returned to its function of the early to late 1930s: transmitting the colonial powers' programming to their countrymen overseas. Great Britain, however, continued to broadcast in Arabic and in Afrikaans, though the latter was discontinued in 1957. The other major powers active in international broadcasting in the early postwar years, the Soviet Union and the United States, were more interested in broadcasting to each other and to Western and Eastern Europe than to Africa. The United States, for its part, would have been engaging in a potentially undiplomatic act had it broadcast competitively to areas where its allies had widespread colonial interests. However, the United States, under the terms of a 1949 agreement with the French, operated transmitting facilities in Tangier, Morocco, primarily for transmissions to the Mediterranean area. An American-backed religious station also operated from Tangier between 1954 and 1959, using a 10-kw. transmitter oriented toward Africa. This was the forerunner of Trans World Radio, one of the major international religious-broadcast services.

The next major entries in the list of international broadcasters for Africa came from within the continent itself, but from two very different directions. In January 1954, Station ELWA ("Eternal Love Winning Africa") began transmissions from Liberia. Station ELWA is supported by the Sudan Interior Mission (see §§ 5.4.1 and 11.2.3). At about the same time, Radio Cairo initiated a major expansion of its international service, with Sub-Saharan and North Africa as two of the principal target areas. Radio Cairo at first used the languages of the African colonial powers, but in addition it soon began to employ such vernacular languages as Swahili. In fact the Egyptian Swahili service, starting as early as 1954, appears to have been the first international broadcasting service in a "native" African language (*Time* 1958). The Egyptian service later took advantage of a language vacuum created by countries which sought to use a single official indigenous language as a compulsive instrument of policy for national unification.

10.2 Postcolonial Scramble for the Ether

The "African decade," which eventually saw virtually every African nation attain independence or self-rule, began in 1957 with the independence of Ghana. This event signaled a new era of international broadcasting to and within Africa. The first newcomers were Radio Moscow and Radio Peking, which began their African services in 1958 and 1959, respectively. Initially, these services were in the dominant European languages—English, French, and Portuguese—but by 1961 Radio Moscow had added Swahili. The BBC also began to broadcast in African languages. It added brief (15 minutes a day, twice a week) services in Swahili, Somali, and Hausa in 1957. In 1960 it took what might be considered, diplomatically, an even bolder step when it introduced special services in French for North, West, and Equatorial Africa. The Voice of America also began special services to Africa at this stage: English to Africa in late 1959, French to Africa in 1960. Swahili was added as a regular VOA service in late 1962, although there had been special broadcast feeds to African stations on an irregular basis at least as early as 1961.

France, Portugal, and Spain continued their policies of broadcasting chiefly in their national languages, although by 1960 Radio Portugal also carried an English service to East Africa of about five hours per week. The two former African colonial powers, Germany and Italy, also initiated broadcast services to Africa. Both Germanies did so at about the same time, East Germany's Radio Berlin International in 1960, West Germany's Deutsche Welle in 1962. Most of the other nations of the Communist Bloc developed modest African services in the period 1959–61, usually featuring English, French, Portuguese, and Arabic. It has been pointed out that "the whole continent came into the full crossfire of international radio propaganda" (Voss 1962, p. 247; translated from the German).

African nations themselves tend to regard international broadcasting as one of the perquisites of nationhood. Ghana, because of her early independence and the pan-African ambitions of her prime minister, the late Kwame Nkrumah, became the first independent black nation in Sub-Saharan Africa to enter this field. External broadcasts in French began in 1959 (*COMBROAD* 1972e, p. 37). In October 1961, Nkrumah dedicated a new, high-powered external short-wave transmitting station, to be used in support of the "complete emancipation of Africa" and the political unification of the continent (see Thompson 1969). To this end Radio Ghana employed French, English, Portuguese, Arabic, Hausa, and Swahili.

Nigeria began a service called Voice of Nigeria in 1962. By early 1963 this service was carrying broadcasts in French, English, Arabic, Hausa, and Swahili. Guinea's Voice of the Revolution started in October 1961; Tanganyika began its Voice of Freedom in late 1962. The latter two differed from the Nigerian and Ghanaian international services in that they chiefly served exiled African nationalist groups, such as those from Portuguese Guinea and Moçambique. They therefore carried very little programming that had anything to do with the nations from which their broadcasts originated. Although they carried programs in English and Portuguese, they also employed languages hitherto unused by international stations, such as Sena, Herero, Zulu, Bambara, Creole, and Wolof.

As the propaganda war in Africa intensified, the number of hours broadcast by the competing services was increased. In the period 1960–66, for example, broadcasts to Africa from the Communist Bloc—USSR, Eastern Europe, Communist China, North Korea, North Vietnam, and Cuba—soared from just under 100 hours weekly to nearly 500 hours weekly, not counting the many hours of Arabic broadcasts to North Africa. The BBC and the Voice of America made less dramatic increases, while France actually reduced her French-language broadcasts in 1964 from 3½ to 1½ hours daily. West Germany's Deutsche Welle, however, expanded its African services and even obtained the consent of the Rwanda government to establish a powerful relay transmitter complex near Kigali. This installation, which began operations in 1965 with a 250-kw. short-wave transmitter—since joined by a second one—vastly strengthened the Deutsche Welle signal in Central and East Africa.

The Chinese People's Republic, the United States, Great Britain, the Netherlands, and several religious organizations also obtained African transmitter sites. Such arrangements generally included the construction of several transmitters, perhaps some studios, and, on one or two occasions, the provision of a large number of radio or television receivers, with at least some of these benefits going to the nation on whose sovereign territory the foreign transmitters were to be erected. As an example, the Germans built Radio Kigali for the Rwanda government in exchange for the right to locate its own relay facilities there. The Chinese People's Republic erected powerful transmitters for Mali, reportedly with the understanding that China be allowed to share in the transmitting time (*Africa Research Bulletin* 1967, p. 831c). The United States began broadcasting Voice of America programs to Africa from its powerful transmitter complex in Liberia in 1963 (§ 5.4). The terms of the Liberia-United States agreement have not been made public, but the renewal of the Voice of America's lease arrangement in Tangier in 1959 allowed the Moroccan government to use the VOA transmitting facilities on a shared-time basis (*New York Times* 1960).

Great Britain may have made a special arrangement with Botswana in late 1965, when the British government established a powerful medium-wave transmitter in Francistown. This installation, intended chiefly to make BBC programs easier to receive in Rhodesia, where unilateral independence had been declared, operated for three years. Apparently the British maneuver was effective, for Rhodesia jammed the Francistown transmissions whenever they dealt with Rhodesian affairs. Officially, the BBC denied responsibility for the installation, but it was public knowledge that the British prime minister had visited Rhodesia shortly before UDI and was reported to be dissatisfied with the quality of BBC reception there (*Times* [London] 1966; *Rundfunk und Fernsehen* 1968; Fellows 1966).

The Netherlands concluded an agreement with the Malagasy Republic in 1970 providing for the construction of two 300-kw. transmitters to relay Radio Nederland programs to listeners in Africa, Asia, and Australia. In return the Dutch were to provide transmitter time over this installation for the Malagasy government and to construct six transmitters throughout the island for the use of Malagasy radio.

Two Protestant international broadcasting stations also managed to secure African locations for their studios and transmitters in the 1960s. Radio Voice of the Gospel (ETLF) was established in Addis Ababa, Ethiopia, in 1961; and Radio CORDAC came on the air from Bujumbura, Burundi, on Christmas Eve, 1963. Both stations have assisted their host countries through staff-training programs, and both broadcast in a number of African languages. In 1972 Trans World Radio was attempting to secure the permission of the Republic of South Africa's government to establish a religiously oriented station within the republic (Bower 1972). These stations are discussed further in § 11.2.3.

With increased international broadcasting activity on the part of several hostile nations, it was logical that the Republic of South Africa, itself often the object of attack from Radio Peking, Radio Moscow, and Tanzania's Voice of Freedom, should counterattack. The South African Broadcasting Corporation had operated a modest external service for Africa since 1952, chiefly in English and Afrikaans. The one 20-kw. transmitter proved inadequate by the mid-1960s. Accordingly, the South African government spent some $5.6 million on a new transmitting installation and inaugurated a new international service called "Radio RSA." It began new services to North America and Europe while increasing its African service to 30 program hours daily, in English, French, and Portuguese, as well as in Swahili and other African languages. Radio RSA's African service took a soft-sell approach, representing South Africa as cooperative in nature and pointing out the benefits of the agreements that had been concluded between Black African states, such as Malawi, and the republic (McKay 1971).

By 1972, then, the air waves over Africa appeared to have become a major battleground for international broadcasting. Each year, additional African nations initiate or expand international broadcasting services. Nearly half of all independent African nations claimed to operate external services, although many of these, such as the Voice of Algeria (formed in 1971) or the Somali Republic's Voice of Somalia, broadcast for only two or three hours daily.

10.3 African Audiences for International Services

In considering the African audience for international broadcasts, one must assess two factors: (1) physical reception, and (2) psychosociological conditions of receptivity. Both factors apply to the audience for international broadcasting anywhere in the world, and the African situation appears to differ from other situations only in degree (see Browne 1971 for a detailed treatment of this subject as applied to Asian audiences).

10.3.1 Physical Aspects of Reception

As for primary reception, two obvious conditions must be fulfilled: the strength of the incoming broadcast signal and the choice of operating frequencies must allow for reasonably clear and dependable listening, and the reception equipment itself must be capable of picking up the signal. Most of the major international broadcasters active in Africa either have transmitters in African locations or are close enough to the continent to make an African location unnecessary; others have increased their transmitting power and signal directivity to the point where they can be reasonably competitive with the other international services. The jamming of incoming signals by African nations is rare. We have noted the Rhodesian jamming of BBC broadcasts (§ 10.2), and the French administration in Algeria jammed Tunisian broadcasts to Algeria at various times in the late stages of the Algerian independence movement. These are highly exceptional cases, however, for jamming is an expensive process which few African broadcasting systems can afford without crippling their own transmission capacities. Thus the African radio listener, if equipped with even a modest shortwave receiver, has a remarkably wide range of services from which to choose if he wants to explore the dial.

In practice, however, the listener's physical choice could be limited by two subfactors: the nature of his set, and his own ability to understand the languages employed by the broadcast services. Most international services broadcasting to or within Africa operate on short wave. The typical radio set in Africa is able to receive several short-wave bands, thanks to the fact that even most domestic services use short-wave transmission for at least part of their broadcasting coverage. The international broadcaster cannot count on being able physically to reach a substantial part of the total population, for even the ubiquitous transistor set has not enabled anything approaching deep saturation in Africa.

The second limiting subfactor is language, since Africa is notorious for its multiplicity of localized tongues (see § 18.1.2). Suffice it to point out here that the international broadcaster must make language choices which, for most target areas, automatically place severe limits on accessibility to target audiences. The choices boil down essentially to one of the few widely spoken African languages such as, Swahili, Hausa, or Arabic, or one of the former colonial metropolitan languages, English, French, Italian, Portuguese, or Spanish. In the one case the broadcaster may be able to reach beyond the cities to segments of the rural, less highly educated population; in the other he will be limited to the urbanized elite. Nevertheless, in addition to one or more European languages, most major international broadcasters seriously interested in reaching African listeners employ one or more African languages. Swahili leads the list, with 18 international services (or, at least, services that can be heard beyond national borders) employing this East African lingua franca, while Hausa is broadcast by at least nine services. Still, one must conclude that, on the basis of language barriers alone, international broadcasters fail to reach the large majority of African populations.

10.3.2 Psychological and Sociological Receptivity

Assuming that an international broadcaster is able to meet the physical prerequisites for reaching audiences in a given geographical area, he must then consider what material his target audiences will accept. The increased availability of domestic radio services, television services, newspapers, magazines, books, and other leisure-time diversions has made it ever more difficult for international broadcast services to capture attention. While these diversions may be less available or accessible in Africa than in many other parts of the world, they are rapidly becoming more available.

Most domestic services are easier to "use" than foreign sources, particularly when the latter are available through short wave only and are on the air for very brief periods daily, as is the case for most African languages.

The first elements of programming strategy employed by the international broadcaster, then, must be the consideration of the screening effects of physical accessibility and language proficiency on his potential audience. Next, he must consider the competitive effect of the domestic media available to the audience and tailor his prospective service accordingly. Only then can he bring his own national or organizational priorities to bear on the form and substance of his program service (see, e.g., Janvier 1962).

A detailed comparative study of "image fluctuations" on the part of citizens in foreign nations led Deutsch and Merritt to conclude that fully 40% of any population simply will not change its mind with respect to any given international event. The majority of the remaining 60% will change only in response to a highly spectacular event (e.g., the Russian intervention in Hungary in 1956) or to an unusual combination of lesser events. Most of those whose minds do change sooner or later lapse into the opinions they had held prior to the event. Less than 15% of any population appears to be susceptible to change under "normal" circumstances, that is, without spectacular or highly unusual combinations of events (Deutsch and Merritt 1965).

Several authors have suggested that certain specific categories of the general population fit into this susceptible 15%. They include students, teachers, government officials, and, to a lesser extent, members of such specialized occupations as military officer, businessman, lawyer, journalist, and doctor. Most of these are well educated, inquisitive, and fairly prosperous and are regarded as "opinion leaders." Many have traveled internationally or maintain contact with people and organizations in foreign countries. If such people are "important" in terms of national or denominational priorities, the fact that they form a minority within the total national population does not really matter to an international broadcaster. If they also use radio frequently, and if their sets can receive foreign broadcasts, the chances of reaching them are favorable (see Deutsch and Merritt 1965; Janis and Smith 1965; Browne 1965). Their reasons for listening to foreign broadcasts vary, of course. They may want (1) to better understand a foreign nation or ideology; (2) to better understand an "enemy" so as to be able to oppose him more successfully; (3) to acquire or improve a language skill; (4) to retain ties with a "mother country" or "second homeland"; (5) to keep abreast of the ideological, political or cultural developments of a certain nation or "way of life" (e.g., Communism, Christianity) so as to be able to better act as a proponent of that nation or ideology; (6) to seek entertainment unavailable through domestic media (e.g., music-request shows; recent jazz or rock recordings); or (7) to apply a corrective to domestic news reports when they are suspected of being incomplete or biased. Several of these purposes could motivate, to varying degrees, the same listener. Some might be antithetical to the goals of certain international broadcasters (e.g., number 2); others would be minimally productive in and of themselves (e.g., number 6).

Among audiences in Africa all these reasons for listening to foreign broadcasts can be found, but number 4 is particularly worth noting, because of Africa's colonial past and the residue in substantial numbers of former colonial civil servants, foreign technicians, doctors, educators, and European-educated Africans. Several of the international broadcasters take this factor into account by providing substantial services in the languages commonly used in the countries to which these persons have ties: English, French, and Portugese, of course, but also German, Russian, and even Mandarin. Numbers 1 and 5, especially as they apply to the attempts made by several religious broadcasters to spread Christianity throughout Africa, are also particularly prominent.

Number 5 admits of one other interpretation when one considers African audiences. Several territories on the continent remain under colonial rule, while two nations—Rhodesia and the Republic of South Africa—are governed by white minorities. Several international broadcasting services seek to reach black listeners in these territories and nations, to strengthen nascent independence movements, or to encourage civil unrest or revolution. These stations, among them Radio Tanzania's Voice of Freedom, Radio Cairo, and Radio Moscow, broadcast in languages seldom used by other international broadcasters.

10.3.3 Audiences in Actuality

To discover how many Africans actually do listen, and, more important, why they listen and what they think about what they hear, is obviously difficult. Two studies conducted on behalf of the United States Information Agency, one in West Africa in 1964, one in East Africa in 1966, indicate that better-educated Africans tended to listen more often to international broadcasts than less well-educated Africans (USIA 1966a, 1966b; see also Smith, 1970–71). A 1970 study by RBL (Research Bureau Limited, a commercial research firm) in Kenya, Tanzania, Uganda, and Ghana indicated that 96% of the Africans included in the survey who owned radio sets could receive short-wave signals (Research Bureau Limited 1970). Both studies indicated that the domestic service of each country was far more likely to be listened to than international stations; that the BBC was the only foreign station, outside of those in neighboring countries (e.g., Radio Tanzania for listeners in Kenya and Uganda) that was likely to be tuned to by more than 50% of the listeners; and that such stations as Radio Moscow, Radio Peking, Radio Cairo, Deutsche Welle, and Radio Berlin International were listened to by no more than 10% (and usually far less) of the radio listening population even on an occasional basis.

Further data come from the analysis of listener mail. Most major international broadcasters engage in mail analysis, and, where the results have been made public, the general profile that emerges of the "African who listens and writes" is of a young, relatively well-educated male. The Voice of America mail count for Africa for the first ten months of 1970 amounted to about 10,650 pieces, not including mail directed specifically to the VOA Worldwide English Service (Voice of America 1970; see also Waldschmidt 1966; USIA 1964b, 1969). Illiteracy, of course, limits both the quantity and the representativeness of mail feedback. In short, the nature of the audience for international broadcasting in Africa remains even more of a mystery than in most other areas of the world.

Ignorance about the size and nature of the African audience notwithstanding, most of the major international broadcasting services continue to direct their attentions toward it, and even to increase those attentions, be it through increased broadcast hours, increased transmitter power, or increased numbers of languages employed, as indicated in § 10.2. Since it is expensive to establish and maintain these services, one must conclude that their sponsors feel they get an adequate return in terms of influence.

10.4 International Services from the West

More than 20 Western nations claim to operate broadcast services intended at least in some measure for African audiences, but only six or seven of these are significant in terms of hours broadcast, and only five use African as well as European languages. Of these five—the BBC, Deutsche Welle, the Voice of America, the International Service of RTB (Belgium), and Radio Nederland—the first three are the most prominent in terms of broadcast hours and scope of programming. The RTB broadcasts, in several Congolese languages and in French, English, and Dutch, are apparently aimed mostly toward Zaïre, the former Belgian Congo. In 1971 Radio Nederland, using English, French, Dutch, Afrikaans, and Portuguese, started transmitting from a new relay installation on Madagascar. A sixth service, one not broadcasting in African languages, is also prominent enough to deserve mention, the French Office de Radiodiffusion-Télévision Française.

10.4.1 BBC External Services

The BBC first introduced African languages (Afrikaans and Arabic excepted) into its African Service in 1957 (§ 12.1.3). In the ensuing years the BBC African Service developed a variety of programs—some daily, some weekly, most of 15–30 minutes' duration—designed particularly for African listeners. In fact, the BBC now offers more specialized programming for Africa than for any other area of the world. Much of this service is informational: "Report on Africa," "African News," "Focus on

Africa," "What the African Papers Say," "The Week in Africa." As an example of the content of such programs, "The Week in Africa" for Saturday, 29 January 1972 comprised a 15-minute report on the Rhodesian situation, including interviews with the British foreign minister and a black Rhodesian M.P. and a report from a BBC correspondent on the scene; a 5-minute report on the meeting of the U.N. Security Council in Addis Ababa; and a 5-minute report on tension in Namibia (South West Africa).

Other BBC African programs deal with economics, in keeping with Great Britain's mission of promoting trade with foreign nations: "Men and their Money; Rich Man, Poor Man" (part of a special series on management and the economy). Specialized programs also include "Break for Women," "This Sporting Life," "The Arts and Africa," "University Report," and "Postmark Africa" (replies to letters sent by African listeners). The BBC also furnishes an entertainment show for African listeners, "The Morning Show" (weekdays, usually 20 or 30 minutes in length); it features popular music, much of it African, and is often hosted by an African disc jockey. Chike Egbuna, a Nigerian, achieved some fame in this capacity (§ 12.1.3). In addition, the BBC broadcasts a great deal of more general material, both to Africa and to other parts of the world, much of it taken directly from the BBC's domestic services. These programs consist of everything from quiz shows to radio dramas, from classical music to cricket and soccer scores.

The USIA West African survey mentioned in § 10.3.3 revealed that over 20% of the sample of adult radio listeners in Accra, Ghana, reported listening to the BBC "daily or almost every day"; the USIA East African survey showed that about 25% of urban adult radio listeners with at least a primary school education made the same claim for their BBC listening; and the RBL survey in East Africa and Ghana indicated that 45% of the sample audience (adult radio listeners in cities or in "bush" areas near cities) listened to the BBC "more or less often." The BBC also received high marks for credibility in the 1966 East Africa survey: 69% of the sample audience expressing any opinion on the subject of credibility felt that one could believe "all" or "most" of what the BBC said (comparable percentages for other services: VOA, 39; Radio Cairo, 38; Radio Moscow, 23; and Radio Peking, 21).

The BBC's French service to Africa amounts to 4¼ hours a day, broken into four widely separated segments. Only 2% of the respondents in the 1964 USIA survey said they listened "daily or almost every day" to this service in Dakar, Senegal, and only 1% in Abidjan, Ivory Coast. The BBC has set up listener panels to provide critiques of its Hausa, Somali, and Swahili services. It reported receiving 16,000 letters in Hausa alone in 1970, but its Research Department declined to release details on this research (*BBC Handbook,* 1971, p. 103).

The BBC's quest for African listeners is helped by its Ascension Island transmitter site, which gives excellent coverage of much of the continent (§ 9.3.2). Moreover, a number of African countries rebroadcast BBC programs. In 1970, for example, Botswana, The Gambia, Lesotho, Liberia, Nigeria, Sierra Leone, and Swaziland all rebroadcast BBC programs on a daily basis (*BBC Handbook* 1972, p. 106). Most important to the BBC's success, however, are long-established policies which have achieved the status of tradition—a low-key approach, completeness and objectivity in news coverage, emphasis on news of Africa, and programming relevant to African tastes and needs.

10.4.2 Voice of America

As we noted in § 10.1, the Voice of America delayed creating an African service until late 1959. Africa became a top-priority area for expansion of State Department, U.S. Agency for International Development, and U.S. Information Agency activities in the Kennedy era. In late 1961, the VOA expanded its English and French services to Africa from 30 minutes to one hour daily and added a 30-minute daily broadcast in Hindi to East Africa. Hindi was dropped in early 1965. In 1962 a 30-minute daily broadcast in Swahili was added. The expansion continued on into the mid-1960s, when it leveled off (see § 5.4.1).

In 1972 the VOA broadcast about 130 hours a week directly to Africa, broken down by VOA language service roughly as follows (in percentages): Regionalized English, 35; English Division to Africa, 32; French to Africa, 21; and Arabic (to North Africa only) and Swahili, 7 each. Seven hours a week of "feeds" (delivered via broadcast transmitters but intended for recording in Africa and subsequent local broadcast by African stations) included English, French, Swahili, and Hausa for East, Southern, West, and Central Africa. The chief daily programs in the major category Regionalized English included "African Safari," 50% news and news-related material, 25% features, and 25% music; "African Panorama," a 50–50 division of news and music; and "Africana," again 50% news, the rest features and music. The daily programs in French included the "Breakfast Show," 35% news, 65% music; "Radio Journal," all news; "Antenne," 25% news, 40% features, and 35% music; and "Radio Journal to North Africa," all news. In addition to direct broadcasts and feeds, VOA supplied an average of more than 60 hours a week of packaged recorded programs, including some in Yoruba, Amharic, Somali, and Portuguese, for use by local African stations; also, USIA posts in Africa produced a small amount of programming for local use in a few countries.

The VOA usually covers the news candidly and in detail, without avoiding items unfavorable to United States policies. The service considers credibility its most important asset despite occasional domestic political repercussions. The general style of the program series mentioned above reflects the informal chattiness of modern American domestic radio-magazine formats. This informality has replaced the VOA's earlier tendency to be rather stodgy and conservative. The change in style was symbolized in 1967 when the VOA adopted as its signature theme a variety of gay, light-hearted orchestrations of "Yankee Doodle," in place of a solemnly orchestrated, hymnlike version of "Columbia, the Gem of the Ocean."

As indicated above, about a third of the VOA's English programs reaching Africa are designed for audiences that are not exclusively African. Perhaps the most significant of these programs is a daily half-hour in "Special English," which limits the announcer to a reading rate of 90 words a minute and to a basic vocabulary of 1,200 words. The VOA believes it to be ideal for those who are just beginning to learn English.

The studies cited earlier indicate that from 8% to 20% of the sample audiences say they listen to the VOA "daily or several times weekly." The VOA also fared quite well in terms of credibility in the 1966 East Africa survey, the one study in which this characteristic was investigated; 34%–45% of the sample audiences in the Anglophone countries where the survey was taken felt that they could believe "all or most" of the news they heard on the VOA. This range was considerably higher than the ranges for Radio Moscow or Radio Peking, but about 30 percentage points less than that for the BBC.

10.4.3 Deutsche Welle

Deutsche Welle's African Service developed later than the African services of most of the other leading international broadcasters, but in the ten years following its first English and French language broadcasts to Africa (August 1962), its transmissions to the continent expanded to the point where the Deutsche Welle was considered a major external voice in Africa. The service is supported by the West German government, but controlled by a politically independent council. The broadcasts of Deutsche Welle to Africa in German occupy a little over two hours a day (plus repeat broadcasts); in English a little over four hours a day (some repeat broadcasts included); in French, a little over four hours a day; in Swahili, about two and a half hours a day; in Hausa, two hours a day; and in Amharic, less than one hour a day. A measure of Deutsche Welle's interest in reaching African listeners is its investment in the powerful and costly relay station near Kigali, Rwanda, mentioned in §§ 4.4 and 10.2.

Underlying West German interest in Africa are at least three motives; promoting trade in a potentially large and expanding industrial market; presenting the West German viewpoint on such issues as the cold-war with East Germany; and capitalizing on such favorable attitudes toward Germany as might exist in certain parts of Africa by reason of Germany's brief colonial rule there several decades ago. There appears to be a certain emotional attachment in the minds of some Germans vis-à-vis Africa, some of which appears to derive from this colonial experience (see also § 6.2.4). Broadcasts to Africa feature a good deal of news and information (technical, economic, cultural, and sociological) about West Germany; commentary on major world events from a West German perspective; and entertainment —chiefly popular music (most of it European, a little of it African, some of it by listener request). There are also newscasts of solely African events, however, and numerous features and interviews concerning African political or cultural figures and developments. Deutsche Welle carries considerable African-oriented material, though less than the BBC or the VOA.

Deutsche Welle's success in reaching African listeners is difficult to judge, but listener mail has been climbing steadily, from 9,262 letters in 1967 to 16,624 letters in 1971 (Deutsche Welle 1972, pp. 103–05). According to the 1966 USIA East African survey (made only a few months after the Kigali relay station opened), only 3% of the sample audience listened to Deutsche Welle programs "daily or nearly every day" (about the same as Radio Moscow); its credibility score on the same survey was 35% (a little below VOA's; half the BBC's). The 1970 RBL survey gave Deutsche Welle a 10% listenership figure, but this included a certain number (exact percentage unspecified) of "less frequent" listeners. In terms of audience appeal much of Deutsche Welle's feature programming seems rather formal in style, the humor tends to be heavy-handed, and news is sometimes full of excessive detail. News coverage is thorough, however, and music-request programs seem to draw good listener response.

10.4.4 Office de Radiodiffusion-Télévision Française

Although France was one of the major colonial powers in Africa, her national broadcasting efforts for the continent in 1971 were surprisingly modest: 1¼ hours a day in English, 3¾ hours a day in French, and 4¾ hours a day in Arabic (for North Africa). Until 1972 the ORTF enjoyed a very favorable transmitter-relay location in Brazzaville, People's Republic of Congo (§ 6.3.1). The 1964 USIA West African survey showed that 6% of the sample population in Dakar and 10% of that in Abidjan listened to ORTF broadcasts (not all of them necessarily relayed by Brazzaville) daily or nearly every day. The 1966 USIA East Africa survey showed that about 12% of the sample populations in Kenya, Uganda, and Tanzania listened to Brazzaville daily or nearly every day, and that about 80% of these listeners said they did so for the music.

Inasmuch as ORTF devotes a relatively small portion of its international broadcasting effort to programs designed specifically for African listeners, it might seem that the French attach little importance to broadcasting to Africa. The assumption would probably be incorrect on two counts: first, the French national radio service, because of its training programs and technical aid arrangements with the radio stations in its former African colonies, arranges for direct placement of tapes, discs, and rebroadcasts; second, the French commonly assume that the primary interest of those who really matter in France's former colonies will be to continue their contact with French culture through ORTF domestic broadcasts (see § 6.1.2). Perhaps this second point also explains why ORTF does not broadcast in any of the African languages that are widely spoken in the former French colonies. In any case, the French appear to make few concessions in dealing with the African radio audience. Efforts by the writer to obtain more information on ORTF programming policies in Africa were unproductive.

10.5 International Services from Communist Sources

All the Communist nations operate international broadcasting services. In 1970, ten Bloc countries broadcast 458 hours a week to Africa in 21 languages other than their own (USIA 1972, p. 7). However, relatively few Bloc countries tailor programs specifically for African audiences. Of those few, three stand out because of the numbers of languages they employed, the hours of programming they transmitted, and their mention by African listeners on the few polls and surveys which have been made public. They are Radio Moscow, Radio Peking, and Radio Berlin International.

10.5.1 Radio Moscow

In October 1972, Moscow directed approximately 157½ hours a week to Sub-Saharan Africa, in 15 languages; and 20 hours a week to North Africa, in two languages. Radio Peace and Progress, a service using Radio Moscow facilities and sponsored by the Union of Journalists of the USSR and other such groups, broadcast an additional 10½ hours a week in three languages. Russian transmitters are powerful, but most of their African programs run for only 15–30 minutes, with gaps of 30 minutes to several hours before the next broadcast in the same language. Newscasts and commentaries dominate the Radio Moscow schedule, with occasional features, popular music (European far more often than African), and party or government declarations and proclamations. A typical newscast on Radio Moscow's English service to Africa, judging by this writer's monitoring in early 1972, may contain items on African events in Moçambique, Angola, Rhodesia, or the Republic of South Africa, and on technical assistance projects involving the USSR and African nations, but rarely are these African items given the lead positions in newscasts.

Both Radio Moscow and Radio Peace and Progress include news concerning the Arab world (particularly the Egyptian-Israeli conflict) in their broadcasts to Africa. Both employ loaded terms in reporting news about Africa—"the Arabs' just cause" against Israel, "racist" or "white supremacist" regimes in South Africa, Rhodesia, and the Portuguese territories—

but to no greater extent than Radio Cairo, Radio Ghana, or the Voice of Freedom in Tanzania. Both rely on clichés and stock phrases. Radio Moscow's share of the audience in the available surveys of radio listenership in Africa is invariably relatively minute. This is understandable if one assumes that the Russian broadcasts appeal primarily to African Communists or Communist sympathizers. Such listeners may find it discreet not to publicize their affiliations, especially since Radio Moscow aims its vernacular broadcasts particularly at areas where Communism is least appreciated by the governments in power—South Africa, the western Congo region, Nigeria, and Senegal (see Hutton-Williams 1971).

10.5.2 Radio Peking

Slightly more than 100 hours a week emanated from Radio Peking to Africa in December 1970. Of the nine languages used, only two—Hausa and Swahili—were indigenous African languages. Many of the broadcasts (notably, those in three Chinese languages, in English, and in Portuguese) were intended for listeners in Africa, Europe, and the Middle East. Broadcasts in English and French enjoy the advantage of being scheduled on several frequencies in relatively long blocks of air time, sometimes as much as four hours. Nevertheless, Radio Peking's effort to reach Africans in the vernacular tongues is obviously more modest than Radio Moscow's. On the basis of the author's very limited monitoring of Radio Peking broadcasts to Africa, it can be said that the comments made about Radio Moscow and Radio Peace and Progress would apply here as well; in fact, Radio Peking's broadcasts seem more heavily devoted to news, editorials (from Chinese newspapers such as the *People's Daily* and the *Red Flag*), and political features (quotations from Chairman Mao, revolutionary songs) than Radio Moscow's. Audience surveys have shown that Radio Peking is rarely listened to *at all* by more than 1% or 2% of the sample populations. In part, the reportedly weak signal strength in much of Africa may account for this, but Radio Peking's heavy-handed use of jargon and tortuous sentence structure, plus the relatively small attention it pays in its newscasts to African affairs, minimizes the palatability of the service.

10.5.3 Radio Berlin International

East Berlin broadcasts relatively few hours per week to Africa (about 71, in December 1970) and uses only four languages—English, French, German, and Swahili. Still, no other Communist source besides Moscow and Peking comes close to matching these figures, and Radio Berlin International is the only Communist station besides Radio Moscow and Radio Peking mentioned by African listeners in the surveys already cited. Its program schedules resemble those of Radio Moscow more than those of Radio Peking, with news, features, and occasional selections of popular music. Its prose style, too, is closer to the Radio Moscow pattern—fairly direct and simple. News items concerning events in Africa are numerous but brief, with news about developments in other parts of the world predominating. Most of the items are handled in a relatively straightforward, unbiased manner. The features, however—at least those heard by the author—appear to be prepared for a more general (i.e., not specifically African) audience. They consist of formal recitations about state agreements, visits, cooperative projects, and the like. For example, "News about the Socialist World," monitored by the author on 7 January 1972, offered three short features and four brief news items, read in formal, prosy style, and they had nothing whatever to do with Africa.

The nature of Radio Berlin International's audience is difficult to discern. The station apologetically declined to provide information in response to a 1972 enquiry by the author, but in 1966 the head of the station's African Service said he felt that its audience included young people, particularly students and workers; young party officials; trade union workers; and clergymen. He also said he felt that the station's African audience particularly wanted information on collective farms in East Germany and on the role of women in East German society (Waldschmidt 1966). The fact that the station broadcasts over several frequencies and in blocks of an hour or more should help attract listeners, but there is little evidence of significant numbers. The 1966 USIA East African survey reported no figures for RBI, meaning that no respondent mentioned it as a station listened to with any regularity; the 1970 RBL East Africa and Ghana survey reported that only 3% of the sample audience listened to the station.

10.6 International Services from African Nations

10.6.1 Radio Ghana

Ghana's external service, Radio Ghana, may carry as much as 110 hours a week of international programming. About half is in English, for Ghana's immediate neighbors. Programs for non–West African listeners consist of music (highlife, Ghanaian folk music, music from South Africa, and Western "pops," etc.); news, extracts from Ghanaian newspapers; features on African poetry and short stories, and on African culture and history; and answers to listener mail. Ghana broadcasts in French (nearly five hours daily, mostly to West Africa), Hausa (one hour daily), Portuguese (90 minutes daily), Swahili (90 minutes daily), and Arabic (45 minutes daily to North Africa, repeated for the Middle East). The service has four 100-kw. and two 250-kw. transmitters which lay down a clear signal over most of Africa. The 1964 USIA West African survey revealed that even in French-speaking Ivory Coast 30% of the sample population listened to Radio Ghana at least occasionally. Ghana's external service claims to receive as many as 200 pieces of mail per day (letter from Sam Armateifio, director of GBC Sound Broadcasting, 30 March 1972).

10.6.2 Voice of Nigeria

The Voice of Nigeria broadcasts approximately 60 hours a week, in English, French, Hausa and Arabic (Swahili was also carried at one time), for the most part to West and North Africa and to Europe. The nature of its programming, as well as its program balance, is much the same as Radio Ghana's. The 1964 USIA West Africa survey showed that the Voice of Nigeria had no listeners among the sample population in the Ivory Coast, but that over 40% of the sample population in Ghana listened to it (or a domestic Nigerian service), as did nearly 20% of that in Togo. The station claims to receive approximately 150 foreign-listener letters a month. There are indications that the Nigerian government feels, in retrospect, that it made ineffectual use of the service in bringing the Nigerian case to the rest of the world during the Nigerian civil war, and that it is preparing to increase transmitter power (see Aluko 1971).

10.6.3. Radio Tanzania

Radio Tanzania operates what amounts to three external services—one in English and one in Swahili for East Africa; and the third, in as many as 13 African (mainly Southern African) languages, for various national-liberation movements. The English and Swahili services include Western and African popular music (some of it by request), news, editorial roundups, and such weekly features as "Sons and Daughters of Africa" (profiles of famous Africans) and "Inside South Africa" (a critical review of events taking place in South Africa). According to the 1966 USIA East Africa survey, for about 70% of the stations's listeners in Kenya and Uganda, music was the main inducement for tuning to the station; for roughly 40%, news. Close to 40% of the sample population in Kenya and Uganda listened to the station "daily or several times weekly."

The service for the national-liberation movements, often known as the "Voice of Freedom," is on the air for 2½ hours each day and features programs produced by national-liberation organizations such as FRELIMO, South West African People's Organization, Zimbabwe African National Union, African National Congress, and National Liberation Movement of Comoro Islands (*COMBROAD* 1972c). The Voice of Freedom is broadcast over one short–wave frequency only, with a transmitter power of 50 kw. Because of Tanzania's favorable physical placement with regard to Southern Africa, the service is able to reach the intended audiences clearly. As evidence of its effectiveness, Radio Tanzania officials cite counterpropaganda from Radio RSA and the lodging of a complaint by the South African minister of information against the Radio Tanzania series "Apartheid in Action" (letter from Tanzanian official, 12 February 1972). Tanzania's more powerful transmitters were bought with a Chinese loan and installed in 1966 by Chinese technicians (see §4.2 for more details on Tanzania's external service).

10.6.4 Lourenço Marques Radio

The Radio Club of Moçambique lists itself as a nonprofit organization (*WRTH* 1972, p. 121), but it "provides facilities" for Lourenço Marques Radio, whose business address for the sale of commercial time is in Johannesburg, South Africa (German Africa Society 1970, p. 249). Its format is simple—virtually nonstop popular music, 24 hours a day. Unlike the other external services mentioned in this chapter, it is motivated more by economics than by politics. Its closest equivalent in Europe would be Radio Luxembourg, which also maintains a business office in the capital city of its chief target area. The station apparently has substantial listenerships in both South Africa and Rhodesia, with somewhat smaller audiences in Malawi and Zambia. A 1971 Zambia survey revealed that about 2½ % of the sample population had listened to Lourenço Marques Radio, mostly because of its nonstop popular music (Mytton 1971a). Its political significance as an international service is the possibility that it may give some Black African listeners a favorable impression of the Portuguese colonial government in Moçambique. The director of the 1971 Zambia survey observed, "No doubt some listeners might be reticent in the present political climate to admit the amount they listen to the radio stations of racist regimes" (Mytton 1971a, p. 59).

10.6.5 Republic of South Africa

Geographically speaking, Radio RSA, the "Voice of South Africa," occupies a particularly advantageous position for reaching African audiences. Its powerful array of two 100-kw. and four 250-kw. transmitters located in a mountainous region near Johannesburg directs strong signals to the north, northeast, and northwest. There are few periods in the day, from early morning to midevening, when RSA's programs cannot be heard in Africa. The English service to Africa is on the air for more than seven hours a day; the French service for five; the Portuguese service for 2½; the Swahili, Chichewa, and Tsonga services for one hour each; and the Afrikaans service for just under one hour.

Only rarely does Radio RSA's propaganda deal directly with the fundamental issue of apartheid; instead, it features stories on the progress of the Bantu states in the republic, and aspects of Bantu cultures. It stresses cooperative projects in which the Republic of South Africa and certain independent African nations, such as Malawi, are engaged. The following from a Radio RSA commentary of 8 May 1969 serves as an example of its technique:

Now there is a new realism, arising to no small extent from Black Africa's increasing experience in affairs of state. Confronted with the realities of government, the more sensible Black leaders are coming to realize more and more that emotionalism is a heavy burden to bear in international relations. Similarly, confronted with unmistakable evidence that cooperation with South Africa engenders prosperity, it must have become clear to Black leaders having the welfare of their people at heart, that there is not much to be gained by aloofness and animosity, especially not in the face of South Africa's consistent willingness to place its vast knowledge and experience at the disposal of the entire continent. [McKay 1971, p. 720]

Much of the Radio RSA schedule is taken up with talks, perhaps as much as 80% of the time in the European-language services, about 60% of the time in the African-language services. The station's newscasts typically place heavy stress on African developments, and their credibility is high because of their completeness and general avoidance of bias (Mc-Kay 1971). Hachten (1971a), who made a special study of the news media in Zambia for his book *Muffled Drums,* told the author that a number of Zambians of his acquaintance listened to Radio RSA newscasts to learn of events in their own country. In a survey conducted by the University of Zambia Institute for African Studies in 1971, 13% of the sample mentioned Radio RSA as one of the foreign stations to which they listened, and most gave its news as the reason for listening (Mytton 1971a). Given the sensitivity of the issue in Zambia it is safe to assume, as the Univerity of Zambia survey suggests, that more listeners resort to Radio RSA than would care to admit to it in a survey conducted by an agency of the Zambian government.

Radio RSA reserves most of its propaganda for its features, particularly its commentaries and its programs on South African history. Features on Bantu culture (e.g., "Journal des Bantous" and on Afrikaner culture provide wedges for propaganda ploys. Listeners interested in Afrikaans can get lessons by radio, both beginning and advanced. Music programming includes popular, Bantu, Afrikaaner *Boeremusiek,* and classical music (often by South Africa's own symphony orchestras).

Thanks to its many program hours, varied schedule, relatively reliable news coverage of African events, and powerful signal, Radio RSA is in a good position to attract a sizable audience throughout much of Africa. Tangible evidence of the extent and nature of its audience is scant, but the station claims it received more than 35,000 letters from African listeners in October 1971, mostly in response to a special competition (letter from Radio RSA, 1 February 1972). The significance of this response may be judged by comparing it with the response—38,600 pieces of mail—to a VOA *worldwide* transistor-radio contest in 1971 (USIA 1971b). The most serious impediment to increasing the size of Radio RSA's African audience is the virulent anti–South Africa stance of most independent African nations. The station cannot buy advertising space in the domestic media of these nations, as the BBC, VOA, Radio Moscow, and others frequently do. Instead it must rely on chance dialing and word-of-mouth publicity to reach new listeners. Nevertheless, Radio RSA's avoidance of hard-line propaganda and its frequent programs about Bantu life and culture, must surprise and even please many African listeners.

10.6.6 Radio Cairo

The Egyptian external services were summarized briefly in § 2.1.4, in which Green describes Radio Cairo as "the flagship of the Arab renaissance." The Egyptian external services hold a special interest because President Nasser mobilized radio, along with the other mass media, into a propaganda instrument unmatched in the whole of Africa and the Middle East. According to Copeland in *The Game of Nations,* United States diplomatic interests lent Nasser the services of Paul Linebarger, "perhaps the leading practitioner of 'black' and 'gray' propaganda in the Western world." Linebarger had made his reputation during World War II; one of his successful devices was seemingly pro-German newscasts whose actual effect was demoralizing to the Germans. He taught Nasser's men the technique of "how to damage hallowed figures . . . while seeming to praise them—a technique the Egyptians still use in Arab world politics" (Copeland 1969, p. 100).

In the early years of the independence decade, Nasser appeared to make a bid for the leadership of the African renaissance as well as the Arab (Ismail 1971). The campaign featured, among many other stratagems, energetic use of radio, television, press, and photography to impress the charismatic Nasser image indelibly on the consciousness of the African world. The leading theme depicted a defiant Nasser boldly challenging the great colonial powers. In radio plays, for example, he might be found "maintaining icy calm before desk-pounding British colonels, then ending the exchange with some devastating punch line delivered in a firm, unemotional voice" (Copeland 1969, p. 200).

Why, then, in the end, did Nasser's bid for African leadership fail? According to Copeland's interpretation of power politics, Nasser in fact never seriously entertained an ambition for that impossible goal. He simply used its potentiality as a threat to squeeze more concessions out of the United States and Russia. Still, the Arab world may have reaped some second-growth benefit from Nasser's germinal propaganda in Africa, insofar as a number of African states, contrary to what would seem to be both their historic and current interest, sided with the Arabs against Israel after the Six-Day War.

The emphasis of the Voice of the Arabs in recent years has been on vernacular language services—in Sindebele, Nyanja, and Shona for Rhodesia; in Lesotho and Zulu for the Republic of South Africa; in Swahili, Amharic, and Somali for the Horn and East Africa; and in Hausa, Wolof, Fulani, Bambara, and Yoruba for West Africa. The service also broadcasts in Lingala to Zaïre and the Congo, and in English, French, Arabic, and Portuguese to, primarily, West Africa (see also § 6.3.2). Most of the vernacular-language services to West, Southern and Central Africa have been added in the last ten years. By the end of 1970, Radio Cairo was broadcasting to Africa for 138 hours a week, and in 19 languages.

Statistics on listener mail to Radio Cairo are not available. When the writer visited Radio Cairo in 1970, his questions regarding listener mail met apologetic evasions. In the USIA West African and East African surveys and the Research Bureau Limited survey, Radio Cairo was rarely mentioned by more than 2%–3% of the sample population as a station to which they listened frequently. Even in Ethiopia, which has a large Arabic-speaking Muslim population, Radio Cairo was reported as "listened to most" by 3.5% (SCOPE 1969, pp. 168, 171). For those East Africans who heard it, its credibility rating was fairly good—38% of those expressing opinions in the USIA survey said that most or all of Cairo's news was trustworthy.

Radio Cairo's external service to Africa is limited by the fact that most of its language services to Africa are on the air briefly (an hour or less, and only once a day) and are transmitted over only one frequency. Cairo also faces problems in securing the services of writers and announcers for some of its African vernacular-language services; many of these announcers and writers were obtained from among the once considerable number of African students studying at Cairo universities, but there were some indications at the time the author visited the station in 1970 that this source of supply, for some languages at least, was drying up.

10.6.7 Other African Services

Several other African nations broadcast internationally, most of them with programs similar to those of Radio Ghana and the Voice of Nigeria, but on more modest schedules. For example, the Voice of African Brotherhood in Lubumbashi, Zaïre, carries six hours a day of programs in French, English, Swahili and Portuguese; Radio Senegal International at Dakar provides one hour a day, with 20 minutes in each of the languages Spanish, Portuguese, and English; Radio Morocco relays several hours a day of its French and Arabic home-service broadcasts but also provides one hour daily in English and 2½ hours daily in Spanish; and Radio Abidjan broadcasts in French and English to Africa and Europe. While Radio Abidjan's French service consists of relays of the home service, its English service (30 minutes to one hour daily) consists of original material, such as "Know the Ivory Coast," a 15-minute program of music and brief vignettes on tourist attractions, major buildings, Ivory Coast industries, etc. Finally, there is a modest, 5-kw. imitation of Radio Lourenço Marques in The Gambia—the Swedish-operated Radio Syd, a commercial station broadcasting to West Africa (mainly Senegal) in English, French, Wolof, and Mandingo, and on the air for 20 hours a day (see § 5.3.2).

10.7 Conclusion: Some Strategic Considerations

We shall conclude this survey of attempts to influence African broadcasting audiences from outside their own national borders with a brief review of some of the principal desiderata which affect the success of such efforts. It can be taken for granted, of course, that no such service will succeed without the physical ability to reach its target area with a reliable signal. Not all administrations appear to realize, however, that this ability does not depend alone on nominal transmitter power and strategic siting. It is not uncommon to find transmitters in Africa being operated far below their rated maximum power; the efficiency of directional antenna arrays can profoundly affect the ultimate signal output; and the choice of suitable frequencies also has an important bearing on the effectiveness of power. Simultaneous transmission on several bands to give listeners a frequency choice in accordance with transient local reception conditions is essential for consistent service; as is shifting to new frequencies when propagation conditions change from season to season and from year to year.

Once assured of physical coverage, an international service should study the programming policies of both domestic and spillover service from immediate neighbors of the target audience. Both choice of languages and choice of content must be considered. Omissions and distortions of content in the available local programming give cues to the kinds of additional program material most likely to find a welcome. A reputation for credibility has crucial importance. The BBC has the reputation of succeeding beyond all other international services, primarily on this single criterion, while even a service like South Africa's RSA, handicapped almost fatally by the policies of the sponsoring government, can still gain listenership by scrupulous attention to completeness and objectivity in news reporting.

Next, an international service must consider the element of psychological relevance in its programming. Audiences naturally tend to be most interested in programs related to their own affairs (USIA 1960b, p. 20). Most of the world's daily hard news, like most of the world's culture in forms readily assimilable into broadcast programming, is distinctly *not* related to African interests. It takes ingenuity to ferret out uniquely African newspegs. Many of the minor international services—and even some of the major ones—simply repeat for Africa the same wire-service copy that target audiences have already heard over local facilities; and they direct toward African audiences, without adaptation, the same bland features designed for European or Asian consumption.

There are many other aspects of psychological relevance in programming. For example, after a few years of African independence, the BBC and the VOA decided that African audiences might like to hear African voices on programs directed toward them—in fact might even resent the "lily-white" complexion of newsreading, announcing, and program hosting. In 1968, the VOA employed a girl disc jockey from Liberia, Ivonne Barclay. Her warm, throaty voice and charmingly accented American slang on "Request Time" made her a celebrity in many Anglophone African cities. In fact the VOA even sent her back to Africa on personal-appearance tours.

Here sensitive programming judgment is needed, for it is easy to err in either direction. Occasional use of African talent could be interpreted as condescension; over-frequent use, on the other hand, would falsify the credentials of a service ultimately designed to represent a particular non-African language and culture. The one item of research information available on this point does not strongly support the assumption that African talent is generally preferred by most African listeners. A 1969 opinion survey among urban Ethiopian students and professionals asked whether the respondents preferred African announcers on non-African stations. Of the 1,150 sample members who said they listened to the radio at least once a week, 60% said it made no difference, and 27% said they actually preferred non-African announcers (SCOPE 1969, p. 249).

Then, too, there is the element of timing. Broadcasting, by its nature, is a service which ideally should be "there" whenever wanted. To inject an isolated 20-minute program into the cacophony of the short-wave bands is likely to be futile: audience building requires, if not continuous round-the-clock service, at least large blocks of time, measured in hours rather than in minutes. And those blocks should be chosen, of course, with due regard both to the living habits of the target population and to the schedules followed by competing services.

Finally, there is the element of audience promotion, which in turn benefits from audience research. Though expensive and often politically difficult to carry out, formal audience research is essential to the rational conduct of international broadcasting services. Among the promotional devices cited in 1962 by the United States Information Agency as used in Communist international broadcasts were: frequent promotional announcements for upcoming programs, with their dial positions given; advertisements in target-area publications; quizzes, polls, forums, and "mailbag" programs stressing current propaganda themes and offering prizes for participation; listener clubs (especially cultivated by East Berlin and Moscow); special broadcasts commemorating anniversaries significant to Africans; and greetings in vernacular languages to friends back home from African students abroad (USIA 1962, pp. 33–34; see also *Communist Affairs* 1964).

It is evident to any short-wave listener that not all broadcasting administrations seriously consider such strategic factors in the conduct of their international services. Many appear to operate by guesswork, counting on sheer chance to deliver listeners. Surely a couple of hundred kilowatts of power must do *some* good (Browne 1965, p. 82)! Considerations of status or prestige are the primary, if unspoken, motivators for some services; no one concerned with them is really prepared to sustain the recurrent costs of converting sheer wattage into effective propaganda.

Nevertheless, the prospect for the 1970s seems to be even more external voices contending for attention in Africa, especially within the continent itself, as the African countries seek to reach both their neighbors and the world beyond with nationalistic and Pan-African viewpoints. The cold-war battle of words between the East and the West may wind down somewhat, or at least expand at a slower rate than that of the 1960s.

On the other hand, religious proselytizing in Africa via broadcasting seems on the eve of significant expansion, even though the more traditional, on-site activities of foreign missionaries have been decreasing. Religious broadcasting across national frontiers represents a specialized field of international broadcasting to which all that has been said in this section about strategies applies. A detailed discussion of this subject will be found in chapter 11.

10.8 United Nations Radio, *by Athmani R. Magoma*

[EDITOR'S NOTE. A special case of international broadcasting is that of the United Nations. Its predecessor, the League of Nations, had a transmitter of its own and produced programs in Geneva from 1932 to 1939 (Codding 1959, p. 66). The United Nations no longer has transmitter facilities of its own, but it still maintains a broadcasting production unit in Geneva. Its main production activities, however, now take place at the New York headquarters, where the author of the following description is stationed.]

The task of United Nations Radio, a part of the Office of Public Information, is to fulfill the objectives laid down by the General Assembly: to inform the world of the activities and functions of the U.N. Organization—to point out, not only its successes, but also its failures and shortcomings. Africa receives all sorts of programs from all parts of the world. Many are completely useless as far as Africa is concerned; they are nothing more than propaganda and counterpropaganda in big-power ideological conflicts. United Nations Radio, on the other hand, provides information which is strictly objective, factual, and above all impartial (Bass 1970). The secretary-general of the United Nations, in his 1971 report reviewing

Athmani R. Magoma is Chief of the African Section, United Nations Radio, New York. He was a pioneer broadcaster of the 1950s in Tanzania when it was still the Tanganyika Trusteeship Territory, and he later worked in London for the BBC African Service and headed Tanzania's external and English services.

and appraising U.N. information policies and activities, emphasized that the entire U.N. information effort must "confine itself to objective information, free from propaganda or proselytizing. . . . U.N. information programmes, no matter to what field they relate or how actively or purposefully they are conducted, must continue to be fashioned and articulated essentially as programmes aimed at explanation and clarification and not exhortation" (United Nations 1971 p. 11).

Virtually all African countries and territories use U.N. programs in one form or another. In 1972, 17 used U.N. material in their television programs; and 43 used U.N. radio features, all but five on a regular basis. The U.N. radio materials for Africa are released in eight languages: Amharic, Arabic, English, French, Portuguese, Somali, Spanish, and Swahili. Most programs are prerecorded, but some are broadcast directly by short wave from New York for rebroadcast by national services in Africa.

There are three main program series in the prerecorded category: (1) "This Week at the United Nations," a weekly digest of major events pertaining to the world organization; (2) "Perspective," an analysis in depth of one particular topic or problem discussed that week in the General Assembly, the Security Council, or one of their committees; and (3) "Scope," a magazine-format program based mainly on material gathered at meetings or by means of interviews, and on descriptions of projects of U.N. agencies throughout the world. Each of these programs runs 15 minutes. The first two are taped and distributed weekly either by diplomatic pouch to U.N. offices in each country or by airmail directly to the stations. "Scope," however, is less topical and so is sent out once a month on disc in sets of four programs per disc.

Summaries of meetings at U.N. headquarters are relayed daily by short wave during the General Assembly, and weekly during interassembly periods. Important General Assembly and Security Council sessions are covered live. The United Nations has no transmission facilities of its own. It depends on facilities leased to it under preferential terms by France, Italy, Switzerland, and the United States. Africa is covered by U.S. shortwave transmitters in Greenville, North Carolina; Tangier, Morocco; and Monrovia, Liberia. African radio organizations either record these live transmissions for delayed broadcast or rebroadcast them directly. Most of them use this service only periodically, when matters of special interest and urgency are up for discussion.

In 1972, the New York staff of U.N. Radio consisted of 37 members— some appointed directly by their governments, others recruited independently but with their appointments subject to the approval of their governments. The facilities of U.N. Radio included seven radio and three television studios in its New York headquarters and three radio studios in Geneva.

11   Religious Broadcasting

In this chapter, the term "religious broadcasting" refers not only to that small percentage of local religious programming routinely scheduled by most broadcast services, but more essentially to international missionary broadcasting. The subject of international missionary broadcasting follows on the heels of the chapter on international political broadcasting because the two enterprises are analogous. Without comparing them invidiously, one may point out that each seeks to persuade and to aid; each varies in style from outright propagandizing/proselytizing to straightforward informing/educating; and each introduces an element from the outside into a nation's broadcast program options—whether in the form of a prepackaged science talk from the BBC or an exhortation from Billy Graham, whether news as the Voice of America sees it or news as the Voice of the Gospel sees it.

11.1 Islam and Christianity, *by Sydney W. Head*

It is estimated that 37% of the African population adheres to ancestral religious faiths, 33% to the Muslim religion, 29% to Christianity, and 2% to other immigrant religions (*Britannica Book of the Year* 1972, p. 613). There is no evidence that the indigenous religions are making converts, but Christians and Muslims vigorously proselytise each other as well as the so-called pagans. Indeed, the literature of some of the Christian fundamentalist sects suggests that they prize the conversion of a Muslim more highly than the conversion of a pagan.

Islam as a missionary force was there first, of course. Once established in the seventh century in North Africa, along the Mediterranean coast, Islam began to follow the trade routes southward, traveling with the caravans across the Sahara and thence down the great western rivers to the Atlantic, and on the dhows down the Red Sea and Indian Ocean coasts. Thus by modern times Islam dominated the first tier of Sub-Saharan states, reaching entirely across the continent—from Mauritania in the west, through Mali, Niger, and Chad to the Sudan in the east. It also reached down the coasts, in the east as far south as Moçambique, in the west as far south as the Ivory Coast.

The continued spread of Islam in more recent times may be ascribed less to organized missionary work from outside the continent than to the adaptability of its propagators and to Islam's relative compatibility with immemorial African folkways. Compared with Christian dogma, Islam's has seemed less destructive of traditional culture and less intolerant of fundamental customs, such as polygamy. Moreover, its advocates have been personally less alien: "Lacking any formal hierarchy . . . with no exclusivistic tradition of expatriate appointment, there was little or no barrier to the recruitment and training of local teachers to spread the faith" (Lewis 1966, p. 28). Christian missionaries, on the other hand, have often impressed the Africans as ethnocentric and obdurate. How Africans themselves perceived missionaries, in one region at least, is interestingly documented in Mobley's study *The Ghanaian's Image of the Missionary* (1970). Nor have sectarian rivalries among Christians gone unmarked by African observers. Once intense—and in places even bitter—these counterproductive antagonisms have been largely submerged in ecumenism, as Robertson's survey in §11.2 shows.

Such exceptions as the early Portuguese coastal missions and the attempts by Jesuits to convert the Ethiopians from their Monophysite belief in the sixteenth and seventeenth centuries aside, Christian missionary work in Africa essentially began in the nineteenth century and was linked with the European exploration of the continent. That Christian missionaries either led the major European explorations of the African interior or followed hard on the heels of lay explorers is of course well known; not so well known perhaps is the ironic fact that European explorers often depended on Arab or Arabicized guides, interpreters, traders, soldiers, straw bosses, and servants. These Europeans brought with them, as an integral part of their baggage, the Qur'an as well as the Bible.

Thus Islam continued to spread osmotically, so to speak, without the benefit of—or apparently the need for—highly organized missionary societies to collect funds in distant lands for the support of outposts in "darkest Africa." With the Arab nationalist revival and with broadcasting, however, came a change. Early in the 1960s, Egypt began using its powerful radio facilities to broadcast an effective blend of religious and political propaganda aimed at Tropical Africa. One of its constant themes associated missionaries with Western imperialism: "Islam, especially in Africa, has found Christianity's Achilles heel, its old secular links with the West, which it exploits mercilessly in making 9,000,000 converts in Africa each year" (Cooley 1967, p. 323). The old secular link of the Arabs with the African slave trade seemed not to impair the argument.

In the absence of adequate census information, one can of course dispute the figure of nine million converts a year, but in the 1950s and early 1960s it was widely accepted in the West that Islam was winning the religious contest in Africa. The growth of Christian missionary radio, however, is credited as one of the factors which more recently have tended to equalize the contest (Aske 1971). In fact, radio has encouraged a counterattack.

The significance of radio for Christian efforts at converting Muslims can hardly be exaggerated. Before radio, Islam's closed society, especially its exclusion of women from public life, made Christian proselytizing virtually impossible. A veteran Christian pastor working in a predominantly Muslim country is quoted as saying he welcomed deaths among his parishioners. In explanation of this startling hyperbole, he went on, "Preaching the Gospel on the street-corners is not allowed. We cannot invite our Muslim neighbors to church. Only when somebody dies do people from the community come to church and we can witness to our faith. But now . . . Radio Voice of the Gospel will proclaim—without police permission or government visa—the Gospel of Christ behind drawn curtains and shut doors" (LWF 1970, p. 91). Another veteran missionary of a different church put it this way: "Each new transistor radio becomes a prospective missionary for Jesus Christ. Gospel broadcasting is new in the lands of Islam. . . . Most important it is private. A person can listen to the radio without stigma or public intimidation" (Reed and Grant 1968, p. 149).

Broadcasting thus takes on a special role in the work of the Christian missionary, a role for which there is no exact parallel in Islam's use of the medium. Egypt's Islamic broadcasts may be regarded as exceptional because of their political motivation. News reports in 1972 spoke of plans to build a short-wave station in West Africa devoted solely to Islamic teaching (*Rundfunk und Fernsehen* 1972a, p. 102), but the announcement came from the small Ahmadiyya sect of Pakistan, known for its anti-Christian propaganda in Africa and for its lack of wide support in the Islamic community because of its unorthodox doctrines (Trimmingham 1964, pp. 109–11).

It seems unlikely that the growth of Christian missionary broadcasting across national boundaries in and to Africa will be countered soon by similar broadcasting activity on the part of Islam. The challenge may come, instead, from changing concepts of the acceptable role of the missionary in maturing independent Africa. The nineteenth-century career missionary, secluded in his bungalow "on the hill," may be no more anachronistic than the foreign white evangelist, secluded in his recording studio in Europe or America, exhorting Africans from afar. "We don't need missionaries any more," a Zaïrian Methodist minister is quoted as saying, "but we need brothers who come and work with us" (Fiske 1972). To those two traditional good works of missionaries, medicine and education, should be added broadcasting—a field which can serve not only those activities, but many others as well. That is the kind of development strongly emphasized by the Lutheran station in Ethiopia, whose policy of active service in such work as agricultural education is described by Aske in § 11.3.

In § 11.2.1 Robertson describes the practice of incorporating Christian religious program elements into the regular schedules of government stations. A comparable religious use of government broadcast facilities occurs, of course, in Islamic countries as well; there, however, religion has official status, or at least close identification with government. The broadcast day opens with recitations from the Qur'an, Friday services are broadcast from a mosque, and major holidays such as the 'Id al Fitr following Ramadan are specially celebrated on radio and television. Some of the transitional states between North Africa and the tropics, where large Muslim populations are found, schedule both Muslim and Christian religious programs.

11.2 Christian Broadcasting in and to Africa, *by E. H. Robertson*

To understand how Christian broadcasting in and to Africa is coordinated, it helps to know something about the two major international religious organizations involved. Roman Catholic broadcasting interests are represented by the Association Catholique Internationale pour la Radiodiffusion et la Télévision. This association has a head office in Switzerland and members in some 30 African states and territories. The World Association for Christian Communication was formed in 1968, when it brought together a number of earlier organizations concerned with broadcasting and other media. Its head office is in London. The WACC is ecumenical, with membership open to individuals as well as to churches, communications agencies, and religious associations. African membership includes some 30 individuals in 12 countries, as well as a dozen Africa-based corporate members, such as the All Africa Conference of Churches (Kenya), the Nigerian Broadcasting Corporation, and TELE-STAR in Zaïre. The WACC has supported with advice, the supplying of expert personnel, and fund raising a number of major projects throughout Africa, several of which are discussed in the ensuing sections.

Christian broadcasting reaches African listeners by means of three main avenues. The most frequent avenue is the government broadcasting service of a given country, which, either at its own expense or with the financial help of the churches, broadcasts a certain amount of devotional or other religious material to its national audience. Less frequently one finds in African countries church-initiated production centers that are outside government broadcasting systems in terms of production control, but still

The Reverend E. H. Robertson is Associate Director, World Association for Christian Communication, London; Secretary General, Ecumenical Satellite Commission. He was formerly Assistant Head of Religious Broadcasting, BBC; and Study Secretary, United Bible Societies, Geneva.

dependent in terms of transmission. Still less frequently one finds complete, independent broadcasting stations supported and controlled by religious bodies; these may be localized stations serving limited areas within given countries, or international stations serving several neighboring countries and even, in a few cases, more than one continent.

11.2.1 Religious Programming on Government Systems

During colonial days it was natural that broadcasting stations established by colonial governments should offer time to representatives of the churches which had done a great deal to explore and open up Africa to Western influences. By the same token, it seemed possible that newly independent nations might feel less inclined to donate time on their national broadcasting systems to such religious organizations. In fact, the opposite happened: "Religious groups have been offered twice to six or seven times as much broadcast time as the colonial governments had allotted them" (Maclin 1966, p. 54). That being the case, it became a question how proffered time could be most usefully employed. What mechanism of program production is most likely to achieve desired results?

The general pattern in English-speaking countries of Africa has been the formation of a department or other unit within a government broadcasting system to be responsible for religious programming. Nigeria set up such a department in 1952, with the support of the main Christian religious bodies of the country, but staffed at the expense of the Nigerian Broadcasting Corporation. The Nigerian practice follows closely the BBC precedent, with such offerings as its morning "Family Prayers," acceptable alike to Roman Catholics, Anglicans, Baptists, Methodists, and the Salvation Army. An alternative approach is that adopted in Zambia, where the Religious Department of the national broadcasting system is staffed by churchmen whose salaries are paid by their respective mission boards, while the Zambian Broadcasting Services provides the production facilities. The choice between these alternative modes of production control troubles churchmen in all of English-speaking Africa: How much control can you get without paying for it?

11.2.2 Production Centers

Multimedia Zambia. The Zambian experience also includes the notion of a production center independent of the national broadcasting system. Multimedia Zambia, founded in 1970 after a long gestation period, co-ordinates the use of the several mass media for religious communication (Carpenter 1971, p. 36). In 1972, Multimedia Zambia included, in addition to the Religion Department of the Zambia Broadcasting Services with its staff of four, a library of audiovisual aids and films staffed by a volunteer, a publicity section with a staff of three, and a publications section with a staff of two. This undertaking, which is totally ecumenical, has strong government support, as shown by the following excerpts from a letter written by the permanent secretary of the ministry which controls broadcasting in Zambia:

> . . . the increased tempo of general development in the country has made the Churches feel the necessity to improve and, where possible, increase their participation and performance in mass communication. Evidence of this can be seen in their efforts to train their communication staff and in the establishment of Multimedia Zambia, which acts not only as a co-ordinating agency, but also as a production centre for material to be channeled into the various avenues of mass communication. The Churches have also now established their own newspaper. . . .
>
> The Churches' communication plans, like their plans in other areas of the social life of Zambia, are in every way Church plans and not Government plans. . . .
>
> The Churches' co-ordinated effort in Multimedia Zambia should complement this Ministry's work in providing suitable locally produced material for use in the communication services. In this way, this particular project does fit in to the overall development plans of the country in this area. [Multimedia Zambia 1972, pp. 3–4]

This letter is also significant for the care with which it defines the limits of freedom allowed the churches: when their work complements that of the government media and coordinates with government plans, the churches are encouraged and actively assisted (see § 7.1.2 for other comments on Multimedia Zambia).

TELE-STAR. There is nothing else quite like TELE-STAR in Africa. Although originally a Catholic foundation, TELE-STAR became fully ecumenical, supported by both the Episcopal Council (Catholic) and the Protestant Council of Zaïre. In 1971–72 it produced over a thousand radio and several hundred television programs for release over the Zaïre national broadcasting system (see § 6.4). These productions were not explicitly religious, though based on Christian principles; they dealt with such educational areas as health, agriculture, youth problems, and the emancipation of women. The subjects meet with Zaïre government approval, for TELE-STAR works in closest collaboration with the national broadcasting system. The radio section of TELE-STAR was inaugurated in 1963 in Lubumbashi, and by 1965 it was being served by five regional production units located at Mbandaka, Kisangani, Luluabourg, Bukavu, and Mbuji-Mayi. Each of these regional studios had a staff of five, one of whom was a European. The main studio had a staff of 21, including two European clergymen with training responsibilities. The television section opened in 1969 in Kinshasa with a staff of 69, including 11 Europeans and 15 Belgian-trained Africans. New production facilities in Kinshasa were inaugurated in 1972 (§ 6.4).

In 1972 the Zaïre government began taking steps to loosen the hold of the church on national social life, the Catholic church having played a prominent role in the country's educational system during colonial times (*New York Times,* 8 May 1972). Apparently in a move to avoid difficulties that might arise from its religious affiliations, in the same year, TELE-STAR converted itself into a secular nonprofit corporation (§ 6.4).

Feeder studios. Radio Voice of the Gospel, Station ETLF, is the Lutheran World Federation's international station in Addis Ababa, Ethiopia (discussed in §§ 11.2.3 and 11.3). It depends for most of its broadcast material on local production studios in its target countries. These studios supply ETLF with radio programs on tape. They are recorded in the local languages, adapted in form and content for local consumption. RVOG uses seven such feeder studios in Africa. The Lutherans sponsor five of them, located in Moshi, Tanzania; Jos and Uyo, Nigeria; Antsirabe, Malagasy Republic; and Addis Ababa, Ethiopia; and two in Cameroon are supported by the World Association for Christian Communication, at N'gaoundéré and Yaoundé. These production studios airmail their taped material to RVOG in Addis Ababa, which in turn sends them back via broadcast. This roundabout procedure is important to the religious groups concerned because it gives them at least relative freedom from government control and supervision, in comparison with the situation of groups entirely dependent upon time donated to them on local government facilities.

The Sudan Interior Mission is the largest evangelical missionary society in Africa, in number of missionaries in the field. Its international station in Liberia, Station ELWA, uses the same feeder-studio technique for obtaining locally relevant broadcast materials. ELWA obtains taped materials from studios in Ethiopia, Guinea, Ivory Coast, Nigeria, Sierra Leone, Tanzania, and Zaïre (ELWA is discussed further in §§ 5.4.1 and 11.2.3).

Other production studios. There are scores of small production studios scattered about Africa, particularly in French-speaking parts of the continent where churches often get time on national broadcasting systems on the condition that they bring in prepackaged programs. Sometimes these production facilities are of the most primitive sort, consisting of no more than a home type of tape recorder set up in a back room. In 1972 the World Association for Christian Communication initiated a survey to ascertain the location, resources, and needs of such minimal production facilities. The WACC also planned to hold a French-speaking regional production workshop every two years.

11.2.3 Church-related Stations in Africa

Church-sponsored local stations have a long history in Africa, especially in the Francophone countries. There the Catholic church often had major official educational responsibilities, sometimes with the help of colonial government subsidies. The number of such stations has declined since independence, however.

Radio CORDAC. One can distinguish three types of church- or mission-related stations: local stations of the type just described, international stations sited within Africa, and international stations sited outside the continent. Among the first group Burundi's Radio CORDAC may be mentioned, although it is to some extent international in scope since it considers that the neighboring states also provide part of its target audience. CORDAC, which is described in more detail in § 4.4.1, is a missionary station with international Protestant support. It devotes about a third of its broadcast time to educational and cultural programming.

ELWA. We have already mentioned the two large, international missionary stations located within Africa—ELWA in Liberia, and RVOG-ETLF in Ethiopia. Both broadcast in a number of languages, both depend primarily on local feeder studios of the type previously described for their program materials, and both beam programs to all parts of Africa and to other continents as well. Their styles differ considerably, however. ELWA ("Eternal Love Winning Africa") is an Evangelical station founded by the Sudan Interior Mission in 1954 near Monrovia, the capital of Liberia (see § 5.4.1). It occupies a hundred acres along the Atlantic shore, donated by the Liberian government in the person of its late president, William S. Tubman. ELWA offers a domestic service for Liberia in English and local languages and an external service aimed at West, Central, and North Africa and the Middle East. As the last two targets suggest, one of the major goals of ELWA is the conversion of Muslims. "No one is more aware of the growth of Islam in recent years than the ELWA staff. The Supreme Islamic Council, headquartered in Cairo with its Al Azhar University, is training and sending out hundreds of missionaries a year" (Reed and Grant 1968, p. 148). In 1968 ELWA installed two new transmitters to strengthen its signal in "the areas of greatest conflict between the Prophet of Allah and the Christ of God" (Reed and Grant 1968, p. 149).

Altogether, the Sudan Interior Mission station broadcasts in some 50 languages, which makes it impossible to sustain a program service in any one language for more than a short period. Most vernacular services are scheduled for only 15 minutes at a time (*WRTH* 1972, p. 117). The station programs features, music, serial dramas, and religious spot announcements. Nearly all the programming has a strong religious content.

RVOG. The second major Africa-based international missionary station, Radio Voice of the Gospel, started in Addis Ababa, Ethiopia, in 1963. Originally, two Protestant groups applied for the franchise from the Ethiopian government; they agreed that the group that received the franchise would share it with the other. The Lutheran World Federation, headquartered in Geneva, Switzerland, won permission of Ethiopia and thus became the owner and operator of RVOG; it promptly granted half its external-service time to the Near East Christian Council. Later the partnership was broadened to include several other international church groups, which achieve a single voice through membership in the Department for Church-related Communication of the World Association for Christian Communication. Thus RVOG has an extremely wide and highly organized base in Africa as well as outside the continent. In 1972 LWF was considering adding television to its local services in Addis Ababa at the request of the Ethiopian government (Volz 1972, 2:1). The technical facilities of RVOG are described in § 3.1.7, and its philosophy of programming in § 11.3.

Although RVOG depends for the bulk of its programming on feeder studios, it produces daily news programs in a dozen languages from its own studios in Addis Ababa. It has a highly competent, professional news department. Much of its programming, as explained by Aske in § 11.3, is aimed at assisting the social and economic development of its listeners. The main feature distinguishing RVOG from similar religious broadcasting organizations is thus a programming policy which gives high prority to what might be called "electronically mediated good works," as well as to evangelism. This emphasis seems to be in keeping with general trends in the missionary movement. As a Catholic church official expressed it, "There is more emphasis on serving the whole man, not simply his spiritual needs. We're preaching Christian values through works of social betterment" (Fiske 1972).

The fulfillment of these programming goals implies a high level of professionalism in writing and production, and another distinguishing feature of ETLF is the intensity of its training effort. Training at the Addis Ababa studios is a year-round affair. Though it is expensive to do so, the managers of feeder studios are brought to Addis Ababa for consultation and brushing up on technique at the ETLF studios once every two years; in the intervening years representatives of the Addis Ababa studio tour the feeder studios to troubleshoot and offer on-the-job training.

FEBA. The Far East Broadcasting Association has a transmitter site in the Seychelles Islands, a British colony in the Indian Ocean off Kenya (§ 9.3.1). Although a thousand miles from the African mainland, the Seychelles are usually classified politically with Africa. FEBA's target areas are India, Pakistan, the Middle East, and the East Coast of Africa (Winter 1971, p. 23).

11.2.4 Church-related Stations outside Africa

Beyond the confines of Africa, two major international religiously oriented stations beam programs into the continent: Vatican State Radio and Trans World Radio.

Radio Vaticana. The Vatican State's service, Radio Vaticana, has been called "the first truly international radio," having been started in 1931 with a 10-kw. short-wave transmitter given to the pope by the inventor of radio himself, Guglielmo Marconi (Onder 1971, p. 43). In 1972 the

Vatican had six short-wave transmitters ranging in power from 25 kw. to 100 kw., as well as medium-wave facilities. The Vatican beamed programs to Africa in Arabic, English, "Ethiopian" (Amharic and Tigrinya, according to Onder), French, and Portuguese.

Trans World Radio. Actually started in Africa, in the international zone of Tangier in 1954, Trans World Radio had to find another site when Morocco became independent. It reached an agreement with Radio Monte Carlo in Monaco to share its transmitter site. In 1971 TWR had two 100-kw. short-wave transmitters there, as well as short-wave transmitters of 50 kw. and 260 kw. and a medium-wave transmitter of 500 kw. on the island of Bonaire in the Netherlands Antilles. Trans World broadcasts religious programming exclusively, much of it consisting of sponsored fundamentalist syndicated series. Its target audiences are mainly in Europe, but as of 1971 it addressed short program services in Arabic and Berber to North Africa, and a daily half-hour program in Zulu to southern Africa (*WRTH* 1972, pp. 78–79). TWR planned a third transmitter site in southern Africa in 1972, from which it intended to broadcast in several local languages of that region (*Rundfunk und Fernsehen* 1971b, p. 373).

Altogether, Africa is well covered by religious broadcasting, from within and from without. It is not evenly distributed, however, and not all the major African languages are used to an adequate extent. The technical facilities exist, however, and it seems doubtful whether there is need, from the Christian broadcaster's point of view, to add substantially to present transmission capacity. The main need in Africa at this stage is not so much hardware as personnel capable of using existing hardware to the best advantage.

11.2.5 Training

The skills required for effective religious broadcasting do not differ fundamentally from those required for other kinds of broadcasting. However, most of the training opportunities open to government employees in Africa are not open to nongovernment personnel, and therefore an urgent need exists for training facilities available to all persons who wish to work in religious broadcasting.

The most important such facility, as of 1972, was the All Africa Conference of Churches Training Centre in Nairobi, Kenya. The center's beginnings go back to 1961, when some 90 delegates from Africa, Europe, and North America met at the Mindolo Ecumenical Center in Zambia to consider how the churches of Africa could make better use of the mass media of communication in their work. After a great deal of committee work and some preliminary trials of courses, the AACC decided that Nairobi seemed to offer the best facilities, the necessary stability, and the convenience in terms of travel to serve as the site for a regional training center. Starting in 1965, the AACC Nairobi center held a radio-production course each year, usually five to six months in duration, with an average of about 15 students in residence the whole time. In the period 1966–71 the center graduated 69 students, representing 26 countries, 19 of them African. The ecumenical nature of the center is attested to by the fact that these students represented no less than 18 Christian denominations, ranging from Ethiopian Orthodox to Assembly of God, from Roman Catholic to Seventh Day Adventist (AACC, May, 1972). Initially, the center's work was confined to radio. It was planned, however, to start installing television studio facilities in 1973, with the next year as the target date for the start of television training. The training center is headed by Canon Yinka Olumide, a highly experienced African broadcaster from the Nigerian Broadcasting Corporation.

Not every prospective trainee can leave his work for six months; nor do all need such extensive and intensive training. To answer these more limited needs, the center offers shorter courses and also sends out members of its staff to conduct such courses at the studios where the trainees already work. To supplement such short-term courses, WACC published a radio training manual, which is widely used in developing countries (Milton 1968).

At the Nairobi training center the common linguistic denominator is English. Similar facilities are needed in the French-speakng area, and the WACC was planning in 1972 to conduct a series of workshops in that area to identify its needs.

There still remains the need for a more sophisticated setting in which to train the future top leaders of communication in Africa. The WACC undertakes the training abroad of about 15 leading communicators from developing countries, mostly Africans, each year. This course takes advantage of the opportunities for training described in chapter 14, such as those provided by the BBC and CEDO, along with attachments to ongoing broadcasting organizations.

The AACC-WACC training activities described here represent only one example, though perhaps the leading one, of such activities. Virtually all the religiously oriented broadcasting activities of any size in Africa, such as those mentioned earlier in this section, have integral training components. In addition, of course, there are many secular government-sponsored training activities.

11.3 A Program Philosophy for Religious Broadcasting, by Sigurd Aske

Free time on national radio and television stations is normally made available for church services and devotions in traditional patterns inherited

Sigurd Aske is General Director, Lutheran World Federation Broadcasting Service, Geneva, and he was the first director of Radio Voice of the Gospel in Addis Ababa.

from colonial days. The churches using such time may have their own underlying broadcast philosophies, but the full freedom to spell out those philosophies, together with the backup power to put them into practice, seems to be a prerogative of the private, church-owned stations. As far as the Roman Catholic church goes, this means Radio Vaticana plus smaller, local stations in Africa. It would be only partly correct to conclude from this pattern that the Roman Catholic church does its most effective broadcasting for Africa from Rome, projecting an image of official spokesmanship. The fact is that the local Roman Catholic stations and, above all, the local Roman Catholic programs, do a far better job of identifying with the cultures and people in the area of broadcast than Radio Vaticana.

Government stations, by alloting free time to the church for programs with predetermined program formats, have, purposely or not, gently ushered church broadcasting away from many of the burning issues in national development, education, and nation building. For the private stations, however, freedom of format, approach, and content is most challenging. The concrete example of Radio Voice of the Gospel in Addis Ababa illustrates a way of meeting this challenge. RVOG is owned and operated by the Lutheran World Federation Broadcasting Service, in affiliation with the World Association for Christian Communication and The Lutheran Hour (for the history of RVOG, see Van Deusen 1968). The station transmits on two 100-kw. short-wave transmitters, feeding specially constructed curtain antennas. It uses 13 languages and directs its signals to the major parts of Africa except the northwest. A smaller, medium-wave transmitter covers Addis Ababa itself (see § 3.1.7).

RVOG's philosophy of broadcasting can be spelled out in the following seven points:

1. With the exception of news (see point 6), all programs are produced locally by the churches in the areas where the programs are heard, rather than produced by the station itself. RVOG has thus avoided two common pitfalls in missionary radio: (a) the building up of a "radio city" type of operation, in which station staff and friends preach to the world; and (b) the importation of sermons by prophets from afar. RVOG accepts no programs made in Europe for European audiences or from America for American audiences.

2. Broadcasts are planned for transmission to a given area only when at least a daily half hour of transmitter time is available, and only when the programs can be transmitted on the same frequency and at the same time each day. For this period each day RVOG becomes that area's own "local" station. The actual location of the transmitters is irrelevant, and perhaps even unknown, to the listeners. What matters is that, with regularity, programs relevant to local needs and produced by the local church are heard in its own area in the listener's own language.

3. The program content is balanced according to what has come to be

known as the "30–70" principle. The "70" indicates that 70% of the total programming is devoted to broad informational, educational subjects, while only 30% is devoted to programming directly evangelistic in character and format. The whole spectrum of program ideas and formats—entertainment, information, and education—has a legitimate place. But all programs attempt to present material appropriate to the listener's own surroundings and relevant to his own problems and interests. Education takes priority over entertainment, to help meet the crying need in Africa, where in some countries far less than 50% of school-age children receive formal education. To these children, and to millions of adults, the mass media, and especially radio, can mean free education not otherwise obtainable, often even at any price, because the facilities simply do not exist.

4. Audience research and audience relations at RVOG warrant a separate department headed by professional staff which attempts to do serious research in the area of listener situation and response. Research findings provide a rational basis for formulating broadcast strategy and program approach (Radio Voice of the Gospel 1972).

5. Training has from the very beginning been part and parcel of RVOG's operation. The station has benefited from wide support, ranging from ITU-sponsored technical courses to scholarships from overseas broadcasting agencies such as the BBC, Radio Nederland, Deutsche Welle, Radio Denmark, and the ORTF of France. The station itself and related church agencies have also provided professional training. Training is, in fact, not looked upon as something extra, but as an ongoing concern, an integral part of the station's operation.

6. News broadcasting serves a large and interested audience, as research studies have amply shown. RVOG's news policy of nonsensational and factual world news tailored to regional audiences is respected and appreciated. Its emphasis on international news, on news without comment, and on news in national focus—all presented by highly professional radio journalists—has established RVOG's reputation in this field. When the United Nations Security Council met in Addis Ababa early in 1972, RVOG was explicitly asked to provide news coverage of its sessions, which for the first time were being held in Africa.

7. Economic development is receiving strong emphasis in the 1970s by RVOG. This important new role has been recognized by the Development Service of the German Evangelical churches, which has made grants to cover about 25% of the station's total operational budget. The station's role in aiding development has also been recognized by the United Nations Economic Commission for Africa, which, after a symposium entitled "Rural Development in Africa," held in Addis Ababa in the summer of 1971, asked RVOG to cooperate with the ECA in the production of special development programs. In 1971 RVOG accordingly began the preparation of a monthly series of 12 programs on such topics as rural water develop-

ment, the improvement of agricultural practices, farmer cooperatives, fish farming, and improved methods of food storage. It was planned that these programs would be aimed at the "decision makers"—influential persons in their respective rural communities who themselves could serve as multipliers by communicating concern and know-how to others.

An excerpt from an internal memo from RVOG's general director to its news staff on the role of RVOG perhaps sums up the station's general program philosophy:

. . . in a very humble way RVOG strives to serve the nations of Africa, the Near East and Asia. Stupendous tasks in the general field of education and nation-building confront all the nations within RVOG's target areas.

Tackling this task, RVOG does so not as a European or an American station, speaking into these areas from the outside. Nor should it be done from a bystander's detached point of view. RVOG is a station located in the very heart of Africa.

The matter of approach can hardly be overemphasized. We do not represent a station delighting in critical analyses of situations with which it is not the least concerned. Each program should breathe insight, understanding, concern. An air of condescending superiority, of cold cleverness or sarcastic smartness must be banned from any program broadcast over RVOG. We want to be of help, and help can only be given in an atmosphere of understanding and genuine sympathy.

There is a growing acceptance of the fact that the new media are the most important education-information channels. Schooling and learning can no longer be confined to a formal, examination-graded, year-limited system. Education is lifelong, the home is the center, and the family becomes more and more involved as the primary unit of society.

Some may conclude that this conception refers more to the future in the Western World than to the present in Africa. If so, they are mistaken. In many ways Kenya and Ethiopia are better suited as the electronic educational community of the future than is the United States or Germany, where for so long the processes of the mechanical age have profoundly affected home life and group activities. The community of the Africa of tomorrow, it seems to me, will be family centered and media focused. It ought to be possible, and may in fact be urgently necessary, to formulate a media-conscious cultural strategy for developing (1) an educational system with decentralization as a conscious goal (not a de facto evil), with the local school functioning as a culture center for the community; and (2) an open, comprehensive, and flexible educational community where the school is more concerned with creating roles than with imparting knowledge. In the light of such goals must the future role of religious broadcasting in Africa be seen.

12   Bilateral Foreign Aid

As the histories of individual broadcasting systems described in part 1 of this book show, virtually all African broadcasting services originated as colonial undertakings. The colonial powers saw to it that their own manufacturers and institutions had either a monopoly or heavily preferential treatment in their colonies. Independence destroyed, or at least weakened, these colonial economic and ideological monopolies. Released from paternalistic tutelage, African leaders found satisfaction in exercising freedom of choice, sometimes perhaps for its own sake, without regard to the relative merits of the ideas or goods selected. Offers of aid from Communist countries were sometimes welcomed, not necessarily because of any commitment to Communist ideology, but for the sheer pleasure of exercising independent choice and (one suspects) of watching former masters squirm.

That these exercises in free choice sometimes backfired is evidenced by the number of diplomats, technicians, and media personnel whom African countries at first welcomed but later expelled. The media represent, of course, a tempting target to any cold-war strategist. In the main however, African governments have been wary of surrendering media control to foreign ideologies—have, in fact, shown a shrewd ability to neutralize them by playing one country against another.

In the postindependence scramble for influence over the mass media, Britain and France continued as major sources of developmental assistance in most of their former colonies. Instead of the piecemeal approach of other countries, France offered more-or-less standardized development packages through a single specialized aid organization, successively SORAFOM, OCORA, and ORTF, as described in § 6.1.3. Among other Western countries Canada, the United States, and West Germany have been particularly active in giving broadcasting assistance. Japan has become a force in African broadcasting as a result of success in marketing transistor radios, some of which are assembled in Africa. Since 1961, NHK, Japan's national broadcasting corporation, has offered annual engineering and programming courses to trainees from developing countries; and toward the end of the

215

1960s Japan began technical-cooperation projects in Africa, notable among which is long-term assistance to the expansion of Uganda's television network, starting in 1968 (letter from Roku Ito, NHK, 3 December 1971). In January 1972 Japan agreed to make a loan to Zambia and to assist in a major overhaul of its information system (*African Journalist* 1973). In November 1972 a Japanese team began a six-week survey in Ghana looking toward major extensions of the television service there.

Among Communist countries, the USSR and Czechoslovakia took an early lead. They particularly favored journalism training and assistance to national news agencies, which gave an excuse for introducing Tass and other Communist, state-controlled news services. For example, Communist advisers gained influence over Kenya's national news agency for a while in the early 1960s, and for a time Tass had priority of place in the official newsfile released by the Ministry of Information. But as an instructor who was teaching in the International Press Institute's journalist-training school in Nairobi at the time remarked, "six months of handling some of the copy which Tass sends out invariably had the effect of levelling the views of any extreme left-winger" (Barton 1969, p. 68). Initial Bloc broadcasting aid in Tropical Africa went to Ghana, Guinea, and Mali. In 1961, nine African countries received media assistance of various kinds from China, Czechoslovakia, East Germany, Poland, and the USSR (USIA 1962, pp. 44–47). Among other recipients of Communist broadcasting aid mentioned in part 1 are Algeria, the Congo, Guinea, Somalia, the Sudan, Tanzania, and Zambia.

The sources and varieties of bilateral aid to African broadcasting are far too numerous to list exhaustively—even if donor and recipient countries were always willing to supply full information. This chapter describes programs of Canada, Great Britain, the United States, and West Germany as examples of bilateral developmental-assistance programs to African broadcasting.

12.1 Great Britain, *by J. F. Wilkinson*

[EDITOR'S NOTE. British assistance to African broadcasting comes from many sources, public and private, some of which are discussed in chapter 14. The most logical and efficient single instrument of official British bilateral aid, however, has been the British Broadcasting Corporation. Its independent status and (formerly, at least) its monopolistic position in some ways made it ideal for the purpose. The BBC could act as the transmission belt for British aid funds without being regarded as an arm of the British government, first vis-à-vis colonial governments, later

J. F. Wilkinson has been Head, BBC African Service, since 1969 and was the first Controller of the Nigerian Northern Regional Service, 1950–56; he was in charge of the Nigerian National Programme, Lagos, 1956–58, and for the next ten years served as African Programme Organiser for the BBC.

vis-à-vis independent African governments. And as the sole source both of all officially sanctioned external broadcasting services and until recently of all domestic services as well, the corporation had the accumulated experience and resources and, perhaps more important, the single-mindedness to perform the aid function with superlative efficiency.]

In 1927, the year before Kenya broadcasting began, there was not a single public-service radio station broadcasting in what we now know as "Black Africa." There is no evidence that a single African on the continent owned a radio set at that time. By 1972 there were 43 national sound-radio services, 21 television services, nearly 15 million radio sets, and a quarter-million television sets.

The BBC's contribution to this growth falls into three main categories: first, the development of direct transmissions to Africa, which have set the professional standard that listeners to BBC News Bulletins and programs appreciate and respect; second, the secondment of experienced BBC staff, who have played a major part in the development of most of the broadcasting services in English-speaking Africa; and third, the provision of training at home and abroad, which is covered in § 14.2.1.

12.1.1 Colonial Broadcasting Policy

The first official recognition of the role the BBC was to play came in 1937 when a committee was set up by the British government under the earl of Plymouth to study colonial broadcasting and to recommend ways of accelerating its development and of coordinating it with the BBC's operations (Great Britain 1937, p. 1). The BBC had been devoting considerable expenditure to what was then called the "Empire Service"—later renamed "Overseas Services"—ascertaining the requirements of listeners, and increasing the power of transmissions so as to secure good reception in all parts of the empire. The audience was mainly composed of expatriates in the old dominions of Australia, Canada, and New Zealand, but the BBC Empire Service was also rebroadcast in Africa by stations in Kenya, Sierra Leone, and the Gold Coast. The Plymouth committee pointed out that in the future this kind of radio service would not serve the needs of the indigenous populations. The committee envisaged colonial broadcasting as providing, not only entertainment, but also enlightenment and education. It strongly recommended that, wherever possible, broadcasting activities should be developed in the colonial territories as a public service by the local governments concerned. It also recommended that every possible use should be made of the BBC's Empire Service.

The committee looked into the question of whether the local governments or individual companies would control colonial broadcasting activities and recommended government control; but it suggested that, for the sake of economy, use might be made of the existing technical facilities of the private firm, Cable and Wireless Limited. It was recognized that in certain dependencies it would, in the long run, be embarrassing for the government to be responsible for all programs broadcast, but that in most dependencies the government would have to be the controlling body. The Plymouth committee did not, however, rule out an organization similar to the BBC, and it suggested setting up advisory committees for educational, public-health, and agricultural programs. Bearing in mind the fact that the Plymouth committee's report was published in 1937, we can fairly say that it was a remarkably farsighted document.

The inquiries the Plymouth committee had suggested and the work of choosing suitable frequencies for the colonial stations were in progress when World War II intervened. Although the war put a stop to the rapid spread of broadcasting as envisaged by the Plymouth committee, it did cause some new stations to be built and others to be strengthened. Broadcasting provided the best means for spreading news about the war's progress. It was, for instance, during the war that the BBC started "Calling West Africa" for African listeners, and that station ZOY in Accra began transmitting special programs for African members of the West African Frontier Force.

It took some time to regain momentum after the war. Not until 1948 did the British Colonial Office ask Britain's colonial governments once more to consider whether their existing arrangements for broadcasting were adequate. It emphasized that broadcasting should be operated by governments as a public service, again stressing the point that broadcasting should be the instrument for the social and educational advancement of the *indigenous* populations of colonial territories. The BBC involvement was now becoming so great that a senior member of staff was seconded to the Colonial Office to act as the liaison point with the BBC and to give professional advice. These secondments continued until 1962, by which time the remaining dependent territories were too few to warrant the retention of the post.

The main problem in establishing and developing local broadcasting services was, of course, that of financing the services. Few African territories could afford to devote more than a limited amount, if any, of their resources to broadcasting. Its potential could not be entirely foreseen, and it was not easy to convince local colonial governments that money should be devoted to something as new as broadcasting when there was a desperate shortage of schools and medical services. In 1949, however, the Colonial Office in London gave the final impetus by granting £1 million from Colonial and Development and Welfare funds for broadcast development. The grant was intended primarily to pay the capital cost of transmitting services, but expenditure on developing listening facilities by whatever means practicable was not ruled out. This and subsequent grants in the period 1949–c. 1960, amounting in all to just under £3 million, were mainly spent on Africa. They laid the foundation of African public-broadcasting services as they exist today.

12.1.2 Development of Colonial Systems

Before a broadcasting service can be established a great deal of technical work must be done; so the BBC's Engineering Division was its first division to become heavily involved in Africa itself. Immediately after World War II, BBC engineers began to conduct surveys which were to have a lasting effect on African broadcasting. In 1949, for example, at the request of the Colonial Office, L. W. Turner, a BBC engineer, and F. A. W. Byron of the Telecommunications Department, Crown Agents for the Colonies, made a technical survey of The Gambia, the Gold Coast, Nigeria, and Sierra Leone. Byron had already installed wired broadcasting systems before World War II in both Sierra Leone and the Gold Coast. The Turner/Byron report visualized an ultimate West African broadcasting corporation based in Accra, but it fully recognized that political and cultural as well as technical considerations required the development of individual services in each territory.

In two other respects this report had a lasting influence on West African broadcasting. It drew attention to the superiority of the individual wireless receiver over the community type of receivers and wired loudspeakers which were then almost the only means of listening for Africans, and so linked up with the pioneering work on a special low-cost receiver, the "Saucepan Special," that had been undertaken in Northern Rhodesia (§ 7.1.1). It also emphasized the importance of professional training and so looked forward to the special courses in broadcast program and engineering techniques that the BBC later arranged, and still arranges, for the African broadcaster; and to the local training schools which are essential parts of the organization of the larger broadcasting services in Africa itself.

The technical surveys having been completed, the practical development of the African broadcasting services began in earnest in the early 1950s, and the BBC became even more heavily involved. The development of broadcasting in Nigeria illustrates the extent of this involvement and the role of the BBC staff concerned.

In 1950, the BBC seconded a senior BBC executive, T. W. Chalmers, experienced in both production and engineering, to Nigeria. He found that the transmitted-radio service in Nigeria was minimal, but that there were a number of local wired-radio distribution services in some of the big townships (§ 5.1.12). These rediffusion stations were run jointly by the Government Public Relations Department, which was responsible for programs, and the Posts and Telegraphs Department, which was responsible for the technical operations. Although the staffs of both these departments had made the most of very slender resources, they were not professional broadcasters and had many other responsibilities. Therefore they were not capable of providing the coordinated driving force needed to create a new broadcasting service. The task, then, was to create a Nigerian broadcasting service run by Nigerians for Nigerians. This meant the purchase of a vast quantity of studio and transmitting equipment, the training of staff, and the rapid development of program services for all parts of Nigeria. In line with the Plymouth committee recommendations, the Nigerian colonial government decided that the broadcasting service in Nigeria should be developed as an independent public-service corporation on the BBC pattern. This was formed in 1956 (see § 5.1.2).

Between 1950 and 1962 nearly 60 BBC staff were seconded to Nigeria, but it was clearly understood from the start that the objective was the complete Nigerianization of the broadcasting service as rapidly as possible. In fact the task was virtually completed by the early sixties, and by then there was a staff of more than 2,000. This was no small achievement, particularly on the part of the Nigerian broadcasters themselves, who took on tremendous responsibilities very quickly and who later had to face very great pressures.

In 1954 a step which a few years later was to have serious consequences was taken. The Nigerian Constitutional Conference, which led to independence, decided that broadcasting should be a "concurrent subject." In other words, it could be the responsibility of both the federal government and the regional governments. In the early 1960s the premiers of the North, East, and West regions each set up radio, and later TV, stations in regional headquarters, in competition with the regional station of the NBC. The regional premiers and their ministers used their services for their own purposes, with no regard for the cost. The standard of NBC regional broadcasting tended to decline, and the result was that the divisive influences in Nigeria were allowed to foment ill-feeling through these new regional stations. It is my belief that this step, which undermined the unifying influence of a single Nigerian broadcasting system, played an important part in leading Nigeria to the tragedy of the 1967–70 civil war (cf. § 5.1.12). This development illustrates the power of radio and the great importance of ensuring that it is in responsible professional hands. Although they have been subjected to immense problems and pressures, there is still a strong team of professional broadcasters in Nigeria, and as I see it they are determined to develop their services in the national interest rather than in narrowly sectional interest.

I have dwelt at some length on Nigeria as an example of the BBC's involvement in Africa, but the BBC was involved similarly, though on a smaller scale, in Botswana, Ghana, The Gambia, Kenya, Lesotho, Malawi, Sierra Leone, Somalia, Tanzania, Uganda, and Zambia. Apart from BBC engineering and program staff (which includes schools broadcasters), news editors, gramophone librarians, studio operators, accountants, copyright experts, and administrators have all served on secondment in African broadcasting services. As their tasks have been completed their numbers have decreased; yet in 1972 10 BBC staff members were on secondment in Africa, and there were indications that requests for BBC experience would continue to be made for some time to come.

12.1.3 Programs Transmitted to Africa

Throughout the period during which broadcasting services in Africa developed the BBC was, of course, improving its own programs and transmission services for listeners in Africa. The BBC's external services are financed by a British government grant-in-aid which is currently about £ 12 million a year. The cost of BBC services to Africa is charged against this figure. The British government prescribes the languages in which the BBC external services broadcast, and the number of hours each language is on the air. Once a service is prescribed and the financial cost determined, the BBC assumes full responsibility for the running of the service and exercises completely independent editorial control of news bulletins and programs. As an integral part of the BBC, the African Service and other external services operate under the same charter as the BBC's domestic services and share the same traditions.

In 1972 the BBC broadcast in Arabic for North Africa; Hausa, West Africa; Swahili, East Africa; Somali, the Horn of Africa; French, Francophone Africa; and English, the whole of Africa. The Arabic service was the oldest and the largest of the 39 language services still being transmitted by the BBC's external services in 1972. Its first transmissions began in January 1938 and consisted of a 15-minute daily period of news and comment, followed by 45 minutes of European music. By 1972 the service was on the air 10 hours a day with news, talks, features, drama, music, and light entertainment. Its audience ranged from the Atlantic coast of Morocco to the Arabian Sea and included the enormous Arabic-speaking population along the coast of North Africa.

The Hausa, Somali, and Swahili services were introduced in 1957, and in 1972 each was on the air one hour a day. In that limited time they concentrated on world and African news, current affairs, and programs of an educational nature. Listener correspondence is encouraged, and in 1972 the Hausa service received more than 1,000 letters per month; the Swahili service's Maarifa Club ("Knowledge Club") had more than 26,000 members.

The French-language service offers 2½ hours a day of special transmissions for Francophone Africa, similar in content to the three African-language services. Listeners in Africa can also hear the BBC's main French-language transmissions that are broadcast to Europe and Africa simultaneously.

By far the largest program service for Africa is provided by the English transmissions of the BBC World Service, which began as the Empire

Service in 1932, became the General Overseas Service in 1947, was renamed the World Service in 1965. The World Service is on the air 24 hours a day, though of course its transmissions are beamed from one time zone to another. The listener in Africa can hear World Service news bulletins, radio newsreels, commentaries, and other current-affairs programs such as "The World Today," as well as a variety of programs on science, industry, education, agriculture, sport, and of course drama, music, and general entertainment.

It is apparent from the foregoing that many departments in the BBC's domestic and external services provide services and programs for African broadcasting systems. Among the 24,000 members of the BBC staff many have made contributions. It is in this larger BBC context that the work of the BBC's African Service should be seen.

English-speaking listeners in Africa can listen to "News of the African World" and other programs produced especially for them by the BBC African Service. The day begins with "The Morning Show," a lively and controversial "getting up and going to work" program which includes everything from popular music to politics. It runs competitions, some serious and some lighthearted, and provides services for listeners who ask for help and advice.

"Focus on Africa," an African current-affairs program, is broadcast three times an afternoon Monday through Friday. It has its own reporters covering almost every African country. With the use of cables and satellite telephone circuits, reports and interviews are recorded and broadcast with astonishing speed.

Traditionally the BBC African Service has done its best to encourage interest in the arts, and most African authors and poets have contributed to "West African Voices," which began in 1948, or to its successor, "Writers Club," which covered the whole continent. This in turn gave way to "The Arts and Africa," a more wide-ranging program dealing with writing, music, painting, sculpture, and the other arts. Similarly, the monthly "African Theatre" 30-minute radio-drama productions have provided opportunities for African playwrights, actors, and actresses to gain experience. The second "African Theatre" competition, held at the beginning of 1972, resulted in the submission of more than 600 plays by writers from almost every country in Africa. Other African Service programs were "University Report," which linked African and other universities together through reports on research projects, conferences, teaching methods, and academic administration; "Men and Their Money," for African businessmen; "Break for Women"; "This Sporting Life," the only regularly scheduled pan-African sports series; "Postmark Africa," to which African listeners send in questions; and regular press conferences and features presenting personalities and subjects of special interest to Africa.

Needless to say, the rapid changes taking place in Africa mean that the program schedules of BBC English- and foreign-language services to Africa have to be constantly reviewed and reassessed, whenever possible upon consultation with professional colleagues in Africa. Many new BBC contributions to radio listening in Africa have resulted from the cooperation that exists with African broadcasting services.

The staff of the African Service consists of about 80 people solely concerned with providing programs for listeners in Africa. Of these between 30 and 40 are broadcasters from Africa, including four who are on the permanent staff of the BBC. Most of them, however, are on short-term contract and work in the language services. They include secondments from broadcasting services in East and West Africa, who return to their parent organizations; and persons recruited directly, many of whom take up broadcasting as a career and later join their national broadcasting services. Those who decide not to do so return home with wider horizons as a result of working overseas. Former BBC staff can be found among African politicians, senior civil servants, businessmen, and university academics. They exert an important influence in the development of African broadcasting systems.

At any given time four or five experienced broadcasters from African broadcasting services are on working/training attachment for periods of six to nine months with the BBC African Service (§ 14.2.1). During this period they become members of staff and are expected to contribute to programs and take responsibility for productions. Attachments are financed by British Government Technical Assistance and the British Council is responsible for the welfare of attachees during their period with the BBC. Nearly all the British program-production staff in the BBC African Service have worked in Africa for long periods, and a number of them have worked in African broadcasting organizations.

Technical improvements in short-wave transmitting stations in the United Kingdom and the bringing into service of our Atlantic Relay Station on Ascension Island in 1966 have enhanced BBC reception in West, Central, and Southern Africa (§ 9.3.2). North Africa is well covered by short- and medium-wave, direct and relayed transmissions via the East Mediterranean Relay Station. East Africa, however, is another story. Until there is a relay station serving that side of the continent the BBC will suffer at the hands of competitors; with many choices available to him, the African listener is no longer prepared to put up with poor reception.

12.1.4 BBC Programs Transmitted by African Stations

Besides transmitting programs directly to African listeners, the BBC sends programs to them indirectly through African broadcasting organizations which use BBC material to augment their own domestic-program schedules. Sometimes this help is in the form of retransmission of timely material, as in the case of the 26 African national services which relayed, that is, rebroadcast, daily BBC news bulletins and the like in 1972. More numerous, however, are programs sent out from the BBC in the form of transcription discs or tapes. The program series "Topical Tapes," for example, is sent out by airmail each week. In 1972 there were 75 broadcasting organizations on the mailing list, 17 of them in Africa. Each user received one or more of the 19 topics available each week, according to his needs. The programs themselves, mainly in magazine format, deal with such topics as international affairs, with special reference to the Commonwealth; literature and the arts; sports; science development; education; and new research on and techniques to improve health, housing, roads, and agriculture in the tropics. The BBC African Service sends out tapes of special interest to African broadcasting services in English, Hausa, and Swahili. The Hausa and Swahili radiotapes are mainly educational, but the English radiotape programs vary greatly in content; besides African current affairs, they cover such subjects as university developments, items for women listeners, African theater, and series dealing with the economic and political development and the history of Africa. Weekly magazine programs "Calling Nigeria," "Calling Ghana," and "Calling Sierra Leone" are sent, and "English-by-Radio" courses, ranging from elementary to advanced levels, are distributed to nine of the French-speaking countries. All these materials are sent out at no cost to the users except for postage and tape stock (since the tapes are not returned). The BBC Transcription Service, on the other hand, although subsidized by government grant-in-aid, makes a charge to cover some of the costs involved. The service provides materials drawn mainly from BBC domestic programming, such as plays, panels, lectures, and music. The service is sold on an annual subscription basis at rates varying widely, depending on the amount and kind of materials needed.

12.1.5 Future Prospects

A number of my broadcasting colleagues in Africa are concerned that, in Black Africa as a whole, professional standards have fallen; and government control of radio and television services causes constant problems. But, although the distribution of newspapers can be completely banned, no one can stop a strong radio signal from crossing boundaries and reaching people who really want to listen. The African listener is in the happy position of being able to choose. He can tune to his own radio station, to neighboring African stations, and to many other external services broadcasting within Africa itself or from outside Africa to the continent. The encouraging fact is that many African listeners do compare (cp. § 10.3.3). Just as people who are involved in current affairs might read half a dozen newspapers every morning and then draw their own conclusions as to the truth, so the African listener can tune to his own radio station, to neighboring countries, to Moscow, Peking, Deutsche Welle, South Africa, the VOA, or the BBC and then form his own opinion as to the truth of any situation. In the process, when he compares the output of other stations with that of his own service, the listener may ask why he can hear news of his own country from abroad before he hears it on his own service. In some cases he never hears it on his own service. At other times he tunes to a neighboring country's station and finds that it is professionally ahead of his own service, and he wants to know why. So for the first time public opinion is having an effect, and politicians are being pressured to cause an improvement in the professional standards of the national broadcasting services in Africa. This is a healthy trend and is naturally welcomed by African professional broadcasters, in their drive to obtain recognition and support. To those of us in the BBC who have been concerned with the development of broadcasting *in* Africa, this is a welcome development. For those of us broadcasting *to* Africa it represents a challenge which must be met, both in program and in engineering terms.

As to future BBC contributions to African broadcasting services, one challenge is of course the development of television, which will in due course become the dominant partner in African broadcasting services, just as it has in Britain and elsewhere. The Western world as a whole, and Britain in particular, is not paying sufficient attention to this inevitable development. Intelligently used and with money behind it, TV could be a major aid to the development of education and general understanding in Africa. As it is, most of the African TV services suffer from lack of funds, poor equipment, and inadequate training. It is true that the BBC/Overseas Development Administration finances some training, but it merely scratches the surface. A much more determined effort is required.

BBC Television Enterprises is increasing its sales of syndicated programs to Africa. Good though these are, one must question their relevance to the real needs of Africa today. The BBC sends its "English-by-Television" courses to Africa and works with the British Council, the Centre for Educational Development Overseas, and the Overseas Development Administration on ideas that will help to provide educational assistance. But the costs of producing "English-by-Television" have to be recovered, and therefore the BBC tends to tailor it for the richer TV services in Europe. Given financial support, the producers could do far more to meet the needs of African television services. More generally, I feel that the production of many more TV programs specifically for African viewers should be treated as a matter of much greater importance than it is at the moment.

12.2 The United States

To itemize the kinds, amounts, and sources of official American aid to African broadcasting would be extraordinarily difficult, first because of the great number of government and quasi-government organizations involved;

second, because none of those chiefly involved appear to have kept systematic records which would enable sorting out broadcasting activities—or even communications activities generally—from all the rest.

Broadly speaking, bilateral American government broadcasting assistance has fallen into four categories: (1) technical development projects, often involving hardware as well as people, financed by the Agency for International Development; (2) day-to-day contacts on a continuing basis with African media in the field, through the United States Information Agency; (3) assignment of specialized personnel for fixed terms, by the Peace Corps; and (4) "exchange of persons," a two-way flow between Africa and America of students, teachers, technicians, experts, and advisers *as individuals,* rather than as human elements in projects or bureaucratic structures.

12.2.1 Agency for International Development, *by Sydney W. Head*

The United States has no government-related, monolithic broadcasting organization to act as its logical pipeline for broadcasting aid as do other aid-giving countries. The Voice of America's brief does not include running training programs or seconding officers to developing countries as does the BBC's, for example. When the VOA was preparing to open its new African relay station in Liberia in 1964 (§ 5.4.1), thought was given to the possibility of using it also as the base for a major regional broadcast training center, but approval for such an addition to the VOA's primary functions could not be obtained from the U.S. government.

The Agency for International Development was left as the main instrument for providing major official assistance to broadcasting in developing countries. Since it is not itself a broadcasting organization, AID depended for expertise on a variety of sources of varying quality. Until about 1967 AID field offices had their own communications-media divisions which spearheaded media projects, but they in turn had to hire short-term specialists or rely on contractors for major undertakings. After 1967 AID depended entirely on contractors for technical assistance in this area. Ostensibly the host country selected the contractor and negotiated the contract. In practice, however, once a host government had agreed to the general goals of an assistance project and had accepted the proposed contractor, AID specified the detailed terms, which were subject to innumerable legal restraints imposed by Congress. An assistance agreement required the host country to make substantial contributions of its own to the project, but these contributions were often in kind or in the form of cash expenditures that would have been necessary even in the absence of the project.

AID tended to approach broadcasting projects rather gingerly, especially when they extended to the general development of national systems rather than being limited to formal educational uses. The foreign-assistance program has always had its congressional enemies, ready to seize on any example of alleged bumbling or misuse of taxpayer funds. The entertainment, propaganda, and commercial aspects of broadcasting offered rich potentialities for such embarrassment ("taxpayers bring 'I Love Lucy' to uncomprehending tribesmen in African bush"). The propaganda aspects of broadcasting offered such potentialities both domestically ("antidemocratic regime propped up by US-supplied media facilities") and internationally ("gift broadcast transmitters used to oppose American policies"). Nor, apparently, were top American-aid strategists ever convinced of the importance of broadcasting as a developmental tool (cp. chap. 15 on the relative value assigned to educational broadcasting). Not surprisingly, therefore, USAID financed few broadcasting projects in Africa, compared with its overall investment in the continent. Most projects date from the late 1950s and early 1960s, the period of initial rapid growth of American diplomatic involvement in Africa. Thereafter AID phased out its communications-media divisions and accepted fewer and fewer requests for aid to broadcasting.

By the 1970s the United States was reducing its total commitment to foreign aid and changing the direction of what remained. In the mid-1960s AID had bilateral assistance programs in 35 African countries; the 1973 proposed AID budget cut this number down to ten, with the other 25 eligible only for minor assistance to "self-help" projects (USAID 1972 p. 36). The new policy limited assistance to "priority development problems," identified as agriculture and food production, population control, health, and low-cost education. It also placed more reliance than hitherto on contributions to multilateral-assistance programs, primarily those of the United Nations. The foreign-assistance law, however, still held the agency responsible for securing popular participation in development. In its presentation to Congress for the fiscal year 1973, AID said,

Central to the legislation is the proposition that the people of developing nations should be involved in decisions that affect their own lives. . . . Popular participation can be increased by such activities as taxation to improve income distribution, land reform and other government policies to assist the small farmer or businessman. . . . It also requires development or strengthening of a wide variety of institutions which perform economic, social and civic functions at all levels of society. [USAID 1972, p. 35]

Nowhere did AID explicitly recognize that the mass media might constitute an institution capable of helping to "maximize popular participation." The agency did, however, seem to recognize the potential value of the educational applications of broadcasting, for it also reported to Congress:

Research and experimentation with curricula, teaching methodology, and *educational technology* is urgently needed. . . . Recent analyses have underscored the need to experiment with the use of *modern communications techniques* . . . to try to spread quality education to more people at a feasible cost. *New technology* can supplement the job of existing teachers. . . . *Mass communication* can assist in both formal and non-formal education . . . [USAID 1972, p. 32; italics added]

Examples of AID projects. AID's assistance to African broadcasting has consisted primarily of supplying technical advisers, backed up by logistic support and a certain amount of equipment—usually types that could be justified as directly contributing to the training and demonstration functions of the advisers. Larger-scale gifts of facilities such as transmitters have been relatively infrequent, and mostly in aid of radio broadcasting. The conspicuous exception to the radio-only rule was the loan in 1959 of about $12 million to Egypt, in American-owned Egyptian funds on deposit in Egypt, for local expenses in building up the Egyptian television network (Dizard 1966, p. 72). The details of the transaction, which led to an Egyptian contract with RCA (see § 2.1.5), were never made public, but it was apparently not an AID-administered project.

A third element in most AID-financed projects provided for "participant trainees"—host-country nationals designated to fill specific jobs in the AID-assisted activity following specialized training abroad, usually in the United States, but sometimes in a third country. Participant training might vary from a technician's course of a few months to a full university-degree program. A host-country national was also normally assigned by the cooperating country as a "counterpart" to work alongside the American adviser or technician and eventually to take over his functions.

The Sudan. Perhaps AID's most comprehensive media effort took place in the Sudan, starting in 1959 and extending for five years, until 1964. The Sudan AID mission's own Communications Media Division carried out most of the project directly, with contractual help that included a three-man team fielded by the National Association of Educational Broadcasters. In the course of this project the Sudanese Information Ministry acquired first-class facilities and trained personnel for every facet of its operation. Equipment included two 50-kw. short-wave and two 100-kw. medium-wave radio transmitters, which more than tripled the Sudan's wattage; 24 especially constructed cinema vans, designed to operate in remote areas devoid of formal roads; complete facilities for professional motion-picture production; equally complete facilities for still photography; printing facilities for the preparation of information materials; new and much enlarged quarters, including provincial information offices; and much more. On the training side, the AID mission brought in specialists to see that equipment was properly installed and that maintenance procedures were set up. More than 70 Sudanese went abroad, mostly to the United States, for specialized training in every aspect of operations and management. The two-year contract with the NAEB provided services of advisers in radio programming, studio engineering, and transmitter engineering.

The unusual comprehensiveness of the Sudan project was primarily due to the exceptional energy and drive of the local AID mission's communications media officer, Michael Guido. He not only maximized AID's input to the media project; he also persuaded the Sudanese government to make even greater investments from its own funds. AID contributed on the order of $1.5 million, while the Sudanese spent about $2.25 million. Guido's tour of duty had ended by the time of the official dedication of the new transmitter site near Khartoum, but in an unusual gesture of appreciation the Sudanese government invited him to the ceremonies and offered free air passage part of the way.

Ethiopia. As described in § 3.1.6, the United States entered into a broadcasting technical-assistance agreement with Ethiopia in 1957. The three major transmitters involved in this project did not actually go on the air until 1966, but in the meantime AID-Ethiopia's Communications Media Division provided a radio adviser in 1960–61 to assist in upgrading Radio Ethiopia's production and programming capacity in anticipation of the greatly enlarged coverage expected from the new transmitters. Little was accomplished, and the adviser wrote a negative report. Four years later, however, AID agreed to finance a three-phase contract much larger in scope and more sophisticated in conception. The contract was awarded to RTV International, a New York-based consulting firm. The first phase began in 1965 with a one-year, one-man, feasibility and planning study; this was followed by a two-year implementation phase during which RTV International provided the Ethiopian Ministry of Information with six advisers, along with training and demonstration equipment and supplies. Four were broadcasting advisers, who covered the fields of management, production, news, and business; and two were press advisers, who assisted with publications (Ethiopian newspapers and magazines are published by the government). The advisory group was reduced to four men during 1969, the final, phasing-out year. There was no participant-training component in the RTV-Ethiopia contract, inasmuch as the German Radio Training Center was being operated at Radio Ethiopia during the same period (see § 14.4).

Nigeria. The Washington County School Board, Hagerstown, Maryland, was chosen as the contractor to help the four educational ministries in Nigeria—those of the Federal Territory and the Eastern, Western, and Northern regions—to upgrade existing radio and television schools programming (See § 15.2.2). Hagerstown was widely known for its extensive use of closed-circuit instructional television in the public schools. Modern Aids to Education, or MATE, as the project was called, supplied 16 specialists during the course of the contract, 1963–68; the highest number in Nigeria at any one time was 10. In addition, MATE employed 16 short-term visiting consultants for specialized services in engineering, research and evaluation, and the like. Equipment supplied under the contract included 200 radio receivers and 75 television receivers; seven videotape recorders; vehicles, generators, sound-recording equipment, photographic gear, graphic materials; and other such backup items. Eight participant trainees went to the United States for study—five in television-receiver maintenance and repair, two in ITV school-studio liaison, and one in production and writing. Two of MATE's goals were to develop a national film library and similar resources for schools broadcasting, and to give advice and training in the development of the ministries' broadcasting units. The task was complicated, first by the involvement of four different ministries, each with varying degrees of commitment to the project; second, by political unrest starting in 1966 (Washington County 1968). Indiana University also had a Nigerian AID-financed contract during most of the Hagerstown period (Indiana University 1967).

Malawi. The University of Missouri contracted to provide a variety of mass-media services to Malawi in the years 1965–70. The focus of the project was the development of the Malawi Broadcasting Corporation and of the Ministry of Agriculture's extension services. More generally, it was to encourage the fullest possible use of the media resources of the country in the interests of national development. Fourteen man-years were supplied by the contractor during the course of the contracts. The basic team consisted of advisers in the areas of radio production, radio advertising, graphics production, agricultural information, and motion-picture production. In addition, four short-term consultants visited the project. AID supplied Malawi with seven medium-wave transmitters of 1 kw.–10 kw. in power, along with interconnecting relay transmitters; two studios; and over $20,000 worth of technical commodities. Fifteen participant trainees from the Malawi Broadcasting Corporation studied radio in the United States, while nine from the Agricultural Ministry Extension Service studied a variety of subjects connected with their work. The final report of the Missouri project indicates that it had an unusual degree of success in meeting its goals (University of Missouri 1970).

12.2.2 United States Information Agency, *by James M. Kushner*

The United States Information Agency plays a part, though not necessarily a conspicuous one, in the activities of many African broadcasting organizations. Known as the "United States Information Service" (USIS) at posts overseas, the USIA tries to influence public attitudes in other nations in support of American foreign-policy objectives. One of its methods is to make itself as useful as possible to the media in a host country. To the extent wanted by the host country, USIA provides it with goods and services, ranging from encyclopaedias to special VOA short-wave feeds in African languages, from sound-effects record libraries to advice on how to solve technical and organizational broadcasting problems, from help in recording folksongs in the hinterland to assistance in conducting seminars on mass communication.

In 1971 USIA had 48 posts in 34 African countries. Africa stood about midway among major regions of the world in terms of USIS budget priorities, according to 1971 congressional hearings at which the agency presented its proposed budget for fiscal 1972 (U.S. Congress 1971, p. 12). Its world requirements for fiscal 1972 were estimated by the agency to be about $67.6 million. The $7.5 million requested for Africa was to be roughly divided as follows: American employee salaries, 45%; local (foreign) employee salaries, 17%; and program activities, 38%.

The budgeted program activities include four basic components: press and publications, film services, information-center operations (by far the most expensive activity), and radio. The last includes local production of programs, adaptation and placement of United States-produced programs, promotion of the Voice of America, and acquisition and maintenance of local broadcast equipment.

USIS posts use a wide variety of methods in meeting their local objectives. They include "media placement," that is, providing materials such as recordings, news stories, still photos, and films for use by local media; operation of free libraries stocked with books and magazines representative of American culture; distribution of books to key institutions; exchange visits of culturally and politically significant groups and individuals; staging of public discussions, lectures, and film showings; and informal personal contacts between USIS media specialists and influential people in the host countries. All these and many more activities are orchestrated by a "Country Plan" which outlines each post's overall requirements and capabilities in terms of the particular local situation in its host country.

The man in charge of a USIS post, the public affairs officer, along with his staff, considers the general climate of opinion regarding the United States in the host country, the country's media resources and needs, the available channels for reaching priority groups within the local population, the capacity of each local medium to carry varying types of messages, and the post's ability to gain access to each medium (Elder 1968, p. 315). All of this means, of course, that USIS assistance to local broadcasting varies greatly from one country to another, just as do other types of assistance such as those administered by the United States Agency for International Development, with which USIA collaborates in technical matters (Rubin 1968, p. 64). One country may need and accept a great deal of direct assistance in the form of materials and advice. If its broadcasting organization, for example, cannot afford essential resources—reference books, an adequate music and sound-effects library, packaged programs on film or tape, a correspondent to report on its ambassador's activities in Washington, or enough tape recorders to cover local events—the gift of such goods and services from the USIS might be welcome. Another country, whose broadcasting organization might have less urgent needs, might be unwilling to place itself under the obligation implied by the acceptance of such gifts; there, the USIS's role would necessarily be more peripheral.

Because of this variability it is not possible to give a realistic view of USIA assistance to African broadcasting systems in a single, composite picture. Instead we have chosen to select a range of actual examples of USIS activities culled from a representative selection of African posts' monthly reports. These suggest the broad spectrum of recurrent, day-to-day USIA activities in countries where USIS assistance is welcomed. It should be understood that isolated examples can do no more than define the agency's role in a limited, operational way.

Broadcasting service. The Voice of America supplements its regular, direct international broadcasts by producing tapes in languages other than those on its broadcast schedule. A Nigerian Broadcasting Corporation program director at Kano, for example, reported that VOA/Hausa tapes fit well into his station's program. Only four languages (Arabic, English, French, and Swahili) were used on VOA direct broadcasts in 1972 to Africa, but material in additional languages was supplied by means of special "feeds." A feed originates in the United States and is sent either by cable or short wave to USIS posts for recording and subsequent placement on domestic radio stations in the host country. Or the short-wave feeds may be picked up directly by the stations themselves.

More common, however, is the donation of prerecorded, packaged VOA radio programs to local stations. In 1972 the following series were sent to African posts (the number of posts is indicated in parentheses): in English: "Radio Newsreel" (14), "Voices of Africa" (11), "New Horizons in Science" (9), "Science Digest" (6), "Africa in Print" (5), "Sierra Leone Newsletter" (1); in French: "Science et progrès" (16), "Antenne USA" (12), "A Propos" (10), "Africa in Print" (6); in Swahili: "Science Features" (3), "Swahili Newsreel" (2), "Calling All Farmers" (1); and in Hausa: "Letter to the Northern States of Nigeria" (2).

During the Apollo 13 space flight, a USIS information officer in Addis Ababa arranged Amharic-language interviews for both Radio Ethiopia and Radio Voice of the Gospel. The South African Broadcasting Corporation rebroadcast live VOA English-language transmissions to its audiences.

VOA occasionally sends specialists on tour to assist local government and media officials. One of these is the VOA music consultant, Leo Sarkisian, an expert on African folk music. During one field trip he worked with Radio Niger to record prize-winning groups of musicians during an annual youth week in Niamey. In the Ivory Coast, at the request of Radio-Télévision Ivoirienne, USIS-Abidjan helped prepare an hour-long Christmas Eve program, "Black Christmas." VOA also supplies the services of American correspondents, both in Africa and elsewhere, to complement local-station coverage of important news events. When the head of state of a host country visits the United States, USIA sees to it that the newsmen in his entourage have every convenience and facility in sending news about the visit to the media back home.

Unlike the BBC, the VOA makes no systematic provision for foreign broadcaster "attachments"—on-the-job assignments of the type described by Seymour in § 14.2.1. Aside from a few attachments of Ethiopian, Kenyan, Tanzanian, and Zambian broadcasters at the VOA in the past, the VOA's temporary foreign-language broadcast personnel are hired from the pool of foreign students at the many educational institutions in the Washington, D.C., area.

Screen Service. While African television stations can get all sorts of syndicated film material from commercial sources, little of this material has any direct relevancy to African culture. The USIA Screen Service not only produces newsfilm but also produces film documentaries and features, many of which serve this need.

Major documentaries and features are produced for the USIA Screen Service by independent producers under contract, or by the USIA's own production team working out of Washington, D.C. At times a USIS post may be able to produce features of special interest to local television stations; for example, USIS-Kampala, in cooperation with Uganda Television, produced a videotape of the Nnyonza Singing Group which was aired in prime time in 1970. The Screen Service sometimes makes arrangements to supply commercial programs of special interest to host-country television stations. Again in Kampala, Uganda Television was able to schedule a Xerox-sponsored CBS news feature, "Of Black America," as a result of such USIA assistance.

USIS posts often assist local educational-television projects. In early 1969, USIS-Abidjan invited the Ivorian minister of education and his staff to view two films describing the progress of ETV in Samoa and the United States. The minister later asked for more information on American ETV experience. USIS-Niamey supplied slides, films, and other materials to Niger's "Télévision scolaire" for a series of lessons designed to acquaint students in Niger with world affairs.

Press and Publications Service. The Press and Publications Service sends to each USIS post a daily radio-teletype wireless file of news, program materials, and background information which is used at many posts as the basis for daily newsletters or bulletins for local distribution. This material is available to local radio and television stations, should they want to use it. This service also supplies photographs which may be useful to local newspapers and television stations. Its Regional Service Center in Beirut offers editorial and printing services and technical advice to USIS posts in the Near East and Africa. USIS posts often send local employees to the center for training.

Information Center Service. Books, exhibits, and other educational supporting materials are distributed by the Information Center Service. In mid-1970, for example, Radio Sierra Leone was given a set of encyclopaedias and professional reference books, along with African-exhibit pictures for its foyer; and USIS-Ibadan presented encyclopaedias to the library of the Nigerian Broadcasting Corporation.

Other services. USIA and individual USIS posts sometimes cross specific media service lines with special forms of assistance. The American Embassy in Lagos telegraphed Washington:

[Nigerian] Government has appointed committee to recommend future organization and management of radio and TV in Nigeria. Committee has asked USIS for material that might be useful as general background information. Following is suggested: (1) An FCC report of examination of radio and TV broadcasting industries including recommendations for changes; (2) the legal instrument that established the FCC; (3) a copy of the broadcasting code that sets forth advertising standards, morality and ethical standards . . . ; (4) a report on problems involved in establishing educational radio and TV in a developing country. . . . [Telegram from American Embassy, Lagos, to USIA, 21 August, 1970]

In May 1970, USIS-Addis Ababa cooperated with the Ethiopian Ministry of Information in presenting a two-day seminar entitled "The Role of Mass Communications in Furthering Economic Development," and in February 1972, the Sudanese Ministry of Information expressed to USIS-Khartoum the interest of Sudan Television in sponsoring a television-production workshop similar to one conducted two years earlier in Zambia by an American expert.

Travel grants. The State Department provides funds for travel grants administered by USIA. These grants enable USIS posts to invite key African media men to visit American stations, networks, advertising agencies, production firms, government departments, training facilities, and the like, according to the grantees' special interests. The programs are not standardized tours, but are individually designed for the grantees. For example, a Sierra Leone Television staff member spent two months visiting places where he could become familiar with American practices in television scenic and graphics design. Other aspects of such individual grants are discussed in § 12.2.4.

It can be seen from these few examples that the USIA's contribution to African broadcasters consists essentially of many small, day-to-day courtesies and practical, operational aids, in response to changing needs and attitudes in each host country. It is thus a highly flexible, long-term, low-key type of assistance, in contrast with the more spectacular, limited-term projects of the Agency for International Development described in § 12.2.1.

12.2.3 The Peace Corps, *by James M. Kushner*

The Peace Corps' first volunteers were sent as teachers to Ghana in 1961. In the following decade more than 50,000 Peace Corps volunteers, or PCV's, participated in a wide range of projects, many of them initiated by individual PCV's in the field as they responded pragmatically to immediate needs. From general "community development" activities these projects turned more and more toward specialized, technical work as the decade went on. In contrast to the Peace Corps' highly publicized participation in Colombian educational television, involving as many as 100 volunteers (see Comstock and Maccoby 1966), its broadcasting projects in Africa have had much lower visibility. They were often informal, sometimes unsuccessful, and never involved PCV's in large groups. This account describes examples of PCV efforts in six countries: Ethiopia, Ivory Coast, Kenya, Liberia, Mauritius, and Swaziland. It is based in the main on information supplied by Peace Corps country-desk officers Bill Sittig, John Hannah, Bill Dawson, and Penny White.

Ethiopia. The Peace Corps sought to become involved with educational television as far back as October 1961, when it unsuccessfully requested clearance for a project in Ethiopia (see § 15.4). Shortly thereafter, the Ethiopian government's Third Five-Year Plan promoted the introduction of educational radio and television, and from 1966 on the Peace Corps was able to assign a few volunteers on a special-placement basis. By the summer of 1968, following the inception of the Mass Media Center by the Ministry of Education, Ethiopia had requested five PCV's to serve as lower-level staff responsible for planning, researching, writing, and producing broadcasts in chemistry, physics, history, geography, mathematics, and science. Working with Ethiopian counterparts, the PCV's were also asked to assess the effectiveness of various program approaches.

Mauritius. Two PCV's were assigned to the island of Mauritius to develop educational television. Hoping for funds from USAID and the American Freedom from Hunger Schools Progress Program, volunteer Joseph Sauder wrote up a formal proposal calling for 30 television receivers and a videotape recorder: "There is every reason to believe that given the proper broadcast facilities and guidance Mauritius could serve as a good example of multi-cultural educational television in action. . . . With a few alterations I think the general Colombian plan could work well in Mauritius" (Sauder's proposal to AID, 9 August 1971, p. 10). A pilot project along the lines proposed was to start in January 1972.

Swaziland. Orientation began in December 1971 for two PCV radio-production advisers assigned to work with the University of Botswana, Lesotho, and Swaziland (located in Lesotho). Their mission was to arrange materials for an adult-education series sponsored by the Swaziland Ministry of Agriculture. The ministry planned to direct these broadcasts to Swazi farmer listening groups. Volunteers were also to conduct field surveys and to monitor the project's effectiveness.

Kenya. A PCV teacher devoted his spare time in 1967 and 1968 to assisting the Schools Broadcasting Division of the Kenya Ministry of Education with field research on educational radio program utilization and on student listening habits. His extensive reports and evaluations of mathematics, science, and history broadcasts included studies of teacher and student attitudes toward program components. His questionnaires and report forms were later adopted as models for general use in Kenya.

Ivory Coast. Inevitably, some projects never get off the ground. One of these was originally proposed in October 1970: Four highly qualified audiovisual specialists were to be assigned to the Ivory Coast Ministry of Education as installers and maintainers of equipment used by the burgeoning Ivorian ETV system (see § 15.5). Training began in March 1971, and after more than three months of intensive language and practical instruction the volunteers arrived at their job sites—only to learn that French advisers were already thoroughly in command and felt no need for the Peace Corps.

Liberia. Volunteer Bob Brandow was assigned as an elementary school teacher in Pleebo, a town of 20,000 in the far southeastern corner of Liberia. He turned an "exotic idea" into one of the Peace Corps' more engaging success stories. Brandow knew nothing about operating a radio station, but he was convinced that a local radio service could further community-development efforts. "What I thought we could do," he recalled, "was get a small army surplus radio transmitter, hook up my battery powered tape recorder and record player and set it all up in the back of Mr. Wilson's bar where we could use his generator." More than two years and innumerable private and governmental contacts later the "Voice of Pleebo" actually went on the air. In December 1972 it was still on the air, run by a team of seven unpaid Liberian volunteers. It had received donations of equipment and supplies from the government station in Monrovia and the Firestone Company, as well as funds raised by the surrounding community. A Pleebo official was quoted as saying, "To let that station close down is to bury Bob Brandow alive. As long as the station runs Bob is alive in our midst" (communication from Peace Corps acting director in Liberia, 12 December 1972).

12.2.4 Exchange of Persons, *by Wayne Towers*

By "exchange of persons" we mean the going of persons, either from Africa to America or vice versa, in their individual capacities rather than as part of structured projects or as government employees in pursuit of their normal duties. The international exchange of persons involves so many United States government branches, government-supported organizations, private foundations, and trade groups that to compile a complete statistical record, even for one continent and one discipline, is probably impossible. The present writer's research among such government and other records as he could gain access to appears to be the first comprehensive effort to

Wayne Towers, while a graduate student at Temple University, received a grant from the Kaltenborn Foundation which enabled him to carry out the research for this paper.

find out the extent to which America-Africa exchange-of-persons activities have aided African broadcasting.

The passage of the Fulbright-Hays Act by Congress in 1961 marked the start of a sharp increase in the level of persons-exchange activities. This law provides federal funds for the support of several categories of U.S. educational personnel in work and study abroad: university lecturers, researchers at various levels, elementary and secondary school teachers, and persons engaged in foreign-language training and area studies. It also provides scholarships for foreign students to come to the United States to study, after nomination by Fulbright commissions in the candidates' own countries. The membership of the commissions includes both United States and host-country citizens.

Another factor which increased American international exchange of persons in the 1960s was growing worldwide interest in educational television. For example, during the fiscal year 1962–63, the U.S. State Department brought 77 foreign broadcasters to the United States on observation tours (Dizard 1966, p. 248); in 1962 the Agency for International Development contracted for the first of its series of ITV support projects, in Nigeria, where ITV experimentation had begun in 1959 (§15.2.2); and the Peace Corps' major ETV effort began in Colombia, South America, in 1961 (§ 12.2.3).

Before these developments, Northwestern University ran a Foreign Journalists Project, almost exclusively devoted to print media, throughout the 1950s (Arpan 1970); Boston University staged international seminars on radio and television in the years 1956–58; and the University of Missouri's School of Journalism offered a program for foreign broadcasting experts in 1955 (Briscoe 1958, pp. 242–46). But American assistance to broadcasting, and particularly to African broadcasting, via exchange of persons was very limited indeed prior to the 1960s.

Although a certain amount of exchange of persons goes on under purely private auspices—programs funded by churches, nonprofit foundations, and commercial interests—the great majority of exchanges are government financed, either directly through the State Department and its subsidiaries, or indirectly through nongovernment organizations working under contract with government funds. Most direct governmental involvement is coordinated by the Council on International Education and Cultural Affairs, which comprises representatives from the State Department; the Health, Education, and Welfare Department; the Agency for International Development; the United States Information Agency; and the Peace Corps. The most active among these have been State and AID. Space does not permit description of all their programs, but some examples of major activities should suffice to give a representative picture.

The State Department's Bureau of Educational and Cultural Affairs (known as "CU") arranges, among other things, for short-term visits to the

United States by middle-level "influentials" under its Leadership Grants program. In 1972, State budgeted about $3.5 million for the African aspect of CU's programs. Two-thirds of this budget was allocated to United States embassies in Africa for Leadership Grants, and one-third was retained for the stateside administration of Africa-wide projects, labor exchanges, women's affairs, and other programs. In Africa, American embassies select for Leadership Grant nomination promising local persons associated with politics, universities, youth, or media activities.

After approval of nominees by CU in Washington, the actual "programming" of the Leadership grantees is turned over to nongovernment organizations, notably the African-American Institute and the Government Affairs Institute. These are nonprofit organizations which are supported mainly by government contracts. It is thought that such private organizations, even though funded by the government, have somewhat more freedom of action and insulation from suspicion of political motives than would government departments trying to accomplish the same ends directly in their own names.

On arrival in Washington, D.C., a grantee's itinerary is worked out in accordance with his specific professional interests. The length of stay is usually about 30 days, during which the grantee may (for example) visit a number of networks and broadcasting stations, advertising agencies, package producers, manufacturing plants, universities, and the like. The tour organizer usually sees to it that a few side trips that will show the United States in a favorable light—visits, for instance, to model examples of United States policies in action, such as the Cuban refugee center in Miami—are included.

Leadership grantees in the media category are nominated by United States Information Service posts overseas (see § 12.2.2). Officers at these posts keep in close personal contact with media personnel in host countries and so can readily identify the up-and-coming young men and women in broadcasting and other media work who hold out promise for future leadership as department heads, directors, assistant ministers, and eventually even as ministers.

Another State Department CU personnel-exchange activity, known as "Multinational Projects," combines visitors from various foreign countries into common-interest groups. This International Visitors Program is co-sponsored by a variety of nongovernment organizations. Examples are the Foreign Journalists Project at Indiana University (1960 ff.); the International Women Broadcasters' Program of American Women in Radio and Television, a professional association (1964 ff.); and the International Broadcast Seminars at Syracuse University in New York State (1961 ff.). In the decade 1961–71, 40 African broadcasters participated in the Syracuse program, which provides grantees with three months in the United States. About one-third of the time is spent on an academic seminar at

Syracuse, one-third on group tours, and one-third on individualized "professional assignments." For example, 15 broadcasters representing 12 countries participated in the 1968 seminar; five were from Africa. The group visited Boston; Hagerstown, Maryland; Los Angeles; New York; and Washington, D.C. Among the Washington stops were the VOA, the FCC, the White House, Congress, and Comsat (Syracuse University 1968).

The AWRT program is designed for women professionally engaged in broadcasting and provides them with a 45-day visit to broadcasting organizations in America. Five women participated in the 1971 program, including one each from Ethiopia, Nigeria, and Upper Volta. They were, respectively, acting head of educational television, executive producer of TV women's and children's programs, and TV program director in their home systems. All participants visited Houston, Texas; Los Angeles; New York; Phoenix, Arizona; San Francisco; and Washington, D.C. Individual visits to other cities were arranged for each participant. (AWRT 1971).

The Fulbright programs, too, are administered largely by nongovernment organizations. The Committee on International Exchange of Persons handles applications for university lecturing and advanced research, while the Institute for International Education handles those for graduate study and predoctoral research abroad. No data could be obtained from these sources on specific fields of teaching or study followed by grantees. It is known, however, that at least some university lecturers have gone to Africa on Fulbright grants to teach communications or communications-related subjects and that others have engaged in research related to communications. Since the African students nominated by Fulbright commissions for study in the United States are usually limited by local ground rules to academic fields regarded as having highest national priority, it is unlikely that broadcasting has often been a subject of study by African Fulbright scholars.

The Agency for International Development provides for a two-way flow of students, teachers, and advisers, but many of these are associated with AID projects and therefore are categorized, for present purposes, not under the exchange-of-persons classification, but under bilateral assistance (§ 12.2.1). AID finances large-scale undergraduate and graduate university scholarship programs through the African-American Institute, which contracts with AID to act as the intermediary between the many American colleges and universities willing to award scholarships to qualified African students and the even larger number of African students anxious to earn degrees at American institutions. AID imposed rather stringent limitations on permissible fields of study, on the basis of the manpower priorities of the African countries concerned, and as usual, communications did not rank high on the priority list. It is therefore doubtful that broadcasting has benefited significantly from the hundreds of degrees granted to Africans under these programs.

In terms of documentary evidence, virtually the only officially available data on exchange of persons with Africa in the broadcasting field, aside from the reports on specific programs like that at Syracuse, consist of material in CU's Washington files. The writer was given access to some of these files by Owen Roberts, deputy director in the Office of African Programs, whose assistance is gratefully acknowledged. The files on individual grantees contain short occupational identifiers enabling recognition of persons connected with broadcasting. Not included in the summary are grantees identified only with the press or with high-level administrative posts peripherally connected with broadcasting. The following numbers must be regarded as only very approximate indicators of the actual flow of persons under CU auspices. In the decade 1961–71, the number of African broadcasters visiting the United States under State Department auspices was 146, distributed as follows: Leadership Grants, 98; Syracuse International Seminars, 40; American Women in Radio and Television, 6; and Indiana University, 2.

In general one may conclude that the lack of statistical data on broadcasting-related studies, teaching, and research, as well as the omission of broadcasting from the approved subjects of study for government-financed college-level scholarship programs, is symptomatic of the low priority of broadcasting among developmental activities supported by United States government funds.

12.3 Canada, by Cynthia E. Bled

12.3.1 Canada's Aid Philosophy

Reflecting the newness of mass-media expansion, the projects identified in this report were effected between 1960 and 1971. The Canadian International Development Agency (CIDA), which coordinates foreign aid from Canada, does not initiate requests for aid, nor does it seek to direct the pattern of a country's development; instead, it responds to requests from countries which have themselves laid out their development plans and assessed their own priorities. CIDA clearly recognizes that aid "may contribute to, detract from, or distort the achievement of the real goals of the society to which it is directed" (CIDA 1969, p. 5). To maximize the social impact of its assistance, CIDA had reduced its emphasis on food and transportation and stepped up its contribution to telecommunications development and to adult education outside the formal educational system.

In 1970 the Canadian Department of Communications held a conference

Cynthia E. Bled is Bibliographical Consultant to the Canadian Council on Urban and Regional Research and Professor of Economics, Algonquin College of Applied Arts and Technology, Ottawa, and was formerly on the staff of the Canadian Broadcasting Corporation Research Department. The author acknowledges the financial assistance of the International Development Research Centre, Ottawa.

to assess the potential contribution of communications in accelerating progress in developing countries. The study report identified a trend in Canada toward communications assistance, due in part to "a growing recognition that communication services, i.e., conventional telecommunications and mass communications, radio and television, in all [their] phases, [are] vital to increasing the rate of economic and social progress in the developing countries." (Canada 1971c, p. 52).

CIDA opposes "aid-tying," the common practice of attaching strings to aid to ensure direct advantages to the donor country, such as requiring that equipment purchased with aid funds be bought from the donor country. At a House of Commons committee hearing on international development assistance, CIDA pointed out that "the practice of tying is now generally recognized to have resulted in serious problems and in general reduction in the value and effectiveness of aid" (Canada 1971b, p. 68). The committee recommended offering "the most liberal terms possible" for repayment of aid loans, and that the Canadian government "should proceed without delay to untie Canadian aid funds for procurement in developing countries" (Canada 1971b, p. 18).

12.3.2 Direction and Extent of Canadian Aid

Canada has adopted the principle of regional concentration in its aid programs. Historical and other links, such as the existence of Canadian diplomatic missions at the time of the establishment of new countries, have in the past been influential in determining the direction of aid. Assistance programs were formally established in Commonwealth Africa in 1959 and in Francophone Africa in 1962. African countries stand to benefit still more in the future from the government's announced intention of pursuing the concept of "social justice" by stepping up economic assistance "to black African states of [southern Africa] to assist them to develop their own institutions and resources" (Canada 1970, p. 20).

The Canadian secretary of state for external affairs has stated that "by providing an outward-looking expression of the bilingual character of Canada, our development assistance role also helps contribute to our sense of internal unity and purpose" (Canada 1970, p. 10). Therefore, all French-speaking Africa, without distinction, is now regarded as an area of aid concentration. Canadian bilateral allocations to Francophone Africa grew from about $C22 million in fiscal 1968–69 to nearly $C51 million in 1971–72. During the same period Commonwealth African allocations increased from about $C26 million to $C36 million (data supplied by CIDA). In the past no special effort was made in CIDA's bookkeeping to single out broadcasting allocations from other fields, such as education. In the general category "communications," however, Canada's bilateral-aid disbursements for fiscal 1968–69 amounted to over $C1.7 million for Commonwealth Africa, none for Francophone Africa (CIDA 1969, p. 32).

The latter has since received significant allocations, as the outline of projects which follows shows.

The government is committed to increasing Canada's contribution to multilateral-aid projects to 25% of total official assistance. The External Affairs Sub-Committee on International Development Assistance pointed out that "Canadian participation in multilateral aid programs cannot be considered complete on the basis of financial contributions alone"; it was vital that "Canadian skills and talents be made available as fully as possible for roles in the operations and secretariats of multilateral aid organizations" (Canada 1970b, p. 32). The Ivory Coast educational-television project, discussed below, illustrates Canada's involvement at the multilateral level.

This report focuses on the role of CIDA as the centralizing body for aid disbursements in Canada. Official development assistance is relatively new in Canada, however. In the past, private and semigovernmental bodies have played a more active role than government in overseas development projects. The voluntary sector alone provides overseas assistance estimated at an average of $C40 million per year (Canada 1971b, p. 14).

Canadian aid to broadcasting in Africa focuses on four areas: school broadcasts; community development through public affairs or extension programs; training programs, either in Africa or Canada; and advisory/feasibility studies.

12.3.3 Educational Broadcasting

In 1966, a team of six experienced Canadian scriptwriters, narrators, and teachers began working with the Kenya Institute of Education, preparing radio broadcasts over the Voice of Kenya for an elaborate in-service course to train unqualified teachers and to develop leadership of qualified teachers at the headmaster's level. The unqualified-teachers radio programs tied in with correspondence instruction through the Correspondence Course Unit at University College, Nairobi. This course responded to an emergency situation and was expected to continue for as long as shortages compelled the use of unqualified teachers.

The headmasters' course occupied one week in April and two weeks in August. It included elements of supervision and administration, school management, child study, English, mathematics, science, history, and geography. Although "in three weeks a headmaster cannot learn how everything related to his position should be done . . . he can be challenged and inspired to recognize the scope of the position, to build a vision of its possibilities and to work with determination towards becoming an enlightened leader in the educational affairs of his school and his community" (Kenya Institute of Education 1970a, p. 1).

The Voice of Kenya Schools Broadcasting Service carried the lessons. The 1970 teacher-training sequence included, not only sessional programs, but also 16 between-sessions programs to assist with correspondence assignments from mid-May to early July. Each sessional broadcast lasted approximately 26 minutes, but teachers' colleges were advised to allot one hour per broadcast to allow for introduction and follow-up. The between-sessions broadcasts approximated 13 minutes each. Tape recordings of all broadcasts could be purchased, and colleges were encouraged to acquire tapes to allow scheduling flexibility.

In some sections of the Unqualified Teachers Course an effort was made to introduce methods adaptable to varying languages of instruction. For one English broadcast in 1970, for example, trainees were issued copies of a picture book, wall charts, and the book "Starting to Read: Teacher's Notes for a Vernacular Reading Programme," with the point made that "these books are designed for use in *any* classroom using the *mother tongue*" (Kenya Institute of Education 1970b). From time to time the lessons attempted to emphasize that good teaching methods apply, regardless of what language is used. The fact that the programs were produced in English only, however, placed a limitation on their impact, and so consideration was being given to the production of a Swahili version of the course.

The Kenya project did not generate local replacements until 1971, when two Kenyans were brought to Canada for training. After a nine-month teacher-training crash course at the Ontario Department of Education in Toronto, the trainees returned home to take over some of the administrative aspects of the program, enabling a start on the phasing out of Canadian personnel, which had of course been planned from the outset.

Eight Canadians began serving in the Ivory Coast in mid-1971. Their role was mainly the conception, elaboration, writing, and printing of the documents needed for teachers and pupils in the Ivorian ITV project, which is described in detail in § 15.5. A significant number of the Ivorian teachers are not advanced much beyond the level of their pupils, so that a simultaneous learning situation exists. A high level of ingenuity is required to prepare programs and accompanying printed materials capable of teaching both the teachers and the taught. This project has the nature of a long-term involvement, although the intention is to train local staff to take over operation of the Canadian-run printing shop within as short a period as possible.

In 1969 Canada responded to proposals to establish a nationwide educational-television project in Niger, aimed primarily at language training but also embracing aspects of community development. The project, referred to generally as "Francophonization," implied countrywide teaching of French via television so as to provide the country with a universal language. In spite of delays the project was not lost sight of, and early in 1972 exploratory meetings were held in Montreal to work out further aspects, with consideration also given to the possibility of radio use in some areas.

In 1969–70, the Canadian University Service Overseas responded to a request from Nigeria for a co-worker on a schools broadcast project over

Kaduna Television. The volunteer wrote scripts and helped direct the program "Straight for English," designed to teach English to the primary grades.

In 1969 a Canadian YWCA officer in Tanzania received a CIDA grant to help test the use of radio as a means of stimulating awareness of social issues. The pilot project consisted of a series of six 15-minute radio broadcasts called "Education for Life." They dealt with the relationship between teenagers and parents, with the focus on rural youth. Problems encountered in preparing, taping, and coordinating this series led to the setting up of a three-week course on radio production by the Adult Education Centre of the YWCA in Tanzania.

12.3.4 Community Development

A basic Canadian contribution in the area of community development was the introduction in 1964 of the Ghana Farm Radio Forum by Helen C. Abell, a rural sociologist, and Jack McPherson of the Canadian Broadcasting Corporation. This project, initiated by UNESCO and supported by the Canadian government, is described in detail in § 15.2.1. Abell, as research director in charge of evaluation, planned, conducted, and reported research on the project, while McPherson worked with a local counterpart on organizing and producing the broadcasts (Coleman, Popku, and Abell 1968). After the experimental phase, the program was continued as a regular feature of its schedule by the Ghana Broadcasting Corporation (§ 5.2.2). "It takes organization and dedication to make it work," explains Abell, but "the radio/TV forum (with organized listening/viewing groups who discuss, comment and act) is the *best tool* yet devised for development programmes" (letter to author, 12 October 1971).

Canada made another contribution to farm-forum development in Africa in 1964, when a Canadian Broadcasting Corporation program supervisor spent a month as instructor and participant at a broadcast seminar on farm radio forums in Kenya under Food and Agricultural Organization auspices. In 1970 the Canadian government made a loan to Kenya for purchasing radio transmitters to achieve wider broadcast coverage.

In 1966, a CIDA-sponsored Canadian Broadcasting Corporation producer was seconded to Madagascar for three months to help in the setting up of an adult-education program, again adopting the technique of the farm radio forum.

A CIDA economic adviser in Tanzania facilitated an integrated program of broadcasting activities there. In 1971, for example, the Canadian government contributed four mobile recording vans for use by Radio Tanzania in rural radio broadcasts. One of the vans is a mobile substudio for relaying programs back to radio headquarters, and three are for recording in the field. The vans were expected to contribute to the development of the *ujamaa* village concept, a cooperative village movement which emphasizes localized development in an effort to counter the migration of rural dwellers to the cities (see § 4.2.1). Programs somewhat along the lines of the farm-forum concept were to be offered, conveying social, political, and agricultural information. The Canadian adviser also arranged the preparation of documentaries using local talent for Radio Tanzania and introduced a daily dramatic radio serial focusing on farming family stories. The scripts were prepared in Swahili by students at the University of Dar es Salaam.

Nongovernment contribution to the development of the *ujamaa* concept was made by a Canadian filmmaker and his team. Starting in mid-1971, they prepared videotapes of interviews with government officials and with the people, the subsequent viewing of which helped in the mutual understanding of ideas and attitudes. Since Tanzania had no television station, a battery-operated television monitor was used for this project. Part of the personnel costs were met by the Canadian University Service Overseas, with the funds channeled through the Canadian Hunger Foundation. The foundation has also received contributions from voluntary groups such as the Canadian Catholic Organization for Development and Peace, and the Victoria and Saskatoon Miles for Millions groups, as well as from private commercial sources such as Whittaker Electronics Limited (Ottawa). This project was deemed highly successful and received additional support from the Norwegian Agency for International Development, the Swedish International Development Authority, and the Danish International Development Agency.

12.3.5 Training

Canada-based training. The range of Canadian institutions associated with the training of African broadcasters varies widely. Most trainees who remain for extended periods are seconded to the Canadian Broadcasting Corporation in the summer to gain practical experience. The pattern of institutional involvement in 1971 is indicated in the following list (the numbers of African trainees are shown in parentheses): *Cameroon:* Algonquin College of Applied Arts and Technology, Ottawa (1); Ryerson Polytechnical Institute, Toronto (1). *Ghana:* Algonquin College of Applied Arts and Technology (1); Saskatchewan Institute of Applied Arts and Science, Saskatoon (1). *Kenya:* Ontario Department of Education, Toronto (2). *Nigeria:* Northern Alberta Institute of Technology, Edmonton (1). *Tanzania:* Centennial College of Applied Arts and Technology, Scarborough, Ontario (2); McGill University, Montreal, Quebec (1).

The Canadian Broadcasting Corporation has no formalized training program for foreign broadcasters, but in response to requests provides ad hoc in-service, on-the-job training to CIDA-supported students. In the decade 1959–69, CBC provided about 80 training months to 190 trainees from 31 developing countries, with courses ranging in length from two weeks to one year (Canada 1971c, p. 20). Since CBC has no facilities for basic training, all trainees have been experienced broadcasters or students with advanced skills. Overseas engineering students are accepted at the corporation's National Training Centre at Engineering Headquarters, Montreal, which provides formal courses for Canadians covering general operations, master control, video, VTR, and audio. Foreign trainees pay no fees, and CIDA or the trainees' home organizations cover travel and living costs. In 1970–71, 12 trainees from Algeria, Cameroon, Ghana, Mali, Rhodesia, Togo, and Zambia received CBC attachments, mostly in the technical field (data supplied by CBC).

Africa-based training. The Canadian Broadcasting Corporation played a formative role in the staffing of Ghana Television, starting in 1961 when a senior corporation technician and a producer went to Ghana to set up studio classroom facilities along with two Ghanaian technicians. In 1963 classes began with ten production trainees, twelve technician trainees, one film student, and one artist trainee. In 1963 and again in 1964 two groups of 22 Ghanaian trainees came to Canada for one year, and during this period three additional corporation men were added to the Accra staff. In addition, six Accra-based film trainees were sent to the corporation studios in Halifax, Nova Scotia, and Winnipeg, Manitoba, for additional training in 1964. By 1965 Ghana Television was on the air (see § 5.2.1).

The Trades Training Centre was established in Accra by CIDA in 1965, when Ghanaian trainees were brought to Canada and Canadian staff sent to the center. The Canadians were all expected to be replaced by local staff during 1972. Enrollment at the center, for 1970–71, was 539 full-time and 1,028 part-time students. Among the training facilities offered was a laboratory for the assembly and repair of radio and television equipment.

Another important Ghana-based training project was the regional Studio Operators Course held at Accra, July–September 1970. This was the first training course held under the auspiecs of the Commonwealth Broadcasting Conference (see § 13.3) and it was fully endorsed by CIDA. It was under the joint guidance of a CBC and a BBC instructor and was attended by trainees from four Commonwealth countries in West Africa (Woodward and Evanyshyn 1971, p. 1).

CIDA assisted a Senegalese training scheme at the Centre d'Études des Sciences et Techniques de l'Information de l'Université de Dakar (CESTI). Initiated in 1968 under the aegis of UNESCO and the Senegalese government, CESTI offered a three-year diploma course in all phases of communications. The first complete year of courses was taught in 1970. The program, as it evolved, provided for one year of liberal-arts courses, followed the second year by courses on information gathering and information transmission through newspapers, radio, and television. The third year provided a unique experience: the student spent three months training in Canada, three months in France, and a further three months in Dakar. In Canada the student would be exposed to "the study of North American industrial society, to the Anglo-Saxon conception of information and of the mass media in general, of the English language, etc."; in France he would "study the European (west and east) industrial society, the French and European press, etc."; and in Senegal, "the relations between the mass media and development, etc." (University of Dakar 1971, p. 8; translated from the French). Canada assumes responsibility for travel to Canada, subsistence, and teaching expenses. The first group of students was due to arrive at the University of Montreal, Quebec, in July 1972.

After a series of financial difficulties, the Senegalese center received the full support of Canada and France in 1971–72, with France contributing most of the administrative budget and teaching staff, Canada contributing staff and equipment. In addition, Canada provides scholarships to neighboring Francophone countries. For 1970–71, scholarships to the center were distributed as follows: Dahomey, 2; Ivory Coast, 13; Mali, 11; Mauritania, 1; Senegal, 4; and Upper Volta, 7.

12.3.6 Advisory/Feasibility Studies

Between 1959 and 1967, 27 CBC advisers were seconded to 10 developing countries in Africa, Asia, and the Caribbean (Canada 1971c, p. 20). Most of these secondments were CIDA supported. In addition to the attachments already mentioned in this report, the CBC and CIDA have made secondments in Africa as follows: *Cameroon*, 1965–66: CIDA sponsored a producer for 16 months to serve as organizer and general adviser in the production of English-language radio broadcasts; *Sierra Leone*, 1969: the CBC sponsored one of its own staff for two weeks to advise on the merger of Sierra Leone radio and television; *Nigeria*, 1969: CIDA sponsored an expert for six weeks to survey existing engineering facilities and to advise the Nigerian Broadcasting Corporation on the expansion of radio services.

While CIDA relies largely on the CBC to supply advisers on broadcasting projects abroad, the agency's own economic advisers also perform important on-the-spot advisory functions. The contribution to broadcasting development in Tanzania by the CIDA economic adviser attached to the Ministry of Information at that country's request has, for example, been noted above. Not only has he served to establish programs and arrange training, but he has also acted as a resource person.

12.4 The Federal Republic of Germany, *by Laura Gläser-Weisser*

12.4.1 German Policy on Aid to the Mass Media

German aid to developing countries sponsored by the Federal Ministry for Economic Cooperation has as its underlying objective the promotion of

Laura Gläser-Weisser is an editor in the German transcription service for developing countries. She was a member of an advisory team for Radio Afghanistan, 1962–66, and an Instructor at the Radio Training Center, Ethiopian Broadcasting Services, 1966–70. Section 12.4.1 was adapted with permission from a policy paper by Dr. Jürgen Sacklowski, Mass Media Department Head, Federal Ministry of Economic Cooperation, Federal Republic of Germany.

economic and social progress so as to improve living conditions in recipient countries. In the specific field of mass media, we try to make people aware of the constructive role the media can play in facilitating social change, in providing guidance for self-help projects, in furthering formal education, in preserving indigenous cultures, and in achieving national integration. Radio and television, along with the other public media, form part of the basic educational system of a country. They can help resolve conflicts within a society and bridge gaps between social groups. They are essential to the formation of public opinion.

However, governments of developing countries usually ask for outside help in setting up technical installations and in gaining technical know-how. We regard this type of assistance as justifiable only if the actual use of the resulting mass-media installations is in keeping with stated objectives of development policy.

Increasingly, we tend to assess proposed projects in terms of the absorptive capacity of the recipient country. Secondary considerations, such as national prestige, should not be the decisive factor. For example, while a technically sophisticated installation for motion-picture production might be impressive, in a given situation it might be much more useful to start wth mobile cinema vans and modest, technically simple production facilities. Television is more glamorous than radio broadcasting, but in many situations radio can serve development objectives much more efficiently.

We believe that the planning and execution of mass-media projects should not be left exclusively to technicians and media professionals. Decisions about such projects are essentially political in nature and must be based on detailed knowledge of the political and social structure of the recipient country. The fact that media installations acquire permanent potentialities for exercising political influence has to be borne in mind when assessing their probable long-term impact on development policy.

The foregoing policy statement finds practical expression in axioms such as the following: (1) The extent to which German aid funds may be used to help create the technical infrastructure of mass media depends on its relationship to the attainment of desired development goals; (2) the task of the German adviser is to determine, not *what* is to be done, but *how* the stated development goals of the recipient country can be achieved; (3) when feasible, projects should be developed on a regional scale, involving several countries; (4) aid should be concentrated on a few highly effective projects, not diluted by an attempt to create a "presence" in a great many countries; (5) the German government should consider financing the current costs of producing programs applicable to development goals when there is a particular need; (6) media projects should be integrated with other German activities, such as agricultural projects; and (7) German-supported media projects for developing nations should be designed to serve the development needs of those nations, not the needs of German information policies. Commercial interests of German industry may not influence the type of development projects selected for German government support, or the kind of technology recommended to implement such projects.

12.4.2 German Government Media Projects

The German government has been involved in media-assistance projects in 17 African countries; in 1972 they were either still ongoing or only recently completed. Five of these projects dealt with television. In general the German emphasis has been on supply of equipment, and on expert advice closely linked to specific developmental goals and practical needs. For example, nine of the seventeen projects provided mobile units, which are invaluable for producing interesting and lively rural and public-affairs programming but are often overlooked in planning less flexible studio installations.

Television. In Morocco the aim is to help expand the scope of the television service by training personnel in the use of mobile units and in the production of films, both with special reference to agricultural development. The training of producers and cameramen began with the initiation of the project in 1971. Two TV mobile units have been supplied. A producer-trainer and a mobile-unit technician help to maximize the usefulness of the mobile units. There is also a radio component in the Moroccan aid project in the form of assistance in further development of the country's FM network. Starting in 1972, this project was to supply four additional FM transmitters and the services of a transmitter engineer.

The use of the mobile TV unit is also stressed in Uganda, where a long-term German government project (1968–75) has supplied a sophisticated mobile van with three cameras and recording facilities, capable of doubling as a small studio to relieve pressure on regular studios as well as acting in its normal mobile capacity. Six German experts man this project: a program adviser, a director, a cameraman, and three technicians. Evidence of the interest of the Uganda Television Service in the mobile-unit operation is the fact that 20 of the UTS staff of 100 were assigned to work with it.

Sudan Television, initiated in Omdurman in 1962 with German government help, received additional aid to build a second station in Wad Medani in 1972 so as to extend the television service in the 1,500 villages of the Gezira scheme for cotton cultivation (see § 3.2.2). Equipment supplied in Wad Medani included the transmitter, two mobile units, and facilities for two studios; personnel included a program adviser and a film technician. Germany has also given assistance to the television systems of Sierra Leone and Zambia.

Radio transmitters. In Malawi a major project in support of radio broadcasting, with emphasis on educational programming, was initiated in 1965 to run through 1972. Equipment included a 100-kw. short-wave transmitter, a mobile unit, four studios, and editing equipment. A program expert was provided for five years, a studio and a transmitter engineer for three years, and a second program specialist for one year. A hundred Malawi broadcasters received on-the-job training from these specialists. The final phase of the project emphasized assistance in improving the station's organizational structure. Marked increases in educational and informational programming and in listener response during the course of this project gave evidence of its effectiveness.

Another major radio project stressing rural development provided Dahomey with a 50-kw. medium-wave transmitter, a mobile unit, and 500 receivers. The receivers were used to equip listening centers for farm radio forums (see § 15.2.1) which attracted 14,000 listener-participants. Three German specialists were provided: a program adviser and studio and transmitter engineers. A similar rural-development project, this time with emphasis on rural radio journalists, was initiated in 1970 in Upper Volta. A 100-kw. medium-wave transmitter was to be provided, along with three studios and portable recording equipment. Technical facilities were to be installed in 1973. Three engineers and a specialist in rural journalism made up the personnel complement. Tunisia received a 100-kw. short-wave transmitter and four studios, along with the services of a transmission engineer and a sound technician. This project was initiated in 1968 but suspended after a year; it was resumed in 1972, however, with another four studios planned by the end of that year.

Rwanda provides an African transmitter site for Deutsche Welle, the external radio service of the German Federal Republic (§ 4.4.2.). Germany gave Rwanda major assistance in the development of its broadcasting service: a 50-kw. short-wave transmitter, three studios, and a mobile unit equipped with a radio link. The first phase of the ten-year aid project started in 1965 with three program advisers; the second phase started in 1967, with the number of program advisers reduced to two, but they were joined in 1968 by two studio technicians. Rwanda's new broadcasting center was opened in 1968, staffed with personnel largely trained by the German advisory team.

A project to aid Gabon radio, scheduled to go into effect in 1973, was to provide a 20-kw. medium-wave transmitter and three technical experts to improve the national radio service in Gabon's northern region. Togo was scheduled to receive a transmitter and the services of an engineer.

Radio production. Several West African Francophone countries received German assistance in the field of radio production. Guinea acquired four radio studios, two mobile units, a studio-transmitter link, and the services of eight experts. This project started in 1965 but was phased out prematurely in 1970 because of political disagreements. Mali received a studio and ten tape recorders, along with the services of a program adviser during the period 1967–71. Niger was scheduled to receive a mobile unit equipped with a radio link and the services of an engineer in 1972. On the other side of the continent, Somalia received an air-conditioned wing for its broadcasting center, comprising four fully equipped studios and a workshop. This project ran from 1966 to 1970, with a program adviser and a studio engineer providing on-the-job training. Somalia's neighbor, Ethiopia, was offered technical facilities for equipping a new eight-studio broadcasting center in 1964, but by 1972 delivery still awaited the erection of the studio building by the Ethiopian government (§ 3.1.6). In the meantime, however, a completely equipped training studio, a dubbing facility, and a workshop were installed in temporary facilities as part of a production training center for Ethiopian radio. Facilities also included a mobile unit and portable tape recorders. Two German instructors and a studio engineer used these facilities to run what amounted to a small radio school during the period 1964–70. This school is described in detail in § 14.4.

12.4.3   Nongovernment Aid

The Friedrich-Ebert Foundation, a nongovernment, nonprofit organization with a special interest in trade unionism, the cooperative movement, adult education, and community development, has supported broadcasting projects in four African countries. In Ghana the foundation financed a major project for the production of educational films and the training of film personnel. Complete 16-mm. cinematography equipment for three production teams, including laboratory and extensive backup facilities such as mobile cinevans, vehicles, and workshops were provided. In 1965, when the project started, it had a staff of 28 experts who were gradually phased out over the years as they trained Ghanaian counterparts. All but five of the expatriate staff had left by late 1972. One immediate by-product of the Ghana project was a series of 72 educational films with both English and French sound tracks, designed for use in Sub-Saharan Africa. Starting in 1971, Kenya also received aid in cinematography from the foundation, but on a smaller scale. The Kenya project provided cinematographic facilities for two production teams. The Tanzania and Uganda aid projects of the foundation deal with the use of radio in adult education, providing facilities for documentary radio production and expert advice.

German Catholic and Protestant church groups participate cooperatively in multilateral assistance to TELE-STAR, the radio and television educational production agency in Zaïre which is described in detail in § 11.2.2. In the period 1962–72 the German churches contributed funds for studio construction and equipment, such as a facility for transferring videotape images to film; and funds for the underwriting of 75 television programs.

13   Multilateral Aid

Since bilateral assistance inevitably brings with it the suspicion—and as likely as not the reality—of self-serving designs by the donor country, there has been growing interest in multilateral sources of aid, especially as the newly independent countries have learned increasingly to perceive motives of "economic imperialism" and "neocolonialism" in aid programs. The United Nations Educational, Scientific and Cultural Organization (UNESCO) has been a prime source of multilateral assistance—not so much through funding, since its financial resources are very limited, as through its role as a disinterested and impartial catalytic agent. Thus, individual nations as well as international organizations such as the World Bank and the United Nations Development Program have no qualms about allowing UNESCO to administer funds on their behalf.

UNESCO is a "specialized agency" of the United Nations whose aim is to promote international cooperation in the spheres mentioned in its title, with a view to furthering world peace. It is considered a "facilitative" organ of the United Nations, which in plain language means it is less given to speechmaking, more oriented toward achievement than the parent body. Its interest in mass media springs from two separate functions they might serve—as a means of international exchange of information, and hence understanding; and as a means of facilitating educational development.

UNESCO's first efforts at helping the media to cultivate international understanding stressed the training of journalists and the removal of impediments to the free flow of information from one country to another. Projects initiated or supported by UNESCO included revision of international copyright agreements, removal of restrictive import duties on educational and scientific materials, reduction of postal and telegraph rates for such materials, and elimination of censorship. As it turned out, however, most new countries opted for censorship and for propagandistic uses of the media. Instead of increased freedom of information in Africa there has been a distinct trend toward more stringent government controls.

UNESCO has therefore turned toward the less controversial roles of the media as weapons in the battle against illiteracy and as devices for ameliorating shortages of basic educational resources.

In the meantime, UNESCO has performed an invaluable documentary service. Its publications may often be "clogged with the obscurantism of international civil-servant prose," as one national civil servant put it (Dizard 1966, p. 240), but as most chapters of this book show, it is almost impossible to write about the mass media on an international scale without resorting to UNESCO sources for essential data. The world picture is updated annually by the *UNESCO Statistical Yearbook*. Between 1949 and 1961 the organization issued a sequence of 20 publications under the series title "Press, Film, and Radio in the World Today." This was succeeded by another series under the general title "Reports and Papers on Mass Communication," started in 1952, and reaching number 66 in the series by 1972. Over the years these publications have dealt more and more with broadcasting subjects. The major items in the series will be found listed in the Bibliography (see also Knight 1970).

As UNESCO moved into the 1970s it devoted increasing attention to the study of space-communication satellites from the legal, technical, social, and educational points of view. In particular it concerns itself with the potentialities of satellites for overcoming the deficiencies of telecommunications infrastructural development in Africa and for serving the needs of educational technology. These studies were initiated some years earlier, in the mid-1960s (see, e.g., UNESCO 1966).

Assistance also comes from another U.N. specialized agency, the International Telecommunication Union. In addition, each region of the world has its own union of national broadcasting administrations. As the earth has grown smaller in terms of easier long-distance communication, these regional unions have taken on increasingly active roles in cooperative ventures. Although broadcasting unions of the developing world are still in the formative stage, they can be expected eventually to bring to their members important benefits such as program exchanges, the improvement of technical standards, the encouragement of enlightened legislation, and regional training schemes.

Classified for purposes of logical exposition in this chapter—along with the regional groupings, yet distinctly apart—stands the Commonwealth Broadcasting Conference. This organization brings together a strange medley of national services, ranging from All India Radio to the Australian Broadcasting Commission, from the Nigerian Broadcasting Corporation to Radio Gambia. Brooding benignly over all is the great mother figure of the BBC. The organization is loose, a typical British improvisation, and yet the shared values and resources are significant.

Finally, as a seemingly even more unlikely inclusion, we have classified the World Bank in the grouping of multilateral sources of aid to African broadcasting. In point of fact, by 1972 the bank had actually committed itself to the support of only one African broadcasting system, but this commitment takes on symbolic meaning as the first concrete evidence that the world of finance takes broadcasting seriously as an important element in the infrastructure of developing nations.

13.1 UNESCO, *by Francis Bebey*

As early as 1947, the United Nations Educational, Scientific and Cultural Organization initiated a global survey of the structure, work, and equipment of news agencies, press, cinema, and radio, and in 1951 a volume in UNESCO's series "Reports on the Facilities of Mass Communication" was published that summarized the state of the mass media in 151 countries and territories, including those in the African continent (UNESCO 1951).

Assistance to the newly independent states of Africa, which started in 1960, can thus be regarded as the continuation of a program which UNESCO has gradually adapted to the specific needs of the continent. This program is intended to help African governments expand the use of mass media as means of information in general, and to promote their educational use within the framework of national development plans. A particularly important aspect of this expansion is the integration of mass media into schemes for adult education and literacy teaching now being carried out in several African countries.

Of all the mass media, however, radio broadcasting has particularly retained the attention of UNESCO. First, almost all African countries possess fairly good radio-broadcasting infrastructures, the technical development of which can be improved either within the countries' own economic possibilities or with relatively limited help from outside; second, the advent and spread of the transistor receiver has made reception of radio programs possible in remote areas; and third, as a medium which uses the spoken word, radio conforms to the African tradition of oral communication and therefore has a particular impact on African audiences. The exceptional significance of radio in modern African life has been repeatedly recognized and emphasized by broadcasters and other communication specialists from the continent attending meetings organized by UNESCO. The organization of such meetings is in itself part of UNESCO's assistance to the development of African broadcasting. Other means of assistance include the provision of services of experts to governments, the granting of fellowships to students in broadcasting, the carrying out of experimental short- or long-term projects connected with the use of radio

Francis Bebey is responsible for the Music Program, UNESCO Development of Culture Division, and was formerly Program Specialist, UNESCO Mass Media Development Division. He is a musician and novelist as well as an internationally known writer and lecturer on African broadcasting.

for development purposes, and the organization of national or regional training courses.

13.1.1 Meetings, Seminars, Training Courses

The first meeting convened by UNESCO to deal with problems related to the development of educational broadcasting in Tropical Africa was held at Moshi, Tanganyika (now Tanzania) in September 1961 (UNESCO 1961a). One aim of the meeting was to provide educators and broadcasters with an opportunity to discuss their possible cooperation for better use of radio for in-school and out-of-school education in the future. This was the first meeting of its kind that had ever been held in Africa, featuring African high-ranking broadcasting staff and educators in search of solutions to their common problems.

As a result of the meeting at Moshi, a training course was organized in Kampala, Uganda, in 1962, attended by 26 participants from the English-speaking countries of the region (Marathey and Bourgeois 1965). In 1963, a similar training course was held in Bamako, Mali, with the attendance of 28 French-speaking African participants (UNESCO 1963a). Both courses were primarily intended to bring together broadcasters and adult-education specialists, offering them the same training, and helping them to consolidate the idea of cooperation in the production and utilization of radio programs of an educational nature. Similar courses have since been organized on a national level in such countries as Mali, Niger, Senegal, Togo, and Uganda.

The recommendations of the 1961 Meeting on Educational Broadcasting in Tropical Africa were submitted to, and fully supported by, participants at the Meeting of Experts on the Development of Information Media in Africa, which was held at UNESCO headquarters in Paris from 24 January to 6 February 1962 (UNESCO 1962). The latter meeting brought together some 200 experts coming from almost all African member states. They devoted a great deal of time to examining various aspects of broadcasting problems in the continent. A general review of the situation at the date of the meeting made it evident to everyone that the expansion of radio broadcasting should have top priority. The participants stressed once again the important role of radio in education, and the necessity of planning its use very carefully.

This feeling has remained unchanged ever since, and the number of people who share it has considerably increased. This is the more true because television seems to have raised financial problems difficult to solve within the economic context of developing nations. UNESCO convened a meeting devoted to the introduction and development of television in Africa in Lagos, Nigeria, 21–29 September 1964 (UNESCO 1964). Television was the basic element of a six-year pilot project concerning the application of new techniques and methods in education which was carried out in Dakar, Senegal, up to 1970. The assessment of this project was still being pursued in 1972. UNESCO is actively engaged in the multilateral educational-television project in Ivory Coast, where the government has decided to install an educational-television network with nationwide coverage (see § 15.5). This project, which started in 1969 after a three-year preparatory period, is conducted by specialists and financed by an unusually large group of sources working together, including the World Bank, the United Nations Development Programme, UNESCO, the United Nations Children's Fund, France, the Federal Republic of Germany, Canada, and the United States. It has its own teacher-training center, a production center for school television programs, a production center for reading material designed to support educational television programs, an evaluation center, and a documentation center. By October 1971, some 446 classrooms in primary schools, comprising a potential audience of 21,500 pupils, had been equipped with television receivers. This experiment is being watched with great interest by observers from other countries with educational problems similar to those of Ivory Coast.

UNESCO held two seminars within the framework of the Dakar pilot project, the preparatory phase of the larger project just described. The Seminar on the Use of the Mass Media for Social Education in Urban Areas of Africa, held in Dakar, 27 January–1 February 1969, was attended by participants from eleven French-speaking Tropical African countries. Subjects discussed included the urban milieu in Africa; social education in urban milieux; and the uses of information media (UNESCO 1969). A second seminar, held in Dakar and Kaolack in 1970, concentrated on the use of information media in rural development in Africa. It was attended by 27 participants from 15 Francophone countries of Africa, 17 observers, and 6 broadcasting experts, who discussed mass communication planning and the integration of mass media in government plans for adult education, literacy teaching, and rural development. This meeting produced an interesting document accounting for national experiments carried out in the respective countries after the meeting at Moshi in 1961 (UNESCO 1970a).

The use of radio broadcasting for educational and development purposes in urban or rural areas has also been the main theme of seminars and training courses organized locally with the assistance of UNESCO experts. In the decade 1962–72, Cameroon, Gabon, Ghana, Kenya, Mali, Nigeria, Senegal, Sierra Leone, Togo, Uganda, Upper Volta, and Zambia have organized national seminars of this kind. Most notable, however, were those held in Togo, where the government, assisted by a UNESCO expert, established a radio school and a rural broadcasting network which was being expanded in 1972 with a view to covering the whole country; and in Upper Volta, where a UNESCO pilot project for women's equality of access to education is substantially based upon the use of radio.

13.1.2 Experts, Projects, Experiments

In the business of "know-how" transfer, the selection and preparation of experts is clearly as important as the objectives and methods of the project itself. In larger projects, while competence and knowledge are the main criteria of selection, there is usually a deliberate attempt to provide a compatible mix of experts so that the variety of experiences in their backgrounds may offer both alternatives and enrichment to the project's execution. In some cases, a new concept of broadcasting use which has been tried and proved in one country will lend itself to direct transfer, with some adaptation, to another. In such projects experts are deliberately chosen from the country where the specific experience has been undergone, and UNESCO will often act as both an intermediary and a partner in fostering bilateral arrangements and in participating itself.

For example, the 1962 Meeting of Experts on the Development of Information Media in Africa, held in Paris, recommended that the experience gained by UNESCO specialists in the field of farm radio forums, a Canadian technique of rural radio which was tried with great success in India starting in 1956, should be applied to Africa (UNESCO 1962). The technique of the farm radio forum constituted an important part of the curricula of the previously mentioned Kampala and Bamako training courses. The implementation of this recommendation, the African Experiment in Radio Forums for Rural Development, was carried out in Ghana from December 1964, to April 1965. The project organization was the responsibility of Ghana Broadcasting Corporation, with the financial and technical cooperation of UNESCO and the government of Canada. Several ministries of the Ghana government contributed by seconding staff to the project. An assessment of this experiment was made by Canadian experts (Coleman, Popku, and Abell 1968).

In Togo, the development of an educational broadcasting service for rural areas was carried out for six years, from 1964 to 1970, with the assistance of a UNESCO expert (Marathey 1968). In early 1966, the government of the Republic of Zambia requested that UNESCO provide the services of a farm-forum organizer for three to four months to survey the existing needs and facilities and to advise on planning and organizing farm forums. A consultant was duly appointed, and, in the light of his recommendations and of the emphasis given by the government to the improvement of agricultural methods and production, further assistance was requested from UNESCO. The result was the assignment of a rural-radio specialist whose contract ran through 1972. At first the specialist's mission had been purely to deal with the organization of farm radio forums, but it expanded into the use of radio broadcasting for literacy teaching, inasmuch as the government of Zambia in 1972 expressed an interest in training a Zambian broadcaster for this purpose. In Senegal, a rural-radio section within the national broadcasting organization has existed since 1966. This most democratic of the educational radio services has drawn the attention of outside observers, for it really gives the floor, so to speak, to farmers and other rural people. Thanks to the radio, they can talk to any government officials, including the president of the republic himself, and explain problems of their professional and everyday life with the certitude that answers will be given to their questions.

More academic in approach are the African Institutes of Mass Communication, one of which has been established within the University of Lagos, Nigeria, with a UNESCO expert as technical adviser. In 1972, UNESCO also provided the assistance of an expert to the Kenya Institute of Mass Communication, Nairobi (§ 14.3.2).

These examples illustrate how UNESCO's work in the broadcasting field encompasses a wide spectrum of activities: meetings, seminars, and advisory and expert services. These not only respond to the expressed needs of specific countries but also create forums where African broadcasters themselves may influence the priorities for the development of the media in their own regions. Cooperation with and assistance to the Union of African National Radio and Television Organizations (§ 13.2.2) is a part of this self-determination policy. Consultation and advice, however, are but frameworks for action; the policies and plans which may evolve from these frameworks can be carried out only by people who understand not only the technology and techniques of broadcasting, but also the where, why, and how of radio and television use. Training, therefore, is the basic ingredient of this program.

UNESCO has made considerable efforts in this field since 1960, not only through the provision of experts' assistance, but also by organizing training courses of a regional or national impact and by granting fellowships to deserving candidates from member states. Fellowships may be awarded for studies in Europe or North America, and also for courses organized in African countries other than the incumbents' own. Regional courses in Bamako, Kampala, and Lagos have been attended by UNESCO fellowship holders.

Specialized subject matters vary from one training course to another. For example, they have included the production of educational radio programs and collective reception (Kampala, Bamako), community reception in rural areas (Lomé, Togo—a training course held within the framework of a long-term project which aimed at setting up a national educational-broadcasting network), and the training of broadcasting trainers (Lagos).

13.1.3 Longer-Term Projects

The role of UNESCO, however, is not limited to immediate-impact activities such as training courses or technical assistance through the services of experts. UNESCO seeks to probe far beyond the immediately useful—and sometimes ephemeral—solutions to current problems; it seeks out the sources of the problems so as to forestall them. This is why UNESCO is making a comprehensive study of the present state of broadcast training and of the problems it poses for all countries of the region. In 1967, UNESCO hired two African broadcasting experts to make a personal survey of West, Central, and East African radio stations (Quarmyne and Bebey 1967). This survey collected recommendations expressed by the very staff members who were operating African radio stations at the time. One such recommendation asked for a training manual based upon the realities of radio operations in the African continent. As a follow-up to this recommendation, UNESCO engaged an international expert well aware of the difficulties connected with broadcasting in Africa. This manual, published in 1971, is being used successfully by training specialists in Africa, who regard it as a valuable tool that helps fill a serious gap in their training regimen (see Aspinall 1971a).

UNESCO's program in communication development recognizes both the achievements of broadcasting and the potential of the media in informing, educating, and involving people in the changes which shape their lives. The scale of communication functions, however, is not diminished by development; quite the contrary. The future calls for more systematic and more intensive planning of communication strategies and the formulation of national policies for the development of communication. In this, communication research to determine both the effectiveness and the effects of communication media—and, in particular, of radio broadcasting—in development programs will be indispensable. For in Africa, as anywhere else, communication is more than information; it is even more than information plus culture plus education plus entertainment. It is more than something added to society, for when the addition is made, society itself gets larger. UNESCO's assistance to African countries in the future will put emphasis on guiding this coextension of communication and society, both from a technical and from a socioeconomic point of view.

13.2 International Broadcasting Unions, by Charles E. Sherman

The term "union" refers in this section to organizations representing national communication administrations, rather than to organizations representing labor. The world-wide union of this kind is the International Telecommunication Union, like UNESCO a specialized agency of the United Nations. In its primary function as coordinator of world telecommunications in general, it serves the African countries as ITU members; but in addition ITU provides African telecommunication administrations with multilateral assistance, some of which has a bearing on broadcasting.

Charles E. Sherman is Associate Professor and Chairman of Radio-TV-Film Division, Communication Arts, University of Wisconsin. He has conducted field research on international broadcasting unions in Western and Eastern Europe and Asia.

African broadcasting administrations also have their own regional organization, the Union of National Radio and Television Organizations, for purposes of mutual assistance specifically in the field of broadcasting. Its acronym, URTNA, derives from the French version of the name. Some African countries also derive multilateral benefits from the Arab States Broadcasting Union, whose membership includes both African and Middle Eastern systems; and from the two European regional organizations, the European Broadcasting Union and the International Radio and Television Organization.

13.2.1 International Telecommunication Union

As the United Nations' intergovernmental body responsible for preparing world and regional administrative conferences relating to technical aspects of telecommunications, the ITU's most direct and important involvement with African broadcasting has been the development of frequency-allocation plans for the continent. Two such plans, one for television and FM and the other for long- and medium-wave frequencies, were drawn up by ITU in Geneva in 1963 and 1966, respectively (ITU 1963, 1966). Aside from such planning conferences, ITU's ongoing activities aimed at improving the technical quality of African broadcasting take the forms of visiting experts, fellowships, training centers, seminars, and equipment. Africa tends to receive more of such ITU assistance than other developing areas of the world. The United Nations Development Program generally funds these activities, with ITU providing expertise and acting as the executing agency.

Visiting experts. Through the cooperation of national telecommunications administrations, experts are detached from their home organizations and sent to requesting African countries to provide on-the-job training, to introduce new techniques and planning methods, and otherwise to strengthen existing services. An ITU expert generally stays in the host country for several years. From 80 to 100 such experts are on duty annually on the African continent (see annual summaries in *Telecommunication Journal*).

This program of secondments appears to be one of ITU's most successful ventures, but it faces increasing difficulty. By the 1970s, the demand for experts doubled, but the supply remained the same. Bureaucratic complications made the supply problem even more difficult: long delays while recruiting went on; adverse factors such as the unattractiveness of some duty stations; special requirements such as knowledge of a specific foreign language, previous experience in conducting training programs, and stringent academic qualifications insisted upon by some recipient countries; then more delays in obtaining host-country approval and the release of the nominee by his national administration (*Telecommunication Journal* 1969b).

Fellowships. In the 1960s approximately 175 Africans a year received UNDP/ITU fellowships to visit developed nations for training or to attend special seminars held in Africa. These fellowships included travel and living expenses, with the ITU acting as the placement agency for the fellowship holders. The nations which hosted most of the trainees were, in order of frequency: the United Kingdom, France, West Germany, Japan, and the United States. In the late 1960s the UNDP reevaluated the fellowship programs, and, while it continued to fund them, it began emphasizing the placement of grantees at training centers in Africa.

Training centers. UNDP was concerned that students receiving training in highly developed nations might not acquire suitable techniques for coping with problems at home. It believed that "even if the problems are the same, their solutions may imply the use of means and techniques much beyond the standards and possibilities of the home country" (*Telecommunication Journal* 1969b, p. 524). To this end, African national training centers were established over the 1964–72 period with UNDP/ITU help in Algeria, Egypt, Ghana, Madagascar, Nigeria, the Sudan, and Zaïre. These centers taught technical phases of telecommunications, and most accepted students from other African countries. The original funding was provided by UNDP in conjunction with the host government and with the understanding that the centers would be supported nationally after approximately five years. In many instances, however, continued UNDP financing has proved necessary even after the initial five years.

Seminars. Until 1968 ITU conducted seminars at its headquarters in Geneva, but thereafter these activities moved more frequently into the field. The seminars were organized as short courses with the aim of updating the technicians' knowledge within a week or two. Lecturers were usually drawn from the developed nations, although on occasion an expert from a developing nation was recruited.

Few seminars dealt with broadcasting matters exclusively. One in 1969 in Dakar, Senegal, concerned the improvement of sound and television broadcasting in Africa; another, involving the planning of African broadcasting systems, was held in Lagos, Nigeria, in 1971. ITU organized both these seminars in collaboration with URTNA (§ 13.2.2). The European Broadcasting Union (§ 13.2.4) also assisted by recruiting lecturers. Engineers received instruction on such subjects as frequency allocation and usage, planning and development, operating and maintenance problems, and recruitment and training. As in the other activities previously mentioned, UNDP provided the funds for the participants (*Telecommunication Journal* 1969a, 1971).

Equipment. Compared with other continents, Africa has few centers for regularly monitoring the frequency spectrum as part of ITU's international-watchdog program. ITU planned to remedy this deficiency by supplying national telecommunications administrations with help in equipping monitoring facilities. The data gathered by these stations would provide a sounder basis for future frequency allocation planning in Africa (*Telecommunication Journal* 1969a, p. 364).

13.2.2 Union of National Radio and Television Organizations of Africa

URTNA was established in September 1962, by 23 African nations. Its headquarters is in Dakar, Senegal, with a separate technical center in Mali. Full membership rights are granted only to African nations, but associate status is available to broadcasting services in other regions (URTNA 1967). Thus the annual meetings of URTNA provide an opportunity for broadcasters from longer-established services outside the continent to exchange information with their African colleagues.

While URTNA's lack of financial resources limits the scope of its activities, it has nevertheless performed valuable services, particularly by cosponsoring activities with other international organizations. We have already noted collaboration in ITU technical seminars (§ 13.2.1). As another example, URTNA arranged for experts from three U.N. agencies —UNESCO, the Food and Agriculture Organization, and the World Health Organization—to participate in the Regional Educational Radio Television Conference in Algeria in 1969.

Equitable copyright legislation for African nations is another matter of concern, especially since established copyright laws tend to favor the developed nations. Working with UNESCO and the European Broadcasting Union, URTNA has attempted to obtain better terms for African nations, which import a great deal of copyrighted material, and to formulate a regional African copyright convention.

In the area of satellite technology, a special committee was created to collect relevant data, and URTNA participated with the other regional unions in a UNESCO meeting which considered broadcasting satellite utilization (UNESCO 1968).

Program-exchange activities are not yet extensive among African broadcasters, but URTNA has arranged the exchange of taped recordings of annual music festivals (Thompson 1971, pp. 232–46).

13.2.3 Arab States Broadcasting Union

Founded in 1968, ASBU has goals similar to those of URTNA. Its membership and purposes, however, are more restricted. It promotes Arab unity and causes, and full membership is granted only to broadcasting organizations of the Arab League states. Of ASBU's 15 full members in 1972, five were African nations—Algeria, Egypt, Libya, Morocco, and Sudan. Somalia was an associate member. ASBU has headquarters in Cairo and a technical center in Khartoum. It seems to be more active and public-relations conscious than its sister African organization, URTNA. For example, the European Broadcasting Union invited all international unions to contribute articles about their activities to the January 1972 issue of *EBU Review* on the occasion of an international conference on satellites. URTNA made no contribution, but ASBU contributed an excellent summary of its history and activities (*EBU Review* 1972).

In 1970, at the request of ASBU, a joint UNESCO-ITU committee studied the possibilities of using satellite communication for broadcast education and other developmental roles in the Arab states (Ploman, Berrada, and Clergerie 1971). The *ASBU Review*, the union's quarterly publication, reported a variety of ambitious hopes and plans discussed at its Fourth General Assembly in 1972, including a regional Arab broadcast training center, an Arab TV news service, and educational broadcasting developments (*ASBU Review*, April 1972).

13.2.4 European Broadcasting Union

EBU, the largest and most productive of the regional broadcasting associations, had 33 full members in 1972, drawn from Western Europe and its fringes, including Algeria, Morocco, and Tunisia. In addition, there were 55 associate members, 18 of them African broadcasting services, in all parts of the world.

In 1962, EBU established an aid program for broadcasting organizations in developing countries, and African nations are its greatest beneficiaries. During the 1960s it held several seminars and conferences in cooperation with URTNA, dealing with technical, legal, and administrative matters. In addition, a score of monographs relating to these subjects were prepared and furnished without cost to African EBU members.

EBU provides technical consultation on request. As examples, its technical representatives met with their African counterparts prior to the 1963 African VHF/UHF Conference, and a delegation led by the director of the EBU Technical Center played a significant role in designing new broadcasting facilities for Tunisia (interview with George Hansen, director, EBU Technical Center, Brussels, July 1970).

Legal matters, especially copyright agreements, pertaining to developing nations are a vital EBU concern, because of two primary considerations: first, EBU's mission of obtaining better terms for all broadcasting organizations in copyright conventions and in relationships with licensers of copyrighted material—mostly music, of course; second, EBU's concern that broadcasting systems of developing nations, which rely so heavily upon copyrighted materials, get special consideration. EBU's director of legal affairs, at the request of Ghana, Kenya, Malawi, South Africa, Tunisia, and Zambia drafted national copyright legislation for consideration by each country's Parliament. When they passed this legislation, he then negotiated, on behalf of some EBU members, new contracts with European authors' societies and the recording industry. EBU supported successful efforts to revise the Berne Convention and the Universal Copy-

right Convention at Paris in July 1971, with particular concern for improving the position of developing nations without unduly harming the
developed ones (Ulmer 1971). During this entire process, EBU's director
of legal affairs watched over the interests of both full and associate members
of the EBU, while participating as a representative in the Kenya delegation
(interview with Madeleine Larrue, assistant to the director, EBU Department of Legal Affairs, Geneva, July 1970).

As to program exchanges, Algeria, Morocco, and Tunisia participate in
EBU's Eurovision regional network, which links them not only to Western
Europe's national systems, but also through EBU to Eastern Europe's
Intervision network and to satellite transmissions from North and South
America and Asia. Eventually similar interconnection may be possible for
African services south of the Sahara, depending on the reduction in the
cost of satellite use or the development of high-quality microwave links
between African countries.

13.2.5 International Radio and Television Organization

Full membership in the OIRT depends upon no geographical or political
considerations; it considers itself to be a true world organization. Nevertheless, its headquarters are in Prague, it consists essentially of nations
aligned with the USSR, and its major sphere of influence is Eastern
Europe. Of the 25 full members in 1972, four were African nations—
Algeria, Egypt, Mali, and the Sudan. Although its statutes provide for
associate members, there were none as of 1972.

OIRT's activities in Africa have not been as extensive as EBU's. The
relations it maintains with URTNA and ASBU have mainly resulted in
arrangements for African broadcasting personnel to receive training in
OIRT member nations. Program exchanges are limited essentially to those
arranged through EBU's Eurovision. The major OIRT contribution in
the program area is radio scripts concerning development problems such as
public health and agriculture (interview with Jaromir Hrebik, secretary-
general, OIRT, Prague, June 1970).

13.3 The Commonwealth Broadcasting Conference, by Kenneth Adam

Nairobi was the ninth headquarters of the Commonwealth Broadcasting
Conference at the end of October 1972. This was the second time the
conference, now meeting in full session once every two years, had accepted
an African invitation. Nigeria was the host in 1965, in Lagos, Jos, and
Kaduna.

It was the writer's good fortune to see this remarkable association of

Kenneth Adam is Overseas Visitor, Temple University School of Communications
and Theater, and as a free-lance journalist contributes regularly to the *Listener* and
Financial Times. He was Director of BBC television networks, 1960–69.

national broadcasting organizations in the Commonwealth grow from six member countries in March 1945 to 37 in 1972, with several more still to come, as Great Britain divests herself of her last colonial territories. I was present at the first conference in London, as publicity officer, when the 19 delegates were easily accommodated in the Council Chamber of Broadcasting House; at the second conference, also in London, in 1952, I was an adviser. I was a full delegate at the conference in Canada, in 1962; Nigeria, 1965; and New Zealand, 1968. They were fascinating experiences, not only of cooperation, hardly argued and won, but of expanding human relationships. Unfortunately, the very size of the conference has proved to some extent its undoing; the old, leisurely progress through the host country, with chances to sample its scenery and its culture over four weeks, has given place to a tight ten-day schedule in a single locale. Nor is it easy to accommodate at least a hundred full delegates, as in Nairobi, with their accompanying legal, educational, and technical experts. The old club atmosphere has given way to a more formal and yet a more extensive exploration of detail.

I speak of a club. In 1945 it was very much a "white man's club," with India alone of the newer countries joining the old family of the United Kingdom—Australia, Canada, New Zealand, and South Africa. It was a family committed to the continued establishment of the "British way of life."

The purpose of the conference was to review the broadcasting work the members had done together through the years of World War II, and to consult on the best ways of continuing and extending collaboration in peacetime. Plenary sessions apart, the two divisions of the conference, program and technical, which were set up in 1945, are followed to this day. The objectives seen as vital to the first conference—exchange of programs between constituent members; pooling of resources and exchange of information, especially of news; cooperation over the broadcasting of great national events within the Commonwealth—have all remained permanently in the minds of the enlarged membership, though for "exchange" it would nowadays be more accurate to substitute "purchase on most favored nation terms," and for "national" to read "international" events. In 1972 for instance, arrangements for covering the Olympic Games in Munich were of greater interest to the broadcasters than the Queen's tour of the Far East. Training, as outlined below, has become in both the engineering and program fields of paramount importance in the intervening quarter-century.

This was a period which coincided with the growth of membership to 37 organizations by 1972, of which the following 14 are in or near Africa: Ghana Broadcasting Corporation, Lesotho National Broadcasting Service, Malawi Broadcasting Corporation, Mauritius Broadcasting Corporation, Nigerian Broadcasting Corporation, Radio Botswana, Radio Gambia,

Radio Seychelles, Radio Tanzania (Dar es Salaam), Radio Uganda and Uganda Television, Sierra Leone Radio and Television, Swaziland Broadcasting Service, Voice of Kenya, and Zambia Broadcasting Service. South Africa would have made a fifteenth African member, but it had withdrawn from the organization.

Ghana was the first African country to be admitted, in 1960, followed in 1963 by Nigeria, Tanzania, Uganda, and Sierra Leone. The first fulltime secretary of the conference was Michael Stephens, an Englishman; the second was John Akar, a Sierra Leonian; the third, and 1972 incumbent, was Alva Clarke, a West Indian.

The conference has a number of continuing committees responsible for mutual-assistance projects; an example of such assistance was a pilot eight-week training course in Accra in 1967, attended by broadcasters from The Gambia, Ghana, Sierra Leone, and Uganda, with British and Canadian instructors (§ 5.2.3). Typically, the training courses are mounted ad hoc and, what is very important, on the spot. A subgroup of the conference was established for Central and Southern Africa, comprising Botswana, Lesotho, Malawi, Swaziland, and Zambia, and its first full meeting in 1971 led to the continuing scrutiny of problems common to those parts of the continent (see King 1971). Moreover, the example of the conference proper inspired other, larger groups, outside as well as inside the Commonwealth, to combine to mutual advantage; and so there is a fertile, if sometimes competitive, crossmembership between the oldest body, the Commonwealth Broadcasting Conference (which even predated the United Nations) and the African, Asian, and European Broadcasting Unions. The Asian union's veteran secretary general, Colonel Sir Charles Moses, was one of the founder members, not only of the Commonwealth Broadcasting Conference, but also of the Union of National Radio and Television Organizations in Africa, and the Caribbean Broadcasting Union.

From the beginning the criterion of membership to which the Commonwealth Broadcasting Conference has clung stubbornly has been one of "public service," but this has been stretched to include, not merely those organizations fully protected in their independence by the license-fee system, but also those less protected (compare the BBC, which is not accountable on a day-to-day basis to Parliament, with the Canadian and Australian equivalents, which are); and to include those wholly dependent on government grants and those which are financed by both public funds and commercial revenues.

The increasing importance of commercial revenue in a decade in which television, the most expensive of the mass media, is opening up all over Africa, has been recognized, so far as developing countries are concerned, since the Jamaica Conference of 1970; but the commercial undertakings in Britain, Australia, and Canada, for instance, have so far been excluded from membership completely. This has given considerable offense to

Britain's Independent Television Authority, which in 1972, with the arrival of commercial radio, became the Independent Broadcasting Authority. This body insists that the parliamentary sanction and the parliamentary obligations under which it operates give it a sufficient identity of endeavor with the majority of the members of the conference, which have mixed systems, to justify its immediate entry. It is unlikely that its moral and professional claim can be indefinitely delayed.

13.4 The World Bank, by James M. Kushner

The term "World Bank" is actually shorthand for a group of financial institutions—the International Development Association, the International Finance Corporation, and the World Bank itself, an informal name for the International Bank for Reconstruction and Development, or IBRD. More than a hundred member nations subscribe to the IBRD, one of whose roles is to provide loans, under favorable conditions, for infrastructure projects in developing countries. An advantage of these loans for developing countries is that they come without the strings, real or imagined, attached to credits offered unilaterally by individual countries.

"Infrastructure projects" have usually been understood as roads, power stations, ports, and the like—the "hard" structures which lay a working foundation for economic progress. Only recently has the bank recognized that a "soft" facility like educational broadcasting could be counted as a part of a developing nation's economic infrastructure. This recognition of the potential developmental role of broadcasting by hard-nosed, unsentimental financiers is a significant breakthrough.

World Bank president Robert McNamara has said that educational broadcasting can "contribute significantly to the learning process and, thereby, help overcome one of the most stubborn bottlenecks in development efforts" (*Finance and Development* 1970). Specifically, the bank believes that the broadcast media "can be highly effective in the introduction of new curricula, in upgrading of teachers and in the most efficient use of the best teachers for the mass of students. They do not hold out the promise of lower costs per student but because they can be highly effective innovating forces, they can, in some cases, provide a much greater educational return for a moderate increase in expenditure" (IBRD 1971, p. 20). The IBRD's first full-scale educational-television investment was made in 1970 in the Ivory Coast (see § 15.5), which in 1970 obtained a $19.1-million loan for educational development—including an integral educational-television component. A great deal of background experimentation preceded this venture into large-scale use of ETV, much of it in Niger (see § 15.2.3.). Although that experiment succeeded on a very small scale, Niger was unable to generate support for extending it to the educational system as a whole.

The Ivory Coast seemed to offer a more promising venue. UNESCO/ World Bank "reconnaissance" missions in 1967 and 1968 determined the feasibility of large-scale application of instructional television there, and in December 1968 the Ivory Coast government formally approached the World Bank for assistance. A bank appraisal mission recommended that a loan be made through its Education Projects Department, and on 27 April 1970 the final loan agreement was concluded (interviews with Shigenari Futagami, mass media specialist, World Bank Education Projects Department). The loan agreement between Ivory Coast and the IBRD refers to "a program to provide on an experimental basis instructional television and, if the results so justify, to extend its use through its educational system."

France had assured support in the form of technical experts, and several bilateral-aid agencies had also promised help. Part of the World Bank loan was earmarked specifically for the construction and furnishing of a production center at Bouaké and a maintenance center at Abidjan by 30 June 1973 (see § 15.5). Interest rates on the loan run 7% on used funds (to be repaid by 15 December 1999) and only 0.75% on funds committed but unused. The terms of the loan require open, competitive international bidding on construction, furnishings, and services derived from bank funds, and the bank must approve the ensuing contracts.

It can be seen from this sequence of events that World Bank loans could hardly be classed as impulsively generous gestures. Financial experts take a long, cold look at the realistic prospects of success for any project they are asked to consider supporting. For example, a UNESCO/World Bank reconnaissance mission went to Niger in 1970 to survey possible projects for educational support; despite the prior success of the Niger television experiment, the mission decided that Niger's fiscal state was too shaky to warrant a loan. A second mission in the same year reported back that Niger's basic telecommunication system—considered an essential infrastructural element on which to base educational television—was entirely inadequate for the purpose.

The fact is that too many educational broadcasting schemes in developing countries have been based more on enthusiasm than on realistic assessments. They have often been ill-conceived, inadequately planned, and chaotically administered. In short, they have not offered sound developmental investment opportunities from a soberly detached, objective viewpoint such as that taken by the bank. Not surprisingly, in early 1972 the bank had no other educational broadcasting projects in Africa under serious consideration. This was not for lack of proposals. We have already mentioned the case of Niger. As another example, Senegal applied for a loan to initiate a rural-radio project but was unable to disentangle the project from politics and so was eventually turned down.

The IBRD's policy toward educational television is well summarized in the following statement from a working paper on education:

Two educational television projects which the Bank has considered—on the Ivory Coast and Niger—bring out sharply the characteristics of this type of development and why the Bank should not rush headlong into it. In the Ivory Coast educational television is being introduced as part of a multi-faceted program . . . and the expected number of students and teachers to be reached constitutes a sufficiently large market to keep unit costs at an acceptable level. In Niger most of these favorable circumstances do not exist . . . expansion of the project for the education system as a whole would require substantial capital and operating expenditure for a small and widely dispersed market which will not be economically justifiable for some years to come. [IBRD 1971, p. 20]

14   Training

14.1 Introduction

Bebey describes in § 13.1.3 how he and A. T. Quarmyne came to visit 19 countries in the course of making a survey of broadcast training in Tropical Africa on behalf of UNESCO. Perhaps because of their subsequent report's pungency and unusual frankness, UNESCO never released it as a formal publication (Quarmyne and Bebey 1967). In this chapter we shall not attempt to do more than to bring up to date and to develop in more detail certain aspects of the subject, for Quarmyne and Bebey's perceptive treatment remains the definitive one, even though not made generally available.

We consider in some detail the major British training institutions and practices because they have had such widespread influence and because their recent history illuminates changing concepts of broadcast training needs in Africa. This emphasis is not meant to discount the activities of other countries. Many of the bilateral- and multilateral-aid projects described in chapters 12 and 13 include significant training components. France's training efforts were discussed in § 6.1.3 in connection with French aid to broadcasting generally. The French metropolitan training center, Studio-École, adopted the logical yet seldom-used device of giving students access to their own on-the-air radio facility, in which "students plan, produce and actually broadcast programmes over a low power radio station which has built up a loyal and highly critical audience in the community surrounding Maisons-Laffitte" (Quarmyne and Bebey 1967, p. 20).

The most significant developments in training since the Quarmyne and Bebey tour have taken place in Africa itself. Training at home, to be fully effective, however, needs to rise above the level of the trade school. Gläser-Weisser reports that the German Radio Training Center in Ethiopia (§ 14.4) found that secondary school graduates simply did not have sufficient background and sophistication to benefit fully from the training program; thereupon the center aimed at recruiting college graduates, making the year-long program essentially a postgraduate course. For the students, however, this fifth year of study is unduly wasteful. The same objective could be reached in four years if students could study broadcasting—and the media generally—as a major undergraduate subject in college.

Of course, at that level the specific skills of the broadcaster are but the tip of the iceberg. They can be brought to bear effectively only if supported by a broad, general education which enables the broadcaster to deal intelligently with the unlimited range of subject matters that enters into broadcast programming. From a survey of media training needs in East Africa and Ethiopia came the suggestion that "a complete and well-conceived program for the development of mass media in East Africa must include a fourth component in addition to broadcasting, film, and journalism training. The fourth component is training in the skillful use of these media in education and development" (Schramm, Nelson, and Sommerlad 1969, p. 125). In § 15.3.1 Nwankwo points out the impossibility of achieving effective information/guidance programs without producers who understand the subject matter, and in § 14.3.2 Scotton stresses the importance of training in general economic and social development for those whose job it will be to use broadcasting to assist such development. After the University of Nairobi Journalism School's first year, the director announced that a new course, Journalism in Development, would be introduced, and that students would be assigned to study ongoing development projects— steps in the right direction, though one wonders why it was necessary to lose even one year in discovering so obvious a need (*African Journalist* 1972b).

College education in broadcasting is also important from the point of view of manpower strategy. Since the primary direct road to preferment and status is through higher education, broadcasting cannot hope to attract the most intelligent, highly motivated types of personnel in the absence of degrees for broadcasters. Nor can broadcasting attain suitable levels of priority in the civil service hierarchy without formal academic status. That African countries are already responding to this need for broadcasting education at the college level is made clear by Scotton's survey later in this chapter.

14.2 British Training

14.2.1 British Broadcasting Corporation, *by Geoffrey Seymour*

By 1972, the BBC had been in public-service broadcasting for 50 years. Over this half-century it pioneered and developed ideas, techniques, and systems for the benefit of its domestic audience; but at the same time it accepted the responsibility of sharing its know-how with broadcasting

Geoffrey Seymour has been BBC Overseas Training Organiser since 1959. He joined the BBC originally in 1947 and has traveled widely in Africa.

organizations overseas that are similarly committed. This was especially so with respect to other members of the Commonwealth, where the BBC may have been involved in consultancy for, or the actual setting up of, the national broadcasting services. Links forged in this way and maintained through such bodies as the Commonwealth Broadcasting Conference (see § 13.3) enable a common language to be spoken when it comes to questions of training.

In Africa the BBC's training links have been strongest, therefore, with the Anglophone countries of the continent, like Botswana, The Gambia, Ghana, Kenya, Lesotho, Malawi, Nigeria, Sierra Leone, Swaziland, Tanzania, Uganda, and Zambia; but the whole continent, north and south of the Sahara, has responded to the offer of BBC assistance in the training field. The BBC has established over the years a wide range of training services, both formal and informal, available to African broadcasters as they are to broadcasters overseas generally. This section will describe those services available in 1972.

At home in Britain formal training courses are mounted for overseas broadcasters from Africa and other parts of the world. Radio courses specially designed for overseas broadcasters were started by the BBC in 1951, and during the years 1951–71 52 courses were held. Of the 505 broadcasters attending them, 293 came from broadcasting organizations in Africa, and 212 from the rest of the world. Previously, overseas broadcasters had been accepted as guests on domestic courses run by the BBC Staff Training Department. Though this practice has diminished considerably since 1951, the occasional place is still given to an overseas guest on a BBC domestic course.

Radio. The Overseas Radio Production Course is held twice a year in London. It consists of ten weeks of instruction on techniques of sound broadcasting, with lectures, demonstrations, discussions, and emphasis on practical work. This is followed by two to three weeks of observer attachment to specialist departments of the BBC. The course is designed for producers or program assistants who have had a year or two of experience working in their own broadcasting organizations. There are 12 places on each course.

The Advanced Overseas Radio Production Course, held once a year in London, started in the spring of 1972, with 13 of the 15 participants from African countries. Lasting 12 weeks, it provides opportunity for the study, at an advanced level and with wide scope for practical work, of one particular area of broadcasting. This will be the course member's own specialist field, such as presentation, drama, or current affairs. The course is designed for producers working in specialist fields, and normally at least four years' working experience is required. There are 12 to 15 places available on this course.

Television. Television courses specially designed for overseas broadcasters were started by the BBC in 1966. Over the period 1966–71, 11 courses were run, attended by 165 overseas broadcasters, 35 from organizations in Africa and 130 from the rest of the world. The practice before these special courses were started was to accept overseas guests on domestic courses run by the BBC Staff Training Department.

The Overseas Television Production Course is held twice a year in London. It lasts 14 weeks and is followed by a period of up to three months of observer attachments to BBC production departments. It covers all aspects of the planning and production of television programs, in the studio and on location, on tape and on film. There are 16 places available on each course, and 12 of the 32 participants in 1971 were from Africa.

Engineering. The BBC started overseas engineering training in 1948. Since then, between 350 and 400 staff members of broadcasting organizations in Africa have attended courses and training attachments in Britain. The training programs have been flexible, since they were designed to take account of the candidate's qualifications in education and experience as well as the employer's requirements. Most of them have combined one or more formal courses, run for the BBC's own staff, with periods of attachment. However, the BBC Engineering Training Centre—located at Evesham, about 100 miles from London—is currently examining means whereby it can devise courses or elements of courses with the special needs of overseas trainees in mind. It looks to the time when, with the steady growth of national training within each country or region, it can support, in conjunction with senior-level engineering training, the preparation of instructors. Places are available for members of overseas broadcasting organizations on any of the BBC's own internal engineering-training courses, which are held at the Engineering Training Centre. They are:

The Technical Assistant and Technical Operator Course, which lasts 12 weeks. Primarily intended for new entrants, it gives an introduction to basic operation and maintenance techniques for broadcasting equipment. Educational systems differ so widely that it is impossible to set specific educational requirements for entrance to the course; all that can be stipulated is "a reasonable standard of education." The earlier parts of the course are common, but each student specializes toward the end in radio or television studios and recordings, transmitters, receivers, or communications.

The Senior Technical Operator Course, in radio or television, lasting nine weeks. It is designed for technical operators of three or four years' experience who can benefit from a wider and deeper study of facilities and techniques in their field of work and related areas.

The "C" Engineering Course, lasting for 14 weeks and divided into two equal parts. The first part deals with the necessary theory, and the second part can be in one of the specialties listed above.

The Direct Entry Engineering Course, consisting of two parts. The first is a five-week introduction to broadcast engineering at a level suitable for graduate engineers, and the second is the seven-week part 2 of the "C" Engineering course in appropriate specialties.

After these courses, on-station attachments are arranged for overseas trainees to areas which will provide experience with equipment and techniques most nearly related to their fields of training. In some areas participation is possible; in others the trainees are merely observers.

Management. The Senior Management Conference, which is residential, is intended for senior management executives. Two such conferences, each lasting six weeks, were held in 1970 and 1971 in association with the Birmingham Graduate Centre for Management Studies. A third conference was planned for 1972. Eighteen of the 46 participants in the first two conferences were African. For middle-management executives, there is the Management of Resources Course, an eight-week course held in London.

Newswriting. A twelve-week course in newswriting for overseas radio journalists is held once a year. The capacity is normally eight places. Practical instruction is given in writing news reports, preparing and recording news items, cutting and editing tapes, and the like. Five of the eight participants in 1971 were from Africa.

Other types of training. Apart from the foregoing formal training courses, there are other means whereby the broadcaster from an organization in Africa can share some of the BBC's know-how at base. There has been, and there continues to be, a steady stream of visitors from overseas, whether to Broadcasting House, the Television Centre, a regional station, or Bush House, where the external services act as a magnet. The BBC's Department of Overseas and Foreign Relations arranges countless ad hoc visits and short attachments, in which there might be a greater or lesser degree of training content.

As long ago as 1958, the BBC African Service at Bush House initiated a system of "working/training" attachments. A producer from a broadcasting organization in Africa works alongside professional colleagues in the African Service in London for a period of three to six months, or even a year; but it is in the context of a totally practical training exercise. This arrangement often follows attendance at one of the formal overseas training courses at the BBC.

All overseas training in the BBC enjoys the advantage of always having the working business of a large organization going on not far away. An expert in almost any field can be called upon instantly. A practical situation can be demonstrated, not merely talked about academically in isolation from the reality.

Training in Africa. So much for the shop window of BBC overseas training at home. As an export commodity to Africa, it has been and still remains in the hands of the individuals who leave their colleagues and working environment behind them and carry their expertise overseas with them. Just as there has been a stream of African visitors to the BBC, so there has been a steady flow of BBC men and women to work in Africa. There must have been few who did not have some element of training in their briefs.

Today, as in the past, there are BBC "experts" ready to answer the call to do a job with a broadcasting organization in Africa. In the area of formal training, the BBC's overseas training organizers, for radio and for television, expect to spend at least part of the year, which is mainly devoted to running courses in Britain, conducting courses overseas or advising in some way. In Africa the ground is new for television, but in radio a number of BBC courses have been conducted on site—in Botswana, The Gambia, Ghana, Kenya, Lesotho, Malawi, Sierra Leone, Tanzania, Uganda, and Zambia.

The BBC is still seconding staff to work as training officers with African broadcasting organizations, continuing a long tradition. Training was either specific or implied in the roles of the hundreds of BBC staff who have occupied executive or advisory posts in African broadcasting organizations since the early 1950s. During 1971, for example, eight program and administrative and five engineering officers were on secondment to African broadcasting organizations. This does not include many visits and short-term consultancies. Of course, these figures were very much higher in the big development years of the late 1950s and early 1960s.

The fact that the BBC continues to provide training opportunities both at home and overseas must surely demonstrate a conviction that there are arguments for, and a place for, both. The trend is certainly toward providing more training at base or regionally, where for the beginner there are definite advantages. The training can be direct, less expensive, and cause less disturbance. But at a later stage in a broadcasting career there can be advantages in a wider horizon. The BBC may be able to help in both cases.

Terms of admission. For all the formal training opportunities the BBC charges tuition fees, which vary from course to course. However, the vast majority of trainees from broadcasting organizations in Africa have had these tuition fees and their travel and maintenance expenses met through technical-assistance awards from the British government. The Special Commonwealth African Assistance Programme and various regional programs have enabled many hundreds of broadcasters from Africa to attend BBC courses.

Applicants for BBC training must be officially nominated by their home broadcasting organization. The BBC does not accept applications from private individuals. Organizations may make direct application to the BBC, but where technical assistance is being sought requests for training are channeled through the local British Council representative, or in certain cases through the local British high commission or embassy.

14.2.2 Centre for Educational Development Overseas, *by Alexander B. Edington*

In 1962, the Centre for Educational Television Overseas (CETO), an independent nonprofit body, was set up in London by four cofounders—the Nuffield Foundation; the Independent (i.e., commercial) Television Companies, acting as a body; the British government, through the then Department of Technical Co-operation, now the Overseas Development Administration; and the British Broadcasting Corporation. Soon after its inception, the Ford Foundation and the Rockefeller Brothers Fund made additional financial support available to CETO.

The most urgent educational-television need at the time was for assistance with the training of personnel. CETO, therefore, instituted training courses on a regular basis in London and also conducted others, on request, in Africa. From the outset CETO courses had the objective of turning out, in the words of a past head of training, "a self-reliant professional." The courses, which had a normal duration of thirteen weeks, were practical in nature and intensive in method, essentially concerned with the training of producers. No direct training was or is given in the more specialized aspects of television such as engineering, graphics, or filmmaking, although individual secondments and attachments to CETO in such specialties have been arranged on an ad hoc basis over the years.

After eight years of pioneer work, CETO merged with two other ongoing British organizations in related fields—the Centre for Curriculum Renewal and Educational Development Overseas, and the Oversea Visual Aids Centre. On 18 March 1970, the name "CETO" went out of existence and "CEDO"—the Centre for Educational Development Overseas—came into being. CETO provided the nucleus for the Broadcasting Division of CEDO, which includes educational radio as well as television.

CEDO has deliberately tried to keep its training environment at a level compatible with the working environment to which trainees will return. Educational broadcasting is very much the poor relation of general broadcasting, and most educational-television programs are produced in the smallest, least well-equipped studios of the broadcasting service. While not compromising high standards of maintenance and efficiency, CEDO's training studios were designed to use the minimum of professional equipment essential to maintain a broadcast standard.

During his ETV course, each trainee writes, produces, and directs pro-

Alexander B. Edington is Director, Information and Research Department, CEDO. He joined CETO in 1965 after serving as Education Officer in Nigeria and was seconded by CETO for a time to Ghana as Broadcasting Adviser.

gram exercises that have an immediate relevance to his own domestic educational situation. These start with simple, single-point concepts and lead up to full-length programs of the type that the trainee might expect to produce on his return home. In addition, each trainee is made aware of the problems of cameramen, floor managers, sound and lighting engineers, and studio hands. In the team exercises all trainees operate in each of these positions. It has been found that in order to provide the individualized courses and schedules that have been a feature of the training given by CEDO, the numbers of trainees must be limited to between 15 and 20 per course.

All Anglophone countries in Africa which possess educational-television services (including the Arab Republic of Egypt and the Sudan) have sent personnel to London for training. Trainees must be sponsored by their appropriate government departments and must plan to return home to work in ETV following their courses. An analysis of the trainees who attended the Centre's courses in educational-television production over the ten years 1962–72 indicates that approximately 80% came from educational backgrounds—inspectors, headmasters, ministry officials, and teachers, The rest came from ministries of information, radio, journalism, and the like. No system of grading is used in the training courses to enable statistical comparisons, but the teaching staff considers that trainees coming with no prior experience of television succeed better than those with experience in entertainment television.

It can be argued that first-level training can most effectively be given on the spot, but because of the limited numbers of personnel needing training from established services it is more cost-efficient to conduct these courses centrally. However, in cases where considerable new developments have taken place in an ETV service, it has proved more effective to send a person or a team of persons to the service to conduct a training course on the spot. Courses of this type have taken place in Egypt, Ethiopia, Ghana, Mauritius, Sierra Leone, Uganda, and Zambia. Another case that justifies on-site training is that of preparing classroom teachers to utilize ETV. Courses essential for the users of the programs must be carried out on the spot because of the large numbers of persons involved, the short duration of each course, and the dependence of each course on access to locally produced educational program material.

Before the formation of CEDO, British assistance to African educational radio had been channeled through the BBC. With the creation of CEDO, the BBC's former head of Schools Broadcasting in Kenya became the head of the CEDO Broadcasting Division's Educational Radio Section. BBC and CEDO, therefore, shared responsibility for the fiftieth Overseas Radio Production Course for Schools Broadcasters, held in 1970, just after the formation of CEDO.

CETO's experience in providing ETV training was drawn upon in developing CEDO's training programs in educational radio. Intensive, practical courses are run regularly in London. Considerable attention is paid to the problems at the reception end—whether in the classroom or the extension center. The relationship of educational radio to the educational system and to other media is also stressed (see Singleton 1971). In addition, some courses have been conducted on the spot—for example, in Ethiopia, Mauritius, and Sierra Leone.

Besides the training courses conducted in London or in Africa, CEDO has involved itself in a variety of cooperative training ventures by seconding members of its staff to assist with or to run regional, subregional, or national courses arranged by international agencies such as UNESCO.

During the pioneering stage of its educational-television work, CETO recognized that in addition to training there was also an urgent need for basic program materials, which in turn might serve a secondary training function. It recognized that complete prepackaged educational series produced abroad would not be adaptable to specific local needs in developing countries. CETO's solution was the concept of a "do-it-yourself" program kit, complete in itself yet just as adaptable as the imagination and resources of local producers allowed. Each kit contained full instructions for producer and technical staff, scripts, and ready-made visual materials, such as captions and silent-film sequences to illustrate key points in the lessons. Each series also contained descriptive material for the education authorities, specimen notes for classroom teachers, and in some cases even samples of workbooks that could be duplicated for distribution to viewers. CETO developed such kits for series of television lessons in basic subjects having a minimum of cultural bias, such as science and mathematics.

CETO designed the kits for use in studios with minimal professional equipment, staff, and facilities. Their aim was in the first instance to provide high-quality television material completely adaptable to the particular pupil and curricular needs of any country or region, but they also served as indirect training devices. The scripts could be translated or paraphrased; local photographs, models, or other visual materials could be substituted for those supplied. None of the kit materials were copyrighted. Local broadcasters and educational authorities were encouraged to modify the kit materials in any way that suited their purposes.

CETO kits answered an immediate need by enabling inexperienced personnel with minimum training to put out programs of acceptable quality, and yet with some degree of local flavor. Like any successful technical adviser, they eventually worked themselves out of a job. As local personnel became more experienced, confident, and resourceful they had less need for ready-made materials. Ghana's use of the geography kits illustrates the pattern. In the first year, the Ghanaian producer followed instructions contained in the kits to the letter. In the second year a number of local modifications and adaptations were introduced. By the third year the local producer had discarded most of the kit material, retaining only a few of the visuals. Thus the kits served their double purpose—first as emergency program materials, second as a practical training exercise for local producers.

Although the kits cost CETO a great deal to produce, it either donated them or "sold" them for a token fee to the developing countries that used them. The cost factor, along with the success of the kits in stimulating independent local production, caused CETO to phase them out in the late 1960s. To a large extent their training function has been taken on by films about the techniques and methodologies of educational television which CEDO now provides.

Another feature of CETO's earlier activities no longer being emphasized by CEDO is the provision, on request, of personnel on a long-term second-ment basis. The Ethiopian Educational Mass Media Center in Addis Ababa (§ 15.4) used the services of a CETO general-production adviser and a film adviser. A production adviser and a utilization adviser were seconded to the Educational Television Service of the Ghana Broadcasting Corporation, and the Kenya Institute of Mass Communications (§ 14.3.2) also used the services of an educational-production adviser.

In 1970–71, CEDO's first year, its expenses amounted to close to a million dollars (CEDO 1971, p. 12). It handled 636 trainees of all kinds in London, and 355 overseas. Specific broadcasting activities included help in the design of new ETV studios in Egypt, seven courses run in London and four overseas, and the previously mentioned secondments in Africa. CEDO's announced schedule of courses for 1972 included five in audiovisual studies, two in educational radio, and four in educational tele-vision. They varied in length from one to 15 weeks, most of them closer to the longer term.

Since its inception CETO had published a quarterly journal, whose files have become an important repository of information and lore about educa-tional broadcasting, especially in developing countries. Published first as *CETO News,* in 1967 it was retitled *Educational Television International.* With the merger of CETO into CEDO the title was changed once more. Starting with the March 1971 issue it became *Educational Broadcasting International* in recognition of the addition of radio to the brief of the Broadcasting Division.

With the advantage of hindsight gained in ten years' experience, it is possible to be somewhat critical of CETO's early response to the immediate demands for training for educational-television staff. That the training given was of a high standard is not in question. Factors that could be questioned however, were the balance and emphasis of the content of this training; the method of selecting trainees; and the general lack of planning, organization, and purpose in the educational administrations from which the trainees came. Indeed, in some situations one could even question the educational relevance of the medium, the decisions which led to its introduction, and the manner of its introduction.

Without doubt one of the most important elements in all training activities is the selection and recruitment of the personnel who will undergo training. In the past insufficient attention was paid to this element. Wastage or nonutilization of training is a luxury that neither the trainees nor the trainers can afford; yet all too frequently the persons nominated have been unsuited to profit from the course of training for which they were selected.

During the earliest CETO courses in the 1960s emphasis was centered almost entirely on educational-television production. Later, much more consideration was given to the organizational implications of using television as an educational tool—the problems of classroom utilization, the relationship of the ETV service to the educational system in general and the curriculum unit of the Ministry of Education in particular, and the relationship of television to other media. CEDO expects to become increasingly involved in providing help in these critically important areas in the 1970s. It will no longer be sufficient first to acquire television or other technological aids to education and then to ask what to do with them. The reverse is required—first, a definition of the educational problems to be solved; then, consideration of the best methods available for solving them.

14.2.3 Thomson Foundation Television College, *by Sydney W. Head*

In a Glasgow suburb in 1962, Lord Thomson of Fleet, the Canadian newspaper and business magnate, set up a residential facility for television training, the Thomson Foundation Television College. This facility complements Thomson Television International, a commercial subsidiary concerned with the sale of television-construction and -management package deals to developing countries (§ 17.3). Attendance at the college is not limited, however, to trainees from stations with which the Thomson organization has commercial connections. The college is an activity of the Thomson Foundation, an endowed charitable trust. Through 1971 it had trained 279 persons from 47 developing countries, and nearly half the trainees were Africans.

Instruction at the college is carried out in well-equipped facilities that include two television studios and three videotape machines. Sixteen-week courses in both production and engineering are offered twice a year, with about 70% of the course time devoted to practical work. A dozen to 15 students participate in each course. They receive scholarships covering all instructional and living expenses; only travel cost to and from the school is not covered by the bursary. Trainees must be professionally employed in television at home and must have television jobs to return to after the course. By the end of 1971, the college had trained 133 Africans: from Nigeria, 37; Ghana, 22; Ethiopia, 14; Zambia, 13; Kenya, 12; Uganda, 10; Libya and Sierra Leone, 7 each; Egypt, 6; Sudan, 2; and Congo, Rhodesia, and South Africa, 1 each.

As an additional service to television systems in developing countries, members of the college staff sometimes go abroad to conduct in-service training programs of three to eight weeks' duration. Such secondments have been made in Africa to Ethiopia, Kenya, Nigeria, Sierra Leone, Uganda, and Zambia. The principal of the college, a veteran of the BBC, points out that these visits are valuable in helping the instructors to appreciate "the incredible limitations imposed upon some of our students" in terms of equipment and budgets (letter from William J. C. Meikle, 7 December 1971).

14.3 Training in Africa, by James F. Scotton

14.3.1 Traditional Methods

Broadcast training in Africa has largely followed patterns long established in Great Britain and France. One pattern has been on-the-job training, with broadcast newcomers learning skills by long apprenticeship at low pay. Many African broadcast executives still believe this is the only way to train professional broadcasters, and a United Nations survey predicted that this system would continue for many years to come (Quarmyne and Bebey 1967, p. 5). Conversations the writer had with broadcasters from ten African countries in both East and West Africa confirm that this attitude was still widely held in 1972.

Rapid Africanization of broadcast staffs in the late 1950s and the 1960s, however, brought great pressure for short courses to prepare Africans to replace Europeans as quickly as possible. The pressing need for African broadcast personnel of all types is suggested by the fact that, between 1950 and 1960, 16 African countries inaugurated new broadcasting services and others greatly expanded existing operations (UNESCO 1963b, p. 7). The old, leisurely apprentice system could not meet this demand, especially in the technical areas. Accordingly, special courses for training engineers and maintenance technicians were set up in Ghana in 1955, in Nigeria in 1957, and in Uganda and other African countries in the 1960s (UNESCO 1962, pp. 34–35).

Local courses for training reporters, announcers, producers, and directors also soon developed. Some were merely informal training sessions. At the Liberian Broadcasting Corporation, for example, the regular operating staff gave lectures or demonstrations when they had the time. Larger organizations, such as the Nigerian and the Ghanaian Broadcasting Corporations, organized more formal courses of study with full-time instructors (see §§ 5.1.11, 5.2.3). These training programs remained heavily practical in orientation, with emphasis on "learning by doing."

James F. Scotton was Dean, Institute of Mass Communications, University of Lagos, 1971–73. He was Research Associate, Makerere University Social Science Research Institute, 1968–70, and has had professional experience in newspaper, wire-service, and public-relations positions.

The recruitment of both technical and production personnel continued to be from among those who had done well in their final examinations at secondary school, the British "O Levels" or the French "Brevet." Ethiopia's Broadcast Training School was unique in that it recruited university graduates for its 12-month course in radio production (see § 14.4). Recruitment was carried on under civil service procedures, in many cases by the civil service itself (Quarmyne and Bebey 1967, p. 10). Little attention was paid to such vital qualifications as talent, aptitude, or even interest; in consequence, individuals with imagination and creativity were rarely attracted (Naesselund 1971b, p. 5). After surveying some of those who had risen through the ranks to reach executive positions in African broadcasting, a UNESCO team commented, "It makes little difference to them whether they are in Broadcasting or in the Public Works Department and they will have no hesitation about transferring at any time for a slightly higher salary. These are men and women meant for civil service careers and can never look upon broadcasting as a profession" (Quarmyne and Bebey 1967, p. 22).

Journalism programs at the secondary school level have been established in several African countries. Emphasis has been on the print media, but interest in broadcast training is growing. The Institute of Journalism in Accra, founded by Kwame Nkrumah in 1958 as the first journalism school in Tropical Africa, includes writing for radio and television in its two-year diploma course (letter and course syllabus from G. F. Dove, acting director, Ghana Institute of Journalism, 4 April 1972). The Publicity Media Institute of the Nyegezi Social Training Centre at Mwanza, Tanzania, has an 18-month sequence which includes writing for broadcasting. Although it is supported by Catholic agencies, the institute's graduates usually take jobs with secular organizations, including government (letter from Rev. O. J. Granville, head, Department of Journalism, Nyegezi Training Centre, 28 March 1972).

In Zambia, the journalism program at the Evelyn Hone College of Further Education, a secondary school, has developed into a two-year sequence offering some broadcast fundamentals, the students having access to radio studios for practical training. The school has prepared a curriculum for a prospective radio-television production course (letter from Joseph Klansky, head, Communications Department, 16 May 1972). There is also a journalism school in Algiers which may develop broadcast training.

In Morocco the Ministry of Information sponsors a journalism training program at the Center for the Development of Journalists. Some instruction in program production is included, and students get practical training in government broadcast studios (letter and course material from Sebti Azedine, director, Center for the Development of Journalists, Rabat, 4 April 1972). In the Ivory Coast the government sponsored a two-year course for production and technical personnel (Quarmyne and Bebey 1967, p. 17).

An increasing amount of broadcast training has been given by Christian church organizations in Africa. Radio Voice of the Gospel, Addis Ababa, has its own training program (§ 11.2.3). Most of the church-sponsored media centers, however, train church workers to produce religious, educational, and cultural material to be used by the government-owned broadcasting stations. The All Africa Conference of Churches offers a six-month course in radio scriptwriting and production in Nairobi (§ 11.2.5), and in Zaïre TELE-STAR holds training sessions at its radio and television studios (§ 11.2.2). There have been moves to increase the scope of both the Zaïre and the Nairobi operations (Healey 1968, pp. 9–10; AMECEA 1971, p. 1). A four-year radio training institute has been started by Protestant missionaries in Burundi (§ 4.4.1).

Short courses in broadcast production have been held at various church centers throughout Africa, such as the MEMA (Modern Evangelical Methods in Africa) Studio in Lilongwe, Malawi. The Rhodesian Episcopal Conference trains priests and lay people in radio and television techniques at its Radio and Television Production Center at Salisbury. An ecumenical radio training center at Yaoundé, Cameroon, to serve many African countries has been proposed (Healey 1969, p. 14). The Catholic Radio and Television Center at Hatch End, England, and the Communications Center at Dublin, Ireland, have offered scholarships to Africans working in the religious broadcast field.

Although there has been little recruitment into African broadcasting above the trainee level, there have been opportunities for additional outside training for broadcasting staff. In Uganda, for example, technical trainees can spend two terms each year at the Uganda Technical College, and the third working at Radio Uganda. For program personnel, the equivalent has been to attend one of the occasional UNESCO broadcasting short courses, such as those held in Kenya, Mali, Senegal, or Uganda. These courses have frequently focused on a particular problem, such as rural development, and have tried to combine classroom with field work (Marathey and Bourgeois 1965, pp. 32–36). Emphasis in such courses has usually been on the print media (UNESCO 1965, pp. 34–42), but later more attention began to be paid to the needs of broadcast personnel; for example, two broadcast workshops were held in Lagos and Nairobi in 1971.

Since 1945, African technical and program personnel have been going in increasing numbers to training courses overseas, particularly in Britain and France, but also in Canada, Eastern Europe, Germany, and the United States. Many of these training programs are discussed in previous sections of this chapter. Broadcasters from French-speaking Africa have attended courses lasting up to 18 months at the Studio-École near Paris, which provides training in newswriting, editing, newscasting, and program production. This school emphasizes the practical application of classroom instruction. The Studio-École also gives some training in broadcast administration and television production.

Some of the training programs established by African broadcasting organizations have developed into broadcast schools, with established curricula and full-time staffs. Such schools can be found in Ghana, Ivory Coast, Kenya, Nigeria, Togo, Uganda, and Zambia. However, Quarmyne and Bebey concluded in their 1967 survey that none of these schools had adequate training facilities at that time (p. 25). Since then the Kenya Institute of Mass Communication has been launched, specifically to train broadcast personnel (§ 14.3.2).

It is axiomatic that the broadcast media provide the best channels for reaching both the scattered rural peoples and the urban population of the continent. For example, the three-year experimental television program designed to provide social education for women in Dakar, Senegal, persuaded representatives from eleven French-speaking nations of Africa to focus on the broadcast media when trying to reach urban populations (UNESCO 1969, pp. 5–10). The same conclusion, with respect to rural populations, was reached by a UNESCO expert who surveyed English-speaking countries in East Africa (Naesselund 1971b, p. 4). Despite the responsibilities these conclusions imply, African broadcasters enter the profession directly from secondary schools, devoid of mature knowledge of development problems. Moreover, the training programs they undertake seldom consider in depth the use of broadcast media in dealing with development problems.

Nevertheless, the justification for allocating funds and manpower to broadcasting, especially television, in Africa comes largely from its potential for helping to solve the many educational, social, and political problems that beset the developing nations (see § 16.1). Broadcasting is not, in fact, providing all the support it should for the attack on these problems. "The capability of broadcasting to play leading roles in the social welfare and development programmes in Africa and in other developing countries has been effectively established. There is, however, very little assistance given today by broadcasting organizations to their countries' development programmes" (Quarmyne and Bebey 1967, p. 28). This conclusion was supported in 1971 when 15 senior broadcasting executives from nine African countries spent two months on a training course at the University of Lagos. The UNESCO course director noted, "The first two weeks, with thought and time given to Broadcasting and National Development, provoked considerable interest; for many participants it was the first time consideration had been given to the use of broadcasting toward specific developmental ends" (Aspinall 1971b, p. 6).

Most African broadcasters, though becoming technically proficient, have simply not had broad training in development problems and the information programs needed to meet them. Thus the full utilization of broadcasting's potential in Africa is frustrated. Several concurrent programs attempt to provide the needed training—UNESCO seminars, short courses at training institutions, and overseas attachments. Some experts, however, insist that the real solution must be university-based training for broadcasters, in African institutions.

14.3.2 Broadcast Training in African Higher Education

There has been a general trend since World War II toward university training in journalism. This development has come slowly in Africa. The first UNESCO training course in Africa for journalists was held in 1961 at the University of Dakar in Senegal. The next year UNESCO held its first training course for African broadcasters in Kampala, Uganda, but it had little connection with nearby Makerere University College. In a 1962 study, however, the United Nations did support mass-communications training programs in a university setting (UNESCO 1965, p. 9). In the late 1960s African universities were just beginning seriously to consider broadcasting as an area for academic attention. Much of that interest originated in education faculties, as they awakened to the potentialities of the broadcast media as helps in solving some of the chronic educational problems of developing countries (see chap. 15).

Broadcasting organizations had already begun to recognize an urgent need for an increasing number of trained specialists. Fourteen territories and countries sent participants to a course on educational broadcasting in Uganda in 1962. When Togo's Radio-École developed a successful program for training radio-club leaders to organize rural-education classes, Mali and Niger sent personnel to learn from their experience (Quarmyne and Bebey 1967, p. 19). Such ad hoc courses, however, could never meet the long-range need for versatile, thoroughly trained communicators in both the print and the broadcast media. Yet many academics as well as journalists continued to question the value of university training in journalism. African universities saw no journalism discipline in the European universities on which they were modeled. African journalists also saw that few European journalists had university training, almost none specifically in journalism. Broadcast officials in particular, beset with immediate problems, thought university programs long-drawn-out and academic. They preferred practical training with its immediate operational benefits (UNESCO 1965, p. 9). Older journalists continue to denigrate the value of a university program which they never followed. The writer, as dean of the Institute of Mass Communications at the University of Lagos in 1971–72, faced this problem in trying to place graduates. Often, middle-range officials, such as subeditors and program producers, regarded university-trained recruits as a threat to their own further advancement and so resisted hiring them.

Beginning in the late 1960s, however, some African universities began to show interest in communications study. This was particularly true in universities with strong links to the United States, where by 1970 journalism training had over a half-century tradition and broadcasting was taught as a major in 180 universities. As early as 1935, the American University in Cairo established a journalism program, and the neighboring University of Cairo started journalism courses in 1939, later offering a four-year degree. These North African curricula emphasized print media, with only a course or two in broadcast newswriting or production technique (UNESCO 1965, p. 24).

The first university in Tropical Africa with a full program in journalism was the University of Nigeria, established at Nsukka in 1960 with American advice and assistance. It offered both three- and four-year degree programs, and the course structure resembled that found in American journalism schools. In addition, the university offered a one-year diploma course in journalism for university graduates in other fields. Five courses in radio-television were taught: a year-long introductory course, three courses on news or script preparation and presentation, and one course on radio-television production and direction. Plans to build a broadcasting studio where students could get practical training were halted by the Nigerian civil war, but the journalism department was reopened after the end of hostilities (interview with Ezenta Eze, acting head, Department of Journalism, University of Nigeria, 17 June 1972).

By 1970 a number of African countries had some type of media training linked with a university-level institution. Some offered courses in broadcasting, but mostly in the technical areas. Little attention was paid to programming needs. In 1970, however, in one of the first steps toward accommodating those needs, Senegal, with help from Canada and other countries, established a three-year diploma course at the University of Dakar—the Center for Information Studies, known as CESTI (§ 12.3.5). There, second-year students spent six hours weekly on broadcast writing and production techniques. In 1972 CESTI had 68 students, all sponsored by Francophone governments (communication from Georges Galipeau, CESTI director, 21 November 1972).

A dozen countries are listed in "Schools of Journalism and Communications Research Centres" (UNESCO 1970c, pp. 3–6), and by 1972 at least three additional programs—one in Cameroon and two in South Africa—were in operation, with another planned in Ghana. It seems clear, however, that two programs at the university level led in the scope of their broadcast training, those at the University of Nairobi in Kenya and the University of Lagos in Nigeria. Broadcast training at the University of Nairobi developed from two separate institutions—the university's School of Journalism and the Kenya Institute of Mass Communication. The School of Journalism opened in 1970 as a permanent successor to the training program operated in Nairobi in the 1960s by the International Press Institute (§ 1.1). The Kenya Institute of Mass Communication

(KIMC) was started in 1965 by the Ministry of Information and Broadcasting, in the first instance to provide technicians for the Voice of Kenya, but ultimately to provide all types of personnel.

The first School of Journalism class at the university consisted of 32 students from nine East African countries, enrolled for a two-year diploma course. The school requires students to have had two years of professional experience, but since it admits some without the Advanced School Certificate, it cannot award degrees. According to information provided by the acting director, "For the purpose of further studies in journalism the diploma is deemed equivalent to a first degree." Most of the students have their fees paid and receive a stipend from sponsoring employers. Half the $100,000-annual budget of the school is provided by Norway, Denmark, and Austria, largely in the form of support of expatriate staff members (proposed syllabus of courses, School of Journalism, University College, Nairobi, undated; letter from Poul Martinsen, 4 November 1971). The Nairobi school originally placed heavy emphasis on the print media and required basic courses in sociology, economics, and law, but because some students had problems with English, a modification of the original syllabus was necessary. Journalism students may take up to 72 hours of class and practical work in radio and television at the KIMC.

The initial emphasis at the KIMC was on technical training; it offered a 36-month course in radio and television engineering. The institute began offering 15-month courses for radio and television production assistants, enrolling 72 students in 1971–72 (Naesselund 1971a, p. 11). The radio syllabus ranges from scriptwriting to directing, from production techniques to audience-survey methods. The television syllabus adds instruction in camera techniques, lighting, and graphics. Broadcasting students spend two months in basic studies, including African history and culture and the uses of mass media in developing societies. With a new building opened in 1969, KIMC acquired fully equipped radio and television studios plus a film unit. UNESCO would like to see KIMC broaden its program and become a center for regional broadcast training more closely linked to the University of Nairobi. Shortages of funds and staff, plus the immediate Kenyan needs for broadcast engineers, were limiting factors in 1972.

The University of Lagos in 1971 offered the only university degree program in Africa which included a substantial amount of broadcast training. The university's Institute of Mass Communications opened in 1967 with a one-year diploma course for experienced journalists. In 1971, the institute graduated the first nine students from its three-year degree program. About half of the 90 degree students and 25 diploma students enrolled in 1972 emphasized broadcast training.

From the start, the institute tried to strike a balance between academic and professional courses, recruiting staff members with both media experience and academic background. At first, practical sessions in broadcast training were held at the studios of the Nigerian Broadcasting Corporation in Lagos, but in 1971 the institute set up a small radio studio on the university campus with the help of equipment provided by the Voice of America. A $300,000-building, to include two radio studios, was scheduled to open in October 1973. A larger, second unit of the institute, to include television facilities, was also planned. Effective January 1973, the institute received a UNESCO grant of more than half a million dollars for overall development. The Lagos institute thus seemed assured of becoming the leading center for media training in Africa.

Institute students take a normal university program in humanities and social sciences in their first two years, plus basic journalism courses. All take a year's course in print media plus a year in the techniques of broadcast media. In their final year, broadcast students take a separate broadcast sequence in studio operations and program production, and in producing news, interview, music, discussion, and public-events programs. Student productions are taped and then played back for class discussion. The campus has been wired for remote pickup of public events, such as sports matches, so that students can gain experience in on-the-scene reporting.

Other universities in Africa have journalism programs, but they continue to emphasize training for the print media. Nevertheless, interest in the broadcast media is growing at the university level. The 1971–72 syllabus of the University of Nigeria, Nsukka, listed two year-long courses in broadcasting, including scriptwriting, announcing, studio techniques, and the direction and production of radio and television programs. A radio studio was to be ready late in 1972, and a broadcast specialist had joined the staff. A shift of the Department of Journalism to Enugu, which has government broadcasting studios, was also being considered.

The American University in Cairo, which awards both bachelor's and master's degrees in journalism, offers only introductory courses in broadcast writing (letter and course description from F. Floyd Shoemaker, director of mass communication, 1 April 1972). At Cairo University, however, a broader program has been developed, in its Institute of Communication. The Departments of Journalism and Publishing, Radio and Television, and Public Relations and Advertising enrolled more than 500 students in 1972. The institute offers two-year diploma and four-year degree courses which include training in broadcast production and technical areas (Luthe 1969; letter from Dean Ibrahim Imam, Institute of Communication, July 1972). The University of Tunis had two two-year sequences at its Institute of Press and Information Sciences, founded in 1967, but by 1972 very little was yet being offered in the broadcast area (letter and course announcement from H. Aleya, director, Institute of Press and Information Sciences, University of Tunis, 10 April 1972).

In French-speaking Tropical Africa, universities at Dakar, Kinshasa, and Yaoundé offer at least some courses for journalists (see § 12.3.5 for details on the Dakar course). In 1972 the Department of Social Communication at the National University of Zaïre, in Kinshasa had 120 students enrolled in a two-year diploma program which included survey courses in radio and television communication—about half the students were considered to be in the Broadcast Production Program, but little or no practical training was given, according to the course description (letter and course description from Jean Lohisse, director, 24 March 1972). The Federal University of Yaoundé, Cameroon, however, planned to include broadcast training for students from several French-speaking countries in its journalism curriculum started in 1970 (interview with Boniface Forbin, Radio Cameroon staff, 16 January 1972).

In 1970, two South African universities, the University of the Orange Free State at Bloemfontein and Rhodes University at Grahamstown, started degree programs emphasizing the print media. At Rhodes, however, third-year students take a year-long course in radio and television journalism, mostly concerned with the writing and presentation of news and documentary programs. These students have access to studios of the South African Broadcasting Corporation for practical training. Rhodes ordered a closed-circuit television system in order to start studio courses well ahead of South Africa's scheduled 1975 introduction of broadcast television (letter from C. A. Giffard, head, Department of Journalism, 13 April 1972).

Further evidence that broadcast training is on the increase in Africa includes the Uganda School of Journalism's establishment, in 1971, in the Institute of Public Administration in Kampala (letter from M. J. Pascoe, Institute of Public Administration, 25 February 1972); the plan of the Center for Continuing Education at Makerere University in Uganda to include a studio for its Mass Media Unit in a building to be constructed in 1973 (interview with Richard Aspinall, UNESCO expert, Lagos, Nigeria, 30 January 1972); and the University of Ghana's 1972 appointment of a man with interests in both broadcast and print media as the first full-time director of its Institute of Journalism and Mass Communication (letter from William Hachten, director of the Institute, 20 May 1972).

A serious problem in establishing university programs in broadcasting is the inadequate theoretical training of many senior African broadcasters with long years of practical experience. They will be prone to oppose such education unless they can see in it benefits for, rather than threats to, themselves. The solution is to offer diploma programs for experienced broadcasters who lack formal educational prerequisites for entry into regular university degree curricula. In this way, the value of university training is likely to be accepted much faster by established broadcasting organizations, and the educational and professional levels of African broadcasters are likely to rise rapidly.

14.4 A German-sponsored Radio Training Center in Ethiopia, *by Laura Gläser-Weisser*

The most ambitious on-site training program sponsored in Africa by the Federal Republic of Germany ran from 1964 to 1970 on the premises of the Ethiopian Broadcasting Service in Addis Ababa (§ 3.1.6). It offered a series of full-time radio courses, each lasting a whole year. The German government provided facilities capable of handling 12 to 15 trainees at a time. They consisted of a well-equipped production studio, a dubbing studio, a workshop, an outside broadcast vehicle, a minibus, tape recorders, a music library, teaching aids, and necessary spare parts. These facilities were manned by two German instructors and a maintenance technician. For its part, the Ethiopian government provided building space, a co-ordinator for the project, and stipends for the students.

Experience with the first group of trainees in 1964–65, which consisted of 11 secondary-school graduates and four students who had completed one year of college, indicated that a higher level of academic preparation was needed if trainees were to benefit fully from the course. The second group, therefore, included three university graduates and four students who had completed three years of college. It developed that college graduates could get more attractive offers elsewhere, and so the college graduates of the third group were offered stipends equivalent to the civil service salaries they could expect as holders of the bachelor's degree. On the whole, the most satisfactory class consisted of a mixture of college graduates and students who had completed several years of college, all of whom were able to pass a difficult entry examination based on general knowledge, creative writing and editing abilities, voice auditions, and psychological tests.

In addition to the specialized instruction provided by the German experts, instruction in such subjects as Amharic, the history and culture of Ethiopia, and English phonetics was provided by visiting lecturers, brought in mostly from the national university. The teaching schedule allotted about a quarter of the time for the visitors' lectures, a quarter for staff lectures on the theory of the mass media, and half for practical production training. The last included visits to factories, agricultural projects, and the like to provide practical occasions for field recording exercises. All trainees were expected to learn how to type. Toward the end of their year trainees were assigned individually to work part of their time with specific departments of Radio Ethiopia; this gave them practical experience in the day-to-day problems of the station and also gave the station officials a chance to appraise their abilities before having to assign them to regular staff positions after graduation. At the close of the course the instructors recommended

Laura Gläser-Weisser served as an instructor at the Radio Training Center, 1966–70.

assignments to specific departments in the broadcasting organization, in keeping with each trainee's individual talents and achievements.

Such specific recommendations were withheld for the one or two marginal students in each class. None were failed outright, partly because of careful advance screening for admission, but perhaps also because failure would have been such a severe penalty. The trainees were, after all, almost equivalent to staff members, once accepted in the course; they received bursaries equivalent to salaries during training and were assured of employment on successful completion. In retrospect, however, one can say that ideally the standard for graduation may have been too lenient. The tendency to retain marginal students is a common failing. Quarmyne and Bebey remark in their survey of broadcasting training in Africa, "Where it is evident that a trainee is unsuitable it should be possible to dismiss him. It must be an essential responsibility of every training centre to sift out undesirables. It is bound to be a more satisfactory approach than paying several years' salary for a low standard of operation and a demoralizing effect on staff" (1967, p. 62).

The original plan had envisioned the Radio Training Center's becoming a permanent facility of the Ethiopian Broadcasting Service. It was expected that the German instructors would have counterparts to work with them and to take over once the original teachers themselves had left. However, the demand for trained operating personnel was too great to allow for the retention of outstanding graduates of the course as counterparts for the instructors. Therefore, after the departure of the German teaching staff in 1970, training activity at the center ceased and the facilities were turned over to regular production functions.

15 Educational Uses of Broadcasting

Robert Nwankwo

[EDITOR'S NOTE. In almost every sphere of developmental activity one finds a need to communicate with large, widely dispersed publics. Nation-wide improvement in education, literacy, health, agricultural practices, and the like involves reaching the general population with effective motivational and informational messages. This process, known as the "diffusion of innovations," has been the subject of a compendious survey which analyzes the results of more than 1,500 published studies concerned with the process of bringing about innovations. One theme that runs all through these studies is the proposition that "communication is essential for social change" (Rogers and Shoemaker 1971, p. 6). Of course, broadcasting represents only one medium of mass communication; in turn, the medium of inter-personal communication must be considered along with the mass media. But among the conceivable means of reaching very large numbers of widely scattered peoples in developing countries at reasonable expense and without unreasonable delay, radio alone has the requisite attributes. Though less able to cope with terrain and distance, television also has unique potentialities for assisting development by multiplying the effectiveness of such limited educational resources as skilled teachers, expensive laboratory equipment, and filmed materials.

It appears, then, that a broadcasting component would automatically form an integral part of *any* comprehensive scheme of national development, and, therefore, that one should be able to document any number of successful applications of broadcasting to the solution of developmental problems. A UNESCO study of broadcasting's educational and developmental role concluded that "it is necessary to consider broadcasting as part of a country's so-called 'infrastructure.' While it is firmly accepted that harbors, roads, railways, waterways, electricity, post, telephone and telegraphic

Robert Nwankwo is Assistant Professor of Journalism, University of Rhode Island. He earned a B.A. degree, First Class Honours, at the University of Nigeria and a Ph.D. at the University of Wisconsin. He was Postdoctoral Fellow, University of Pennsylvania, 1970–71.

services belong to the infrastructure, for which funds must be invested which do not necessarily yield immediate and clearly identifiable results, it is not generally recognized that broadcasting . . . belongs to the same category" (UNESCO 1967, p. 12).

The fact is, however, that development planners usually ignore broadcasting; or, if they consider it at all, they treat it as a minor component. One can search in vain through any number of African five-year plans for mention of broadcasting as a vital, integrated component of development strategies. Experimental applications of broadcasting to help solve specific educational-development problems have been tried, but they have generally been half-hearted in concept and mediocre in outcome. A sober analysis by top experts published in 1967 concluded: "The fact is that most uses of the educational media throughout the world are quite insignificant parts of the total educational effort . . . their full potential has never been tested" (Schramm et al. 1967, p. 16). Five years and many experimental educational-broadcasting projects later, the even more negative conclusion was that "educational technology is still in a primitive state everywhere in the world. Its history to date has been marked with false starts, inflated expectations, and assorted misunderstandings" (Tickton 1972, p. 103). This chapter will explore some of the reasons for this failure to live up to initial promise.]

15.1 Modes of Application and Their Differentiation

The application of broadcasting—whether radio or television—to developmental problems falls into three generally recognized modalities: (1) information/guidance elements within *general* programming; and, outside the usual context of general programming, (2) adult-education programming and (3) instructional programming (see Schramm et al. 1967 for a detailed analysis of the last two). These terms are not entirely self-explanatory, nor do they define completely watertight compartments. For example, all three often deal with the same general subject matter, but in characteristically different ways: public-health principles can serve equally well as the subject matter for occasional information/guidance talks, for a series of adult-education lessons, or for a complete, formalized course designed for reception in the conventional classroom. On the other hand, a series of formalized lessons on physics would not be a likely subject for either information/guidance or adult-education programming.

No satisfactory term has been found to designate what we have awkwardly named "information/guidance elements within general programming." This phrase refers to a type of informational and motivational programming found in the domestic services of all developing countries. It seeks explicitly, though informally, to help the general audience to understand and appreciate the world around it, and to advise and exhort audience members to adopt attitudes and practices desired by the national leadership. It includes news and public affairs as well as programs dealing with explicitly developmental subjects such as health and agriculture. Information/guidance programs are generally subsumed under the heading of "nation building" and as such often take on a distinct political coloration. Mytton describes this process at work in the programming of Radio Tanzania (§ 4.2.3), for example. It often becomes a fine point whether ideological coloration, especially in news and public-affairs subjects, should more accurately be called propaganda. "Instructional broadcasting," by contrast, refers to systematic instruction in conventional school subjects designed for reception in the classroom. Adult education usually falls between these two—more formal and systematized than information/guidance programming, but generally less so than instructional programming.

The chief factors distinguishing these three types of educational broadcasting one from another are (1) subject matter, and organizational relationships among the programs in a series; (2) definition of target audience; (3) production style; (4) scheduling; (5) conditions of reception; (6) the amount and kind of feedback employed; and (7) assignment of responsibility.

15.1.1 Content and Its Organization

A UNESCO guidebook lists the following as representative of actual adult-education broadcast series on rural and community development topics:

General problems. Example: the role of agriculture in the overall economy of the country.
Community life. Example: women's organizations.
Rural and agricultural economics. Example: cooperative marketing.
Modern agriculture. Example: crop storage.
Dealing with environmental conditions. Example: floods.
Health and nutrition. Example: maternal and child care.
Family life. Example: premarital and marital guidance.
Family planning. Example: contraception and physiology.
Home interests. Example: home dressmaking.
Consumer's education. Example: savings.
Education. Example: How does the school function?
Civics. Example: administration of justice.
General knowledge and outlook. Example: the cultural heritage of the nation (Waniewicz 1972, pp. 123–27).

This list, better than any abstract description, reveals the thrust of adult-education programming in developing countries. It also shows clearly that the same subject matters could as easily serve for information/guidance programming in a general service. One difference is that adult-education programming tends to be more highly organized, with each element in a program series bearing a logical and systematic relationship to the preceding and following elements, while in information/guidance series each program stands, essentially, as a comprehensible independent entity, with only a broad topical relationship binding the programs in a series together.

Instructional programming, by contrast, would not be likely to use many of these subject matters. Instead, it typically deals with such basic subjects of ordinary school curricula as languages, mathematics, geography, sciences, and history. And of course the programs in an instructional series are tightly articulated one with another, to the extent that an isolated program might be incomprehensible to a student who had not followed the sequence from the beginning.

Literacy training might almost be considered a separate, fourth mode of educational broadcasting, for it is a universal need in developing countries and one posing its own special problems. One cannot teach reading and writing in a vacuum, however. There must be something to read and write *about,* and so literacy projects normally include the study of some basic subject matter along with literacy, both as a motivator and as a way of inculcating useful information and desired attitudes.

15.1.2 Target Audience

The general service of a broadcasting system has the duty of serving the population at large. This implies serving a heterogeneous audience, whose members cannot be assumed to have either a preestablished, focused interest in the subject matter or common bonds of background, experience, and motivation. It is also a noncaptive audience; to win it, the programs must be both comprehensible and attractively presented.

Adult-education programs, on the other hand, are designed for relatively homogeneous, "molecular" subaudiences, whose members have common educational backgrounds, interests, and motivations. Usually, the participants are expected to gather in groups for listening or viewing, and to participate in preliminary and follow-up activities—all of which differentiates this audience from the "atomistic" general-service audience.

Instructional-broadcasting audiences, it goes without saying, *are* captive audiences, which are limited in size, strongly homogeneous, and subject to powerful motivational forces.

15.1.3 Production Style

Much of what has been said about subject matter and target audiences has a highly practical bearing on writing, producing, and performing. While there is no reason to suppose that the production of instructional and adult-education broadcasting requires unique skills fundamentally different from those needed for the production of general programming, production style must be adapted to subject matter and to audience. Production for general audiences involves the art of popularization, in the best sense of that word. The heterogeneity of the audience, the exposure of the audience to competing stimuli, and the basically weak attention-holding power of the impersonal box—the radio or television receiver—all have important implications for the popularizer. He must consider word choice and sentence structure, the understandability of concepts, and the need to capture attention initially and to restimulate it periodically. If his audience were live, immediate feedback would serve as a guide for future programming. The special skill of the broadcast writer, producer, and performer is to simulate immediate feedback from his own imagination. He must *anticipate* the audience's questions, the points at which interest will flag, the stages at which reminders of the previously laid groundwork must be introduced. At the same time he must avoid talking down, over-simplification, and trivialization.

The educational broadcaster faces precisely the same problems as the popularizer, but with differences in degree. He can make assumptions about his audience's vocabulary, level of understanding, amount of prior knowledge, and degree of motivation. But within these assumptions his problems remain those of the general-service producer—he must still consider the individual differences among students, the lack of immediate feedback, and the impersonality of the receiving set.

15.1.4 Scheduling

Information/guidance programs other than news and public-affairs programs are generally scheduled no more than once a week, rarely as often as daily. Systematic education requires frequent review and reinforcement, however, so that adult-education series tend to be scheduled two or three times a week and instructional programs as often as five time a week. Information/guidance programming is scheduled as part of the established general service; adult-education programs to some extent, and instructional programs to a much larger extent, tend to be scheduled so that they will not interfere with the general service—either day-parts not normally part of the general-service schedule are used, or separate transmission facilities. Conflicting schedule requirements of the several kinds of service can cause troublesome disagreements. The availability of both adult-education and instructional audiences is limited to specific hours, and when these times conflict with the needs of the general service, education is likely to be the loser. This conflict of interests was one of the reasons for the disappointing results obtained from pioneer TV instructional-programming projects in Nigeria (§ 15.2.2).

15.1.5 Reception Conditions

The general audience receives broadcasts under unpredictable listening or viewing conditions, whereas adult education usually, and schools broadcasting always, involves controlled, structured reception conditions. Lack of control over reception conditions means that information/guidance programs have to compete more strenuously with rival stimuli which may either prevent potential members from joining the audience at all or distract attention at any moment throughout the program. These circumstances place heavy demands on the skills of the writer, producer, and performer. They also place limits on the amount of assimilable material that can be packed into a given time period. Reception conditions quite profoundly affect every aspect of programming and production.

15.1.6 Feedback

Immediate feedback, as we have just said, is a problem equally for educational and for general-service broadcasters. The two receive quite different types of *delayed* feedback, however. Research provides relatively little feedback on the audiences of African general services, as indicated in § 16.1. The programmer must depend on fragmentary information and sheer intuition. The audiences for adult-education and instructional programming, however, participate in group listening and watching at known locations and so can be much more easily studied.

15.1.7 Assignment of Responsibility

Information/guidance programming is normally a responsibility of the national broadcasting service itself, that is, of broadcasters as such. Programmers and producers normally strive for a suitable balance among program types, a fair representation of various national interests, and an appropriate degree of popularization. In practice, however, they may lack the required authoritativeness to control subject-matter experts; some ministries may have more influence than others in obtaining time and services from the broadcasting organization; and some outside organizations may insist on doing their own programming and production, whether or not they have the necessary judgment and skills (see § 4.2.5). Nevertheless, the responsibility for the information/guidance type of programming clearly belongs, at least in theory, to the broadcasting organization itself.

Adult education poses a more complex problem. Many different government ministries or departments as well as private organizations may have a direct interest in the subject matter of adult education. Moreover, a well-designed adult-education project involves important functioning elements not normally the responsibility of the broadcaster, such as the organizing of local audience groups and group leaders, provision of listening or viewing facilities, and preparation of supplementary printed materials. According to the 1972 UNESCO guidebook on adult educational broadcasting,

it happens quite often that in one single country the agency responsible for development is concerned with education in the field of community development; the Ministry of Agriculture deals with the popularization of agriculture knowledge, the Ministry of Health is concerned with health education and family planning, the Ministry of Education has often two or more parallel agencies, each dealing separately with such fields as formal education of adults, higher education, literacy teaching, youth activities, etc.; the Ministry of Defence is concerned with general education in the Armed Forces. In addition some non-governmental organizations, like trade unions, women's organizations . . . carry out educational activities of their own. Often one agency does not even know what the other is doing in the same locality. [Waniewicz 1972, pp. 44–45]

Instructional broadcasting, since it goes into the schools as a coordinated part of the official curriculum, suffers little of this confusion: it is clearly the business of the Ministry of Education or its equivalent. The main problem of coordination likely to arise concerns the terms and conditions upon which the educational authorities will be given access to transmission and production facilities controlled by the broadcasting authority, assuming the educational authorities do not have their own separate facilities.

15.2 Some Practical Examples

The field of educational broadcasting as it stood generally, in 1965, was surveyed in a series of publications financed by the United States Agency for International Development and published by UNESCO: *The New Media: Memo to Educational Planners,* a synthesizing volume by Schramm et al. (1967), and three volumes of detailed case studies (UNESCO-IIEP 1967). The case studies included five African projects—in Algeria, Ivory Coast, Niger, Nigeria, and Togo.

Every African broadcasting system has made at least some attempts at educational broadcasting. Not many, however, have appreciably reduced the problems they were intended to help solve. In 1972 only a project in the Ivory Coast seemed sufficiently well financed and broad-gauge in conception to offer the promise of major achievements. The reasons for the low level of achievement we shall examine later. First, let us review a few projects.

15.2.1 Transplanting Farm Forums: Ghana

First in Canada in the 1940s and then in India in the 1950s, an especially imaginative and effective means of using radio broadcasting to assist rural development evolved—the farm radio forum (Schramm et al. 1967, pp. 107–34). This concept led to a now generally accepted hypothesis of diffusion research, that "the effects of mass media channels, especially among peasants in less developed countries, are greater when these media are coupled with interpersonal communication channels" (Rogers and Shoemaker 1971, p. 263). In brief, the linking of the two channels is achieved by organizing listeners to radio rural-development programs into small groups which use the programs as the bases for discussions leading to local decisions on courses of action suggested by the programs.

To test whether the format would work in yet another cultural setting and to discover what local adaptations might be required, UNESCO sponsored the Ghana Farm Radio Forum Project in 1964–65 (Coleman, Popku, and Abell 1968). Ghana had been using the more conventional types of farm programs since 1956, and each rural community in the country already had a development committee established. Reflecting the multiple responsibilities discussed in § 15.1.7, nearly a dozen Ghanaian organizations participated, including the Ghana Broadcasting Corporation; the Ministries of Education, Agriculture, Health, and Social Welfare and Community Development; the National Women's Council; the national organization of farmers' cooperatives; and the University of Ghana Sociology Department. Canada made important contributions to the project, as described by Bled in § 12.3.4.

In several regions of Ghana where a common language, Akan, could be used, 40 villages were designated, within which 60 farm forums were organized. Each forum consisted of 20 members, selected by local headmen with guidance from the experimenters so that forums would be representative of their villages in sex, education, and occupation. Listening to receiving sets provided by the government, the 40 organized forums heard a weekly series of 20 half-hour radio programs on such topics as problems of crop storage, family budgeting, agricultural loans and subsidies, and nutrition. The format of the programs varied in accordance with the needs of the topics; some parts were in the form of straight talks, others in the form of playlets. Discussants had printed guidebooks on the topics, so that the total experience combined three media—radio, print, and face-to-face discussion.

The discussion sessions served several important purposes: (1) they brought subjects down to the local level, thus overcoming one of the built-in disadvantages of broadcasting as a mass medium, that of delivering identical messages indiscriminately to all varieties of listeners or viewers; (2) they gave the villagers a sense of responsibility and self-reliance, by allowing them to participate in decision making; and (3) they provided the experimenters with feedback which could be applied to subsequent programs with minimum delay. Sometimes, in fact, the experimenters recorded the discussions and edited them for playback over the air the next week, which enhanced even further the villagers' sense of participation.

An integral research component was a vital element in the project—not merely as a follow-up, but as a part of the original design. Both villages and villagers were selected for their representativeness, and matching nonforum villages were selected at the same time to provide a control group (see § 16.3.3 for more details on the research design). Interviews with a representative sample of participants before and after they had been exposed to the experience established the effectiveness of the farm-forum technique. A valuable side benefit of the experiment was that it revealed the kinds of local problems such projects can expect to encounter. The forum concept is now routinely accepted as an element in the format of most rural adult-education projects utilizing radio and television.

15.2.2 Pioneering ITV: Nigeria

Nigeria pioneered, not only television, but also instructional television, in Sub-Saharan Africa. The Western Region of Nigeria used educational television first, in 1959, with Northern Nigeria following in 1961, and the federal National Broadcasting Corporation in 1965. The Nigerian experience provides a classic illustration of all the problems which usually beset such projects. The introduction of every television system in Africa was rationalized as an educational investment, but the commercial firms from abroad, which in the early years won contracts for installing facilities and managing stations, were interested in recouping their loans and so tended to put more stress on programming that would attract audiences for advertisers than on educational programming. In both the Western and Northern regions of Nigeria, "one of the strongest points in support of the campaign for a regional station was that it would help to solve the region's educational problems. In both regions, once the stations were obtained, however, their management and the original political proponents of television became less interested in educational uses. . . . The result has been a series of difficult relationships and negotiations between the people responsible for the educational programmes and the people re-sponsible for the commercial stations" (Schramm et al. 1967, pp. 30–31). Nevertheless, the project attracted favorable attention from the U.S. Agency for International Development, which in 1962 made the first of a series of agreements to help develop Nigerian ITV. Between 1964, when work actually began, and 1967, AID invested nearly $900,000 in the Nigerian project (Dizard 1966, p. 248).

The undertaking was beset by a "cloud of horrendous difficulties" (Schramm et al. 1967, p. 32). Aside from the difficulty of prying loose sufficient time at suitable hours from commercially minded station man-agements, frequent power failures interrupted transmission or reception, or both; as many as half the receiving sets destined for schools were broken in the course of delivery to distant points; at times three-quarters of the school sets were out of order. Even when ITV programs did get through to the classrooms, they had little impact, for they were at first conceived merely as enrichment, not as instruments of direct teaching. Some of the British expatriate teachers, who still held many positions, resented the American presence and did not attempt to conceal their contempt for the whole idea of educational television. Despite heroic efforts by the proponents of ITV, these early attempts in Nigeria must be regarded in retrospect as failures. AID became disenchanted, and therefore reluctant to invest more American funds in foreign educational-broadcasting projects. With the benefit of hindsight, the best that can be said for the Nigerian ITV experiences of the early 1960s is that they constituted a graphic lesson in how not to go about establishing educational television.

15.2.3 First Success with ITV: Niger

Nigeria first approached educational television with a view to using it, not as a truly functional teaching device, but as source of supplementary enrichment for teaching already being carried out in the traditional classroom. This approach, even if ideally successful, does nothing to solve the underlying problem of teacher shortages. Niger, Nigeria's inland neighbor to the north, provided "the first instance of an African country using TV to give young students complete instruction and it was the first time a TV classroom monitor [i.e., supervisor] was implemented to offset a chronic lack of qualified teachers" (Academy for Educational Development 1972, p. 76).

The Niger experiment began in 1964 as a pilot ITV project limited to 22 one-room schools near the capital, Niamey; it reached 800 primary school children—less than 1% of the total school population. Teaching was focused on the mastery of the French language, and all lessons were broadcast in French, even though the pupils had not had prior experience with the language. The older students received, typically, four 14-minute telelessons a day, five days a week. The classroom *moniteurs* had only sixth-grade educations and received only three months of prior training to prepare them for overseeing the reception of the telelessons and for following them up with activities prescribed in a guidebook.

The initial results seemed highly favorable: no dropouts from the teleschools, versus a 25% dropout rate in regular schools; and the telescholars demonstrated much better mastery of French than children in ordinary classes. Even more remarkable, perhaps, the television classes made a sharp break with the severely authoritarian tradition of French education. Instead of stressing rote learning, telelessons and their follow-up exercises stressed pupil participation and problem-solving approaches. The minimally educated classroom *moniteurs* succeeded remarkably well despite the brevity of their training. It has been said that "probably the most important thing [they] learned was to simply love their classroom children" (Academy for Educational Development 1972, p. 78). Unfortunately, the experiment was scheduled to be completed by the fall of 1972, with no financing in sight for its expansion on a national basis. As an important side effect, however, the Niger experiment encouraged the Ivory Coast to go into a similar type of ITV program on a national scale (§ 15.5).

15.2.4 A Ministation for ETV: Senegal

In direct contrast to the commercial example of Nigeria cited in § 15.2.2, the television station in Senegal's capital, Dakar, was initiated purely for educational uses. In general, the Francophone countries did not share the Anglophone countries' experience with private commercial firms as station installers and managers. This was both because of the all-encompassing influence of SORAFOM, OCORA, and ORTF, the French agencies successively in charge of broadcasting developments overseas (see § 6.1.3), and because the French ignored the commercial aspects of television and emphasized its educational aspects. The non-commercial outlook may have been dictated by the desperate state of education in the French ex-colonies and the meager prospects of realizing any profit from commercial television operations.

Senegal's station, built on a very modest scale with the help of UNESCO in 1965, was used for a six-year experiment in adult education; there was no intention of its offering a general service. It was a project in miniature, with a transmitter of but 50 w. and only a baker's-dozen sets at the beginning. Though the rich expatriate French, Portuguese, and Lebanese in flourishing Dakar could doubtless have given substantial support to conventional entertainment television, the Senegalese government opted to bypass this affluent audience and to design TV exclusively for the underprivileged. Another unusual feature of the Senegalese project was the fact that it used Wolof, an unwritten local language, exclusively. To produce a playlet, for example, producers would give the Senegalese actors the outline of the story in French, and the actors would then improvise dialogue in Wolof.

The project is described in detail, along with the results of research on its effectiveness, in a UNESCO report, *Television and the Social Education of Women* (Fougeyrollas 1967). The first pilot programs were aimed at an audience of 500 mostly illiterate urban women, organized into 10 TV viewing clubs. The programs dealt with health, nutrition, and general culture. Not only did the women gain in factual understanding about such things as malaria and dysentery; they also gained in self-confidence: "Television through its power of group formation acts as a catalytic agent well beyond the contents of its programs" (p. 6). As in the radio farm-forum design, the members of the teleclubs discussed the subjects of the programs after they were over—a feature held to be of "decisive importance" in the effectiveness of the project (p. 9).

15.2.5 Literacy Training: Tunisia

In 1969 UNESCO made a survey among its member states to get information on the use of broadcasting for adult literacy training. Eighteen African countries filled out the questionnaire, though doubtless a number of others also had used broadcasting for this purpose. Tunisia's project was selected for detailed description in the UNESCO report (Maddison 1971, pp.

61–68). Tunisia already had a conventional classroom project in Arabic literacy training which handled some 40,000 adults annually; starting in 1968, both radio and television were used to form additional study groups. Whether meeting in a conventional classroom or in an improvised television receiving center, students received instruction for an hour and a half each evening, five days a week. A half-hour's instructional-television program was followed by an hour's discussion and practice, and a 15-minute supplementary radio broadcast was scheduled the morning after each television lesson. Some viewing groups assembled at formally organized centers, each comprising 20 students and supervised by a qualified teacher; others at "semi-directed" centers, supervised by representatives of cooperating national organizations (some classes were organized in prisons, barracks, and factories); and still others at "family centers."

Responsibility for the project was shared by the Tunisian Radio and Television Organization and the national Institute for Adult Education. Many other national organizations, representing special-interest groups, such as family planners, agriculturalists, nutritionists, economists, and psychologists, cooperated by sending representatives to weekly meetings at which the subjects and treatments of upcoming lessons were discussed. The broadcasting organization scheduled the literacy lessons, which also dealt with such subjects as arithmetic and history, as part of its general service. The programs apparently avoided an unduly pedantic style, because research indicated that many literates also watched them for their information and entertainment values.

Feedback came from weekly reports sent in by the leaders at the viewing centers, as well as from periodic tests and a year-end questionnaire filled out by the students. Producers received the weekly critiques promptly, so that they could make corrections and adjustments in subsequent programs without undue delay. The student's questionnaire consisted of a five-point scale ranging from "very good" to "very bad." Points on the scale were represented by caricature drawings of faces displaying the appropriate expression for each position. The experimenters commented, "Quite obviously, the object of this opinion poll is not simply to obtain information. The object is, above all, to teach the students, for whom television is still something of a mystery, to react to what is presented to them by this device . . . and also to teach them to be selective and finally to make them feel that they have to take part not only in determining the direction to be followed by these courses, but also, through this simple exercise, in the general life of their country" (Maddison 1971, p. 67).

15.3 The Unfulfilled Promise

Obviously, much ingenuity and dedicated work have gone into projects such as those described in the preceding section. Yet their impact has been minuscule in comparison with the magnitude of the problems they attacked. For example, the UNESCO report on literacy training points out that the largest number of trainees reached by any of the projects surveyed was 70,000, and most reached far fewer—this in contrast to the 8 million illiterates remaining to be trained (Maddison 1971, pp. 34–35). According to Schramm et al. (1967, pp. 16, 109), "most uses of the educational media throughout the world are quite insignificant parts of the total educational effort," and "in only a relatively few places have the media been used as full partners in education, been woven into the system, and used seriously and fully to attack urgent problems." These strictures apply as well to developed as to undeveloped countries (see Commission on Instructional Technology 1970). In this section we will explore briefly some of the reasons for this failure in terms of the African experience with broadcasting.

15.3.1 Limiting Factors: Information/Guidance Programming

Schramm was writing in the quotation above about formal education. The informal education intended to be achieved by what we have called "information/guidance programming within general programming" has likewise been largely ineffectual, for reasons which also affect most kinds of more formal educational programming.

One reason is simply the fact that not everybody has access to a receiver. As the descriptions of the individual national systems in the first part of this book repeatedly point out, transmission facilities tend to be arbitrarily concentrated where they are least needed—in the vicinity of capital cities, which themselves are often located peripherally rather than centrally. Therefore, ordinary inexpensive receivers get either no domestic service or only intermittent, low-quality signals in many parts of Africa. But much more important than limitations on transmission facilities are limitations on receiving facilities. They, too, tend to be concentrated in urban areas. Limited circulation can be ascribed, at least in part, to government shortsightedness in placing high tariffs on broadcast receivers and component parts that often double their original cost. In some countries receiver license fees represent another government-imposed barrier to the fullest possible broadcast circulation. Instead of making it more difficult than it need be to own a receiver, governments might well consider it in their own interest to encourage the growth of circulation—not only by removing such artificial financial impediments, but also by more positive measures, such as subsidizing receivers, batteries, replacement parts, and repair facilities (see Waniewicz 1972, pp. 48, 102). Ministries of information could well count among their most valuable officers roving technicians whose job is to help people solve problems of reception and set maintenance. One study estimated, for example, that up to 20% of the sets in rural areas were not in operating condition (Mytton 1972b, p. 25).

A second limiting factor on the effectiveness of information/guidance programming is the lack of systematic feedback. Almost no broad-gauge research is done to obtain realistic guidance for programmers, performers, and producers responsible for information/guidance programs. They depend, perforce, on the most unreliable sources of information—letters from the audience and the opinions of their friends and neighbors. Even these questionable sources are bypassed when program decisions are made by simple government fiat, on the basis of the personal whims of individual officials (see § 16.1). While the general lack of effectiveness of much information/guidance programming is obvious from the low level of response, the all-important question Why? is rarely asked. Those in responsible positions in the broadcasting service simply do not have enough objective information about signal characteristics, set distribution, audience habits, program comprehensibility, and the like to do anything about systematically improving the effectiveness of their programming.

A third factor is the built-in human limitations of most broadcasting services. In the past, as Scotton points out (§ 14.3.2), broadcasting personnel in Africa have had no special education in the field of economic and social development. This does not imply that broadcasters themselves must be qualified economists, sociologists, agronomists, and the like; but it does mean they need sufficient general knowledge to deal effectively with the people who are qualified experts. Kenya's minister of finance complained at a 1972 seminar in Nairobi that reporters sent to interview him had no idea what to talk about: "I am appalled by the level of information of the majority of men and women who run our press in Eastern Africa . . . if you are being interviewed by press people or television people about any of the problems we are grappling with, you straight away notice that the people who are interviewing you have no access at any time to the primary sources of information regarding the subject on which they want to interview you . . . you are reduced to being questioned on a very shallow basis about gossip of the town" (Kibaki 1972, p. 3). Nor is it an adequate solution to employ expert outside contributors or personnel from the ministry or specialized agency concerned; the broadcaster must still bring to bear his own expertise and authority as a broadcaster to see to it that content specialists organize their materials and adapt their modes of presentation to suit the needs of radio or television.

A fourth problem is the gap between urban culture and rural culture—a gap which seems, if anything, to have grown wider since independence. Broadcasting personnel usually live and work in the most urbanized locale possible, the capital of the country. Their appreciation of how best to communicate with the many rural subcultures of their own country may become increasingly inadequate. Not infrequently broadcast personnel become infected with an attitude of condescension toward the benighted peasants of the hinterland, an attitude encouraged by the arbitrary, authoritarian way in which leading government officials sometimes exploit broadcasting (§ 16.1).

Finally, broadcasters tend to overcompartmentalize information/

guidance programming. The minister of health comes to the station to secure cooperation in a new campaign to control malaria, let us say. Both the health people and the broadcasting people are likely to think automatically of a series of weekly 30-minute programs. But possibly the messages the health people want to get across do not lend themselves to filling up 30-minute chunks of time interestingly at rather infrequent intervals. Possibly the messages could be more effectively incorporated in 30-*second* time segments 20 or 30 times a day every day. Possibly they could better be worked into existing programs with established audiences—into music, news, variety, or game programs. Overrigid organizational structure and inflexible operational methods in broadcasting tend to discourage this kind of programming inventiveness.

15.3.2 Limiting Factors: Instructional Programming

In one sense, broadcasters responsible for information/guidance programming are fortunate, compared with those responsible for instructional programming. As was pointed out in the previous section, in the absence of systematic feedback, the relative success or failure of the former is not conspicuously evident. But when it comes to converting illiterates into literates, decreasing school dropouts, compensating for lack of teachers, or stimulating improved academic achievement, we are dealing with measurable quantities; and statistics concerning them are routinely gathered by governmental education departments. Judged by these statistics, the performance of instructional broadcasting in the 1960s clearly did not live up to its promise. As late as 1972 it could be authoritatively said that the history of instructional broadcasting "has been marked with false starts, inflated expectations, and assorted misunderstandings about its potential and the requisites to its success" (Academy for Educational Development 1972, p. 109).

Responses to this indictment take divergent directions. The young Turks of educational philosophy tend to see the whole enterprise of "developed" countries' trying to turn "underdeveloped" countries into replicas of themselves as being fundamentally wrong–headed. This view is discussed further in §18.4.3. The educational establishment sees the problem as one of simply applying technology more efficiently. This is the view of the U.S. Agency for International Development, for example. After the embarrassment of its early fiascos (§15.2.2), AID drew back from further commitments to ITV projects themselves and turned, instead, toward research aimed at finding out what went wrong and what to do about it. "What went wrong" is the subject of the previously mentioned *Memo to Educational Planners* (Schramm et al. 1967) and its accompanying three volumes of case studies (UNESCO-IIEP 1967). Subsequently, AID undertook a series entitled "Studies in Educational Technology for Development." In that connection, AID contracted with the Academy for Educational Development in Washington, D.C., to produce a handbook and an illustrative film for presentation to educational leaders in developing countries (Academy for Educational Development 1972). These distill the changed concepts about broadcasting and education which evolved during the 1960s and which had been adumbrated in the UNESCO series.

In brief, the new doctrine advocates a concept derived from engineering, a "systems approach," to the uses of "educational technology"—the term preferred to "educational broadcasting" and its variants because the revised concept embraces *all* the possible technological aids applicable to education. The systems concept can perhaps best be first understood in terms of its opposite—the approach which merely added broadcasting, or any other technologically novel device, to an existing educational system as a superficial adjunct, without ever questioning the adequacy of the system itself. One of the most common symptoms of this "nonsystems" approach is the making of decisions about broadcasting facilities *before* making decisions about how they will be employed educationally. As the International Bank for Reconstruction and Development put it, "A serious danger in educational television is that hardware installation will precede the program planning and production, organization and teacher training and equipment maintenance which are essential to the effective utilization of hardware. This danger is heightened by the promotional efforts of suppliers and the tendency of governments to view these media as short cuts to educational development, which makes them susceptible to high pressure salesmanship" (IBRD 1971, p. 20).

The new doctrine insists that the introduction of educational technology as a systems component requires top-to-bottom reevaluation of the total system. Conventional wisdom must be challenged at every turn. The advantages of this approach, as summarized by Schramm et al. (1967, pp. 163–64), are: (1) that objectives must be explicitly defined at the outset; (2) that all the functioning parts of the educational process must be identified, and their working relationships determined; (3) that results—the output of the system—must be systematically analyzed to see whether the objectives are being truly reached; (4) that costs can thus be analyzed in terms of results and efficiency determined; and (5) that innovations in the educational system as a whole can be facilitated.

Perhaps the last point is the most interesting one, because it brings us back to an underlying dilemma. It was pointed out in chapter 12 that aid-recipient countries tend to prefer hardware to software; they welcome gifts of the means, but prefer to decide on the ends independently of outside pressures. In effect, the World Bank, AID, and other agencies which subscribe to the new doctrine of educational technology have rejected that viewpoint. They see hardware coming last, objectives first. This implied degree of foreign involvement in so fundamental an aspect of nationhood as the system of education is not something that can be easily accepted by a developing country that is at all sensitive about its autonomy.

On a simpler—and one might perhaps even say less doctrinaire—level, the underlying problem revealed by the analysis of experiments with instructional broadcasting is inadequate *organization*. One can readily perceive, from the descriptions of instructional projects in § 15.2, that the successful implementation of such broadcasting projects requires a high degree of organization and coordination. All instructional broadcasting experience reinforces the axiom that what goes on at the receiving end is just as important as what goes on at the transmitting end. This means that two separate groups of complex activities, each involving a wide variety of skills, equipment, and logistical supports, have to be coordinated in accordance with a fixed timetable. Often, several different government authorities not accustomed to working together have to cooperate. The production of programs, training of studio teachers, indoctrination of classroom teachers, preparation of supportive printed materials, reproduction and timely distribution of those materials, delivery of receivers, maintenance of receivers, administration and processing of tests, feeding back of the results of testing to producers, coordinating class and broadcast schedules, provisions for emergency power failures—these are some of the component activities which have to be closely interwoven into a continuous sequence. Failure of any link in the long chain can seriously compromise the whole undertaking.

Lack of the capacity to sustain this kind of organized activity is one of the most characteristic weaknesses of developing countries. Many well-trained, conscientious individuals of the highest competence may be available; but their potentialities are never fully realized for lack of a coherent organization to provide them with a stable, productive working environment. This problem, of fundamental importance in all broadcasting enterprises, is discussed further in connection with training in § 18.3.3. Each of the educational broadcasting projects mentioned in § 15.2 could provide illustrative examples, but let us take just one, the first in the series, the farm-forum experiment in Ghana. Successful though this experiment was within its restrictive framework of only 20 programs, Abell, the Canadian technical adviser who assessed the project stated flatly: "The need for constant and consistent attention to the organizational and administrative aspects of operating Farm Radio Forums is the *chief lesson* which was taught by the entire project. . . . No expansion of Farm Radio Forums in Ghana is recommended until *known organizational problems* have been resolved" (Coleman, Popku, and Abell 1968, pp. 47, 48; italics added). A technical adviser does not publish negative comments of this sort casually; we can be sure that the organizational problems must have indeed been severe, to receive this much notice. A careful reading of the adviser's report makes this clear. In fact, a good portion of the research was nullified because of organizational failures. Among specific operational problems mentioned were lack of reliable transportation, failure to pay allowances as scheduled, failure to transmit printed materials on time, failure to maintain receivers, mishandling of requests for information, and failure to delegate responsibility so as to enable work to progress without delay (Coleman, Popku, and Abell 1968 p. 48). These lapses may seem petty, individually considered, but their cumulative effect on anything as dependent on timeliness and tight coordination as a farm-forum project can be fatally disruptive.

To return to the systems concept, it is basically a particular way of look-ing at organization. To achieve any fundamental amelioration of organiza-tional defects does, in the final analysis, usually require far-reaching changes—changes that may well seem revolutionary to those with a vested interest in the status quo. The failure of a promised vehicle or paycheck to appear on cue is but a symptom of broader, underlying organizational problems—the proverbial tip of the iceberg. In that sense the systems approach correctly diagnoses the central problem of successfully applying broadcasting and other media technologies to developmental goals.

[EDITOR'S NOTE. In the two case histories that follow, the foregoing prin-ciples can be readily traced. The first case, that of the Mass Media Center in Ethiopia, illustrates some of the advantages of an organizational change which brings together the several technologies under a single administra-tion; at the same time, one can also see in this case—more by reading between the lines than from explicit description—examples of organiza-tional weaknesses and their consequences. The second case, that of the national ITV system in the Ivory Coast, is the prize exhibit of the systems doctrine. Here is one country, at least, which was willing to put ends before means and to accept, on an unprecedented scale, outside involve-ment in their determination. In the course of a decade the cost of the project may amount to half a billion dollars, and if it succeeds as planned it will completely revolutionize public education in the Ivory Coast.]

15.4 Case History: Ethiopia's Mass Media Center, *by John Gartley*

[EDITOR'S NOTE. Phoenixlike, a flourishing center for applied educational technology in Ethiopia has sprung from the ashes of an earlier attempt at such a center that failed. In the late 1950s the U.S. Agency for Inter-national Development invested in a Ministry of Education audiovisual production center, located at the site of a small teacher-training college in the capital, Addis Ababa. The center was fully equipped with machinery for economical local production of textbooks, manuals, wall posters, charts, and other graphic materials; it had film and sound-production facilities; and Ethiopian teachers were sent to the United States to learn production

John Gartley is on the Faculty of Speech and Theater, Montclair State College, New Jersey. He worked for three years at the Ethiopian Mass Media Center, first as Peace Corps Volunteeer, later as a United States AID grantee.

and utilization techniques. The idea was to equip the Ethiopian Ministry of Education to harness the potentialities of educational technology for multiplying the effectiveness of Ethiopia's very limited educational resources. It was doubtless a sound idea, but ahead of its time, for as the American advisers completed their tours, the center faded away. The printing machines were dismantled and sent elsewhere, the audiovisual specialists left their studies and went into other fields, and the center finally closed down.

Then came television. Ethiopian television, which the Ministry of Information opened in November 1964 (see § 3.1.3 for details) was rationalized from the outset as needed primarily for education. It did not start as an education medium, however, partly because of the problems of coordination between the Ministries of Information and Education, partly because the latter needed time to sort out all the advice showered upon it by foreign experts and agencies. At one point, for example, Peace Corps representatives proposed making Ethiopia the definitive testing ground for African educational television; a massive pilot experiment in Ethiopia was to do for Africa what the Peace Corps' Colombia ETV project was supposed to do for South America. This ambitious plan faded away, perhaps for the same reason that the earlier audiovisual production center had faded—it may have been in advance of its time.

In any event, when educational television did finally start in Ethiopia, about a year after the public television service opened, its scale was modest; and though there was some American input, British rather than American experts were the prime movers. Eventually, as the ETV operation expanded, it took over all the quarters once occupied by the AID-sponsored audiovisual production center. Other activities of the educational media gravitated toward the same place, so that ultimately the center concept was revitalized, albeit in altered form. As a final touch of symbolism, the story of the emergence of the Mass Media Center is narrated here by a participant who originally went to the center as an American Peace Corps volunteer.]

All during 1964, Ministry of Education planning for the start of Ethiopian educational television went forward. It involved negotiations with the Ministry of Information over the use of, and reimbursement for, studio time; coordination with local schools; provision for office and production space for newly appointed Ministry of Education television personnel and for experts from overseas; arrangements for obtaining and distributing receivers to participating schools; appointment of, and specialized training for, key Ethiopian personnel; and innumerable other details. All this put a heavy strain on a ministry already severely taxed by all the educational problems of a developing country near the bottom of the per capita income table.

In April of 1964, the first Ethiopian ETV specialist, Abdu Mozayen, went to London to attend a course at the Centre for Educational Television Overseas (§ 14.2.2). While he was abroad, a second staff member, Rahel Mekuria, who had recently returned from England with a degree in education, was appointed. During her first year her work consisted mainly in preparing programs for future broadcast, since on-the-air work had not yet started. Ultimately, Ato Abdu became administrator of the Mass Media Center, and Woizero Rahel became head of the Ethiopian Educational Television Service.

15.4.1 Educational Television Service Initiated

In October 1965, the educational service went on the air. Two programs were telecast daily to fifteen secondary schools in Addis Ababa. Since recording facilities were not available, programs had to go out live; and not having its own studios, ETV had to use the Ministry of Information's small studio, located high in Addis Ababa's City Hall, some four miles from the ETV offices at the Teacher Training Institute. These production conditions were far from ideal, but enthusiastic reactions from students and teachers alike during that first year persuaded the Ministry of Education it was on the right track. The next year, both the schedule of televised courses and the number of schools reached were increased. Courses included English (grades 1–3, 9, and 10), French (grades 9 and 10), geography (grades 5 and 6), biology (grade 10), health (grades 7 and 8), and physics (grades 11 and 12). A gift of 20 more receivers enabled the expansion of the receiving schools by that number.

Nevertheless, fundamental policy and logistic problems remained to be solved. For example, it had not yet been decided whether the thrust of the programs should be toward direct teaching or only toward enrichment; some teachers and headmasters had mistaken concepts about such basic matters as providing the necessary physical accommodations for television classes, matching class schedules with television schedules, following proper utilization procedures in the classroom, and feeding back prescribed evaluation data (Mozayen 1967). Such fundamental problems were compounded by shortages of production staff and of production facilities, as well as by inadequate planning to anticipate the innumerable roadblocks which a complex new undertaking of this kind was bound to encounter.

By the 1967–68 school year, however, many of the most pressing problems had been solved. In the schools, for example, headmasters had made the necessary adjustments in their class schedules to coordinate them with the transmission schedules; and parent groups had voluntarily bought chairs to equip viewing rooms. The ETV service itself had acquired additional staff. The service now transmitted three lessons each morning to 50 schools with a student population of 48,000. The extension of television to more schools was helped by the donation of 15 more receivers by Britain. Donated sets were distributed to government schools, but private schools wanting to participate had to buy their own sets. In June 1968, eight private schools had done so, and 55 government schools were equipped, for a total of 63 participating institutions—all, of course, in the Addis Ababa area, to which the TV signal was confined. Three years before, ETV had reached only 15 schools.

15.4.2 Mass Media Center Established

By 1967 the Ministry of Education felt that the prospect of extending ETV to more schools justified a major expansion of production facilities. Up to this point, Ethiopian ETV had been allotted only limited office and production space in the Teacher Training Institute compound. In December 1968, the entire campus was turned over to ETV and related Ministry of Education projects, such as literacy training, educational radio, and conventional audiovisual activities. In short, all the ministry's activities involving educational technology were grouped together at one place under a single administrator. Thus was born the Mass Media Center.

The expansion made it possible to add six more offices for ETV producers; research and library facilities; a materials production center for photography, graphics, and duplication; and a television studio and control room. Equipment for the studio was provided by the Ethiopian Ministry of Education, the British Overseas Development Ministry, and USAID. It included three plumbicon cameras, a document viewer, two telecine chains, and a videotape recorder. ETV continued to use the Ministry of Information transmitter, but starting in March 1969 instructional programs were relayed four miles by microwave link from the Mass Media Center to the City Hall (Blezard 1969, p. 212). This arrangement solved at a stroke the many problems of working in the cramped and overburdened Ministry of Information production facilities.

It is symptomatic, perhaps, that educational television came into systematic use in Ethiopia before educational radio, though radio had, of course, been in general use for many more years than television. New facilities for educational radio located at the Mass Media Center included two studios with control rooms, and an announce booth. The master plan called for three years of closed-circuit testing and evaluation of program materials before the phasing in of special educational transmission facilities, separate from the facilities of Radio Ethiopia, the Ministry of Information service.

In the meantime, Radio Ethiopia was being used, in 1972, to release taped programs associated with a UNESCO literacy campaign, which had been several years under development. The UNESCO offices and materials-production facilities had been incorporated into the Mass Media Center when it was set up in 1968. Another aspect of the center's activity involves conventional projectors, tape recorders, and related audiovisual equipment for classroom use. In 1972 the center began functioning as the base for the maintenance and distribution of such equipment for government schools in the Addis Ababa area.

Like the earlier center, the Mass Media Center also went into the printing business, for it began preparing and reproducing guidebooks covering the lesson series in both radio and television. These were distributed to all teachers using the programs. In 1972 the center was also planning to print student workbooks which were to be made available to every pupil using the lessons sent out by radio.

The watershed year of 1968, when the Mass Media Center was formally established, also saw a marked increase in personnel resources. New foreign advisory staff included two British Council television officers, two Centre for Educational Television Overseas advisers, two British Overseas Development Ministry advisers, and seven Peace Corps volunteers. In September 1968, the staff (national and foreign) totaled 74—only four years after Abdu Mozayen's lone journey to CETO in London.

Ethiopian ETV evolved special production-training programs for its own personnel. The first course, run during the summer of 1971, consisted of four classes: (1) basic television production for new producers; (2) advanced television production for producers already working at the Mass Media Center; (3) educational-materials production; and (4) technical operations, for all studio technicians. The personnel of the center felt that these training courses had unique advantages because of their intensiveness and their location at the very site where the trainees would be working in the future. This meant that the equipment, the ancillary facilities, and in fact the total working environment of the training phase exactly matched those the trainees would encounter in the working phase (see Gartley and Pendred 1971).

In 1971, Ethiopian ETV planned to transmit five programs daily to grades 3–8, with emphasis on direct teaching rather than merely enrichment. The lessons broadcast to elementary schools averaged 15 minutes in length, while those to junior secondary schools averaged 20 minutes. The acquisition of two videotape recorders had enabled prerecording of all programs, which covered areas in science, mathematics, the social sciences, and language learning. Each lesson was based on the standard Ministry of Education curriculum and was scheduled to fit the varying time schedules of the schools. Later the ministry required the schools to adopt uniform time schedules. For 1972 three additional TV lessons a day were planned, which meant that by 1973 educational television would be able to serve all eight periods of the school day.

Ethiopian ETV primarily serves in-school education. Nevertheless, it expanded its services in 1970 to include some adult education as well. Each week, members of the ETV staff produced five programs which were aired as part of the TV service of the Ministry of Information, from 7:00 P.M. to 7:30 P.M. They dealt with language learning, history, health, and geography. The programs were received in homes and places of business; no community viewing centers or teleclubs were being contemplated in 1972, nor were audience data available.

In 1971 the Ministry of Information extended the range of the Addis Ababa television station by means of repeaters, enabling coverage of a series of rapidly growing towns and villages to the south of the city over a distance of about 120 miles. This brought additional schools within reach of Ethiopian ETV, increasing the potentiality to a student population of about 160,000. The British and Japanese governments promised an additional 125 receivers for schools in the expanded area of transmission. Another repeater transmitter was planned for Mount Entoto, the high ridge to the north above Addis Ababa which effectively cuts off the television signal from the City Hall transmitter in that direction.

Even this would, of course, extend educational television to no more than a tiny fraction of the Ethiopian Empire. Ethiopia is one of the larger African countries in area—approximating the combined areas of Texas, Oklahoma, and New Mexico (*Fact Book* 1970, p. 214). It is, moreover, rugged and mountainous, presenting an extremely difficult terrain to cover effectively with line-of-sight signals. True, the central region, in the neighborhood of Addis Ababa, is where 55% of the student population lives. But this merely means that educational television is reaching the part of the school population already best served, rather than the more educationally deprived parts for which television could make some compensation.

15.4.3 ETV Research

Ethiopian ETV has a small but active research unit, known as the Liaison and Evaluation Office. The three-member staff of this office visits schools, conducts utilization demonstrations, coordinates set maintenance, collects teacher-evaluation forms, and—in cooperation with the British Council and Haile Selassie I University—administers tests to determine the success of lesson points, program procedures, and conventions of presentation.

The testing procedures recommended by the Liaison and Evaluation Office had to conform to rather strict criteria of feasibility: among other things, tests had to be easy to administer; to require limited time for preparation and processing; and to be easy to evaluate by personnel not highly trained in statistics and educational research methodology. The British Council in Addis Ababa and the Liaison and Evaluation Office at the Mass Media Center cooperated during the 1967–69 period in developing and administering such tests in two areas: (1) student comprehension of the material taught in the televised English-language programs; and (2) the effect of production and graphics conventions in all programs. The latter tests were developed because it was realized that television-presentation conventions developed and proved successful in one country or culture are not necessarily intelligible in another country or culture (for details see Sherrington and Gartley 1969; Gartley 1971).

15.4.4 Educational Radio

Ethiopian Educational Radio, as noted above, is a more recent producing member of the Mass Media Center than television. In October 1969, many schools in the empire were forced to go on a shift system because of unanticipated increases in enrollment and teacher shortages. The Ministry of Education, needing an empirewide medium, asked for radio lessons for direct teaching to schools where adequately trained teachers could not be provided.

By 1972, the Educational Radio Service was releasing four daily lessons in the social sciences, Amharic, and English, using the Ministry of Information's radio network of both short-wave and medium-wave transmitters (see § 3.1.1). These lessons were being used by all of Ethiopia's 53 secondary schools and by elementary schools in the central and southern portions of the empire. By 1973 the Ministry of Education hoped to acquire additional medium-wave transmitters of its own in the extreme south, where radio coverage was limited to short wave.

Unfortunately, little is known objectively about the effectiveness of this effort at systematic educational use of radio in Ethiopia. The wide dispersal of participating schools made it more difficult to secure feedback on educational radio than to secure it for television. Then, too, no additional funds were allotted for radio research, so that the small Liaison and Evaluation Unit at the Mass Media Center was not able to extend its activities to include radio.

15.5 Case Study: Ivory Coast ETV, *by Stephen H. Grant*

Education in the Ivory Coast is plagued with all the classic problems of developing countries: room in the schools for only a fraction of the children of school age, an exceedingly high dropout rate for those who do start school, a high percentage of repeaters, a grossly uneven distribution of educational facilities geographically, inadequate teaching quality, and bookish curricula ill-adapted to the practical needs of the country.

15.5.1 A Radical Solution

The Ivory Coast has chosen to try a radical solution to all these problems— a top-to-bottom reform of the whole public educational system, built around the use of educational television. In preparation, a massive study was

Stephen H. Grant is a Fellow of the Center for International Education, University of Massachusetts, and he was a UNESCO consultant on teacher training, 1970–71, and on ETV evaluation, 1971–72, Ivory Coast ETV project.

undertaken covering all aspects of television teaching, both practical and theoretical. Eight volumes had been published by mid-1972 (Ivory Coast 1969–).

The willingness of the Ivory Coast to commit itself both to thorough-going educational reform and to major monetary investment elicited external aid from several sources. The total budget for the first five years of the ETV project, 1969–73, was nearly $24 million, of which the Ivory Coast itself put up one-third from its own resources. The rest came from French technical assistance ($7.4 million), a World Bank loan ($3.05 million), the UNESCO/United Nations Development Program ($2.7 million), Canada ($1.7 million), and UNICEF ($1 million). Subsequently, the United States also contributed to the evaluation aspect of the project. By 1980, if all goes according to plan, every grade school classroom in the country will have a television set, and televised lessons will reach a school population of a million primary pupils. Within this period the Ivory Coast hopes to double the number of children in its primary and secondary schools (Tickton 1972, p. 102).

Only one-third of the schools in the Ivory Coast have mains electrical power supply—one of the major technological roadblocks such a comprehensive television-teaching program encounters in a developing country. Initially, at least, this problem was successfully met in the Ivory Coast by the use of battery-operated receivers. French-manufactured wet batteries similar to those used in automobiles were employed, in sets of 32 batteries for each receiver. The batteries had an expected useful life of a year and a half. For the first year French aid supplied the batteries, and the results were highly satisfactory. Battery operation is known to be much more expensive than mains operation, though comparative figures were not available to the writer. The real feasibility test will come when the recurrent cost of battery replacement has to be regularly met from the Ministry of Education's own operating budget.

15.5.2 Five Publics

The first public to be reached by Ivory Coast ETV consists of preservice teachers. Since 1969 close to a thousand Ivorians have been trained each year to become a new brand of primary school teacher (see Grant 1971). New elements in their curriculum include audiovisual instruction, programmed instruction, group dynamics, rural leadership development, intensive French-language preparation, and the new mathematics. The second public comprises in-service teachers, who are brought back periodically to the project center at Bouaké, the country's second city, for "recycling." More than 13,000 such teachers, from both public and private primary schools, were scheduled to receive weekly retraining lessons by television and radio in 1972–73.

The third public is the primary school population itself. During 1971–72, the first year of this phase of the ETV project, 20,000 first-graders in the southern part of the country saw three fifteen-minute televised lessons each morning: French language, mathematics, and "basic education," that is, expression by means of song, dance, gymnastics, painting, clay modeling, and the like. Television brings direct teaching, which the classroom teacher complements for the rest of the period with related drills and elaborations based directly upon the TV lessons. Classroom teachers have the benefit of guides prepared by the TV production group, introducing vocabulary, structures, and concepts, and including suggestions about how local teachers can exploit the TV lessons in the classroom. In 1972 these guidance materials were delivered by car every three months to the 450 teachers in the territory covered by the television signal at that time. Each year the television-production staff, largely French, will remake up for one half of the previous year's broadcast lessons and also prepare broadcasts for the following grade; by 1977 the complete cycle of public primary school grades should have a televised component.

The fourth target public will consist of those students who leave primary school without qualifying for secondary school—the large majority of those leaving primary school, in fact. They will be offered a two-year post-primary television course in trades they can use in rural settings. The adult population constitutes the fifth public, for which literacy-training programs will be developed, utilizing the school TV reception points. This range of targets has to be reached over a single-channel national network, which already broadcasts its own general-interest programs for nearly five hours each day (§ 6.2.2). The possibility of adding a second channel was under discussion in 1972, so that two different ETV lessons could be distributed simultaneously.

TV programs for teachers have been inspired by two sources: suggestions devised by the production staff concerning preparation and follow-up of the televised lessons; and reactions by teachers in the field who either propose solutions to problems which can be shared by other teachers or who ask for supplementary information. The latter situation is exemplified by the following incident: when classroom teachers were asked to add painting to the curriculum as a creative, nonverbal skill, some wrote to the ETV Production Center, complaining that they had no painting materials. The production staff thereupon prepared a special program showing how one can grind up readily available local materials (charcoal, chalk, termite mounds), sift them, mix them into a paste with water, and create "paint."

Nearly all the TV lessons for first-graders developed in the Ivory Coast have reflected indigenous images. In studying French the youngsters see films showing, for example, an Ivorian mother and her child on a shopping trip. The children follow a carefully constructed series of exercises of ascending difficulty, while being told by the teleteacher to "listen and repeat," then to "listen and answer" as the shopping dialogue progresses.

In arithmetic the televiewers see other children like themselves in an out-door setting, manipulating piles of leaves, seeds, or bottle caps, learning basic mathematical classifications and set construction. The classroom teacher is asked to assemble similar objects and to use them in exploiting the lessons of the television demonstrations.

15.5.3 Evaluation: Pros and Cons

In 1972 the Ivory Coast project was still in its early operational stages. As a case study it offered both positive and negative lessons. The following evaluative comments should be understood as some of the writer's sub-jective impressions, not at this stage as scientifically validated assessments.

On the positive side, one of the impressive features of the project is the way it meshes integrally with the country's development goals as set forth by the Ministry of Planning. Furthermore, the television component of the educational system is no mere frill to dress up traditional practices; rather, it has stimulated far-reaching reforms, involving new principles and revised attitudes. The use of television means that a higher standard of instruction will be made generally available; at the same time a corps of new, and retrained, classroom teachers will be available to exploit the TV lessons effectively. The government has decided to employ automatic promotion to higher grades, in the hope that pupils will not only stay in school but will also actively participate in learning processes having direct relevance to their future lives in the Ivory Coast.

Another positive value of the TV teaching system is the unique arrange-ment which places the TV production center in the same location as the main Ivorian teacher-training school, in Bouaké. This proximity makes it easy to familiarize future teachers with both the philosophy and the me-chanics behind TV lesson construction and production.

On the negative side, chief among the disappointments has been the low number of nationals working in the ETV project. Of a total staff of over 200 (161 in production and 42 in teacher training), only 52% were Ivorian, and most of those occupied subordinate positions. Original plan-ning called for a much more significant level of Ivorian participation, with a steady reduction in expatriate staff. The Ivorian directors of the project, however, have claimed they could not find suitable counterparts for the foreign specialists. Until 1972 not a single top-level Ivorian official in the Ministry of Education devoted his full time to managing the project. In that year, however, the minister of education (the fourth since the project's inception in 1969) named a special deputy to this task.

Second, suggestions have often been made for launching a comprehensive public-information campaign to explain the project to those it most affects. There is evidence to suggest that potential student-teachers, parents, gov-ernment cadres, and particularly teachers in the field fail to grasp the basic purposes of the program which will so radically change their national educational system. Lack of information and misinformation have caused fear and resistance in many instances.

Third in the list of negative impressions is the awkward position of expatriate staff members. Ideally, as a mercenary force offering technical expertise locally unavailable, a foreign staff should carry out a program delineated by the host government. For this project, however, the host government has officially requested that the expatriates also formulate the objectives. It is hard to justify this function as an expatriate prerogative.

Fourth, early contacts were made to obtain funds for a built-in component of research and evaluation; yet not until 1972 was support obtained, from UNESCO and the American government. The only criterion upon which all three of the comparable major previous ETV projects had been rated "poor" was that of evaluation (Ivory Coast 1969–, vol. 3). Despite the announced intention to include a "complete and continuous evaluation" component in the project, this vital factor has received only minor attention. A complete scientific appraisal of the Ivorian experiment with ETV would be of the greatest interest to all other developing countries, for the Ivory Coast project is a crucial testing ground for African education and educational television. It has been called "the world's most ambitious educational project to date" (Tickton 1972, p. 102), and on its success or failure may largely depend the future willingness of the developed countries to continue supporting the use of television as a means of overcoming Africa's educational problems.

16　Research

Sydney W. Head

16.1 Role of Research

Conventional wisdom regards broadcasting as a one-way street, a medium which sends messages monologically instead of carrying on a dialogue, as in face-to-face or even telephonic communication. Though literally true in an engineering sense, this conception is only superficially true in a social sense. Certainly broadcasting does not create immediate and continuous feedback, which is defined as "the control of a system by reinserting into the system the result of its performance" (Wiener 1950, p. 71). Nevertheless, broadcasting does receive delayed and intermittent feedback, and that feedback does have an impact on its performance. Broadcasters, in other words, not only send messages out; they also take messages in. True, the intake may vary greatly in quality, significance, immediacy, and frequency; but it does occur. Broadcasters—whether managers, writers, producers, or performers—do not, after all, live in a social vacuum. Inevitably some forms of feedback reach them and affect their future conduct.

At one extreme, feedback might consist of praise or censure from a minister of information, the comments of friends, gossip overheard in bars, or an occasional letter from a listener of consequence; at the other extreme it might consist of sophisticated and expensive investigations of representative samples of the total audience. The problem, then, is not the complete absence of feedback in broadcasting, but the absence of feedback representative of the audience as a whole. The messages that come in tend to be from a very narrow segment of the audience—from people in authority, particularly; and, more generally, from people in the same social milieu as the broadcaster. The great mass of the audience has no input to the feedback system in the absence of deliberate efforts on the part of broadcasting management to create channels of return communication. Creating return channels is one role of research.

Gifted broadcasters, it is true, develop sensitive antennae which enable them to anticipate audience responses intuitively, but no national broadcasting service can afford to rely on intuition alone for basic management decisions. Research is essential because of the very nature of broadcasting and must be regarded as an integral part of the system. This is a proposition which few African broadcasting managers would be likely to deny; yet it more often receives lip service than active response. Research and audience promotion should be regularly budgeted activities, counted as equally essential with programming and engineering—for they themselves can be justified in the final analysis only in terms of their ultimate effects.

The lack of research sponsored by African broadcasting systems themselves (rather than by *users* of the systems, such as advertisers) cannot be ascribed entirely to financial limitations and the special problems of conducting broadcasting research in developing countries (see § 16.5). Part of the reason for the lack is that officials of some governments still tend to regard broadcasting as a one-way medium. They see it as a means of issuing directives, orders, fiats, or edicts, rather than a means of establishing a dialogue. They see it as a way of imposing conformity, rather than as a means of developing consensus; as a weapon of propaganda, rather than as an avenue of enlightenment. Such officials use the national broadcasting service as a personal megaphone, rather than as a device for responding to the wants and needs of those at the receiving end. This one-way approach on the part of high officials demeans broadcasters as professionals—though their generally low status is also a function of the recruitment and training process (see § 18.3). The minister of public works would not be likely to tell an engineer how to build a bridge, nor the minister of health to tell a surgeon how to perform an operation; but these same officials would be quite likely to tell a broadcaster how to conduct a campaign. When broadcasting is mishandled in this way, any money spent on research would be money wasted. The truth is that, in some political contexts, nobody really *wants* to know the facts that would be uncovered by audience research (cf. § 16.6.2).

This indifference is the more unfortunate because developing countries, even more than industrialized ones, imperatively need research to justify moneys spent on broadcasting systems. Schramm, in his well-known vade mecum on the use of mass media in national development, makes the case for the essentiality of research. He points out, for example, that it can help ensure that desired messages will be delivered efficiently and successfully, thus preventing costly failures which developing economies can ill afford; it can bridge the cultural gap between broadcaster and audience, which increasingly separates the two; it can keep the broadcaster abreast of rapidly changing audience needs and outlooks; and it can help "make the process of change as efficient and as little disruptive as possible" (Schramm 1964, pp. 176–78).

16.2 Development of Research

A British Colonial Office committee reported in 1943 that "there is no detailed and systematic evidence of the effects of different types of programmes upon the listeners" (Great Britain 1943, p. 38). A decade later the situation in British Africa was much the same, for Fraenkel, in his report on effects research he conducted for the Central African Broadcasting Station (§ 7.1.1) in the early 1950s, wrote, "On the whole vast continent of Africa no one was doing any research of this sort. Various governments and Colonial Offices were now starting to pour tens of thousands of pounds into new transmitters and studios, but nobody thought it worthwhile to spend a penny to find out what was understood" (Fraenkel 1959, p. 142). Since then, millions more have been poured into new broadcasting hardware in Africa; yet the situation with regard to research budgets remains much the same. Fraenkel's research problem had nothing to do with today's most common concerns—coverage, circulation, audience demographics, and program preferences. Quite simply, he started with essentially zero quantities in all these dimensions. The "Saucepan Special" low-cost battery radio (§ 7.1.1) created an audience ab ovo. Receiver-sales and licensing records enabled the tabulation of the audience as it grew, just as did similar records for television audiences two decades later. At that stage African radio-set owners "thought of themselves as an elite group, almost as an exclusive club," and they cooperated readily with researchers (Fraenkel 1959, p. 136).

Fraenkel concentrated on problems of program intelligibility and recall: To what extent were useful messages in local languages actually getting across? How well were they remembered? When he found that "only a very small proportion of the listeners had a proper grasp of what had been broadcast," he turned to the analysis of reasons for misunderstanding (Fraenkel 1959, p. 141). One of the early insights derived from these investigations was the extent to which radio communication is culture-bound. The CABS tried using public-service announcements in the form of the proverbial sayings which are a convention of Central African traditional speech. The statement "The fly, though small, is dangerous" failed completely to carry its health message; instead, African listeners interpreted it to mean, "Though the Europeans are few, yet they are powerful . . . we'll never be able to drive them out of the country" (p. 153). A family serial based on the soap-opera format likewise failed, for "no European could write such plays and make them sound plausible" (p. 154). The most effective format turned out to be single-concept playlets written by African members of the CABS staff.

We have dwelt on these early investigations, not only because they have intrinsic historical interest, but also because they point up the fact that broadcasting research includes much besides the counting of sets and heads. Intelligibility studies of the type Fraenkel used have obvious relevance to all forms of educational and information/guidance programming. Their reciprocals are studies designed to pretest program materials before investments are made in large-scale campaigns or the preparation of educational lessons. These, and many other types of research, derive their special importance from their implications for the role of broadcasting in development. A UNESCO-sponsored meeting of research experts concluded:

The mass media are an integral part of national development; indeed they have a leadership role to play in this field. Therefore, the primary concern of the researcher for some time to come will be to relate communication to nation-building. Subjects to be taken up for continuing study will include: the promotion of national unity; the role of communication in developmental campaigns relating to agriculture, health, education, family planning, adult literacy. . . . Studies of the effectiveness of the media in relation to their full cost will . . . be crucial in guiding governments in the allocation of their communication services. Research is also essential to broaden the motivational base necessary for wider public participation in nation-building. [UNESCO 1970b, p. 28]

16.3 External Sponsorship

Little research of the kinds that UNESCO experts described had been undertaken by 1972. This is not to say there had been no research. In fact, there had been a good deal, but not from the broad perspective of national development as outlined by the UNESCO committee. Rather it had been conducted at the behest of interests external or peripheral to the national broadcasting services, by organizations with limited objectives— advertisers, manufacturers, foreign governments, sponsors of specific educational broadcasting projects, religious broadcasters. A complete collection of all such studies might in fact provide a valuable bank of research data; unfortunately most sponsors guard their research findings about African broadcasting as jealously as ancient sea captains exploring the African coast guarded their charts. The scattering of available materials up to 1965 was summarized in a journal article by Bled (1969). Since then the main new development has been the growing involvement of African universities and national statistical institutions in the field of broadcasting research.

16.3.1 Advertiser-oriented Research

Advertising interests, including at times the advertising departments of national broadcasting services, routinely employ commercial research organizations to conduct audience surveys. Blair (1965) surveyed this field as it was in the early 1960s. As a current example, the Research Bureau Limited of London has offices in Nigeria, Ghana, and Kenya, and associates in South Africa and Francophone Africa, and it completed ten studies in seven countries in Anglophone Africa during the period 1963–72. All were multimedia studies confined to urban areas, with sample sizes ranging from 600 to 12,000-plus (letter from the director of overseas operations, RBL, 14 April 1972). However, RBL's French associate reported that their clients refused "not only to tell anything about the research made, but even . . . to disclose their very names and the countries in which we operated" (letter from the research director, Société d'Études Commerciales et Documentaires, Paris, 6 June 1972). A Swiss firm, SCOPE, has formed a Research Department for Developing Countries and has conducted surveys in Ethiopia and Zaïre (see § 3.1.5).

Typically, advertisers want to know the number of sets in a market; the size of the audience and its chief demographic characteristics; program and language preferences; and variations in audience size by time of day. Though useful for station sales departments, most such surveys have limited value for management generally because they usually confine their inquiries to urban areas, where the primary market for advertised products is found. The management of a national service, however, should be even *more* concerned about the rural areas, where the great majority of the population is found, and where, moreover, the greater need for broadcasting service exists.

As an example of survey practice, we may consider one survey conducted for Kenya by Associated Business Consultants (East Africa) in 1969, some results of which were noted in § 4.1.4. A sample representing 56 locations of high population density was selected; 40% of the 5,320 adult respondents were urban and 60% were rural residents. The sample design called for overlay grids, which were used to select, by probability methods, either blocks in urban areas or starting points in rural areas. This method in itself implies the availability of accurate, up-to-date maps and census data, which Kenya, better than most other African countries, can provide. The selection of specific urban households was controlled by specifying the interviewer's direction of movement and the intervals between dwellings, and in rural areas interviewers simply traveled a compass course. In each selected household an individual respondent was selected from a roster of household members. Interviewers used four local languages as well as English. Telephone checks and reinterviews of 15% of the respondents authenticated the interviewers' reports. The conduct of the survey required 150 field workers, selected according to education and personal qualities. University students did the editing, which university graduates supervised (Associated Business Consultants 1969).

16.3.2 Foreign Government Sponsorship

Foreign governments with substantial international broadcasting activities carry out research in major friendly target countries, either directly through embassy staffs or indirectly through commercial research firms. Sometimes broadcasting systems such as the BBC, the VOA, and Deutsche Welle exchange information or join forces to reduce costs. Foreign broadcasting organizations want to know about opinions and media habits in target countries for guidance in choosing effective programming, scheduling, and production techniques. The approval of the host country has to be obtained, of course; a common inducement offered by the broadcasting organization is the promise to share its findings with the host government. If the foreign government is not on good terms with the target country's government, less reliable data such as listener letters, reports of travelers, intelligence from third-country embassies, and reactions by the target country's own media must be used.

The principal publicly available collection of research data on African broadcasting in English has been, at least until the 1970s, the United States Information Agency's reports of research studies it has sponsored. In the past these studies have been classified, initially, and released only after the lapse of several years, though nothing in their content appeared to warrant classification. By 1972, however, these restraints had been relaxed: "We seem to be moving closer to the realization that most of these reports can serve more than one audience" (letter from the chief of the Near East and Africa Division, USIA Office of Research and Assessment). Elsewhere, nondisclosure seems to be the general rule, with governments as with sponsors of private research. The BBC, for example, declined to provide any information about its research activities beyond what can be read in the BBC's annual handbook (letter from head of BBC External Audience Research, 8 July 1971).

USIA issued two bibliographies of its reports made public through 1970 (USIA 1964a, 1971a). The first, covering the period March 1955–July 1964 had no separate African section, but it did list three reports on African media. As the first, and almost the only, reports of their kind, they have been very widely quoted. Two of the three drew upon the same research project, a radio study in West Africa (USIA 1960b, 1961). The agency characterized the study as "the first large-scale public opinion survey ever undertaken in West Africa" and as "the first major USIA effort in that crucial area" (USIA 1960b, p. i). Its sample population comprised approximately 1,000 adult Africans in each of four cities—Abidjan, Accra, Dakar, and Lagos. Interviewing was conducted by French and British companies associated with the American Gallup Poll organization. Among other data obtained from the interviews, it was found that listening was somewhat higher in the Anglophone cities; that from a third to a half of the respondents listened outside their homes; that peak listening hours differed considerably from one city to another; and that the Anglophone respondents listened more frequently to the VOA than the Francophone respondents.

The third of these pioneer research reports, "Media Use among Africans in Nairobi, Kenya," is an account of a survey conducted in 1962 by a local Nairobi firm, Marco Surveys (USIA 1963). This was a small-scale urban survey of 175 adult Africans, representing 87% of the sample as originally designed. Selection was based on an area probability sample of households, and the questions concerned print media and films as well as radio. If the sample was representative of Nairobi's population, and if its responses were reported fully, at that early date few African listeners in Nairobi were exposed to foreign radio influences, for the 73% who reported listening to a specific service mentioned only the Kenya Broadcasting Company's African Service.

The second USIA bibliography, carrying the list forward from 1964 to January 1970, contains a section of 21 African studies, though only two deal specifically with broadcasting (USIA 1971a). The available USIA reports on broadcasting in Africa are unique sources of information, as their frequent citation in this book as well as in others indicates (see esp. chap. 10). Like the advertisers', however, the USIA's interest normally lies more with the urban elite than with the rural majority, so that we still cannot be sure what its reports tell us about the media habits of the mass audience.

16.3.3 Educational Sponsorship

Every use of broadcasting for adult and formal education needs research on two levels: (1) Production personnel need the guidance of feedback from the reception center or the classroom. (2) Project planners and responsible officials need more formal, longer-term research findings to establish whether or not the project as a whole is meeting its goals. Gartley touches on an instance of the first of these in § 15.4.3, in which he describes research at the Ethiopian Mass Media Center; and of course such feedback forms an integral component in the farm-forum concept (§ 15.2.1). Despite the obviousness of these research needs, they seem to have been overlooked or insufficiently fulfilled in a surprising number of cases. In § 15.5.3 Grant points out the inadequacy of research in the initial stages of Africa's biggest instructional-television project. And the extensive AID-financed educational-broadcasting project in Nigeria described in § 15.2.2, though programmed to include a research component from the beginning, had five different research specialists in as many years and finally had to have an outside research organization analyze data collected by the operational team itself (Washington County 1968). The last example, an almost farcical case of bureaucratic confusion, perhaps hints at the root problem: once again everyone pays lip service to the indispensability of research, but somehow the conviction is not compelling enough to guarantee that the necessary advance planning and funding will take place.

An example of how such research should and can be built into an educational project as an operational component from the earliest planning stages was provided by the Ghana Farm Radio Forum Project, described in § 15.2.1. Abell, the Canadian rural sociologist assigned to assess the outcome of the experiment, conducted a "before and after" study to ascertain whether the experimental groups which participated in the radio forums gained significantly in contrast to people who did not hear the broadcasts at all, and to others who heard the broadcasts but not under the structured conditions of the forum situation (Coleman, Popku, and Abell 1968). For the results of the experiment to have national significance, it was essential that the experimental group represent the rural population of the country as a whole; likewise, for the before-after measurements to have significance, it was necessary to select statistically meaningful samples from among both participants and nonparticipants. Furthermore, the content of the broadcasts themselves had to lend itself to inducing measurable audience effects. The researcher spent over a year on the project, although the actual broadcasts extended over only 20 weeks. Thus the requirements of research were taken into consideration throughout the planning stage as well as the operational and postoperational stages.

As an example of the integrated use of research in Francophone Africa, one may cite the Senegal pilot experiment in the use of television to aid in the social development of urban women, described in § 15.2.4. UNESCO contracted with the Centre de Recherches Psycho-Sociologiques at the University of Dakar to make an evaluation study (Fougeyrollas 1967). Again a before-after analysis was used, based in this case upon a probability sample of 99 women drawn from the 500 scheduled to take the course. These formed a panel, which was interviewed before and after exposure to the television lessons. The first survey established the attitudes already. prevailing among the women on the particular nutrition and hygiene subjects that were to be covered in the telecasts. The second survey measured the degree of change in attitudes that had occurred by the end of the course. Ten percent of the panel members had dropped out before the end, but this was held not to affect the statistical significance of the results. As an example of the shift in attitudes, in the first survey 41% of the sample correctly identified the mosquito as the transmitter of malaria. In the second survey 76% made the correct identification. In the pretelevision survey 50% had no opinion on this subject, while in the posttelevision survey only 8% had no opinion. At the same time, the number with the *wrong* opinion rose from zero to 16%. The investigator regarded this as a gain, however, ascribing the wrong answers to increased confidence on the part of the women as a by-product of the group-viewing and discussion experiences.

16.3.4 Religious Broadcasters

Both their cost-consciousness and their sense of mission have made the more responsible religious broadcasters sensitive to the need for research

(§ 11.3). ELWA in Liberia (§ 11.2.3) claimed to have made the "first mass audience survey of radio by African missions" (*ICB Bulletin* 1971, p. 4). Radio Voice of the Gospel in Ethiopia (§ 3.1.7) had an active research department from its inception. After completing minor local surveys, it undertook a major national study in 1971 (Radio Voice of the Gospel 1972). This survey used a national rural-urban sample of 20,000 adult respondents, who were questioned by a team of 52 interviewers selected from among "several hundred" candidates. Twelve members of the interview team were girls—an interesting departure since it was generally understood that women could not be successfully used as interviewers in Africa. After disposing of the usual questions about respondents' basic listening habits and demographic characteristics the RVOG survey focused specifically on its station image and opinions about its own programming and production practices (communication from RVOG audience research director, 20 June 1972).

16.4 Self-Study

The research activities discussed in the preceding section involve sponsors *external* to the medium as a national service. They use broadcasting to achieve specific, limited ends, but they are not generally responsible for achieving the broad spectrum of goals of a national broadcasting service. The more mature of the African services have begun to sponsor their own research, though often it, too, has had the narrow focus of interest implied by the special needs of their commercial departments. In the 1970s, however, a new trend began as African universities and statistical organizations developed their research capabilities. For example, Nigeria set up the National Mass Communications Council in 1972 at the University of Lagos, with plans for establishing an information clearing house (*Newsletter* 1972). Such a repository could be invaluable in extending the usefulness of individual research efforts such as those described in this chapter.

The Ghana Broadcasting Corporation has had a research department since 1956, which has depended for most of that time on panels of listeners as a source of information about audience response (see description in § 5.2.2). In 1968 GBC commissioned its first major study, employing a British commercial research firm. In 1971, by contrast, GBC started a large-scale survey on its own with the cooperation of the University of Ghana's Adult Education Institute, Statistical Research Institute, and Sociology Department. For the first time a study was to be made of the country as a whole, rural as well as urban; a sample of 10,000 was planned, with 130 university students conducting the interviews. The tabulation of the results was expected to be completed in 1972 (Kugblenu 1972; *This is GBC* 1971).

Of the several such cooperative ventures, the most significant has been one shared by the Zambia Broadcasting Services and the University of Zambia's Institute for African Studies, formerly the Rhodes-Livingstone Institute. The ZBS sponsored the three-year project, which started in 1970, and paid the costs the first two years, but the University of Zambia took on the third year's expenses when ZBS suffered a budget cut. The project in its entirety cost over $50,000. As Powell pointed out in § 7.1.2, the Zambian project holds a particular interest because of the thread of continuity which connects it directly with the pioneer research work at the Central African Broadcasting Station reported by Fraenkel (§ 16.2).

Previously, the only audience study at the disposal of the ZBS had been a conventional urban commercial survey made in 1965 for the station's sales department by a South African market-research firm. The ZBS/ University of Zambia project is actually a mass-media survey, dealing with press and films as well as radio and television, but of course broadcasting receives the most attention because it is by far the most widely used medium. The survey's sample design called for 5,000 interviews, stretched over a period of 12 months (Mytton 1971b). The following description is based on Mytton's third report (1972a). The chief topics of study were: (1) the use of local languages in broadcasting, (2) mass-media coverage and circulation, (3) news dissemination and assimilation, (4) program preferences, (5) the impact of specific educational broadcasts, and (6) competition from foreign stations. Quota sampling was used because of the difficulty of using pure random sampling in rural areas. Census data enabled random choice of sampling units in urban areas; in the country stratified cluster sampling was employed, with stratification according to age, sex, and land use.

Some of the findings of the Zambian study have already been reported in § 7.1.2. An interesting element in the study was a series of questions designed to test news assimilation. Respondents were asked about events recently salient in the news and presumably of intense interest—for example, the death of Egypt's President Nasser. Of the respondents in Lusaka, the capital, 59% replied they had not heard of the event; in Kasama, a town in the remote northern part of the country, 89% had not heard the news. In the capital, of those who *had* heard of Nasser's death, about 72% said they had learned about it from the radio. The report concluded that "high level of exposure to the mass media and in particular to radio did not necessarily mean a high level of knowledge of news events" (Mytton 1972a, p. 51).

On the complex and important problem of multilingualism in broadcasting, the Zambia study produced a number of significant insights. Even the definition of what constitutes a separate language becomes a problem, because speakers tend to identify closely related dialects as entirely separate languages. This feeling, it was found, could in part be traced back to the fact that, while different ethnic groups may use related languages, their cultures may differ considerably. ZBS had tended to program from the point of view of one particular cultural group among the several sharing a basic language, leaving the other groups feeling deprived even though they could understand the programs. As the researcher pointed out, this cultural bias is equivalent to designing English-language programs of interest only to Englishmen (Mytton 1971a, p. 6). Other useful observations in the report touch on news vocabulary, news translation into vernacular languages, factors that make for program popularity, the use of various kinds of music, the organization of production functions at ZBS, personnel problems arising from the civil service status of government broadcasters, and the role of public relations in broadcast operations. In sum, the ZBS/University of Zambia study provides a mine of useful insights for African broadcasters generally, for they share many of the same problems.

16.5 Methodological Problems

The Zambia project also provides illuminating examples of the problems endemic to broadcasting research, especially survey research, in Africa. The most intractable of these problems is the lack of what might be called "information infrastructure," which includes the virtually limitless amounts of detailed and constantly updated economic and demographic data already available at no cost to researchers in industrialized countries (see § 16.6.1 for further discussion of this concept). These include, for example, readymade sampling frames representative of relatively complete populations, such as telephone directories, city directories, voter registration rolls, membership lists; and, in some ways most important, the people's accumulated experience of surveys and their candor in answering questions freely and in giving frank opinions.

At the scholarly level, problems specific to broadcasting research in Africa have been ignored. For example, a 1973 publication bearing the inclusive-sounding title, *Survey Research in Africa* makes no reference to research on mass communication (O'Barr, Spain, and Tessler 1973). A handbook on marketing research in developing countries, published in 1971, reviews the more superficial operational problems and practical ways of dealing with them (Kracmar 1971). An earlier but more scholarly analysis points out that in some countries "lack of census data and the unreliability of existing statistics make it difficult to apply any but the most primitive sampling designs" (Wilson 1958, p. 230). As African national statistical services develop, this problem is being ameliorated somewhat, but the information infrastructure will remain sketchy for a long time to come. Surveying rural populations adequately still poses severe language and transportation as well as sampling difficulties. The Zambia survey, for example, required travel of "more than 70,000 miles . . . by Land Rover, bicycle, motor launch, canoe and on foot" (Mytton 1972b, p. 24). Few survey research designs budget for such an array of transport facilities!

The factor of unfamiliarity with polling and survey interviews, while troublesome enough even in the urban African environment, adds still another discouragement to coverage of rural populations. Although refusal rates are low, according to Wilson, so is the probability of getting candid answers; the interviewer must, in a sense, first teach each respondent how to be interviewed (1958, p. 233). One must bear in mind that it is almost impossible for a broadcasting-survey interviewer in an African country to present himself to the interviewee as a private person: since the interviewee knows broadcasting is a government activity, he automatically assumes that anyone asking questions about it must represent government. In Zambia many interviewees "refused to express an opinion or favoured the status quo"; research assistants "often reported having encountered hostility and suspicion" because of presumed political or government connections (Mytton 1971b, p. 33). For this reason Mytton believes that it is impossible to get highly reliable data on foreign-station listening in a situation where such listening could be politically sensitive (p. 59). Fraenkel encountered similar problems and relates examples of skillful concealment of purpose by African interviewers who worked for the Central African Broadcasting Station. For instance, the interviewer would take a radio battery (for a "Saucepan Special") with him to the interview:

> "It's probably flat," most of them said.
> "Try it out. . . . Have you got a set?"
> "No, I listen at my brother's."
> "Why not buy one. You can start with the battery. They broadcast programmes in just about every language. What's yours?" [Fraenkel 1959, pp. 139–40]

The problem of formulating written questions in African languages has been less frequently discussed (cf. Head 1968, pp. 91–92). Foreign researchers themselves rarely understand vernaculars into which their questionnaires have to be translated for use in the field. They may take it for granted that the questions, so carefully planned, tested, and refined in their own languages, will survive translation intact. This assumption overlooks two sources of error: (1) Most African translators into non-literary languages are used to making rough paraphrases rather than precise translations (see § 18.2.2). (2) In any event, a kind of questionnaire jargon has grown up in English and other major languages which has no counterpart in African languages—nor can one count on the existence of identical ways of expressing, for example, a concept such as scalar values. Even back-translation can be misleading unless translators are selected for their representativeness with regard to the target population.

16.6 Needed Research

As the preceding section suggests, Africa needs methodological studies of broadcasting research. Established sampling methods currently used in highly developed societies, for example, rely on an information infrastructure not yet available in most of Africa. Nor can it be safely assumed that established research techniques can be exported to Africa without adaptation. The 1969 UNESCO conference on media research raised the question "whether developing countries can effectively use techniques of research developed in industrialized nations or whether they should attempt to evolve techniques more suitable to their own needs and conditions, based on and adapted from the broader methodology already available" (UNESCO 1970b, p. 29). What if, for example, it turned out that, because of the problems of conventional interviewing mentioned in § 16.5, some other method of data gathering should be used in rural areas? Testing assumptions about media use, two researchers experimented with a "diary-keeper" observational technique in rural Nigeria. Trained diary keepers observed the communication behavior of 128 subjects over a 12-month period. They found that claimed radio listening was much overstated; in fact, "most of the subjects in this study did not listen to radio at all. Of 16,500 usable diaries accumulated during the year, radio listening shows up on only 161 of them—less than 1%" (Axinn and Axinn 1969, p. 322). The researchers concluded that "interviews at one point in time are less than adequate in assessing communication habits" (p. 406). Possibly the few subjects of this study were not representative of their region's population, and their region may have been exceptional; but this kind of methodological inquiry needs to be pursued further before one can rest easy with the direct transfer of specific research techniques from one cultural environment to another.

16.6.1 Information Infrastructure

Preliminary to formal methodological studies, however, should come a move to collect and make available existing data of the types described in this chapter—a service which organizations like the Nigerian National Mass Communications Council, mentioned in § 16.4, could perform. Such centers could also develop standards of reporting. As it is, research reports often fail to disclose *all* the relevant facts about the methods used in gathering and processing data. Without these facts meaningful interpretation and assessment are impossible. Forms of presentation vary widely, often confusing and even misleading the reader. Broadcasting organizations and ministries of information could be asked to subscribe to uniform disclosure and reporting standards, which all officially endorsed broadcasting research would be required to meet. A precedent exists in the United States government's imposition of such requirements on American national rating services as an aspect of fair-trading practice.

On the substantive side, the first research need is for the most elementary types of data, such as how many sets there are in use and how much they are used. The urgency of this need is illustrated by all-too-common contradictory reports. For example, the 1972 *World Radio-TV Handbook* lists Kenya as having 200,000 radio receivers, while on an adjoining page in the same issue the Voice of Kenya's overseas sales representative firm claims 774,000, a figure evidently based on the 1969 survey described in § 16.3.1. UNESCO's 1971 *Statistical Yearbook* reported 500,000 for 1969. Such discrepancies in the most fundamental measurements are commonplace in the absence of statistically reliable methods of estimation and of standardized methods of reporting.

Another category of basic information that needs to be gathered, organized, and made available concerns the legal frameworks and the policies, facilities, organization, programming, and procedures of the individual national broadcasting services. As the present book unfortunately demonstrates, it is exceedingly difficult to obtain current, complete, objective, and comparable data on most African systems. Again, regional clearinghouses to collect, process, analyze, and store such data could be of great mutual benefit to the systems involved. An immense reservoir of transferable wisdom about solutions to common problems must surely exist untapped for want of such clearinghouses. Something of this kind was adumbrated at the 1962 all-Africa media meeting organized by UNESCO in Paris, the official report of which suggested that "valuable information which could be gathered by researchers might be legislation, statutes and conventions concerning mass communication and the manner of their implementation. Studies might also be made of successful management practices" (UNESCO 1962, p. 41). Seven years later, however, a meeting of research experts convened by UNESCO complained that "very little seems to be known about how the media are actually being used now in developing countries" (UNESCO 1970b, p. 12).

The same group quoted recommendations based on the results of British research, to the effect that studies should be made of how programs are produced and what forces impinge upon the production process, thereby affecting the output of the medium:

Our research has shown that it is important to know how media producers . . . see their role, and to have information about their values, attitudes, aims, conventions, intentions, working conditions and general background. Patterns of recruitment should also be examined.

The products of the mass media, and therefore the effects, depend (at least in part) on the prevailing system of ownership, control and support. Research . . . should investigate the relationships between programming and control. [UNESCO 1970b, p. 18]

The kinds of preliminary research so far reviewed in this section—collection and analysis of prior studies, investigation of disclosure and reporting standards for future studies, methodological studies of basic problems of sampling procedures for estimating circulation, and collection and analysis of information about current conditions and practices—would help supply some of the information infrastructure on which to base more sophisticated investigations. Crucial among these would be studies of the effects of general domestic services, as distinguished from the effects of specialized educational services. For "it should be noted that much of the research in the developing countries has been concerned with educational, instructional or developmental problems. The influence of the media in the wider socio-cultural field has not been given the attention it deserves" (UNESCO 1970b, p. 12).

16.6.2 Developmental Role of Media

Ultimately, asking questions about media and their effects brings one to a confrontation with the fundamental question, "What, if any, role do the mass media have in development?" Here we enter a realm of theoretical research, concerning the diffusion of innovations, well above the levels of pragmatic investigation discussed so far. The introduction to chapter 15 alludes to this rapidly growing field of communications research, but the theoretical case has not yet been made for mass communication as a prime mover in the development process. McNelly summarizes scholarly opinion neatly by positing four positions: the null, the enthusiastic, the cautious, and the pragmatic. He believes the weight of evidence favors the pragmatic position: "For communication strategists this position says in effect . . . 'Try it and see if it works.' For researchers this position implies a disposition to seek empirical evidence in the field uninhibited by rigid assumptions; to accept evidence of the effects of mass communication in other cultures even though it may be out of harmony with seemingly well-established theoretical models" (McNelly, 1970, p. 161).

A great deal depends, of course, on the stage of development a society has reached. There may be a critical developmental turning point which must be reached before the mass media can bring their potential leverage to bear effectively. In § 16.1 we pointed out that in certain political contexts nobody at the top really wants to know the facts about audiences that research might uncover. Going somewhat further, Merrill (1971, p. 240) has argued rather persuasively that early in the developmental process national leadership *does not really want a mass media system*" (Merrill's italics). He argues that before a society reaches the "transitional" stage of development, mass media are essentially irrelevant; only "elite lines of communication" really matter. The kind of personal exploitation of broadcasting by officials mentioned in § 16.1 could well be characterized as an elitist use of the medium. Merrill continues:

In fact, the leadership elite feels that mass communication is a danger—not an asset . . . little attention is given to the masses—to their participation in government, in [sic] their literacy, in their "right to know" and all such things. All this comes at a later stage, when the nation is fairly well-established, stable, and has what is considered by the elite a viable political and economic base.

   . . . The general assumption is: the people can't rule themselves in a traditional society; they don't even expect to. And, say the elite, we can't encourage them through mass communication *to expect to.* [p. 240; Merrill's italics]

Merrill concludes by suggesting that the present answer to the question "What effect do the mass media have on development?" should be an adaptation of Harold Lasswell's famous sentence about media study generally, namely: *What media in what society at what stage of development have what effect on what aspects of the nation?* Still more skeptical views have been advanced—views which question the ethical as well as the pragmatic foundation of communications development, especially as it is promoted by foreign aid. These views are discussed in § 18.4.3.

17 Broadcasting and Commerce

Sydney W. Head

Past studies of African broadcasting have almost entirely neglected its commercial aspect. Virtually nothing has been published, for example, about the sources, manufacture, assembly, distribution, and sale in Africa of receiving sets and other equipment; and efforts to interest manufacturers in contributing to this book met with negative response. Little if anything has been written about the costs of station operation, the economics of program syndication, or the growth of broadcast advertising in Africa. The German Africa Society published a handbook of commercial rate-card information in 1970, but aside from this, only fragments of information were obtainable from trade journals and station representative firms.

17.1 Broadcast Advertising

Of the 58 radio systems treated in this book, 41 sold advertising in 1971. Countries offering more than one service usually designated one in particular as the commercial service, leaving the others free of advertising content. Of the 28 television systems, 16 sold advertising. No national system appeared able to sustain itself on advertising alone, and many had abandoned the effort to collect receiver license fees, especially for radio; this left direct government subventions as the main source of funds for operating broadcasting systems. Egypt seems to be the only country which has resorted to a special tax—in this case a tax on electrical-power consumption—to support broadcasting (§ 2.1.3).

17.1.1 Commercial Efficiency

In every instance that has come to the writer's attention, when an African system sought competent outside advice on how to increase advertising revenue, billings have gone up—often dramatically. Ethiopia, Kenya, and Malawi, for example, increased their revenues severalfold (§§ 4.1.5, 12.2.1). With the possible exception of South Africa, it seems likely that no government-controlled broadcasting system in Africa realizes its full earning potential over the long run. Why this shortfall?

To start with, most radio services were organized and tutored by the predecessors of the ORTF and by the BBC—neither of them experienced or sympathetic with commercialism in broadcasting. A weak start could have been overcome in time, of course; but a more fundamental impediment has been the divorce of earning from spending. Most African governments require advertising revenue to be deposited to the general treasury, while the broadcasting systems that earn the revenue operate on inflexible annual budgetary appropriations. The powerful engine of economic self-interest stands idle, its motivational energies untapped. The University of Missouri AID project in Malawi introduced some of the standard commercial motivators such as talent fees, with immediate positive results:

. . . the fact that the presenter was in effect personally earning revenue for his organization plus the variety of materials introduced by commercial operations leads to more professional standards of presentation. Staff members . . . displayed considerable more polish and skill in presentation when commercial elements were involved . . . it seems desirable to exploit commercial possibilities as a motivational tool even when advertising revenue is not essential to the operation of a communications service. [University of Missouri 1970, p. 8]

As matters usually stand, however, civil service appointees constituting broadcasting staffs neither gain nor lose from commercial operations; in consequence, they tend to treat commercial duties with indifference. Indeed, in situations where most local economic activity is in the hands of non-Africans, staff attitude toward commercials may well be downright hostile. Indifference alone, however, is enough to produce a laxness devastating to commercial effectiveness. Salesmen may tend to sit behind desks, instead of pounding pavements in search of business—as civil servants they may actually consider vigorous selling and account servicing demeaning; commercial continuity may be badly written or translated and sloppily produced; production personnel may present commercials ineffectively and miss scheduled spots with indifference; traffic personnel—if indeed a traffic department exists—may be careless in scheduling makeups, providing proof-of-performance, and keeping track of contract dates; and sales-department clerks may not bother to send out billings promptly. With all this, sales promotion languishes, and the overseas sales representative tries in vain to get up-to-date information. These retrograde tendencies might be abruptly reversed if salesmen worked on commission, if production personnel earned talent fees, and if the staff as a whole stood to earn bonuses from improved sales efficiency.

But operating personnel can hardly be held responsible for adopting a casual attitude toward commercial aspects of broadcasting when, as often happens, the government itself sets the tone. Arbitrary orders from above to shift schedules around and to cancel or substitute programs without notice cause breaches of commercial contracts—perfectly legal, of course, since the government's interest must always come first, but nevertheless demoralizing. In most cases, professional management, if given the opportunity, could accomplish the end in view less disruptively. Commercial clients, used to being regarded with some deference by advertising media, find it difficult to adjust to frequent reminders that they are allowed to pay for broadcast advertising only on sufferance, and that carefully planned campaigns are subject to unforeseen and arbitrary preemptions.

A few purely commercial broadcasting enterprises do exist in Africa. The oldest, dating back to 1935, is Lourenço Marques Radio, a Moçambique station located not far from the border of South Africa, to which it directs its programming. Sales and programming are controlled from within South Africa. This operation is described in more detail in § 9.2.4. Apparently inspired by the success of Lourenço Marques Radio, an American entrepreneur has started a somewhat similar across-the-border commercial venture in Swaziland (§ 8.4.1). A smaller foreign commercial station, Radio Syd, exists in The Gambia, also aimed primarily at neighboring countries (§ 5.3.2). Still another variant of this commercial stratagem is Tanzania's Swahili commercial service; in this case a *government* commercial station seeks to capitalize on audiences beyond its borders by scheduling popular entertainment aimed at the large Swahili-speaking population of the entire East African region (see § 4.2.3). A number of private "radio clubs" operate commercially in Portuguese territories, but do not realize enough revenue to be self-supporting (§ 9.2.2).

17.1.2 Advertising Agencies

Another impediment to achieving maximum commercial revenue is the lack—or ineffectiveness—of advertising agencies. Agencies offering a full range of services, including research and production, can contribute to programming variety as well as to advertising volume, as pointed out by Roberts in § 4.1.3. The most effective agencies in this regard are likely to be affiliated with major international concerns such as Britain's SSC&B-Lintas International, the largest international agency, which has branches in Ghana, Nigeria, and Sierra Leone.

The annual survey by *Advertising Age* for 1972 indicates that at that time internationally recognized agencies existed in only ten African countries: Egypt, Ghana, Malawi, Morocco, Rhodesia, Sierra Leone, and Zambia each had one; Kenya, 2; Nigeria, 4; and South Africa, 13 (*Advertising Age* 1972). The South African agencies' combined billings for all media of $95 million put them in a category apart; this figure was more than triple the total billings of all international agencies in all the other nine African countries combined. The international agencies in the nine African countries besides South Africa derived an average of 30% of their billings from radio, 18% from television. The range, however, was considerable: In Sierra Leone radio accounted for 61% of total billings; in Egypt, only 10%. In Morocco television accounted for 35%; in Kenya, only 2%. Agencies in both the North African countries Egypt and Morocco billed more television than radio advertising; and in Rhodesia 26% of total billings were in radio, 21% in television.

17.1.3 Limits on Revenue Potential

It must be conceded, however, that even at its potential maximum, advertising income would still not pay the full cost of government-commercial systems in Africa. South African broadcasting probably approaches the maximum, and yet according to a 1969 estimate, the press accounted for over 71% of South Africa's total advertising revenue, radio for only 8% (Streek 1971, p. 12). The extent of this discrepancy makes one suspect that radio may still be somewhat undersold there, but the underlying lesson is nevertheless clear: the consumer market exists basically in the urban areas, where literacy is high and newspapers are available. Despite its size, the rural audience, which only radio reaches, has little purchasing power or access to the marketing network. National broadcasting services must, nevertheless, serve this commercially nonproductive audience. Governments require still other types of commercially nonviable services, such as external services, for political reasons. A system subject to purely commercial motivations would, of course, simply concentrate broadcasting services in urban areas and neglect all the rest. So it would be unreasonable to expect a broadcasting system in a developing country to be commercially self-sustaining. Indeed, if there were such a system one would be justified in suspecting a priori that it must be failing to provide an adequate service to the population as a whole.

From the point of view of the most efficient use of limited funds, broadcasting systems could nevertheless benefit from cost-accounting procedures. These could be rationalized if government-commercial systems divided their operations into (1) commercially self-supporting services, and (2) government-underwritten noncommercial services. The government would pay the actual costs of the commercially nonviable services it requires. The commercially supported services would expand or retrench independently in accordance with market conditions. This method of organizing a national service would permit meaningful cost accounting, would encourage more efficient use of available funds, and would allow for the flexibility essential for fullest exploitation of commercial potentials.

17.2 Commercial Practice

The German Africa Society handbook of 1969 rate-card information previously mentioned, though titled *Commercial Radio in Africa,* covers both radio and television (German Africa Society 1970). It contains data on systems in 55 countries and territories, representing more than 100 different commercial services; radio and television were counted as a single service where both were available. The society states in its preface that the 1970 volume will "be followed in regular intervals by revised editions," but inquiries about plans for the next edition elicited no response. The following generalizations about commercial practices are based upon the 1969 data.

17.2.1 Salience of Commercials

A generally conservative policy seemed to be followed in setting the number of announcements or the amount of commercial time allowed per hour. The Sudan, with the most conservative policy, allowed only three minutes an hour, and at the other extreme Radio Clube of Angola allowed 27 spots an hour for "already prepared programs." Several stations limited the number of permissible product mentions. Rhodesia radio allowed seven per 30-second spot; Uganda, five.

Many stations limited to specific short segments the times when commercials could be scheduled. Zaïre television specified 7:35 P.M.–7:45 P.M. and 8:15 P.M.–8:30 P.M.; Rwanda listed only 11:45 A.M.–12:45 P.M.; Mogadishu, 1:15 P.M.–1:25 P.M. and 5:25 P.M.–5:30 P.M.; and Gabon, "before and after news." Some countries forbade commercials on certain days or at certain hours. The Central African Republic allowed no commercials on its ten annual public holidays; Uganda, none on Good Friday, Easter Sunday, and Christmas; Western Nigeria-Ibadan, none between 11:30 A.M. and 2:00 P.M. Double-spotting was specifically ruled out by Zambia but not mentioned in other rate cards. No stations seemed explicitly to follow such American practices as specifying different maximum commercial-time standards for day and night, and exceptions to standard commercial time limits for certain types of programs.

17.2.2 Rate Policies

Most radio stations used two or more time classifications in setting their advertising rates, but because of their short schedules many television stations offered a single rate. Evening prime radio times varied considerably, starting between 4:30 and 8:00 and ending between 8:15 and 11:00. Tanzania and Uganda were exceptional in terminating prime time as late as 11:00.

Quantity or frequency discounts were almost universally offered, more usually the former, and the maximum discount rate ranged for the most part from a low of 10% to a high of 25%. Zaïre's 40% and Réunion radio's 30% were exceptionally high. Agency commissions were universally allowed, usually at 15% of air-time charges, although a few systems, such as Malawi and Zambia, allowed 16.5%. Kenya had a sliding scale, with rates, depending on how promptly payment was made, going from a high of 16.5% (for payment within 45 days) to a low of 10%.

Most stations seemed to offer spots on a rotating basis, with markups for preferred positions. In general the preferred-position markup varied from a low of 10% in Liberia to a high of 50% for Lourenço Marques. News adjacencies, where mentioned, were usually marked up 20%–25%. Rhodesia had an unusual news-adjacency requirement—the sale of spots only in before-and-after pairs. Another unusual type of markup was that of Angola Radio Club, which charged 50% more for the weekend than for weekdays. Cameroon advertisers were warned of a government tax markup of nearly 10%.

Differentials between local and national rates were not mentioned except by Mauritius, which charged twice the rate for imported products as for local products—an unusual way of differentiating, since the pattern of product distribution rather than product origin is the immediate economic basis for differentiation. Tanzania also provided for "local" and "casual" announcements, for which there was a fixed rate, allowing only 15-second spots for cash, with no discounts, commissions, or bulk purchasing. Presumably the rate cards published in the German Africa Society volume were intended for international trade and so may have omitted to mention such special concessions usually made for local advertisers. Certainly a need exists for a low-priced, easily negotiated class of announcements for small, local, retail shops and even for "personals" such as death notices and inquiries after missing persons.

Package deals do not seem to figure largely in African commercial broadcasting practice. The main exception noted was South Africa. For example, its regional FM networks offer "snap campaign" packages consisting of 18 30-second spots distributed throughout the schedule over a three-day period.

17.2.3 Miscellaneous Rate-Card Provisions

Sponsorship. In addition to spots and participations, many stations offered sponsorship to advertisers. Malawi and Uganda mentioned news specifically as sponsorable, for which the latter's markup rate was 25%.

Services. Listings of production and other services vary according to the size and sophistication of the station. Because of polylingualism, many stations mentioned translation fees: Malawi radio would translate a 30-second spot for $1.20, Nigerian federal radio for $4.20. Nigeria listed jingle writing among its services—about $44 for writing a one-minute jingle and $280 for producing it. Fees for the use of staff talent were sometimes listed: in Malawi a radio-staff voice cost a minimum of $1.20 for a spot or $2.40 for a sponsored program of 25 minutes or less. Rhodesia radio was unusual for listing rates for the use of a piano ($2.80 for the first hour) and for the use of an outside broadcasting unit ($14.00 per hour).

Representation. The remoteness of African stations from the main offices of international advertisers would seem to make overseas sales representatives rather important adjuncts to local sales departments. Only 15 countries listed representatives, however, and only a dozen firms, located in Frankfurt, London, Munich, New York, Paris, and Toronto, were mentioned. Liberia was unique in listing *four* representatives, and the Nigerian Broadcasting Corporation in listing its *own* London sales office. Little Rwanda's Munich representative offered to prepare spots that blended Swahili, French, and English—from which "arises a kind of language puzzle" (German Africa Society 1970, p. 219).

17.3 Construction and Management Contracts

The government-to-government assistance programs discussed in chapters 12 and 13 necessarily relied on contracts with commercial firms to provide equipment and installation services. In this chapter we are concerned with similar contracts, but made directly between African governments and commercial organizations. Though ostensibly purely commercial transactions, they sometimes involved foreign governments somewhat ambiguously in the background. For example, Egypt contracted with the Radio Corporation of America for its original television and receiver-assembly facilities; but Egypt relied on a long-term loan of moneys deposited to the United States government's account in Egypt, representing accumulated payments for surplus-food shipments from America (§§ 2.1.5, 12.2.1).

Since African governments could not ordinarily expend cash for new television stations or major radio installations, it devolved upon the private contracting organizations to arrange for loans. Contractors thereupon usually became part-owners of the enterprises. This financial stake gave them added leverage in obtaining management or management-consulting contracts after the installations were completed. One of the contractor's ongoing jobs would be to act as purchasing agent abroad for spare parts and for syndicated program materials.

The pioneer television station in Tropical Africa started at Ibadan in October 1959, as the result of joint investment by the regional government of Western Nigeria and a British company, Rediffusion. As its name suggests, Rediffusion has an interest in the system of redistributing programs by wire to subscribers who pay a monthly fee. At one time the British Colonial Office considered wired radio as a possible solution to the problem of making radio programs accessible to urban Africans in the Colonies. Operating through local subsidiaries, Rediffusion developed several Colonial wired radio systems, including those in Ghana (§ 5.2.1), Nigeria (§ 5.1.12), and South Africa (§ 8.1.2). Rediffusion also participated in development of Liberian television (§ 5.4.1). Although in 1965 the South African government cancelled Rediffusion's license for the wired system it operated in Orlando Township, the company retained the hope of being able to move into the modern-day version of wired radio—cable television—in South Africa with the start-up of video service there (letter from A. J. S. Taylor, May 14, 1973).

In 1962 Granada Television, one of the independent television-program contractors in Britain's commercial system, teamed with a British equipment manufacturer to install and manage both radio and television for Nigeria's Northern Region at Kaduna. The British concerns each had a quarter-interest, the regional government a half.

The most active British firm in the business of building and operating television stations on behalf of developing governments, however, has been Thomson Television International, one of the scores of firms owned by Lord Thomson of Fleet, the Canadian newspaper tycoon. At about the same time that Thomson conceived the idea of a specialized company for this purpose he also set up the Thomson Foundation with a £5-million endowment. The foundation has provided training for many African television personnel, as described in § 14.2.3. These activities, in turn, benefited from the fact that Thomson also owns Scottish Television, another of the independent program contractors in Britain. Thomson Television International was connected, either as part-owner or as management contractor, with the launching of television in Ethiopia, Kenya, Mauritius, Rhodesia, and Sierra Leone. In some of these projects, the Thomson organization formed consortia with other competing organizations and other investors; the case of Kenya is a good example (§ 4.1.1). Thomson himself, though famed for hard-headed commercialism, appears to have justified these commercially unpromising African ventures on ideological rather than on business grounds. In his review of operations of The Thomson Organisation in 1964, he wrote that but for his intervention,. "a number of newly formed nations of the world would have been obliged to turn for assistance to . . . the Communist bloc" (Ainsley 1968, p. 237).

A subsidiary of the Radio Corporation of America, NBC International, participated as a member of some of the communications consortia in Africa. We have already mentioned in this section RCA's involvement with the start of television in Egypt. If we add to that NBC International's contract with the federal government of Nigeria, we can say that, prior to the 1970s, the American electronics company had a decisive hand in the two biggest television projects in African television. Unlike its British competitors, NBC International refrained as a matter of policy from investing in government-owned stations (Tyler 1966, p. 59). NBC International contracted in 1962 to build a television station in Lagos for the federal Nigerian government at a cost of over $2 million. The American company managed the station for five years, during which time it trained Nigerians to take over all positions. According to the head of the 16-man American team, on his arrival in Lagos 10,000 Nigerians applied for jobs in television, from among whom 200 were chosen (Bower 1964, p. 106).

Production started on 1 April 1962, with a garage used as a studio and a mobile unit as a control room. The handsome permanent facilities completed a year later included two large studios and videotape recorders. NBC International withdrew on schedule at the end of its five years, and in April 1967 the television station was merged with the federal radio system under the Nigerian Broadcasting Corporation.

In retrospect it can be said that, while investment by foreign companies in African government-owned broadcasting systems answered a temporary need, it did not prove successful commercially. Partnership between foreign private commercial enterprise and government in as sensitive an area as public communication resulted in an uneasy relationship at best. In addition to the inevitable conflict between political and commercial interests, television advertising progressed more slowly in Africa than its more optimistic investors originally anticipated. The failure to reach promised levels of commercial income was disappointing to governments and private investors alike. Sooner or later—in most cases sooner—governments bought out or forced out their erstwhile partners and assumed sole responsibility.

Part 3   Conclusion

18 An Agenda for Further Study

Sydney W. Head

In looking back over the ground traversed in this survey, the critical reader will be aware of uneven coverage—some topics rather fully explored, some only tentatively, some by-passed altogether. From the more thoroughly surveyed subjects it may be possible to gain useful insights and suggestions for future study, and from those only partially surveyed, at least some signposts indicating areas for further investigation; even the lacunae can serve a purpose in calling attention to areas which urgently need to be reconnoitered. Perhaps the most useful conclusion, then, would be a summing up in a form which may serve to suggest needed routes and promising byways for research and investigation. We have organized these comments and suggestions roughly according to the general plan of the book, dealing first with topics which arise from analyses of individual broadcasting systems, then with topics suggested by the broader, intersystem chapters.

18.1 Audience-building Strategies

Realizing optimum benefits from the existence of given facilities for broadcast transmission and production depends on the existence of receiving components, normally supplied voluntarily by the general public. This supply depends both on economic and on motivational factors. People must have the money to buy receivers, but they must also want to spend it on receivers and on their operation and maintenance, rather than on something else. Creating this essential want is the function of programming, some aspects of which we discuss in § 18.2. In the present section we consider economic and other strategies external to programming which also affect audience growth.

18.1.1 Artificial Impediments to Audience Growth

Governments tend to emphasize the transmission end of the broadcasting system in their fiscal planning and to leave the receiving end pretty much

347

to take care of itself. The Uganda Second Five-Year Plan puts the case succinctly, in stating that "it is the technology and the economics of the small receiver rather than the big transmitters which is the major determinant of broadcasting systems. There is not much point in spending money on broadcasting unless many, and preferably the majority, of people can listen in" (Uganda 1966, p. 124). Governments have not generally acted vigorously upon this principle; yet circulation could be significantly enlarged by price reductions well within the realm of possibility. In Uganda, for example, a 30% drop in the price of radio receivers was accompanied by a 100% increase in sales (Uganda 1966, pp. 124–25).

True, there is a general trend in Africa toward the abolition of one economic impediment—receiver license fees. Among countries that have been mentioned as abolishing fees are Senegal (1963), Malawi (1966), Tanzania (1969), and Kenya (1970). Mytton estimated that there were 200,000 unlicensed radios operating in Zambia (Mytton 1972a, p. 89). The abolition of license fees, however, has come about because of the conviction, not so much that they are undesirable, as that they are uncollectible. The latter was especially obvious after miniaturization of radios made detection of unauthorized use almost impossible.

The blunt fact is that for developing countries receiver license fees are indefensible. They are discriminatory and counterproductive. They place one more artificial impediment in the way of audience growth and cost more to collect than they are worth. Insofar as the broadcasting system functions as an agent of government, rather than as an independent system responsible to the audience, licensing also seems ethically unjustifiable. For television the economic case against license fees may be less clear-cut. The high cost of sets presumes purchasers capable of paying fees, and limitations on distribution may make actual collection feasible. In principle, however, it seems that, if broadcasting is a defensible expense for a developing country, it would serve its own interest best by eliminating all possible economic impediments to audience growth in both radio and television.

Most countries, however, impose even more severe economic impediments than license fees by levying high import duties on receivers, usually about 50% of cost, insurance, and freight. UNESCO's 1962 all-Africa meeting on media development "felt strongly that broadcasting should not be considered a luxury but a vital necessity in the development of the country" (UNESCO 1962, p. 25). The meeting accordingly endorsed the reduction of import duties on sets destined specifically for educational uses; but it was not able to bring itself to the point of recommending the complete abolition of both license fees and import duties on all receivers.

The Malagasy Republic showed what a vigorous campaign of audience building, with appropriate financial inducements, could accomplish. This campaign included, in addition to elimination of duty and license fees on radio receivers, provision for consumer credit (§ 9.1.1). Sierra Leone is said to have pioneered in making general provision for credit buying of radios (Northern Rhodesia's earlier "Saucepan Special" scheme provided credit only for civil servants). Over a period of 20 years, Sierra Leone had built up a 5,000-subscriber wired rediffusion service, but in 1964 the government began to phase out the system and to encourage replacement of the speaker boxes with off-the-air receivers: "Subscribers can obtain reliable sets through the government and pay for them by installments. This is the first large-scale hire-purchase scheme in West Africa and was received enthusiastically; in the first few months of the service 2,900 sets were purchased" (Blair 1965, p. 127).

As an alternative to the sale of receivers, public listening or viewing facilities are often suggested. They must be regarded as a stop-gap measure, however, except in highly organized listening/viewing situations such as farm forums or formal adult-education courses. In the 1940s Franklin experimented with community radio-listening posts in Northern Rhodesia and reported his disillusionment:

The receiver is often not properly looked after. Speaker horns get out of alignment, sets get wheezy and so on. Listeners soon lose interest under such conditions. . . . Even when the receiver is regularly and properly operated in a welfare hall, the hall usually has appalling acoustic properties and is crowded with children who want to shout, women who want to dance and scream out gossip across the hall, youths who just want to hear a loud noise "from the box" and a few serious listeners who would like to shoot everybody else in sight. Similar conditions apply to open air country listening. [Franklin 1949, pp. 3–4]

Subsequent experiences in unorganized radio listening generally seemed to confirm Franklin's conclusions. But organized "radio clubs," characteristic of Francophone West Africa, have succeeded under government supervision. Television community receivers, too, seem to have been used with some success, necessarily also under supervision. Cassirer (1971a) has outlined the view that community reception under controlled conditions provides a number of positive educational benefits. This whole subject should be studied further, to determine whether improved and innovative methods for arranging group reception of general programming would add substantial numbers to the audience and act as a motivator to set purchasing.

Getting sets into the hands of the public solves only half the problem, in any event. Education in their proper use and provision for prompt and economical replacement of batteries and parts and for repair services are equally essential. Research in Zambia indicated that a high proportion of existing sets must be counted as inoperative. The same study showed that virtually no short-wave sets were equipped with external antennas, which means that they could realize only a small fraction of their potential usefulness as receivers (Mytton 1972a, p. 70).

Among the many questions concerning the economic aspects of audience building that could be usefully studied are: What is the present status of financial impediments to offering receivers at the cheapest possible price? Does the law facilitate hire-purchase arrangements fair to both buyer and seller? What steps have governments taken to make it easy and inexpensive to obtain batteries, replacement parts, and servicing? How might broadcasting administrations train people in the more efficient use of existing receivers? What can be learned from campaigns to increase circulation?

18.1.2   Polylingualism

The fragmentation of its potential national audience into separate linguistic groups drastically lowers the efficiency of a broadcasting system. So severe is this fragmentation in Africa that many countries have adopted a European language as the standard, which automatically cuts off access to most of the broadcasting service for most of the population.

European languages have special historical ties in the 58 states and territories surveyed here as follows: English, 24; French, 24; Portuguese, 6; Spanish, 4; Italian, 2. This tabulation counts two European languages in each of four countries—in Cameroon and Egypt, English and French; in Morocco, French and Spanish; in Somalia, English and Italian. Arabic is the principal language of six independent countries and is said to be spoken by more Africans than any other language (van den Berghe 1968, p. 49). The Arabic-speaking North African countries are, for all practical purposes, monolingual, although various dialects of Berber are still spoken and French is still much used (Gallagher 1968, p. 134). Only four small independent countries—Lesotho, Malagasy Republic, Rwanda, and Somalia—have indigenous languages that are approximately universal.

As to vernaculars, broadcast schedules change so frequently that an accurate count of their use is impossible. Some administrations simply report "vernaculars" instead of listing languages by name, or fail to mention minor languages at all. A survey made in 1960 listed 109 languages used by radio and 72 used by print media (Huth 1960, p. 18). In Appendix 5 we list 196 languages as being used in broadcasting in 1972 by African systems, of which 173 are African languages.

Sierra Leone represents a linguistic compromise adopted by a system limited to only one "channel": In 1972, 60%–70% of its programming was in English, most of the rest in four major vernaculars; in addition, however, two weekly half-hour programs were devoted to news summaries in *nine* other vernaculars—an average of about six minutes a week for each language. Kenya typifies the compromise possible when resources permit allotting transmission facilities and production personnel to a complete independent vernacular "channel." The Voice of Kenya in 1972 offered a full service in a European language (English); a full service in a lingua franca (Swahili); and a regionalized, segmented service in some of the vernaculars. The last, fragmented into 14 different tongues, is still at best a form of tokenism. Indeed, according to 1972 press reports, the Kenya information minister was considering recommending the elimination of the vernacular service altogether. Neighboring Tanzania, where a larger percentage of the population understand Swahili, had already seized the nettle by standardizing on Swahili from the outset of its independence. East Africa is exceptional in having such a relatively acceptable common denominator available—a widely used lingua franca with indigenous roots. Even so, Swahili, too, has its opponents, who argue, for example, that it has been the language used by slave traders and colonial exploiters (the pros and cons are summarized by Nsibambi 1971, pp. 69–71).

Moyo indicates in § 4.3.2 how politics affected the proliferation of broadcasting languages in Uganda. At the Seminar on Mass Media and Linguistics in East Africa held in Kampala in 1967, the then president of Uganda announced the addition of ten more tribal languages to Radio Uganda's schedule—at the same time frankly admitting political motivation (Nsibambi 1971, p. 62). Mytton's research in Zambia, which looked more deeply into the language problem as it affects broadcasting than had previous audience studies, found that minority peoples demanded vernacular broadcasts not only for reasons of pride and status; they also demanded them because they feared extinction of their mother tongues. They thought broadcasting would save their languages and at the same time pass on the memory of ancestral life to the younger generation (Mytton 1972a, pp. 62–63). Some governments nevertheless insist on confining most of their domestic broadcasting to a single language, as a way of reinforcing a sense of national unity; and sometimes, also, as a way of enforcing the hegemony of a ruling ethnic group. Either way, government leaders face a dilemma: whether to allow broadcast languages to proliferate for the sake of preserving traditional cultures, winning the loyalty of minority groups, and reaching a maximum audience—at the risk of encouraging tribalism and separatism; or whether to standardize on a single broadcast language for the sake of emphasizing nationhood—at the risk of hastening the disappearance of local cultures, alienating minority groups, and failing to communicate with the very people in whom the central government most needs to inculcate an understanding of its intentions.

Ethnocentrism, racial pride, and cultural separatism are on the rise in the world generally. That trend favors polylingualism in African broadcasting. Practical considerations, however, argue for fewer languages, not more. The fragmentation of limited transmitter time into 15 or 20 separate language segments makes it impossible to build a comprehensive broadcasting service. One would need as many sets of duplicated facilities and duplicated teams of production personnel as languages broadcast—obviously an impossible economic burden. In fact there is reason to believe that even many of the existing short vernacular segments, often consisting of news translations only, or news plus some music, suffer because of inadequacies in production (see, e.g., § 18.2.2 on translation into vernaculars).

It is true that minority groups tend to place a high value on even fragments of service. A commentator on international religious broadcasting—a genre which tends toward the programming of very short vernacular segments—remarked, "The loyalty of language groups to their own programs, even for only *one 15-minute programme weekly,* can be remarkable, and people will go to great lengths to be able to listen" (Maclin 1966, p. 56; italics added). But language loyalty, no matter how intense, is no substitute for adequate uninterrupted air time in which to develop a full-scale broadcasting service.

Broadcasting, as the one universal medium, clearly has to assume the role of unifier. The fragmentation of a national service into many truncated subservices violates the nature of broadcasting as a mass medium, casting away its most precious asset. In the best interests of domestic national broadcasting services, therefore, it appears that, ideally, no more languages should be employed than can be produced and transmitted simultaneously on a full schedule with a full range of programming. This means, in effect, limitation to perhaps three languages at the most. There should be ways of helping to preserve minority cultures within the framework of major-language programming. How radio service can help to satisfy this need for cultural diversity and at the same time help to preserve a sense of cultural unity is a question for serious study.

18.1.3 Localized Service

Paradoxically, the argument for reducing the number of broadcast languages to take advantage of broadcasting's potentiality as a unifying force runs exactly counter to the argument for exploiting another unique potentiality of the medium—that of providing both local and national services through a single instrumentality. The individual domestic station is, by its nature, essentially a local medium; but any number of local stations can be interconnected to form a network, which converts individual stations into a national medium. It is relatively easy to serve one function or the other—local or national—but to serve both involves more sophisticated technology and organization.

From the standpoint of audience motivation, localism is vital, since people's interests naturally center first on themselves and their immediate environments. This parochialism must be especially true in traditional rural societies, which tend to have little interest in anything beyond their own surroundings. According to one observer, villagers "will not listen to any music that does not come from within a few miles' radius of their homes. Beyond that all is 'rubbish—not fit for human beings' " (Fraenkel 1959, p. 145). For such listeners, programming which reflects only broad national concerns can hold little fascination. The news that the president received a newly appointed ambassador from some far-off country at ceremonies in the presidential palace in the far-off capital is of little interest compared with the fact that a newly appointed local official has taken some action which directly affects the lives of one's self and one's neighbors. At the same time, it is also important to know that there *is* a national leader who *does* receive representatives from foreign places. Thus any fully developed national broadcasting system must incorporate elements of both national and local coverage.

It should be noted that, while provisions for vernacular programs described in the preceding section make concessions to regional or local needs, the systems descriptions we have presented clearly indicate that most such programming is centrally controlled and produced; where local or regional transmitters exist, they nearly always simply repeat the national program service. Vernacular programs may be localized, insofar as they contain local music gathered on field recording expeditions, but they can reflect contemporary local interests and current affairs only minimally, if at all.

Exceptions among the independent national systems are Nigeria, South Africa, and Zaïre; and among the dependent territories, Angola, the Canary Islands, and Moçambique. Nigeria's case is particularly significant because of its combination of federal-regional broadcasting and its history of regional factionalism. Apparently from the first the British intended the federal broadcasting system to serve as a unifying force. Wilkinson regards the separate regional governments' broadcasting services in Nigeria as having been "divisive influences" which helped precipitate the Nigerian civil war (§ 12.1.2). It is important to note that even before the regional governments developed broadcasting the federal system itself was providing regional services, and that this aspect of the federal system *declined when faced with competition* introduced by services separately owned and operated by the regional governments.

On the basis of experience, most African governments are not likely to regard autonomous or even semiautonomous regional broadcasting services as politically expedient (see app. 2). This circumstance constitutes a fundamental dilemma for African broadcasting development. This problem of what might be called "broadcasting statesmanship" deserves special study. On the one hand, one might try to determine historically the actual extent to which regional broadcasting may have influenced separatist movements; on the other, one might explore ways in which the legitimate needs and interests of local audiences might be genuinely served without expensive and potentially hazardous decentralization of the national broadcasting facilities.

18.1.4 Legal Status of Broadcasting

The success of a trained cadre of professional broadcasters depends upon how free they are to employ what they know to be effective programming strategies and production tactics. Their degree of freedom from interference, in turn, depends among other things on the legal status of the broadcasting system. Our systems studies neglected almost completely to describe and analyze the law of broadcasting in Africa, which remains a major topic for future explorations, as suggested in § 16.6.1. It is evident that, nominally at least, two patterns of government control generally prevail—a reflection, of course, of the practice of the two major colonial powers. In Francophone countries broadcasting has always come under direct government supervision; in the Anglophone group an attempt was made to insulate broadcasting from day-to-day government intervention by setting up statutory corporations. Some governments rid themselves of what they saw as these encumbrances to sovereignty soon after independence; Kenya and Tanzania are good examples (§§ 4.1.1, 4.2.1). The systems of Egypt, Ghana, Liberia, Malawi, Mauritius, Nigeria, Rhodesia, South Africa, and Tunisia retain corporate identity, at least in name.

No hint is given in our survey as to the degree of effectiveness of these legalistic distinctions in providing a shield against interference in routine broadcasting operations by government officials outside the broadcasting organization. It would be disingenuous to pretend that broadcasting systems in Africa could expect corporate status to guarantee anything like the degree of independence enjoyed by the BBC, the archetypical model for such systems. One-party states and military regimes conceive the function of broadcasting in much different terms (see app. 2 on broadcasting and political crises). But more limited objectives than the BBC's would still be worth striving for. Corporate status would be beneficial if it merely exempted broadcasting from bureaucratic control by inappropriate governmental civil service and fiscal procedures. It would be even more valuable if it cushioned operations from direct intervention in day-to-day operations by government officials outside the broadcasting organization. Such insulation could do much to enhance the professional credibility of broadcasting managers, to improve staff morale, and to reduce needless disruptions to the service. It should be understood that the point here is not to challenge either the right or the power of a government to dictate how its own facilities are to be used; rather it is to suggest that the ends in view, whatever they may be, can probably be reached more effectively and efficiently by informing professional broadcasters of the goals the government hopes to reach and leaving it to the broadcasters to work out the best ways of reaching them.

It would be valuable to know in detail to what extent and in what ways the ten systems mentioned above actually benefit from their corporate status, if at all. Such knowledge might give new impetus to the concept, which despite setbacks seems not to be entirely a dead issue. The Ethiopian government saw merit in a similar idea and adopted it in 1968; unsuccessful recommendations to the Somali and Sierra Leone governments were made as recently as 1968 and 1970 respectively.

18.2 Aspects of Programming

All other audience-building stratagems being optimally employed, in the final analysis programming itself remains the ultimate motivator. A dramatic example is related by Fanon (1965, pp. 82–83), who tells how French radio in Algeria prior to the start of the revolution had little meaning for indigenous Algerians, except as a symbol of alien domination. When the revolution began, however, broadcasts from neighboring Arab countries and from the Voice of Fighting Algeria transformed the meaning of radio. When plans for the clandestine revolutionary radio service were announced, "in less than twenty days the entire stock of radio sets was bought up," and a completely new trade in second-hand radios began in the traditional markets.

18.2.1 Quality and Motivation

Our summaries of national systems tell us little about the quality of programming and production. All systems schedule "information, education, and entertainment." All systems shape these general types of content into specific programs by using established formats. Descriptions of programming in terms of types, formats, hours, and percentages reveal only the barest essentials. In such terms, one service seems much like another. We need critiques that tell us how and why two programs identical in type, format, and length differ qualitatively—why one motivates audiences and another falls flat. Regional- and continental-program prize festivals might be one stimulus to critical analysis. Such devices are essential to compensate for the lack of domestic competition. "The treadmill of broadcast production by tenured civil servants can have a deadly effect on morale and creativeness. It is all too easy to slip into dull, repetitive routines and to fail to make that extra effort which alert and timely programming and production always demand . . . the most effective antidote to this retrograde tendency is competition" (Head 1972, pp. 15–16). Research on ways of assessing quality and of developing a sense of competition—or some substitute drive—within the context of monopolistic systems would be extremely worthwhile.

18.2.2 News

The common practice of assigning the task of news preparation exclusively to a government news agency or information department, independent of the broadcasting organization, debilitates, not only news, but broadcasting itself. It enfeebles the broadcasting organization by amputating one of its most important functions, it usually results in bad copy because the material is not adapted to oral delivery, and it eliminates the possibility of healthy competition among the local media. A survey of such news practices and of experience with various forms of broadcast news control in Africa would be desirable.

Tanzania's facing up to the dullness that results when newsmen are forced (or, perchance, force themselves, out of a mistaken sense of duty) to report the activities of political leaders irrespective of their newsworthiness deserves special notice (§ 4.2.3). This is one of many aspects of news treatment which cause broadcasting to be regarded as a mere propaganda organ rather than as a responsible and credible news medium. Objective evidence of the actual effects of counterproductive news practices is needed. Certainly every audience survey which asks questions about listeners' program preferences proves anew—if indeed the obvious needed proof—that many radio listeners resort to "comparison shopping," which renders censorship futile. Wilkinson makes the point very well in § 12.1.5; he reminds us that, while newspapers and magazines can be banned, air waves from the outside cannot.

Mytton calls attention to a widespread problem which has been almost totally neglected: the failure to accord vernacular translators the status and pay their demanding job should warrant. Referring to Zambia, he goes so far as to say that the inadequacies of translation into vernaculars "constitute the most serious barrier to the better dissemination of news in the country" (Mytton 1972a, p. 93). Vernacular translators generally stand at the bottom of the job-status ladder and yet are expected to transform complex and sophisticated concepts accurately into languages which have no vocabulary for such concepts—this without the aid of dictionaries, thesauri, or specialized linquistic training. Because of the prestige often associated with the mastery of a European language—especially if the language is French—continuing to deal in the vernaculars was once actually counted as a vocational drawback. An observer in Dakar noted, "one reason for the inadequacies of the vernacular transmissions is that they are entrusted to the lowest-paid and least-educated personnel of the station. Work in the French-speaking departments is considered by African employees as a promotion" (*Africa Report* 1960, p. 8). Station officials—not to speak of foreign advisers—often themselves have no mastery of vernacular languages used in broadcasting, so that the grossest inadequacies of translation may pass undetected. A seminar in East Africa on mass-media communication recommended the establishment of a linguistic research center, whose functions would include the training of translators (*East Africa Journal* 1967, p. 18). There is indeed an urgent need for study of translation problems, for the preparation of a variety of translation aids, for standardization of neologisms, for courses in the art of translation, and for the professionalization of the translator's occupation. Studies should be made, too, of the newswriting style employed in the language used for preparation of the general newsfile (Mytton 1972a, p. 93). Research on All India Radio newscasts, as an example, established that few Hindi-speaking rural listeners could follow the sophisticated Hindi style employed by urban newswriters (Ornstein 1964, p. 212).

18.2.3 Indigenous Arts

The UNESCO-sponsored conference of 1964 on the introduction of television into Africa resolved that "adequate facilities should be provided not
only for presenting studio programmes, but, by means of mobile videotape
recording and film units, for presenting programmes reflecting the life of the
people throughout the country" (UNESCO 1964, p. 3). This resolution
carried forward a long-established radio tradition of field recording.
Fraenkel describes arduous field recording trips in what is now Zambia.
They required two truckloads of equipment, until the advent of lightweight
tape-recording facilities made the task much easier. These forays resulted
in the accumulation of "the largest library of African music in the world"
(Fraenkel 1959, p. 216). Ironically, in 1972 Zambia radio had to cancel
all such recording tours because of their expense; moreover, the historic
collection itself was in danger of physical deterioration (Mytton 1972a,
p. 67).

Field recording of traditional artists remains one of the most important
potential sources of program material for African stations, and one still
not sufficiently exploited. Recording tours into remote areas, whether for
radio or television, have important side benefits. They help to bridge the
cultural gap between the life of the cities and traditional rural life, to
preserve the fading cultural heritage of minority ethnic groups and to give
those groups a sense of participation in national life via the broadcasting
service, to correct the cultural distortions caused by urbanism and commercialization of entertainment, and to create an archive of irreplaceable
historical material. A well-known African musician comments that both
radio and television "have been heavily influenced by urban tastes. The
leading international gramophone record companies have branches all over
Africa, but they are principally interested in the music popular among the
record-buying public of Africa, which exists chiefly in the urban and semi-
urban areas. As a result they promote third-rate specimens of Westernized
pop music while first-rate examples of both traditional and neo-traditional
music are almost completely disregarded" (Euba 1970, p. 25). The urban
outlook of the average broadcaster makes him susceptible to this promotional influence, while the majority audience in the countryside has little
chance to make its preferences known.

Fraenkel tells an illuminating anecdote illustrative of this point. Noting
that the character of a music-request program at the Lusaka station had
abruptly changed from "citified" to more traditional music, he found that
a producer had observed that the announcer who chose the requests from
piles of correspondence "rapidly selected a handful of letters that were
neatly written or typed and ignored those more difficult to decipher." The
producer thereupon went through the discarded pile of almost illegible
request letters and found that the less-educated rural listeners from whom
they came overwhelmingly preferred traditional music (Fraenkel 1959,

p. 138). This difference has since been borne out in several studies; one in Zambia, for example, established that the majority of listeners felt there was insufficient traditional Zambian music on the radio, and it pointed out that "from the humanist point of view," the country people, with no optional access to commercial recordings and to record players, deserved to be given priority by the radio service (Mytton 1972a, pp. 67, 69).

African broadcasting systems might advantageously invest more in mobile equipment, less in monumental "broadcasting houses" in capital cities; the West German government seems to have realized this need and has stressed the use of outside broadcasting units in its assistance programs (§ 12.4). Future studies might be directed toward discovering, through actual field experience, the most economical and efficient combinations of equipment for both audio and video field recording; and the best techniques for organizing and conducting field recording tours. Research on the feasibility of adopting international technical standards for original recordings and for archival storage and indexing would be desirable. Such standards would facilitate international exchange of program materials and of archival indexes.

18.2.4 Status of Artists

Closely related to programming problems are those concerning the status of artists, especially musicians and composers (traditionally one and the same). In the absence of unions, commercial syndication, and means for protecting copyrights and performing rights, popular artists have no chance of earning incomes commensurate with their popularity. Worse, a singer or dancer in many African societies suffers the indignity of being classed socially about on the level of players in Shakespeare's time. As Adam, the historian of Somali broadcasting, puts the case:

Even though people realise that there is a place for artists and their entertainment in society, and the people eagerly lap up the output of these artists, there is need for a change in the public attitude toward these people. A large proportion of the society does not whole-heartedly accept entertainment as an absolutely respectable profession. There is still a lingering suspicion that singing and loose morals go in step and that artists stand for the worst in society—drinking parties, dancing, and haunting of public bars. The Government, while using their talents, does little to help in improving their status. . . . Their wages are low and their copyrights are flouted by all and sundry. [Somalia 1968, p. 24]

Adam traces the history of the pioneer radio singers in Somalia. The first of these, Abdullahi Gharshe, sacrificed a good civil service job and endured social ostracism and pressure from his own family. Dalis, the first woman radio singer, was "booed, derided and laughed at by the public." Adam credits her with breaking down the social barrier which hitherto had prevented respectable women from performing in public (Somalia 1968, p. 22).

Conditions vary, of course, from one culture to another. Euba (1970, p. 26), writing presumably of West Africa, speaks of the "new position of social importance occupied by musicians" and points out that "creative artists are gradually becoming distinguished from performing artists." An enduring problem, though, is the absence of suitable career ladders for artists in the civil service. An artist reaches a certain salary level and can advance no further, no matter how talented or popular he may be; his only road to advancement is away from his art and into administration (this point is discussed at greater length in § 18.3.2). A study of the evolution of African broadcasting artists and of their conditions of employment would be of great historical value and interest. In many countries, as in Somalia, it would still be possible to record the experiences and achievements of the first performers on radio and television. Also of interest would be a study of how broadcasting either helps traditional arts and artists or, alternatively, overwhelms them with alien forms and styles.

18.3 Personnel Recruitment, Training, and Utilization

18.3.1 Overseas Training

The innumerable overseas scholarship, training, attachment, and orientation programs which siphon off African broadcasting personnel and keep their organizations in a state of disruption constitute an unconscionable abuse of foreign technical-aid programs. Embassies appear to compete on a "body count" basis—the more host-country personnel they ship home for training programs the higher their efficiency ratings, irrespective of the qualifications of the trainees or the quality and relevance of their overseas experience. Some embassy officials are not above a little arm twisting—"After all we've done for your broadcasting system the least you can do is to give us one or two trainees." The fact is, there are far more offers than suitable candidates. Broadcasting organizations, often already handicapped by essential leaves-of-absence of key men, have to scrape the bottom of the barrel and recommend totally unqualified personnel. In other cases, as Quarmyne and Bebey put it, "training programs are looked upon as rewards for seniority." As for on-the-job training with foreign broadcasting organizations: "In their present form, most attachments . . . give officers a holiday and return them home confused while their organizations suffer by losing their services during the period of attachment" (Quarmyne and Bebey 1967, pp. 44, 54).

Some overseas training programs, so-called, put the trainee at the mercy of instructors no more advanced in broadcasting expertise than the trainee's own colleagues at home. Often he has to waste much of his training period trying to learn a new language which has no probable future value to him and which in any event he never masters sufficiently to allow it to become the vehicle of anything but the most elementary ideas.

This is not to deny that legitimate overseas training and attachment programs exist, such as those described in chapter 14. However, responsible training specialists have come to agree, in principle at least, that it no longer makes sense to take the young African broadcasting recruit out of his own environment and to attempt training him in a foreign environment, except possibly under very limited and special circumstances such as those discussed by Edington in § 14.2.2. Overseas training has a useful function, but mainly for the few highly experienced broadcasters with sufficient maturity both to profit from their foreign contacts and to preserve their own identities. See Kolade's statement of Nigeria's criteria in § 5.1.11.

18.3.2 University Broadcasting Education

Chapter 14 sets forth arguments for professionalizing the study of broadcasting by making it a college-degree program in African institutions (§§ 14.1, 14.3.2). This move would help immensely to build up the self-confidence and the status of the African broadcaster. It would solve many existing disciplinary and performance problems and help the medium come closer to realizing its potentialities. Unfortunately, little has been done to adapt college-level broadcasting education to the needs of Africa. Foreign educational advisers have in the main simply transferred to Africa the same approach to education in mass communication they know at home. The conventional journalism curriculum—West European, East European, or American—has about as much direct relevance to African needs as Ptolemaic astronomy. Yet even for Europe's and America's needs a more coherent approach to communication has been recognized as desirable. A British specialist in journalism education suggests that "there is sufficient in common between the jobs of reporters, writers, subeditors, researchers, current affairs producers on radio and television, photojournalism, public relations men, copy writers and graphic designers in advertising, for there to be common elements in their basic professional training and education and that colleges should develop courses embracing these communications activities rather than that each profession should pursue its educational programme in complete isolation from its colleagues" (Dodge 1972, p. 14). For Africa one would add such jobs as those of government information officer and educational-media specialist, and expand the range of radio and television functions (still, be it noted, curiously restricted even in this argument for comprehensiveness!).

The challenge, of course, is to find teachers willing to forsake their comfortable specializations, ready to take the risks and to undergo the hard work of becoming media generalists. We are constantly being warned that alien techniques, methods, institutions cannot be exported to Africa without appropriate modification. Here is an opportunity for creative adaptation. Africa's lack of information infrastructure (§ 16.6.1), Africa's need to use media in coping with problems of economic and social development, Africa's special political demands upon the media—all cry out for innovative curriculum design.

18.3.3   Capacity to Utilize Trained Personnel

Foreign-aid strategies often seem to have been based on a somewhat naïve faith in training as a panacea. But as a Thomson Foundation official put it, "there is little use in showing a bright young man new ideas, if a tired old man sits on his back when he returns home" (Rowlands 1971). The finest training imaginable avails little without an organizational framework in which it can be put to work.

Broadcasting preeminently involves *organized* activity, which requires a high degree of coordination among a variety of specialists—engineers, managers, clerks, writers, performers, producers, accountants, artists, translators, journalists, and others. Individuals as individuals—no matter how well trained, how talented, how skilled they may be—cannot bring their personal qualities to bear without the cooperation of others. In the absence of a suitable working organization and creative climate, the highly trained broadcaster finds himself frustrated and demoralized. All the typical symptoms of the "returnee" syndrome ensue.

Speaking of overseas "participant training" linked with a USAID project, for example, an American educator observed that when a trainee returns "he finds that he is out of touch. He has changed. He is frustrated. He often becomes discouraged and seeks other work. . . . It has been our experience, often reinforced by association with other technicians and trainees, that a serious side effect of training abroad is the aura of 'expertise' which the trainee feels he has acquired. This seems to give him the notion he need only 'supervise' rather than roll up his sleeves and work" (Washington County 1968, p. IV-A-4). In such situations one cannot in fairness hold the trainee responsible. He responds predictably to the situation of finding himself, after intense personal effort, equipped to do a job which his own organization makes impossible.

Part of the organizational problem arises from the fact that civil service traditions tend to govern all organizations which employ civil servants, no matter how inappropriate such a framework may be. In § 4.1.5 Roberts described the unavailing efforts of a foreign advisory group to get the Kenya broadcasting organization to free itself from the inflexible control of the civil service. The advisers reported that the civil service control of recruitment, appointment, and setting of salary scales and promotion standards "has a tendency to discourage individual initiative and effort, while condoning mediocrity and inefficiency. . . . Flagrant disobedience and disrespect for authority are allowed under the present Civil Service regulations to go unpunished, while at the same time no provision is made for rewarding those who perform their duties in an exemplary manner" (RTV International 1970, p. 1). Such findings have been too frequently confirmed to leave room for the argument that the case is exceptional or that the advisers are hypercritical. Quarmyne and Bebey, themselves experienced African broadcasters, recommended that recruitment should be more flexible and should emphasize "talent, creative ability, and aptitude for broadcasting" and "the special affinity and loyalty to broadcasting upon which creativity in the medium heavily depends"—none of which conventional civil service criteria are designed to measure. Of the 20 recommendations in their study, three concern "general inefficiency and irresponsibility," which they characterize as "one of the biggest problems" of African broadcasting (Quarmyne and Bebey 1967, pp. 39, 62, 64, 68). Mytton points out that in Zambian broadcasting a man reaches a point in his career "beyond which he cannot be promoted and still remain a broadcaster"; some of Africa's most distinguished broadcasters have been lost to the medium because they had to become administrators or forever run in place. He continues: "on matters of pay, overtime, the appointment and dismissal of staff, the provision of transport, the purchase of essential equipment, and on many other matters the ZBS administration is governed by civil service rules that in almost every respect are out of place in a broadcasting service" (Mytton 1972a, p. 100).

USAID participant trainees frequently failed to put their specialized overseas training to effective use on their return because civil services had no job specifications covering their new skills. Thus television maintenance men, of crucial importance to the success of an educational-television project in Nigeria, came back after training in America only to be transferred to another ministry entirely or to remain in educational broadcasting without tools, transportation, or prospects of advancement—all because as far as the civil service was concerned the job of television repairman simply did not yet exist (Washington County 1968, p. IV-A-5).

One solution to this organizational problem may be the kind of autonomous status achieved by the Ethiopian Broadcasting Service (§ 3.1.4). However, freedom from the dictates of civil service by no means guarantees automatic improvement. Quarmyne and Bebey (1967, p. 38) deplore civil service recruitment practices as "condemning many training schemes to failure even before they start," but they are still more disturbed by the fact that some broadcasting organizations continue to use the same procedures even after being freed from civil service control. They emphasize that broadcasting has its own unique demands, requiring a unique organization capable of melding together a unique amalgam of engineering, artistic, business, and managerial skills.

18.4 Problems Inherent in Foreign Aid

Foreign technical assistance almost invariably causes tensions, especially in a field like public communication. Higher government officials are sensitive to possibilities of foreign intrusion into the substantive aspects of the national communication system—not always without reason. Operational personnel are likely to interpret the very fact of accepting assistance as a public admission of inadequacy or failure. Both the foreign adviser and his local counterpart must therefore endure an uneasy relationship in which things are rarely what they seem.

18.4.1 Aid Tying and Donor Ethnocentrism

Built-in economic and ideological biases almost inevitably infect even the most well-intentioned forms of bilateral aid. On the economic side, most such aid comes with "tying" provisos which obligate the recipient to buy goods from the donor country, ship in its bottoms, employ its technicians, and so on. A British adviser is not likely to recommend using an Overseas Development Ministry grant to purchase an RCA transmitter; much less is an American adviser likely to recommend buying a Unimog vehicle with Agency for International Development funds. The American State Department boasts that "ninety-nine percent of our aid commodity purchases are made in the United States" (USDOS 1972, p. 2).

That aid tying is seriously disadvantageous to the recipient country is well recognized; see, for instance, the opinion of the Canadian International Development Research Center quoted in § 12.3.1. It can mean the recipient pays higher prices than necessary or is forced to accept unsuitable equipment, and it can create endless future problems of maintenance and parts replacement. If one could penetrate into all the storerooms and warehouses in Africa where disused broadcasting equipment has been lodged and make an inventory of the items in need of only minor repair and replacement parts, their cumulative value would doubtless come to many millions of dollars.

Aid technicians become acutely aware of such problems when delays in shipment and customs clearance hold up essential tools and equipment for their projects. These delays are the more exasperating when the very items needed could be bought locally were not their purchase forbidden because they had not been manufactured by the donor country. An American technician responsible for setting up an educational-media center in Sierra Leone complained that "it is unreasonable that items essential to the success of a program which are available on the shelves of the [local shops] cannot be purchased immediately" (Indiana University 1967). It is not unheard of for a technician to complete his entire tour of duty and return home before some of the essential equipment he was supposed to use arrives at the project site.

On the ideological side, a donor country necessarily approaches the subject of aid from the standpoint of a given economic and political philosophy. It has to justify the giving in terms understandable and acceptable to a ruling party, to an elected legislative body, and sometimes even to the electorate at large. Justification means relating specific aid projects to larger developmental goals of a sort consistent with the donor country's philosophy. Note how the West German Ministry of Economic Cooperation emphasizes its government's concern with relating the gift of media facilities to the achievement of development-policy goals (§ 12.4.1). The recipient country is likely to welcome the gift of equipment—transmitters, antenna arrays, studios, microwave links, mobile units. Help in installing the equipment and getting it into working order is usually recognized as essential, and even help in training technical and operating personnel may be desired. But there, many a recipient country would like the matter to end. The donor country's involvement in the internal affairs of the recipient country is likely to seem at best paternalistic, at worst self-serving and exploitative. Yet this is precisely the point where the donor country's real interest is likely to begin. It may feel legitimately concerned that the *use* made of the facilities, once installed and in working order, will be in keeping with its own conception of the recipient country's needs. The donor views facilities not as ends in themselves, but as means to ends. How are the new broadcasting facilities going to help to explain the next five-year plan to the general public and to motivate enthusiastic support? How will they serve the educational system by improving the distribution of schools broadcasts (see § 15.3.2)?

Even on the level of hardware, the donor country's experts have difficulty in completely freeing themselves from the influences of their own national life-style and their natural wish to "show the flag." As a result their advice often misses the mark. They may overload the recipient system with expensive and showy equipment in excess of actual needs. Disproportionate operational and maintenance costs then compound the problems of an already underbudgeted system. Vehicles lie idle for lack of fuel, tires, or spare parts; powerful transmitters designed to work 24 hours a day go on the air for only a few hours at a time at less than rated maximum power; and simple talk programs waste space, electricity, and equipment occupying huge studios designed for symphony orchestra concerts and elaborate dramatic productions never produced.

18.4.2 Defective Reciprocation

Assistance agreements necessarily involve reciprocal undertakings. Problems inherent in the ethnocentrism and self-interestedness of the donor country may be compounded by defects in the host country's reciprocation. One of the essential reciprocal requirements of any assistance project is likely to be provision of "counterparts"—host-country nationals who work alongside visiting experts and carry on after they leave. Suitable counterpart personnel may not be easy for the host country to supply, and the foreign adviser may find himself with no counterpart to advise. He is then faced with the dilemma of deciding whether to try to force the issue by standing pat, or to avoid wasted time by converting his role from an advisory to an operational one. For example, the personnel recruited for the USAID instructional-television project in Nigeria (§ 15.2.2) found that top officials in one of the regional ministries involved never had committed themselves wholeheartedly to the project. No counterparts were assigned, and the foreign advisory personnel found themselves doing all the work themselves. A graphic artist, for instance, worked alone for 18 months; two weeks before his departure at the close of his contract, the regional ministry finally assigned a counterpart to work with him (Washington County 1968, p. IV-A-2). End-of-tour reports provide an almost inexhaustible mine of such examples of waste. Foreign experts often have little chance to bring their expertise to bear because so much of their limited time is lost in trying to find housing, transportation, office space, and supplies; to clear commodities through customs; to obtain essential personnel, budget, and operational decisions; and so on and on.

Of course many such problems—individually petty, but devastating in their cumulative effect—must be regarded as the inevitable by-product of undevelopedness. "If you didn't have such problems you wouldn't be here" is the cheerfully unhelpful stock reply. But oftentimes more than simple inefficiency is involved. Fiscal forecasts made at the time the aid agreement was signed may have been overoptimistic, and when the time comes for the recipient country to pay its share, the money may not be available. Failures of reciprocation can also arise out of the deliberate withholding of promised support. One government official may be more enthusiastic about the project than another official of equal influence. The project may be imposed from above on a reluctant, uninformed, or suspicious broadcasting staff; conversely, operating personnel may see the project favorably in terms of its technical and professional value, while higher government officials may see it less favorably in terms of its political implications. Generally speaking, it is far easier for upper-echelon officials to negotiate agreements than for the operating personnel to accept the threat to their status and self-esteem implicit in reform or modernization.

18.4.3 Are the Premises Wrong?

So profoundly contradictory are some failures of reciprocation that even these explanations may seem inadequate to foreign observers. They are tempted to look for a deeper, underlying malaise as the cause for this inexplicable drive toward nonachievement. A British broadcasting adviser who left an African post in 1972 admitting that his mission had been a total failure was quoted as saying privately, "These people resent outside advice and want to do things their way, no matter how bad that way is." Perhaps on later reflection he would have amended the second clause to read "no matter how bad that way *seems to us*." Implicitly, he was raising an intensely practical yet fundamental question which has come increasingly to the fore: Is perhaps the whole approach to foreign aid to developing countries based on false premises?

A writer on the "amorality of power politics" who tends to see the relations among nations in the most cynical light possible distinguishes between two viewpoints about foreign aid—that of the "High Roader" and that of the "Low Roader." The High Roader confidently believes that all nations really *want* a "better" economic and social life, that "better" means patterned after industrialized models, and that foreign aid really *can* help confer these benefits. The Low Roader, however, is skeptical: "The reason why the prospects for such countries are so bleak . . . regardless of the amounts of aid poured in, is that their peoples have become dropouts—dropouts from a system to which they can never belong except as second-class citizens . . . peoples of the under-developed countries are *frustrated to the point of irrationality* and . . . Western policy which assumes that they will act in their best interests is bound to fail" (Copeland 1969, p. 150; italics added).

Curiously enough, the conclusion reached by the cynic is not so very different from that reached by the idealist. The ethical validity of foreign aid to developing countries, as practiced hitherto, as well as its pragmatic value, is being brought into question. Take the case of educational technology as an example. Some educational critics regard the efforts of UNESCO and foreign-aid donors to harness the media to educational development in the Third World as not only completely futile, but even positively harmful. The opposing viewpoints were ventilated in a series of articles and comments in 1971 and 1972. Cassirer (1971b), who retired from UNESCO in 1972 after a distinguished career in the field of adult education, spoke for the established position. He was opposed by Gueulette (1971), a young adult-education theorist of the new school of thought. The latter's viewpoint brought a surprising outpouring of favorable comment (*Mass Media/Adult Education* 1972). Gueulette argued that if critics can find so much seriously wrong with American schools—and few critics fail to find serious faults, even if they disagree on what they are and how to deal with them—American educators can only harm developing countries by advising them on how to run *their* educational systems. He regards current educational practice as "schooled behavior," a form of thought control, and the export of these methods as a way of perpetuating autocratic authoritarian governments. The new "systems approach" to media technology in education, described in § 15.3.2, he characterizes as merely "the latest absurdity."

A professor of communications characterized the attitude of the industrialized nations toward the introduction of modern media into developing countries as the "somewhat arrogant notion that peoples of poor countries have innocent and impressionable minds. They are like Sleeping Beauties waiting to be awakened by the kiss of an electronic Prince" (Riegel 1972, p. 9). He points out that despite increased communication in and among developing countries and between them and the rest of the world there are no signs of a corresponding increase in mutual understanding. UNESCO has been operating all along, however, on the premise that exactly the opposite would happen. The reason it has not, as Riegel sees it, is unbridled nationalism: "Communications in developing countries is a particularly clear example of the subversion by nationalism of noble intentions" (p. 14).

One need not subscribe unreservedly to such challenges as these to conventional wisdom to recognize in them an element of truth. We have only to reflect on technology's demonstrated capacity for damaging the social and physical environment, its amorality, its tendency to usurp control. Experience of technology in the industrially advanced world gives ample reason for concern about its impact on the developing world. In the light of that experience, faith in the inevitability of social benefits arising from technological development seems simplistic, while unquestioning endorsement of technological aid regardless of its long-term human consequences seems irresponsible.

18.5 Two Technical Questions

As we pointed out in § 18.1.3, national broadcasting systems rely for coverage on two separate but closely related technical functions: one, direct dissemination of programs to the general public via individual broadcast transmitters; two, interconnection of such transmitters to form networks, so as to broaden the geographic range of dissemination. As we have seen in the individual systems descriptions, not all African countries can afford the ideal fulfillment of these functions. In many cases all transmitters are concentrated in a few high-population centers, with distant parts of the country having to rely on sky-wave propagation—an unsatisfactory source for a domestic service (see §§ A1.3.2, A1.4.4). And even though transmitters may be dispersed, in many cases microwave relay facilities do not exist—or if they exist are too expensive to use for broadcast station interconnection. Stations distant from the program's originating point have to take sky-wave signals off the air and rebroadcast them—again a far from satisfactory solution, since the quality of such rebroadcasts falls below the quality expected in domestic broadcasting. Two technical developments hold out promise of ultimately ameliorating these problems, though their timing remains in doubt.

18.5.1 Frequency Modulation: The Coming Thing?

A score of countries and territories of Africa had about 400 FM transmitters in operation in 1972—but 85% were concentrated in one country, South Africa. Orlik describes how FM is used there to enable local and regional services in several languages for the whole nation (§ 8.1.3). The Canary Islands also have a rather complete FM system. Otherwise, FM stations in Africa serve primarily as relays or as experiments. Yet for many countries, especially those near the equator, FM is the only way to get truly national coverage. Barghausen indicates in § A1.3 how medium-wave propagation in Africa suffers from special disabilities. Moreover, limitations on the frequency spectrum, combined with the large number of countries requiring channel allocations, restrict the number of medium-wave stations which can be accommodated.

For example, a technical survey has established that the MF channels allotted to Kenya by international agreement are too few to enable good medium-wave coverage for the whole country. The "only suitable technical solution," according to the survey, would be to adopt FM as the standard. It was estimated that 36 main FM station sites, with some supplementation from smaller stations, could blanket the country. The cost of installing a comprehensive two-channel national FM network was estimated at about $12 million, not including the cost of sites, roads, and power lines (Swedish Telecommunication Consulting AB 1972, 1:50). Both capital and operating costs might well be less for FM than for medium-wave transmitters if the object is complete, full-time coverage with a broadcast-quality signal. As the standards of service rise, African countries must turn increasingly to FM for domestic broadcasting.

A side effect of standardizing on FM for domestic broadcasting might have policy implications in some situations: the cheapest receivers would be FM-only sets, unable to pick up distant short-wave signals. Encouraging the purchase of such receivers would, in the course of time, effectively reduce short-wave listening to foreign stations. This has been suggested as amounting to a "subtle form of censorship" (Hachten 1971a, p. 267).

18.5.2 Satellites: How Soon?

Building up the terrestrial telecommunications infrastructure needed for national and international broadcast-relay networks is a slow and expensive process. It could take generations to complete. The prospect of resorting to satellites to bypass this stage completely has great appeal and has been the subject of much discussion—not all of it realistic. Barghausen concludes his analysis of technical aspects of the broadcasting spectrum in § A1.6 by pointing out that, while the use of satellites in Africa presents no special technical problems, their use would raise serious economic and political questions.

Three types of broadcast uses for satellites generally are foreseen: (1) long-distance relays between continents which could enable (for example) any African country equipped with an earth station to plug into the Eurovision network; (2) distribution relays, which would enable one large country or a group of contiguous countries to distribute programs via satellite to earth stations located at major population centers—without regard either to their distance from the source or to the nature of the intervening terrain; and (3) broadcasting satellites, which would bypass conventional terrestrial broadcast facilities by reaching down directly to community or to home receivers.

The first of these uses, the long-distance international relay, is represented by Intelsat, a multinational consortium whose membership by mid-1972 comprised more than 80 investing countries, 19 of them in Africa. A U.S. statutory corporation, Comsat, operates the system under contract. Forty of the member countries had earth stations, and 25 more could participate in the use of Comsat facilities via ground connections to earth stations in other nearby countries (Ploman 1972, p. 14). African ground stations already linked with the Comsat system in 1972 were located in Algeria, Ascension Island, Canary Islands, Kenya, Malagasy Republic, Morocco, Nigeria, Senegal, and Zaïre. The Kenya station also represents Tanzania and Uganda, both being connected by land line to the earth station at Longonot, Kenya. The East African station does not receive television, but the Canary Islands started receiving direct telecasts from Spain via satellite in mid-1971. By the end of that year the islands' television stations had broadcast over 500 hours of daily news and educational programming relayed to them from Madrid (ITU 1972, p. 61). Zaïre's ground station is capable of picking up Eurovision, and so Zaïre television was able to carry the Apollo 15 Mission telecasts and the 1972 Olympic games. Nigeria's ground station capability included: two-way exchange of live television with the United States; conversion from PAL color to NTSC color and vice-versa; and recording of television programs for later transmission to other countries (ITU 1973, p. 108). Other African countries and territories with plans for ground stations linking them to the Comsat system within the 1972–74 period include Angola, Cameroon, Ethiopia, Gabon, Ivory Coast, Moçambique, South Africa, the Sudan, and Zambia (ITU 1972).

It should be understood that these existing and planned ground stations do not necessarily betoken a wholesale easement of the problems of long-distance broadcasting distribution. Most of the facilities are designed to accommodate telephone and telegraph circuits, not television. When one considers that in 1972 it cost on the order of $30,000 an hour to relay television programs between Europe and America via Comsat facilities, it becomes obvious that costs will have to come down considerably before African television systems can make routine use of intercontinental satellite relays.

The second type of satellite use, the distribution relay, has saved Russia the installation of thousands of miles of microwave relay routes and hundreds of relay stations in achieving national television coverage (Ploman 1972, p. 14). African television systems, however, are on the air for so few hours a day and reach so few sets that, in terms of present needs, the costs of distribution satellites for broadcasting could hardly be justified. Nor does it seem likely that schedules and audiences will expand enough to justify their use in the near future.

The third type of application, the broadcast satellite which sends its signals directly to relatively simple community receiving stations, or even to home receivers, had not yet been put to regular use in 1972, although prototype community receiver antenna/adapters had been tested, with estimates of cost on a mass-produced basis on the order of $150 each

(Ploman 1972, p. 19). In 1971 a joint UNESCO-ITU mission, at the request of the Arab States Broadcasting Union and individual countries, made a study of how such a system might be applied to educational and developmental problems in North Africa (Ploman, Berrada, and Clergerie 1971). A similar exploratory team made a survey of Tropical Africa in 1972; it estimated that a hypothetical system designed primarily to assist education would be capable of carrying both educational and general television programming directly to schools and community centers, without using intervening terrestrial television broadcast stations. The system capabilities would include simultaneous broadcast of several programs, with the voice component optionally available in as many languages as might be required. An exciting prospect, but the head of the survey team cautioned unofficially, "It is obvious that the cost of such a system, particularly the software aspects, is enormous. It can therefore only become a viable undertaking if the African nations jointly want to operate the system and adjust their educational planning to a point where 40% of all instruction can be given by television. Only on that basis might there actually be a saving in the educational budgets which are, at present, stretched to the maximum" (letter from A. G. W. Timmers, ITU, 13 June 1972).

Thus we see that both the distribution and the direct-broadcast type of satellite relay require very large areas of coverage to be economically feasible. Such wide coverage implies the need for political cooperation, and politics may raise even more barriers than economics. "No communications undertaking, however, innovative its technology or universal its social potential, can rise above or aspire higher, than its mundane base in the politics of segmented national sovereignties" (Riegel 1972, p. 7). Suppose a group of countries did succeed in overcoming nationalistic distrust and in developing an economically viable plan for cooperative support of a direct-broadcast type of satellite. The very existence of such a system would create still more political problems. Once a country makes itself accessible by installing facilities for countrywide direct reception from its own satellite, it immediately becomes a potential target for *other* countries' satellites. Foreign satellites could relay messages which the receiving country could not control and which it might regard as inimical to its interests. The result would be analogous to radio reception from distant foreign sources on short-wave receivers, but on a much heightened level. Even that type of intrusion from the outside is sometimes regarded as so threatening as to require laws against tuning to foreign stations and against possession of short-wave receivers, as well as to justify costly jamming operations to blot out the offending signals. Television, with its greater audience impact, and satellites with their potentialities for enabling clearer reception, would be regarded as much more dangerous.

Such fears refer not only to deliberate subversion and conscious propaganda, but to communication generally. For example, such a seemingly innocuous program as "Sesame Street," which was being distributed by conventional means to nearly 40 foreign countries in 1973, seven of them in Africa, has been roundly condemned. A commentator in an Ethiopian newspaper wrote: "As Africans living in a non-American environment and as Africans to whom English happens to be a second language—our children's needs have obviously very little in common with those of the kids that we see going to school on Sesame Street and talking an unintelligible language" (quoted in Newsom 1973, p. 82). And a Russian commenting in a Moscow newspaper on a criticism of "Sesame Street," said: "With that type of program, imperialism is seeking to penetrate into other people's homes, even if doors and windows are tightly locked. The passkey is to be global television" (*New York Times* 1973).

Unsolicited satellite relays could be particularly unwelcome in Africa, where nationalistic sensitivities are exacerbated by border disputes, liberation movements, separatist factions, and suspicions of neocolonialism. Accordingly, African countries supported the USSR in 1972 in both the United Nations and UNESCO on motions proposing to restrict broadcasting via satellites (Naesselund 1973). The United States vigorously opposed these moves against what it considered to be the principle of free exchange of information (see Stanton 1972). The proposed rule would make it a principle of international law that a country should have the right to jam unwanted satellite broadcasts, and even to destroy offending satellites. Whatever view one takes of the desirability of such a law from the theoretical viewpoint, widespread support for it indicates that practical politics will severely inhibit full international utilization of satellite technology for a long time to come.

Appendixes

Technical Problems of Spectrum Utilization

Alfred F. Barghausen

A1.1 The Radio Spectrum

The usable radio frequency spectrum extends from about 1×10^3 Hz. to 1×10^{11} Hz. By "usable" we mean capable of transmitting information of a man-made rather than a natural origin. The International Telecommunication Union (§ 13.2.1) has the responsibility for the allocation of the radio frequency spectrum for all communication purposes. Currently, the ITU has allocated only that portion of the usable radio frequency spectrum extending from 1×10^4 Hz. to 4×10^{10} Hz. (ITU 1968). It is subdivided into eight frequency ranges, as shown in table 1.

For purposes of frequency allocation, the ITU divides the world into three major regions, each with a Tropical Zone subregion. Africa falls in Region 1, which includes, in addition to the Tropical Zone, subregions called the European Broadcasting Area and the European Maritime Area. Africa is included in Region 1, with a Tropical Zone subregion between latitudes 30°N and 35°S that includes all of Libya; the other North African countries lie in the European Broadcasting Area and European Maritime Area subregions. Frequencies are allocated by bands for specific services on either a worldwide or a regional basis. The services, such as broadcasting, fixed, mobile, and navigational services, are assigned as primary, permitted, or secondary in various bands. Primary and permitted services have equal rights, except in the preparation of frequency plans, in which primary services have prior choice of frequencies. Secondary services are assigned as either primary or permitted services throughout the radio spectrum, as shown in table 2 (ITU 1968).

The 2,300 kHz.–2,498 kHz. range in Band 6 and the first four frequency ranges in Band 7 are allocated for broadcasting only in the Tropical Zone.

Alfred F. Barghausen is Program Leader, Spectrum Utilization Division, Institute for Telecommunication Sciences, Office of Telecommunications, U.S. Department of Commerce. From 1970 to 1972 he was the U.S. member of CCIR Interim Working Party 6/4, concerned with sky-wave propagation at frequencies between approximately 150 kHz. and 1,500 kHz.

TABLE 1

FREQUENCY BANDS ALLOCATED TO THE RADIO SERVICES

Band Number	Frequency Range [a]	Adjectival Description
4	3–30 kHz.	VLF (Very Low Frequency)
5	30–300 kHz.	LF (Low Frequency)
6	300–3,000 kHz.	MF (Medium Frequency)
7	3–30 MHz.	HF (High Frequency)
8	30–300 MHz.	VHF (Very High Frequency)
9	300–3,000 MHz.	UHF (Ultra High Frequency)
10	3–30 GHz.	SHF (Super High Frequency)
11	30–300 GHz.	EHF (Extremely High Frequency)

a. Abbreviations: k=kilo (10^3), M=mega (10^6), G=giga (10^9).

These are shared with other services, such as fixed and mobile services. The allocations contain many excepted provisions requested by various telecommunication administrations (see ITU 1968). The use of Band 5 for sound broadcasting is permitted only in Region 1, and, in practice, except for a few stations in North Africa, almost all stations operating on these low frequencies are located in Europe.

Two significant broadcasting conferences affecting Africa have taken place which are worthy of note. The first resulted in the Regional Agreement for the African Broadcasting Area concerning the Use of Frequencies by the Broadcasting Service in the Very High Frequency and Ultra High Frequency Bands, signed by 34 delegations and adopted in 1964 (ITU 1963). The second produced the Regional Agreement concerning the Use of Frequencies by the Broadcasting Service in the Medium Frequency Band in the African Broadcasting Area, signed by 36 delegations and adopted in 1968 (ITU 1966). Both agreements concern the specific assignment, in

TABLE 2

ITU ALLOCATIONS TO THE BROADCASTING SERVICES WITHIN REGION 1

Band Number	Frequency Range	Type of Broadcasting
5	150–255 kHz.	Sound (AM)
6	525–1,605 kHz.	Sound (AM)
	2,300–2,498 kHz.	Sound (AM)
7 [a]	3,200–26,100 kHz.	Sound (AM)
8	41–68 MHz.	Television
	87.5–100 MHz.	Sound (FM)
	174–223 MHz.	Television
9	470–960 MHz.	Television
11	11.7–12.7 GHz.	Unknown

a. Includes 12 separate frequency ranges authorized within band.

accordance with the best available technical data, of frequencies in Bands 6, 7, and 8 to the various administrations in Africa. The addition of new stations and changes in existing assignments must be coordinated according to the technical provisions of these agreements.

A1.2 The Broadcasting Service

Radio broadcasting is radio transmissions intended for general reception within geographic areas, as distinguished from radio communications directed to specific receiving stations. The ITU defines a broadcasting service as including sound transmissions, television transmissions, or other types of transmissions such as standard time and frequency transmissions (ITU 1968).

For purposes of frequency assignment and determination of effective range, the service-area concept is used for all broadcasting services. Broadcast service areas can be described accurately only by statistical methods, that is, by calculating the fraction of the locations within a specified area at which a specified grade (quality) of service is available for a given fraction or more of the time (Barghausen, Finney, and Fisher 1967; CCIR 1970c). It is possible to determine statistically the ratios of wanted signal power to interfering signal power necessary to produce sound or picture of a quality acceptable to observers in the presence of various types of interference, such as atmospheric noise, man-made noise, and other stations. This is done for each type of interference and for various grades of service (excellent, fine, passable, marginal, inferior, and unstable), by using a number of observers under controlled conditions. The ratio accepted by half of the observers is chosen for a given grade of service and type of interference. Since the signal may vary with time, it is also necessary to specify the fraction of time during which the acceptance ratio must be exceeded to define completely a given grade of service at a particular location. The location probability is then defined as the probability of receiving this quality of service for a given part of the time or more (CCIR 1970c).

In broadcasting, service areas are usually shown by isoservice contours. These contours describe areas of equal service availability, rather than limits of service for the broadcasting system. The broadcasting system is defined as the transmitter and its antenna, the receiver and its antenna, and the radio propagation medium. In any given area within the isoservice contour only a fraction of the population (the location probability times the population density) is expected to have a service of a given quality available for a given fraction of the time or more. The fraction representing the location probability varies from area to area and, of course, tends to decrease with increasing distance from the transmitter. Quality of service does not change abruptly, as might be inferred from a map showing isoservice contours, but shades gradually from service of high quality to service of low quality.

In a broadcasting system the information transmitted should be reproduced as accurately as possible at reception. This depends on the receiver and antenna characteristics, and the characteristics of the radio propagation medium. The receiver and antenna are under the control of the listener, whereas the propagation characteristics depend upon the type of medium. The general communication medium is the space between the earth and the ionosphere, and we are concerned with three principal propagation modes: the ground-wave, or surface-wave, mode; the tropospheric mode; and the ionospheric, or sky-wave, mode. All these modes are involved in the broadcasting service, and their radio frequency characteristics contribute to a degradation in quality of service. Therefore, we shall discuss broadcasting services in terms of assigned frequency bands and propagation characteristics, with particular attention to technical problems in Africa. Since broadcasting in the low-frequency range is not permitted or useful in Africa, except as noted by a few limited assignments in the Mediterranean subregion (see § 2.2.4), its technical problems as a potential broadcasting service will not be discussed.

A1.3 Medium-Frequency Broadcasting

Since about 1960 the use of medium frequencies in Band 6 for broadcasting has become very popular in the African area. The reasons for this are the relatively good quality of service available from moderate-power stations to large areas, and the highly developed engineering level the experience of using Band 6 has achieved in the European and North American areas. As mentioned earlier, the first coordinated frequency plan for MF broadcasting in Africa was enacted in 1968. Adherence to this plan is recommended if an efficient broadcasting service is to be achieved in all countries.

On medium frequencies, both the ground-wave and the sky-wave propagation modes are important. Depending on the radiated power and other factors, as we shall see, good-quality reception is simultaneously available at moderate distances (80 km.–250 km.) by the ground wave and at long distances (1,200 km.–3,000 km.) by the sky wave. Because of high energy absorption by the ionosphere, however, the sky waves produce useful broadcast signals only during the hours of darkness. During this period and at intermediate distances (200 km.–400 km.), fading—caused by interference between the ground wave and a time-delayed sky wave—often seriously deteriorates the aural quality of the received broadcast signals. It is convenient to define the signals propagated by ground wave as forming a "primary" service area, and those propagated by sky wave as forming a "secondary" service area, since the latter service, as we shall see, is available only at night and is of a lower quality because of the mode of propagation (FCC 1972).

A1.3.1 Ground-Wave Primary Service Area

The ground wave can be defined as that part of the total received signal which has not been reflected from the ionosphere or the troposphere. The propagation of the ground wave is primarily dependent on three parameters: the frequency, the electrical properties of the earth, and the wave polarization. If these parameters are known, the total signal induced by the ground wave may be calculated to a high degree of accuracy. At this point it is important to note that vertical wave polarization is used exclusively by all medium-frequency broadcast stations. This is because the presence of a conducting earth suppresses the propagation of horizontally polarized waves due to the cancellation effects between the parallel electric vector and the induced ground currents. Later, we shall see that vertical polarization has a serious effect on the secondary sky-wave service of broadcast stations in Africa on certain medium frequencies. In practice, the frequency and the wave polarization are known, but the electrical properties of the earth are a combination of two complex quantities—called the "conductivity" and "dielectric constant"—which, in the absence of measurements, can only be estimated. The relative effect of these two quantities depends on the radio frequency. At medium frequencies, conductivity has the greater influence.

To determine the primary service area of a broadcast station, some knowledge of the ground conductivity is essential. It is insufficient to classify the conductivity in broad descriptive terms, such as good, fair, or poor, or in broader terms, such as a single value for all land areas. These general classifications may be sufficient for some administrative purposes, but their indiscriminate use for technical evaluation can result in errors of hundreds of square kilometers in the predicted total service area. For Africa, conductivity estimates have been based solely on surface vegetation, and a map of specific values is included with the technical standards of the 1968 regional agreement. Such estimates are believed to be much too low in some areas; actual primary service areas are expected to be quite different from those calculated from these values. This is because surface vegetation alone, except when the receiver is immersed in dense jungle foliage, is insufficient for estimating the conductivity; other factors, such as the type, thickness, and condition of soils and rocks, the terrain roughness and land-water features, and, to a lesser extent, the climate, must also be considered. South Africa has made an extensive measurement survey using medium-frequency test signals and has established very reliable values of conductivity in its region (Vice 1954). Similar procedures could be used in other countries to better define the important primary service areas of MF broadcast stations. This would assist administrations in the design of networks which would provide an acceptable service to all their geographical areas or to population areas with a minimum of duplication and without excessive transmitter power or number of stations.

As discussed earlier, the service area of a broadcast station is the area within which a satisfactory grade of service is available for a given fraction or more of the time in the presence of interference from atmospheric noise, man-made noise, and other stations. Signals propagated via the ground-wave mode are essentially constant; that is, at a fixed distance from the transmitter, the signal strength—or amplitude—does not vary with time. However, the interference with which the desired signal must compete does vary, except for other undesired ground-wave signals from cochannel or adjacent channel stations, with time of day and season of the year. In Africa, especially in the equatorial region, atmospheric noise due primarily to local thunderstorm activity is the most predominant type of noise in the MF range, although man-made noise in large-city, business-industrial areas may be a factor from time to time. The highest average atmospheric noise levels are encountered during the period from 4 P.M. to midnight local time in the equatorial zone, between about latitude 20°N and latitude 15°S, from September through February (CCIR 1964). In general, signal-strength levels in the equatorial zone must be two to four times higher to provide the same quality of service as that available in other African regions. This area is shown in figure 1, together with other important areas which will be discussed later.

A1.3.2 Sky-Wave Secondary Service Area

Broadcast stations in the MF band have an additional service area at night, owing to reflections from the ionosphere. The ionosphere is a region of ionized gases which surrounds the earth. It is composed of gas molecules and atoms from which electrons are detached by ultra-violet light or X-rays from the sun. That part of the ionosphere important to radio-wave propagation is divided into four layers, according to height and intensity, called the D, E, F1, and F2 regions. The intensity (electron density) and its variation with time are the important properties of the four regions for radio communication. The number of regions, their heights, and their intensities vary from hour to hour, day to day, month to month, season to season, and year to year. The highest radio frequency reflected from each of the four regions is called the critical frequency of the layer. As the frequency is increased above the critical frequency, the radio energy passes through the region; unless reflected by a higher region, it is radiated into space.

The D and E regions determine the presence or absence of a sky-wave secondary area for a medium-frequency broadcasting station. The F region may provide a secondary service when the critical frequency of the E layer falls to a low value and the propagation path is relatively short. The highest critical frequencies are present during daylight hours, since the sun's radiation is the controlling influence on the regions' electron densities.

D-region ionization is usually insufficient to support the reflection of medium-frequency waves; however, it does cause considerable absorption of the waves as they penetrate to higher regions. Absorption is the process whereby part of the wave energy is dissipated by collisions of the excited electrons with molecules of air. During daylight hours ionization in the D region results in almost total absorption of medium-frequency waves. At night most of the ionization and, consequently, absorption in the D region disappears, and medium-frequency waves are reflected from the E layer and propagated to long distances. Thus, the sky-wave signal strength necessary to produce a secondary service has a marked increase from day to night because of this reduction in ionospheric absorption. This increase begins near sunset and reaches its highest value near midnight local time. Near sunrise, the absorption effect of the D region begins, and the signal strength decreases rapidly to its low daytime value. These low daytime values are of negligible importance to broadcasting, since they are of insufficient strength to overcome the interference from atmospheric or man-made noise.

Other factors which affect the loss in power, and thus the extent of the secondary service area from sky-wave transmissions, may be grouped into five major categories as follows: (1) antenna radiation losses; (2) spatial, or distance, loss caused by the spreading of the wave; (3) multipath fading losses; (4) defocusing losses in reflection from a curved or wavy ionosphere; and (5) polarization coupling losses. The effects of the first two categories are easily determined and also apply to ground waves. Categories 3 and 4 are not easily ascertained but can be estimated, and they apply to all sky-wave transmission in any frequency range and area (Barghausen 1966). On the other hand, losses due to category 5 are unique to medium-frequency sky-wave propagation and, most important, to broadcasting in all low-latitude areas.

This polarization coupling loss and its impact on the MF sound-broadcasting service in Africa are briefly explained as follows: A propagated radio wave of any polarization, upon entering the ionosphere, involves a redistribution of energy into two components called the ordinary and extraordinary waves (Budden 1961). This redistribution of energy depends on four factors: (a) the magnetic dip latitude, (b) the frequency, (c) the propagation direction, and (d) the transmitting antenna polarization. It has been shown by both theory and experiment that vertically polarized sky-wave transmissions on paths in an east-west or west-east direction near the magnetic dip equator are almost totally absorbed if the operating frequency is near the gyromagnetic frequency (Phillips and Knight 1965; Barghausen 1966). In equatorial latitudes the gyromagnetic frequency, that is, the frequency of rotation of ions about the earth's magnetic field

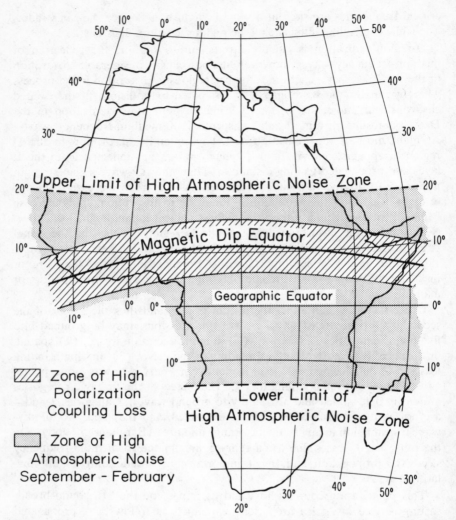

Fig. 1. Magnetic dip equator and zones of high MF sky-wave losses and high atmospheric noise.

lines, is in the range 800 kHz.–900 kHz., or near the center of the MF broadcast band. Thus, sky-wave propagation along the magnetic dip equator at or near this frequency, with vertical polarization, will excite the extraordinary wave component and result in high attenuation, that is, heavy absorption. Conversely, vertically polarized sky waves propagated in a north or south direction out of the equatorial zone will be affected only by normal ionospheric absorption. On the other hand, the use of horizontal polarization would couple all the radiated energy into the ordinary wave component, and sky-wave fields would be quite high and useful as a secondary broadcasting service to great distances. However, as discussed in § A1.3.1, the primary ground-wave service would be severely restricted because of the nature of propagation of horizontally polarized waves over the surface of the earth.

Figure 1 shows the location of the magnetic dip equator and the area within which polarization coupling losses are expected to limit the night-time secondary service area of MF broadcast stations in an east-west or west-east direction. Broadcast stations operating in this area on frequencies from about 700 kHz. to 1,100 kHz. should expect restricted secondary service coverage, in comparison with stations operating on frequencies below and above this range.

There are other natural effects on MF sky-wave transmissions which should be noted, since they, too, affect the quality of service, and thus the choice of sound-broadcasting systems administrations may want to use. These are: (1) magnetic activity effects, and (2) the phase of the 11-year sunspot cycle (Barghausen and Lillie 1965). Figure 2 shows a 9-year continuous record of sky-wave monthly median-signal strengths based on daily hourly values corresponding to midnight at the path midpoint for a 700-kHz. transmission over a 700-km. path. To show the influence of magnetic and sunspot activity, 12-month running means of the planetary magnetic index and the relative Zurich sunspot numbers are also plotted. It is clear that higher signal strengths, and consequently better secondary service, are available during the low sunspot phase of the solar cycle and that increasing magnetic activity, particularly during periods of low solar activity, decreases the signal strength and reduces the quality of a secondary service. The short-term effect of magnetic activity is illustrated in figure 3. Shown is a daily record of the signal strength for the same station and distance as used above, but for a magnetically quiet and a magnetically disturbed day. Notice the lower signal strength and increased fading of the sky-wave transmission during the disturbed day, and also the low daytime levels during both days. This effect may last for six or seven days after the disturbance begins. Although the example was obtained on a middle-latitude path, the effect is the same in other latitudes; it is more severe in the polar regions and perhaps slightly less, though not significantly, in equatorial latitudes.

A1.3.3 Summary

In summary, technical considerations for African sound-broadcasting systems operating on medium frequencies are:

1. MF broadcasting provides both a primary service, via the ground wave, to moderate distances; and a secondary service, via the sky wave (only at night), to long distances.

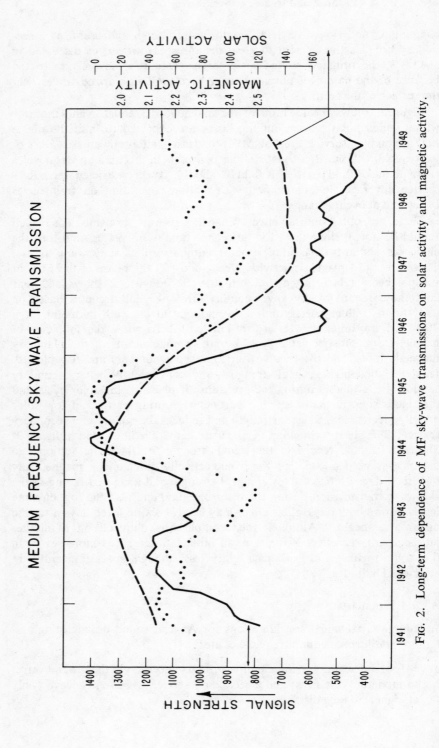

FIG. 2. Long-term dependence of MF sky-wave transmissions on solar activity and magnetic activity.

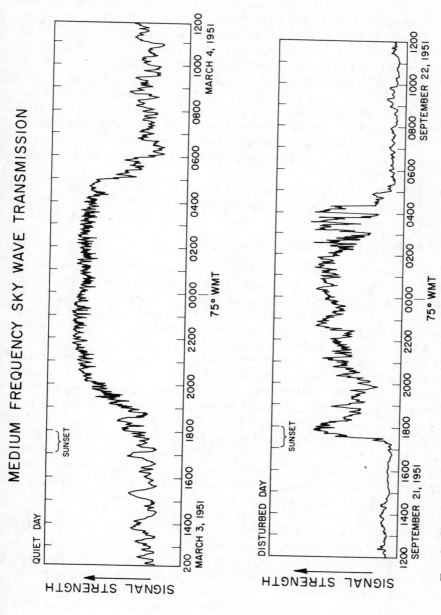

Fig. 3. Signal-strength recordings showing effects of magnetic activity on MF sky-wave transmissions.

2. To determine the extent of the primary service area for effective network planning, better estimates of the ground constants in Africa are needed.
3. During the period September through February the necessary signal strengths to overcome high atmospheric noise levels must be two to four times higher in the equatorial zone than in other areas. This applies to both the primary and the secondary service.
4. Broadcast stations using vertical polarization and operating on frequencies from about 700 kHz. to 1,100 kHz. in an area within about ± 10 degrees of the magnetic dip equator will experience severe restriction in nighttime secondary service coverage in east or west directions.
5. The use of horizontal polarization to overcome the effects of point 4 above essentially eliminates the ground-wave primary service area and is not recommended.
6. The secondary service area of all broadcast stations will be reduced during periods of high solar activity and high magnetic activity.

A1.4 High-Frequency Broadcasting

Since about 1935 high-frequency broadcasting, popularly known as "short-wave broadcasting," has been an important service in Africa. At present, it is the only available means of long-distance broadcasting with a usable quality of service. As we shall see, however, this quality of service is rarely entirely satisfactory, in comparison with other sound-broadcasting methods.

All 12 frequency ranges within Band 7 are allocated to sound broadcasting in Region 1. Included are four frequency ranges, in the lower part of the band, for use only in the Tropical Zone (essentially all of Africa) that are shared with other services. Since atmospheric noise decreases with increasing frequency, these allocations were made to supplement the loss of low-frequency broadcasting methods which cannot overcome the high atmospheric noise levels in the Tropical Zone. In addition, at the time of the allocations, the regions in Africa included extensive sparsely populated, underdeveloped territories, administered by a single country, that could only be served by high-power, long-distance methods of sound broadcasting.

In the HF range the ionosphere is at its highest efficiency for reflecting electromagnetic energy. Therefore, the sky wave is the principal propagation mode for providing HF broadcasting services. An acceptable HF service via the ground-wave mode rarely exceeds 50 km., because of the poor conducting properties of the earth in this frequency range. Optimum sky-wave propagation is achieved by horizontal polarization using antennas having directional properties.

Sky-wave propagation in this frequency range is similar to that described for MF broadcasting. As we have seen, the most important characteristic property of each of the four ionospheric regions is its critical frequency. Maximum critical frequencies occur in the F region and are dependent on time of day, season of the year, phase of the solar cycle, and geographical location. Values for propagation to 4,000 km. range from about 4 MHz. to 40 MHz., with the highest values occurring in the high phase of the solar cycle. For any transmission path the highest frequency returned to the earth after reflection from the ionosphere for 50% of the days in the month at a specific time of day is called the "maximum usable frequency" (MUF). It is this characteristic parameter of the ionosphere which is used to determine the choice of frequencies for HF broadcasting purposes. Worldwide maps of this parameter for each hour of the day and month of the year and for low, medium, or high phases of the solar cycle are available, together with accepted procedures for their use, from the International Frequency Registration Board of the ITU.

Because of the complex nature of sky-wave propagation, the diversity of broadcasting-service requirements, and the fluctuation in spectrum usage, there is no simple method for selecting optimum frequencies to insure coverage of a particular area. There are many procedures and methods used by various administrations, and the reader is referred to documents of the CCIR (1970a–1970i) for specific information. In general, several different transmitter frequencies, or a frequency complement, must be used throughout the broadcast day in order to provide a continuous service to a given area. As noted above, however, we must also have a different frequency complement to account for seasonal and solar-cycle changes in the MUF. The IFRB coordinates all HF broadcasting assignments from frequency requests submitted by each member administration. On the basis of these requests, specific frequency schedules are made for each of four broadcast seasons (see ITU 1968, art. 10). The purpose of these broadcast schedules is to keep interference between stations at a minimum in the desired service area. Coordination among one or more administrations in selecting frequencies is strongly recommended prior to IFRB notification.

Generally, the characteristic properties of sky-wave propagation in Band 7 are similar in all world areas. In some areas, however, these properties are more pronounced and consequently have a more serious effect on the quality of service. In low-latitude areas these are: (a) equatorial sporadic E, (b) spread F, and (c) F region ionization. It is essential that African administrations have some knowledge of these properties and their effect on HF transmissions when they consider the potential of this method of sound broadcasting. In addition, although atmospheric noise decreases with increasing frequency, it is still quite high and is often the limiting factor for a satisfactory quality of service, especially in the equatorial zone (CCIR 1964).

A1.4.1 Equatorial Sporadic E

Sporadic E propagation is defined as a comparatively strong and protracted transmission, lasting several minutes to several hours, returned from the

E region of the ionosphere by some mechanism other than the normal reflection process from the daytime regular E layer (Smith 1957). Sporadic E, as the name implies, is variable, occurring at irregular time intervals in all world areas (Whitehead 1970). The region of ionization is on the order of several kilometers—comparatively thin compared to the tens of kilometers' thickness of the normal E and F regions. Its density, however, is high. This last characteristic results in high critical frequencies and may either totally reflect or partly reflect energy up to and beyond 75 MHz. This can be both helpful or harmful to broadcasting. For example, total reflection may block propagation from a more favorable F region mode and thus reduce the extent of the service area. Partially reflected energy can cause serious fading, and reduce the quality of service, by interference with the regular mode. On the other hand, the presence of a sporadic E layer can extend the useful frequency range for broadcasting services, especially in the low-latitude areas.

Equatorial sporadic E is a regular daytime occurrence which does not exhibit any seasonal variation (CCIR 1970f). It is centered on the magnetic dip equator (see fig. 1) and regularly supports propagation on frequencies as high as 50 MHz. It is most efficient for propagation paths in a north or south direction.

A1.4.2 Low-Latitude Spread F

A serious problem associated with HF broadcasting in equatorial latitudes is the effect of "flutter fading." This phenomenon, first observed in India (Rao and Somayajuler 1949), and further investigated in Africa (Barghausen, Jacobs, and Lillie 1963; Davies and Barghausen 1966), causes severe fading and distortion on broadcast transmissions. It is closely associated with the occurrence of spread F, which appears as a spreading of echoes over a wide range of frequencies and heights on vertical-incidence sounding records (Booker and Wells 1938; Osborne 1952). In oblique transmissions "flutter fading" is characterized by large and rapid frequency changes that may be observed with special recording devices.

An extensive study made in 1972 gives the probability of spread F occurrence on a worldwide basis (Davis 1972). This study shows that its characteristics in low latitudes are (a) that it occurs almost entirely within the period 6 P.M.–6 A.M. local time, (b) that maximum occurrence is in the period June through September for the hours after local sunset until local midnight, and (c) that higher probabilities occur during the high phase of the 11-year solar cycle.

A1.4.3. Low-Latitude Regular F Region

The formation of the regular daytime F region (Wright 1960) shows a minimum electron density centered on the magnetic dip equator, with two maxima on either side at about $\pm 30°$ magnetic dip latitude (see fig. 1). The consequence of this phenomenon is that propagation along and transverse to the magnetic dip equator can be appreciably different. For example, broadcast stations located north or south of the dip equator can be expected to achieve a better service into higher latitudes across the equator during daytime hours because propagation takes place via the electron density maxima without intermediate ground reflections. Also, higher frequencies can be used in north or south directions than in east or west directions for the same time period. The presence of these low-latitude propagation phenomena adds to the problem of frequency planning unless it is properly recognized and taken into account.

A1.4.4 Summary

The technical considerations for African sound-broadcasting systems operating on high frequencies may be summarized as follows:

1. An HF broadcasting service is rarely entirely satisfactory, because of variations in the propagation medium.
2. Directional antennas and complements of frequencies are necessary to insure adequate and continuous coverage of a desired service area.
3. HF broadcasting is subject to severe intereference from other stations because of current practices in frequency management. This is due, in part, to (a) lack of knowledge about the propagation medium, (b) inadequate use of known characteristic properties of HF propagation in frequency planning, and (c) insufficient number of channels to meet demands.
4. HF is recommended for international sound broadcasting, since it is currently the only available method of long-distance broadcasting during both day and night hours; but HF broadcasting is not a satisfactory domestic broadcasting service for most African countries.
5. In Africa, daytime equatorial sporadic E may radically change the service area of stations in the vicinity ($\pm 10°$) of the magnetic dip equator.
6. The occurrence of spread F gives rise to "flutter fading," which degrades the quality of service from HF stations in low latitudes during early nighttime hours. When possible, the use of higher frequencies in the HF band is recommended, to minimize this effect.
7. For the same operating frequency, service areas in north or south directions across the magnetic dip equator are much larger than in east or west directions.
8. In the equatorial zone, atmospheric noise is often the limiting factor for a satisfactory quality of service.

A1.5 Broadcasting at Very-High and Ultra-High Frequencies

Technical problems associated with broadcasting in Band 8 (VHF) and
Band 9 (UHF) are similar, since the principal propagation mechanism in
each is the tropospheric mode. There are some differences, however, which
are important to broadcasting in Africa, and these will be discussed in detail.
As shown in table 2, Band 8 is used to provide both a sound- (FM) broadcast service and a television-broadcast service. Band 9 is used exclusively
for television broadcasting.

Frequency assignments are made according to the provisions of the 1964
VHF-UHF African regional agreement mentioned in § A1.1. The plan uses
a lattice overlay of geographical areas in assigning available frequency
channels. The size and geometrical configuration of the lattice (triangular,
square, rectangular, etc.) are determined by technical considerations involving transmitter power, height of transmitting antenna above surrounding
terrain, protection ratios for specified grades of service, and propagation
characteristics. Once these factors are properly applied, a suitable theoretical lattice is designed, and channels are assigned at appropriate intersections
(see § 8.1.3 for a practical application). In practice some slight distortion
of the theoretical lattice may be necessary if it is to fit some schemes for
network planning. The plans adopted for Africa provide at least three
FM services throughout the entire continent. Television-broadcast services,
on the other hand, presented several different problems (*EBU Review*
1963). In Band 8, for instance, some television services in African countries had begun prior to the 1964 agreement and were using two different
transmission systems (CCIR 1970e). Therefore, the plan developed was
based upon channel-by-channel negotiations between countries. In Band 9,
a quadrilateral lattice was used which provided at least two television
services throughout the entire continent for the range 470 MHz.–790 MHz.
The range 790 MHz.–960 MHz. was not allocated at this time.

A1.5.1 Factors Affecting FM and Television

The propagation of broadcast transmissions in the VHF range is primarily
affected by the characteristics of the lower atmosphere and the terrain
profile. Propagation takes place via two component waves called a "direct
wave" and a "ground-reflected wave." The direct-wave component undergoes refraction in the atmosphere, and the ground-reflected wave undergoes
a reversal in phase which either reinforces or tends to cancel the resultant
signal at the receiver. Thus, both the atmosphere and the terrain profile
play important roles in establishing the broadcast service area. Essentially,
the service area is limited to "line-of-sight" coverage, although some service
is available slightly beyond line-of-sight by diffraction over the bulge of the
earth. Therefore, transmitting antennas should be located on tall buildings,
towers, or tops of mountains.

Since it is not feasible to obtain accurate terrain profile information for every possible receiver location in a broadcast area, it is necessary to use a location-probability concept (discussed in § A1.2) in defining a service area. Signal levels will vary randomly over a number of locations within a relatively small area and may be characterized by a normal distribution of signal levels about a mean or a median value and by a standard deviation. By means of such curves, service areas are derived as a function of path distance, carrier frequency, antenna height, and terrain irregularity expressed by suitable parameters.

Variations of broadcast signals with time (time variability) are caused by changes in the properties of the atmosphere, that is, the refractive index structure. In order to account for these long-term variations, which may last from several hours to several days or more, known worldwide meteorological conditions and their effects on radio propagation were examined and climatic regions were defined (CCIR 1970d). To define the broadcast service area, two estimates are combined: one of time variability in broadcast transmissions, based on available measurements within the various climatic regions of the world (Rice et al. 1967); the other of factors which account for terrain irregularities.

In Africa, a wide range of meteorological conditions exists. Six different climate regions were identified in the 1964 VHF-UHF agreement. In general, for the same conditions of transmitter power, antenna height, and terrain type, the service areas of sound and television stations in Band 8 will be smallest in the Sahara Desert region, largest in the temperate Mediterranean region, and about the same size in all other climate regions.

As noted earlier, the effect of atmospheric noise on broadcast transmissions decreases with increasing frequency, so that in the Band 8 frequency range it is of little consequence. However, noise from unintended man-made sources, such as auto ignition systems and industrial-domestic equipment, becomes a nuisance, and for signal levels to provide a satisfactory grade of service, they should be ten times higher in large cities than in rural areas (CCIR 1970a).

FM sound broadcasting has grown considerably in North America and Europe in the past 20 years. Many experts believe it is superior to AM service. Although service areas are greater in medium-frequency AM sound broadcasting, especially at night, the higher quality of FM service makes it the best sound-broadcasting method for the Tropical Zone.

In Africa the only unique technical problem in the use of television in Band 8 is the effect of sporadic E propagation in low latitudes. We have given several general characteristics of this type of propagation in § A1.4.1, noting that partial reflection of electromagnetic energy can occur up to and beyond 75 MHz. Although of little consequence in the FM band (87.5 MHz.–100 MHz.), it is of serious concern to television broadcasting in the range 41 MHz.–68 MHz. (Smith 1957; Davis, Smith, and Ellyett 1959).

This is especially true in the area centered on the magnetic dip equator ($\pm 10°$), and for the lowest two VHF television channels. During daytime hours signals will be propagated to distances of the order of 1,000 km.–2,000 km., although the signal levels are insufficient for a broadcast service; they will, however, cause severe cochannel interference to other authorized stations.

A1.5.2 UHF Television

Band 9 frequencies were allocated to the television-broadcast service in the 1950s to accommodate the demand for additional channels in North America and Europe. The allocation of additional channels in Band 8 was not feasible, owing to the heavy usage of these frequencies for other radio services, notably aeronautical, radionavigation, fixed, and mobile.

In general, and under normal propagation conditions, the quality of service of UHF television transmissions is the same as that at VHF; however, for the same power and antenna height, the service area is smaller because of the increase in propagation losses with increasing frequency. In addition, the shielding effects of trees, buildings, and terrain are more severe at these frequencies, though usually they are important only at the limits of the service area, often referred to as the "fringe area."

At Band 9 frequencies the most important abnormal propagation condition is that associated with atmospheric ducts. The ducting condition, or the trapping of radio energy, occurs when the refraction, or bending, of the electromagnetic energy exceeds the normal bending; it is then called "superrefraction" (Bean et al. 1966; Bean and Dutton 1966). Under this condition television signals are trapped and propagated to long distances, similar to sporadic E reflections at VHF; or the fading of long-term signal power occurs, which alternately improves or degrades the quality of service as signal-strength conditions at the receiver location change with time. Meteorological conditions that support this propagation mechanism commonly take the form of marked departures from median conditions. Superrefractive conditions occur over a limited range of elevation (layers) at, or above, the earth's surface. In most cases, they can be associated with known meteorological processes and described in terms of typical geographical locations and weather conditions recognizable to the systems engineer. They also behave typically in terms of meteorological measurements available from weather stations and can be systematized for quick reference (Dougherty 1968).

Superrefractive conditions, which give rise to ducting, occur most often in the early night hours. Clear skies and light surface winds permit considerable cooling of the earth's surface, which can cause the formation of a temperature inversion (an increase of temperature with height) and produce a strong refractive gradient near the surface. An analysis of African climatic conditions shows that this occurs most often in the period between October and March in an area of West and Central Africa about 5°N–20°N of the geographic equator (Bean et al. 1966). Thus, in this area (Cameroon, Central African Republic, Chad, Dahomey, Gambia, Ghana, Guinea, Ivory Coast, Liberia, Mali, Mauritania, Niger, Nigeria, Senegal, Sierra Leone, Togo, and Upper Volta), these abnormal conditions can be expected to prevail for longer periods and to have a more serious effect on television services during the prime early nighttime hours than in other climatic regions.

A1.5.3 Summary

Technical factors of importance to VHF and UHF sound or television broadcasting in Africa may be summarized as follows:

1. VHF sound broadcasting using frequency modulation (FM) is superior in quality of service, in comparison with amplitude modulation (AM) in the MF and HF bands, especially in the Tropical Zone during periods of high atmospheric noise.
2. Although more transmitting stations are required to provide an FM sound-broadcasting service over a large area, compared with the number required by other methods of sound broadcasting, recent technical developments make this an economically feasible service.
3. Television broadcasting using the lowest VHF channels (41 MHz.–68 MHz.) is expected to cause and receive severe interference in an area centered on the magnetic dip equator ($\pm 10°$), because of sporadic E propagation effects. The use of VHF assignments in the range 174 MHz.–223 MHz. is recommended.
4. In the early nighttime hours between October and March, UHF television stations assigned to West and Central African countries are expected to experience a degradation in quality of service because of abnormal meteorological conditions. In this area VHF assignments in the range 174 MHz.–223 MHz. are recommended.

A1.6 Satellite Broadcasting

The advent of proved satellite technology offers new opportunities for broadcasting. The ITU Administrative Space Conference in 1963 defined the Broadcasting-Satellite Service as "a space service in which signals transmitted or re-transmitted by space stations, or transmitted by reflection from objects in orbit around the Earth, are intended for direct reception by the general public" (ITU 1968).

In 1971 the ITU organized the World Administrative Radio Conference on Space Telecommunications, which set forth specific frequency allocations in Bands 7–10 for the Broadcasting-Satellite Service. The CCIR conducted a detailed study in 1971 of all technical factors associated with satellite broadcasting and concluded that Band 9 (above 1,000 MHz.) and the lower part of Band 10 (near 3 GHz.) are optimal for satellite broadcasting because of the lower values of atmospheric attenuation, scintillation (signal variations due to high electron concentrations in the ionosphere), and radio noise from natural sources (atmospheric and cosmic).

There are no known unique technical considerations in Africa for the utilization of satellite broadcasting. In this context satellite broadcasting implies (1) direct broadcast to individual homes or vehicles, (2) broadcast to community receiving terminals for further distribution to homes by cable or for rebroadcast to homes or vehicles, and (3) distribution services to conventional terrestrial broadcast stations. Indeed, it is anticipated that satellite broadcast services of any type will be somewhat better in low-latitude areas when synchronous orbits are used, since these positions are directly over the geographic equator. In this way, satellite "look-angles" from earth locations are vertical or almost vertical, and maximum use of receiving-antenna pattern discrimination against unwanted terrestrial noise or signals is achieved. The reader is referred to reports of the CCIR (1970b, 1970g–1970i) for a comprehensive treatment of technical factors common to all satellite broadcasting services.

The potential of this technique for providing the highest quality of sound and television services is apparent; however, coupled with economic considerations, the apprehension that satellite broadcasting might be exploited for political, commercial, religious, or other propaganda purposes may delay its effective implementation for a considerable period of time.

Broadcasting and Political Crisis

William A. Hachten

[EDITOR'S NOTE. Difficult though it may be to find published information about operational details of African broadcasting systems, we often read news of Africa that comes to us only because it was released by radio, the first—and for a time the only—contact with the outside world in time of crisis. Broadcasting assumes this role only temporarily. Nevertheless, that potentiality for taking center stage colors attitudes and policies toward the medium at other times as well. Professor Hachten in the following essay points out some examples and some of the implications of this special political function of broadcasting.]

In the first decade of *uhuru*, governments of over half of the new nations have been changed at least once through military force or other extralegal means. Some, including Ghana, Nigeria, and Sierra Leone, have had several coups. Dahomey, with six successful coups since independence, holds the record. In 1969, Ghana provided a rare example of orderly change in an African government when the military junta voluntarily gave up power to a popularly elected civilian government. However, a military coup put an end to that government in January 1972. Elections in Africa do take place, but no leader or party has been deprived of power by the vote alone.

During the frequent times of acute political crisis, radio broadcasting has played a significant role. In his brilliant little book, *Coup D'État: A Practical Handbook,* Luttwak (1968) provides a detailed and Machiavellian guide for taking over a nation. As he put it, "Control over the flow of information emanating from the political center will be our foremost weapon in the establishing of our authority after the coup. The seizure of the main means of mass communication will thus be a task of crucial importance" (p. 117). Radio broadcasting is most certainly that "main means of mass communication" in Africa, and becomes an essential factor

William A. Hachten is Professor of Journalism and Mass Communication at the University of Wisconsin-Madison and author of *Muffled Drums: The News Media in Africa* (1971).

in any extralegal struggle for power. For example, in the successful coup in Dahomey on 19 December 1969, led by Lieutenant Colonel Maurice Douandete, the army chief of staff, the insurgents first seized the radio station at 8:00 A.M. Only afterward did they storm the presidental palace and kidnap President Emile Zinsou.

Often, the radio station itself becomes the locus of the violence accompanying insurrections. In Morocco's bloody but unsuccessful coup in 1971, military insurgents seized the main broadcasting station at Rabat, claimed the king was dead, and proclaimed a revolutionary republic. Forces loyal to King Hassan put down the rebellion after a seven-hour battle for the radio station itself in which 150 rebels were killed and 700 captured.

On 23 May 1970, about 30 rebel soldiers led by an army lieutenant seized Brazzaville Radio in the Congo and announced the ouster of President Marien Ngoubai. Loyalist troops surrounded the radio station with tanks and, after a brief fire fight, recaptured it. The attempted takeover failed.

That same radio station had figured in another power struggle ten years earlier. At a critical stage in the contest for Congo-Leopoldville (now Zaïre) in 1960, Joseph Kasavubu gained the upper hand over Patrice Lumumba when his fellow Bakongo, Abbe Youlou, gave Kasavubu access to powerful Radio Brazzaville while the United Nations forces were denying Lumumba the use of the Leopoldville station across the Congo River (Ferkiss 1966, p. 114).

Insurgents head first for the radio station because if the populace can be made to believe the government has toppled, the coup is a long way toward succeeding. This principle is not lost on incumbent leaders; the radio station is often one of the best-guarded installations in an African capital. Because of broadcasting's physical centralization and its organization as a government monopoly, there is usually but one key installation to seize.

Radio is the only mass medium capable of quickly reaching a significant portion of the population. More than any other medium, radio is associated with the voice of the nation and speaks with peculiarly direct authority. A new leader or his mouthpiece can talk directly to the people, using the full range of emotional overtones. Also, of course, radio has a unique ability to sound an alarm when trouble threatens (Hachten 1971a, p. 23). In societies where the oral tradition is still strong, radio—the "immediate medium"—has great impact. Listeners tend to conceive it as literally the government itself speaking.

Any group trying to seize power must quickly obtain control of radio broadcasting to establish its authority as the new de facto government. The civilian population then is usually left with no alternative but to accept the fait accompli and to follow the directives of the "voice of government" issuing from their transistor radios. So for political reasons, radio must be controlled, if only to deny it to one's enemies. The power to broadcast also implies the power not to broadcast. Although the word of the death of Gamal Abdel Nasser spread quickly around the world, Radio Cairo waited five long hours before telling the news to the Egyptian public.

At times pirate broadcasts are used to good effect. During the Algerian war of liberation the OAS, the faction fighting to keep Algeria French, constantly used clandestine radio broadcasts to confuse and demoralize the French government and the Algerians. The most notorious feat of the OAS was the interruption of the 1:00 P.M. television newscast in Oran by the blowing up of the power lines supplying the transmitter. Immediately an OAS sound transmitter came on the air on the same frequency as the television sound. "The surprise was total, and the effect enormous . . . within hours the city was talking of nothing else. The government had been made a laughing stock. . . . At very little risk the OAS had scored a major psychological coup" (Hennissart 1970, p. 185). When Ethiopian army officers attempted a coup in 1960, during Emperor Haile Selassie's absence from the country, one of their first targets was the government radio station in Addis Ababa. However, they failed to take full propaganda advantage which control over the station gave them. When the emperor returned the air force set up a jury-rigged transmitter which effectively countered the insurgents' propaganda line (Greenfield 1965, p. 417).

Compared with broadcasting, local newspapers play a passive and secondary role. Political crisis produces great uncertainty and ambiguity, and since they are not sure who the government head may be next week, newspapers are often reluctant to report what many people already know to be true. During one attempted coup d'état, the French-owned *Dakar-Matin,* Senegal's only daily, suspended publication altogether for several days, until it saw which way events were moving.

Nor does television yet play a significant role in African political crises, mainly because the signal range is usually confined to the immediate environs of the capital. In any event the tiny audiences are often predominantly non-African. Nevertheless, television has occasionally been used in a crisis. King Hassan, immediately after the 1971 coup attempt was crushed, made a dramatic late-night television broadcast to the Moroccan people. His audience was restricted to at most 300,000 urban elites in a nation with a population of more than 15 million, but that audience doubtless included virtually every Moroccan of substantial political consequence.

When an African government comes under siege, officials almost universally tend to cut off or suppress the flow of news, despite the obvious public need for reassurance at such times. The more serious and immediate the threat, the less the likelihood of news about it reaching the news media. There are several reasons for this: the lack of public-relations acumen by government officials; the timidity and vulnerability of independent media; and the official attitude that "security" requires that no information be

given out. What results, of course, is an information vacuum. This dangerous vacuum actually invites filling by insurgents broadcasting from a captured radio station.

In the confused and rumor-ridden situation that accompanies a political
crisis, when the government and the local media fail to provide any hard
news, usually the best way to find out what has happened locally is to turn
on a short-wave radio and listen to an international broadcast from BBC
World Service, Voice of America, or a similar source. Audience studies
have found that the overseas broadcasts of the major powers have significant
African audiences, with the BBC preferred in the Anglophonic nations and
the French ORTF favored in Francophonic countries (see § 10.4). Although daily newspapers and periodicals printed in London, Paris, and
other centers supplement the local press in most African capitals, they are
usually seized or banned during a crisis.

Such a time clearly reveals the weakness and inadequacy of the African
news media as independent, reliable sources of objective information as the
West understands their role. But as tools or instruments of government,
the media are significant indeed. Broadcasting, especially, has become an
indispensable means of control and governance, even though officials often
seem to use broadcasting clumsily during times of crisis.

Historical and Demographic Data: Independent States

Nation	Date of Independence	Starting Date Radio	Starting Date TV	Official Language(s)	Literacy Percent	Per Capita GNP in $U.S.
Algeria	1962	1925	1956	Arabic	25	275
Botswana	1966	1965	None	English	20	94
Burundi	1962	1960	None	Kirundi/French	10	60
Cameroon	1960	1941	None	English/French	10–15	150
Central African Republic	1960	1958	None	French	5–10	130
Chad	1960	1955	None	French	5–10	70
Congo	1960	1960	1963	French	20	220
Dahomey	1960	1953	None	French	20	70
Egypt	1922	1926	1960	Arabic	30	188
Equatorial Guinea	1968	None	1968	Spanish	20	290
Ethiopia	Not colonized	1941	1964	Amharic	5	67
Gabon	1960	1959	1963	French	12	325
Gambia	1965	1962	None	English	10	100
Ghana	1957	1935	1965	English	25	262
Guinea	1958	1956	None	French	5–10	104
Ivory Coast	1960	1949	1963	French	30	308
Kenya	1963	1928	1962	English/Swahili	20–25	137
Lesotho	1966	1964	None	Sesotho/English	na	100
Liberia	1847	1959	1964	English	22	196
Libya	1951	1957	1968	Arabic	27	1,601
Malagasy Republic	1960	1931	1967	Malagasy/French	39	106
Malawi	1964	1964	None	English/Chichewe	15	64
Mali	1960	1957	None	French	5	90
Mauritania	1960	1957	None	French/Arabic	1–5	140
Mauritius	1968	1944	1965	English	61	230

Nation	Date of Independence	Starting Date Radio	Starting Date TV	Official Language(s)	Literacy Percent	Per Capita GNP in $U.S.
Morocco	1952	?	1962	Arabic	14	203
Niger	1960	1958	1965	French	5	90
Nigeria	1960	1949	1959	English	25	200
Rhodesia, Southern	(UDI 1965)	1932	1960	English	25–30	255
Rwanda	1962	1965	None	Kinyarwanda/French	10	40
Senegal	1960	1939	1965	French	5–10	186
Sierra Leone	1961	1955	1963	English	10	...
Somalia	1960	1941	None	Somali	5	63
South Africa	1931	1920	None	Afrikaans/English	100 (Whites) 35 (Africans)	740
Sudan	1956	1940	1963	Arabic	10–15	113
Swaziland	1968	1966	None	English/Siswati	36	180
Tanzania	1961	1951	None	Swahili	15–20	98
Togo	1960	1953	None	French	5–10	124
Tunisia	1956	1930	1966	Arabic	30	242
Uganda	1962	1953	1963	English	20–40	116
Upper Volta	1960	1959	1963	French	5–10	50
Zaïre	1960	1940	1966	6 languages	35–40	101
Zambia	1964	1941	1961	English	28	398

SOURCES: Cols. 1, 4, 5, and 6 from USDOS 1972; col. 2 from Bebey 1963, *Africa South of the Sahara* 1972, and local informants; col. 3 from *Television Factbook*, vol. 42, 1972–73, and local informants.

Summary of System Facilities

The following table covers all independent stations and dependent territories on the mainland of Africa. Data on foreign government and missionary stations are not included. Systems statistics constantly change, of course, as the systems themselve grow and evolve. The table should be taken as a rough benchmark for their state of development as of about 1972 and as a broadly valid basis for intersystem comparisons.

Data come in the first instance from the *World Radio-TV Handbook* (*WRTH*, 1973). They were cross-checked against *Broadcasting Stations of the World* (FBIS 1972–73), and *Television Factbook* (1972–73). Other information came from the personal knowledge of local informants, contributors, and the editor. In addition, each administration was invited to provide corrections. Only major unresolved differences in details have been footnoted.

FM and TV transmitters are listed by sites only, inasmuch as their direct-wave propagation is limited essentially to the line-of-sight distance between antenna and horizon. Aggregate transmitter power is given for medium- and short-wave transmitters because power has special significance for long-distance sky-wave reception. Power aggregates are only nominal, however, since transmitters are often operated at below full rated power.

Short-wave transmitters are switched from one frequency to another as propagation conditions change. Sometimes transmitter complements are reported solely in terms of the frequencies employed. This accounting means that the same transmitter may be listed repeatedly, as many times as the different frequencies on which it operates. *WRTH* data vary—some administrations report the number and power of their transmitters separately from the list of frequencies employed; others report lists of frequencies only. The actual number of short-wave transmitters in use can as a rule be deduced from operating schedules, but errors either of understatement or overstatement may have occurred.

In the TV transmitter sites column of the table, plus signs connect primary and low-power repeater sites. In the language column the plus sign indicates that in addition to named languages others are mentioned as "vernaculars" or "dialects." The latter may be assumed in most cases to occupy very little air time. For names of languages see Appendix 5.

Receiver data for TV are in most cases reasonably accurate, but radio data tend to be unreliable. Some reports are based on license data alone, some on estimates alone, some on combinations of indicators. None can account accurately for contraband imports, and sample surveys are too fragmentary and infrequent to be of much help.

Nation or Territory	Transmitters Aggregate Power MW kw.	SW kw.	No. of Sites AM	FM	TV	Languages	Receivers (000's) Radio	TV	Commercial
Afars and Issas	8	4	1	0	1	4	10	3	...
Algeria	3,312 [a]	640	12	0	7+13	4	700	150	...
Angola	160	460	12	9	0	3+9	110	...	R
Botswana	50	20	1	1	0	2	30	...	...
Burundi	1	35	1	0	0	5	100	...	...
Cameroon	21	85	4	0	0	2+	216	...	R
C.A.R.	1	130	1	1	0	5	60	...	R
Chad	1	64	1	0	1	9	70	...	R
Congo	4+	179+	2	0	0	4	70	2	R, TV
Dahomey	51	34	3	0	0	2+	85 [b]	...	R
Egypt	2,820	2,000 [c]	10	0	24+10	36	5,000	575	R, TV
Equatorial Guinea	0	15	2	0	1 [d]	6	75	500 [d]	...
Ethiopia	251	120	3	0	1+2	9	170 [e]	9	R, TV
Gabon	40	124	2	0	2	1	90	5	R
Gambia	0	3.5	1	1	0	6	60	...	
Ghana	0	1,005	2	3	7+4	10	775	25	R, TV
Guinea	100	122	1	0	0	7	100	...	
Ivory Coast	10	135	2	4	4+3	8	200	8	R
Kenya	280	130	3	3	4	16	500	37	R, TV
Lesotho	10	10	1	1	0	2	10	10	R

Nation or Territory	Transmitters					Languages	Receivers (000's)		Commercial
	Aggregate Power		No. of Sites						
	MW kw.	SW kw.	AM	FM	TV		Radio	TV	
Liberia	10	10	1	0	1+2	1+	250	8	R, TV
Libya	2,175	200	6	1	2	4	100	3	..
Malagasy Rep.	11	92	1	0	1+3	3	501	5	R, TV
Malawi	16	130	10	2	0	2	110	..	R
Mali	64	172	2	0	0	8	75	..	..
Mauritania	20	34	1	0	0	5	80	..	R
Mauritius	10	10	1	0	1+3	4	84	23	R, TV
Moçambique	188	593	5	2	0	15	110	1	R
Morocco [t]	1,702	295	12	3	9+5	7	1,500	225	..
Niger	2	8	10	0	1	7	100	5	R
Nigeria	819	611	18	7	7	30	1,550	75	R, TV
Port. Guinea	100	10	1	0	0	1	9	..	..
Rhodesia	118	230	7	0	4	4	215[g]	60[g]	R, TV
Rwanda	0	50	1	1	0	4	50[h]	..	R
Senegal	233	175	8	0	1	11	280[i]	2	R, TV
Sierra Leone	10	10	1	0	1	15	50[j]	5	R
Somalia	0	70	2	0	0	8	60	..	R
South Africa	153	2,080	10	86	0	20	2,350[k]	..	R
Span. Sahara	10	55	2	0	0	2+	12[l]	..	..
Sudan	250	380	1	0	2	9	100	60	R, TV
Swaziland	10	0	1	1		2	50		R

											R
Togo	20	100		2		0	0	6	6	225[m]	…	…
Tunisia	805	250		1	2	0	0	6	6	46	…	…
Uganda	423	7.5		2	6	0	7	3	23	400	80	R, TV
Upper Volta	2	8		6	2	0	5	23	275	15		R, TV
Zaïre	661	370		2	0	1	14	90	100[n]	6.5[n]		R, TV
Zambia	50	152.5		8	3	3	7	11+	100	20		R, TV

a. Includes a 1,500-kw. long-wave transmitter.

b. 1970 data from UNESCO *Statistical Yearbook, 1972; WRTH* has no data.

c. Estimated. Egypt lists 65 short-wave frequencies in use.

d. No TV listed for Equatorial Guinea in *WRTH.* Data from *Television Factbook, 1972–73.*

e. Ethiopia claims 1.5 million radio receivers.

f. Data do not include Spanish enclaves of Ceuta, Melilla, and Sidi Ifni.

g. RBS reports issuing 174,000 radio and 60,000 television receiver licenses in 1973.

h. In 1973 Radio Rwanda claimed 150,000 radio receivers.

i. Senegal claims 2 million radio sets and 3,000 TV sets (August, 1973).

j. Sierra Leone claims 700,000 radio receivers.

k. South Africa claims 4.6 million radio receivers, including Namibia (South-West Africa).

l. 1970 data from UNESCO *Statistical Yearbook, 1972; WRTH* has no data.

m. Mytton (§ 4.2.4) estimates Tanzania has 500,000 radio receivers. Zanzibar data not included.

n. In 1973 the Zaïre Department of National Orientation claimed 8 million radio and 500,000 television receivers.

Languages Used in Broadcasting

A definitive list of broadcast languages cannot be made because of constantly shifting schedules of minor languages. Vernacular broadcasts by guerilla movements and similar propaganda efforts are particularly subject to change. The present list is based on the *World Radio-TV Handbook* for 1973, extensively supplemented with information from local informants and personal knowledge of contributors. Even so, a number of languages listed simply as "vernaculars" or "dialects" have not been identified by name. Spelling and alphabetizing of African languages has been standardized according to the system used by Welmers in a checklist published in *Current Trends in Linguistics* (Welmers 1971). Not all appear in that list in recognizable form, however. No attempt has been made to sort out alternative names or dialect variants. Language names linked by slashes are closely related dialects treated as single languages for purposes of broadcasting. Designation of official national languages, indicated by italicizing the country names, follows the U.S. Department of State listing (USDOS 1972).

Language	Used in Broadcasting by
Afar	Ethiopia, F.T.A.I., Somalia
Afrikaans	Moçambique, *South Africa* (with English), Tanzania
Ajauna	Moçambique
Akan	Ghana
Alur	Uganda
Amharic	Egypt, *Ethiopia,* Somalia
Annobones	Equatorial Guinea
Arabic	*Algeria,* Cameroon, C.A.R., Chad, *Egypt,* Ethiopia, F.T.A.I., Ghana, Guinea, *Libya, Mauritania* (with French), *Morocco,* Nigeria, Senegal, Seychelles, Somalia, *Sudan, Tunisia,* Uganda
Armenian	Egypt
Ateso	Uganda
Attie	Ivory Coast
Bambara	Egypt, Guinea, Mali, Senegal
Baoule	Ivory Coast

Language	Used in Broadcasting by
Baria	Sudan
Basari	Togo
iBembe	Burundi, Zambia
Bengali	Egypt
Berber	Morocco
Beri	Niger
Bete	Ivory Coast
Birom	Nigeria
Boran	Kenya
Bubi	Equatorial Guinea
chiChewa	*Malawi* (with English), South Africa
Chinese	Mauritius
Chinunque	(see chi Nyungwe)
Chuabo	Moçambique
Combe	Equatorial Guinea
Comorian	Comoro Is.
Creole (French)	Seychelles
Dagbane	Ghana
Dankale	Egypt
Dhopadohla	Uganda
Dida	Ivory Coast
Dinka	Sudan
Dioula	Ivory Coast
Djerma	Niger
Dutch	South Africa
Ebue	Ivory Coast
Edo	Nigeria
Efik	Nigeria
Ejagham	Nigeria
Ekpeye	Nigeria
English	Angola, *Ascension I., Botswana,* Burundi, *Cameroon* (with French), Canary Is., C.A.R., Egypt, Equatorial Guinea, Ethiopia, *Gambia, Ghana,* Iyory Coast, *Kenya,* (with Swahili), *Lesotho* (with seSotho), *Liberia,* Libya, Madeira, Malagasy R., *Malawi* (with chiChewa), *Mali, Mauritius,* Morocco, Moçambique, Niger, *Nigeria, Rhodesia,* Rwanda, Senegal, *Seychelles, Sierra Leone, Somalia, South Africa* (with Afrikaans), *St. Helena,* Sudan, *Swaziland* (with isiSwazi), *Tanzania,* Togo, *Tristan Da Cunha, Uganda, Zambia*
Ewe	Ghana
Fang/Pamue	Equatorial Guinea, Ghana
Fante (Fanti)	(see Akan)
French	Algeria, Angola, *Burundi* (with kiRundi), *Cameroon* (with English), *C.A.R., Chad, Comoro Is., Congo, Dahomey,* Egypt, Ethiopia, *F.T.A.I., Gabon,* Gambia, Ghana, *Guinea, Ivory Coast,* Kenya, Lesotho, Liberia, Libya, Madeira, *Malagasy R.* (with Malagasy), *Mali, Mauritania* (with Arabic), Mauritius, Morocco, Moçambique, *Niger,* Nigeria, *Réunion, Rwanda* (with ikinyaRwanda), *Senegal,* Seychelles, South Africa, *Togo,* Uganda, *Upper Volta, Zaïre* (with 5 African languages)

Language	Used in Broadcasting by
Fula	Gambia, Sierra Leone
Fulani (Fulfulde)	Cameroon, Chad, Egypt, Nigeria
Ga	Ghana
Galla (Gallinya)	Ethiopia, Somalia
luGanda	Uganda
German	Egypt, South Africa
Gokana	Nigeria
Gorane	Chad
Gourmantche	Upper Volta
Gouro	Ivory Coast
Gourounsi	Upper Volta
Greek	Egypt
Hassania	Spanish Sahara
Hausa	Cameroon, Egypt, Ghana, Niger, Nigeria, Togo
Hebrew	Egypt
ochiHerero	South Africa
Hindi	Egypt
Hindustani	Kenya, Mauritius
Ibo (Igbo)	Nigeria
Idoma	Nigeria
Igala	Nigeria
Igbira	Nigeria
Ijo	Nigeria
Ikwerre	Nigeria
Indonesian	Egypt
Isoko	Nigeria
Italian	Egypt, Libya, Somalia, Tunisia
Itsekiri	Nigeria
Jola	Gambia
Kabyl	Algeria
Kakwa	Sudan, Uganda
Kalabari	Nigeria
Kalenjin	Kenya
kiKamba	Kenya
Kanembo	Chad
Kanuri	Nigeria
Kaonde	Zambia
Karamojong	Uganda
Khana	Nigeria
Kikuyu	Kenya
Kissi	Sierra Leone
Kisii	Kenya
Kolokuma	Nigeria
kiKongo	Congo, Zaïre
oluKonjo	Uganda
Kono	Sierra Leone
Koranko	Sierra Leone
Krio	Sierra Leone
Kuman	Uganda
Kupsbiny	Uganda

Language	Used in Broadcasting by
ikiKuria	Kenya
Limba	Sierra Leone
Loko	Sierra Leone
siLozi	Zambia
chiLuchasi	Zambia
Lugbarra	Uganda
Luhya	Kenya
chiLunda	Zambia
Luo	Kenya, Uganda
Luvale	Zambia
iMakua	Moçambique
Malagasy	*Malagasy Republic*
Malay	Egypt
Malinke	Guinea
Mandingo	Senegal, Sierra Leone
Mandinka	Gambia
Mandjak	Guinea
Marka	Mali
Masai	Kenya
Masa	Chad
luMasaba	Uganda
Mbunda	Angola, Zambia
Mende	Sierra Leone
kiMeru	Kenya
Moba	Togo
Motti(?)	Ivory Coast
Mundang	Chad
Munukutuba	Congo
Nama	South Africa
isiNdebele	Egypt, Rhodesia
Nembe	Nigeria
liNgala	C.A.R., Congo, Egypt, Zaïre
Nuer	Sudan
Nupe	Nigeria
chiNyanja	Egypt, Moçambique, Rhodesia, Tanzania, Zambia
oruNyoro/ oruToro	Uganda
chiNyungwe	Moçambique
Nzeme	Ghana
Okrike	Nigeria
Ovambo	South Africa
Persian	Egypt
Peul	Mali, Niger, Upper Volta
Poular	Morocco
Pushto	Egypt
Portuguese	Algeria, *Angola,* Cape Verde I., Egypt, Ghana, *Madeira, Moçambique, Portuguese Guinea, São Tomé e Principe,* Senegal, South Africa, Tanzania, Zaïre, Zambia
shiRonga	Moçambique
kiRundi	*Burundi* (with French)

Language	Used in Broadcasting by
Runyakole/ Rugiga	Uganda
Russian	Egypt
kinyaRwanda	*Rwanda* (with French)
oluSamia/ Lunyole/luGwe	Uganda
Sango	C.A.R.
Sara	Chad
Sarahuleh	Gambia
Sarakole	Mauritania, Senegal
Sebei	Uganda
chiSena	Moçambique
Senufo	Ivory Coast, Upper Volta
Serere	Senegal
Shangana	Moçambique
Shangaul	Moçambique
Sherbro	Sierra Leone
Shilluk	Sudan
Shoe	Cameroon
Shona	Egypt, Rhodesia
Shuaile	Moçambique
oluSoga	Uganda
Somali	Egypt, Ethiopia, F.T.A.I., Kenya, *Somalia,* Sudan
Sonrai	Mali
seSotho	Egypt, *Lesotho* (with English), South Africa
Spanish	Canary Is., *Equatorial Guinea,* Egypt, Mali, Morocco, *Spanish Sahara*
Susu	Sierra Leone
kiSwahili	Burundi, Egypt, Ghana, *Kenya* (with English), Rwanda, Somalia, South Africa, *Tanzania,* Zaïre
isiSwati	*Swaziland* (with English)
Swedish	Canary Is.
Tamasheq	Mali, Niger
Tambouri	Chad
Teso	Kenya
Thai	Egypt
Temne	Sierra Leone
Tigre	Ethiopia
Tigrinya	Ethiopia
Tiv	Nigeria
Toucouleur	Mauritania, Senegal
Tshiluba	Zaïre
shiTsonga	South Africa, Zambia
seTswana	Botswana, South Africa
Turkana	Kenya
Turkish	Egypt
Twi	(see Akan)
Urdu	Egypt
Urhobo	Nigeria
chiVenda	South Africa

Language	Used in Broadcasting by
Wolof	Egypt, Gambia, Guinea, Mauritania, Morocco, Senegal
isiXhosa	South Africa
Yakuba	Ivory Coast
Yalunka	Sierra Leone
Yoruba	Dahomey, Egypt, Nigeria
Zande	Sudan
isiZulu	Egypt, South Africa, Tanzania

Bibliography

Bibliography

This bibliography lists only sources cited in the text. Items of a personal and ephemeral nature such as letters and conversations are cited in the text but not listed in the bibliography.

AACC (All Africa Conference of Churches). 1972. "Past Students of A.A.C.C. Training Centre." Mimeographed. Nairobi: AACC, 10 May.

Abshire, David M., and Samuels, Michael A. 1969. *Portuguese Africa: A Handbook*. New York: Praeger.

Academy for Educational Development. 1972. "Educational Technology and the Developing Countries: A Handbook." Produced for the United States Agency for International Development. Loose-leaf. Washington, D.C.: Academy for Educational Development.

Adjangba, Moise. 1968. "L'université radiophonique de Guitarama." *Interstages* (Brussels) 47 (April):14–16.

Advertising Age (New York). 1972. "Profiles of Agencies around the World: Billings, Income, New Accounts." 27 March, pp. 29–94.

Africa Report (Special Issue) (New York). 1960. "Information Media in Mali." 5, no. 9 (September):8–10.

Africa Research Bulletin (Exeter). 1967. "Mali-China (CPR) Radio Transmitter." 4, no. 6 (July):831.

———. 1972a. "Dahomey: New Transmitter." 9, no. 4 (May):2458.

———. 1972b. "UR Tanzania Zanzibar: Agreement for TV Network." 9, no. 4 (May):2459.

———. 1972c. "Latin Script Adopted." 9, no. 10 (November):2650–51.

Africa South of the Sahara. Annual. London: Europa Publications.

African Journalist (Zurich). 1972a. "Africa's 'People Gap.'" 4 (June):1.

———. 1972b. "Training: Practical, or Academic?" 4 (June):9.

———. 1973. "Big Zambia Media Complex." 8 (June):5.

Ainsley, Rosalynde. 1968. *The Press in Africa: Communications Past and Present*. New York: Walker & Co.

Aluko, Olajide. 1971. "The Civil War and Nigerian Foreign Policy." *Political Quarterly* (London) 42:177–90.

Amande, Yapo R. 1963. "L'information en Afrique." *Connaissance de l'Afrique* (Paris), November–December, pp. 3–6.

AMECEA (Association of the Members of the Episcopal Conferences of Eastern Africa). 1971. "Recommendations of the AMECEA Communications Meeting." Mimeographed. Nairobi: AMECEA.

Amira, Charles. 1972. "All African Trade Fair." *COMBROAD* (London) 15:52–53.

Andrews, Linton. 1963. *Problems of an Editor*. London: Oxford University Press.

Arpan, Floyd G. 1970. "Address List, Foreign Journalists Project, U.S. Department of State, 1956–1970." Mimeographed. Bloomington: Indiana University.

Asare, J. K. 1968. "The Role of Engineering in GBC-TV." *Radio and TV Times* (Accra), 26 July, p. 13.

ASBU Review (Cairo). Quarterly. Publication of Arab States Broadcasting Union.

Aske, Sigurd. 1971. "Africa: Christian Continent by 2,000?" *International Christian Broadcasters Bulletin* (Colorado Springs), February, pp. 1, 8.

Aspinall, Richard P. 1971a. *Radio Programme Production: A Manual for Training*. Paris: UNESCO.

————. 1971b. "The Training of Broadcasters in Africa." No. MC/00352/0302. Mimeographed. Paris: UNESCO.

Assoicated Business Consultants (East Africa). 1969. *An Audience Survey Report in Kenya*. Two parts. Prepared for Kenya Ministry of Information and Broadcasting.

————. 1972. "An Audience Survey Report in Uganda." Mimeographed. Kampala: Ministry of Information and Broadcasting.

Awori, Moody. 1964. "Covering the Kenya Independence Celebration." *EBU Review* (Geneva) 87B (September):17–20.

AWRT (American Women in Radio and Television). 1971. "International Women Broadcasters United States Visit." Mimeographed. AWRT.

Axinn, George H., and Axinn, Nancy W. 1969. "Communication among the Nsukka Igbo: A Folk-Village Society." *Journalism Quarterly* 46 (Summer):320–24, 406.

Bancolle, H. R., and Chande, T. C. 1970. "Country Report: Tanzania." In "Proceedings of the Rural Broadcasting Workshop, 2nd to 7th November, 1970." Mimeographed. Lusaka: Ministry of Rural Development.

Barghausen, A. F. 1966. "Medium Frequency Sky Wave Propagation in Middle and Low Latitudes." *Proceedings of the IEEE,* Transactions on Broadcasting BC 12 (June):1–14.

Barghausen, A. F.; Finney, J. W.; and Fisher, R. W. 1967. "Radio Broadcasting on Medium Frequencies." *Broadcast Engineering* (Kansas City, Mo.), October, pp. 20–38.

Barghausen, A. F.; Jacobs, G.; and Lillie, D. A. 1963. "HF Propagation Characteristics in Equatorial Latitudes." In *1963 PTGAG International Symposium on Space Telecommunications, Boulder, Colorado,* pp. 37–41. New York: IEEE.

Barghausen, A. F., and Lillie, D. A. 1965. "Some Evidence of the Influence of Long-Term Magnetic Activity on Medium Frequency Sky Wave Propagation." *Proceedings of the IEEE* 53 (December):2115–16.

Barton, Frank. 1969. *African Assignment: The Story of IPI's Six-Year Training Programme in Tropical Africa.* Zurich: International Press Institute.

Bass, Abraham Z. 1970. "The Impartiality of UN Radio." *Gazette (Deventer)* 16, no. 3:171–78.

BBC (British Broadcasting Corporation). Annual. *BBC Handbook.* London: BBC.

BBC Record. 1968. "Libyan Television: BBC Help at Launching." 63 (December):1–2.

Bean, B. R.; Cahoon, B. A.; Samson, C. A.; and Thayer, G. D. 1966. "A World Atlas of Atmospheric Radio Refractivity." ESSA Monograph no. 1. Washington, D.C.: Department of Commerce.

Bean, B. R., and Dutton, E. J. 1966. "Radio Meteorology." NBS Monograph no. 92. Washington, D.C.: Department of Commerce.

Bebey, Francis. 1963. *La radiodiffusion en Afrique noire.* Paris: Editions St. Paul.

Blair, Thomas L. 1965. *Africa: A Market Profile.* London: Business Publications.

Bled, Cynthia. 1969. "Review of Audience Research in Some Developing Countries of Africa." *Journal of Broadcasting* 13, no. 2 (Spring): 167–80.

Blezard, Dennis. 1969. "A New Educational Mass Media Centre for Addis Ababa." *Educational Television International* (London) 3, no. 3 (September):211–13.

Booker, H. G., and Wells, H. W. 1938. "Scattering of Radio Waves by the F Region of the Ionosphere." *Terrestrial Magnetism and Atmospheric Electricity* 43:249–56.

Botswana. 1969. Ministry of Home Affairs. "Information Media: Policy Directive." Mimeographed. Gaberones: Ministry of Home Affairs, 7 January.

Bower, Alex. 1972. "DXing the New Voices of Africa." *Electronics Illustrated* 15 (May):34–35.

Bower, Roger. 1964. "In Nigeria Talent Is Easiest Problem." *Broadcasting,* 25 May, pp. 106–7.

Briscoe, J. B. 1958. "The Exchange of Broadcasters as an Approach to

International Understanding." *Journal of Broadcasting* 2, no. 3 (Summer):241–46.

Britannica Book of the Year. Annual. Chicago: Encyclopedia Britannica.

Browne, Donald R. 1963. "Radio Guinea: A Voice of Independent Africa." *Journal of Broadcasting* (Philadelphia) 7, no. 2 (Spring): 113–22.

———. 1965. "The Limits of the Limitless Medium: International Broadcasting." *Journalism Quarterly* 42:82–86.

———. 1971. "International Radio Broadcasting: Who Listens." ERIC Document ED 050 581 (September).

Budden, K. G. 1961. *Radio Waves in the Ionosphere.* London: Cambridge University Press.

Canada. 1970. Department of External Affairs. *United Nations: Foreign Policy for Canadians.* Ottawa: Queen's Printer.

———. 1971a. House of Commons. *Minutes of Proceedings and Evidence of the Sub-committee on International Development Assistance of the Standing Committee on External Affairs and National Defence.* 3d sess., 28th Parl., 1970, Issue no. 4, October–December 1970. Ottawa: Queen's Printer.

———. 1971b. ———. *Proceedings of the Committee on External Affairs and National Defence, Sub-committee on International Development Assistance.* 3d sess., 28th Parl., 1970–71, Issue no. 29. Ottawa: Queen's Printer.

———. 1971c. Department of Communications. *Telecommission: Communications and the Canadian Assistance Programme for Developing Countries.* Report of the Telecommunications Study 3 (b). Ottawa: Information Canada.

Carpenter, David. 1971a. "A New Development in Religious Broadcasting." *COMBROAD* (London) 11 (April–June):35–36.

———. 1971b. "Zambia Broadcasting Services: New Transmitter Site." *COMBROAD* (London) 13 (October–December):42.

Cassirer, Henry R. 1971a. "Listening/Viewing Groups: Challenge and Obstacles." *Educational Broadcasting International* (London) 5, no. 1 (March):19–23.

———. 1971b. "The Use of Mass Media in Adult Education in Countries outside the U.S. and Canada: A Literature Review." *Mass Media/Adult Education* 33 (June–July):1–12.

CCIR (International Radio Consultative Committee). 1964. "World Distribution and Characteristics of Atmospheric Radio Noise." Report 322. Geneva: International Telecommunication Union.

———. 1970a. "Standards for Frequency-Modulation Sound Broadcasting in Band 8 (VHF)." Recommendation 412. Geneva: International Telecommunication Union.

———. 1970b. "Feasibility of Sound and Television Broadcasting from

Satellites." Report 215–2. Geneva: International Telecommunication Union.

————. 1970c. "Measurement of Field Strength for VHF (Metric) and UHF (Decimetric) Broadcast Services, Including Television." Report 228–1. Geneva: International Telecommunication Union.

————. 1970d. "Estimation of Tropospheric-Wave Transmission Loss." Report 244–2. Geneva: International Telecommunication Union.

————. 1970e. "Characteristics of Monochrome Television Systems." Report 308–2. Geneva: International Telecommunication Union.

————. 1970f. "Special Problems of HF Radio Communication Associated with the Equatorial Ionosphere." Report 343–1. Geneva: International Telecommunication Union.

————. 1970g. "Feasibility of Direct Broadcasting from Satellites." Report 473. Geneva: International Telecommunication Union.

————. 1970h. "Broadcasting Satellite Service (Sound Broadcasting)." Report 474. Geneva: International Telecommunication Union.

————. 1970i. "Broadcasting-Satellite Service (Television)." Report 475. Geneva: International Telecommunication Union.

CEDO (Centre for Educational Development Overseas). 1971. *First Annual Report, 18th March 1970–31st March 1971*. London: CEDO.

Chad. 1966. "Le premier plan quinquennial de developpement économique et social du Tschad, 1966–1970." Fort Lamy: Government Printer.

Chakroun, Abdallah. 1972. "Maghrebvision." *EBU Review* (Geneva) 23, no. 6 (November):39–42.

Chalmers, T. W. 1962. "Report on a Survey for a Broadcasting Station in Nyasaland." Mimeographed. Zomba: Government of Nyasaland.

Checchi and Co. (Washington, D.C.). 1965. "Report to the Board of Directors of the Liberian Broadcasting Corporation." September.

Chilangwa, Wilfred B. 1970. "The Growth of Educational Television in Zambia." *Educational Television International* (London) 4, no. 1 (March):66–69.

CIDA (Canadian International Development Agency). 1969. *CIDA Annual Review, 1969*. Ottawa: Queen's Printer.

————. "Broadcasts Used to Train Teachers: Canadians Try New Technique to Help Kenya's Teachers." *International Development* 3, no. 2 (February):6.

Clarke, A. G. 1972. "Training and the Commonwealth Fund." *COMBROAD* (London) 14 (January–March):1–4.

Codding, George A., Jr. 1959. *Broadcasting without Barriers*. Paris: UNESCO.

Coleman, W. F.; Popku, A. A.; and Abell, Helen C. 1968. *An African Experiment in Radio Forums for Rural Development: Ghana, 1964–*

1965. Reports and Papers on Mass Communication no. 51. Paris: UNESCO.

Collett, H. O. 1964. "VHF/FM Sound Broadcasting in the Republic of South Africa." Pt. 1, "General Considerations." *EBU Review* (Geneva) 84A (April):55–57.

COMBROAD (London). 1972a. "Lesotho National Broadcasting Service." 14 (January–March):47.

———. 1972b. "Staff Training." 14 (January–March):54.

———. 1972c. "Radio Tanzania, Dar es Salaam: Additional Transmissions." 15 (April–June):42.

———. 1972d. "New Men at the Top." 16 (July–September):44.

———. 1972e. "Eleventh Anniversary of External Service." 17 (October–December):37–38.

———. 1973. "Lesotho National Broadcasting Service: Year of Achievement." 18 (January–March):58.

Commission on Instructional Technology. 1970. *To Improve Learning: A Report to the President and the Congress of the United States*. House Committee on Education and Labor. Washington, D.C.: Government Printing Office.

Communist Affairs. 1964. 2:29. "Communist Radio Propaganda in Africa."

Comstock, George, and Maccoby, Nathan. 1966. *The Peace Corps Educational Television Project in Colombia: Two Years of Research*. 12 vols. Stanford, Calif.: Institute of Communications Research.

Conateh, Swaebou. 1971. "Decimal Currency: RG's Campaign." *COMBROAD* (London) 13 (October–December):42–43.

———. 1972a. "General Gowon Opens Radio Gambia." *COMBROAD* (London) 11 (April–June):29–31.

———. 1972b. "History of Radio Gambia." *COMBROAD* (London) 12 (July–September):41–43.

Condon, John C. 1968. "Some Guidelines for Mass Communications Research in East Africa." *Gazette* (Deventer) 14, no. 2:141–51.

Cooley, John K. 1967. *Baal, Christ, and Mohammed: Religion and Revolution in North Africa*. London: John Murray.

Cooperative Education Centre (Moshi, Tanzania). 1968. *Annual Report, 1967*. Moshi: Cooperative Education Centre.

Copeland, Miles. 1969. *The Game of Nations: The Amorality of Power Politics*. New York: Simon & Schuster.

Crowder, Michael. 1966. *The Story of Nigeria*. Rev. ed. London: Faber & Faber.

Curran, Charles. 1972. "The BBC at Fifty." *COMBROAD* (London) 16 (July–September):3–8.

da Piedade, H. 1963. "Radio Dahomey: The First Ten Years." *EBU Review* (Geneva) 78B (March):6–7.

Darling, Peter. 1970. "On the Carpet: VOK: An Image Problem." *Sunday Nation* (Nairobi), 30 August, pp. 13, 15.

Darlington, Charles, and Darlington, Alice. 1968. *African Betrayal.* New York: David McKay Co.

da Silva, Margarida Moreira. 1968. "The ENR: Portugal's Official Radio Station." *EBU Review* (Geneva) 109B (May):12–16.

Davies, K., and Barghausen, A. F. 1966. "The Effect of Spread F on the Propagation of Radio Waves near the Equator." In *Spread F and Its Effect upon Radiowave Propagation and Communications,* edited by P. Newman. Maidenhead, England: Technivision.

Davis, Griffith J. 1970. "The Challenge of Educational Technology in Underdeveloped Countries." *Audiovisual Instruction* 15, no. 3 (March): 64–67.

Davis, R. M., Jr. 1972. "The Occurrence of Spread F and Its Effect on HF Propagation." Office of Telecommunications, Research and Engineering Report no. 28. Washington, D.C.: Department of Commerce.

Davis, R. M.; Smith, E. K.; and Ellyett, C. D. 1959. "Sporadic E at VHF in the U.S.A." *Proceedings of the IEEE (IRE)* 47 (May):762–69.

Dean, A. M. 1962. "Unique Organisation of the New Kenya Broadcasting Organisation." *EBU Review* (Geneva) 72B (March):32.

de Blij, Harm J. 1971. *Geography: Regions and Concepts.* New York: Wiley.

Deutsch, Karl W., and Merritt, Richard L. 1965. "Effects of Events on International Images." In *International Behavior,* edited by Herbert C. Kelman. New York: Holt, Rinehart & Winston.

Deutsche Welle. 1972. *Handbuch, 1972.* Cologne: Deutsche Welle.

Diamond, Robert A., and Fouquet, David. 1972. "American Military Aid to Ethiopia—and Eritrean Insurgency." *Africa Today* 19, no. 1:27–43.

Dizard, Wilson P. 1966. *Television: A World View.* Syracuse, N.Y.: Syracuse University Press.

Dodge, John. 1972. "Wanted: A Body Representing All Communications." *IPI Report* (Zurich), May/June, pp. 14–15.

Donald, A. H. 1971. "Born in a Prison Cell." *COMBROAD* (London) 13:38–39.

Dougherty, H. T. 1968. "A Survey of Microwave Fading Mechanisms, Remedies, and Applications." ESSA Technical Report ERL 69-WPL 4. Washington, D.C.: Government Printing Office.

Drury, Allen. 1967. *A Very Strange Society.* New York: Trident Press.

Duvignaud, Jean. 1970. *Change at Shebika: Report from a North African Village.* New York: Pantheon.

East Africa Journal (Nairobi). 1967. "Mass Media and Linguistic Communication in East Africa." Summary and conclusions of Seminar on Mass Media Communication, Makerere, Kampala. May, pp. 16–18.

EBU Review (Brussels and Geneva). 1963. "The African VHF/UHF Broadcasting Conference." 80A (August):154–61.

———. 1964. "The Voice of Kenya." 88B (November):45.

———. 1971. "Opening of an HF Transmitting Station." 129A (October):219–20.

———. 1972. "The Arab Broadcasting Union in Brief." 23 (January): 21.

———. 1973. "New Long-Wave Transmitter." 137 (February):81.

EBU Technical Committee. 1972. *Low-Budget Television Service.* Technical Monograph no. 3112. Brussels: EBU.

Elder, Robert E. 1968. *The Information Machine: The United States Information Agency and American Foreign Policy.* Syracuse, N.Y.: Syracuse University Press.

Eisele, Frederick R. et al. 1965. *Area Handbook for Morocco.* American University Foreign Area Studies, DA Pam. 550–49. Washington, D.C.: Government Printing Office.

Elias, T. O. 1971. "The Contribution of Telecommunications and Direct Satellite Broadcasting to Technical Assistance and Nation-Building in the 'New' Countries: An African Viewpoint." In *The International Law of Communications,* edited by Edward McWhinney, pp. 122–37. Dobbs Ferry, N.Y.: Oceana Press.

Emery, Walter B. 1971. "Selected Studies of Broadcast Censorship in Five Countries." *Quarterly Journal of Speech* 57, no. 3 (October):259–65.

Ethiopia. 1963. Imperial Board of Telecommunications. *Telecommunications in Ethiopia: An Historical Review, 1894–1962.* Addis Ababa: IBTE.

———. 1966. Ministry of Information. *Ethiopian Broadcasting Services: Radio and Television Program Schedules, November, 1966.* Addis Ababa: Ministry of Information.

Ettlinger, Harold. 1943. *The Axis on the Air.* Indianapolis, Ind.: Bobbs-Merrill.

Euba, Akin. 1970. "Music Adapts to a Changed World." *Africa Report,* November, pp. 24–27.

Factbook of the Countries of the World. 1970. Background notes reprinted from materials published by the U.S. Department of State. New York: Crown.

Fanon, Frantz. 1965. *Studies in a Dying Colonialism.* New York: Monthly Review Press.

FBIS (Foreign Broadcasting Information Service). 1972. *Broadcasting Stations of the World.* 4 vols. 25th ed. Corrected to 1 July 1972. Washington, D.C.: Government Printing Office.

FCC (Federal Communications Commission). 1972. "Rules and Regulations," Pt. 71, "Radio Broadcast Services." Washington, D.C.: FCC.

Fellows, Lawrence. 1966. "BBC Ordered to End Its Operations in Rhodesia." *New York Times,* 6 April, p. 17.

Ferkiss, Victor C. 1966. *Africa's Search for Identity.* New York: George Braziller.

Finance and Development. 1970. "World Bank Assists Educational TV." 7, no. 2 (June):59.

Findley, Joseph W. O., Jr. 1973. "The Sierra Leone Broadcasting Service." *SLBS Record* 1 (July):1–14.

Fiske, Edward B. 1972. "Missionaries: Why the Call Has Fallen Off." *New York Times,* 12 March, p. 8E.

Fougeyrollas, Pierre. 1967. *Television and the Social Education of Women: A First Report on the Unesco-Senegal Pilot Project at Dakar.* Reports and Papers on Mass Communication no. 50. Paris: UNESCO.

Fraenkel, Peter. 1959. *Wayaleshi: Radio in Central Africa.* London: Weidenfeld & Nicholson.

Franklin, H. 1949. *Report on the Development of Broadcasting to Africans in Central Africa.* Lusaka: Government Printer.

———. 1950. *Report on "The Saucepan Special": The Poor Man's Radio for Rural Populations.* Lusaka: Government Printer.

Frost, J. M. See *WRTH.*

Gallagher, Charles F. 1968. "North African Problems and Prospects: Language and Identity." In *Language Problems of Developing Nations,* edited by Joshua A. Fishman, Charles A. Ferguson, and Jyotirindra Das Gupta, pp. 129–50. New York: Wiley.

Gambia. 1971. *Estimates of Recurrent Revenue and Expenditure with the Development Expenditure, 1971–1972.* Bathurst: Government Printer.

Gartley, John. 1971. "A Procedure to Test Understanding Gained from Instructional Television Programs in Developing Countries." Ph.D. dissertation, University of Michigan.

Gartley, John, and Pendred, Piers. 1971. "Training for Educational Television and Basic Production Training in Ethiopia." *Educational Broadcasting International* (London) 5, no. 4 (December):269–71.

Gaskill, Gordon. 1942. "Voice of Victory." *American Magazine* 134 (December):35.

German Africa Society. 1970. *Commercial Radio in Africa.* Bonn: German Africa Society.

Ghana. N.d. *This Is Ghana Television.* Tema: State Publishing Corp.

———. 1971. *Annual Estimates for 1971–1972.* Accra: Ghana Publishing Corp.

Ghana Information Services. 1965. *Facts on Ghana.* New York: Ghana Information Services.

Ghanaian Times (Accra). 1972. "Varsity Will Now Train Journalists." 4 January, p. 1.

Ginesy, Robert. 1968. "L'information dans les pays en voie de développement l'Afrique francophone." *Institut français de presse,* 7 October 1968, pp. 30–33.

Grant, Douglas. 1965. "Television in Liberia: A Sturdy Newcomer." *EBU Review* (Geneva) 90B (March):20–22.

Grant, Stephen H. 1971. "Educational TV Comes to the Ivory Coast." *Africa Report,* February, pp. 32–33.

Great Britain. 1937. Colonial Office. *Broadcasting Services in the Colonies: Interim Report* ("Plymouth Report"). Colonial no. 139. London: His Majesty's Stationery Office.

———. 1943. ———. *Mass Education in African Society.* Report of the Adult and Mass Education Sub-committee. Colonial no. 186. London: His Majesty's Stationery Office.

———. 1956. ———. *Handbook on Broadcasting Services in the Colonies.* 8th ed. London: Colonial Office.

Green, Timothy. 1972. *The Universal Eye: The World of Television.* New York: Stein & Day.

Greenfield, Richard. 1965. *Ethiopia: A New Political History.* New York: Praeger.

Gueulette, David G. 1971. "The Mass Media in Adult Education in the Developing Countries: A Literature Review." *Mass Media/Adult Education* 34 (August–November):1–9.

Guillard, Jean, 1963. "Gabon Broadcasting and Television Service." *EBU Review* (Geneva) 81B (September):14–15.

Hachten, William A. 1971a. *Muffled Drums: The News Media in Africa.* Ames: Iowa State University Press.

———, comp. 1971b. *Mass Communication in Africa: An Annotated Bibliography.* Madison: Center for International Communications Studies, University of Wisconsin.

Hailey, Lord. 1957. *An African Survey: A Study of Problems Arising in Africa South of the Sahara.* Revised 1956. London: Oxford University Press.

Head, Sydney W. 1968. "The Beginnings of Broadcast Audience Research in Ethiopia." *Journal of Ethiopian Studies* (Addis Ababa) 6, no. 2 (July):77–92.

———. 1972. *Broadcasting in America: A Survey of Television and Radio.* 2d rev. ed. Boston: Houghton Mifflin.

Headland, Frederick H. 1965. "The Malawi Broadcasting Corporation." *EBU Review* (Geneva) 89B (January):24–26.

Healey, Joseph G. 1968. "Survey of Social Communications in Africa." Mimeographed. Nairobi: Association of the Members of the Episcopal Conference of Eastern Africa.

———. 1969. "Survey of Social Communications in Africa: Report No. 2." Mimeographed. Nairobi: Association of the Members of the Episcopal Conference of Eastern Africa.

Henissart, Paul. 1970. *Wolves in the City: The Death of French Algiers.* New York: Simon & Schuster.

Herrick, Allison B. et al. 1967. *Area Handbook for Angola.* American University Foreign Area Studies. Washington, D.C.: Government Printing Office.

————. 1969. *Area Handbook for Mozambique.* American University Foreign Area Studies. Washington, D.C.: Government Printing Office.

Hobbs, Ian. 1971. "French Fury at TV Decision." *Sunday Times* (Johannesburg), 31 October.

Huth, Arno G. 1937. *La radiodiffusion: Puissance mondiale.* Paris: Librarie Gallimard.

————. [1960]. *Communications Media in Tropical Africa.* Washington, D.C.: International Cooperation Administration.

Hutton-Williams, Brett. 1971. "Words as Weapons." *Bulletin of the Africa Institute of South Africa* (Pretoria) 9:217–22.

IBRD (International Bank for Reconstruction and Development). 1971. "Education: Sector Working Paper." Washington, D.C.: IBRD.

ICB Bulletin. 1971. "News Around the World." September, p. 4.

————. 1973. "News Around the World." 2d Quarter, p. 5.

Indiana University. 1967. *Communications Media Project in Nigeria, 1959–1965: Final Report.* Bloomington: Indiana University.

Industries et travaux d'Outre-Mer (Paris). 1968. "Le plan quinquennial 1966–1970 des territoires d'Outre-Mer." 16 (January):16–19.

Interstages (Brussels). 1968a. "Aide financière pour la télévision malgache." 46 (February):24.

————. 1968b. "MERA construit les premier postes de radio rwandais." 47 (April):16–19.

————. 1971. "La radiodiffusion tèlévision marocaine." 70 (February): 4–14.

Ismail, Tareq Y. 1971. *The UAR in Africa: Egypt's Policy under Nasser.* Evanston, Ill.: Northwestern University Press.

ITU (International Telecommunication Union). 1963. *African VHF/ UHF Broadcasting Conference.* Regional agreement for the African broadcasting area. Final protocol, resolutions, and recommendations. Geneva: ITU.

————. 1966. *African LF/MF Broadcasting Conference, Geneva, 1966.* Regional agreement for the African broadcasting area. Protocol, final protocol, resolutions. Geneva: ITU.

————. 1968. *Radio Regulations.* Geneva: ITU.

————. 1972. "Eleventh Report on Telecommunication and the Peaceful Uses of Outer Space." ITU Booklet no. 10. Geneva: ITU.

————. 1973. "Twelfth Report on Telecommunication and the Peaceful Uses of Outer Space." ITU Booklet no. 11. Geneva: ITU.

Ivory Coast. 1969–. Ministry of Education. *Programme d'éducation télévisuelle, 1968–1980.* 8 vols. Paris: Ministry of Education.

Janis, Irving L., and Smith, Brewster M. 1965. "Effects of Education and Persuasion on National and International Images." In *International Behavior,* edited by Herbert C. Kelman, chap. 6. New York: Holt, Rinehart & Winston.

Janvier, Jacques. 1962. "A New Policy toward Short-Wave Broadcasts to Central Africa." *Oversea Quarterly* (London) 3:114–15.

Johnson, Willard R. 1965. "The Cameroun Federation: Political Union between England and French-Speaking Africa." In *French-Speaking Africa: A Search for Identity,* edited by William H. Lewis. New York: Walker & Co.

Kaplan, Irving et al. 1969a. *Area Handbook for Zambia.* American University Foreign Area Studies, DA Pam. 550–75. Washington, D.C.: Government Printing Office.

————. 1969b. *Area Handbook for Somalia.* American University Foreign Area Studies, DA Pam. 550–86. Washington, D.C.: Government Printing Office.

Kenya Colony and Protectorate. 1954. *Report of Kenya Broadcasting Commission, June, 1954.* Nairobi: Government Printer.

————. 1961. *Kenya Gazette Supplement: Ordinances, 1961.* Nairobi: Government Printer.

Kenya Institute of Education. 1970a. "In-Service Course: Headmasters-Tutors Handbook." Mimeographed. Nairobi: Institute of Education.

————. 1970b. "In-Service Course: Unqualified Teachers—Syllabus (April)." Mimeographed. Nairobi: Institute of Education.

Kibaki, Mwai. 1972. "Tough Talking from a Cabinet Minister." Address to International Press Institute Seminar, Nairobi, 1972. *African Journalist* (Zurich) 4 (June):3–5.

King, Peter M. 1971. "Report on the First Commonwealth Sub-Regional Broadcasting Conference for Central and Southern Africa." *Educational Broadcasting International* (London) 5, no. 4 (December):289–90.

Knight, Robert P. 1970. "UNESCO's International Communication Activities." In *International Communication: Media, Channels, Functions,* edited by Heinz-Dietrich Fischer and John C. Merrill, pp. 219–26. New York: Hastings House.

Kracmar, John Z. 1971. *Marketing Research in the Developing Countries: A Handbook.* Praeger Special Studies in International Economics and Development. New York: Praeger.

Kucera, Geoffrey Z. 1968. "Broadcasting in Africa: A Study of Belgian, British, and French Colonial Policies." Ph.D. dissertation, Michigan State University.

Kugblenu, John. 1972. "1971 Audience Research Project." *COMBROAD* (London) 14 (January–March):50–51.

Laves, Walter H. C., and Thomson, Charles A. 1957. *UNESCO: Purpose, Progress, Prospects.* Bloomington: Indiana University Press.

Le Figaro (Paris). 1972 . "La D.A.E.C. deux ans après. . . ." 18 January, p. 21.

Legum, Colin. 1971a. "The Mass Media: Institutions of the African Political System." In *Reporting Africa,* edited by Olav Stokke, pp. 27–38. Uppsala: Scandinavian Institute of African Studies.

————. 1971b. "Tanzania." In *Africa Contemporary Record, 1970– 1971,* edited by Colin Legum. London: Rex Collinge.

Le Vine, Victor T. 1971. *The Cameroon Federal Republic.* Rev. ed. Ithaca, N.Y.: Cornell University Press.

Lewis, I. M., ed. 1966. *Islam in Tropical Africa.* Studies presented and discussed at the Fifth International African Seminar, Ahmadu Bello University, Zaria, January 1964. London: Oxford University Press.

Libyan Arab Republic. 1970. Ministry of Information. *Achievements of the 1st of September Revolution.* Tripoli: Ministry of Information.

Lipsky, George A. 1962. *Ethiopia: Its People, Its Society, Its Culture.* New Haven, Conn.: HRAF Press.

Loya, A. 1962. "Radio Propaganda of the United Arab Republic: An Analysis." *Middle Eastern Affairs* (London) 13, no. 4 (April):98–110.

Luthe, H. O. 1969. "Consultant Report, Institute of Mass Communication, Cairo University." Mimeographed. Paris: UNESCO.

Luttwak, Edward. 1968. *Coup d'état: A Practical Handbook.* New York: Fawcett American Library.

LWF (Lutheran World Federation). 1970. Broadcasting Service. *Report, 1963–1969.* Prepared for the Fifth Assembly of the Lutheran World Federation, Brazil, 1970. Geneva: LWF.

McDonald, Gordon C. et al. 1969. *Area Handbook for Burundi.* American University Foreign Area Studies. Washington, D.C.: Government Printing Office.

————. 1971a. *Area Handbook for the Democratic Republic of the Congo.* American University Foreign Area Studies. Washington, D.C.: Government Printing Office.

————. 1971b. *Area Handbook for People's Republic of the Congo (Congo-Brazzaville).* American University Foreign Area Studies, DA Pam. no. 55–91. Washington, D.C.: Government Printing Office.

Mackay, Ian K. 1964. *Broadcasting in Nigeria.* Ibadan: University Press.

McKay, Vernon. 1971. "The Propaganda Battle for Zambia." *Africa Today* 18, no. 2:18–26.

Maclin, H. T. 1966. "Religious Broadcasting in Africa." *EBU Review* (Geneva) 97B (May):53–58.

McNelly, John T. 1970. "Mass Communication in the Development Process." In *International Communication: Media, Channels, Functions,* edited by Heinz-Dietrich Fischer and John C. Merrill, pp. 158–65. New York: Hastings House.

Maddison, John. 1971. *Radio and Television in Literacy: A Survey of the Use of the Broadcasting Media in Combating Illiteracy among Adults.* Reports and Papers on Mass Communication no. 62. Paris: UNESCO.

Malawi. 1964. *Malawi Broadcasting Corporation Ordinance, 1963.* Zomba: Government Printer.

———. 1971. National Statistical Office. *Radio Listenership Survey, August, 1970–January, 1971.* Zomba: Government Printer.

Marathey, R. M. 1968. "Togo: Radio éducative, January, 1964–March, 1968." Mimeographed. Paris: UNESCO.

Marathey, R. M., and Bourgeois, Michel. 1965. "Training for Rural Broadcasting in Africa." In *Radio Broadcasting Serves Rural Development,* pt. 2, pp. 32–50. Paris: UNESCO.

Marco Surveys. 1965. "A Media Effectiveness Survey." Prepared for Radio Uganda. Nairobi: Marco Surveys.

———. 1966. *Public Opinion Poll. No. 14: Comparative Change in Public Opinion, 1964–1966.* Nairobi: Marco Surveys.

Maro, Violet. 1971. "Training of Instructors," and "Departmental Reorganization." *COMBROAD* (London) 11 (April–June):33.

Marshall, J. L. 1969. *Technical Improvements to Radio Broadcasting Nigeria.* Lagos: Federal Ministry of Information.

Mass Media/Adult Education. 1972. "Commentary." 35 (Summer): 5–10; 36 (Fall):6–13.

MBC (Malawi Broadcasting Corporation). 1967. "Third Annual Report and Statement of Accounts for the Year Ended 31st December 1966." Mimeographed. Blantyre: MBC.

———. 1969. "Malawi Broadcasting Corporation Survey: Phase One (Preliminary)." Mimeographed. Blantyre: MBC.

———. 1970a. "Rate Schedule Number Eight." Mimeographed. Blantyre: MBC.

———. 1970b. "Sixth Annual Report and Statement of Accounts for the Year Ended 31st December 1969." Mimeographed. Blantyre: MBC.

———. 1971. "Seventh Annual Report and Statement of Accounts for the Year Ended 31st December 1970." Mimeographed. Blantyre: MBC.

Merrill, John C. 1971. "The Role of the Mass Media in National Development: An Open Question for Speculation." *Gazette* (Deventer) 17, no. 4:236–42.

Middle East and North Africa, 1971–1972. 1972. London: Europa Publications.

Millar, James. 1972. "Three Years in Sierra Leone." *COMBROAD* (London) 16 (July–September):35–37.

Milton, Ralph. 1968. *Radio Programming*. London: World Association for Christian Communication.

Mlatie, Stephen. 1969. "Radio in Rural Development." In *Seminar on Radio in Rural Development*. Berlin: Foundation for Developing Countries.

Mobley, Harris W. 1970. *The Ghanaian's Image of the Missionary: An Analysis of the Published Critiques of Christian Missionaries by Ghanaians, 1897–1965*. Leiden: E. J. Brill.

Mozayen, Abdu. 1967. "Ethiopian Schools Television: Comments on Schools Reports." Addis Ababa: Ministry of Education and Fine Arts.

Multimedia Zambia. 1972. "With One Voice: Report for 1971." Lusaka: Multimedia Zambia.

Mumanyi, Arnold. 1971. "Training Institute." *COMBROAD* (London) 12 (July–September):36–37.

Mytton, Graham L. 1968. "Tanzania: The Problems of Mass Media Development." *Gazette* (Deventer) 14, no. 2:89–100.

———. 1970. "Mass Media and TANU: Information Flow in Tanzania and Its Relevance to Development." In *Proceedings of the 1st Annual Conference of the Provisional Council for Social Sciences in East Africa*. Dar es Salaam: University of Dar es Salaam.

———. [1971]a. "National Mass Media Audience Survey: The Major Towns." Zambia Broadcasting Services Research Project, Research Reports and Papers no. 2. Mimeographed. Lusaka: University of Zambia Institute for African Studies.

———. 1971b. "Audience Research in Zambia." *COMBROAD* (London) 11 (April–June):5–6.

———. 1972a. "Report on the National Mass Media Audience Survey, 1970–1971." Zambia Broadcasting Services Research Project, Research Reports and Papers no. 3. Mimeographed. Lusaka: University of Zambia Institute for African Studies.

———. 1972b. "Audience Research in Zambia." *COMBROAD* (London) 16 (July–September):24–25.

NAEB (National Association of Educational Broadcasters). 1968. *Educational Television and Educational Development in Tunisia*. Prepared for the Agency for International Development. Washington, D.C.: NAEB.

Naesselund, Gunnar R. 1971a. "Report on a Mission to the Kenya Institute of Mass Communication, May 15–24, 1971." No. MC/1628/5/7/71. Mimeographed. Paris: UNESCO.

———. 1971b. "Report on a Mission to Kenya, Tanzania, Zambia, Uganda, May 15–June 2, 1971." Mimeographed. Paris: UNESCO.

———. 1973. "International Problems of Television via Satellite: A Major Debate at UNESCO's Recent General Conference." *UNESCO Courier* (Paris), February, pp. 21–23.

Natesh, A. M. 1971. "Radio Farm Forum in Zambia." *COMBROAD* (London) 13 (October–December):19–21.

———. 1972. *Organisation of Literacy Broadcasting in Zambia: A Manual.* Lusaka: Republic of Zambia.

Negarit Gazeta (Addis Ababa). 1962. "Order No. 28 of 1962, to Amend the Central Personnel Agency and Public Service Order." 22, no. 6 (19 December):33–69.

———. 1966. "Order No. 46 of 1966, to Define the Powers and Duties of Our Ministers." 25, no. 23 (27 July):131–45.

———. 1968. "Order No. 50 of 1968, to Provide for the Creation of the Ethiopian Broadcasting Service." 27, no. 15 (6 June):90–93.

———. 1971. "Proclamation No. 286 of 1971: Budget Proclamation for the Government Services." 30, no. 25 (20 July):192–226.

Nelson, Harold D. et al. 1972. *Area Handbook for Chad.* American University Foreign Area Studies Series. DA Pam. 550–159. Washington, D.C.: Government Printing Office.

New York Times. 1927. "New Radio Station for French Equatorial Africa." 19 May, p. 32.

———. 1960. "France Objects to Ban on Use of VOA by Third Party." 7 January, p. 9.

———. 1972. "Mobutu Gives an Ultimatum to Catholics." 8 March, p. 3.

———. 1973. "Soviet Assails 'Sesame Street' as Imperialistic." 17 August, p. 6.

Newsletter. Nigerian National Mass Communications Council. Issued irregularly in Lagos, starting 15 June, 1972.

Newsom, Carroll V. 1973. "Communication Satellites: A New Hazard to World Cultures." *Educational Broadcasting Review* 7, no. 2 (April): 77–85.

Nigeria (Federal Republic). 1970. *Nigeria Handbook, 1970.* Lagos: Federal Ministry of Information.

Nigerian Broadcasting Corporation. 1967. *NBC: Ten Years of Service.* Lagos: NBC.

———. 1972. *Radio Broadcasts to Schools: Annual Programme Guide, 1972.* Lagos: NBC.

Nsibambi, Apolo. 1971. "Language Policy in Uganda: An Investigation into Costs and Politics." *African Affairs* (London) 70 (January):62–71.

Nugent, John P. 1967. "A New Light for the Dark Continent." *TV Guide,* 18 February, pp. 18–21.

Nyerere, Julius K. 1969. *Freedom and Socialism: Uhuru na Ujamaa.* Dar es Salaam: Oxford University Press.

Nyrop, Richard F. et al. 1969. *Area Handbook for Rwanda.* American University Foreign Area Studies. Washington, D.C.: Government Printing Office.

———. 1972. *Area Handbook for Morocco.* American University Foreign Area Studies. Washington, D.C.: Government Printing Office.

O'Barr, William M.; Spain, David H.; and Tessler, Mark A., eds. 1973. *Survey Research in Africa: Its Applications and Limits.* Evanston, Ill.: Northwestern University Press.

Olusola, Segun. 1971. "What Does an African Expect from Film and Television?" Paper prepared for Seminar on Television and Society, Berlin.

Onder, James J. 1971. "The Sad State of Vatican Radio." *Educational Broadcasting Review* 5, no. 4 (August):43–53.

Ornstein, Jacob. 1964. "Africa Seeks a Common Language." *Review of Politics* 26 (April):205–14.

Osborne, B. W. 1952. "Note on Ionospheric Condition Which May Affect Tropical Broadcasting after Sunset." *Journal of the British IRE* (London) 12:110.

Patrick, P. E. 1962. "Broadcasting in the Republic of South Africa." *EBU Review* (Geneva) 73B (May):13–16.

Patterson, Sheila. 1957. *The Last Trek.* London: Routledge & Kegan Paul.

Phillips, G. D., and Knight, D. 1965. "Effects of Polarization on a Medium Frequency Sky-Wave Service, Including the Case of Multi-Hop Paths." *Proceedings of the IEE* (London) 112 (January): 31–39.

Ploman, Edward. 1972. *A Guide To Satellite Communication.* Reports and Papers on Mass Communication no. 66. Paris: UNESCO.

Ploman, E. W.; Berrada, A.; and Clergerie, B. 1971. "The Use of Satellite Communication for Education and National Development in Arab States." Mimeographed. Paris: UNESCO.

Pohle, Heinz. 1955. *Der Rundfunk als Instrument der Politik.* Hamburg: Hans Bredow Institut.

Powdermaker, Hortense. 1962. *Coppertown: Changing Africa—the Human Situation on the Rhodesian Copperbelt.* New York: Harper & Row.

Powell, Jon T. 1969. "U.S. Television and Southern Rhodesia: An Issue of Basic Rights." *Federal Communications Bar Journal* 23, no. 2: 122–39.

Quarmyne, A. T., and Bebey, F. 1967. "Training for Radio and Television in Africa." No. COM/WS/64. Mimeographed. Paris: UNESCO.

Radio and TV Times (Accra). 1970a. "Course for Radio Operators at GBC." 7 August, pp. 12–13.

———. 1970b. "Rural Broadcasting: Accra is Venue for Training Centre." 30 October, pp. 12–13.

Radio Voice of the Gospel. 1972. Department of Audience Research. *Report on Audience Research in Ethiopia.* Geneva: Lutheran World Federation Broadcasting Service.

Rao, N. S. Subba, and Somayajuler, Y. V. 1949. "A Peculiar Type of Rapid Fading in Radio Reception." *Nature* (London) 163 (March): 442–43.

RBC (Rhodesian Broadcasting Corporation). 1970. "Broadcasting in the Seventies." Salisbury: Government Printer.

————. 1971. *Seventh Annual Report, 1970–71.* Salisbury: Government Printer.

Reed, James R. 1970. "The Interaction of Government, Private Enterprise, and Voluntary Agencies in the Development of Broadcasting in the Republic of Liberia from 1950 to 1970: An Historical and Descriptive Study." Master's thesis, Temple University.

Reed, Jane, and Grant, Jim. 1968. *Voice under Every Palm: The Story of Radio Station ELWA.* Grand Rapids, Mich.: Zondervan.

Reese, Howard C. et al. 1970. *Area Handbook for the Republic of Tunisia.* American University Foreign Area Studies. Prepared by Systems Research Corp. Washington, D.C.: Government Printing Office.

Remtulla, Khatun, and Barrett, Hugh. 1971. "Toward Mass Education." In "Third Conference of the African Adult Education Association, April 19–24, 1971." Mimeographed. Dar es Salaam: University of Dar es Salaam.

Research Bureau Limited. 1970. "Media Exposure and Image Enquiry." Prepared for the German Consortium. London: Research Bureau Limited.

Rhodesia Television Limited. 1971. "Rhodesia Television Limited: Reports and Accounts, June 30, 1971." Salisbury: Rhodesia Television Limited.

Rice, P. L.; Longley, A. G.; Norton, K. A.; and Barsis, A. P. 1967. "Transmission Loss Predictions for Tropospheric Communications Circuits." 2 vols. NBS Technical Note no. 101 (rev.). Washington, D.C.: Department of Commerce.

Riegel, Oscar W. 1972. "Communications and Nations." In *Studies of Broadcasting: An International Annual of Broadcasting Science,* edited by H. Eguchi and H. Ichinohe, pp. 5–26. Tokyo: Nippon Hoso Kyokai.

Rimmerman, M., and Olusola, Segun. 1961. "1961 Lalupon Omi Adio Communications Project: Case Study of the Impact of TV on a Nigerian Village." Mimeographed. Syracuse, N.Y.: Syracuse University.

Rogers, Everett M., and Shoemaker, F. Floyd. 1971. *Communication of Innovations: A Cross-Cultural Approach.* 2d ed. New York: Free Press.

Roos, Gideon. 1954. "Broadcasting in South Africa." *Finance and Trade Review* (Pretoria) 1 (July):38–48.

Rosenthal, Eric, ed. 1961. *Encyclopedia of Southern Africa.* New York: Frederick Warne & Co.

Rowlands, D. G. H. 1971. "Journalism Training in the Third World." Address at International Press Institute meeting, Helsinki.

RTD (Radio Tanzania Dar es Salaam). 1968. "Radio and Television Services of National Development." Mimeographed. Dar es Salaam: RTD.

————. 1972a. "Frequency Schedules Effective 16th April 1972." Mimeographed. Dar es Salaam: RTD.

————. 1972b. "Utaratibu wa Vipindi kwa Wiki ya 19." Mimeographed. Dar es Salaam: RTD.

RTV International. 1970. *V.O.K. Development Project: Final Report.* New York: RTV International.

Rubin, Ronald I. *The Objectives of the U.S. Information Agency: Controversies and Analysis.* New York: Praeger.

Rundfunk und Fernsehen (Hamburg). 1968. "Botswana." 16:335.

————. 1971a. "Kenia Hörfunk." 19:224.

————. 1971b. "Swasiland: Hörfunk." 19:373.

————. 1972a. "Afrika Allgemein." 20:102.

————. 1972b. 'Madagaskar Hörfunk." 20:103.

————. 1972c. "Kenia Allgemein." 20:102.

————. 1972d. "Kongo Fernsehen." 20:102.

SABC (South African Broadcasting Corporation). 1962. "SABC Annual Report, 1961." *EBU Review* (Brussels) 75A (October):237–38.

Salisbury, Reg. 1973. "Radio Botswana: Schools Broadcasting." *COMBROAD* (London) 18 (January–March):51.

Sarikoki, I. M. 1967. "Educational Broadcasting 1967: Secretary's Progress Report to the Advisory Committee." Dar es Salaam: RTD.

SAUK/SABC Bulletin (Johannesburg). 1967. "To Stimulate, to Inform, and to Entertain." 15 May, p. 42.

————. 1968. "The Reverend Matthew." 5 February, p. 42.

Schaar, Stuart H. 1968. "The Mass Media in Morocco." *American Universities Field Staff Reports, North Africa Series* 14, no. 2.

Schnaible, Raimund. 1967. *Missbrauchte Mikrofone.* Vienna: Europa Verlag.

Schramm, Wilbur. 1964. *Mass Media and National Development: The Role of Information in the Developing Countries.* Stanford, Calif.: Stanford University Press.

Schramm, Wilbur et al. 1967. *The New Media: Memo to Educational Planners.* Based on a research project financed through a contract with the U.S. Agency for International Development. Paris: UNESCO-International Institute for Educational Planning.

Schramm, Wilbur; Nelson, Lyle M.; and Sommerlad, E. Lloyd. 1969. *A Plan for Developing Training for the Mass Media in East Africa.* Report to U.S. Agency for International Development, UNESCO, and the Governments of the Nations of East Africa. Rev. rept.

SCOPE. 1969. Market and Opinion Research. *Media Survey in Ethiopia.* Lucerne: SCOPE.

Shaaban, Mahmoud. 1971. Address delivered at Seminar on Rural Broadcasting, Arab States Broadcasting Union, Cairo, 27 November–16 December 1971.

Sherrington, Richard, and Gartley, John. 1969. "Evaluation and Testing in Educational Television in Ethiopia." *Educational Television International* (London) 3, no. 2 (July):152–55.

Singleton, Thomas. 1971. "CEDO Moves into Educational Radio: A Definition of Purpose." *Educational Broadcasting International* (London) 5, no. 1 (March):28–31.

SIPRI (Stockholm International Peace Research Institute). 1971. *The Arms Trade with the Third World.* New York: Humanities Press.

Smith, Don D. 1970–71. "Student Audiences for International Broadcasts." *Journal of Broadcasting* (Philadelphia) 15:69–70.

Smith, E. K. 1957. "Worldwide Occurrence of Sporadic-E." NBS Circular no. 582. Washington, D.C.: Department of Commerce.

Somalia. 1968. Ministry of Information. *The Development of Broadcasting in Somalia.* Compiled by Suleiman Mohammed Adam. Mogadishu: Government Printing Press.

Stanton, Frank. 1972. "Will They Stop Our Satellites?" *New York Times,* 22 October, p. D23.

Stevens, B. J. 1964. "VHF/FM Sound Broadcasting in the Republic of South Africa." Pt. 2; "Network Design." *EBU Review* (Geneva) 84A (April):58–62.

Stoddard, Theodore L. et al. 1971. *Area Handbook for the Indian Ocean Territories.* Prepared for the American University by the Institute for Cross-Cultural Research. DA Pam. 150–154. Washington, D.C.: Government Printing Office.

Stokke, Olav. 1971. "Mass Communications in Africa: Freedoms and Functions." In *Reporting Africa,* edited by Olav Stokke, pp. 65–115. New York: Africana Publishing Co.

Streek, F. E. 1971. "Media Research in South Africa." *Communications in Africa* (Grahamstown) 1, no. 1 (May):11–18.

Svendsen, Knut, and Teisen, Merete. 1969. *Self-reliant Tanzania.* Dar es Salaam: Tanzania Publishing House.

Swedish Telecommunication Consulting AB. 1972. *Systems Survey for the National Broadcasting and Information Networks: Final Report.* 4 vols. Prepared for the Republic of Kenya Ministry of Information and Broadcasting.

Syracuse University. 1968. "Final Report: 1968 Multi-national Foreign Broadcasters Project." Mimeographed. Syracuse, N.Y.: Syracuse University.

Tanganyika. 1967. *Five-Year Plan for Economic and Social Development, 1st July 1964–30th June 1969.* 2 vols. Dar es Salaam: Government Printer.

Tanganyika Broadcasting Corporation. 1960. "Audience Survey Report, May, 1960." Mimeographed. Nairobi: Market Research Company of East Africa.

TANU (Tanganyika African National Union). 1967. *Arusha Declaration.* Dar es Salaam: TANU.

Tanzania. Annual. *Estimates of Revenue and Expenditure* [title varies]. Dar es Salaam: Government Printer.

————. Sessional. *Parliamentary Debates.* Dar es Salaam: Government Printer.

————. 1969. *Second Five-Year Development Plan for Economic and Social Development, 1st July, 1969–30th June, 1974.* 5 vols. Dar es Salaam: Government Printer.

Telecommunication Journal (Geneva). 1969a. "Dakar: First ITU Seminar on Improvement of Sound and Television Broadcasting in Africa." 36, no. 8 (August):360–65.

————. 1969b. "Some Statistics and General Information on the Implementation of Projects Administered by the ITU." 36, no. 11 (November):523–27.

————. 1970. "Telecommunications and Education." 37, no. 7 (July):67.

————. 1971. "Seminar on the Planning of Broadcasting Systems in Africa." 38, no. 7 (July):507–8.

Television Factbook. Annual. Washington, D.C.: Television Digest.

This Is GBC (Accra). 1971. "Radio and Television Audience Research." 1, no. 1 (25 September):1, 8.

Thomas, Mégnassan. 1969. "Les problèmes de l'information en Dahomey." *Interstages* (Brussels) 55 (1 April):1–11.

Thomasi, Marcel L. 1970. "A Report on Broadcasting in The Gambia, 1942–1970." Mimeographed. Bathurst: Information and Broadcasting Department.

Thompson, Marion E. 1971. "A Study of International Television Programming within the Structure of Global Communications." Ph.D. dissertation, University of Wisconsin.

Thompson, Virginia, and Adloff, Richard. 1960. *The Emerging States of French Equatorial Africa.* Stanford, Calif.: Stanford University Press.

————. 1968. *Djibouti and the Horn of Africa.* Stanford, Calif.: Stanford University Press.

Thompson, Willard. 1969. *Ghana's Foreign Policy, 1957–1966.* Princeton, N.J.: Princeton University Press.

Tickton, Sidney G. 1972. "Instructional Technology in the Developing World." *Educational Broadcasting Review* 6, no. 2 (April):97–104.

Time. 1958. "Voice of Venom." 3 March, pp. 28–29.

————. 1971. "Foreign Aid: Scrambling to the Rescue." 15 November, pp. 13–15.

Times (London). 1966. "Salisbury Jams New Radio." 26 July, p. 9.

Trimmingham, J. Spencer. 1964. *Islam in East Africa.* Oxford: Clarendon Press.

Twining, E. F.; Brashern, W. K.; and Richards, C. A. L. 1939. *Broadcasting Investigations.* Entebbe: Government Printer.

Tyler, Ralph. 1966. "Television around the World." *Television Magazine,* October, p. 32.

Uganda. 1959. Ministry of Information and Broadcasting. *Uganda Information Report: Annual Report for 1958.* Entebbe: Government Printer.

———. [1966]. *Work for Progress: The Second Five-Year Plan, 1966–1971.* [Entebbe: Government Printer].

———. 1971. *Uganda's Third Five-Year Plan, 1971/2–1975/6.* Entebbe: Government Printer.

———. 1972. "Problems Arising from Bringing into Service the Medium Wave Regional Broadcasting Transmitters." Report and Recommendations of the Sub-Committee Appointed by The Permanent Secretary of the Ministry of Information and Broadcasting. Mimeographed. Kampala: Ministry of Information and Broadcasting.

Ullendorf, Edward. 1960. *The Ethiopians: An Introduction to Country and People.* London: Oxford University Press.

Ulmer, Eugen. 1971. "The Revisions of the Copyright Conventions." *EBU Review* (Geneva) 130B (November):86–98.

UNESCO (United Nations Educational, Scientific and Cultural Organization). Annual. *Statistical Yearbook.* Paris: UNESCO.

———. 1951. *Press, Film, Radio.* Reports on the Facilities of Mass Communication no. 5. Paris: UNESCO.

———. 1961a. "Report of the Meeting on Educational Broadcasting in Tropical Africa, Moshi, Tanganyika, 11–16 September, 1961." MC/43. Paris: UNESCO.

———. 1961b. *Mass Media in Developing Countries.* Reports and Papers on Mass Communication no. 33. Paris: UNESCO.

———. 1962. *Developing Information Media in Africa: Press, Radio, Film, Television.* Reports and Papers on Mass Communication no. 37. Paris: UNESCO.

———. 1963a. "Stage d'études sur le radiodiffusion éducative, Bamako, Mali, 18 Novembre–23 Decembre 1963: Documents de travail." Paris: UNESCO.

———. 1963b. *Statistics on Radio and Television, 1950–1960.* Paris: UNESCO.

———. 1964. "Meeting on the Introduction and Development of Television in Africa, Lagos, Nigeria, 21–29 September 1964." MC/51. Paris: UNESCO.

———. 1965. *Professional Training for Mass Communication.* Reports and Papers on Mass Communication no. 45. Paris: UNESCO.

———. 1966. "Meeting of Experts on the Use of Space Communication by the Mass Media, Paris, 6–10 December 1965." UNESCO/MC/52. Paris: UNESCO.

———. 1967. *Radio and Television in the Service of Education and*

Development in Asia. Reports and Papers on Mass Communication no. 49. Paris: UNESCO.

————. 1968. "Meeting of Experts on the Use of Space Communication for Broadcasting, 24–26 January, 1968." Paris: UNESCO.

————. 1969. "Seminar on the Use of the Mass Media for Social Education in Urban Areas of Africa, Dakar, 27 January–1 February 1969: Final Report." Paris: UNESCO.

————. 1970a. "Colloque sur l'emploi des moyens d'information pour le développement rural en Afrique, Dakar/Kaolack, Sénégal, 2–8 Decembre 1970: Rapport final." Paris: UNESCO.

————. 1970b. *Mass Media in Society: The Need of Research.* Reports and Papers on Mass Communication no. 59. Paris: UNESCO.

————. 1970c. "Schools of Journalism and Communications Research Centres." Com/WS/134. Mimeographed. Paris: UNESCO.

————. 1971. "Educational Broadcasting in Eastern Africa." Report from a UNESCO Workshop in Nairobi, Kenya, 16 November–11 December 1970. Paris: UNESCO.

UNESCO-International Institute for Educational Planning. 1967. *New Educational Media in Action: Case Studies for Planners.* 3 vols. Paris: UNESCO–IIEP.

United Nations. 1971. "Report of the Secretary General." A/C.5/1320/ Rev. 1. New York: United Nations.

University of Dakar. [1971]. Centre d'études des sciences et téchniques de l'information. "Organisation des études de la 3d année du C.E.S.T.I.: Avant projet." Mimeographed. Dakar: University of Dakar.

University of Dar es Salaam. 1972. Institute of Adult Education. "Preliminary Results of the Evaluation of 'Wakati wa Furaha'." Mimeographed. Dar es Salaam: Institute of Adult Education.

University of Missouri. 1970. *Final Report: Malawi Communications Project.* Contract AID/AFR 353. Columbia: University of Missouri.

University of Wisconsin. 1969. "Radio Correspondence Education: End of Tour Report of Arthur S. Krival, Chief of Party." Contract AID/ AFR 482. Mimeographed. Madison: University of Wisconsin.

URTNA (Union of National Radio and Television Organizations). 1967. *Statutes.* Dakar: URTNA.

USAID (United States Agency for International Development). 1972. *Introduction to FY 1973: Development and Humanitarian Assistance.* Program Presentation to Congress. Washington, D.C.: AID.

U.S. Congress. 1971. House, Committee on Appropriations. *Departments of State, Justice, and Commerce, the Judiciary, and Related Agencies: Hearing on Appropriations for 1972.* Pt. 4. 92d Cong., 1st Sess.

USDOS (United States Department of State). 1971. "Background Notes: Angola." Washington, D.C.: Government Printing Office.

————. 1972. "The U.S. Role in African Development." *Current Foreign Policy,* August.

USIA (United States Information Agency). 1960a. Research and Reference Service. "Overseas Television Developments." Mimeographed. Washington, D.C.: USIA.

————. 1960b. ————. "Radio Listening in Four West African Cities." No. PMS-43. Mimeographed. Washington, D.C.: USIA.

————. 1961. ————. "Basic Attitudes and General Communication Habits in Four West African Capitals." No. PMS-51. Mimeographed. Washington, D.C.: USIA.

————. 1962. ————. "Communist Propaganda Activities in Africa, 1961." Mimeographed. Washington, D.C.: USIA.

————. 1963. ————. "Media Use among Africans in Nairobi, Kenya." R-91-63. Mimeographed. Washington, D.C.: USIA.

————. [1964]a. ————. "A Listing of Unclassified USIA Survey Research Reports, March 1955–July 1964." Mimeographed. Washington, D.C.: USIA.

————. 1964b. ————. "Voice of America Transistor Contest: French to Africa." No. R-72-64. Washington, D.C.: USIA.

————. 1966a. Office of Policy and Research. "Mass Media Habits in West Africa." No. R-64-66. Washington, D.C.: USIA.

————. 1966b. ————. "East Africa Media Survey" Pt. 1, "Comparative Media Use and Listening to Foreign Radio Stations." No. R-122-66. Mimeographed. Washington, D.C.: USIA.

————. 1969. ————. "Analysis of Letters: Swahili Service 'Lucky Bag' Contest." No. R-72-64. Mimeographed. Washington, D.C.: USIA.

————. 1971a. Office of Research and Assessment. "USIA Survey Research Reports Declassified Between August 1964 and January 1970." Mimeographed. Washington, D.C.: USIA.

————. 1971b. ————. Memorandum M-24-71. Mimeographed. Washington, D.C.: USIA.

————. 1972. ————. "Important Developments in Communist World Broadcasting." No. R-1-72. Mimeographed. Washington, D.C.: USIA.

van den Berghe, Pierre L. 1968. "Africa's Language Problem: Too Many, Too Late!" *Trans-Action* 6 (November):48–54.

Van Deusen, Robert E. 1968. "A Study of a Church-related International Broadcasting Project in Addis Ababa, Ethiopia." Ph.D. dissertation, American University.

Vice, R. W. "A Survey of Ground Wave Propagation Conditions in South Africa." *IEE Transactions of South Africa* (Marshalltown) 45 (April): 139–50.

Voice of America. 1970. "Audience Mail Report." No. 7010. Washington, D.C.: VOA, October.

————, 1971. Africa Division. "Factsheet." Mimeographed. Washington, D.C.: VOA, December.

Volz, Paul M. 1971. 1972. "Television in Africa Study Project." Progress Reports 1 and 2. Mimeographed. Nairobi: LWF Broadcasting Service, January 1971 and February 1972.

Voss, Harald. 1962. *Rundfunk und Fernsehen in Afrika.* Cologne: Verlag Deutscher Wirtschaftsdienst.

Waldschmidt, Julius. 1966. "Radio Broadcasts for Africa." *Radio-Television* (Prague) 4:24.

Waniewicz, Ignacy. 1972. *Broadcasting for Adult Education: A Guidebook to Worldwide Experience.* Paris: UNESCO.

Washington County. [1968.] Board of Education. *Modern Aids to Education Project: Final Report, 1963–1968.* Project 620–11–690–208. USAID/Nigerian Ministries of Education/Washington County, Maryland. Hagerstown, Md.: Board of Education.

Weekly Spectator (Accra). 1972. "Plan for More and Cheaper Radios." 18 March, p. 1.

Welmers, William E. 1971. "Checklist of African Language and Dialect Names." In *Current Trends in Linguistics,* vol. 7, edited by Thomas A. Sebeok, pp. 759–900. The Hague: Mouton.

Welsh, Brian W. W. 1968. "Educational Broadcasting in Tanzania." *Gazette* (Deventer) 14, no. 2:111–28.

————, ed. 1969–70. *A Handbook for Scriptwriters of Adult Education Broadcasts.* 2 vols. Dar es Salaam: Institute of Adult Education.

West Africa (London, 1970). "Commercial Radio Law." 19–25 December.

West African Annual 1970. Lagos: John West Publishing Co.

Whitehead, J. D. 1970. "Production and Prediction of Sporadic E." *Review of Geophysics and Space Physics* 8:65.

Wiener, Norbert. 1950. *The Human Use of Human Beings.* Boston: Houghton Mifflin.

Williams, J. Grenfell. 1950. *Radio in Fundamental Education in Undeveloped Areas.* Press, Film and Radio in the World Today Series. Paris: UNESCO.

Williams, P. O. R. 1967. "Radio: The Best Medium of Communication." *SAUK/SABC Bulletin* (Johannesburg), 24 April, p. 2.

Wilson, Elmo C. 1958. "Problems of Survey Research in Modernizing Areas." *Public Opinion Quarterly* (New York) 22, no. 3 (Fall):230–34.

Winter, David. 1971. *Seychelles Calling.* Woking, Surrey: Far East Broadcasting Association.

Wolfers, Michael. 1972. "Africa's Showpiece for Democracy Prepares for an Election." *Times* (London), Overseas Section, 27 January, p. 9.

Woodward, Julian, and Evanyshyn, Stan. 1971. "Ghana Project." *COMBROAD* (London) 10 (January–March):1–5.

Wright, J. W. 1960. "A Model of the F-Region above h_{max} F2." *Journal of Geophysical Research* 65:185–91.

WRTH (*World Radio-TV Handbook*). Annual. Edited by J. M. Frost. New York: Billboard Publications.

Zambia. 1972. *Estimates of Revenue and Expenditure*. Lusaka: Government Printer.

ZBS (Zambia Broadcasting Services). 1969. "Zambia Broadcasting Services." Lusaka: ZBS.

Index

Index

Adult education, 293–98
—in: Gambia, 101; Lesotho, 235; Niger, 302–3; Senegal, 284; Tanzania, 68–69; Zambia, 129
Advertising, 336–42. *See also* Lourenço Marques Radio
—agencies: Havas, 112; in Francophone countries, 112; Informations et Publicité, 112; in Kenya, 58; in Rhodesia, 135; SSC&B-Lintas International, 338
—in: Egypt, 21–22, 23, 26; Gambia, 97; Ghana, 89, 90; Kenya, 54, 56, 58, 60; Malawi, 133, 135; Moçambique, 160, 164; Nigeria, 81, 84–85; Rhodesia, 131, 132; Somalia, 52; South Africa, 143; Sudan, 48; Swaziland, 152; Tanzania, 54; Zambia, 128, 129–30
—sponsorship, 135–36, 341
African-American Institute, 238, 239
Africanization, 60, 88, 116, 123, 135, 220, 281
Agencies. *See* Advertising agencies; News agencies
Agency for International Development (AID), 226–30
—broadcasting policies of, 226–27, 306
—in: Ethiopia, 38–39, 45, 229, 309–10, 312; Kenya, 60; Malawi, 230; Nigeria, 229–30, 237, 300–301, 364–65; Sudan, 47, 228–29
—and participant trainees, 361–62
Agricultural programs. *See* Rural broadcasting
Ahmadiyya sect, 203
Aid, foreign: bilateral, 110–11, 215–51, 270–81, 290–91 (*See also names of individual donor countries*); and donor ethnocentricism, 363; and ideology, 363–64; multilateral, 252–69; problems of, 61, 362–67
Aid-tying, 241, 363
Algeria: broadcasting in, 16, 31–34, 180, 261; satellite station in, 369
All Africa Conference of Churches, 204, 210–11, 283
All African Trade Fair, 58
All India Radio, 356
American Forces Radio and Television Service (AFRTS), 6, 29, 39
Angola: broadcasting in, 161–63, 340, 341; satellite station in, 369
Arabic (language), as unifier, 15
Arab States Broadcasting Union (ASBU), 20, 28, 260, 262, 370
Artists, status of, 101, 358–59
Arts, African: in broadcasting, 44, 58, 66, 91, 101, 106, 108, 116, 126, 131, 222, 357–59
Arusha Declaration, 62–63
Ascension Island: broadcasting on, 167, 223, 186; satellite station on, 369
Asian Broadcasting Union (ABU), 83
Asians, in Africa, 54, 55, 56, 74, 150, 164, 170
Atmospheric noise, 380, 386, 391
Audience research. *See* Research
Audiences: impediments to growth of, 347–50; mail to broadcasters from, 137, 185, 188, 192, 194–95, 196, 221; promotion of international services to, 195, 198
Australia, aid: to Ghana, 93; to Nigeria, 87

Barclay, Ivonne, 198
Batteries: radio, 95, 126, 304; television, 316
BBC. *See* British Broadcasting Corporation
BBC Television Enterprises, 225
BBC Transcription Service, 137, 224
Bechuanaland, 153
Belgium: aid to Zaïre, 124; colonial policies of, 112, 123; external service of, 184
Berne Convention, 263
Botswana: BBC relay station in, 179; broadcasting in, 153–54, 275
Bourgiba, Habib, 31
British Broadcasting Corporation (BBC), 216–25
—African Service of, 176, 184–86, 221–23, 274
—aid to: Botswana, 153; Ethiopia, 213; Gambia, 275; Ghana, 95; Kenya, 59, 275; Lesotho, 275; Libya, 29; Malawi, 138, 275; Nigeria, 87; religious broadcasters, 211; Sierra Leone, 105, 275; Swaziland, 152; Tanzania, 275
—audience for: Africa, 185, 398; Ethiopia, 43, 44; Ghana, 185; Kenya, 59; Uganda, 73
—and CEDO, 276
—colonial policies of, 175–77
—Empire Service of, 217, 221–22
—as model, 63, 141, 205
—rebroadcasts of: Africa, 223–24; Botswana, 153, 186; Ethiopia, 40; Gambia, 186; Lesotho, 153, 186; Liberia, 104, 186; Malawi, 134; Nigeria, 186; Sierra Leone, 104, 186; Swaziland, 151, 186
—relay stations of, 102, 167–68, 179, 186, 223
—research by, 325
—training by, 223, 271–76
British Council, 50, 223, 276, 313, 314
British Overseas Development Ministry, 312, 313
British Volunteer Service Overseas, aid to Malawi, 138
Broadcasting, role of
—in Arab societies, 16
—in development, 9, 63, 227–28, 241, 259, 284–85, 292–93, 334–35
—in independence movements: Africa, 178; Algeria, 16–17, 31–32, 355, 397; Angola, 163; Egypt, 35, 183; Guinea, 178; Libya, 29; Mali, 179; Morocco, 179; North Africa vs. Tropical Africa, 7–8; Portuguese territories, 158, 166; Tanzania, 65–66, 178, 183, 192; Tunisia, 31; Zambia, 129
—in nationalism, 370–71
—in political crises, 395–98
—and press, 3–5, 108–9, 397
—as unifier, 18, 220, 351–52. *See also* Federal systems; Centralization of broadcasting; Decentralization of broadcasting; Local and regional broadcasting
Bulgaria, program exports of to Egypt, 26
Burundi, broadcasting in, 73, 75–77, 110, 208, 283

Cable television, South African, 150, 342–43
Cameroon, broadcasting in, 105–6, 245, 283, 286, 289
Canada, aid
—philosophy of, 240
—to: Africa, 215, 240–47; Algeria, 246; Cameroon, 245, 246; Ghana, 244, 245, 246; Ivory Coast, 242, 243, 247, 316; Kenya, 57, 242–43, 244, 245, 251; Malagasy Republic, 244; Malawi, 249; Mali, 246, 250; Mauritania, 247; Morocco, 249; Niger, 243, 250, 253; Nigeria, 87, 243–44, 245, 247; Rhodesia, 246; Rwanda, 250; Senegal, 246, 247, 286; Sierra Leone, 249; Somalia, 251; Sudan, 249; Tanzania, 70, 244, 245, 251; Togo, 246; Uganda, 249, 251; Upper Volta, 247; Zambia, 246, 249, 251
Canadian Broadcasting Corporation, 94, 245–46
Canadian International Development Agency (CIDA), 240–42
Canary Islands: broadcasting in, 170; satellite station in, 369
Cape Verde Islands, broadcasting in, 166
Censorship, 4, 58, 252, 397. *See also* News policies
Center for Information Studies (CESTI), 246–47, 286

Central African Federation, 127, 133–34

Central African Republic, broadcasting in, 121, 340

Centralization of broadcasting, 10, 109, 353

Centralization of facilities: in Central African Federation, 127–28; in Moçambique, 164; in Uganda, 72; in Zambia, 128

Centre for Educational Development Overseas (CEDO), 59, 211, 275, 276–80, 311

CETO. *See* Centre for Educational Development Overseas

Ceuta, 34, 171

Chad, broadcasting in, 121

China
—aid to: Africa, 216; Mali, 179; Togo, 118; Tanzania, 193; Zambia, 128
—audience for broadcasts: Africa, 190; Ethiopia, 43; Kenya, 59; Uganda, 73
—external service of, 177, 178, 179, 190
—relay station of in Mali, 179

Cinema. *See* Motion pictures

Civil service, 42, 60–61, 97, 282, 337, 361–62

Closed-circuit television: in Ethiopia, 40; in Ghana, 93; in Nigeria, 229; in South Africa, 147, 149, 150; in Swaziland, 152

Colonial broadcasting
—in: Central African Federation, 127–28; Chad, 121; Ethiopia, 38, 44; French Equatorial Africa, 107–11; French West Africa, 107–11, 113–14; Gambia, 219, 220; Ghana, 78, 218, 219, 220; Kenya, 54–56; Malagasy Republic, 155; Malawi, 125, 127; Mali, 118; Nigeria, 80, 82, 87–88, 219–20; Northern Rhodesia, 125–27; Sierra Leone, 219, 220; Somalia, 50–51, 127; Uganda, 73; Zaïre, 122; Zambia, 125–28
—policies: British, 108–9, 175–76, 217–21; French, 108–9, 176–77
—and religion, 205
—use of wired radio in, 342

Colonial Development and Welfare Fund, 218

Color television: in Rhodesia, 133; in South Africa, 150

Committee on International Exchange of Persons (U.S.), 239

Commonwealth Broadcasting Conference, 83, 94, 104, 246, 253, 264–67

Community development, 244–45

Community reception: of radio, 12, 36, 59, 82, 116, 134, 137, 219, 250, 349; of television, 12, 27, 36, 49, 75

Comoro Islands, broadcasting in, 170

Comsat, 368–69

Congo, broadcasting in, 119–21, 188, 280, 396

Consortia, 55–56, 342

Construction and management contracts, 342–44

Copyright, 252; and Universal Copyright Convention, 263–64

CORDAC, 75, 76, 179, 208

Corporate status of broadcasting
—in: Egypt, 18–19; Ethiopia, 41–43, 362; Ghana, 89; Kenya, 55–56; Liberia, 102; Malawi, 133, 135; Mauritius, 156; Nigeria, 80, 87–88, 220; Rhodesia, 131; Sierra Leone, 105; South Africa, 141; Tanganyika, 63; Tunisia, 354
—value of, 354

Council on International Education and Cultural Affairs (U.S.), 237

Counterparts in aid projects, 228, 364–65

Coups d'état and broadcasting, 20, 395–97

Credibility: of BBC, 185, 197; of Radio Cairo, 196; of VOA, 187

Cuba, external service of, 178

Czechoslovakia, aid: to Africa, 216; to Algeria, 33; to Guinea, 116; to Sudan, 47, 49

Dahomey, broadcasting in, 117, 247, 250, 396

Decentralization of broadcasting: in Ivory Coast, 115; in Morocco, 34; in Nigeria, 353; in Portuguese territories, 353; in South Africa, 353; in Zaïre, 113, 123, 353

Denmark, aid to RVOG, 213

Deutsche Welle. *See* Germany, West

Development. *See* Broadcasting, role of, in development

Directional antennas, 197
Ducting, effect of on television signal propagation, 392–93

East African Economic Community, 53
Educational broadcasting, 292–319
—in: Algeria, 33–34; Botswana, 154; Egypt, 24, 26–27; Ethiopia, 40, 309–15; Gabon, 122; Gambia, 101; Ivory Coast, 112, 115, 243, 267–69, 315–19; Kenya, 57, 235, 242–43; Malawi, 138–39; Moçambique, 164; Muslim society, 16; Niger, 243, 267–69, 301; Nigeria, 83–84, 229, 243, 300; Rhodesia, 133; Rwanda, 77; Senegal, 114, 302; Sudan, 48, 49–50; Tanzania, 66, 68–69, 244; Uganda, 74; Zaïre, 124; Zambia, 129, 130
—production style of, 295–96
—responsibility for, 297–98
—systems approach to, 280, 307
—training for: at CEDO, 276–80; at Thomson Foundation Television College, 280–81
Egypt
—aid from: CEDO, 277, 279, 280; ITU, 261; Thomson Foundation, 280; U.S., 24, 228, 342
—aid to: Nigeria, 87; Sudan, 48, 49
—broadcasting in, 17–28, 203, 286, 288, 339
—external service of: to Africa, 16–17, 177, 183, 195, 196, 202; to Ethiopia, 43; to Middle East, 23; to Sudan, 23
Engineering function, separation from programming function, 41–42, 48, 49, 96–97
ELWA, 177, 207, 208, 328
Equatorial Guinea, broadcasting in, 157
Ethiopia. See also Radio Voice of the Gospel
—aid from: Canada, 251; Great Britain, 277, 278, 280, 288, 311, 312, 313, 314, 343; UNESCO, 312; U.S., 38–39, 45, 229, 232, 234, 309, 310, 312, 313; West Germany, 44–45, 290–91
—autonomy of broadcasting in, 41–43, 362
—broadcasting in, 37–46, 59, 328, 343, 362, 397
—Mass Media Center in, 40, 235, 279, 309–14

—Radio Training Center in, 44–45, 282, 290–91
—satellite station in, 369
European Broadcasting Union (EBU), 15, 33, 83, 260, 262, 263–64

Fanon, Frantz, 16, 31, 355
Far East Broadcasting Association, 167, 209
Farm Radio Forum, 69, 244–45, 257, 298–300, 308–9. See also Rural broadcasting
Federal systems: Cameroon, 105–6; Central African Federation, 127–28; East Africa, 53; French Equatorial Africa, 120; Nigeria, 79–80, 220, 353
Feedback, 184, 296, 297, 299, 303, 304–5, 306, 320–21
"Feeds," VOA, 186, 230, 232
FM (Frequency Modulation)
—allocation plan for, 260, 262, 390
—future prospects for, 367–68
—as indirect censor, 368
—propagation of, 390–92
—use of: Africa, 8; Angola, 162; Cape Verde Islands, 166; Gambia, 99; Kenya, 368; Madeira, 166, 171; Malawi, 134; Moçambique, 164; Morocco, 35; Portuguese territories, 159; Rhodesia, 132; São Tomé, 166; Sierra Leone, 105; South Africa, 8, 143–44, 145, 147, 150, 152; Swaziland, 151; Zaïre, 123
Food and Agriculture Organization (FAO), 262
Ford Foundation, 276
Foreign (non-African) stations
—on African soil: American, 6, 102–4, 177, 179; British, 6, 179; Chinese, 179; Dutch, 6, 156, 179, 184; French, 6, 109, 110, 120, 168, 176, 188, 398; West German, 6, 77, 178, 179, 187
—listeners to: in Africa, 180–84, 187, 188, 190–93, 195, 196, 224–25; in Ethiopia, 43, 44; in Ghana, 185; in Ivory Coast, 188, 191; in Kenya, 59; in Senegal, 188; in Uganda, 73; in Zambia, 131
France. See also OCORA; ORTF; SORAFOM
—aid policies of, 110–11

—aid to: Africa, 215, 261; Burundi, 75–76; Sudan, 48
—language policies of, 177–78
French Equatorial Africa, 112, 119–22
French Territory of Afars and Issas (FTAI), 39, 51, 168–70
French West Africa, 107–19
Friedrich Ebert Foundation, 92

Gabon: broadcasting in, 122, 250, 340; satellite station in, 369
Gambia, broadcasting in, 96–97, 98–102, 275
German colonies, 53, 75, 105, 116
Germany, East: aid to Africa, 116, 216; broadcasts to Africa, 178, 190, 191
Germany, West
—aid policy, 247
—aid to: Africa, 215, 247–51, 261; Dahomey, 117, 250; Ethiopia, 44–45, 251, 270, 290–91; Gabon, 250; Ghana, 95, 251; Guinea, 250; Kenya, 59, 60, 251; Lesotho, 153; Malawi, 136, 138, 249; Mali, 250; Morocco, 249; Niger, 250–51; Nigeria, 87; RVOG, 213; Rwanda, 250; Sierra Leone, 249; Somalia, 51, 251; Sudan, 49, 249; Tanzania, 251; Togo, 116; Tunisia, 250; Uganda, 249, 251; Upper Volta, 250; Zaïre, 124, 251; Zambia, 249
—external service of, 43, 59, 177–78, 187–88
—relay station of, in Rwanda, 77, 178–79, 187
Ghana
—aid from: Australia, 93, BBC, 275; Canada, 93, 94, 245, 251, 299; CEDO, 277, 278; East Germany, 93; Great Britain, 94; Italy, 93; Netherlands, 95; Nigeria, 95; ORTF, 95; Thomson Foundation, 95, 280; West Germany, 94; UNESCO, 93, 257, 299–300; U.S., 95
—broadcasting in, 7, 78, 89–95, 185, 219, 220, 298–300, 395
—external service of, 178, 191–92
—research in, 91–92, 325, 327, 328
—training in, 93–95, 261, 275, 277, 278–79, 281, 284, 286, 289
Government Affairs Institute (U.S.), 238

Government control of broadcasting: compared with press, 4; exceptions to, 6
Granada Television, in Nigeria, 343
Great Britain, aid from, 49, 99, 104, 138, 153, 216–25, 261, 312, 313, 314; "indirect rule" by, 109. See also British Broadcasting Corporation; British Council
Griots, 101, 106
Ground conductivity, 8, 81, 379, 386
Ground-wave propagation, 379–80, 383, 386
Group listening/viewing. See Community reception
Guinea, broadcasting in, 110, 115–16, 178, 250

Haile Selassie I, 38, 40, 397
Hassan, King (Morocco), 397
High-frequency broadcasting, 386–89
Hungary: aid to Sudan, 48; program exports to Egypt, 26

Imperialism. See Colonial broadcasting
Independence movements. See Broadcasting, role of, in independence movements
India, audience for broadcasts in Uganda, 73
Information/guidance programs, 271, 293–98, 304
Information infrastructure, research on, 332–34
Institute for International Education (U.S.), 239
Institute of Mass Communications: in Ghana, 289; in Kenya, 60, 219, 258, 279, 284, 286–87; in Nigeria, 87, 258, 287–88
Instructional television (ITV). See Educational broadcasting
Intermedia (commercial station), 151–52
International Bank for Reconstruction and Development (IBRD). See World Bank
International broadcasting. See also Foreign stations
—audiences for, 59, 73, 180–85, 188, 190, 191, 194, 196, 197–99
—during colonial period, 175–80

International broadcasting—Continued
—originators of: African stations, 191–97; Communist stations, 189–91; U.N. Radio, 199–200; Western stations, 184–89
International Press Institute, 5, 216
International Radio and Television Organization (OIRT), 260, 264
International Telecommunication Union (ITU), 8, 41, 213, 253, 260–63, 370; allocation of frequencies by, 143–44, 375–77, 390, 393–94
International Visitors Program (U.S.), 238
International Women Broadcasters' Program of American Women in Radio and Television, 238, 239
Ionosphere, 380–89, 394
Islam, 15–16, 22, 37, 85, 91, 112, 201–4, 208
Israel aid, to Malawi, 138
Italy: aid to Ethiopia, 43; broadcasts to Africa, 176, 177–78; external service, 177–78
Ivory Coast: broadcasting in, 114–15, 188, 191, 196–97, 232, 233, 282, 284, 325; educational television project in, 112, 236, 247, 256, 267–69, 309, 315–19; satellite station in, 369

Jamming: by French in Algeria, 32, 180–81; by Rhodesia, 179, 180
Japan, aid: to Africa, 215–16; to Ethiopia, 314; to Ghana, 91, 95; to Nigeria, 87; to Sudan, 49; to Uganda, 74

Kenya: aid to, 244, 245, 251, 258, 275, 280, 283; broadcasting in, 48, 54–61, 73, 242, 271, 284, 324, 325–26, 339, 340, 343, 350–51, 361, 368; Institute of Mass Communications in, 60, 219, 258, 279, 284, 286–87; satellite station in, 369
Kenyatta, Jomo, 56
Korea, North: international service, 178

Lakeland Radio, 139
Language policy
—in: Africa, 350–53; Angola, 162; Cameroon, 105–6; Francophone countries, 108; Gabon, 122; Gambia, 99;

Kenya, 59, 350–51; Malagasy Republic, 155; Malawi, 136; Moçambique, 165; Nigeria, 78, 82–83; Portuguese territories, 158; Rhodesia, 132; Sierra Leone, 350; Somalia, 50; South Africa, 141–43, 150; Tanzania, 66; Uganda, 6, 72–74, 351; Zaïre, 123; Zambia, 126–27, 128–29, 130–31, 351
—of: BBC, 221; China, 190; international broadcasters, 176–77, 181, 183, 184; ORTF, 189; Radio Cairo, 195–96; VOA, 186
—research on, 329–30
—statistics on, 350
Law, broadcasting and: in Africa, 7, 353–55; copyright, 262–64; in Egypt, 19; research on, 333
Leasing of facilities: in Malawi, 139; in Rhodesia, 132
Lebanon, aid: to Sudan, 48
Lesotho, broadcasting in, 152–53, 235, 275
Liberia, broadcasting in, 102–4, 179, 207, 208, 281, 328, 341
Libya, broadcasting in, 28–29, 280
License fees, receiver
—abolition of, 304, 348
—in: Angola, 161; Egypt, 20, 24; Ghana, 89; Kenya, 56; Malawi, 135; Nigeria, 80–81; Rhodesia, 131; Rwanda, 77; South Africa, 141, 145; Sudan, 48; Tanzania, 68; Togo, 116; Zambia, 128
Literacy training, 295
—in: Algeria, 33; Ethiopia, 312; Ivory Coast, 317; Muslim society, 16; Tunisia, 30, 302–3; Zambia, 129
—status of, 303–4
Local and regional broadcasting
—importance of, 352–53
—in: Ethiopia, 40; Kenya, 57–58; Moçambique, 164; Nigeria, 7, 41, 83, 85, 220; South Africa, 144–45, 147, 150; Uganda, 71–72; Zaïre, 123
Long-wave (low frequency) transmission: in Africa, 378; in Algeria, 33; in Morocco, 35
Lourenço Marques Radio, 164, 193, 338, 341

Madagascar. See Malagasy Republic
Madeira, broadcasting in, 166

Maghreb: broadcasting in, 28–36; description of, 15–16, 28
Malagasy Republic: broadcasting in, 110, 155–56, 179, 261, 348; satellite station in, 369
Malawi, broadcasting in, 125–27, 133–39, 249–50, 275, 285, 340, 341; external service to citizens abroad, 137
Mali, broadcasting in, 117–18, 179, 246, 250, 283
Management practices, research on, 333
Mauritania, broadcasting in, 118, 247, 277, 278
Mauritius, broadcasting in, 156–57, 277, 288, 341, 343
Medium-frequency broadcasting, technical characteristics of, 378–83
Melilla, broadcasting in, 171
Military broadcasting stations, 6, 29, 38, 39, 51, 55, 151
Mindolo Ecumenical Center (Zambia), 210
Missionaries, 201–4. See also Religion and broadcasting
Mobile units, 136, 244, 249, 250, 251, 341, 344, 357–58
Moçambique: broadcasting in, 6, 159, 163; satellite station in, 369; student-operated station in, 165
Monitoring services, 90, 134, 137, 261–62
Morocco: broadcasting in, 16, 34–36, 179, 249, 282, 339, 396, 397; satellite station in, 369
Motion pictures
—production of: Egypt, 17, 25; Gambia, 101; Malawi, 138; Sudan, 49
—training for: Ghana, 94, 251; Kenya, 60, 251, 287
Multimedia Zambia, 129, 205

Netherlands
—African relay station of, 156, 179
—aid to: Ghana, 95; Lesotho, 153; Nigeria, 87; Malagasy Republic, 179; RVOG, 213
—external service of, 178, 179, 184
News
—agencies: Agence France Presse, 11, 76; Kenya, 216; Malawi, 137; Middle East, 49; New China, 11; Reuters, 11,

137, 160; Tass, 11, 76, 216; UPI, 11, 160; VisNews, 11, 49
—assimilation of, 329
—credibility of, 185, 187, 188, 196, 197
—as information/guidance, 293–94
—policy (countries): Botswana, 154; Egypt, 22, 26; Gambia, 97; Portuguese territories, 159–60; Sierra Leone, 105; South Africa, 94, 146, 197; Tanzania, 67–68, 356; Zambia, 356
—policy (stations): BBC, 186; Radio Berlin International, 191; Radio Moscow, 189–90; Radio Peking, 19; RVOG, 213; VOA, 186
—as propaganda, 293
—production of, 11, 105, 137, 142, 355–56
—role of in crises, 397–98
—service, of USIA, 233
Niger, broadcasting in, 118–19, 243, 250–51
Nigeria
—aid from: Canada, 245, 247; Thomson Foundation, 280; UNESCO, 258, 288; U.S., 232, 233, 234, 300–301, 364–65
—broadcasting in, 78–89, 205, 261, 281, 284, 301, 328, 340, 341, 342–44, 395
—external service of, 85, 178, 192
—Institute of Mass Communications in, 87, 258, 285, 287–88
—National Mass Communications Council of, 328, 332
—satellite station in, 369
Nkrumah, Kwame, 78, 90, 116, 178, 282
Norway, aid to Tanzania from, 245
NTSC color system, 369
Nyasaland. See Malawi
Nyerere, Julius, 63

OCORA, 111, 120, 123, 156, 215, 302
OIRT, 264
ORTF (Office de Radiodiffusion-Télévision Française), 33, 95, 111, 112, 168, 169, 170, 188–89, 213, 215, 302, 398
Organization de l'Armée Secrète (OAS), 31–32, 397
Organization of African Unity (OAU), 40, 66
Outside contributors, 100, 305

Pakistan, external service of, 73
PAL color system, 149, 150, 369
Participant trainees, 228, 230, 361–62
Peace Corps: in Ethiopia, 235, 310; in Ghana, 234; in Guinea, 116; in Ivory Coast, 236; in Kenya, 235; in Liberia, 236; in Malawi, 138; in Mauritius, 235; in Switzerland, 235
Personnel. See Artists, status of; Civil service
Pirate stations, 32, 97, 397
Poland, aid to Africa, 216
Polarization, signal, 381–83, 386
Politics and broadcasting, 6, 7, 10, 11, 62–64, 66–68, 136, 141–43, 146, 148–50, 293, 395–98. See also International broadcasting; Language policy; Nkrumah
Polylingualism. See Language policy
Portugal: dependencies of, 157–66; external service of, 177; relay station of in São Tomé, 166
Portuguese Guinea, broadcasting in, 166
Press vs. broadcasting, 3, 4, 5, 11, 108–9, 397
Primary service area, definition of, 380
Private ownership of stations: Algeria, 32; Canary Islands, 170; Congo, 120; Egypt, 18; Gambia, 97–98; Liberia, 103–4; Madeira, 171; Moçambique, 6; Morocco, 35; Portuguese territories, 158, 159, 162–63; South Africa, 141, 142; Swaziland, 151–52; Zaïre, 122–23; Zambia, 130
Production: centers, 46, 76, 106, 121, 206, 207, 208, 209; services, sale of, 135, 138, 341
Program exchanges: Commonwealth Broadcasting Conference, 265; EBU, 264; Gambia, 100; Moçambique, 160; Nigeria, 83; OIRT, 264; URTNA, 262
Programming: block in Malawi, 136; quality of, 355
Programs, imported. See also Rebroadcasting
—by: Algeria, 33; Egypt, 26; Ethiopia, 40–41; Francophone countries, 111–12; F.T.A.I., 168–69; Gambia, 100; Ghana, 90; Kenya, 58; Malawi, 137; Moçambique, 160; Nigeria, 83, 85–86; Rhodesia, 132–33; Tanzania, 67; Tunisia, 30; Zambia, 130

—from: Arab world, 49; BBC, 26, 40, 59–60, 90, 223–24, 225; Bulgaria, 26; Czechoslovakia, 26; EBU, 33; France, 33, 189; U.N., 200; U.S., 26, 40, 49–50, 85–86, 90, 231–33
Propaganda: Cold War, 178; Egyptian, 16–17, 25–26, 121, 202; Portuguese, 159, 163, 165; Somali, 51; South African, 146, 193, 194, 195; Spanish, 170; World War II, 109, 110, 123, 176. See also Broadcasting, role of, in independence movements; International broadcasting
Propagation: effect of meteorological conditions on, 391, 392; radio, 8, 197, 378–93; superpower, 8–9, 29, 35
Public reception centers. See Community reception

Qur'an, 22, 91, 202, 204

Radio, ubiquity of, 16, 31, 168
Radio Brazzaville, 109, 110, 120, 176, 188, 396
Radio clubs, 159, 164–65, 166, 338, 349
Radio Corporation of America (RCA), 24, 228, 342, 343–44
Radio Luxembourg, 193
Radio Peace and Progress, 189
Radio Syd, 97–98, 197, 338
Radio Vaticana, 100, 209, 210–11
Radio Voice of the Gospel (RVOG), 45–46, 179, 203, 207, 208, 209, 212–14, 283, 328
Rebroadcasting of programs: BBC, 100, 104, 151, 153, 186, 217, 223–24; Deutsche Welle, 100; ORTF, 100, 170; Radio Moscow, 100, 104; Radio Nederland, 100; Radio Vaticana, 100; Senegal, 100; U.N. Radio, 100, 200; VOA, 100, 104. See also Programs, imported
Receivers: cost of, 18, 95, 134, 150, 161, 169, 348, 369; credit purchase of, 155, 248–49, 348–50; duty on, 31, 155–56; maintenance of, 103, 300, 304, 309, 349; production of, 24, 65, 95, 134–35, 149–50; ratio to population of, 9, 12; short-wave, 10, 12, 181, 183; subsidization of, 134, 304; taxes on, 95, 135, 161, 304, 348; urban concentration of, 304. See also License fees, receiver; Saucepan Special

Reception of foreign stations. *See* Foreign stations

Rediffusion. *See* Wired radio

Rediffusion, Ltd., 102, 103, 342–43

Regional broadcasting. *See* Local and regional broadcasting

Relays. *See* Rebroadcasting

Relay stations, international, 30, 33, 36, 102, 103, 166, 167, 170–71, 179, 188, 226

Religion and broadcasting: Christianity, 201–14, 283; Islam, 15–16, 91, 202–4; stations, 45–46, 75, 76–77, 100, 102–3, 124–25, 129, 152–53, 159, 162, 165, 167, 177, 179, 199, 203, 207–12, 283, 328

Research, 320–35

—by: advertisers, 183, 323–24; Central African Broadcasting Station, 322, 329; educational interests, 326–27; foreign governments, 43, 183–84, 324–26; religious interests, 327–28

—in: Ethiopia, 43–44, 46, 198, 314; Gambia, 99; Ghana, 91–92, 328; Ivory Coast, 319; Kenya, 58–59, 325–26; Malawi, 136; Niger, 328; Nigeria, 86, 328; Senegal, 325, 327; Tanzania, 68; West Africa, 325; Zambia, 130–31, 328–30

—on: communication, 259; diffusion of innovations, 298; educational broadcasting, 235, 299–300, 314; farm forums, 327; intelligibility, 322–23; international audiences, 183–84, 185, 188, 194; introduction of television, 150–51; media role in development, 327, 334

Réunion, broadcasting on, 169, 340

Revenue, unusual sources of: in Egypt, 20; in Malawi, 135, 138–39

Rhodesia, broadcasting in, 131–33, 246, 280, 283, 339, 340, 341, 343

Rhodesia, Northern. *See* Zambia

Rockefeller Brothers Fund, 276

RTV International, 54, 60–61

Rural broadcasting, 7, 10, 21, 69, 92–93, 101, 129, 137, 154, 244–45, 257, 268, 298–300, 305, 308, 309

Rwanda, broadcasting in, 73, 75 ,77, 110, 178–79, 187, 250, 340, 342

Saint Helena, broadcasting on, 167

São Tomé and Principe, broadcasting on, 166

Satellites: cost of, 369–70; frequencies allocated to, 393–94; ground stations for, 369; potentialities of, 18, 27, 263, 370–71, 394; study of, 253, 262; types of, 368

Saucepan Special, 123, 126, 219, 322

Scheduling: intermittent, 10; of educational programs, 296; of international services, 196, 198; of religious programs, 212

SECAM color system, 24, 149

Senegal: aid to, 113–14, 246, 247, 257–58, 268, 283, 286, 289, 302, 392; broadcasting in, 98, 100, 113–14, 188, 196, 246, 285–86, 289, 325, 327; satellite station in, 369

Service-area concept, 377–78

Service distribution factor, 9

"Sesame Street," 371

Seychelles, broadcasting in, 167, 209

Short wave: propagation, 386; reception, 12, 386, 389

Sidi Ifni, broadcasting in, 171

Sierra Leone: aid to, 233, 249, 275, 278, 280; broadcasting in, 104–5, 277, 278, 339, 343, 349, 350, 395

Sky-wave propagation, 8, 380–83, 386–89

Somalia, broadcasting in, 43, 50–52, 59, 127, 180, 251, 340, 358

SORAFOM, 106, 110–11, 113–14, 118, 120, 121, 122, 155, 215, 302

South Africa, 140–51

—aid: to Malawi, 138; from Thomson Foundation, 280, 286; from USIA, 232

—broadcasting in, 140–51, 289, 339, 342–43

—external service of, 146, 180, 193–95, 197

—satellite station in, 369

Southern Rhodesia. *See* Rhodesia

Soviet Union

—aid to: Africa, 216; Chad, 121; Somalia, 51

—external service of, 43, 59, 73, 176, 177–78, 189–90

—influence of, in Egypt, 26

Spain: dependencies of, 170–71; external service of, 177; relay station of, 170–71

Spanish Sahara, broadcasting in, 170
"Special English," use of by VOA, 187
Spectrum, radio: allocations to broadcasting, 377–78; divisions of, 375–77
Studio-École de Maisons-Laffitte, 110, 270, 283
Sudan: broadcasting in, 43, 44, 46–50, 234, 249, 261, 280; satellite station in, 369
Sudan Interior Mission, 103, 177, 207
Sunspot cycle, 383
Survey research. See Research
Swaziland, broadcasting in, 151–52
Sweden, aid to Tanzania from, 70, 245
Syndication. See Programs, imported
Syracuse University International Broadcast Seminars, 238, 239

"Talk radio," two-way format, 154
Tanganyika, 62, 63. See also Tanzania
TANU (Tanganyika African National Union), 63–64, 66
Tanzania: aid to, 244, 245, 251, 275; broadcasting in, 62–71, 73, 275, 282, 338, 341, 352; external services of, 65–66, 178, 180, 183, 192–93
TELE-STAR, 123–24, 204, 206–7, 251, 283
Television, propagation of, 390–91
Terrain profile, effect on FM and TV of, 390
Thomson Foundation Television College, 95, 280–81, 343
Thomson Television International, 40, 280, 343
Togo: aid to, 246, 256, 257; broadcasting in, 116–17, 284, 285
Training. See also Universities and broadcasting
—aid from: BBC, 271–76; Canada, 245–47; CEDO, 276–80; Commonwealth Broadcasting Conference, 265–67; Czechoslovakia, 216; France, 110, 270; ITU, 260–61; Japan, 215; OIRT, 264; Soviet Union, 216; Thomson Foundation, 280–81; UNESCO, 255–56, 283; U.S., 226, 228, 230, 233, 234, 236–40, 361; West Germany, 44–45, 270, 282, 290–91
—in: Africa, 281–91; Botswana, 275; Burundi, 283; Cameroon, 283, 286;

Egypt, 27; Ethiopia, 270, 282, 290–91; Gambia, 91, 93; Ivory Coast, 282, 284; Kenya, 59–61, 275, 281; Nigeria, 86–87, 261, 281, 285–88; Rhodesia, 283; Senegal, 246–47, 286; Sierra Leone, 275, 277, 278; Sudan, 48–49, 261; Tanzania, 70–71, 275, 282; Togo, 284–85; Tunisia, 288; Uganda, 275, 277, 283, 284; Zaïre, 261; Zambia, 275, 277, 282, 284
—and motion picture production, 60, 94, 251, 287
—and religious broadcasting, 45, 210–11, 213
Translation: of interview protocols, 331; of news, 356
Transmitter sites/area ratio, 9, 12
Trans World Radio, 177, 179, 210
Tristan da Cunha, broadcasting on, 168
Tropical zone, 375–76; radio propagation in, 386, 391
Tunisia, broadcasting in, 30–31, 264, 302

Uganda: aid to, 233, 249, 251; broadcasting in, 59, 71–75, 283, 284, 285, 289, 340, 341, 351
Ujamaa villages, 63, 64, 69–71, 244
Ultra-high frequency propagation, 392–93
UNESCO (United Nations Educational, Scientific and Cultural Organization), 252–59
—aid from: to Algeria, 33–34; to Ethiopia, 312; to Ghana, 93, 299; to ITU, 370; to Ivory Coast, 256, 316; to Kenya, 283; to Libya, 29; to Mali, 283; to Nigeria, 258, 288; to Senegal, 114, 246, 257, 283, 302; to Somalia, 51; to Togo, 256, 257; to Uganda, 283; to URTNA, 262
—Meeting of Experts on the Development of Information Media in Africa, 257
—studies and reports of, 9, 27, 253, 254–55, 259, 263, 270, 302, 323
Union of African National Radio and Television Organizations (URTNA), 83, 258, 260, 261, 262, 263
United Nations: Economic Commission for Africa, 40, 213; Radio, 199–200; sanctions, 131, 132–33, 149

United States, aid to African broadcasting, 215, 225–26, 261; in Egypt, 228; in Ghana, 95; in Ivory Coast, 316; in Kenya, 57; in Malawi, 138; in Zaïre, 124. *See also* Agency for International Development; Peace Corps; United States Information Agency; Voice of America

United States Department of State, 237–38, 363

United States Information Agency (USIA)

—aid to: Africa, 186, 230–32; Ethiopia, 232, 234; Ivory Coast, 232, 233; Niger, 233; Nigeria, 232, 234; Sierra Leone, 233; South Africa, 232; Sudan, 234; Uganda, 233

—research by, 43, 183–84, 185, 191, 192, 196, 325–26

—travel grants by, 234, 237

· United States Information Service (USIS), 230, 231, 238

Universities and broadcasting

—in Africa: Cameroon, 289; Egypt, 286, 288; Ethiopia, 314; Ghana, 94, 289, 328; Kenya, 60, 242, 271, 285–87; Lesotho, 235; Malagasy Republic, 156; Nigeria, 284, 285–88; Senegal, 246, 285–86, 289, 327; South Africa, 289; Sudan, 48; Tanzania, 69; Tunisia, 288; Uganda, 285, 289; Zaïre, 289; Zambia, 62, 130, 194, 329

—outside Africa, 138, 238–39, 240, 245

Upper Volta, broadcasting in, 119, 247, 250

USSR. *See* Soviet Union

Vernaculars in broadcasting. *See* Language policy

Very-high frequency propagation, 390–92

VisNews, 11, 49

Voice of America (VOA), 36, 54, 59, 176–77, 178, 179; African Service of, 186–87; audience for in Africa, 43, 73, 184, 187; "feeds" by, 186, 230, 232; listener mail, 194; Monrovia relay station, 102, 103; Tangier relay station, 36; training by, 226, 233; use of African talent, 198

Voice of the Arabs. *See* Egypt, external service of

Wired radio: in Ghana, 89, 90, 91, 219; in Malagasy Republic, 156; in Nigeria, 87, 219; in Sierra Leone, 104, 219, 349; in South Africa, 143, 342–43; in Togo, 116; in Zaïre, 123

World Association for Christian Communication, 204, 207, 209

World Bank, 41, 253, 267–69, 316

World Health Organization (WHO), 262

World War II and broadcasting, 109, 110, 122–23, 125–26, 176, 218

Zaïre: broadcasting in, 73, 109, 110, 112–13, 122–24, 196, 206–7, 261, 289, 324, 340; satellite station in, 369

Zambia: aid to, 246, 249, 251, 257, 275, 277, 280; broadcasting in, 62, 125–31, 205–6, 282, 284, 328–30, 340, 348, 356, 357, 358, 362; satellite station in, 369

Zanzibar, broadcasting in, 53, 62, 70–71